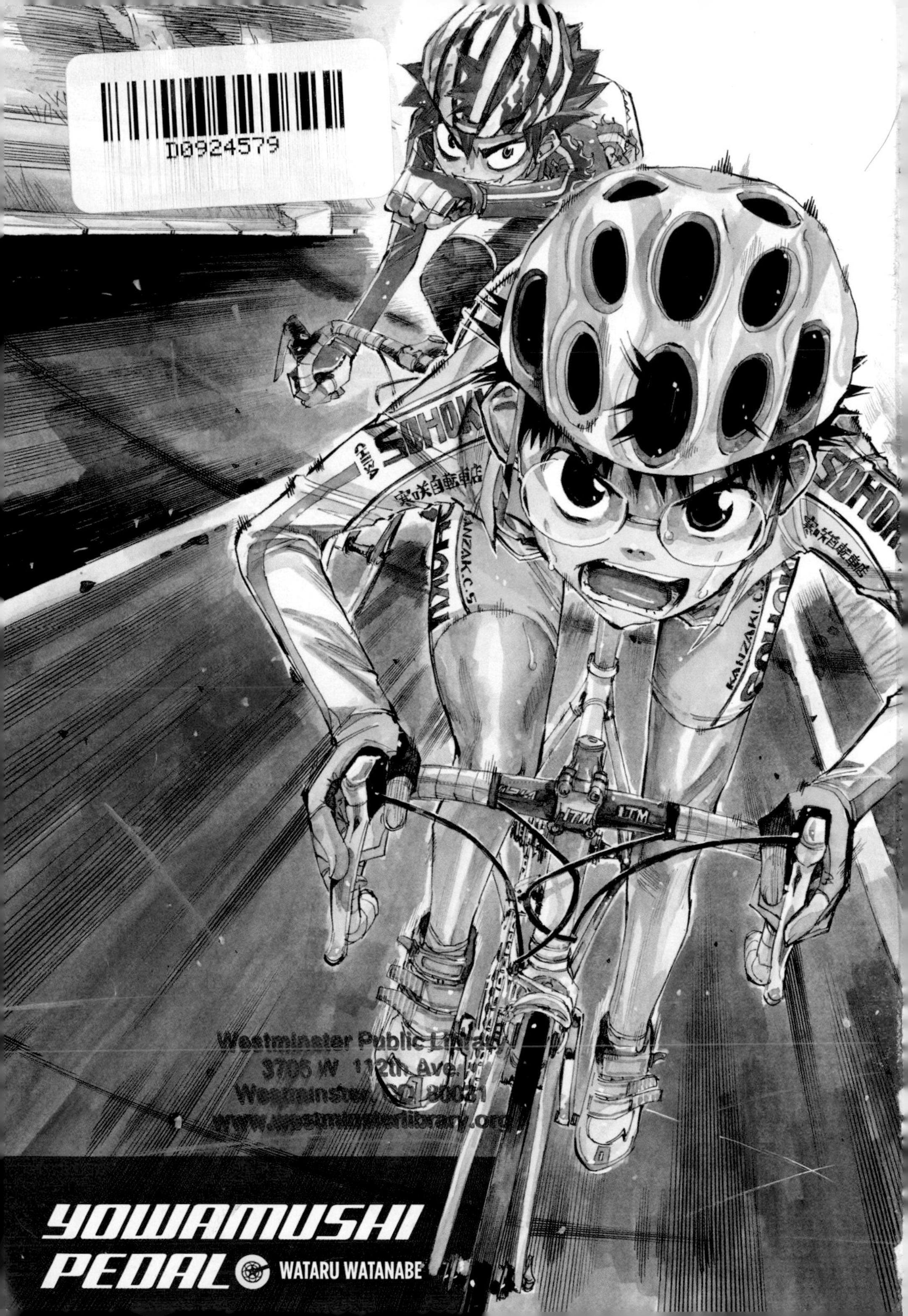
SOHOKU
CHIBA
寒咲自転車店
KANZAKI.C.S
ITM

YOWAMUSHI PEDAL

WATARU WATANABE

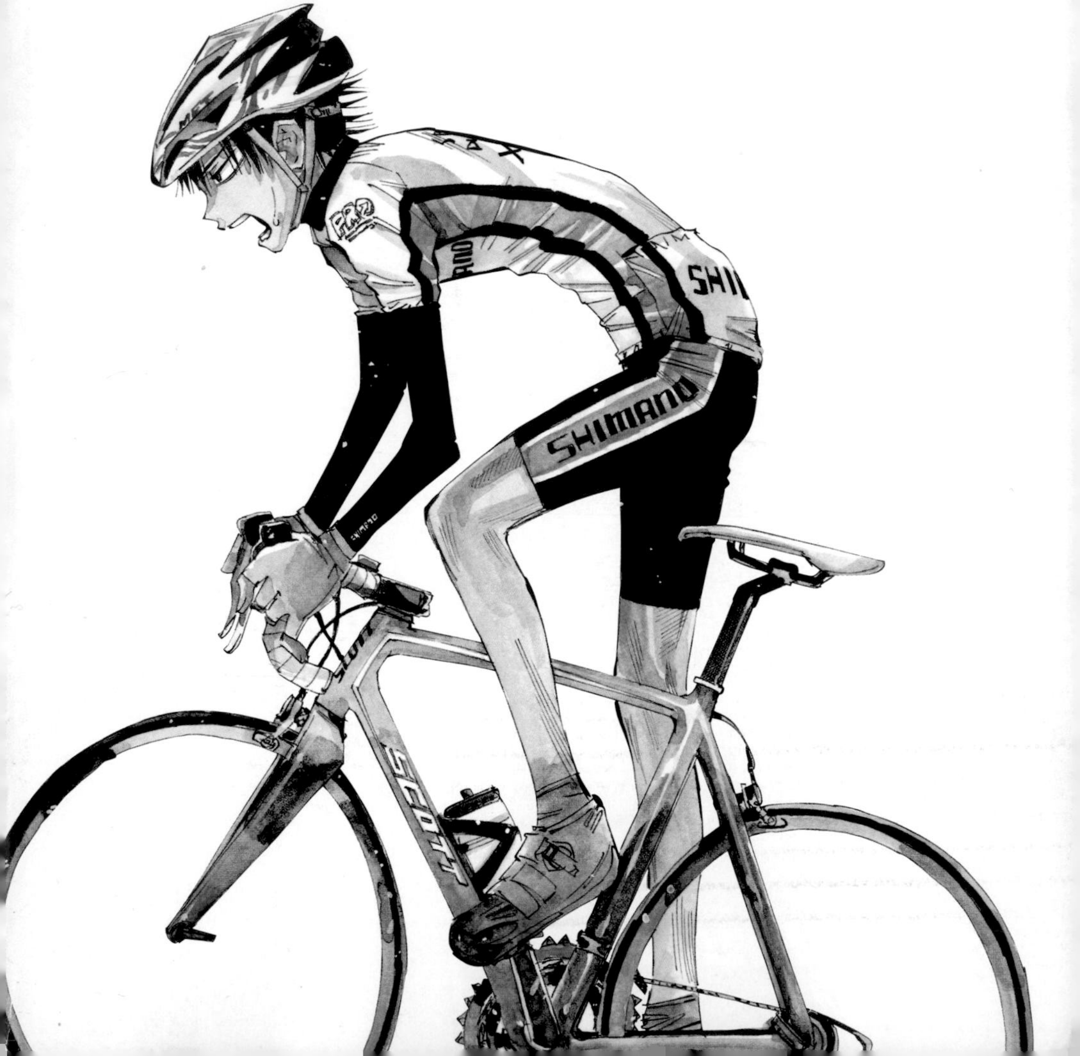
SHI
SHIMANO
SHIMANO
SCOTT

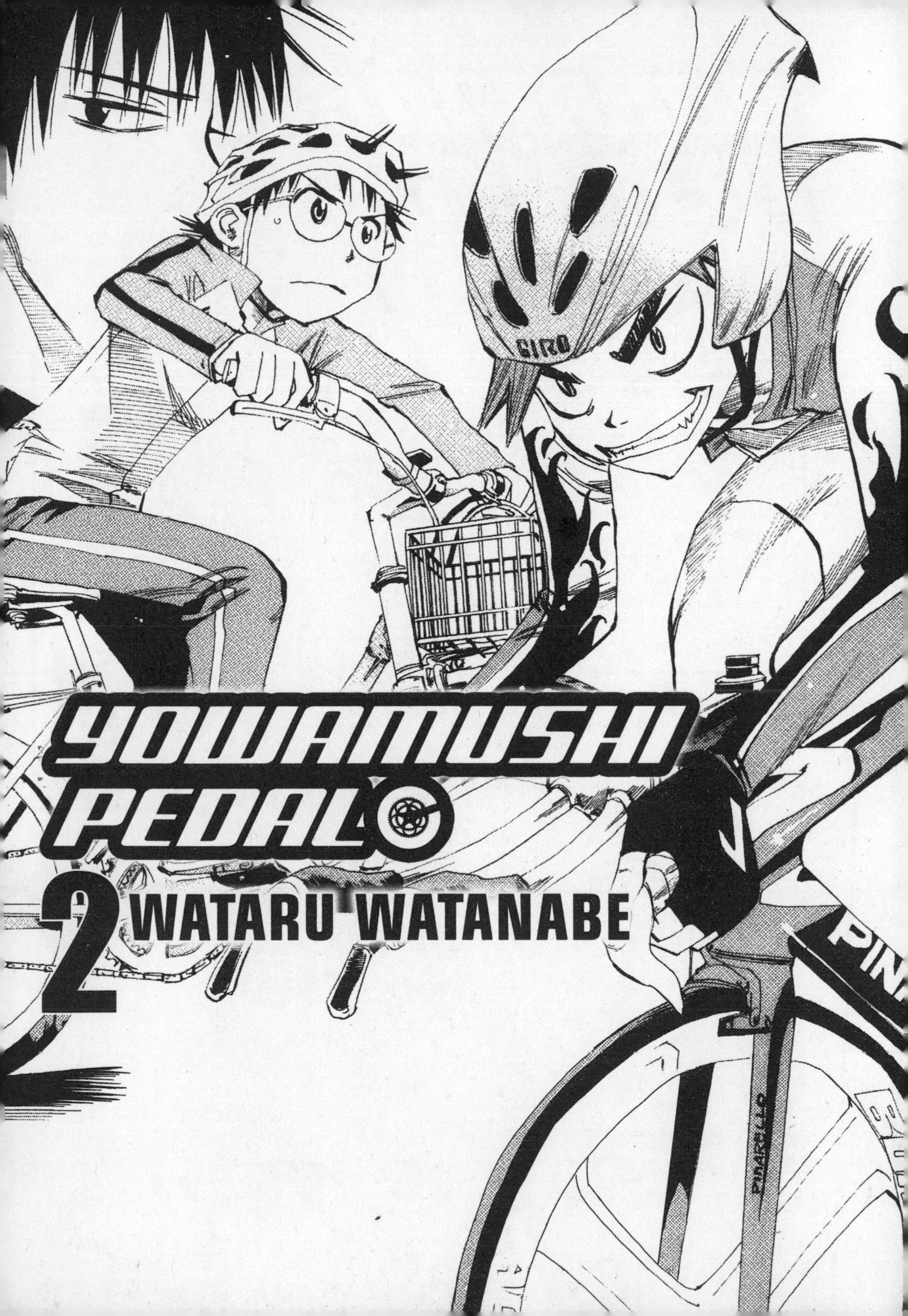
YOWAMUSHI PEDAL
2
WATARU WATANABE

YOWAMUSHI PEDAL

STORY & CHARACTER INTRODUCTION

SAKAMICHI ONODA

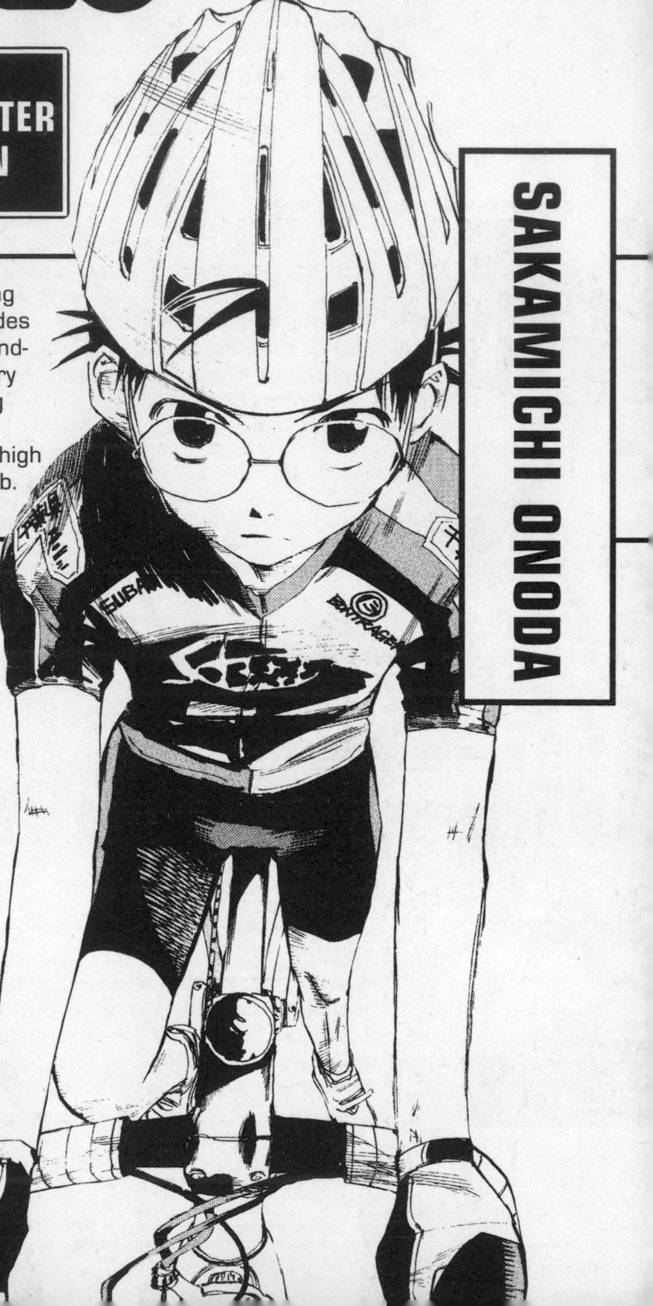

Sakamichi is an anime-loving high school student who rides his mommy bike 90km round-trip up extreme slopes every week to visit Akiba. Hearing that he has potential as a cyclist, Sakamichi joins his high school's Bicycle Racing Club.

DATA ON ONODA

Preferred Bike: Mommy Bike (maker unknown)

Cycling Style: High Cadence Racer

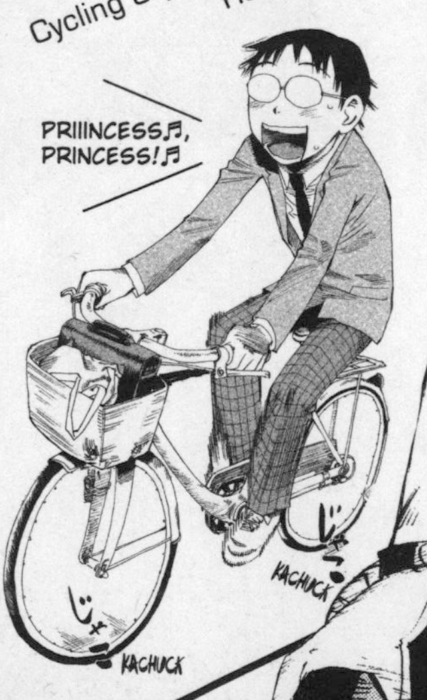
PRIIINCESS♬, PRINCESS!♬
KACHUCK
KACHUCK

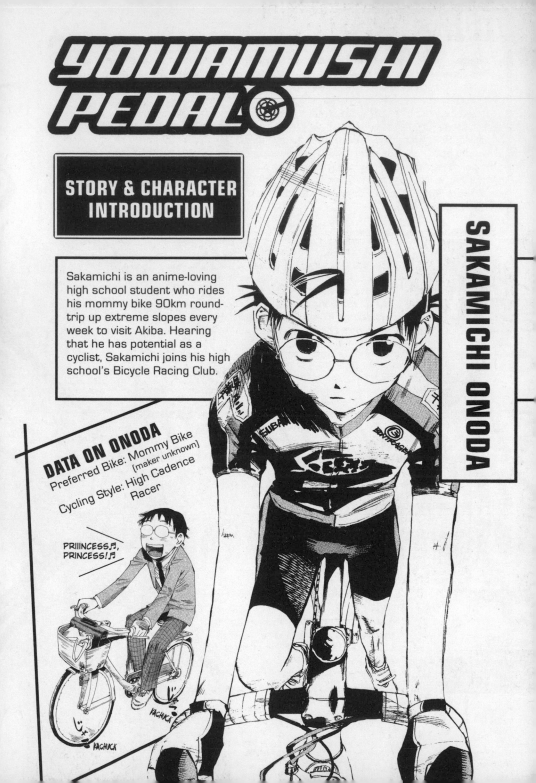

STORY

Despite a narrow loss against Imaizumi during their race up the steep Rear Gate slope, Sakamichi gets a taste of the thrill of bicycle racing for the first time. Later, during a visit to Akiba, he makes the acquaintance of a red-haired bicyclist with an Osakan accent named Naruko. When Sakamichi's bike is hit by a carelessly thrown cigarette butt, Naruko is enraged and insists Sakamichi join him in biking after the cigarette-tosser—who is in a moving car. During the wild chase with Naruko, Sakamichi fully realizes how much fun riding bicycles can be. The following day, the boys run into each other and realize they coincidentally go to the same school! Sakamichi decides to join the Bicycle Racing Club along with Naruko. However, what awaits him there is a Welcome Race pitting all the first-year members against one another! What lies in store for Sakamichi during his first real race!?

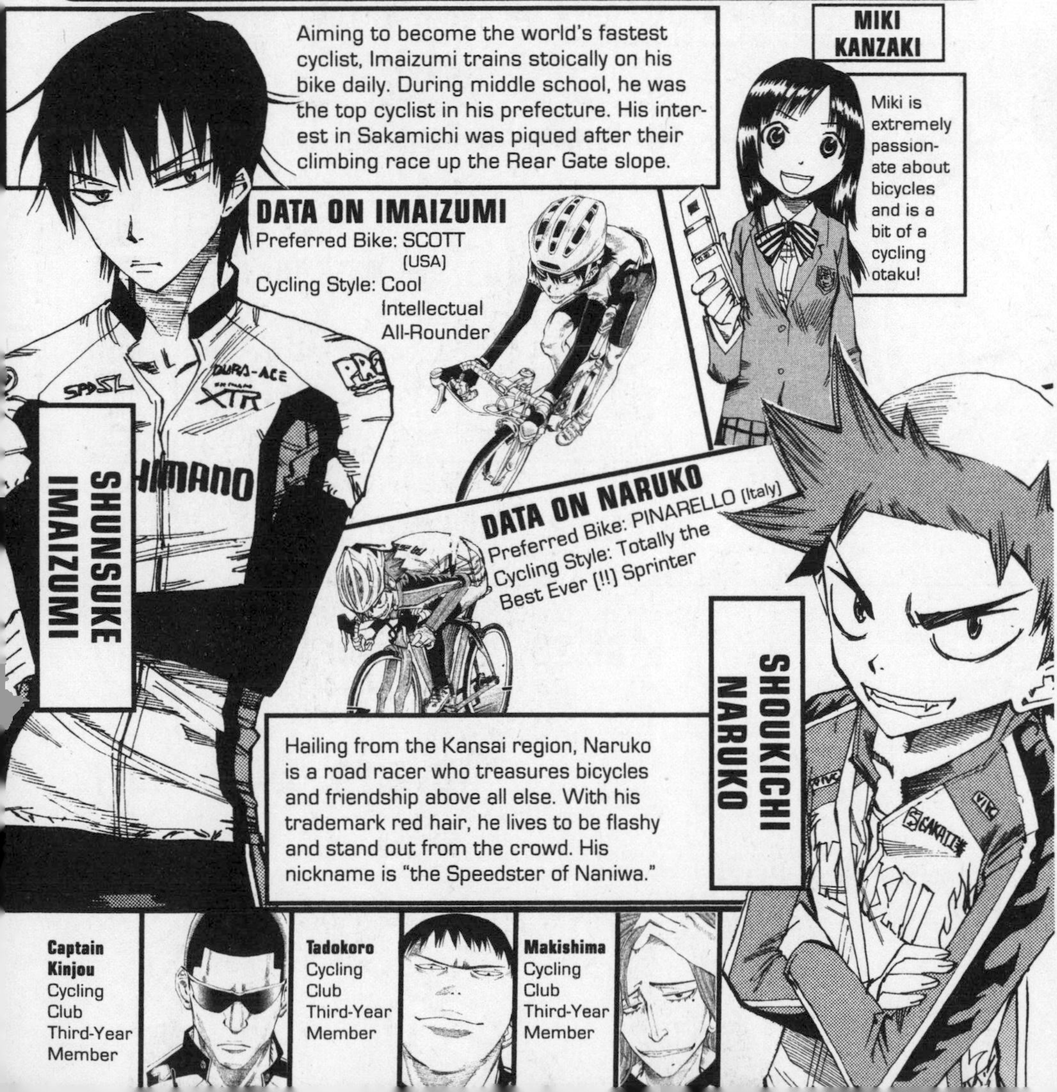

SHUNSUKE IMAIZUMI

Aiming to become the world's fastest cyclist, Imaizumi trains stoically on his bike daily. During middle school, he was the top cyclist in his prefecture. His interest in Sakamichi was piqued after their climbing race up the Rear Gate slope.

DATA ON IMAIZUMI
Preferred Bike: SCOTT (USA)
Cycling Style: Cool Intellectual All-Rounder

MIKI KANZAKI

Miki is extremely passionate about bicycles and is a bit of a cycling otaku!

SHOUKICHI NARUKO

DATA ON NARUKO
Preferred Bike: PINARELLO (Italy)
Cycling Style: Totally the Best Ever (!!) Sprinter

Hailing from the Kansai region, Naruko is a road racer who treasures bicycles and friendship above all else. With his trademark red hair, he lives to be flashy and stand out from the crowd. His nickname is "the Speedster of Naniwa."

Captain Kinjou
Cycling Club Third-Year Member

Tadokoro
Cycling Club Third-Year Member

Makishima
Cycling Club Third-Year Member

VOL.2 YOWAMUSHI PEDAL
CONTENTS

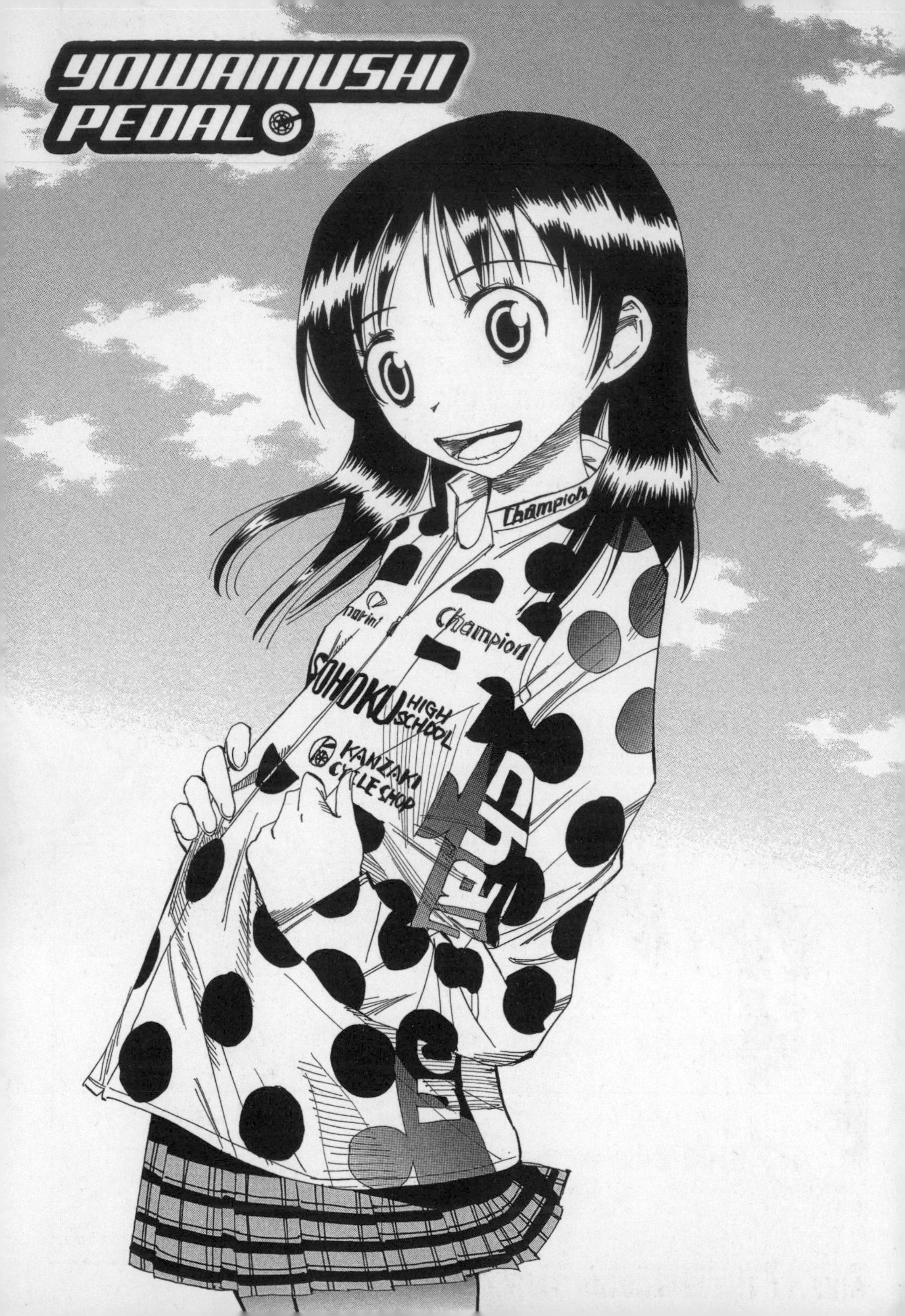
YOWAMUSHI PEDAL
Champion
Champion
SOHOKU HIGH SCHOOL
KANZAKI CYCLE SHOP

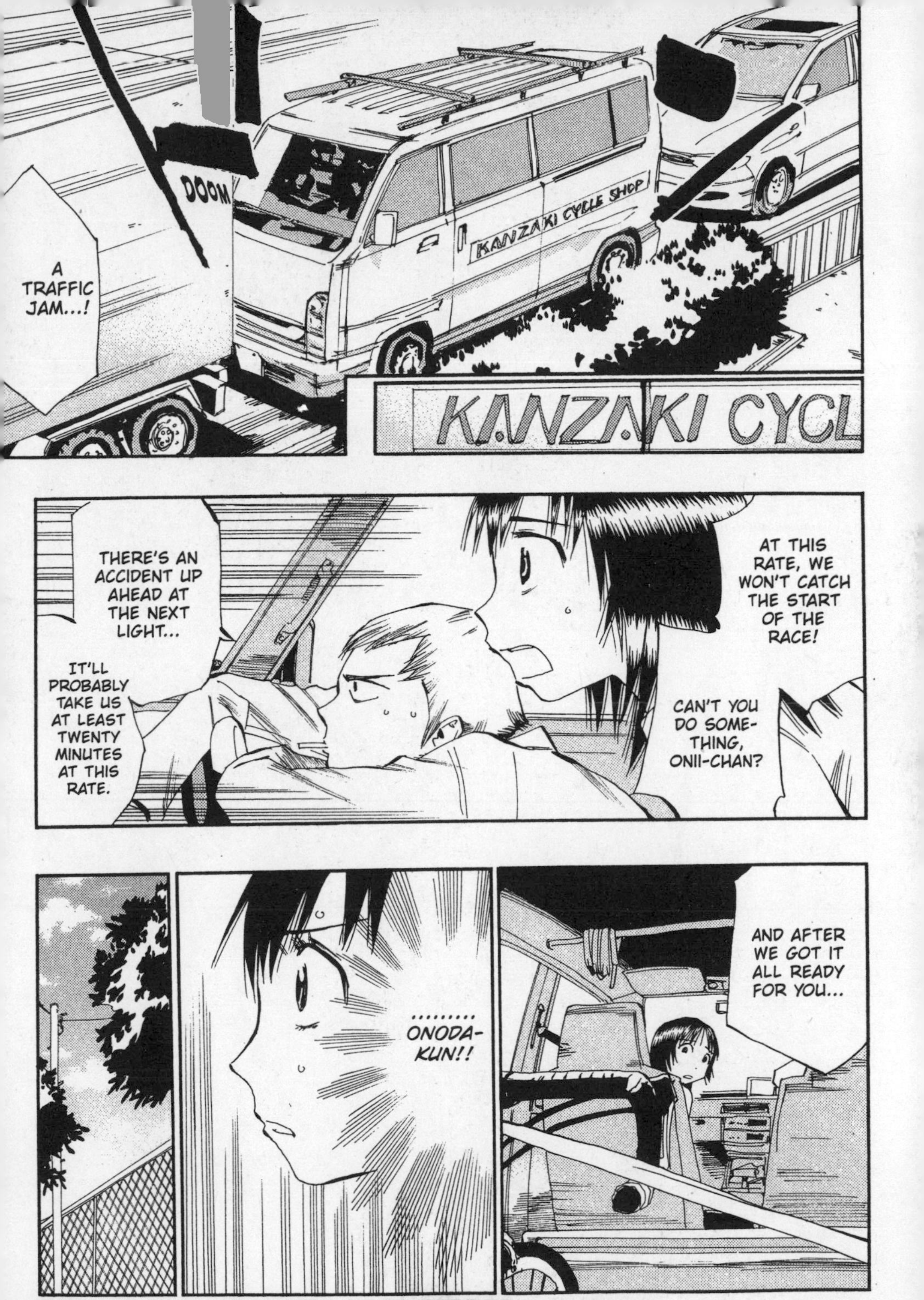
KANZAKI CYCLE SHOP
DOOM
A TRAFFIC JAM...!
KANZAKI CYCL
AT THIS RATE, WE WON'T CATCH THE START OF THE RACE!
CAN'T YOU DO SOME-THING, ONII-CHAN?
THERE'S AN ACCIDENT UP AHEAD AT THE NEXT LIGHT...
IT'LL PROBABLY TAKE US AT LEAST TWENTY MINUTES AT THIS RATE.
AND AFTER WE GOT IT ALL READY FOR YOU...
.... ONODA-KUN!!

RIDE.17 THE WELCOME RACE STARTS

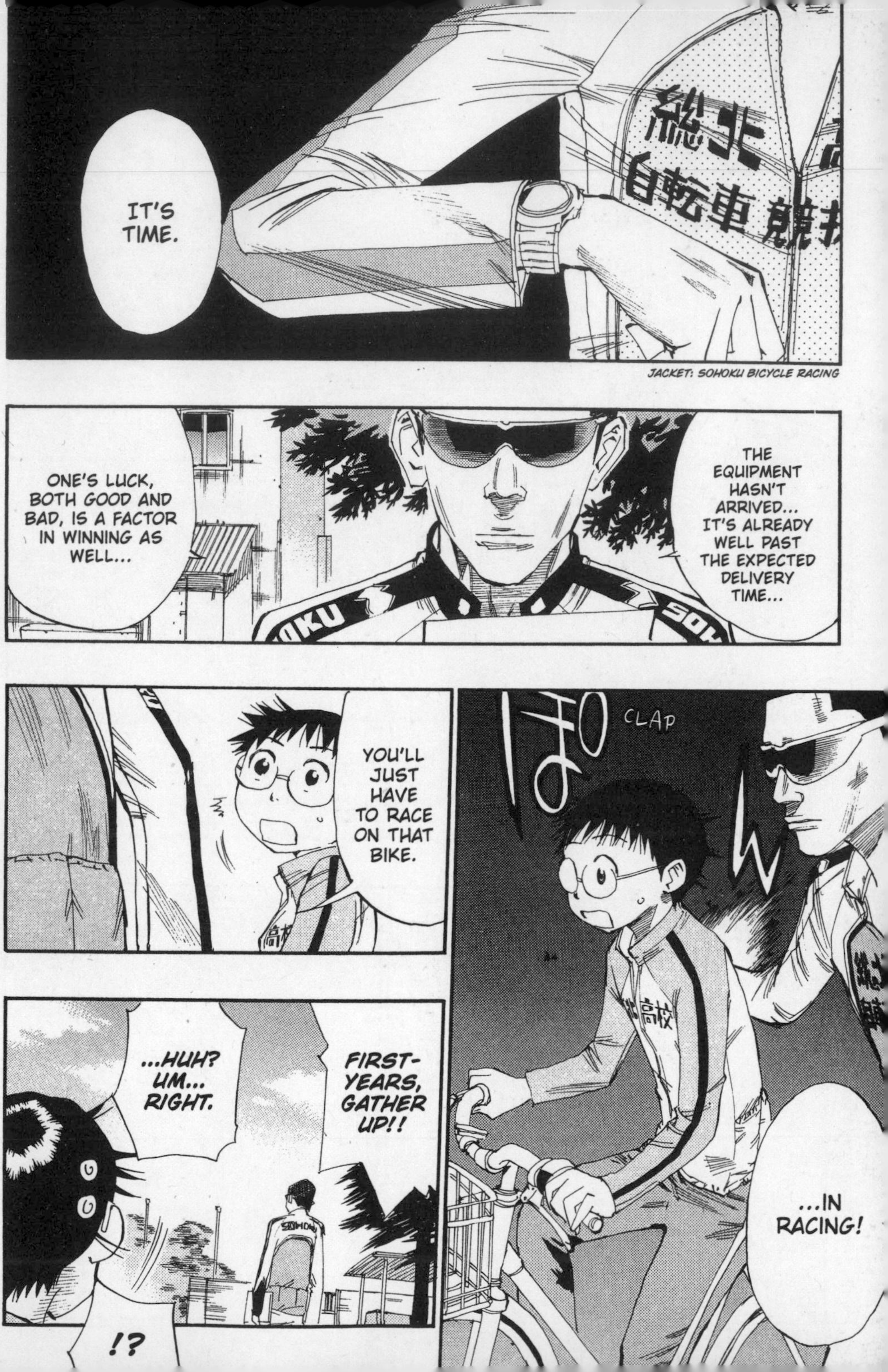
IT'S TIME.
JACKET: SOHOKU BICYCLE RACING
THE EQUIPMENT HASN'T ARRIVED... IT'S ALREADY WELL PAST THE EXPECTED DELIVERY TIME...
ONE'S LUCK, BOTH GOOD AND BAD, IS A FACTOR IN WINNING AS WELL...
CLAP
...IN RACING!
YOU'LL JUST HAVE TO RACE ON THAT BIKE.
FIRST-YEARS, GATHER UP!!
...HUH? UM... RIGHT.
!?

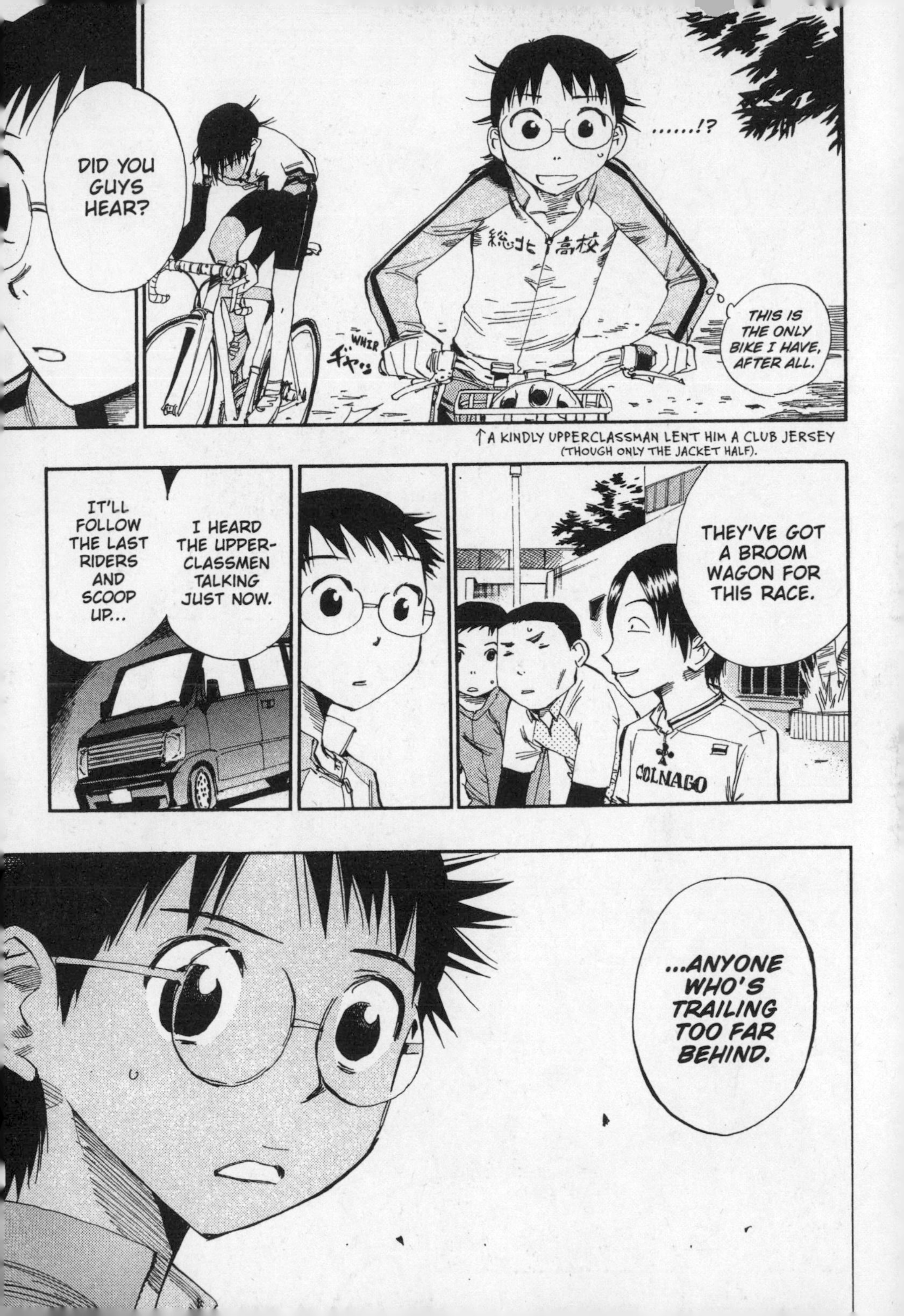
......!?
THIS IS THE ONLY BIKE I HAVE, AFTER ALL.
↑A KINDLY UPPERCLASSMAN LENT HIM A CLUB JERSEY (THOUGH ONLY THE JACKET HALF).
WHIR
DID YOU GUYS HEAR?
THEY'VE GOT A BROOM WAGON FOR THIS RACE.
COLNAGO
I HEARD THE UPPER-CLASSMEN TALKING JUST NOW.
IT'LL FOLLOW THE LAST RIDERS AND SCOOP UP...
...ANYONE WHO'S TRAILING TOO FAR BEHIND.

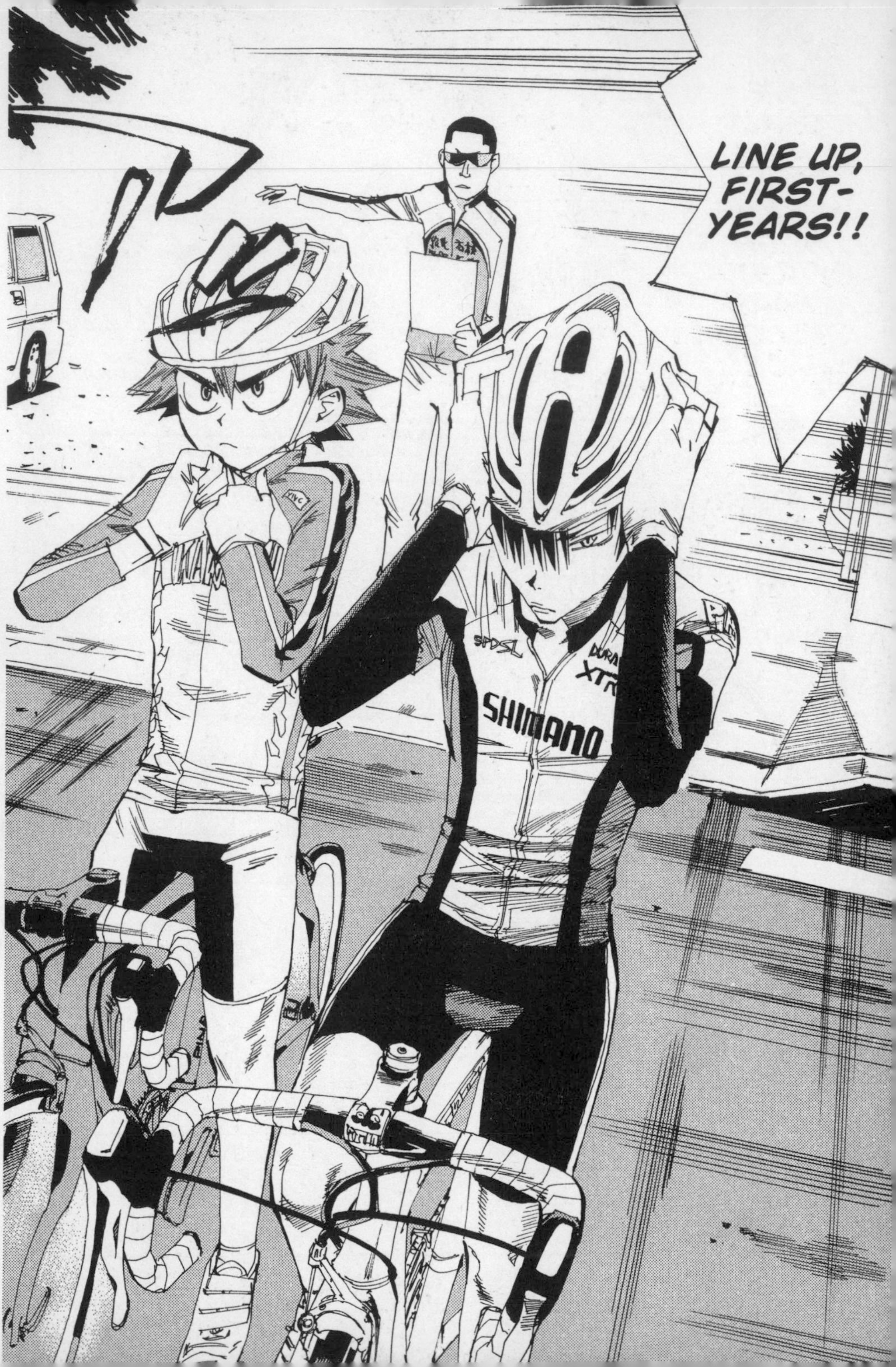
LINE UP, FIRST-YEARS!!

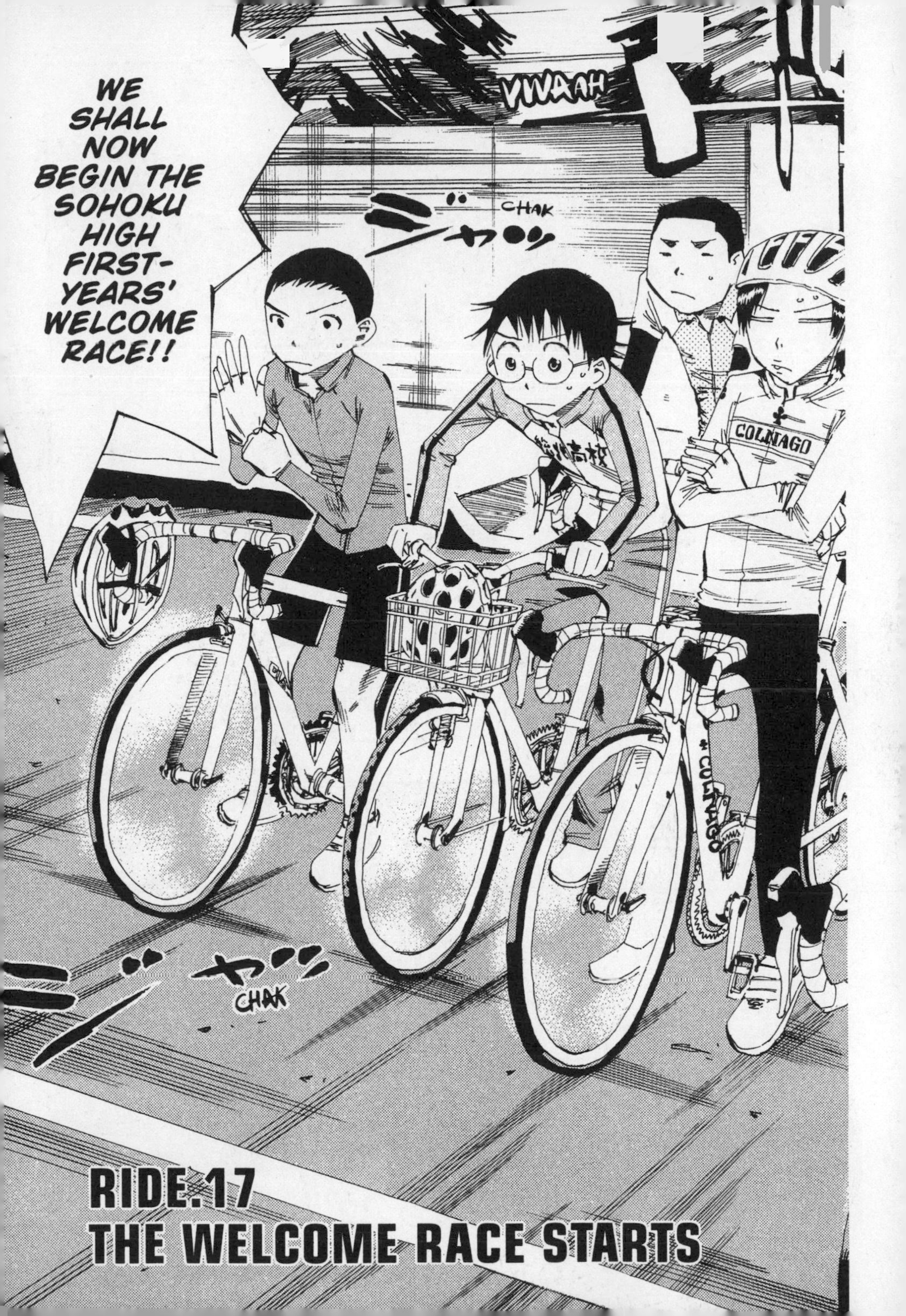
VWAAH
WE SHALL NOW BEGIN THE SOHOKU HIGH FIRST-YEARS' WELCOME RACE!!
CHAK
COLNAGO
CHAK

RIDE.17 THE WELCOME RACE STARTS

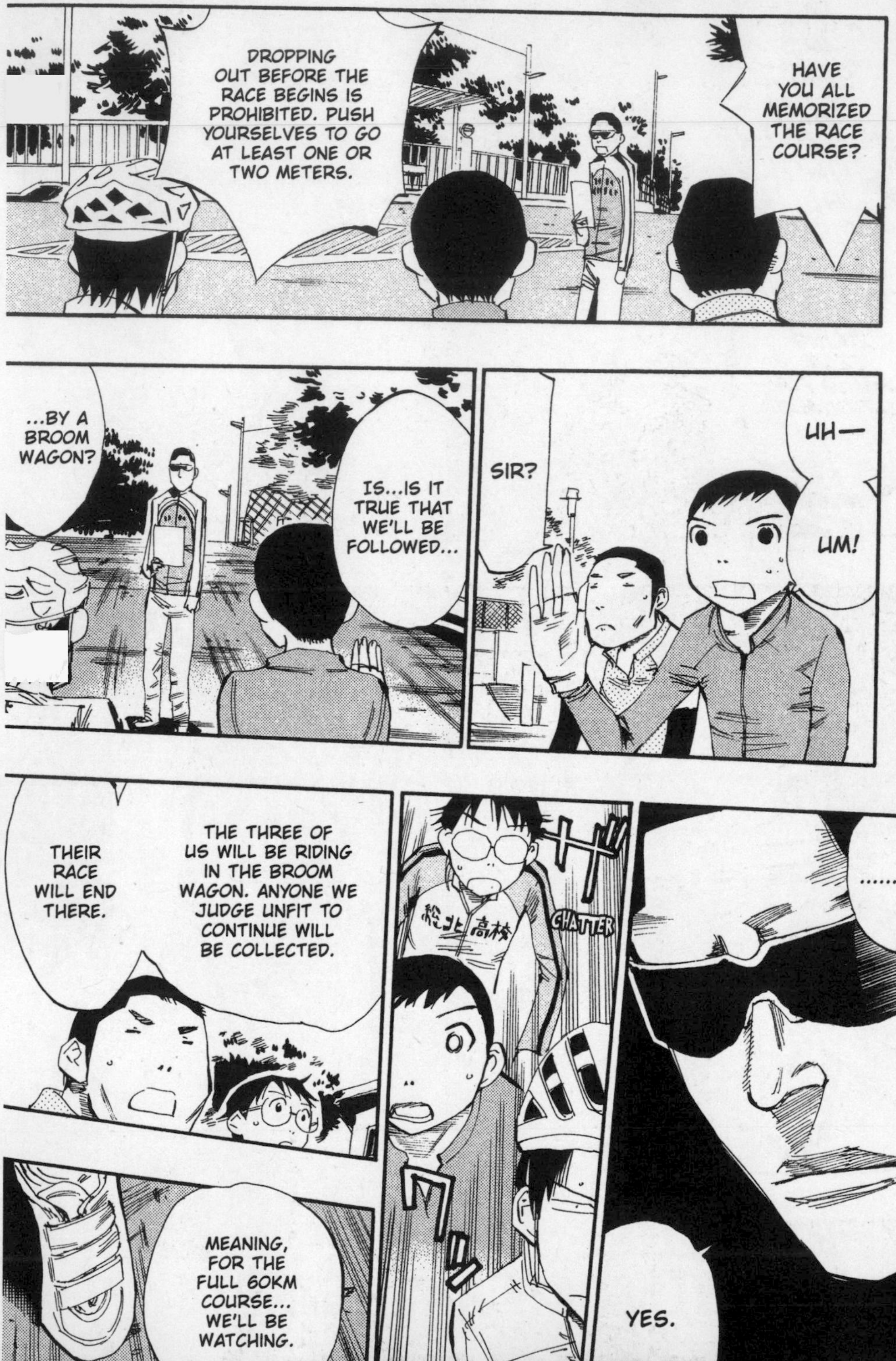
HAVE YOU ALL MEMORIZED THE RACE COURSE?
DROPPING OUT BEFORE THE RACE BEGINS IS PROHIBITED. PUSH YOURSELVES TO GO AT LEAST ONE OR TWO METERS.
UH—
UM!
SIR?
IS...IS IT TRUE THAT WE'LL BE FOLLOWED...
...BY A BROOM WAGON?
....
YES.
総北高校
CHATTER
THE THREE OF US WILL BE RIDING IN THE BROOM WAGON. ANYONE WE JUDGE UNFIT TO CONTINUE WILL BE COLLECTED.
THEIR RACE WILL END THERE.
MEANING, FOR THE FULL 60KM COURSE... WE'LL BE WATCHING.

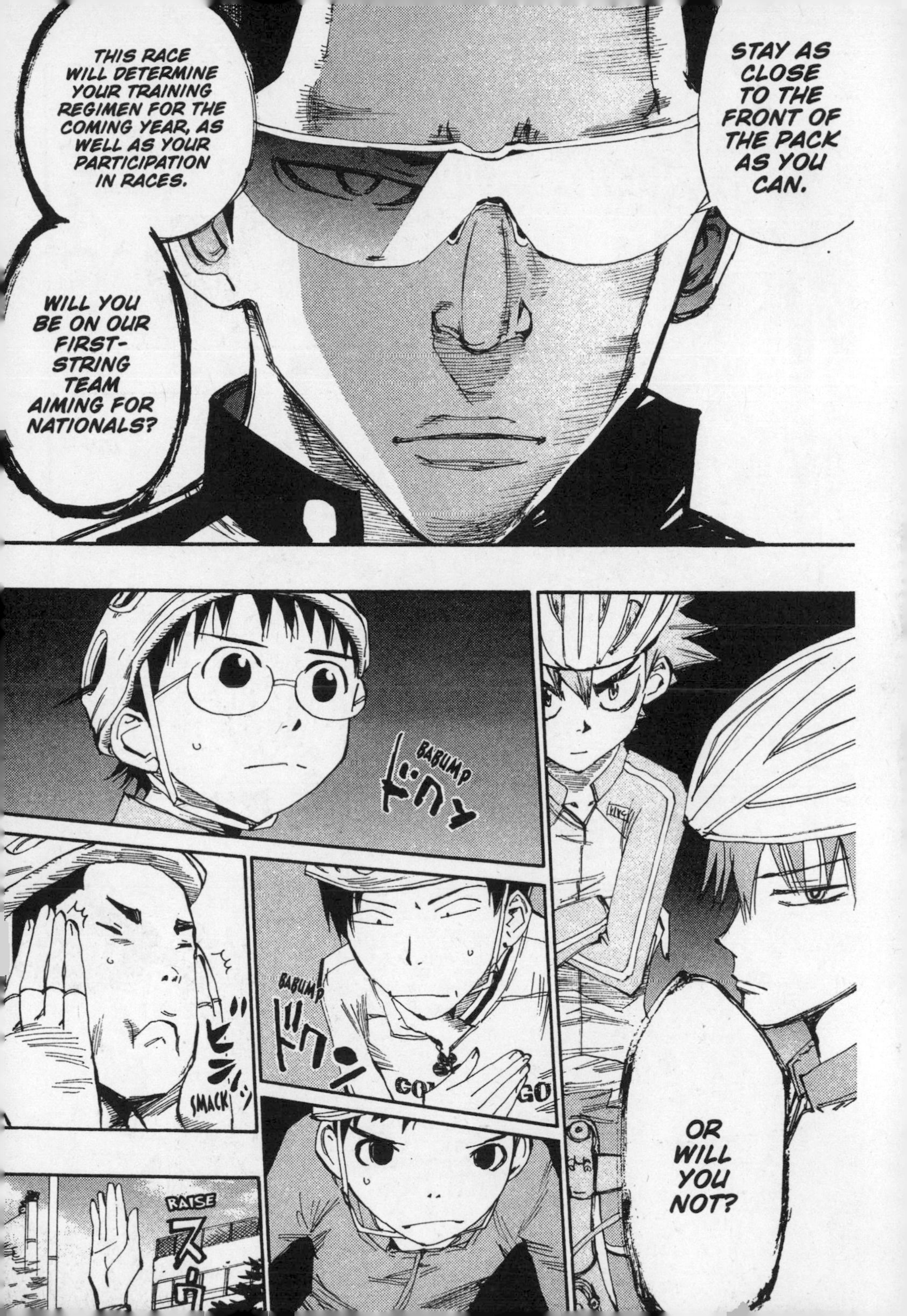
STAY AS CLOSE TO THE FRONT OF THE PACK AS YOU CAN.
THIS RACE WILL DETERMINE YOUR TRAINING REGIMEN FOR THE COMING YEAR, AS WELL AS YOUR PARTICIPATION IN RACES.
WILL YOU BE ON OUR FIRST-STRING TEAM AIMING FOR NATIONALS?
OR WILL YOU NOT?
BABUMP
ドクン
BABUMP
ドクン
SMACK
RAISE

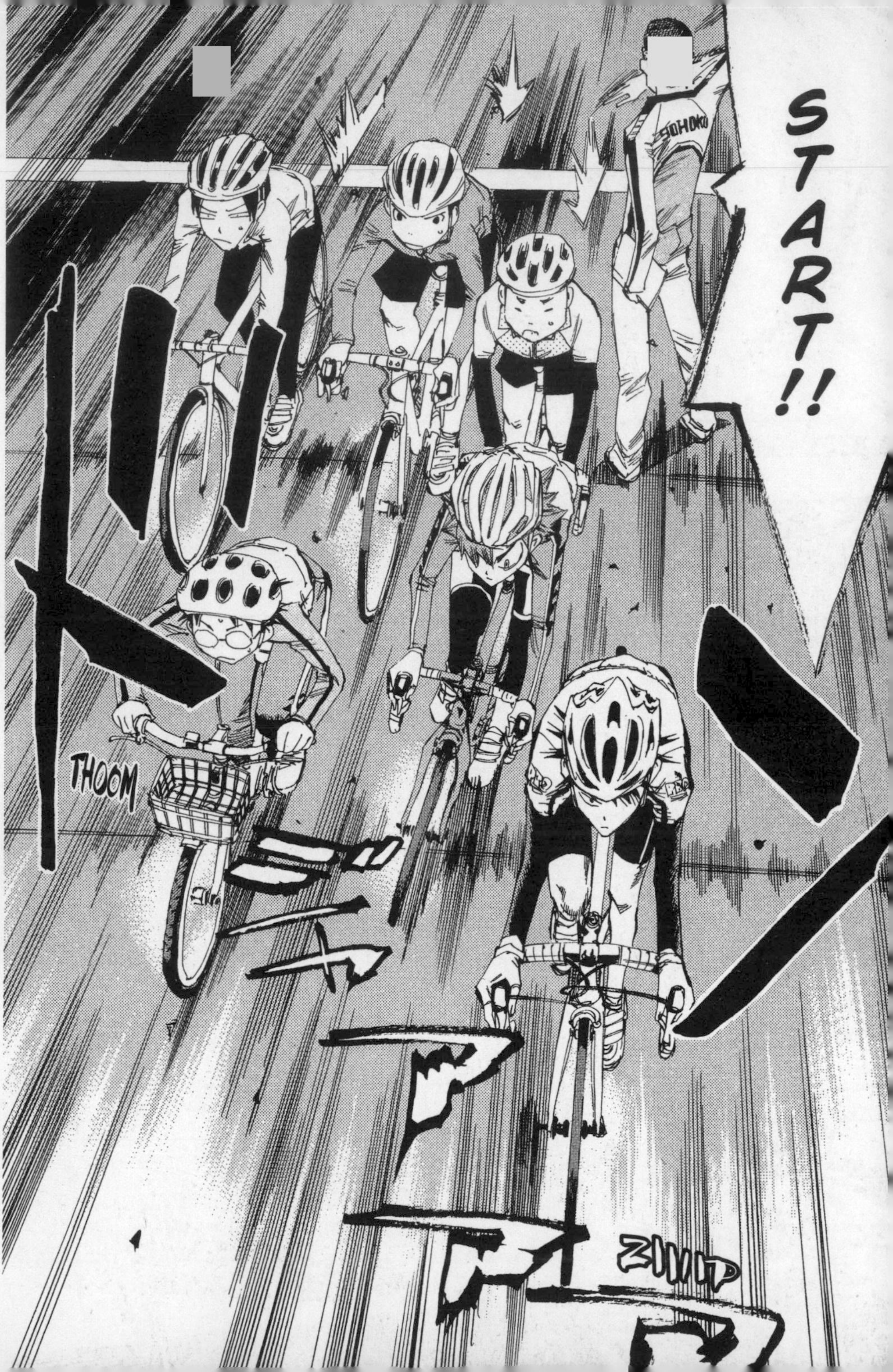
START!!
SOHOKU
THOOM
ZWIP

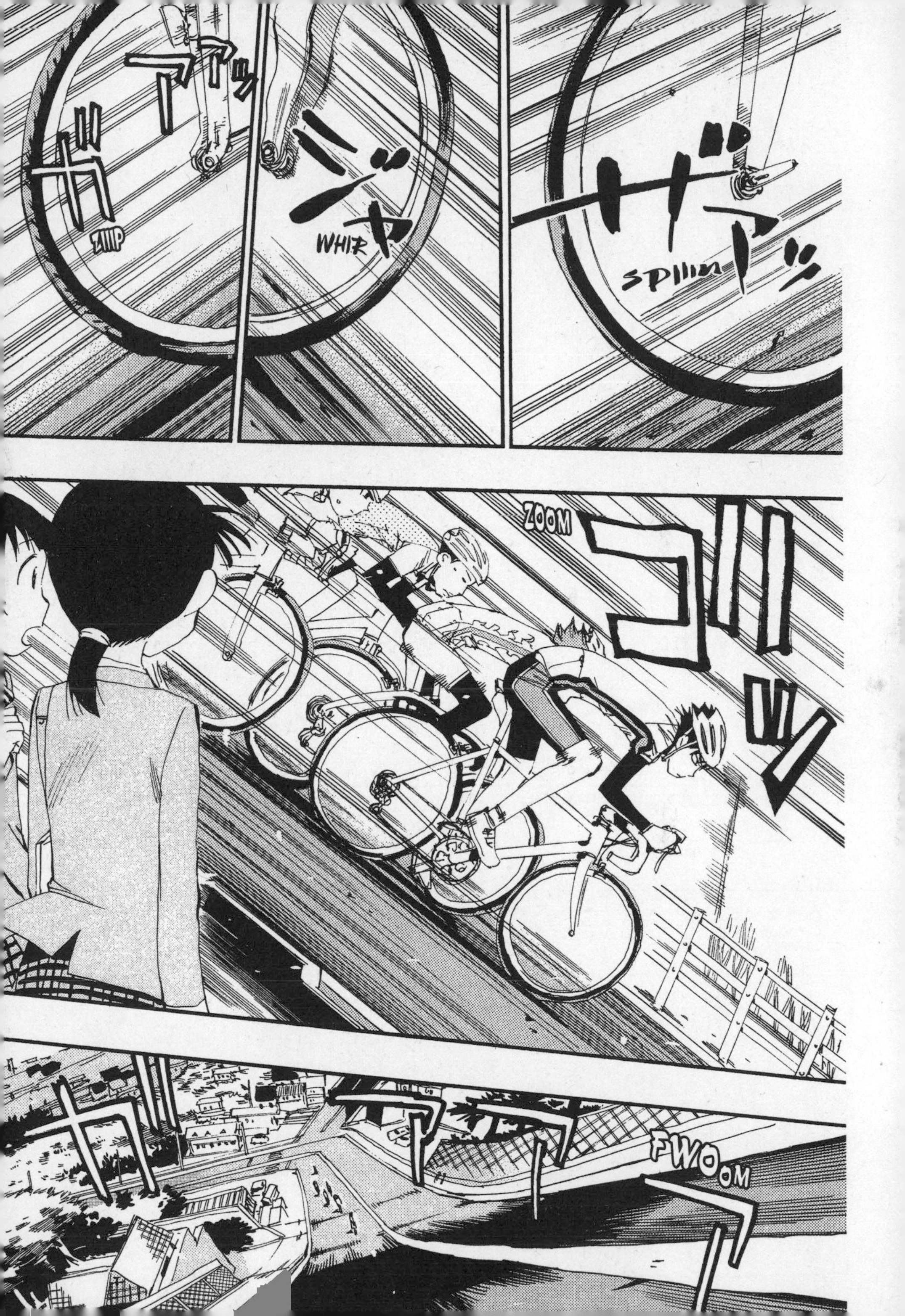

ザアアッ
SPIIIIN
ジャ
WHIR
ガアアッ
ZIP
ゴオオッ
ZOOM
FWOoom

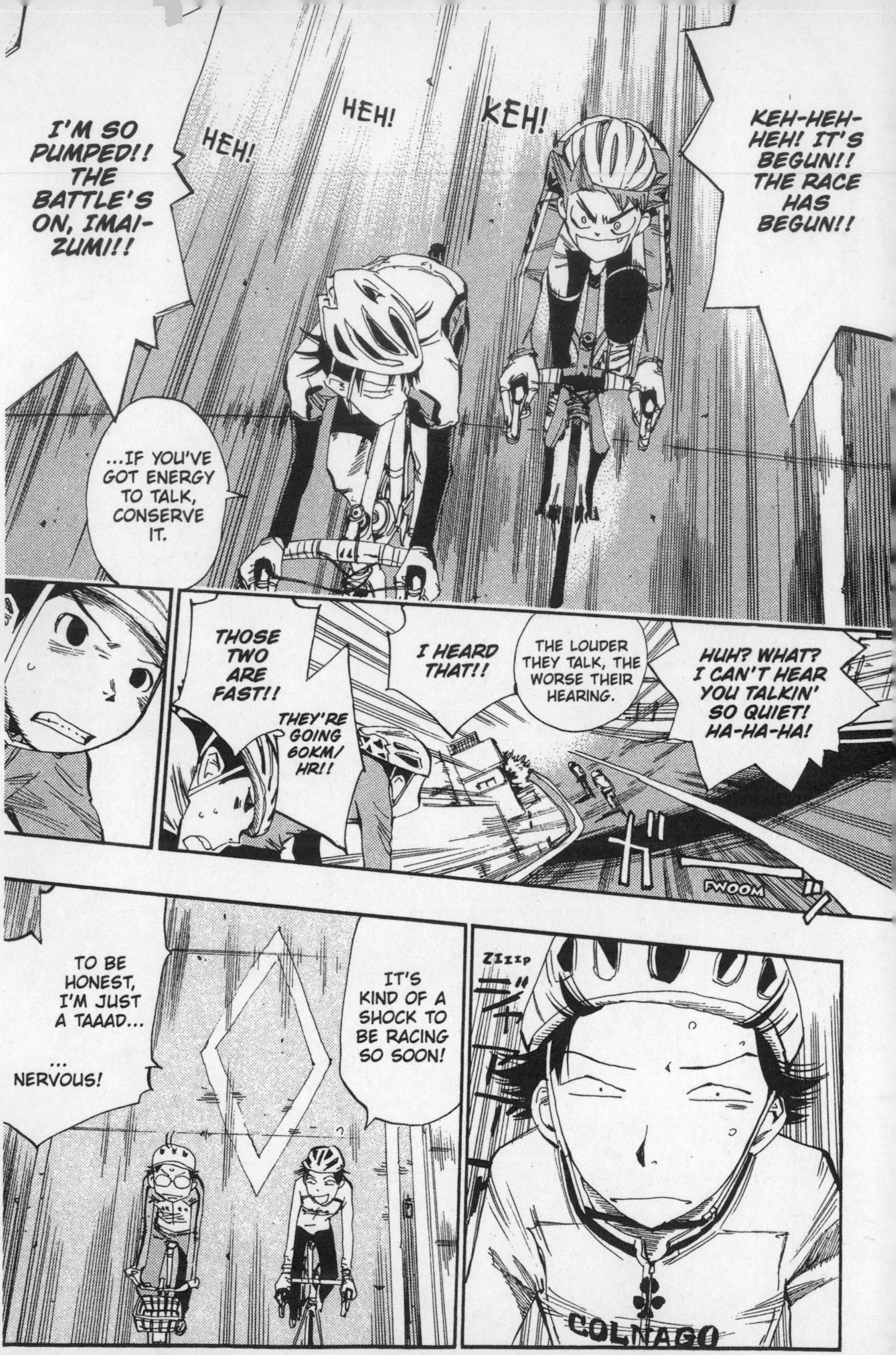
KEH-HEH-HEH! IT'S BEGUN!! THE RACE HAS BEGUN!!
KEH!
HEH!
HEH!
I'M SO PUMPED!! THE BATTLE'S ON, IMAI-ZUMI!!
...IF YOU'VE GOT ENERGY TO TALK, CONSERVE IT.
HUH? WHAT? I CAN'T HEAR YOU TALKIN' SO QUIET! HA-HA-HA!
THE LOUDER THEY TALK, THE WORSE THEIR HEARING.
I HEARD THAT!!
THOSE TWO ARE FAST!!
THEY'RE GOING 60KM/HR!!
FWOOM
ZIIIp
IT'S KIND OF A SHOCK TO BE RACING SO SOON!
TO BE HONEST, I'M JUST A TAAAD...
... NERVOUS!
COLNAGO

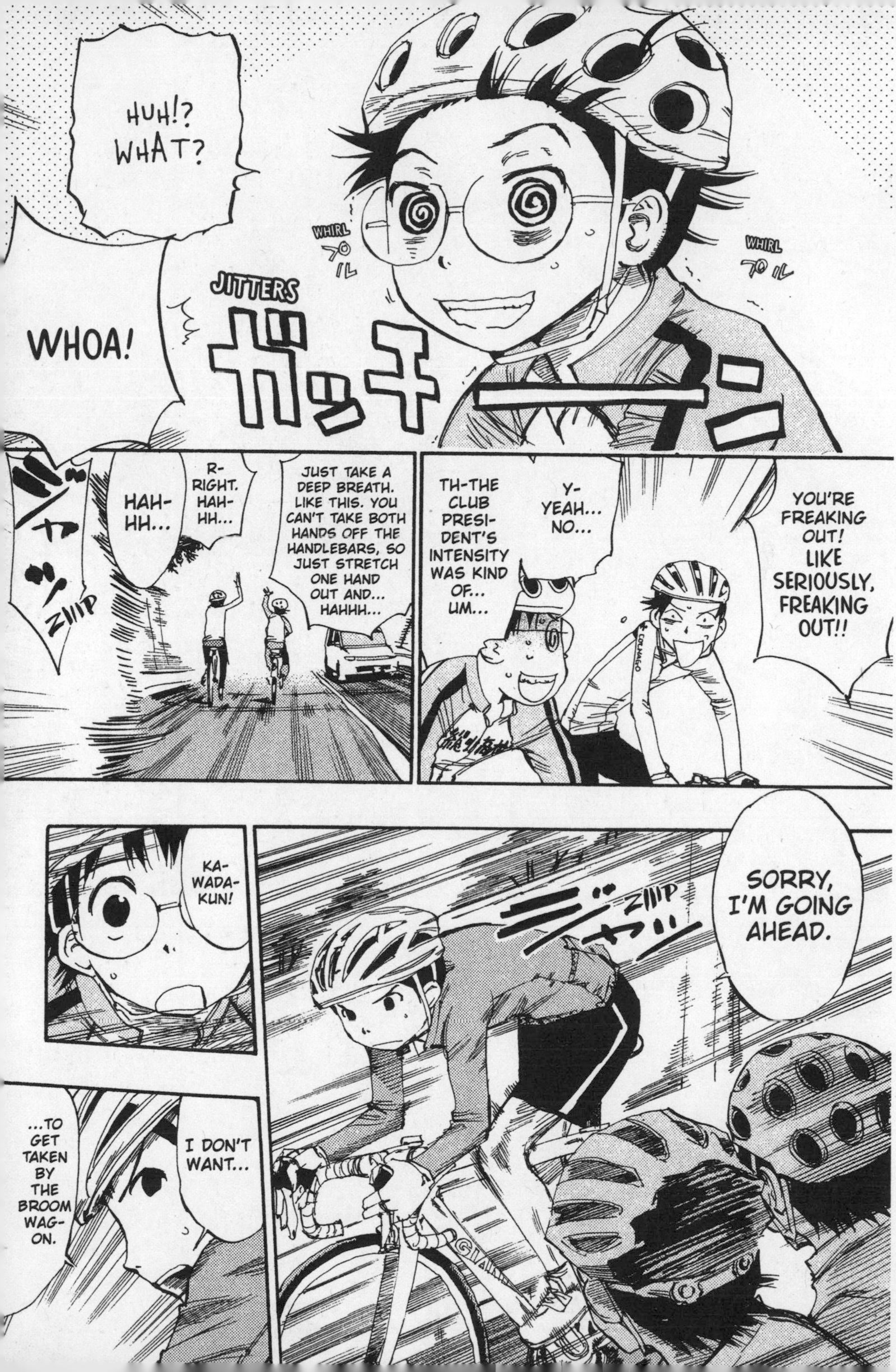
WHIRL
WHIRL
HUH!? WHAT?
JITTERS
WHOA!
YOU'RE FREAKING OUT! LIKE SERIOUSLY, FREAKING OUT!!
Y-YEAH... NO...
TH-THE CLUB PRESIDENT'S INTENSITY WAS KIND OF... UM...
JUST TAKE A DEEP BREATH. LIKE THIS. YOU CAN'T TAKE BOTH HANDS OFF THE HANDLEBARS, SO JUST STRETCH ONE HAND OUT AND... HAHHH...
R-RIGHT. HAH-HH...
HAH-HH...
ZIIIP
SORRY, I'M GOING AHEAD.
ZIIIP
KA-WADA-KUN!
I DON'T WANT...
...TO GET TAKEN BY THE BROOM WAG-ON.

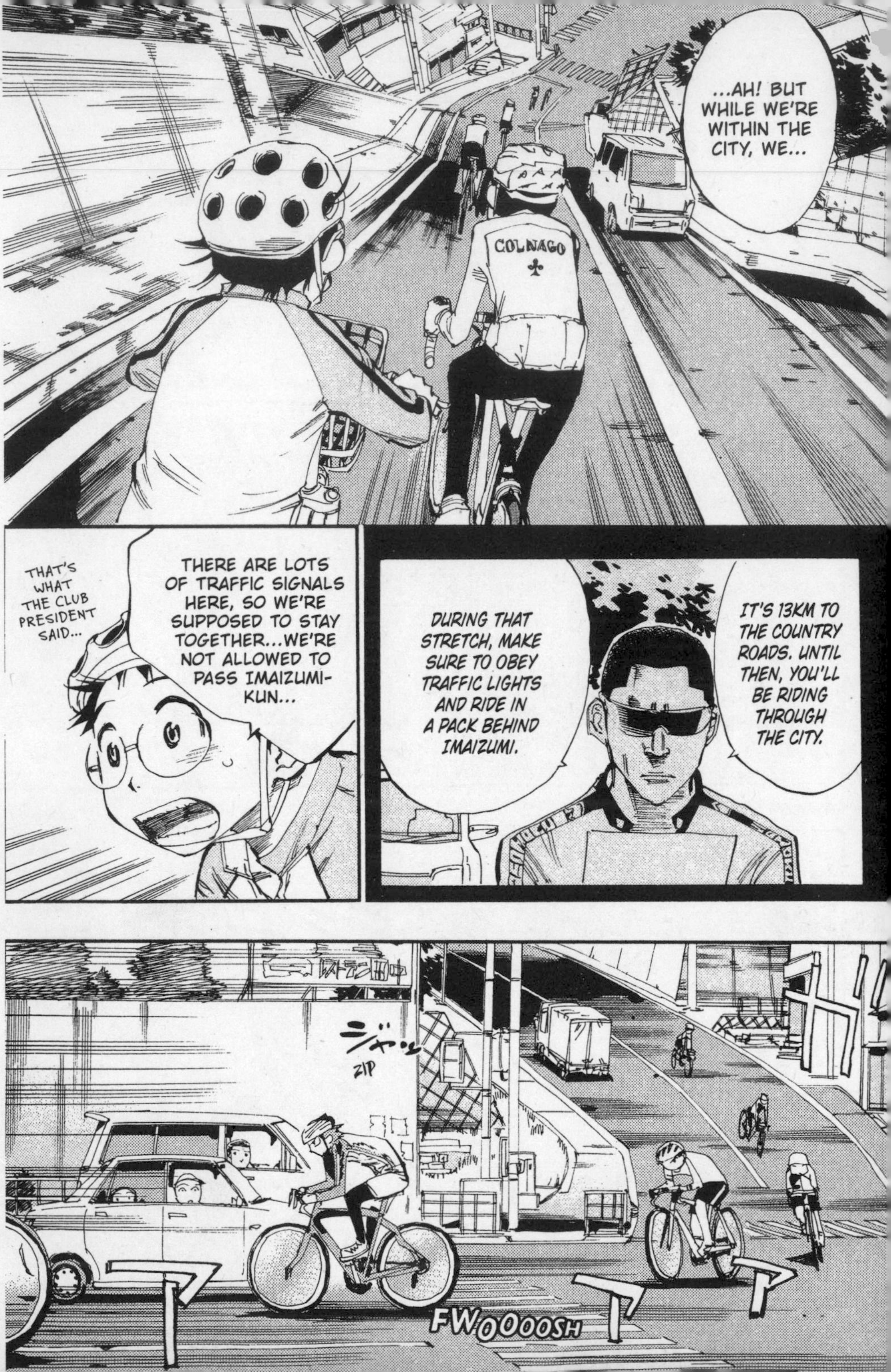
...AH! BUT WHILE WE'RE WITHIN THE CITY, WE...
IT'S 13KM TO THE COUNTRY ROADS. UNTIL THEN, YOU'LL BE RIDING THROUGH THE CITY.
DURING THAT STRETCH, MAKE SURE TO OBEY TRAFFIC LIGHTS AND RIDE IN A PACK BEHIND IMAIZUMI.
THERE ARE LOTS OF TRAFFIC SIGNALS HERE, SO WE'RE SUPPOSED TO STAY TOGETHER...WE'RE NOT ALLOWED TO PASS IMAIZUMI-KUN...
THAT'S WHAT THE CLUB PRESIDENT SAID...
ジャッ
ZIP
FWOOOOSH

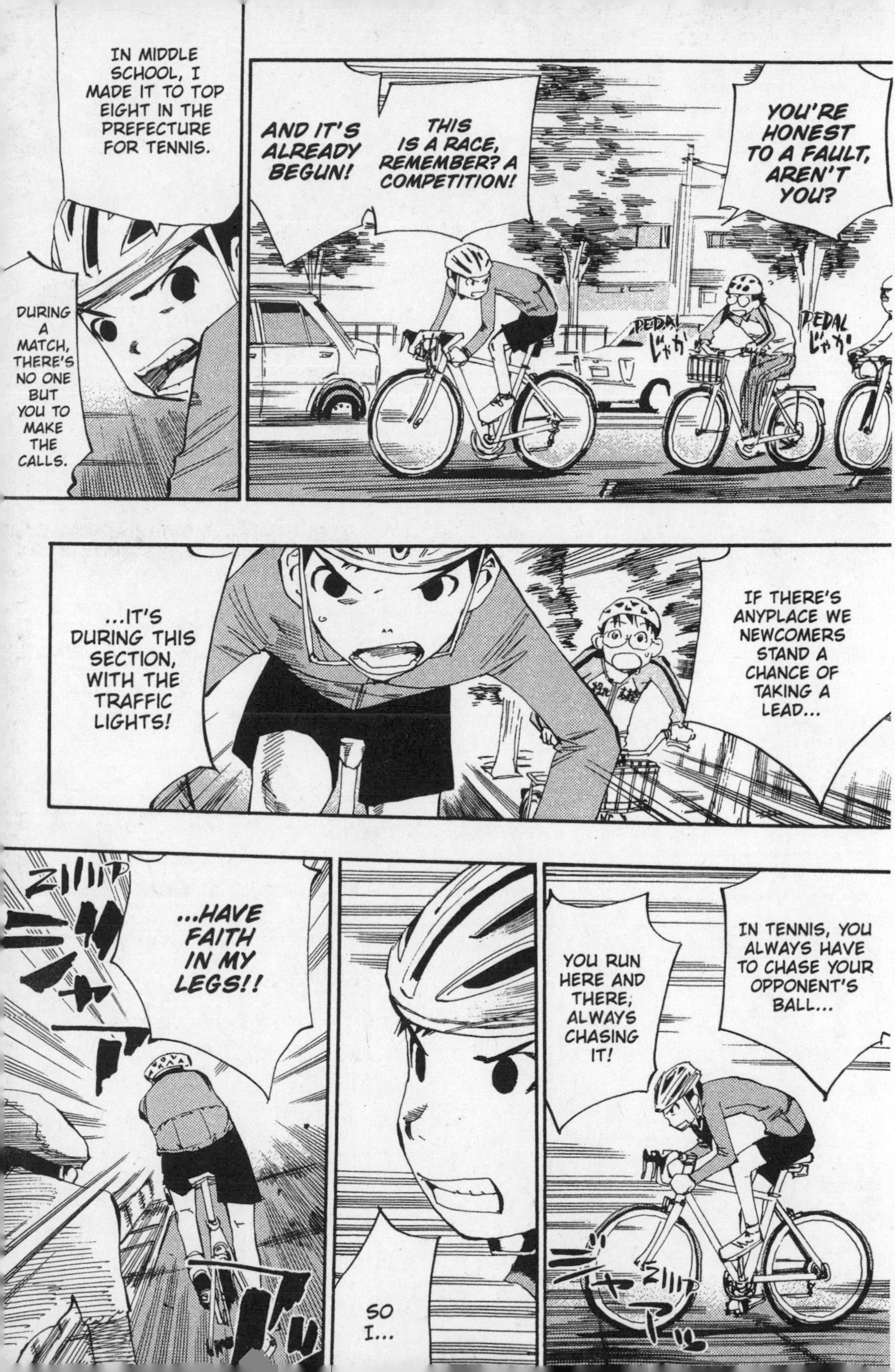
YOU'RE HONEST TO A FAULT, AREN'T YOU?
THIS IS A RACE, REMEMBER? A COMPETITION!
AND IT'S ALREADY BEGUN!
PEDAL
PEDAL
IN MIDDLE SCHOOL, I MADE IT TO TOP EIGHT IN THE PREFECTURE FOR TENNIS.
DURING A MATCH, THERE'S NO ONE BUT YOU TO MAKE THE CALLS.
IF THERE'S ANYPLACE WE NEWCOMERS STAND A CHANCE OF TAKING A LEAD...
...IT'S DURING THIS SECTION, WITH THE TRAFFIC LIGHTS!
IN TENNIS, YOU ALWAYS HAVE TO CHASE YOUR OPPONENT'S BALL...
YOU RUN HERE AND THERE, ALWAYS CHASING IT!
ZIIIP
SO I...
...HAVE FAITH IN MY LEGS!!
ZIIIP

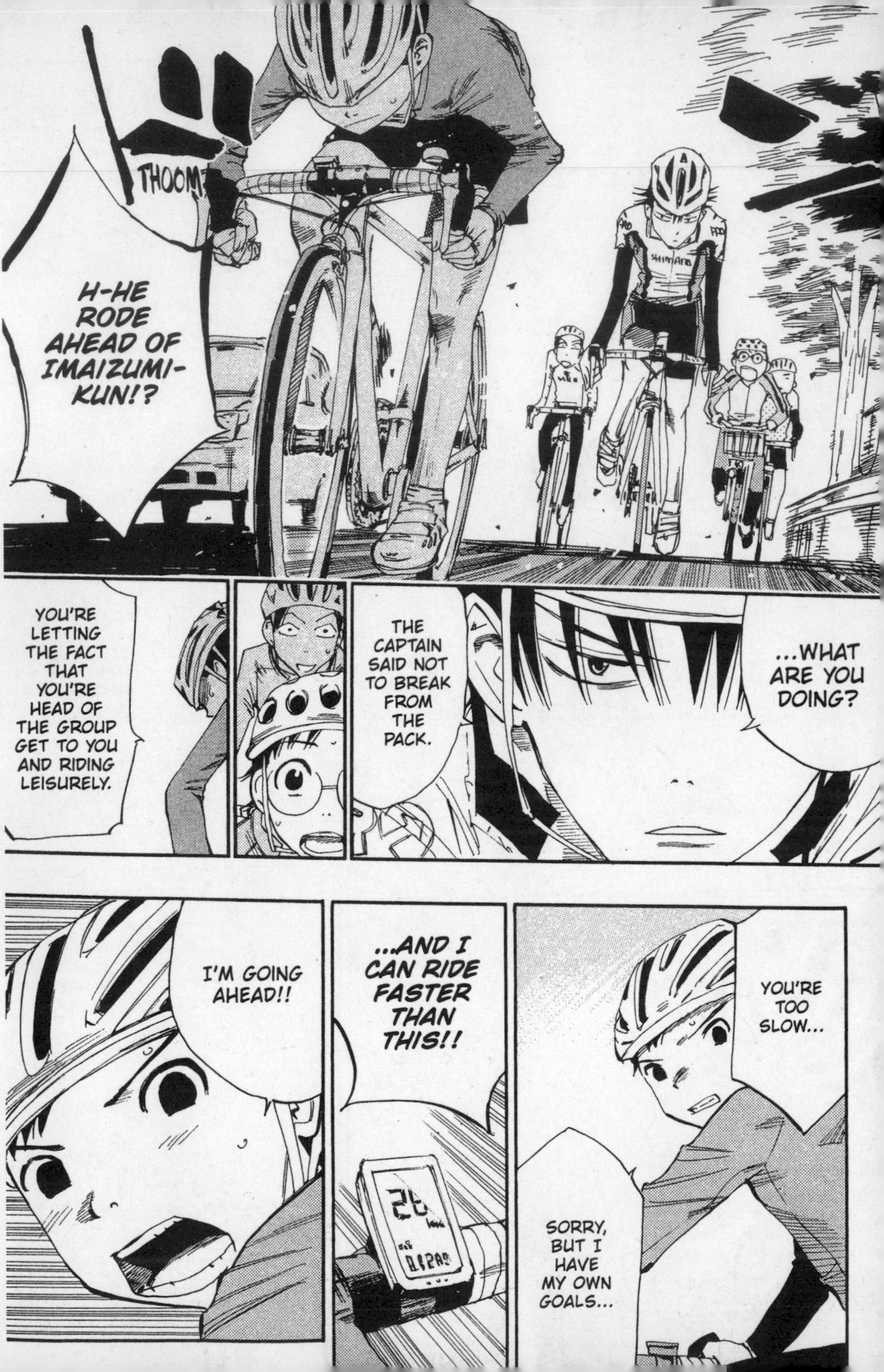
THOOM!
H-HE RODE AHEAD OF IMAIZUMI-KUN!?
...WHAT ARE YOU DOING?
THE CAPTAIN SAID NOT TO BREAK FROM THE PACK.
YOU'RE LETTING THE FACT THAT YOU'RE HEAD OF THE GROUP GET TO YOU AND RIDING LEISURELY.
YOU'RE TOO SLOW...
SORRY, BUT I HAVE MY OWN GOALS...
...AND I CAN RIDE FASTER THAN THIS!!
I'M GOING AHEAD!!

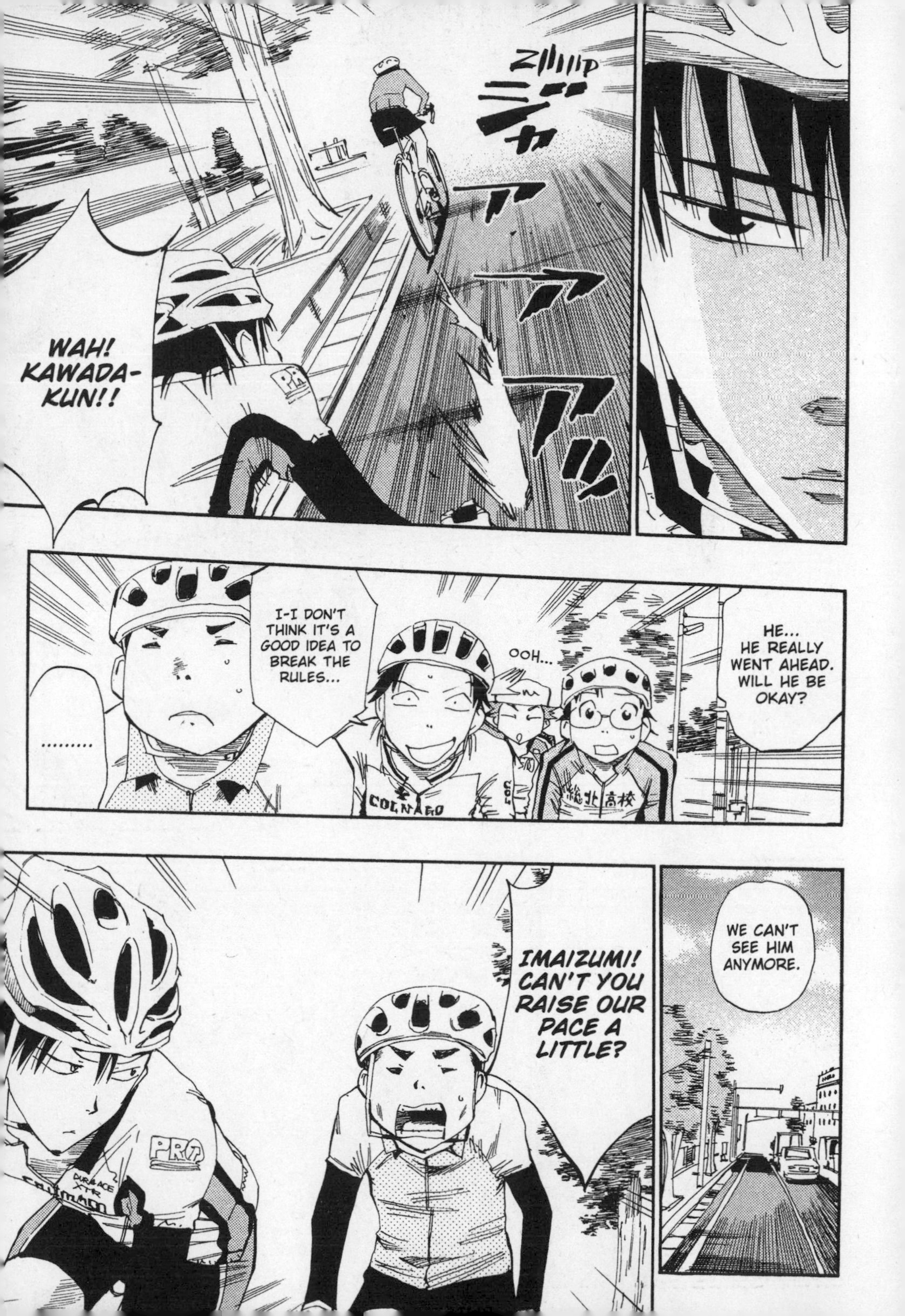
ZIIIIP
WAH! KAWADA-KUN!!
HE... HE REALLY WENT AHEAD. WILL HE BE OKAY?
OOH...
I-I DON'T THINK IT'S A GOOD IDEA TO BREAK THE RULES...
....
WE CAN'T SEE HIM ANYMORE.
IMAIZUMI! CAN'T YOU RAISE OUR PACE A LITTLE?

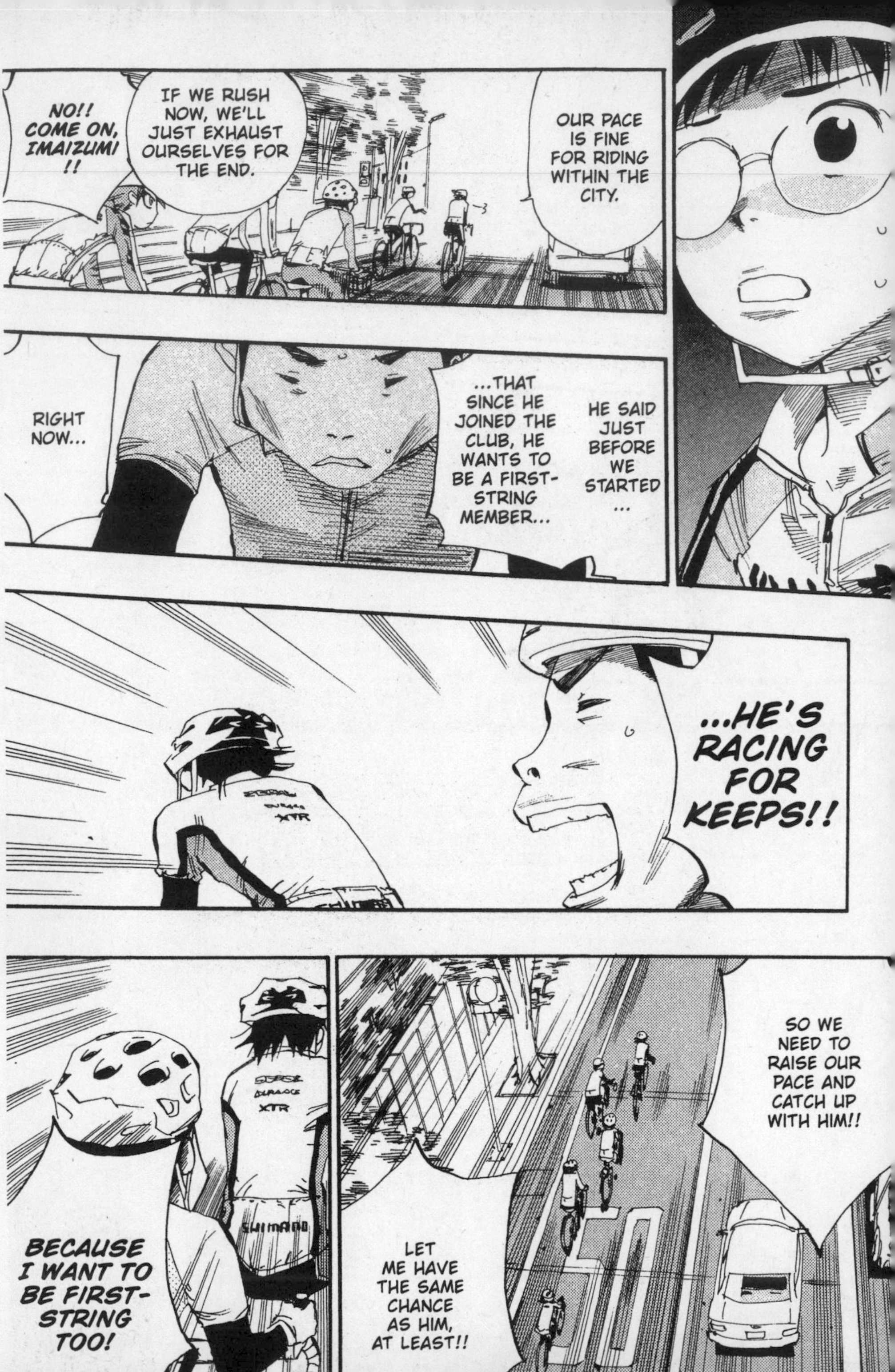
OUR PACE IS FINE FOR RIDING WITHIN THE CITY.
IF WE RUSH NOW, WE'LL JUST EXHAUST OURSELVES FOR THE END.
NO!! COME ON, IMAIZUMI!!
HE SAID JUST BEFORE WE STARTED...
...THAT SINCE HE JOINED THE CLUB, HE WANTS TO BE A FIRST-STRING MEMBER...
RIGHT NOW...
...HE'S RACING FOR KEEPS!!
SO WE NEED TO RAISE OUR PACE AND CATCH UP WITH HIM!!
LET ME HAVE THE SAME CHANCE AS HIM, AT LEAST!!
BECAUSE I WANT TO BE FIRST-STRING TOO!

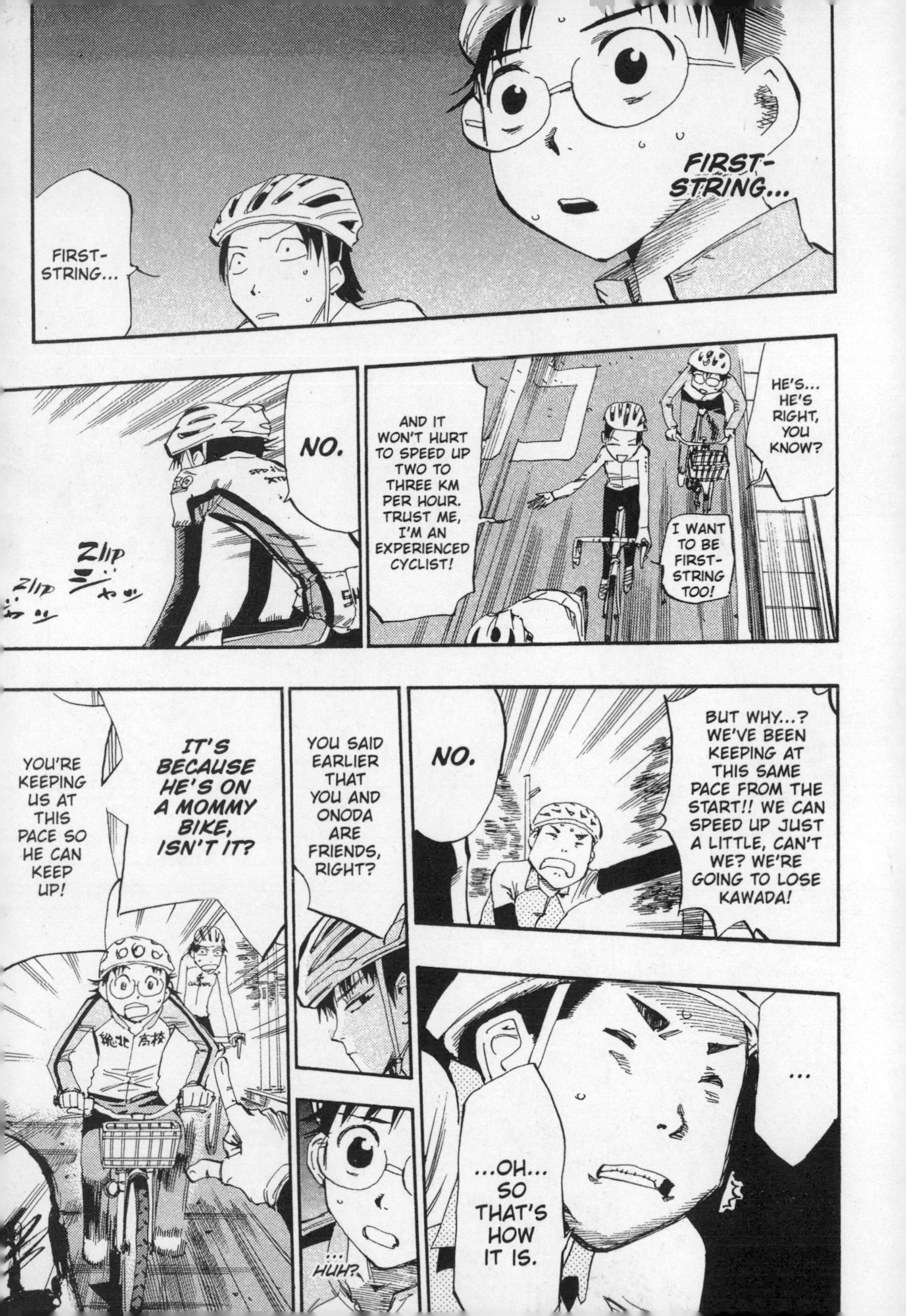
FIRST-STRING...
FIRST-STRING...
HE'S... HE'S RIGHT, YOU KNOW?
I WANT TO BE FIRST-STRING TOO!
AND IT WON'T HURT TO SPEED UP TWO TO THREE KM PER HOUR. TRUST ME, I'M AN EXPERIENCED CYCLIST!
NO.
ZIIP
ZIIP
BUT WHY...? WE'VE BEEN KEEPING AT THIS SAME PACE FROM THE START!! WE CAN SPEED UP JUST A LITTLE, CAN'T WE? WE'RE GOING TO LOSE KAWADA!
NO.
YOU SAID EARLIER THAT YOU AND ONODA ARE FRIENDS, RIGHT?
IT'S BECAUSE HE'S ON A MOMMY BIKE, ISN'T IT?
YOU'RE KEEPING US AT THIS PACE SO HE CAN KEEP UP!
...
...OH... SO THAT'S HOW IT IS.
...HUH?

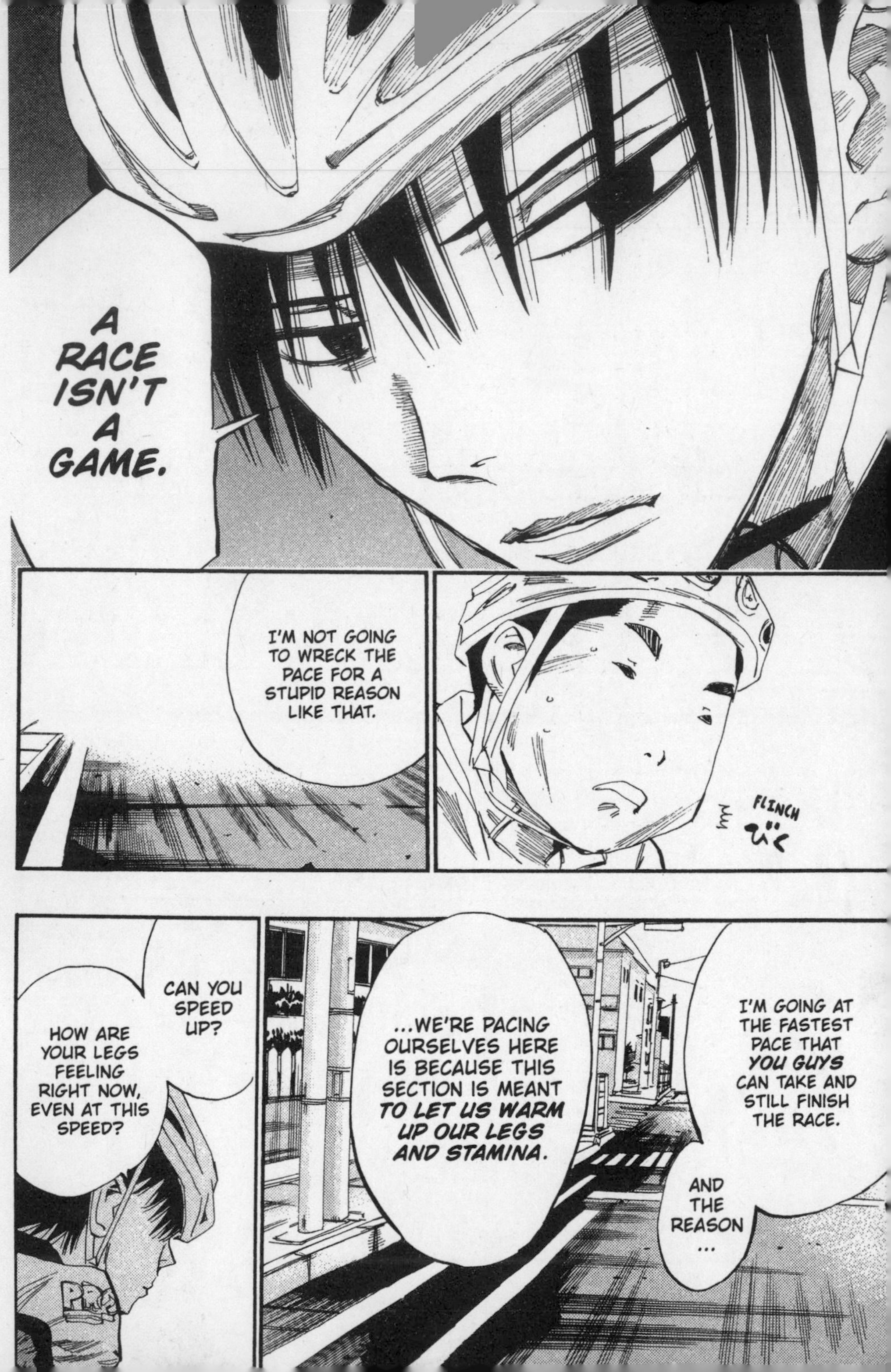
A RACE ISN'T A GAME.
FLINCH
びく
I'M NOT GOING TO WRECK THE PACE FOR A STUPID REASON LIKE THAT.
I'M GOING AT THE FASTEST PACE THAT YOU GUYS CAN TAKE AND STILL FINISH THE RACE.
AND THE REASON ...
...WE'RE PACING OURSELVES HERE IS BECAUSE THIS SECTION IS MEANT TO LET US WARM UP OUR LEGS AND STAMINA.
CAN YOU SPEED UP?
HOW ARE YOUR LEGS FEELING RIGHT NOW, EVEN AT THIS SPEED?

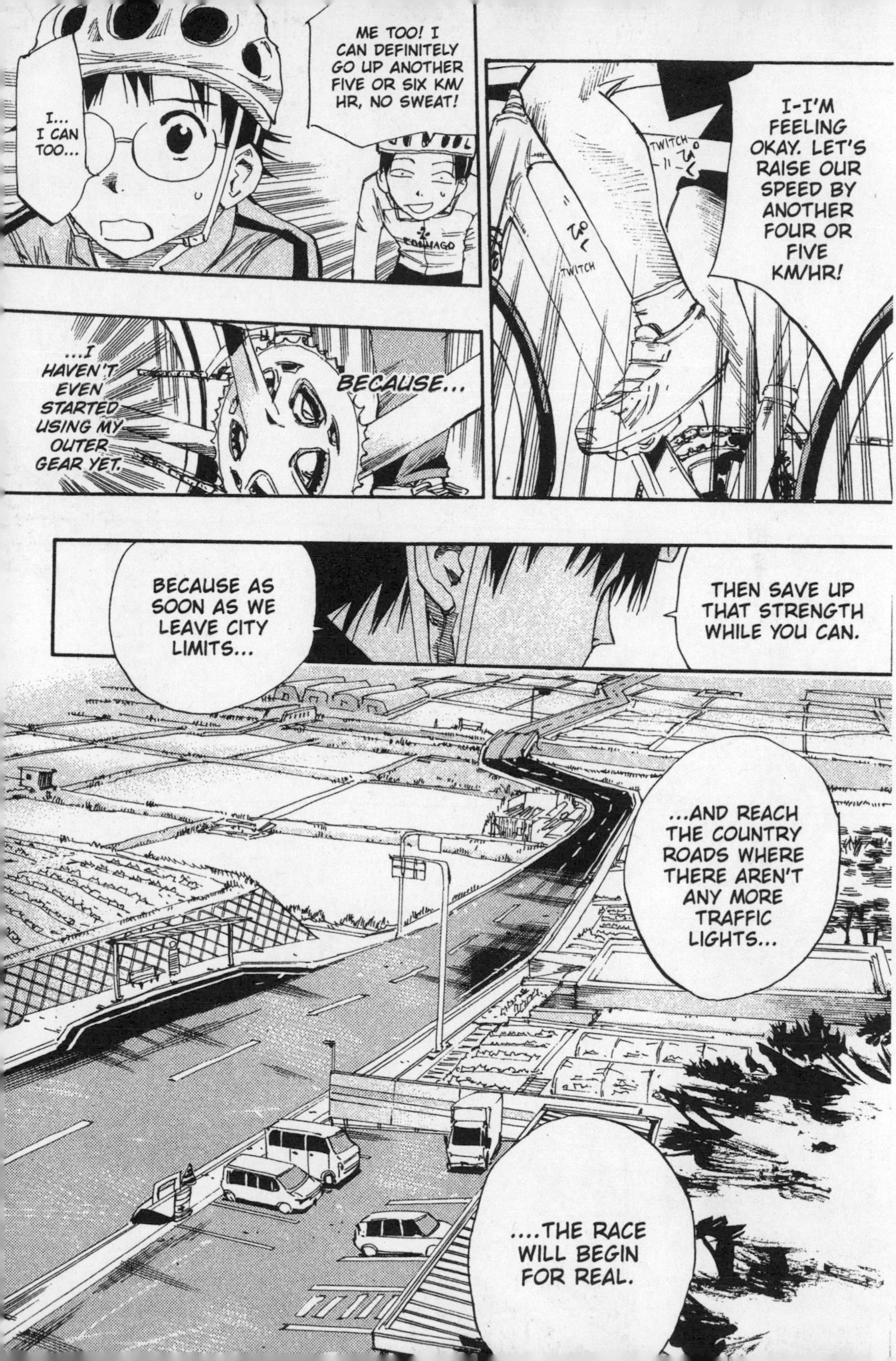
TWITCH
I-I'M FEELING OKAY. LET'S RAISE OUR SPEED BY ANOTHER FOUR OR FIVE KM/HR!
TWITCH
ME TOO! I CAN DEFINITELY GO UP ANOTHER FIVE OR SIX KM/HR, NO SWEAT!
I... I CAN TOO...
BECAUSE...
...I HAVEN'T EVEN STARTED USING MY OUTER GEAR YET.
THEN SAVE UP THAT STRENGTH WHILE YOU CAN.
BECAUSE AS SOON AS WE LEAVE CITY LIMITS...
...AND REACH THE COUNTRY ROADS WHERE THERE AREN'T ANY MORE TRAFFIC LIGHTS...
....THE RACE WILL BEGIN FOR REAL.

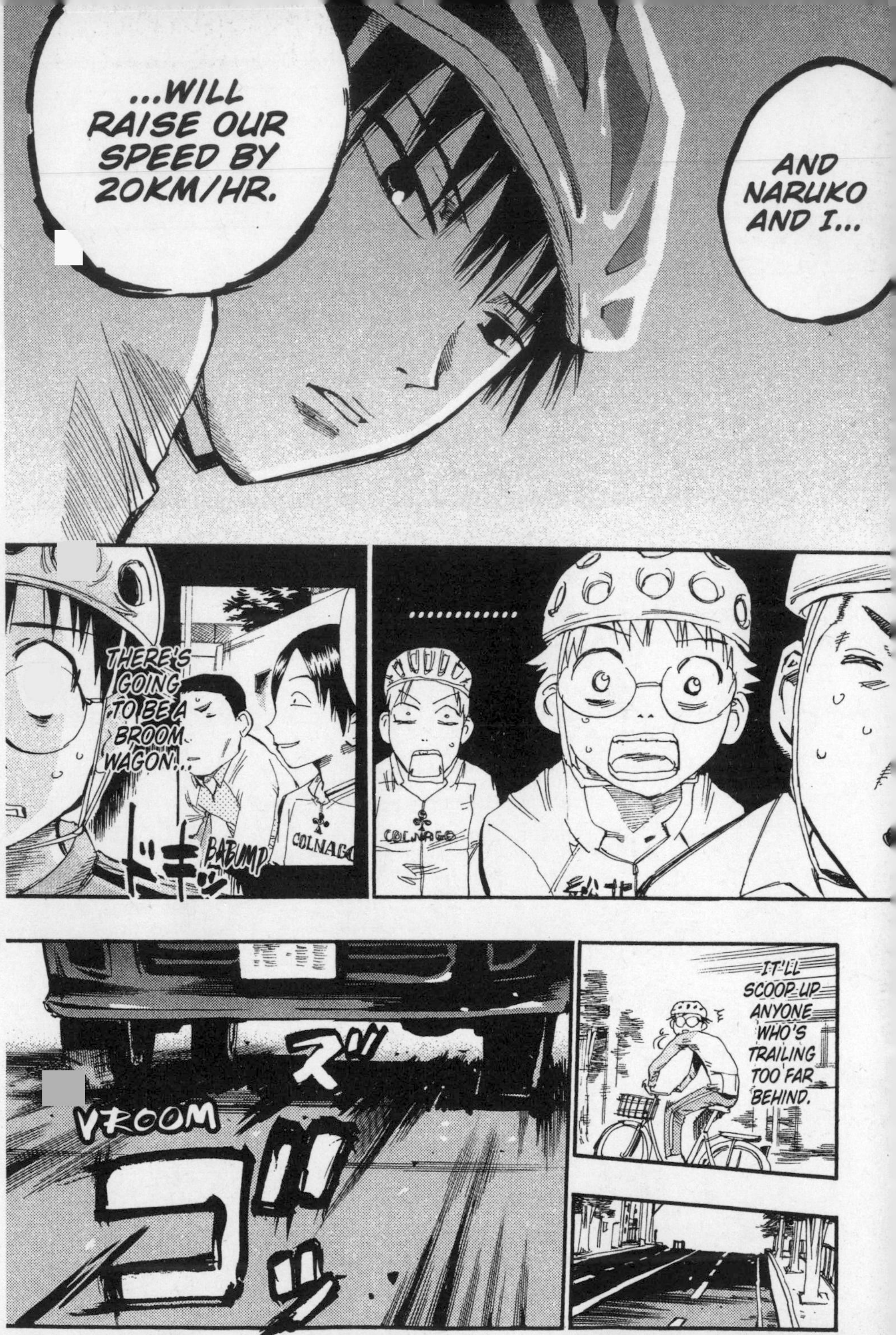
AND NARUKO AND I...
...WILL RAISE OUR SPEED BY 20KM/HR.
....
THERE'S GOING TO BE A BROOM WAGON...
BABUMP
IT'LL SCOOP UP ANYONE WHO'S TRAILING TOO FAR BEHIND.
VROOM

RIDE.18 TEARING THROUGH THE FIRST STAGE!

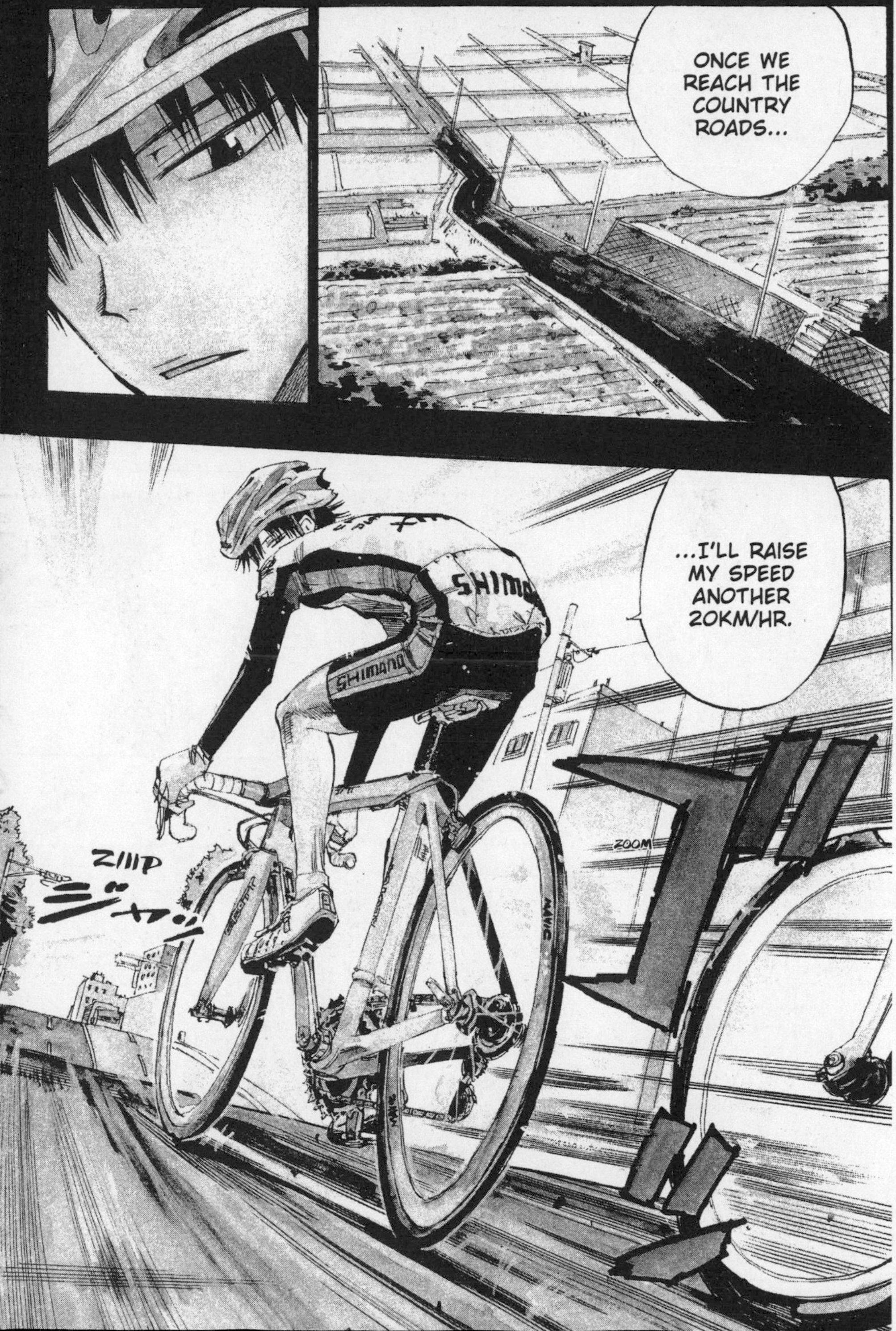
ONCE WE REACH THE COUNTRY ROADS...
...I'LL RAISE MY SPEED ANOTHER 20KM/HR.
ZOOM
ZIIIP

RIDE.18 TEARING THROUGH THE FIRST STAGE!

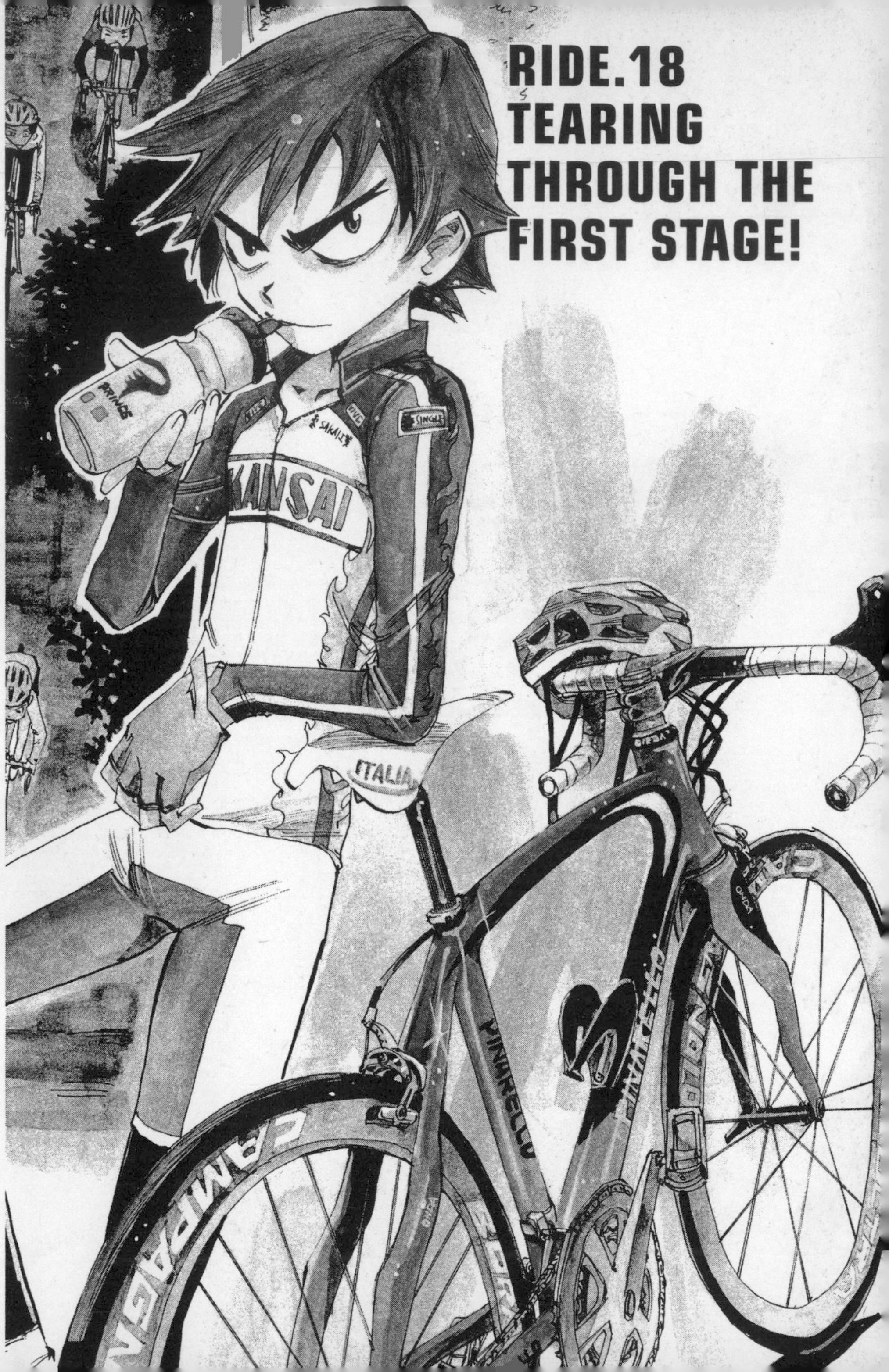
SINGLE
KANSAI
ITALIA

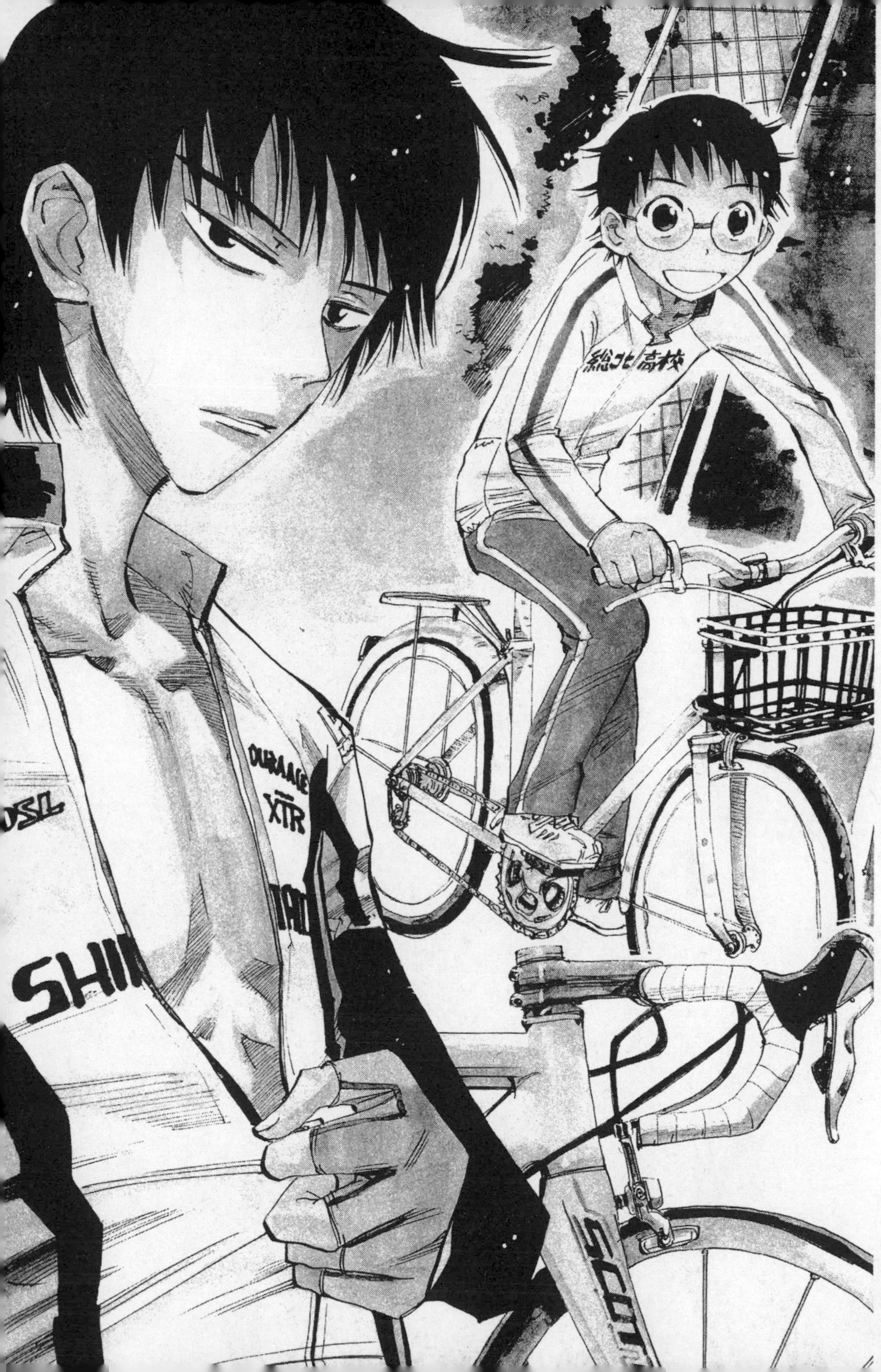
総北高校
XTR
SHI

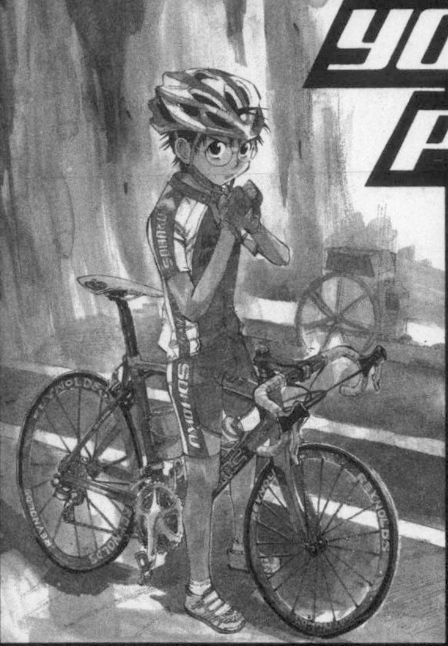

YOWAMUSHI PEDAL 2

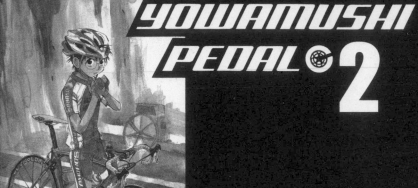

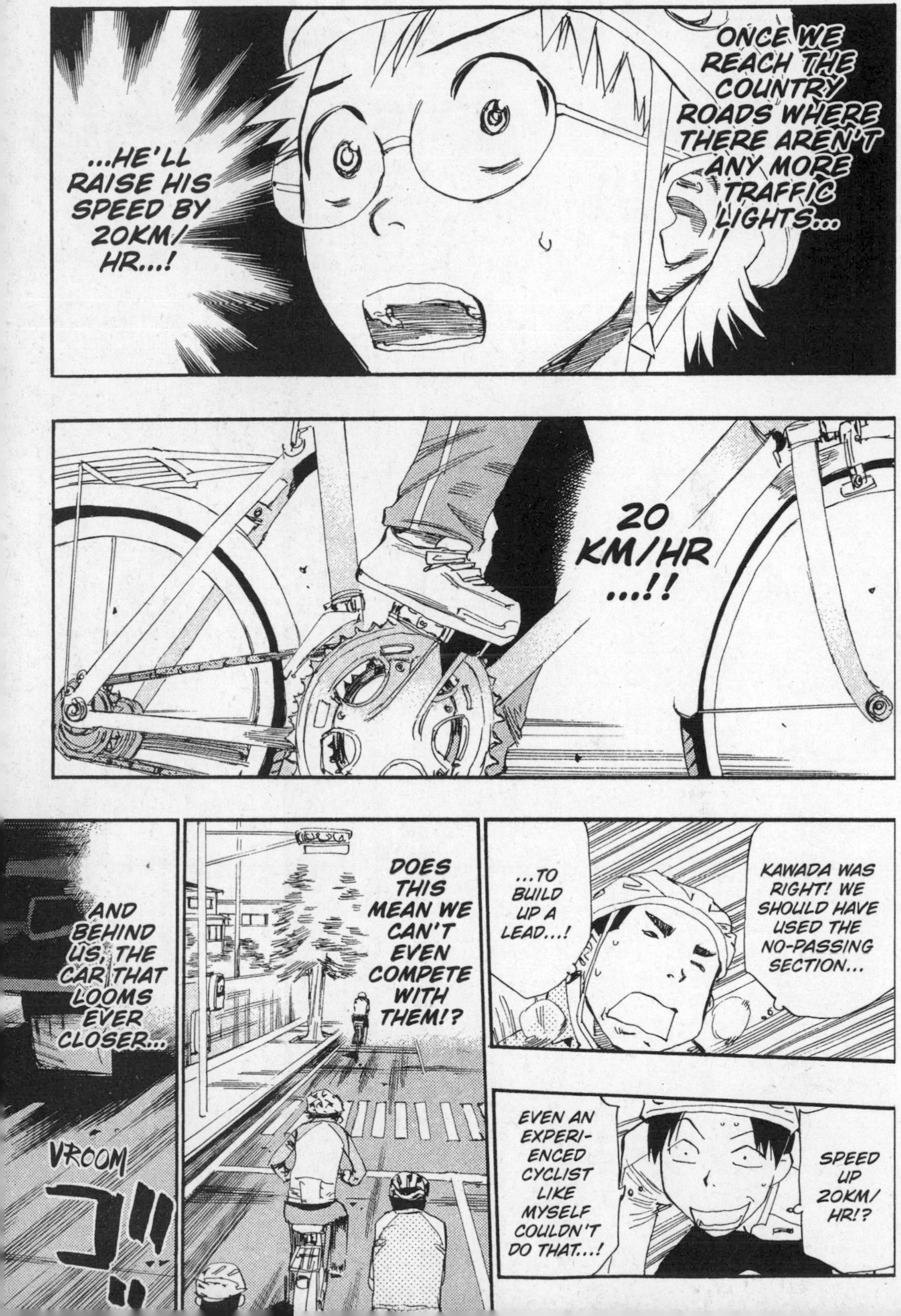
ONCE WE REACH THE COUNTRY ROADS WHERE THERE AREN'T ANY MORE TRAFFIC LIGHTS...
...HE'LL RAISE HIS SPEED BY 20KM/HR...!
20 KM/HR ...!!
KAWADA WAS RIGHT! WE SHOULD HAVE USED THE NO-PASSING SECTION...
...TO BUILD UP A LEAD...!
SPEED UP 20KM/HR!?
EVEN AN EXPERIENCED CYCLIST LIKE MYSELF COULDN'T DO THAT...!
DOES THIS MEAN WE CAN'T EVEN COMPETE WITH THEM!?
AND BEHIND US, THE CAR THAT LOOMS EVER CLOSER...
VROOM
ゴ!!

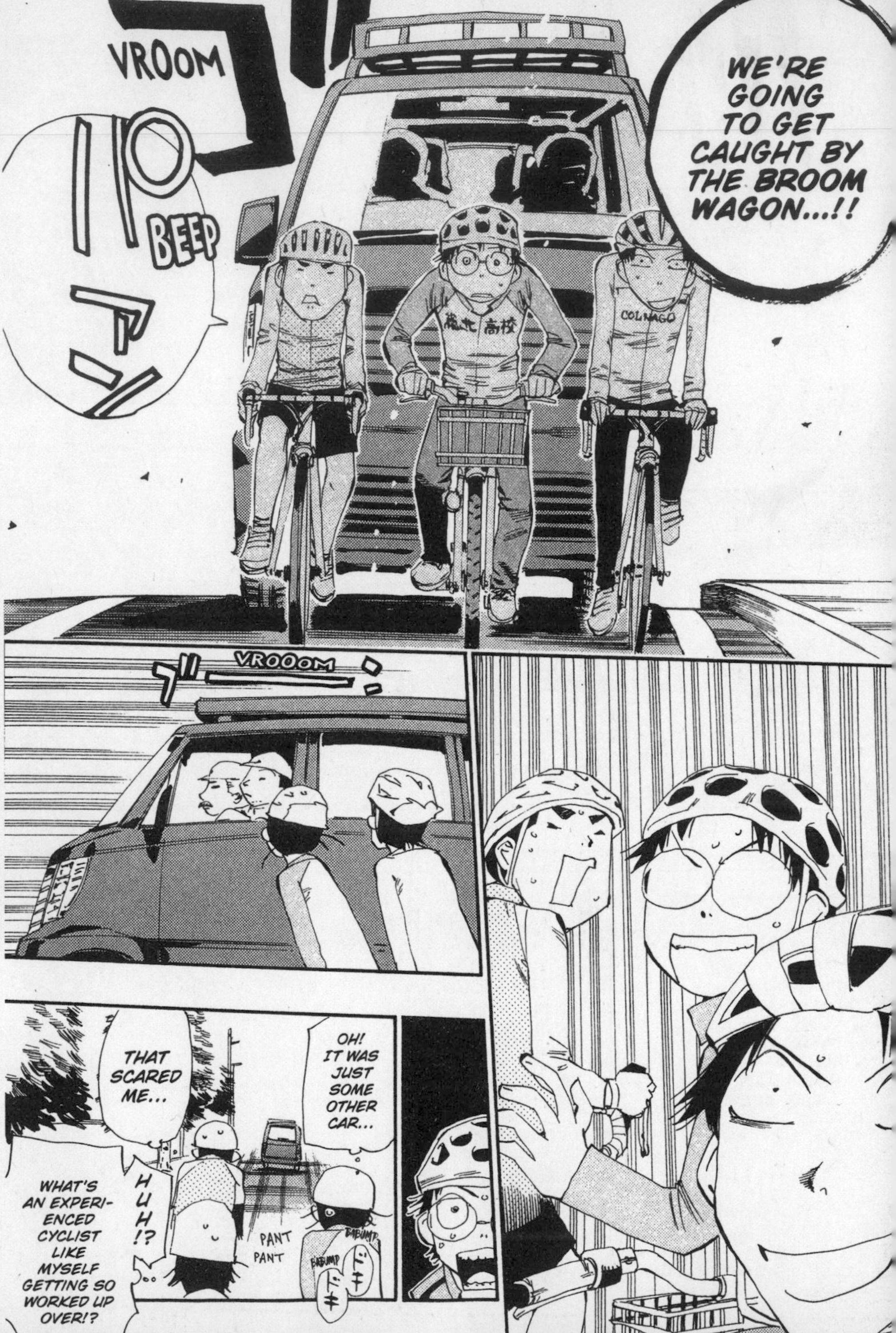
WE'RE GOING TO GET CAUGHT BY THE BROOM WAGON...!!
VROOM
BEEP
VROOOM
OH! IT WAS JUST SOME OTHER CAR...
THAT SCARED ME...
BABUMP
BABUMP
PANT PANT
HUH!?
WHAT'S AN EXPERIENCED CYCLIST LIKE MYSELF GETTING SO WORKED UP OVER!?

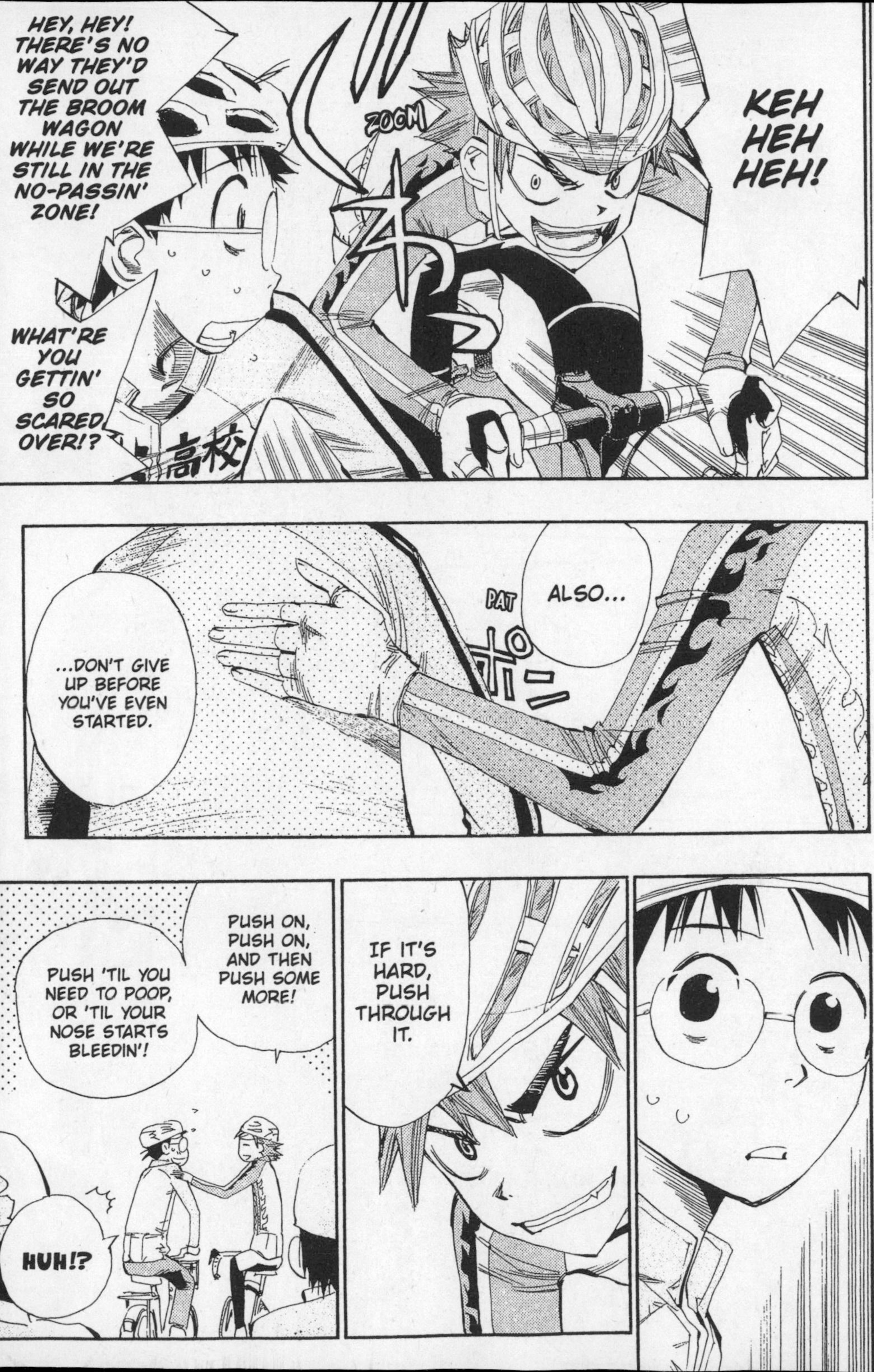
KEH HEH HEH!
ZOOM
HEY, HEY! THERE'S NO WAY THEY'D SEND OUT THE BROOM WAGON WHILE WE'RE STILL IN THE NO-PASSIN' ZONE!
WHAT'RE YOU GETTIN' SO SCARED OVER!?
ALSO...
PAT
...DON'T GIVE UP BEFORE YOU'VE EVEN STARTED.
IF IT'S HARD, PUSH THROUGH IT.
PUSH ON, PUSH ON, AND THEN PUSH SOME MORE!
PUSH 'TIL YOU NEED TO POOP, OR 'TIL YOUR NOSE STARTS BLEEDIN'!
HUH!?

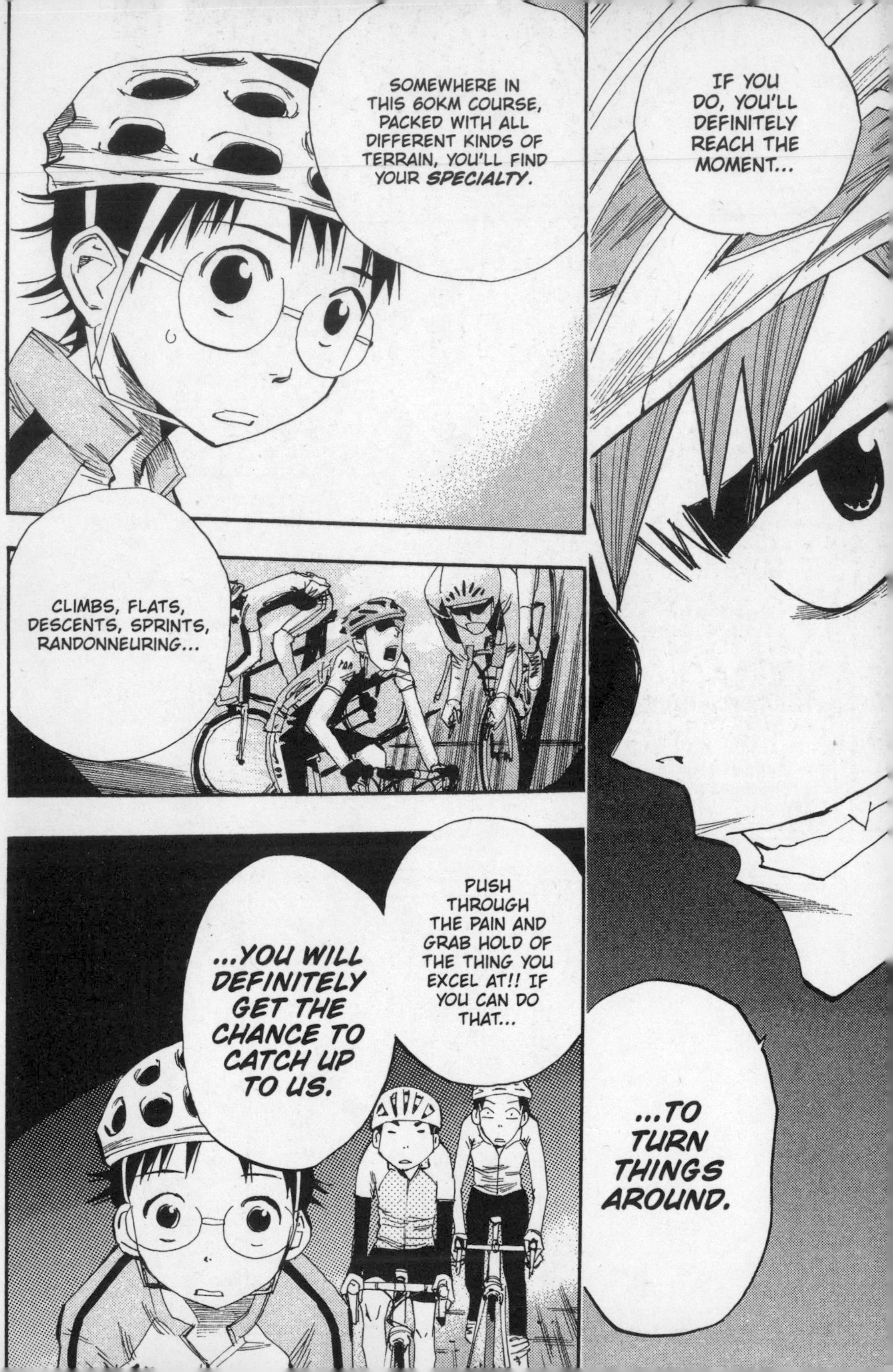
IF YOU DO, YOU'LL DEFINITELY REACH THE MOMENT...
...TO TURN THINGS AROUND.
SOMEWHERE IN THIS 60KM COURSE, PACKED WITH ALL DIFFERENT KINDS OF TERRAIN, YOU'LL FIND YOUR *SPECIALTY*.
CLIMBS, FLATS, DESCENTS, SPRINTS, RANDONNEURING...
PUSH THROUGH THE PAIN AND GRAB HOLD OF THE THING YOU EXCEL AT!! IF YOU CAN DO THAT...
...YOU WILL DEFINITELY GET THE CHANCE TO CATCH UP TO US.

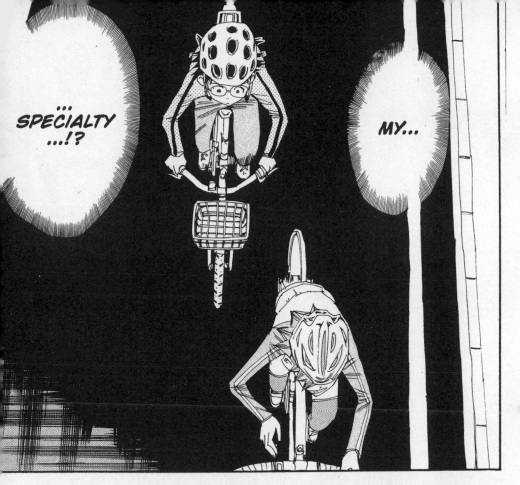

SPECÏALTY
...!?

MY...

KATHUMP

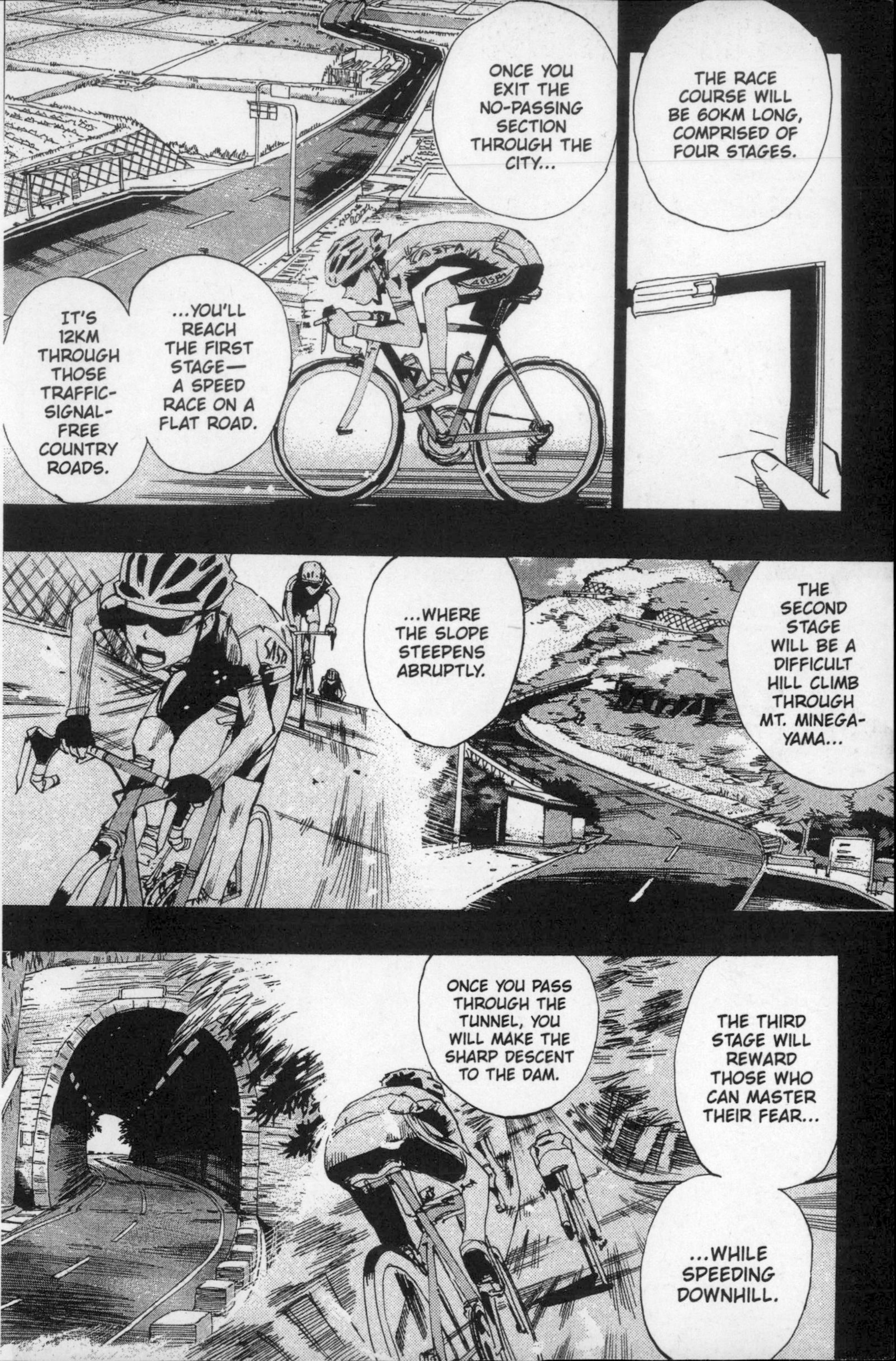
THE RACE COURSE WILL BE 60KM LONG, COMPRISED OF FOUR STAGES.
ONCE YOU EXIT THE NO-PASSING SECTION THROUGH THE CITY...
...YOU'LL REACH THE FIRST STAGE—A SPEED RACE ON A FLAT ROAD.
IT'S 12KM THROUGH THOSE TRAFFIC-SIGNAL-FREE COUNTRY ROADS.
THE SECOND STAGE WILL BE A DIFFICULT HILL CLIMB THROUGH MT. MINEGAYAMA...
...WHERE THE SLOPE STEEPENS ABRUPTLY.
THE THIRD STAGE WILL REWARD THOSE WHO CAN MASTER THEIR FEAR...
...WHILE SPEEDING DOWNHILL.
ONCE YOU PASS THROUGH THE TUNNEL, YOU WILL MAKE THE SHARP DESCENT TO THE DAM.

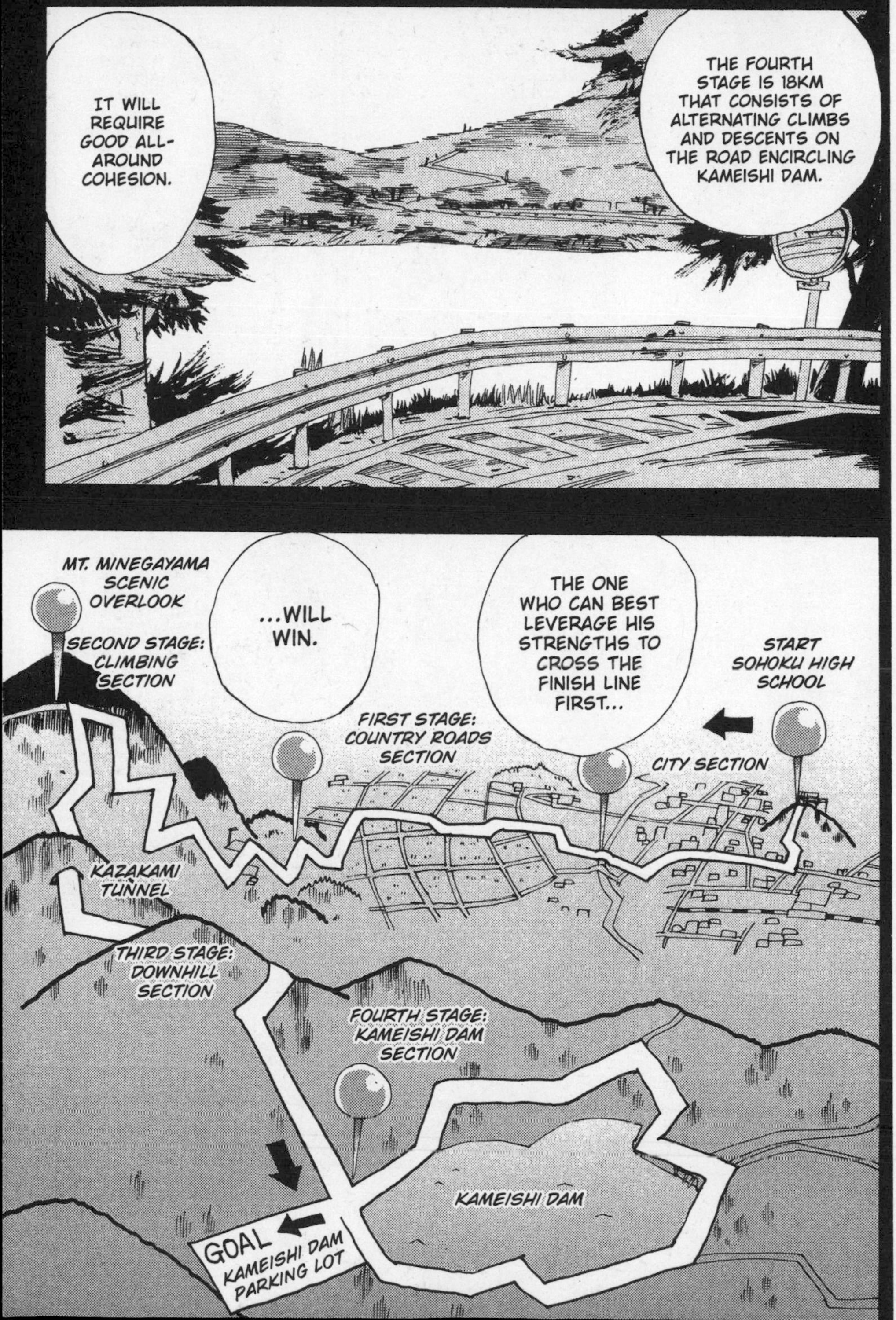
THE FOURTH STAGE IS 18KM THAT CONSISTS OF ALTERNATING CLIMBS AND DESCENTS ON THE ROAD ENCIRCLING KAMEISHI DAM.
IT WILL REQUIRE GOOD ALL-AROUND COHESION.
THE ONE WHO CAN BEST LEVERAGE HIS STRENGTHS TO CROSS THE FINISH LINE FIRST...
...WILL WIN.
START SOHOKU HIGH SCHOOL
CITY SECTION
FIRST STAGE: COUNTRY ROADS SECTION
MT. MINEGAYAMA SCENIC OVERLOOK
SECOND STAGE: CLIMBING SECTION
KAZAKAMI TUNNEL
THIRD STAGE: DOWNHILL SECTION
FOURTH STAGE: KAMEISHI DAM SECTION
KAMEISHI DAM
GOAL
KAMEISHI DAM PARKING LOT

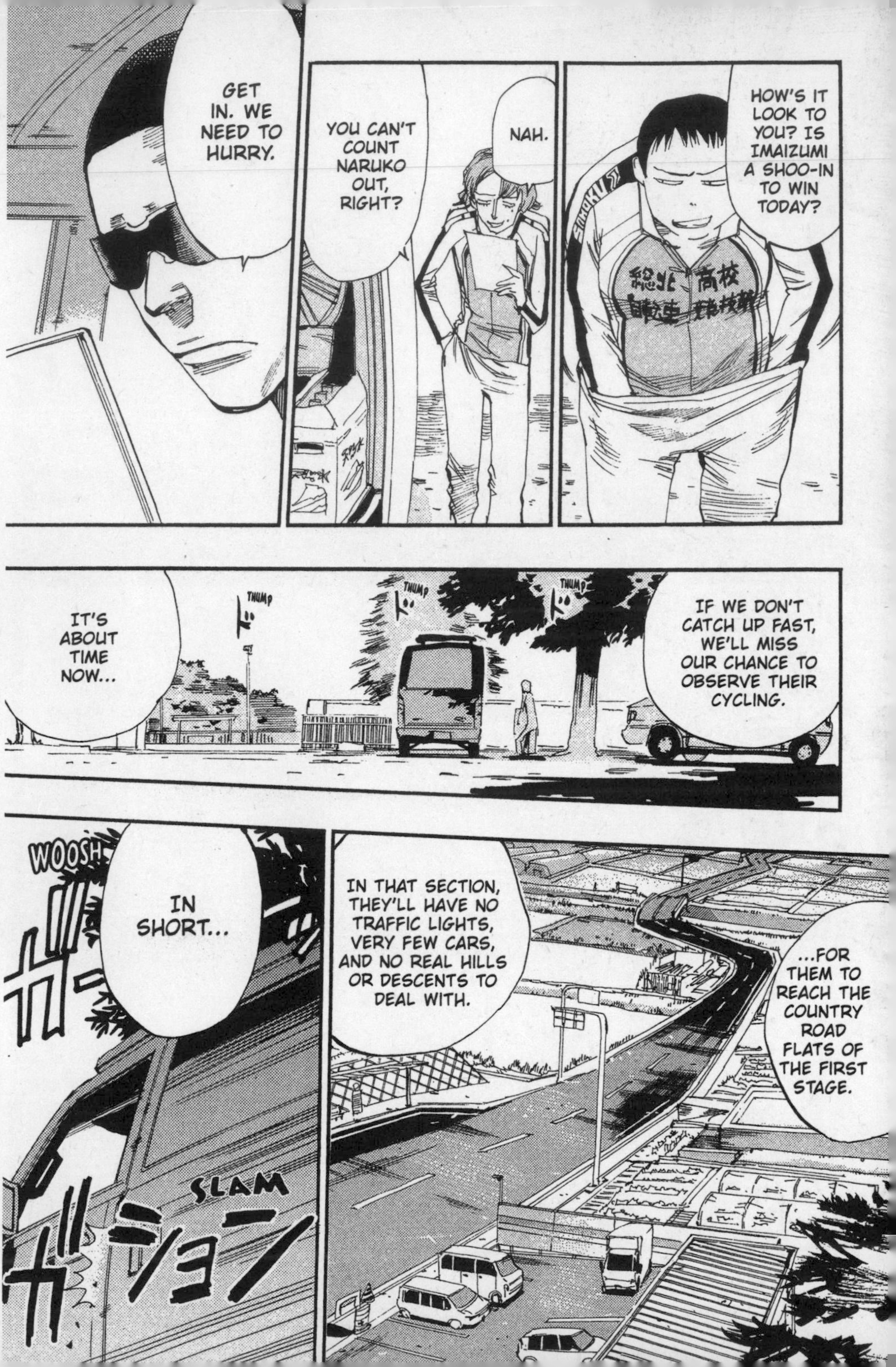
HOW'S IT LOOK TO YOU? IS IMAIZUMI A SHOO-IN TO WIN TODAY?
総北高校
自転車競技部
NAH.
YOU CAN'T COUNT NARUKO OUT, RIGHT?
GET IN. WE NEED TO HURRY.
IF WE DON'T CATCH UP FAST, WE'LL MISS OUR CHANCE TO OBSERVE THEIR CYCLING.
THUMP
ド
THUMP
ド
THUMP
ド
IT'S ABOUT TIME NOW...
...FOR THEM TO REACH THE COUNTRY ROAD FLATS OF THE FIRST STAGE.
IN THAT SECTION, THEY'LL HAVE NO TRAFFIC LIGHTS, VERY FEW CARS, AND NO REAL HILLS OR DESCENTS TO DEAL WITH.
IN SHORT...
WOOSH
SLAM

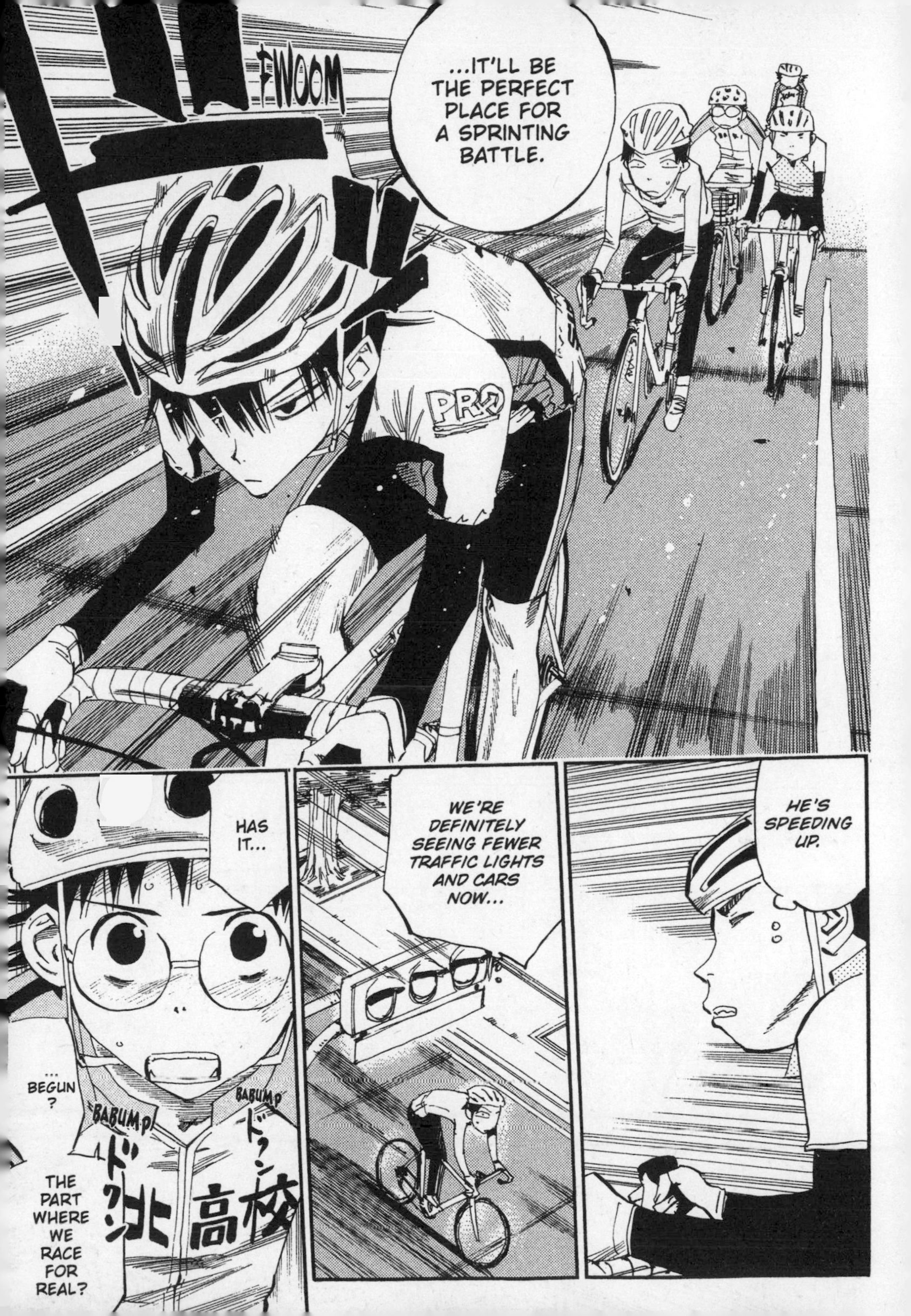
FWOOM
...IT'LL BE THE PERFECT PLACE FOR A SPRINTING BATTLE.
HE'S SPEEDING UP.
WE'RE DEFINITELY SEEING FEWER TRAFFIC LIGHTS AND CARS NOW...
HAS IT...
...BEGUN?
BABUMP
BABUMP
THE PART WHERE WE RACE FOR REAL?

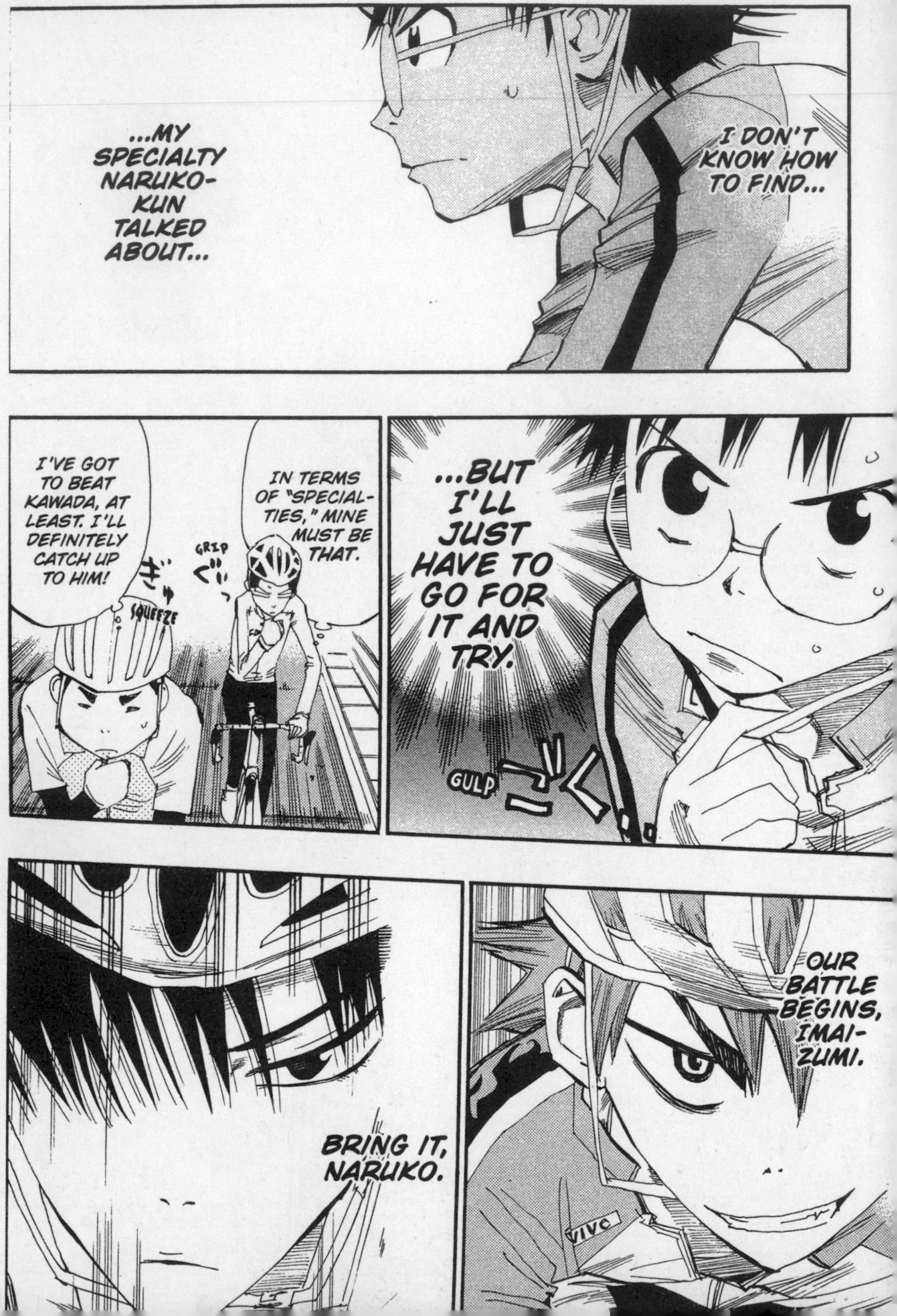
I DON'T KNOW HOW TO FIND...
...MY SPECIALTY NARUKO-KUN TALKED ABOUT...
...BUT I'LL JUST HAVE TO GO FOR IT AND TRY.
GULP
IN TERMS OF "SPECIAL-TIES," MINE MUST BE THAT.
GRIP
I'VE GOT TO BEAT KAWADA, AT LEAST. I'LL DEFINITELY CATCH UP TO HIM!
SQUEEZE
OUR BATTLE BEGINS, IMAI-ZUMI.
BRING IT, NARUKO.

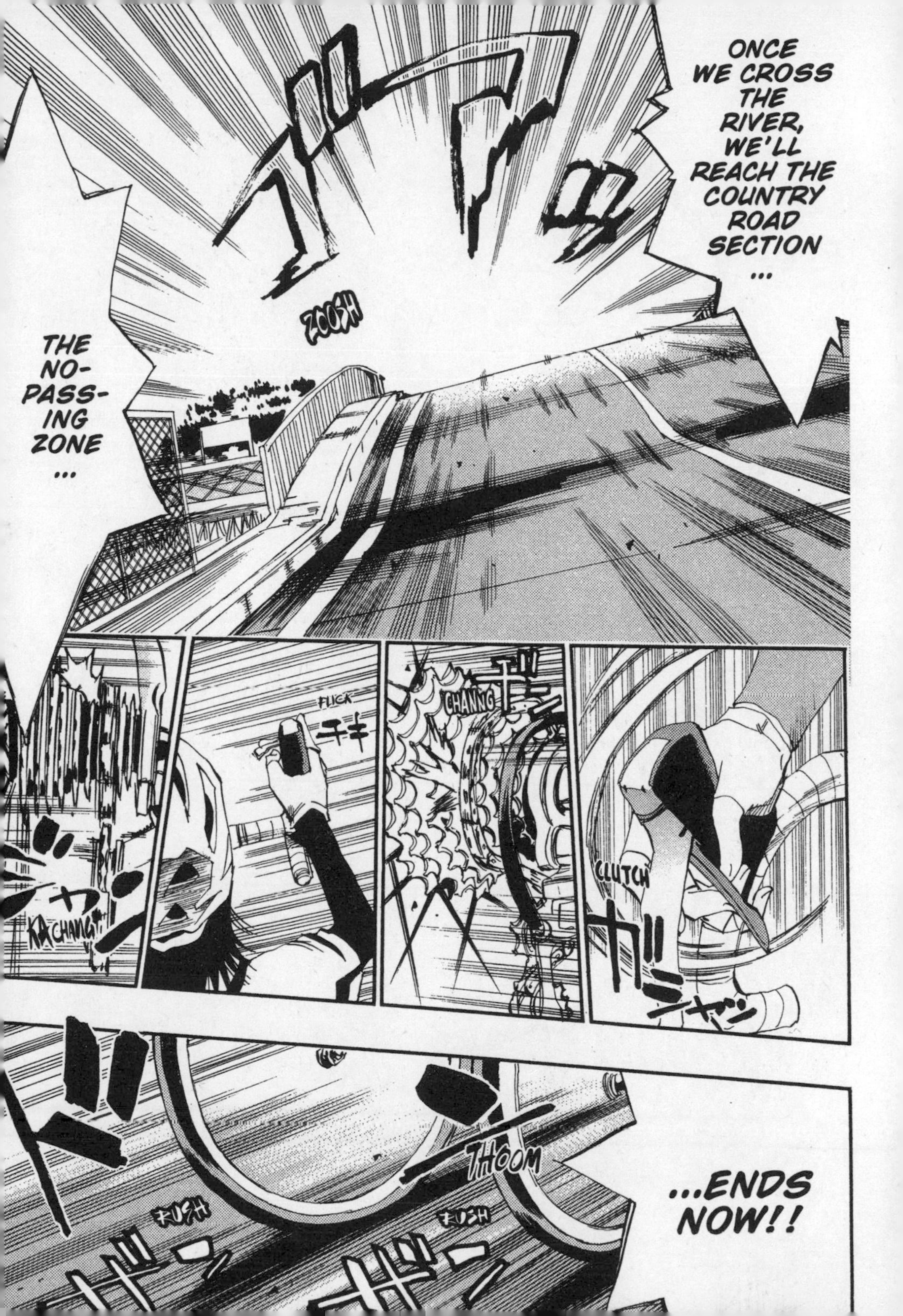
ONCE WE CROSS THE RIVER, WE'LL REACH THE COUNTRY ROAD SECTION...
ZOOSH
THE NO-PASSING ZONE...
CLUTCH
CHANNG
FLICK
KACHANG!
THOOM
...ENDS NOW!!
RUSH
RUSH

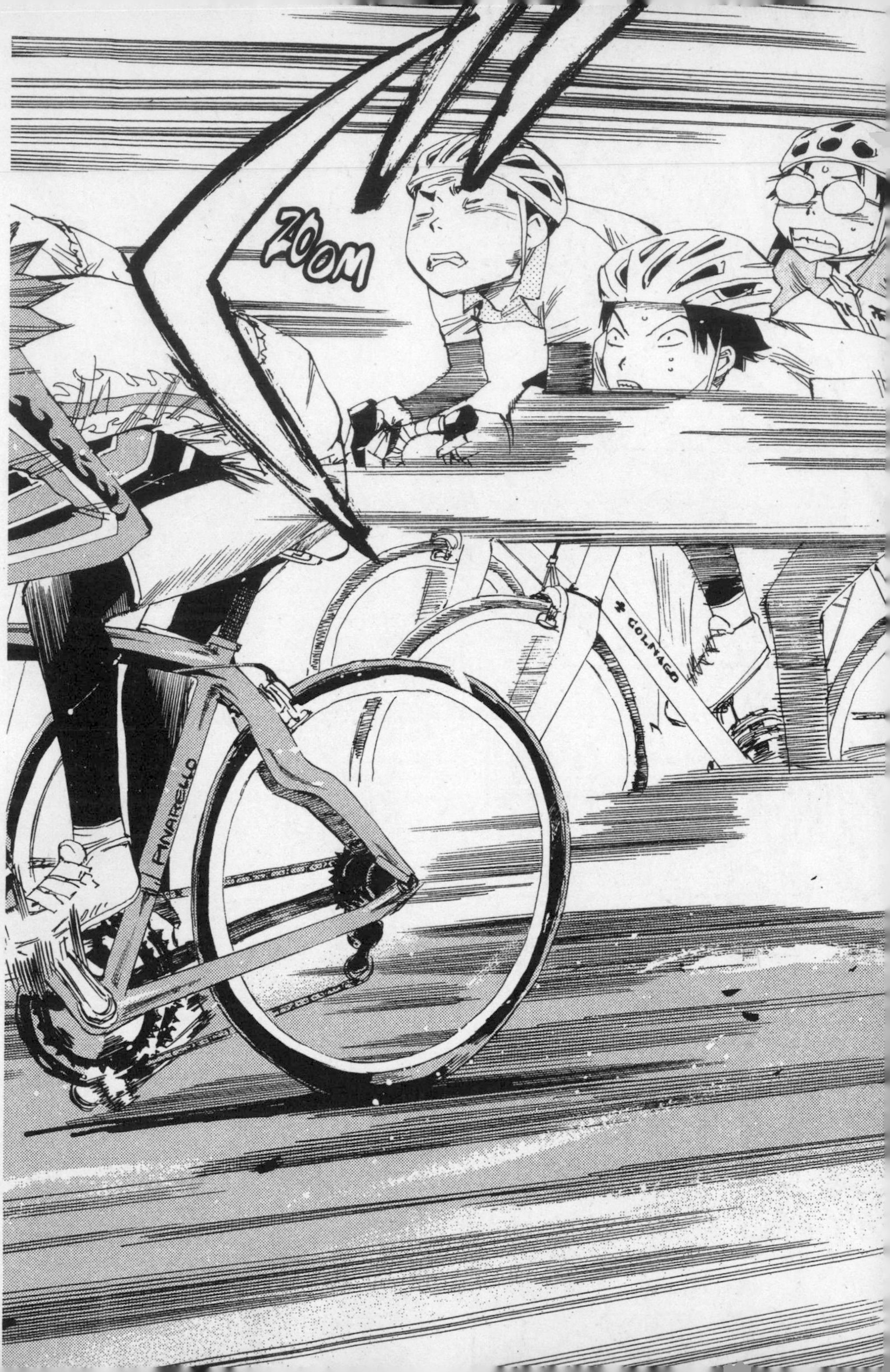
ZOOM
COLNAGO
PINARELLO

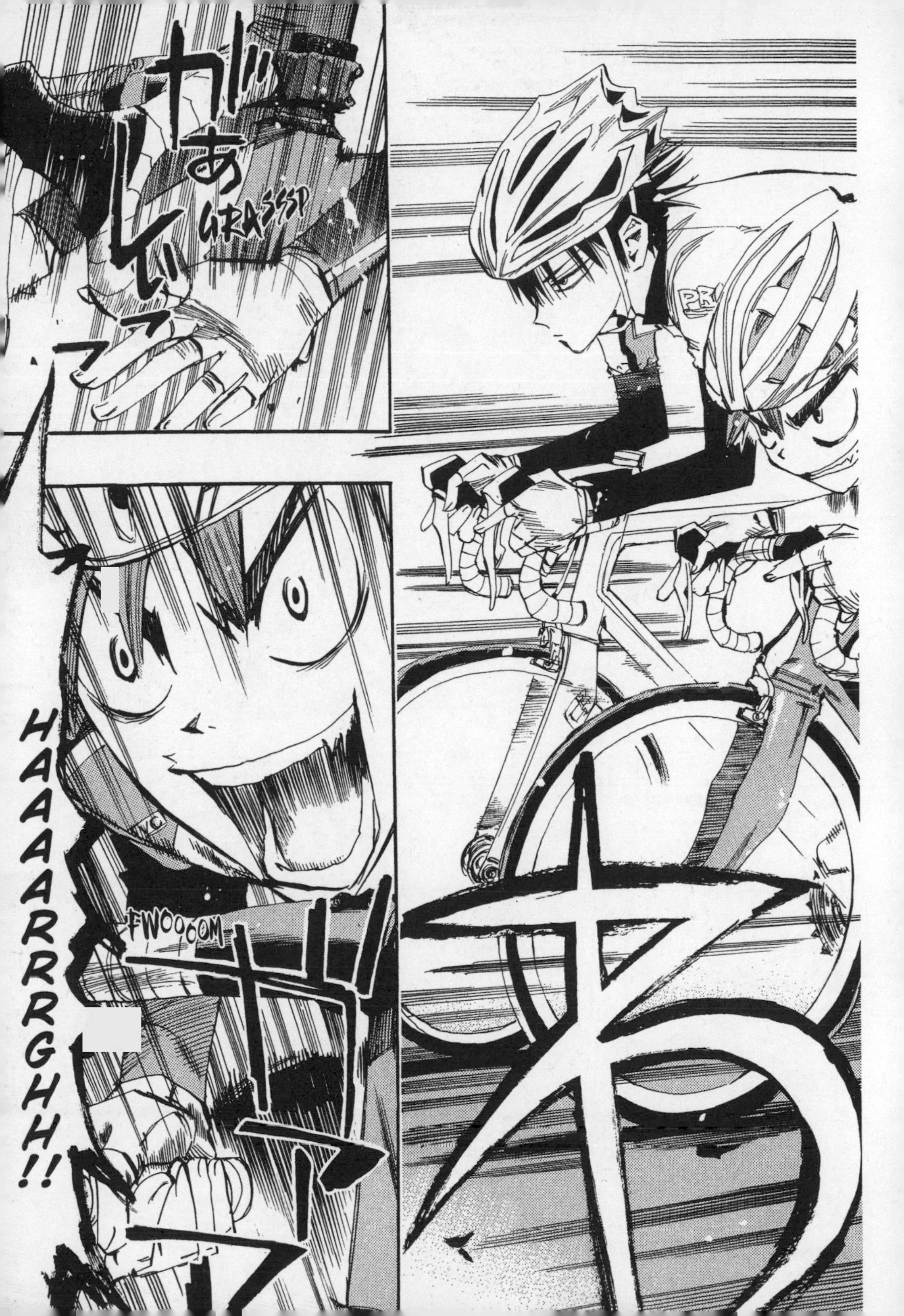
GRASSSP
FWOOOOM
HAAAARRRGHH!!

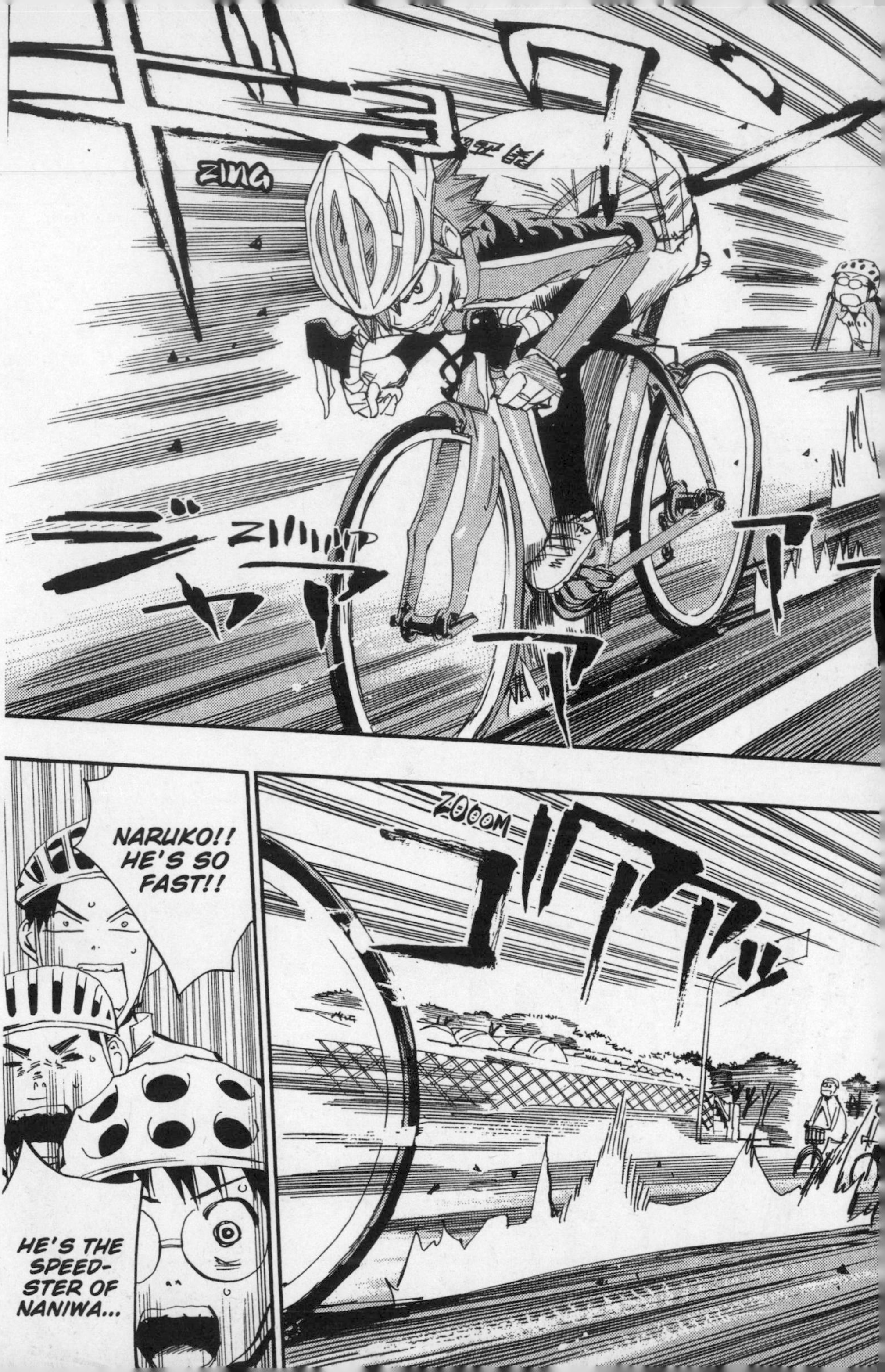
ZING
ZIIIIIIP
ZOOOM
NARUKO!! HE'S SO FAST!!
HE'S THE SPEED-STER OF NANIWA...

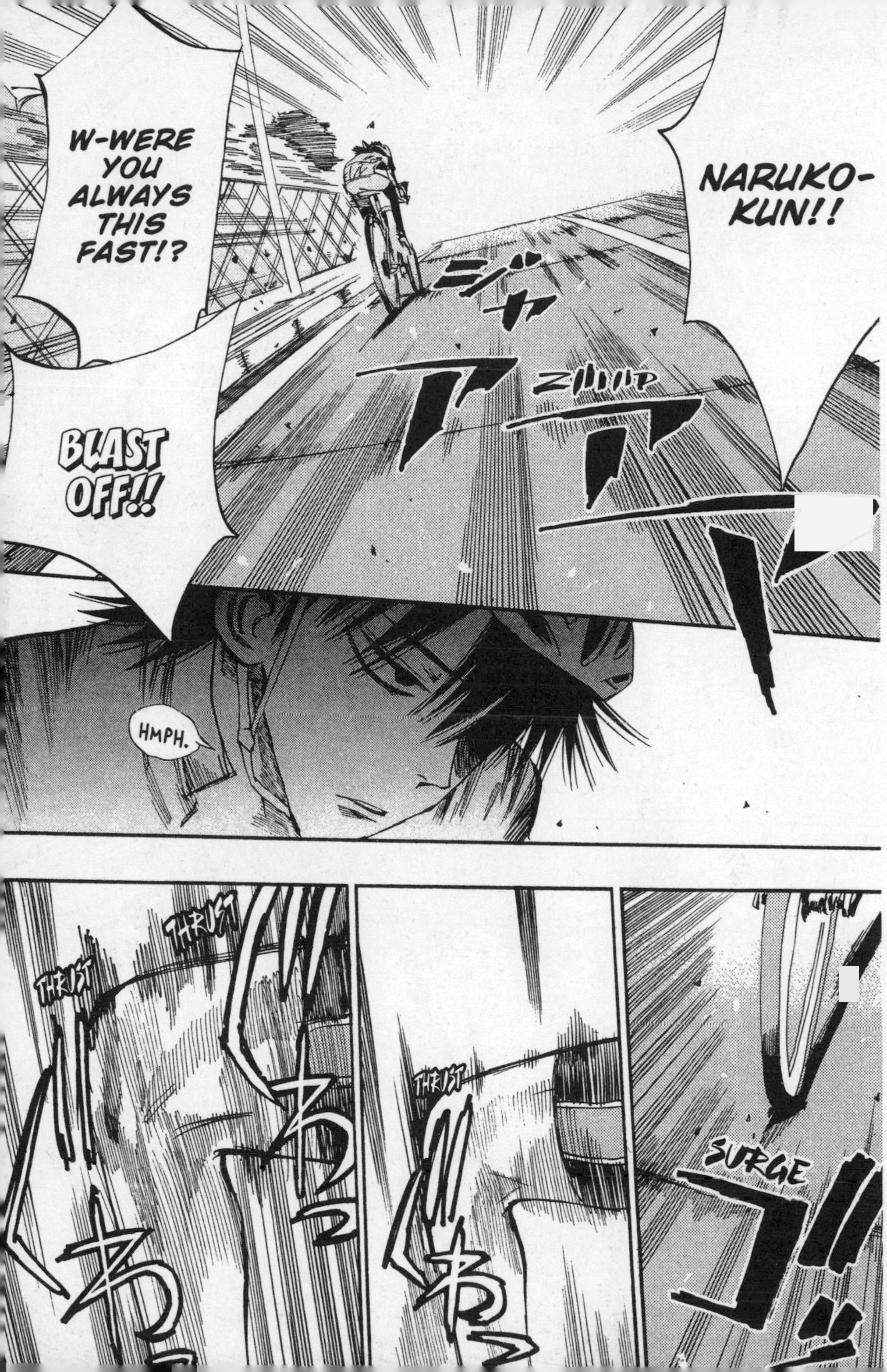
NARUKO-KUN!!
W-WERE YOU ALWAYS THIS FAST!?
ZIIIIP
BLAST OFF!!
HMPH.
SURGE
THRUST
THRUST
THRUST

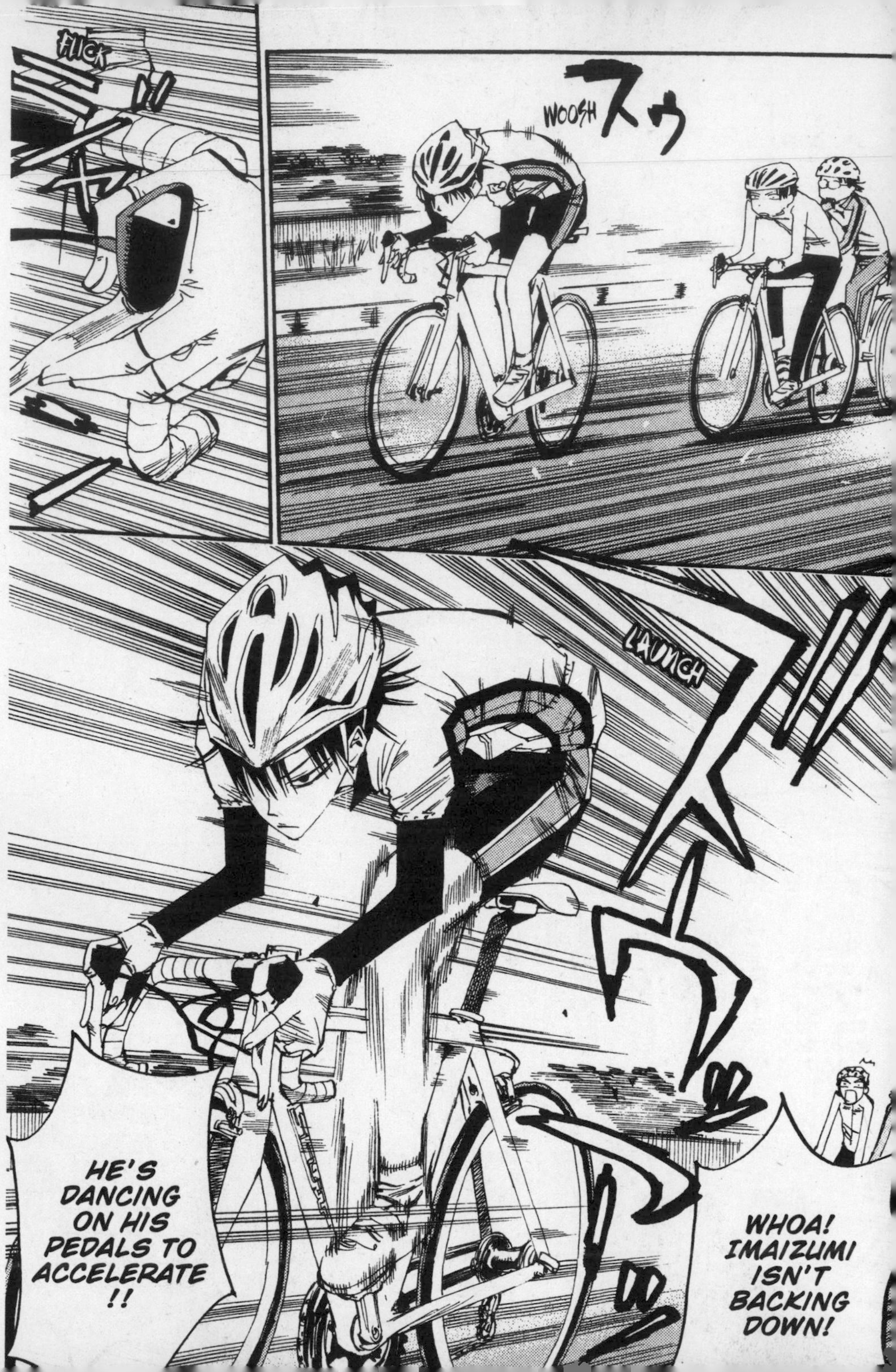
WOOSH
スゥ
FLICK
LAUNCH
WHOA! IMAIZUMI ISN'T BACKING DOWN!
HE'S DANCING ON HIS PEDALS TO ACCELERATE!!

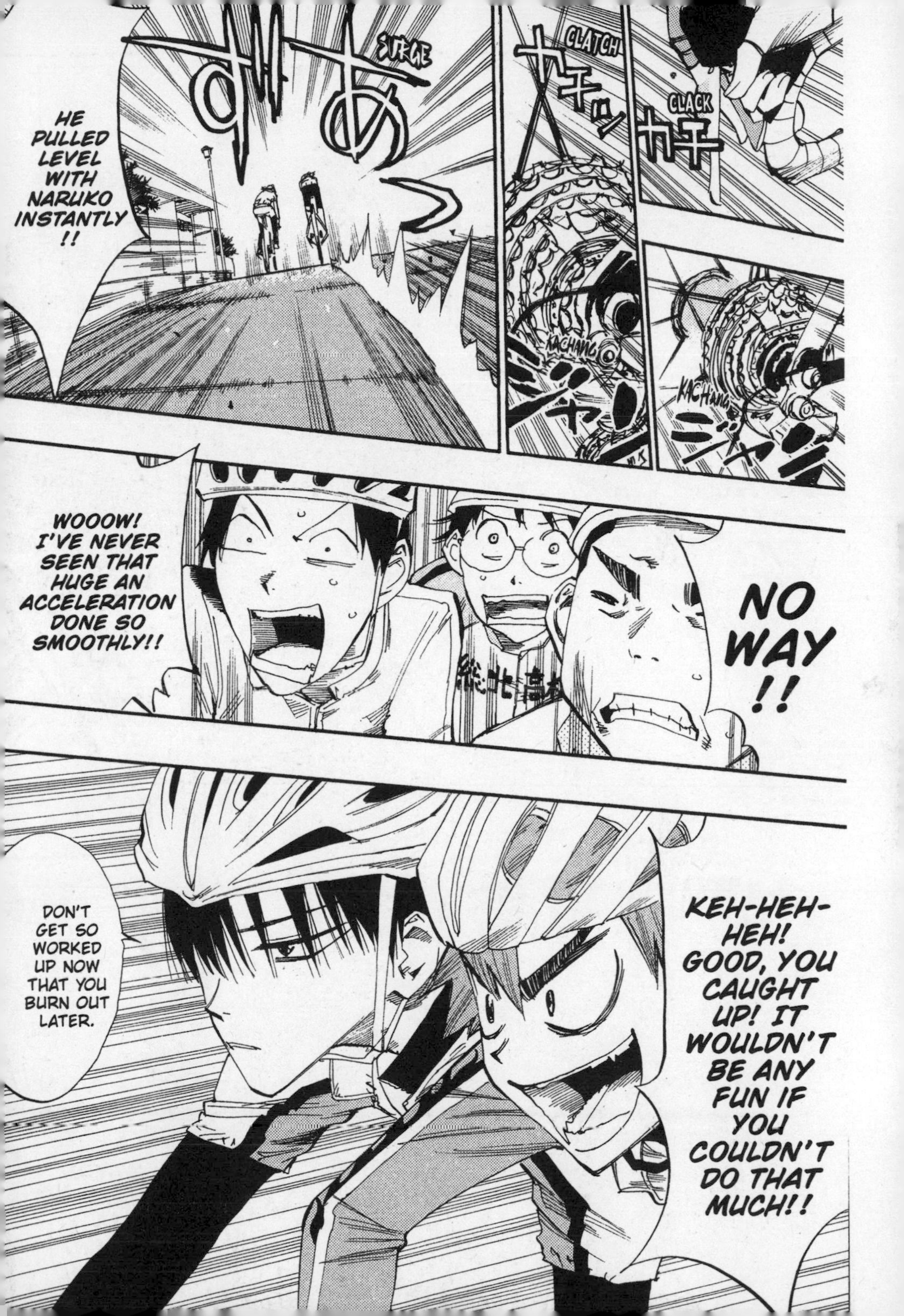

CLACK
KACHANG
CLATCH
KACHANG
SURGE
HE PULLED LEVEL WITH NARUKO INSTANTLY!!
NO WAY!!
WOOOW! I'VE NEVER SEEN THAT HUGE AN ACCELERATION DONE SO SMOOTHLY!!
KEH-HEH-HEH! GOOD, YOU CAUGHT UP! IT WOULDN'T BE ANY FUN IF YOU COULDN'T DO THAT MUCH!!
DON'T GET SO WORKED UP NOW THAT YOU BURN OUT LATER.

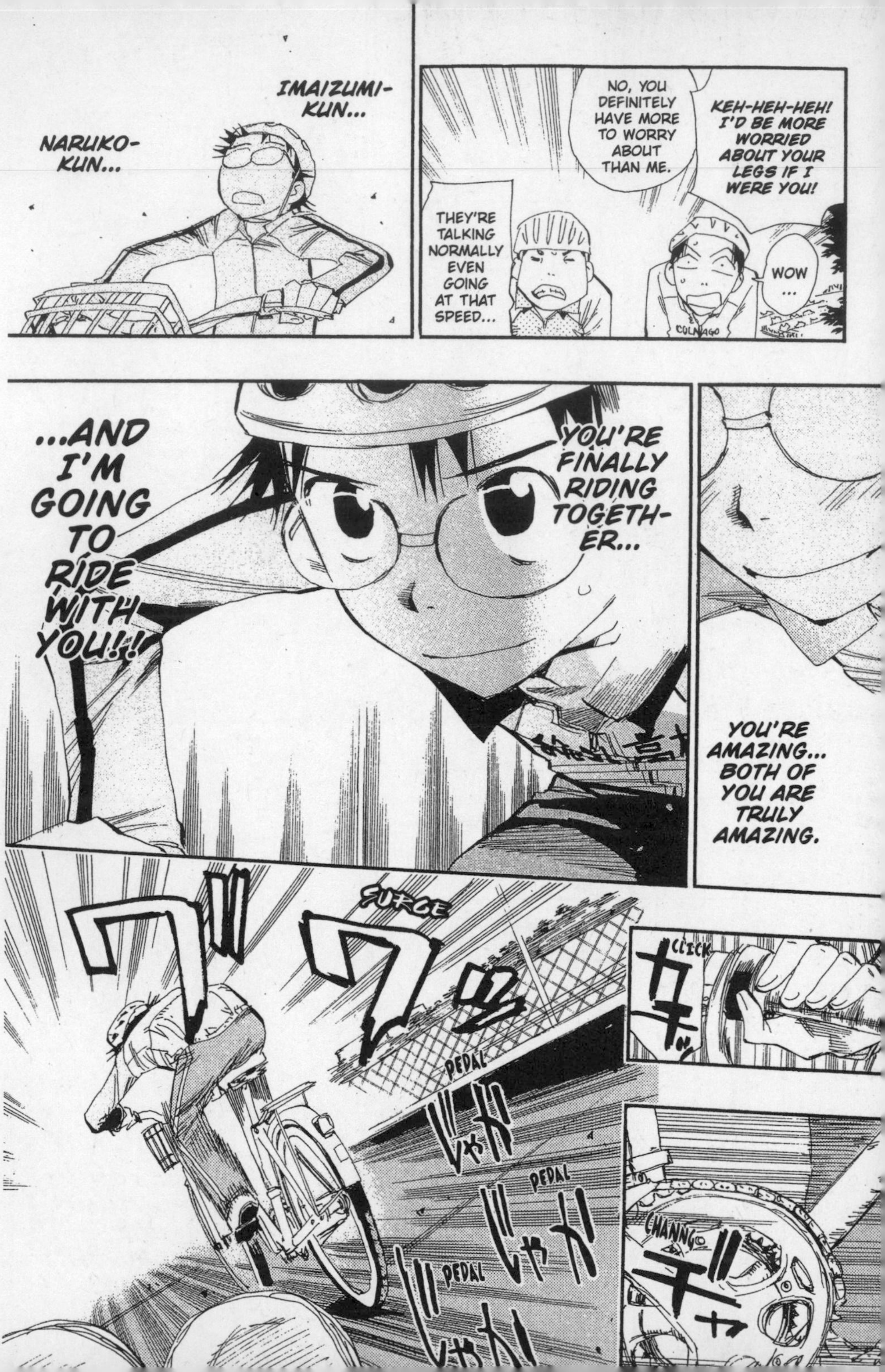
KEH-HEH-HEH! I'D BE MORE WORRIED ABOUT YOUR LEGS IF I WERE YOU!
NO, YOU DEFINITELY HAVE MORE TO WORRY ABOUT THAN ME.
WOW ...
THEY'RE TALKING NORMALLY EVEN GOING AT THAT SPEED...
COLNAGO
IMAIZUMI-KUN...
NARUKO-KUN...
YOU'RE AMAZING... BOTH OF YOU ARE TRULY AMAZING.
YOU'RE FINALLY RIDING TOGETH-ER...
...AND I'M GOING TO RIDE WITH YOU!!
CLICK
CHANNG
SURGE
PEDAL
PEDAL
PEDAL

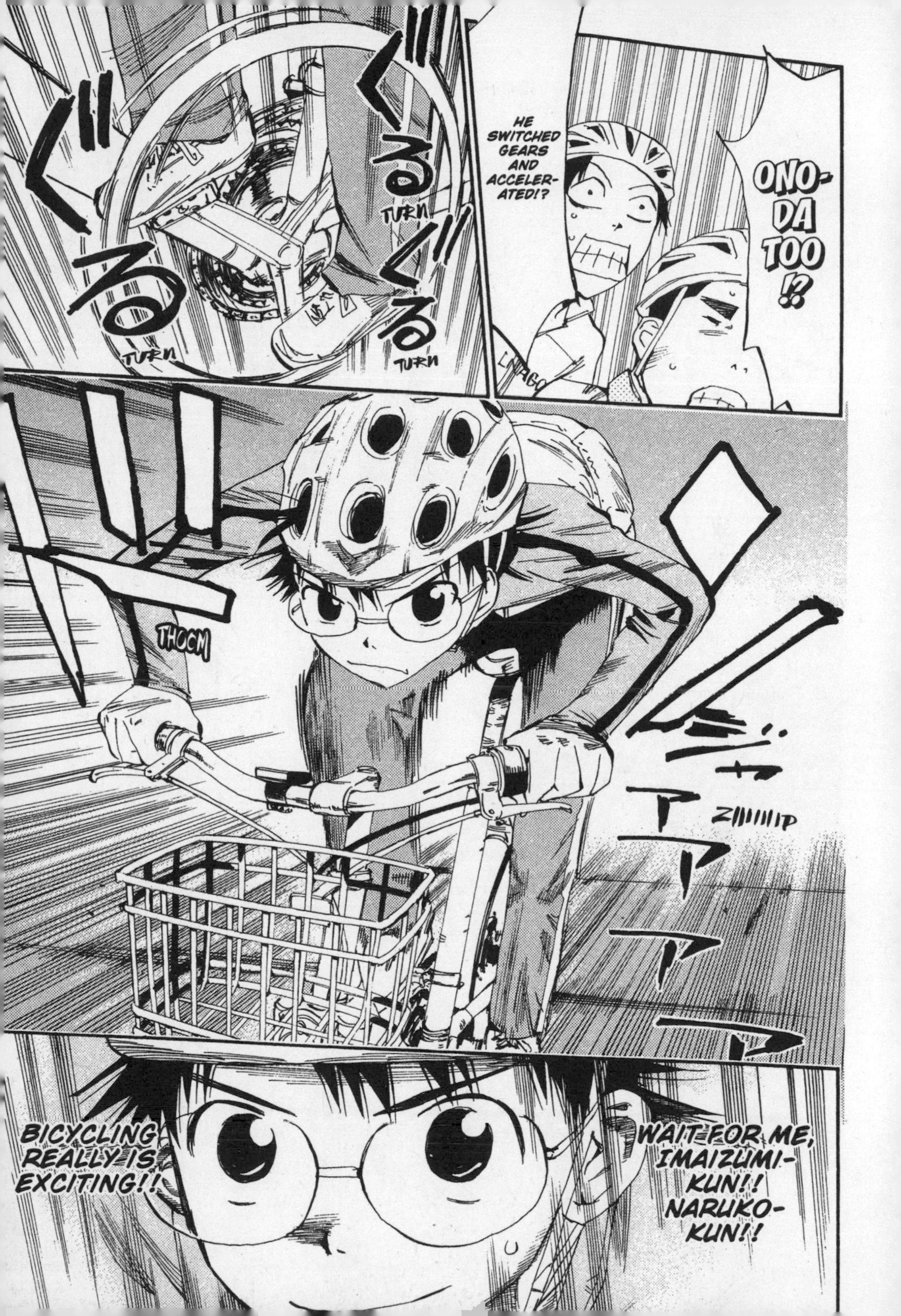
ONO-DA TOO!?
HE SWITCHED GEARS AND ACCELERATED!?
ぐる
TURN
ぐる
TURN
ぐる
TURN
THOOM
ZIIIIIIP
WAIT FOR ME, IMAIZUMI-KUN!! NARUKO-KUN!!
BICYCLING REALLY IS EXCITING!!

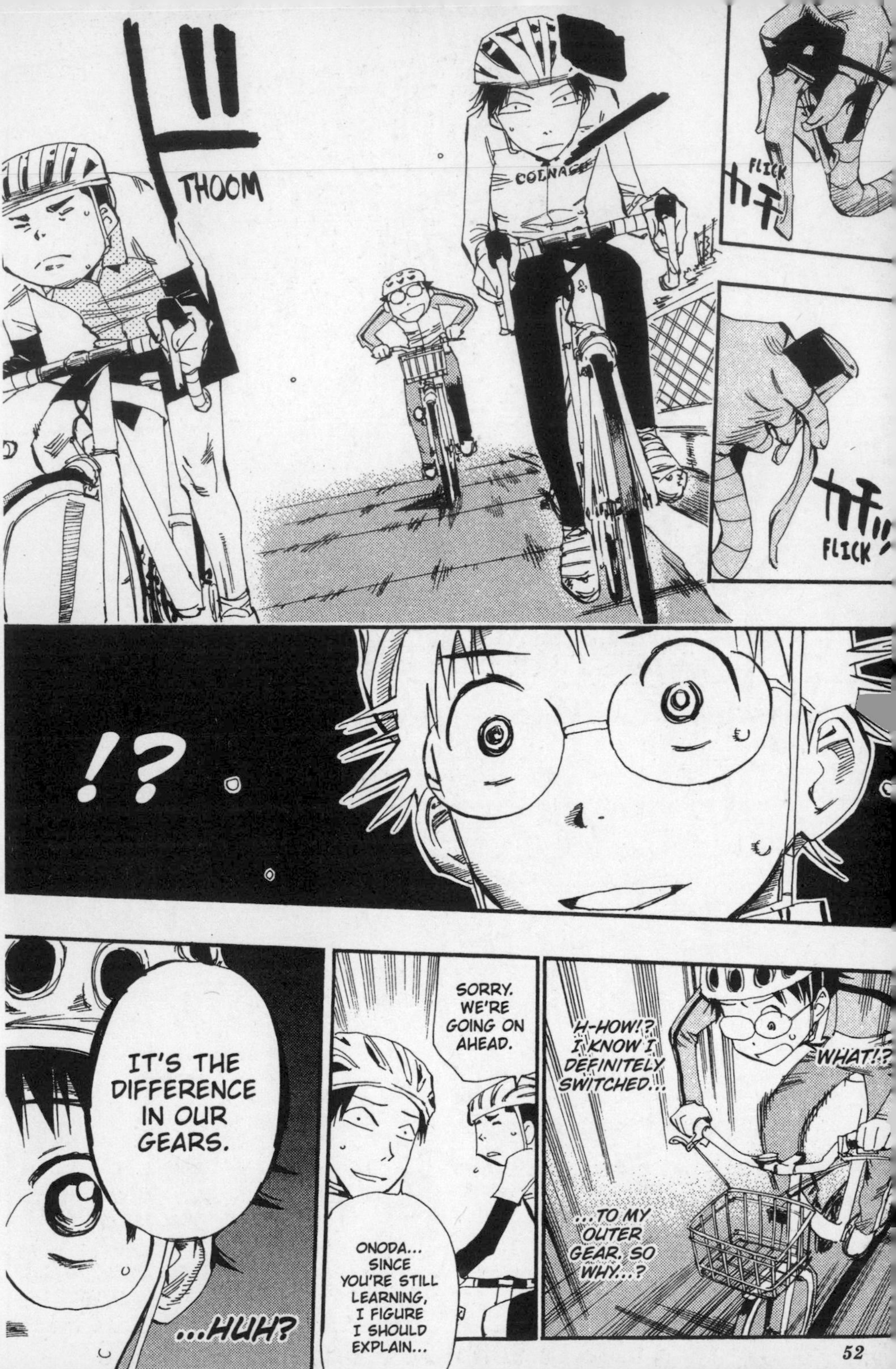
カチ
FLICK
カチ!!
FLICK
ド
THOOM
!?
WHAT!?
H-HOW!? I KNOW I DEFINITELY SWITCHED...
...TO MY OUTER GEAR. SO WHY...?
SORRY. WE'RE GOING ON AHEAD.
ONODA... SINCE YOU'RE STILL LEARNING, I FIGURE I SHOULD EXPLAIN...
IT'S THE DIFFERENCE IN OUR GEARS.
...HUH?

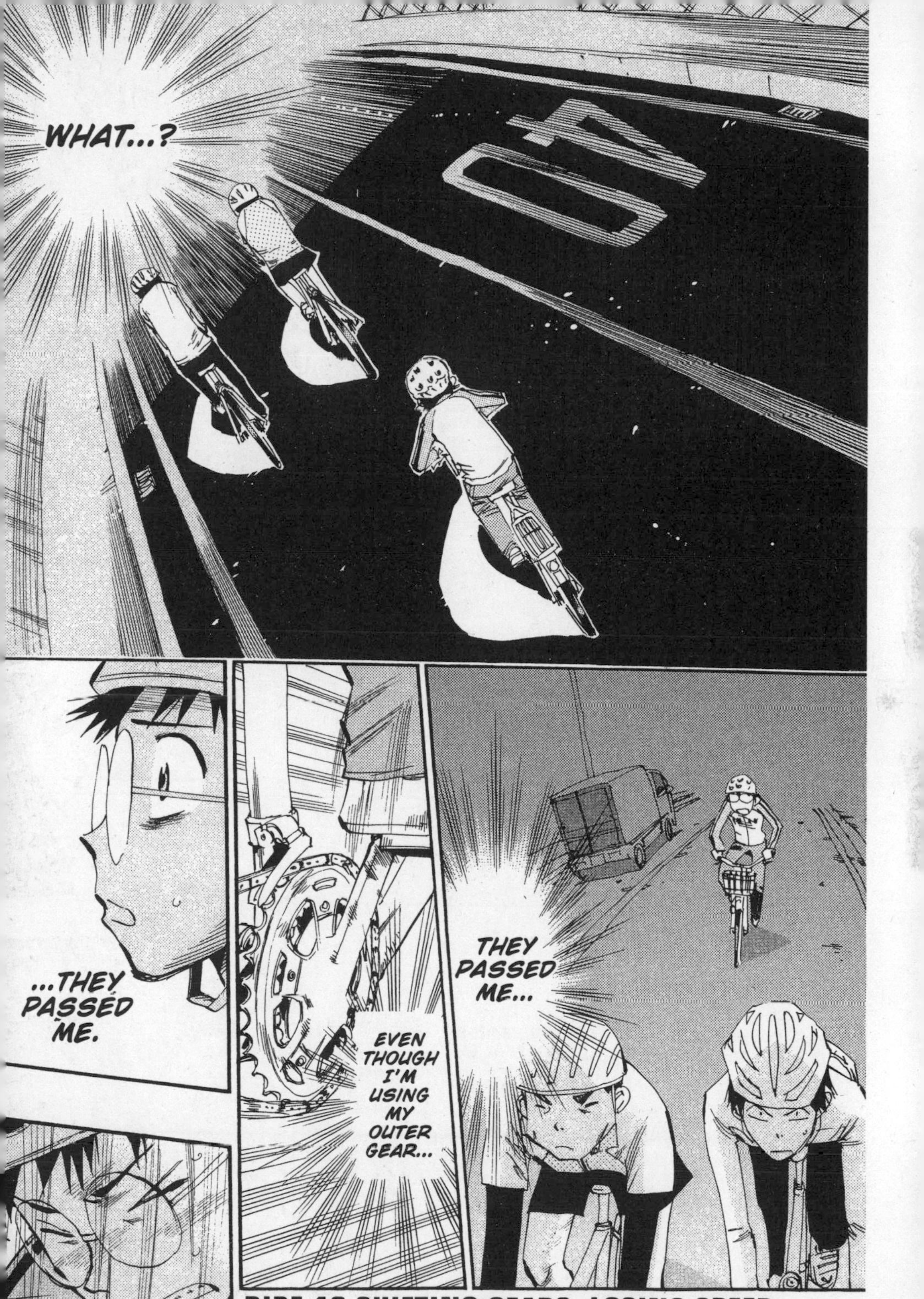
WHAT...?
THEY PASSED ME...
EVEN THOUGH I'M USING MY OUTER GEAR...
...THEY PASSED ME.

RIDE.19 SHIFTING GEARS, LOSING SPEED

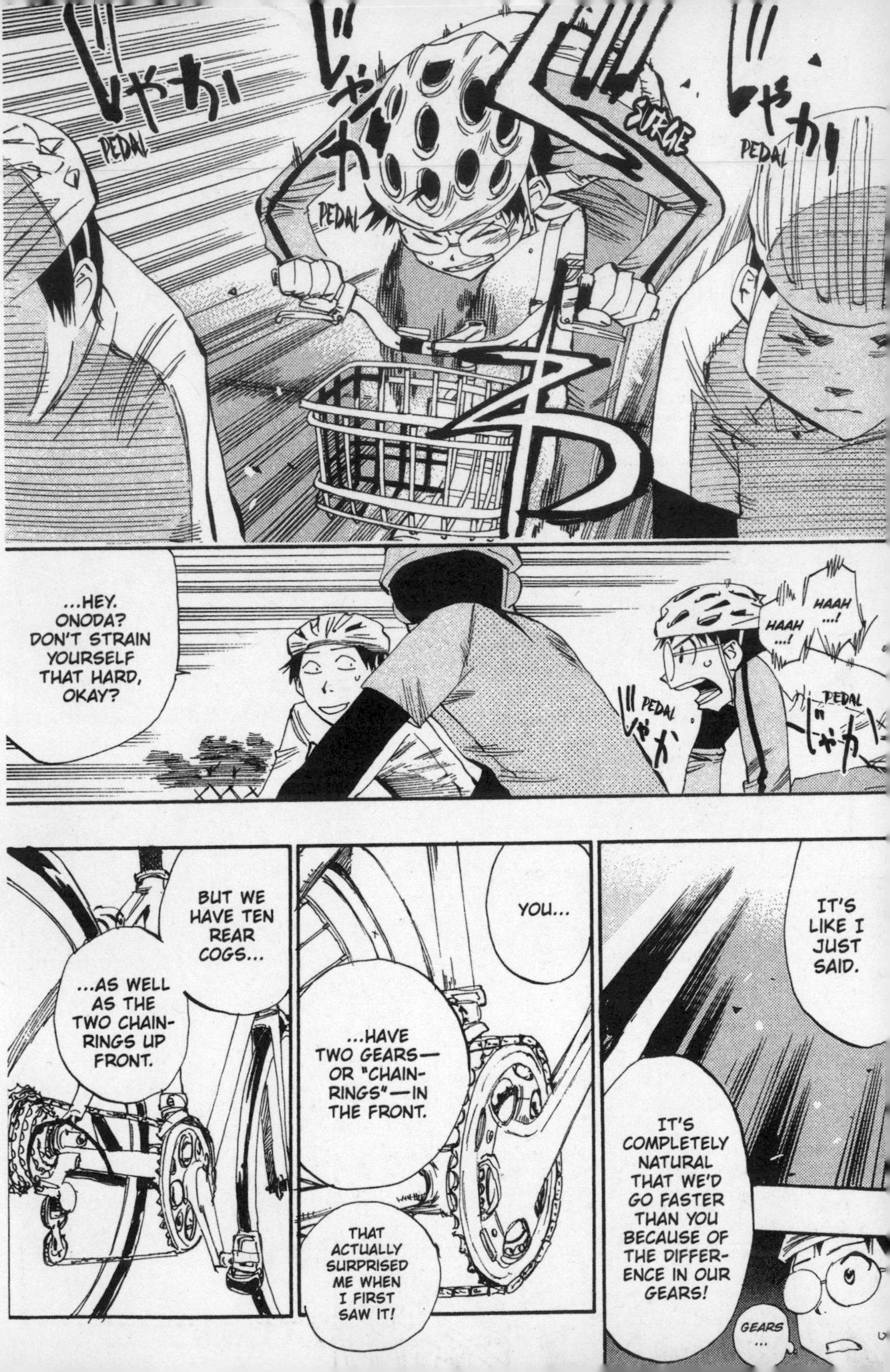
じゃか
PEDAL
SURGE
じゃか
PEDAL
じゃか
PEDAL
HAAH ...!
HAAH ...!
じゃか
PEDAL
じゃか
PEDAL
...HEY. ONODA? DON'T STRAIN YOURSELF THAT HARD, OKAY?
IT'S LIKE I JUST SAID.
IT'S COMPLETELY NATURAL THAT WE'D GO FASTER THAN YOU BECAUSE OF THE DIFFERENCE IN OUR GEARS!
GEARS ...
YOU...
...HAVE TWO GEARS—OR "CHAINRINGS"—IN THE FRONT.
THAT ACTUALLY SURPRISED ME WHEN I FIRST SAW IT!
BUT WE HAVE TEN REAR COGS...
...AS WELL AS THE TWO CHAINRINGS UP FRONT.

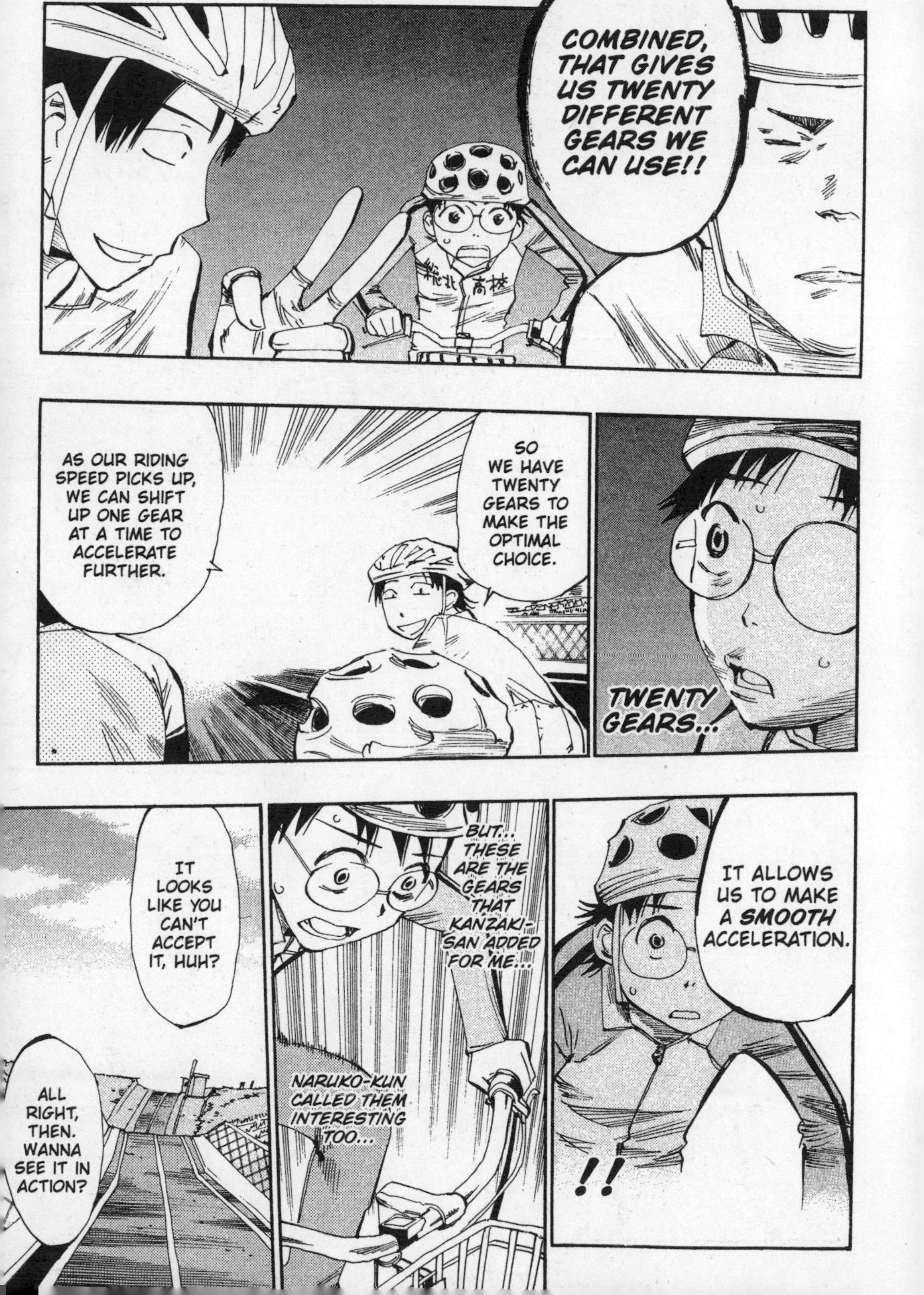
COMBINED, THAT GIVES US TWENTY DIFFERENT GEARS WE CAN USE!!
TWENTY GEARS...
SO WE HAVE TWENTY GEARS TO MAKE THE OPTIMAL CHOICE.
AS OUR RIDING SPEED PICKS UP, WE CAN SHIFT UP ONE GEAR AT A TIME TO ACCELERATE FURTHER.
IT ALLOWS US TO MAKE A ***SMOOTH*** ACCELERATION.
!!
BUT... THESE ARE THE GEARS THAT KANZAKI-SAN ADDED FOR ME...
NARUKO-KUN CALLED THEM INTERESTING TOO...
IT LOOKS LIKE YOU CAN'T ACCEPT IT, HUH?
ALL RIGHT, THEN. WANNA SEE IT IN ACTION?

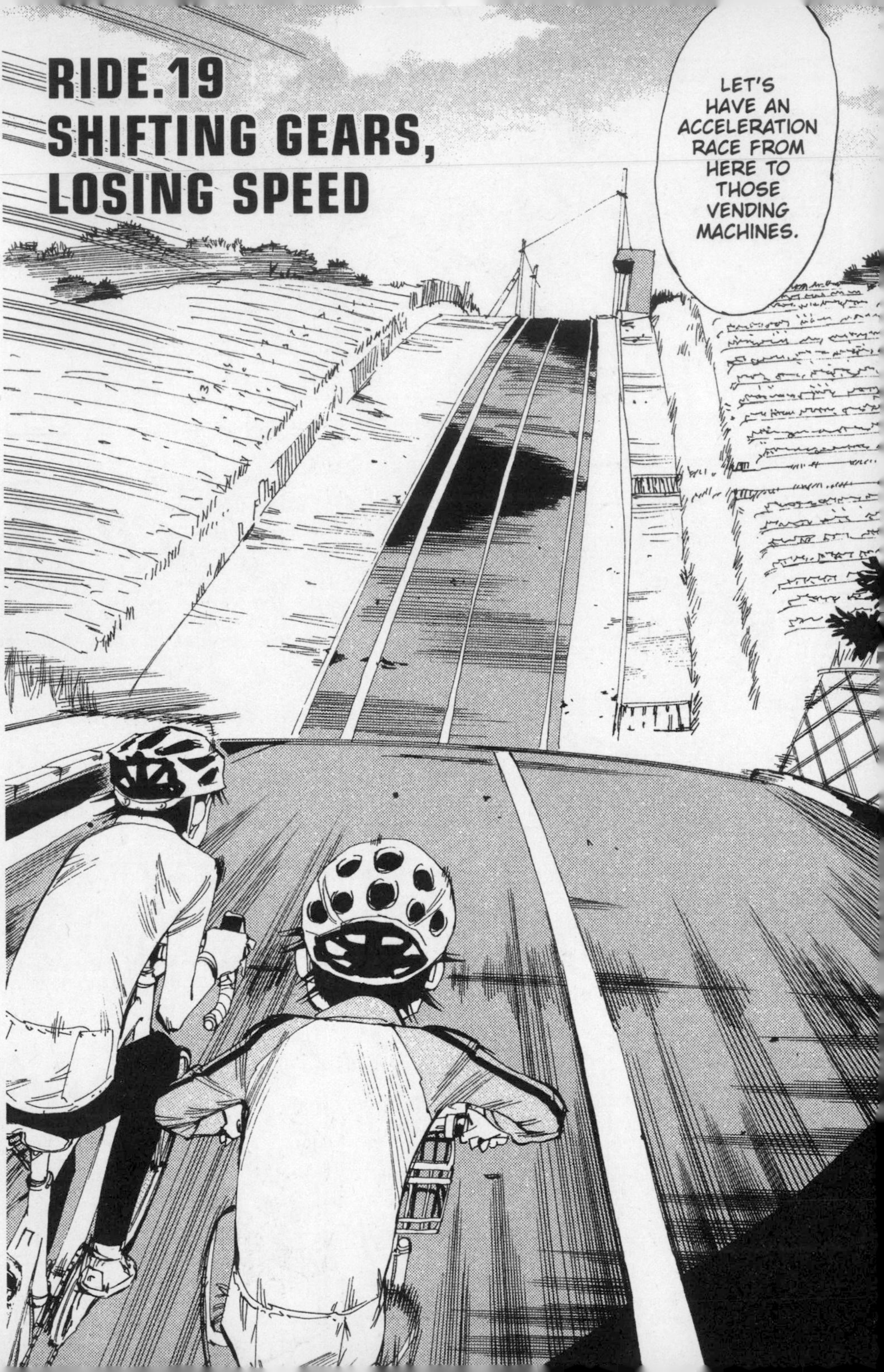
RIDE.19
SHIFTING GEARS, LOSING SPEED
LET'S HAVE AN ACCELERATION RACE FROM HERE TO THOSE VENDING MACHINES.

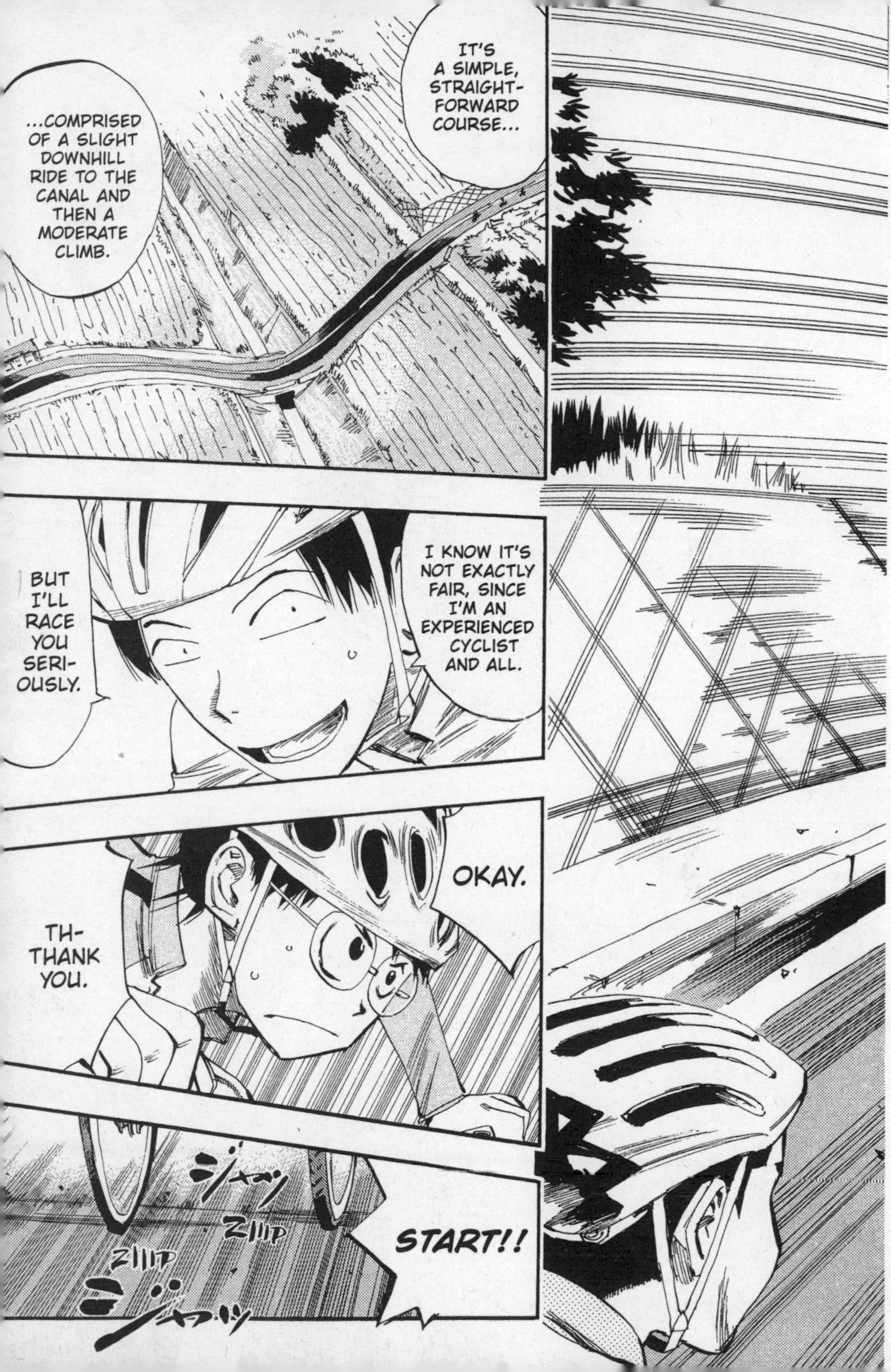
IT'S A SIMPLE, STRAIGHT-FORWARD COURSE...
...COMPRISED OF A SLIGHT DOWNHILL RIDE TO THE CANAL AND THEN A MODERATE CLIMB.
I KNOW IT'S NOT EXACTLY FAIR, SINCE I'M AN EXPERIENCED CYCLIST AND ALL.
BUT I'LL RACE YOU SERI-OUSLY.
OKAY.
TH-THANK YOU.
START!!
ZIIIP
ZIIIP

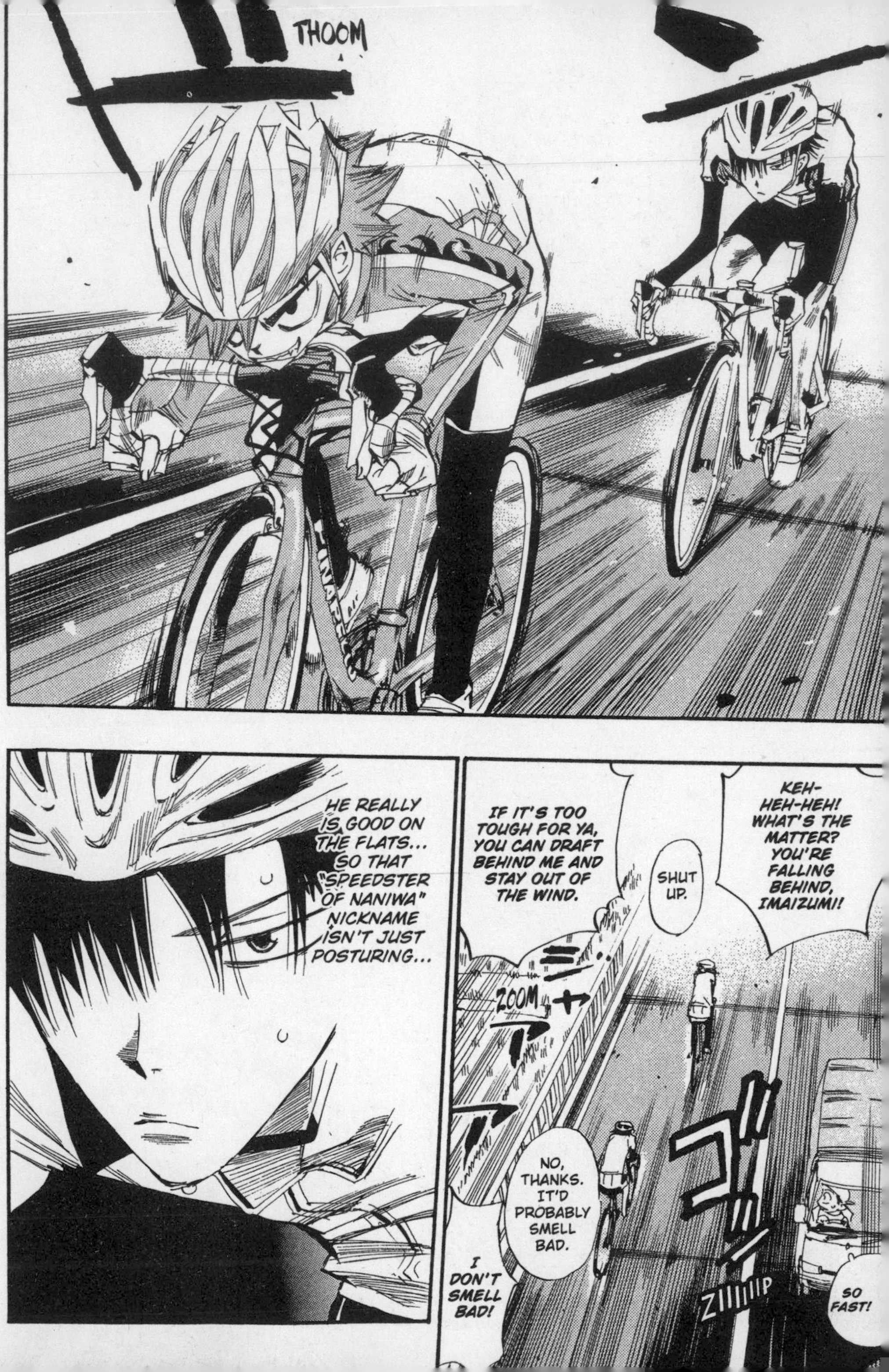
THOOM
KEH-HEH-HEH! WHAT'S THE MATTER? YOU'RE FALLING BEHIND, IMAIZUMI!
SHUT UP.
IF IT'S TOO TOUGH FOR YA, YOU CAN DRAFT BEHIND ME AND STAY OUT OF THE WIND.
ZOOM
SO FAST!
ZIIIIIP
NO, THANKS. IT'D PROBABLY SMELL BAD.
I DON'T SMELL BAD!
HE REALLY IS GOOD ON THE FLATS... SO THAT "SPEEDSTER OF NANIWA" NICKNAME ISN'T JUST POSTURING...

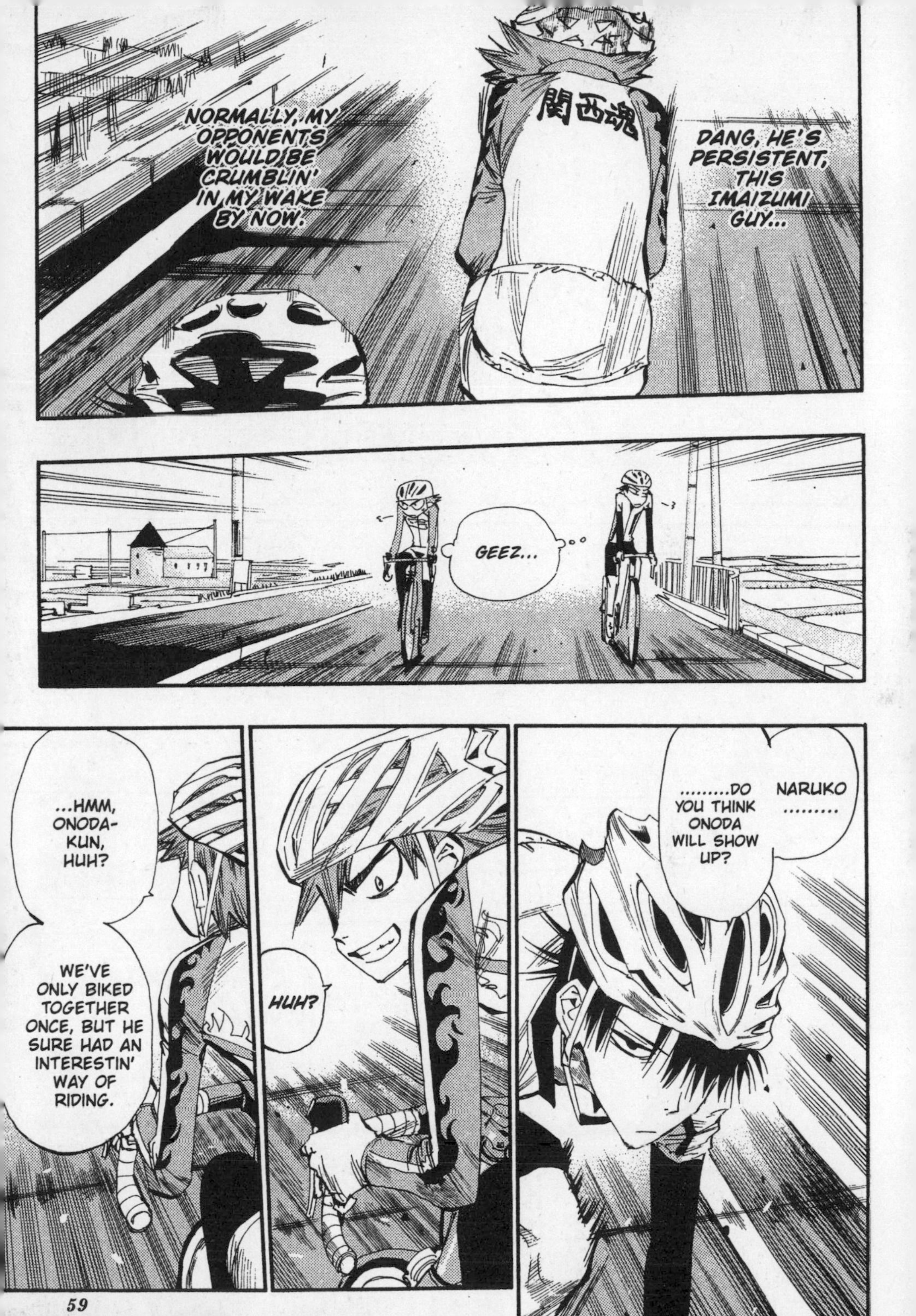
DANG, HE'S PERSISTENT, THIS IMAIZUMI GUY...
NORMALLY, MY OPPONENTS WOULD BE CRUMBLIN' IN MY WAKE BY NOW.
GEEZ...
NARUKO.........
.........DO YOU THINK ONODA WILL SHOW UP?
HUH?
...HMM, ONODA-KUN, HUH?
WE'VE ONLY BIKED TOGETHER ONCE, BUT HE SURE HAD AN INTERESTIN' WAY OF RIDING.

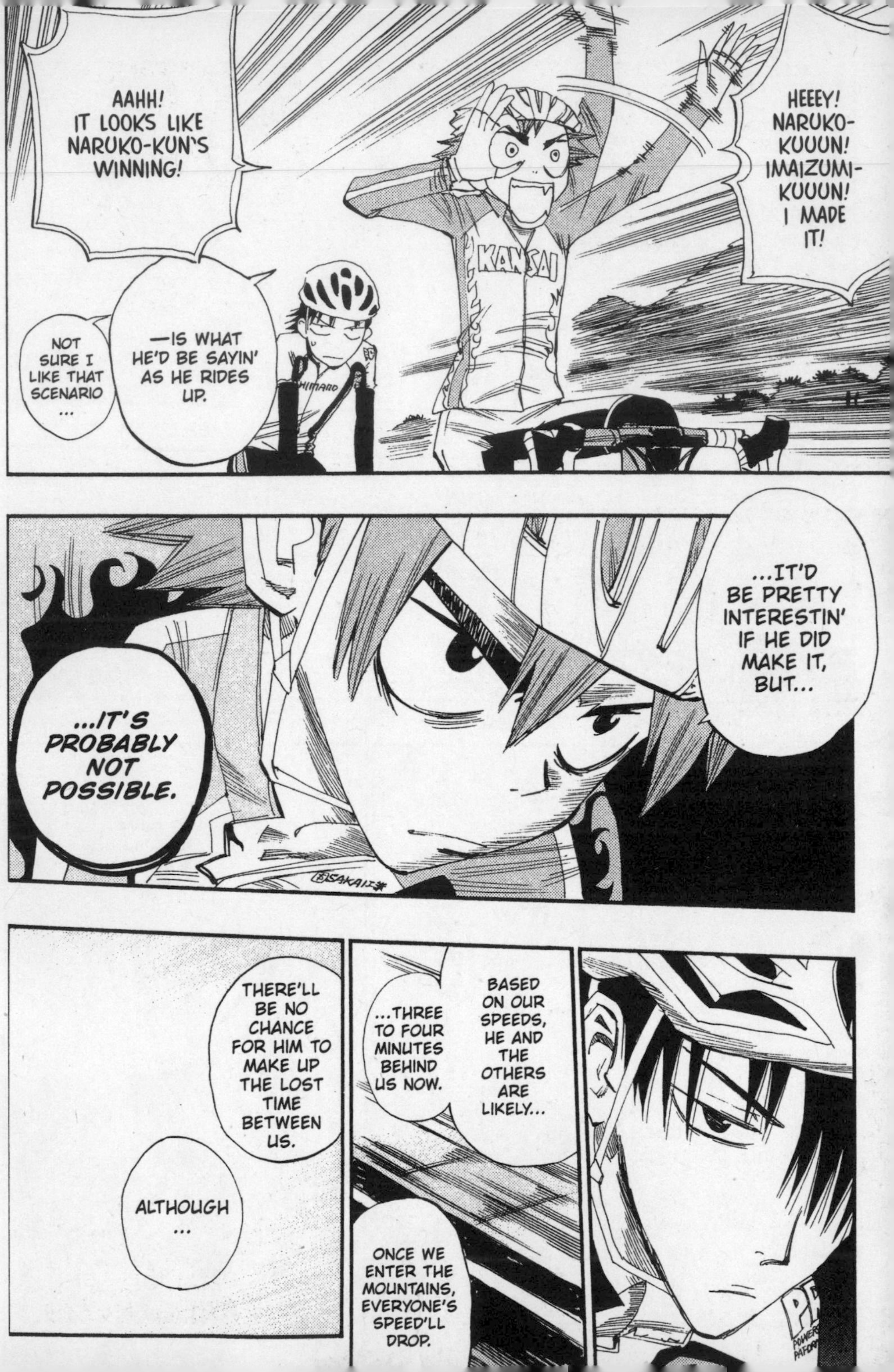
HEEEY! NARUKO-KUUUN! IMAIZUMI-KUUUN! I MADE IT!
AAHH! IT LOOKS LIKE NARUKO-KUN'S WINNING!
—IS WHAT HE'D BE SAYIN' AS HE RIDES UP.
NOT SURE I LIKE THAT SCENARIO...
...IT'D BE PRETTY INTERESTIN' IF HE DID MAKE IT, BUT...
...IT'S PROBABLY NOT POSSIBLE.
BASED ON OUR SPEEDS, HE AND THE OTHERS ARE LIKELY...
...THREE TO FOUR MINUTES BEHIND US NOW.
ONCE WE ENTER THE MOUNTAINS, EVERYONE'S SPEED'LL DROP.
THERE'LL BE NO CHANCE FOR HIM TO MAKE UP THE LOST TIME BETWEEN US.
ALTHOUGH...

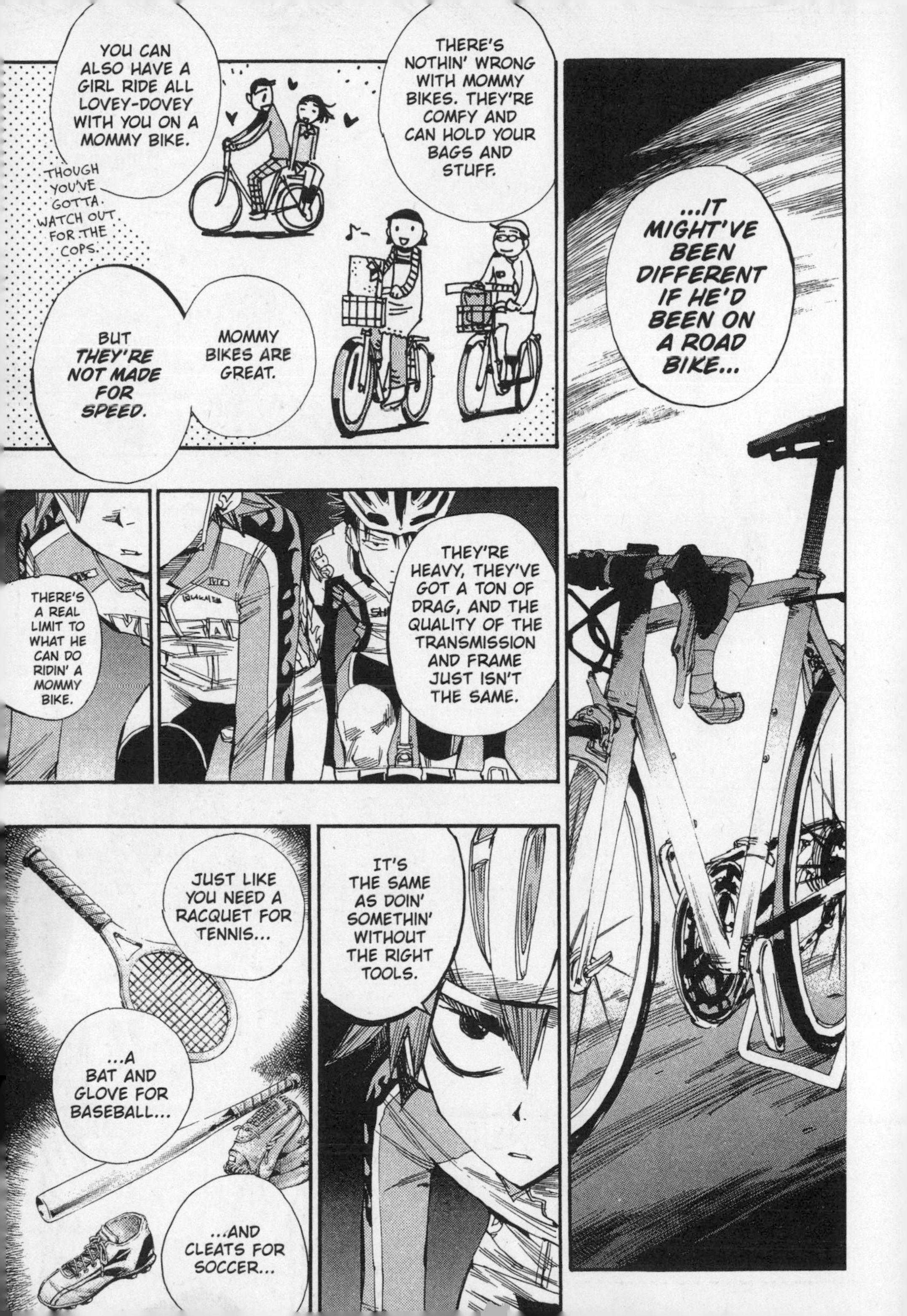
...IT MIGHT'VE BEEN DIFFERENT IF HE'D BEEN ON A ROAD BIKE...
THERE'S NOTHIN' WRONG WITH MOMMY BIKES. THEY'RE COMFY AND CAN HOLD YOUR BAGS AND STUFF.
YOU CAN ALSO HAVE A GIRL RIDE ALL LOVEY-DOVEY WITH YOU ON A MOMMY BIKE.
THOUGH YOU'VE GOTTA WATCH OUT FOR THE COPS.
MOMMY BIKES ARE GREAT.
BUT THEY'RE NOT MADE FOR SPEED.
THEY'RE HEAVY, THEY'VE GOT A TON OF DRAG, AND THE QUALITY OF THE TRANSMISSION AND FRAME JUST ISN'T THE SAME.
THERE'S A REAL LIMIT TO WHAT HE CAN DO RIDIN' A MOMMY BIKE.
IT'S THE SAME AS DOIN' SOMETHIN' WITHOUT THE RIGHT TOOLS.
JUST LIKE YOU NEED A RACQUET FOR TENNIS...
...A BAT AND GLOVE FOR BASEBALL...
...AND CLEATS FOR SOCCER...

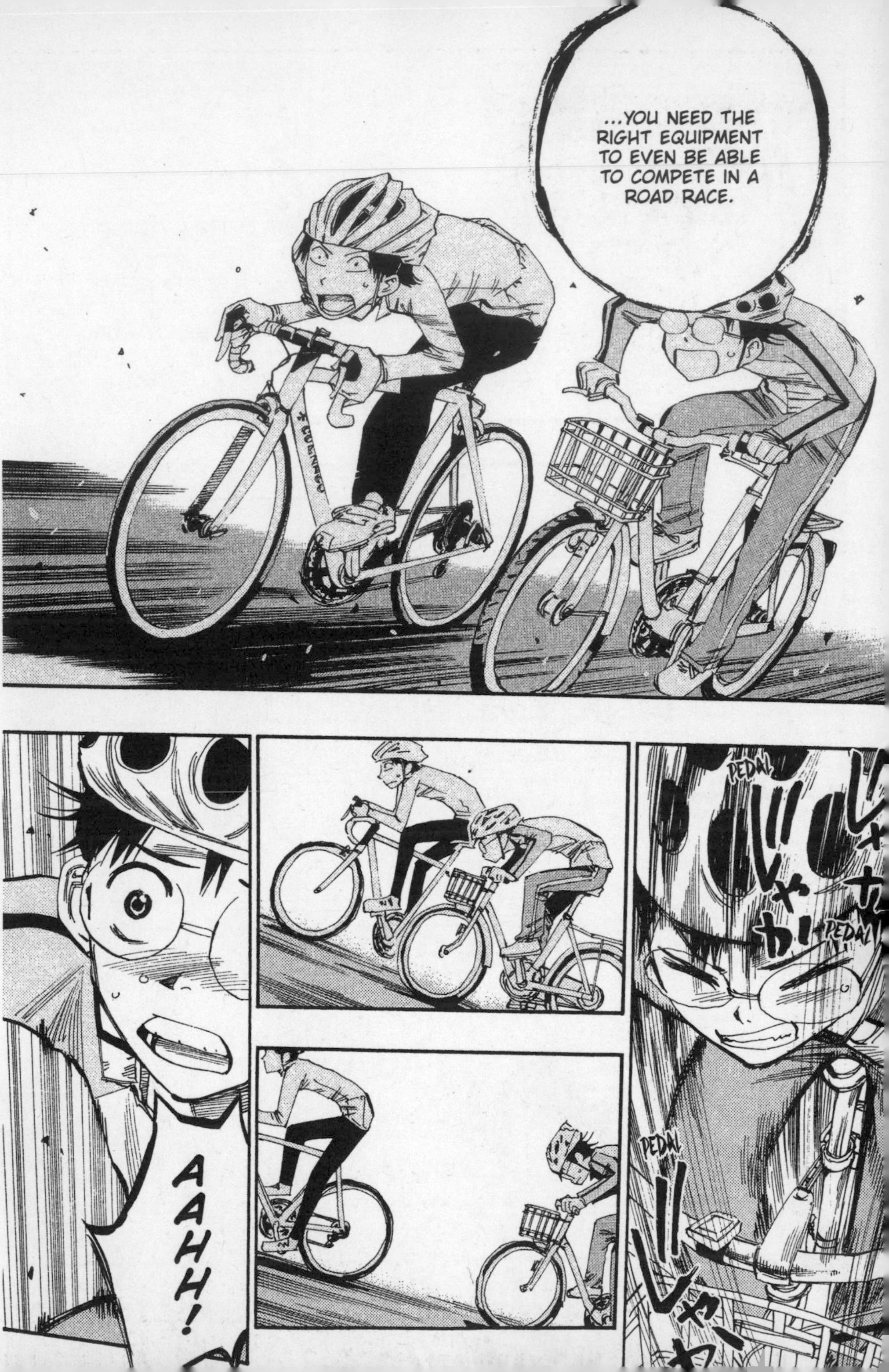
...YOU NEED THE RIGHT EQUIPMENT TO EVEN BE ABLE TO COMPETE IN A ROAD RACE.
PEDAL
PEDAL
PEDAL
AAHH!

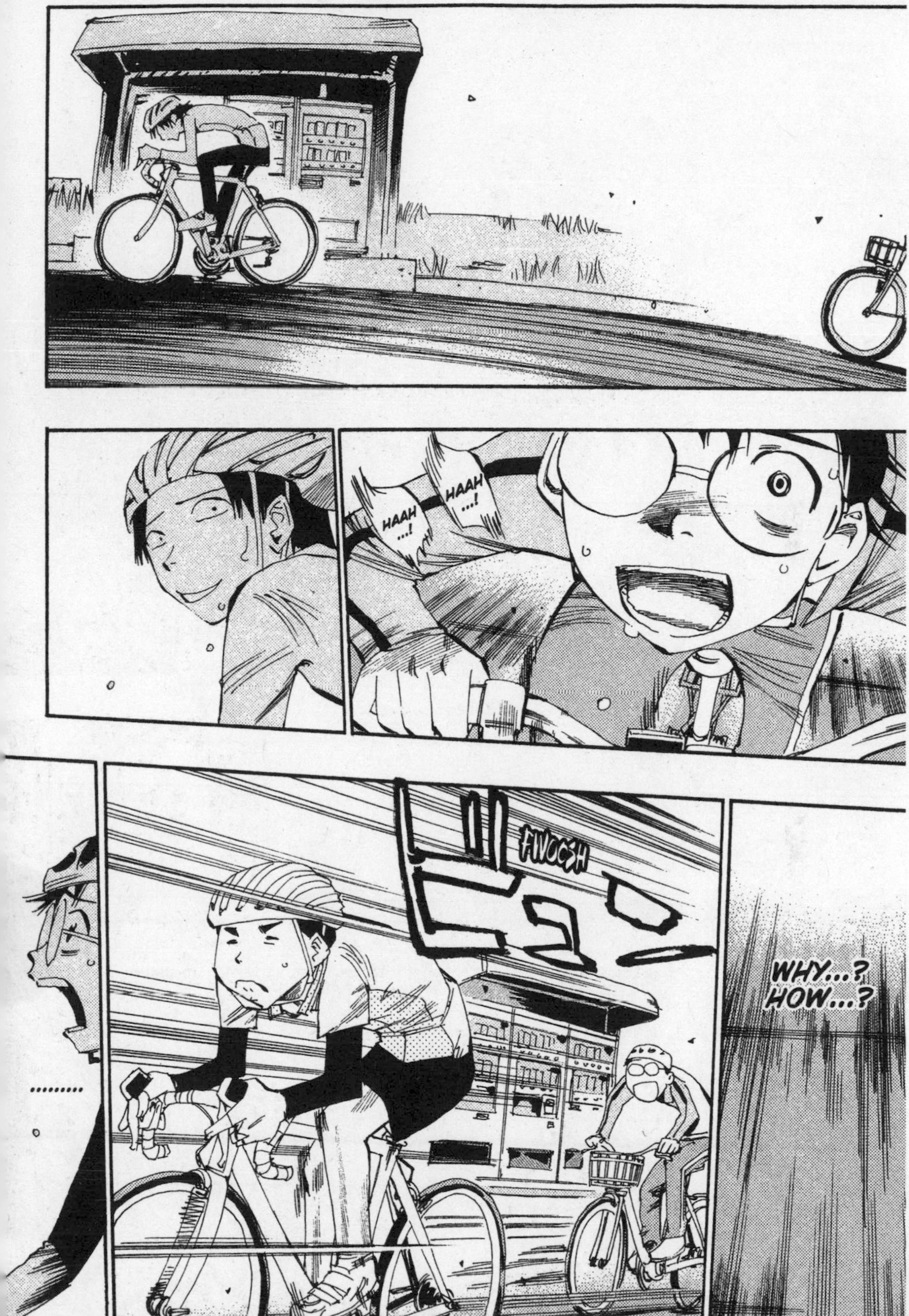
HAAH ...!
HAAH ...!
WHY...? HOW...?
FWOOSH
....

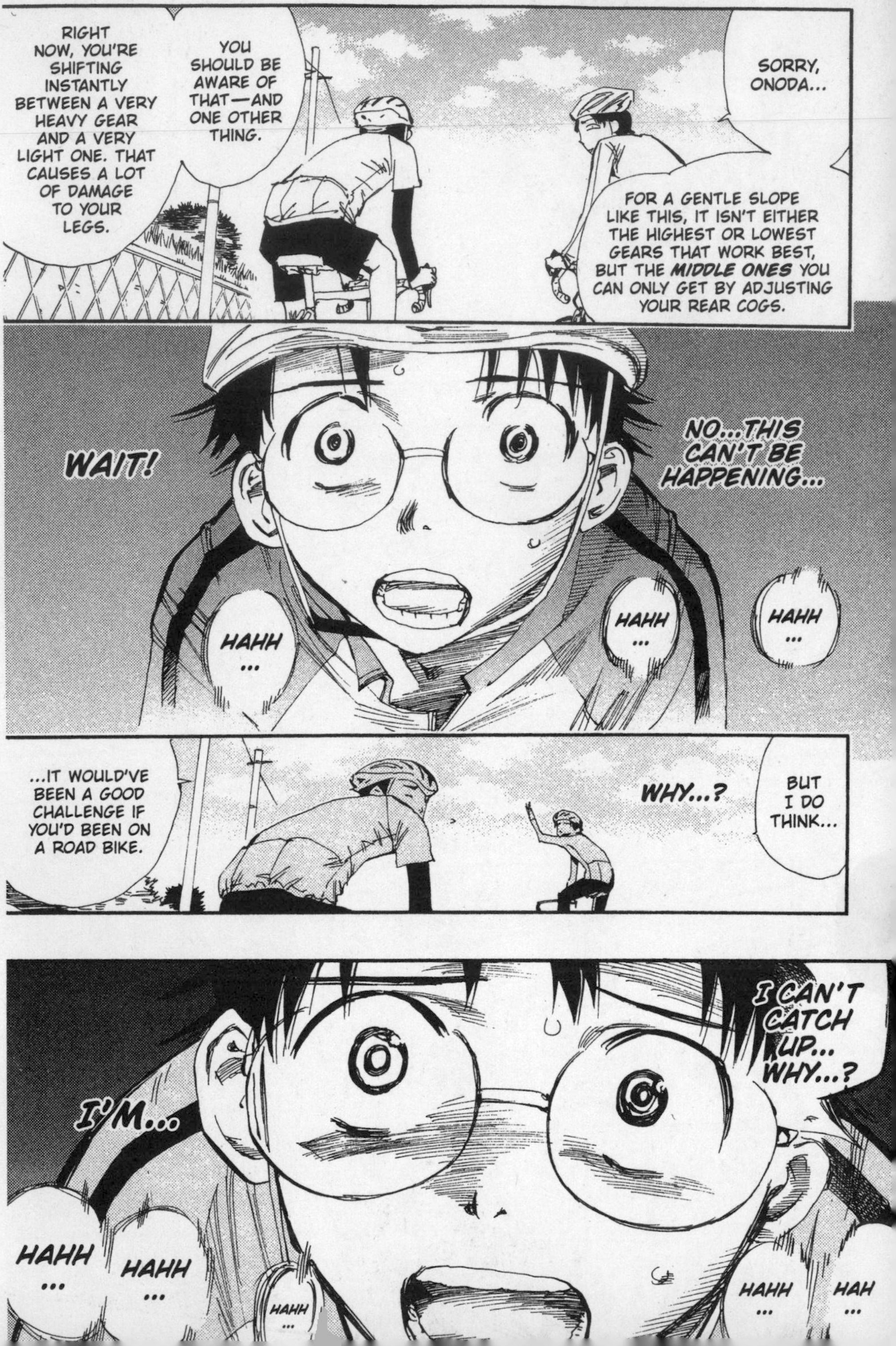
SORRY, ONODA...
RIGHT NOW, YOU'RE SHIFTING INSTANTLY BETWEEN A VERY HEAVY GEAR AND A VERY LIGHT ONE. THAT CAUSES A LOT OF DAMAGE TO YOUR LEGS.
YOU SHOULD BE AWARE OF THAT—AND ONE OTHER THING.
FOR A GENTLE SLOPE LIKE THIS, IT ISN'T EITHER THE HIGHEST OR LOWEST GEARS THAT WORK BEST, BUT THE ***MIDDLE ONES*** YOU CAN ONLY GET BY ADJUSTING YOUR REAR COGS.
NO...THIS CAN'T BE HAPPENING...
WAIT!
HAHH...
HAHH...
HAHH...
BUT I DO THINK...
WHY...?
...IT WOULD'VE BEEN A GOOD CHALLENGE IF YOU'D BEEN ON A ROAD BIKE.
I CAN'T CATCH UP... WHY...?
I'M...
HAH...
HAHH...
HAHH...
HAHH...
HAHH...

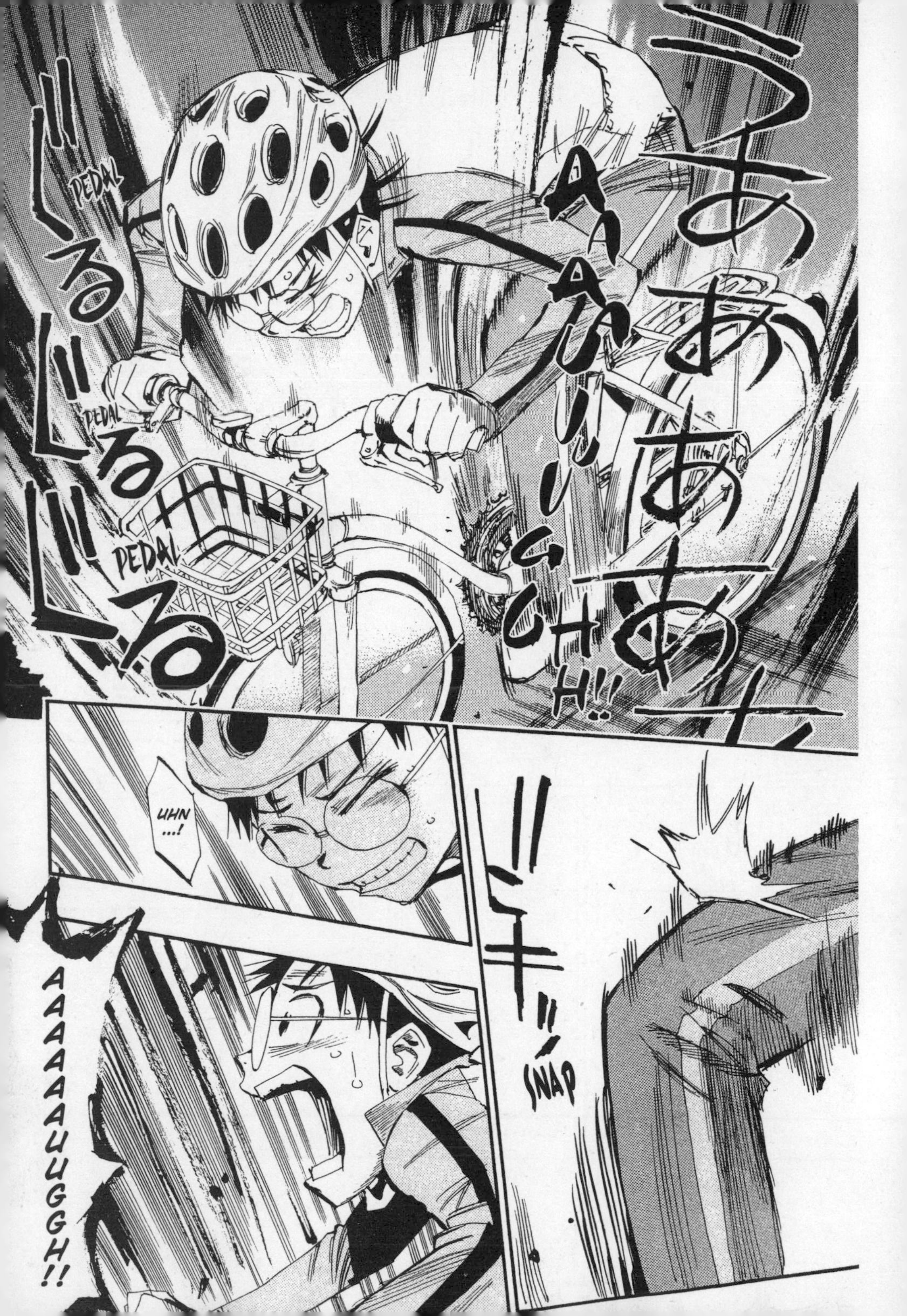
AAAGGHH!!
PEDAL
PEDAL
PEDAL
SNAP
UHN ...!
AAAAAAUUGGH!!

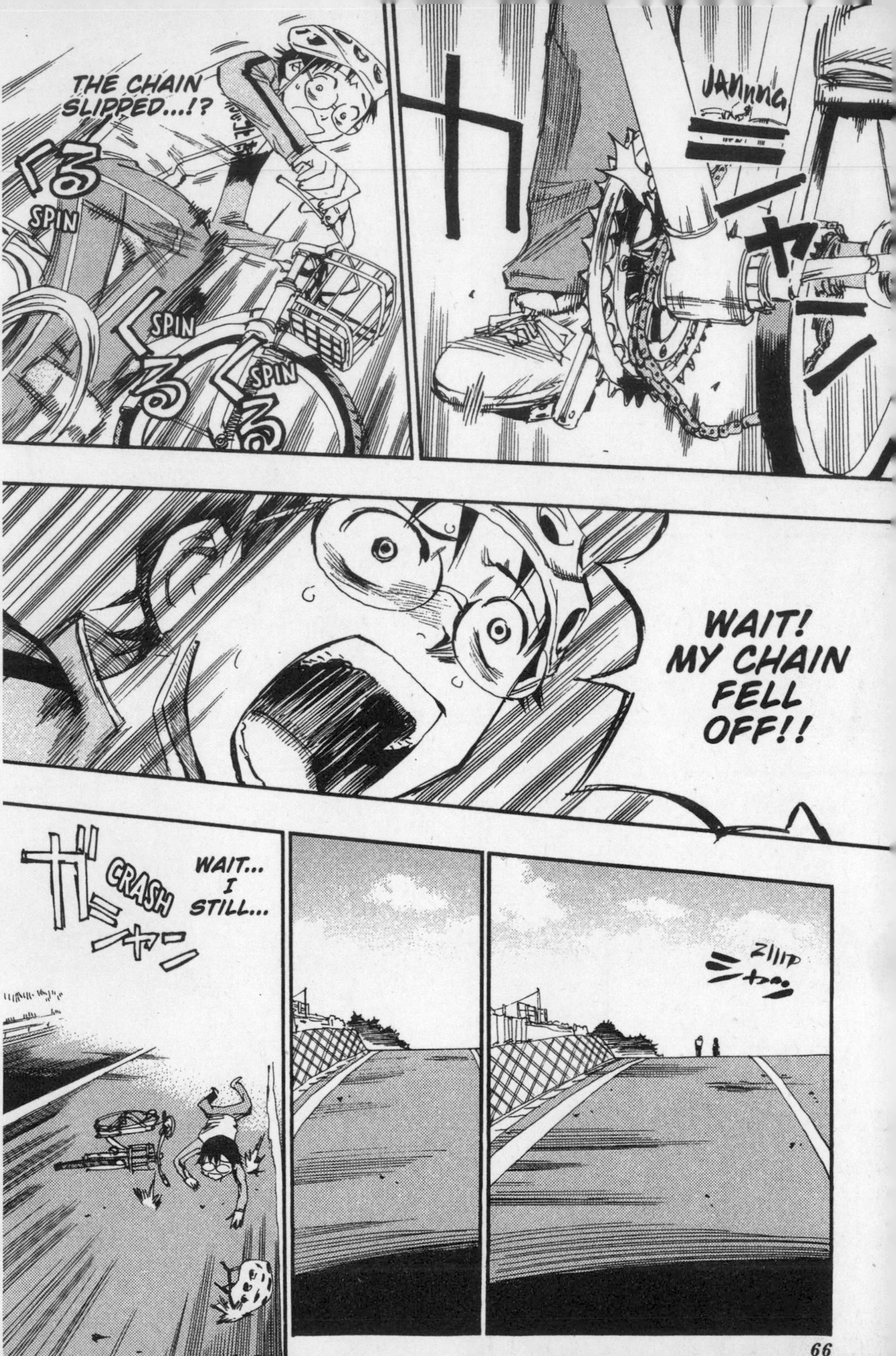
JANnnG
THE CHAIN SLIPPED...!?
SPIN
SPIN
SPIN
WAIT! MY CHAIN FELL OFF!!
ZIIIP
CRASH
WAIT... I STILL...

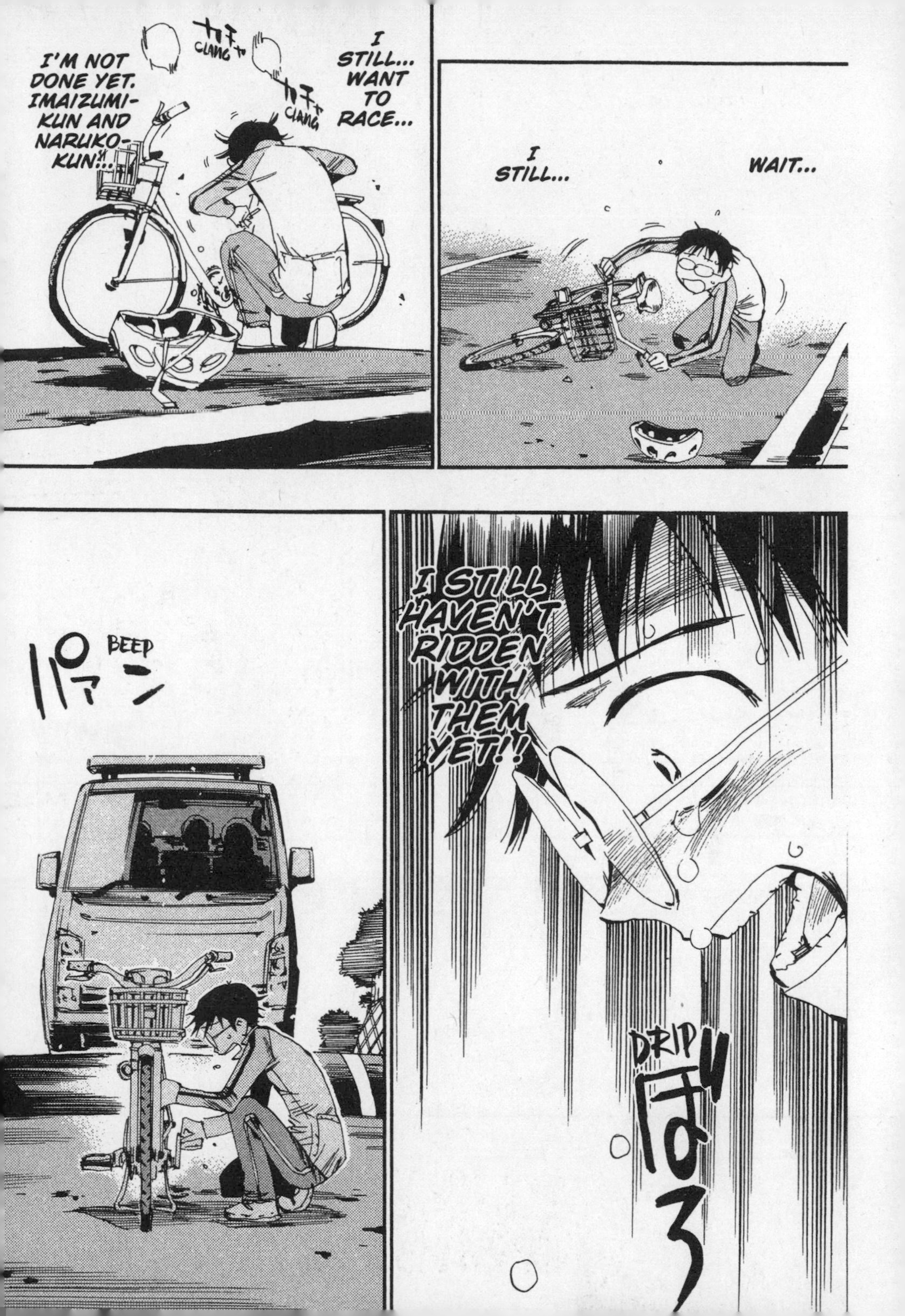

I STILL...
WAIT...
I STILL... WANT TO RACE...
CLANG
CLANG
I'M NOT DONE YET. IMAIZUMI-KUN AND NARUKO-KUN...
I STILL HAVEN'T RIDDEN WITH THEM YET!!
DRIP
BEEP

HAHH...

THE BROOM WAGON...

Onoda.

KRICK

Stop.

LEAN

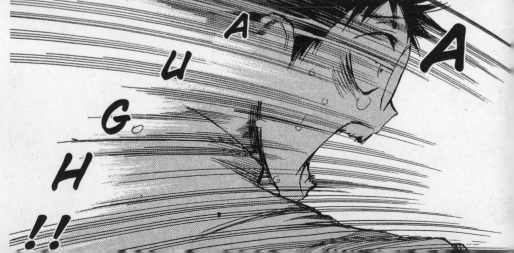

AUGH!!

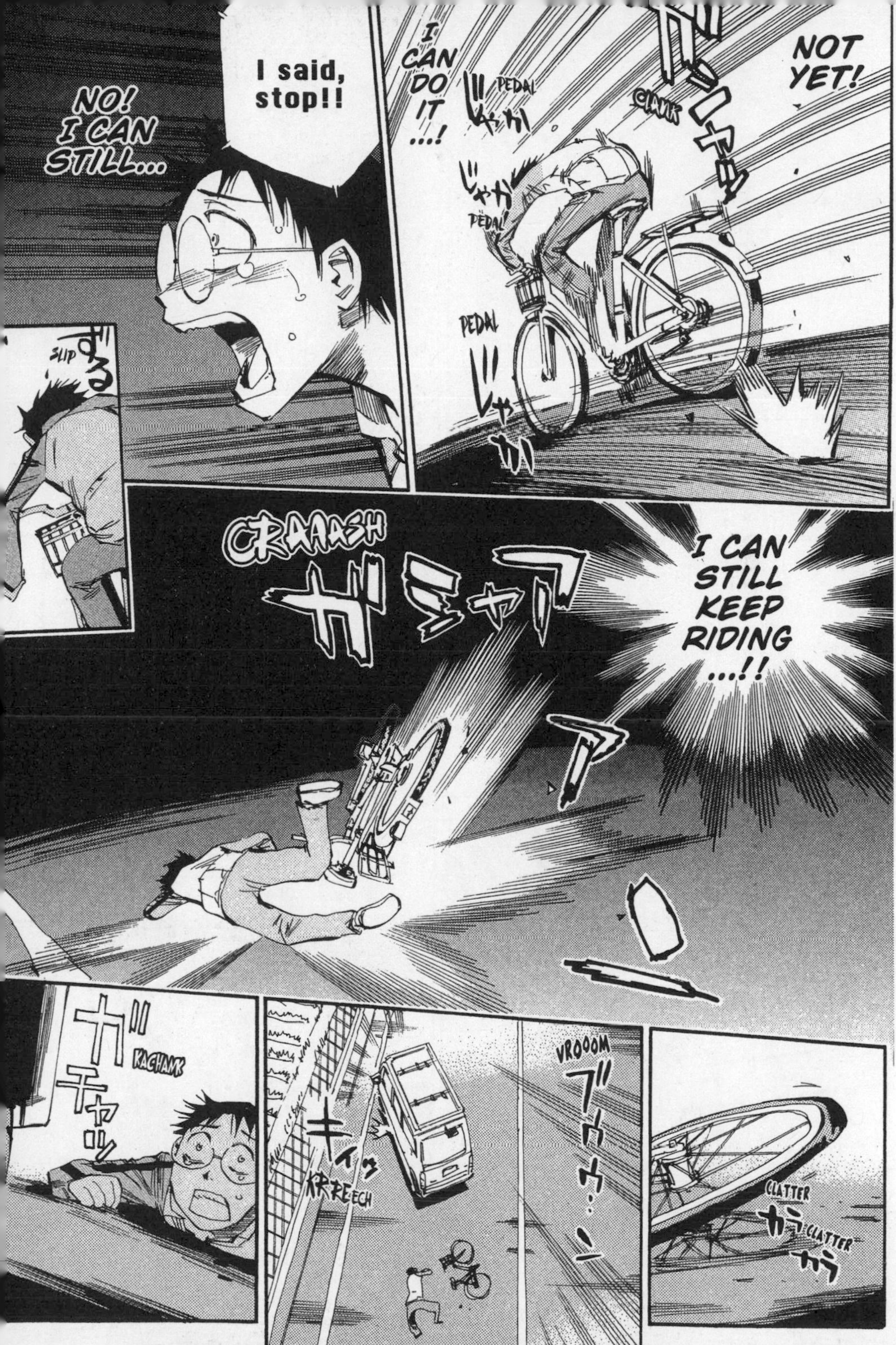
NOT YET!
CLANK
I CAN DO IT ...!
PEDAL
PEDAL
PEDAL
I said, stop!!
NO! I CAN STILL...
SLIP
I CAN STILL KEEP RIDING ...!!
CRAAASH
CLATTER
CLATTER
VROOOM
KRREECH
KACHANK

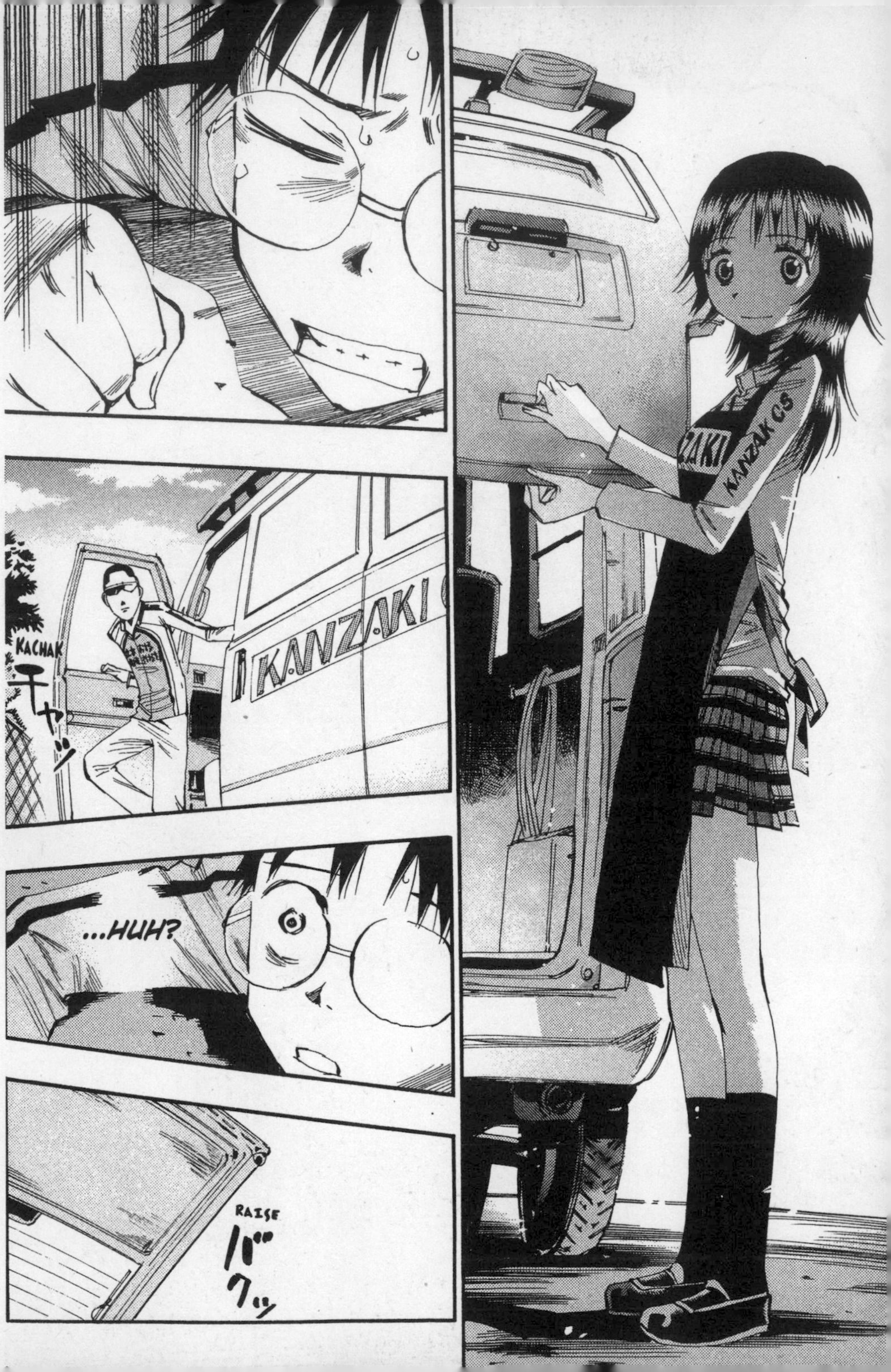
KACHAK
チャッ
KANZAKI
...HUH?
RAISE
バクッ

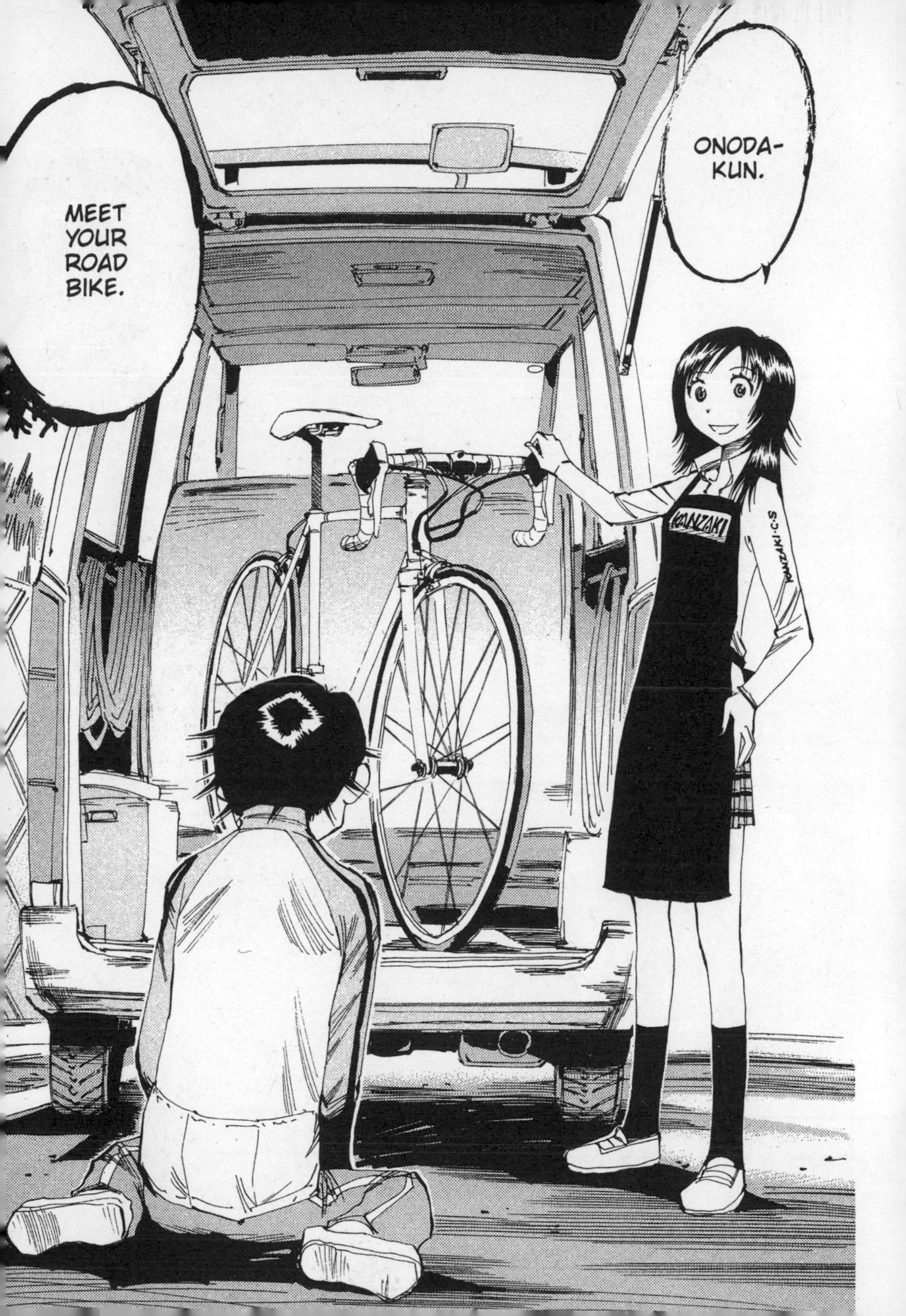
ONODA-KUN.
MEET YOUR ROAD BIKE.
KANZAKI
KANZAKI-C.S

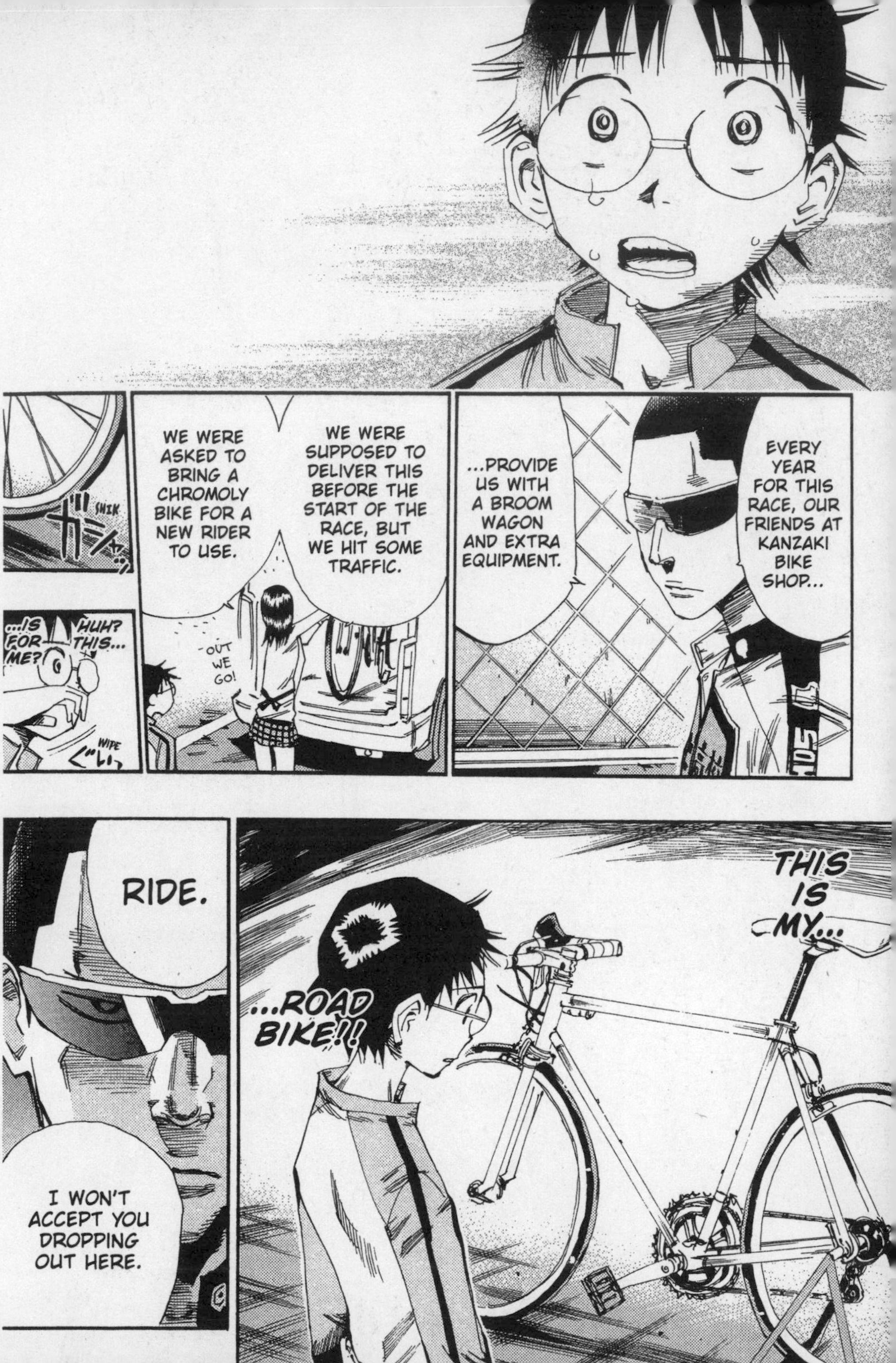
EVERY YEAR FOR THIS RACE, OUR FRIENDS AT KANZAKI BIKE SHOP...
...PROVIDE US WITH A BROOM WAGON AND EXTRA EQUIPMENT.
WE WERE SUPPOSED TO DELIVER THIS BEFORE THE START OF THE RACE, BUT WE HIT SOME TRAFFIC.
WE WERE ASKED TO BRING A CHROMOLY BIKE FOR A NEW RIDER TO USE.
OUT WE GO!
SHIK
HUH? THIS...
...IS FOR ME?
WIPE
THIS IS MY...
...ROAD BIKE!!
RIDE.
I WON'T ACCEPT YOU DROPPING OUT HERE.

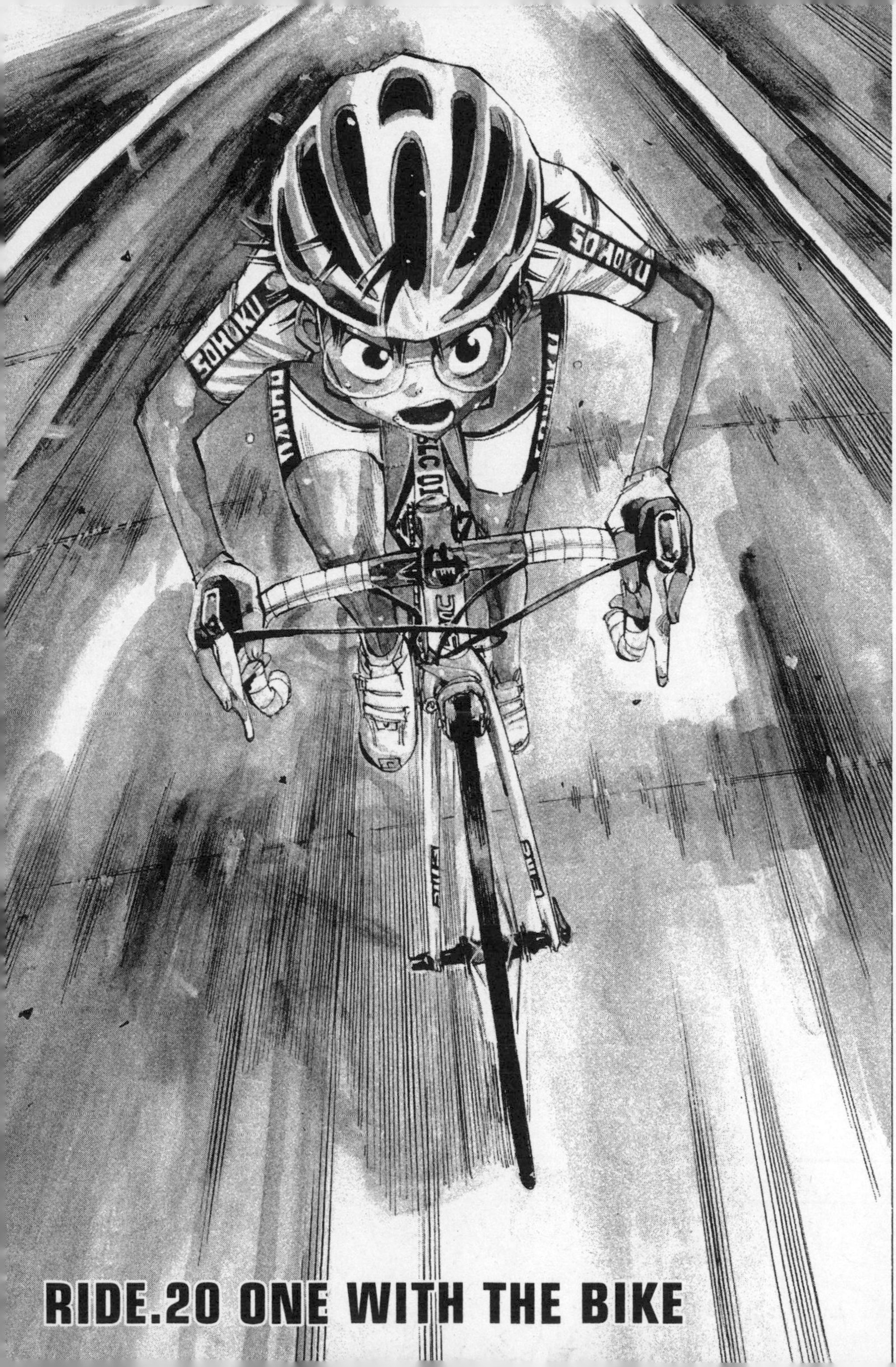
SOHOKU

RIDE.20 ONE WITH THE BIKE

YOWAMUSHI PEDAL 2

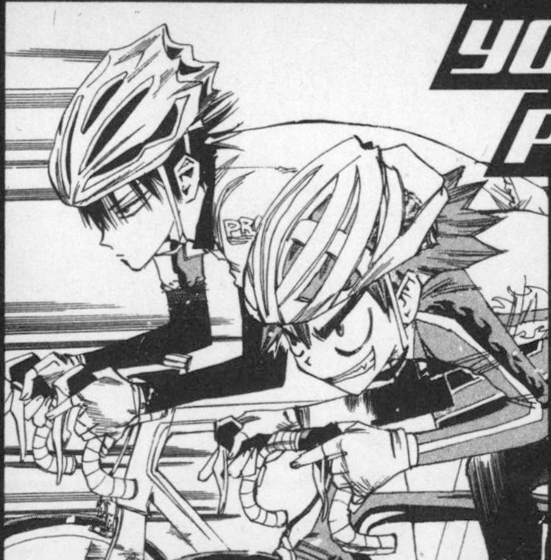

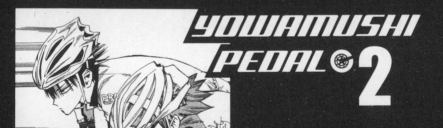

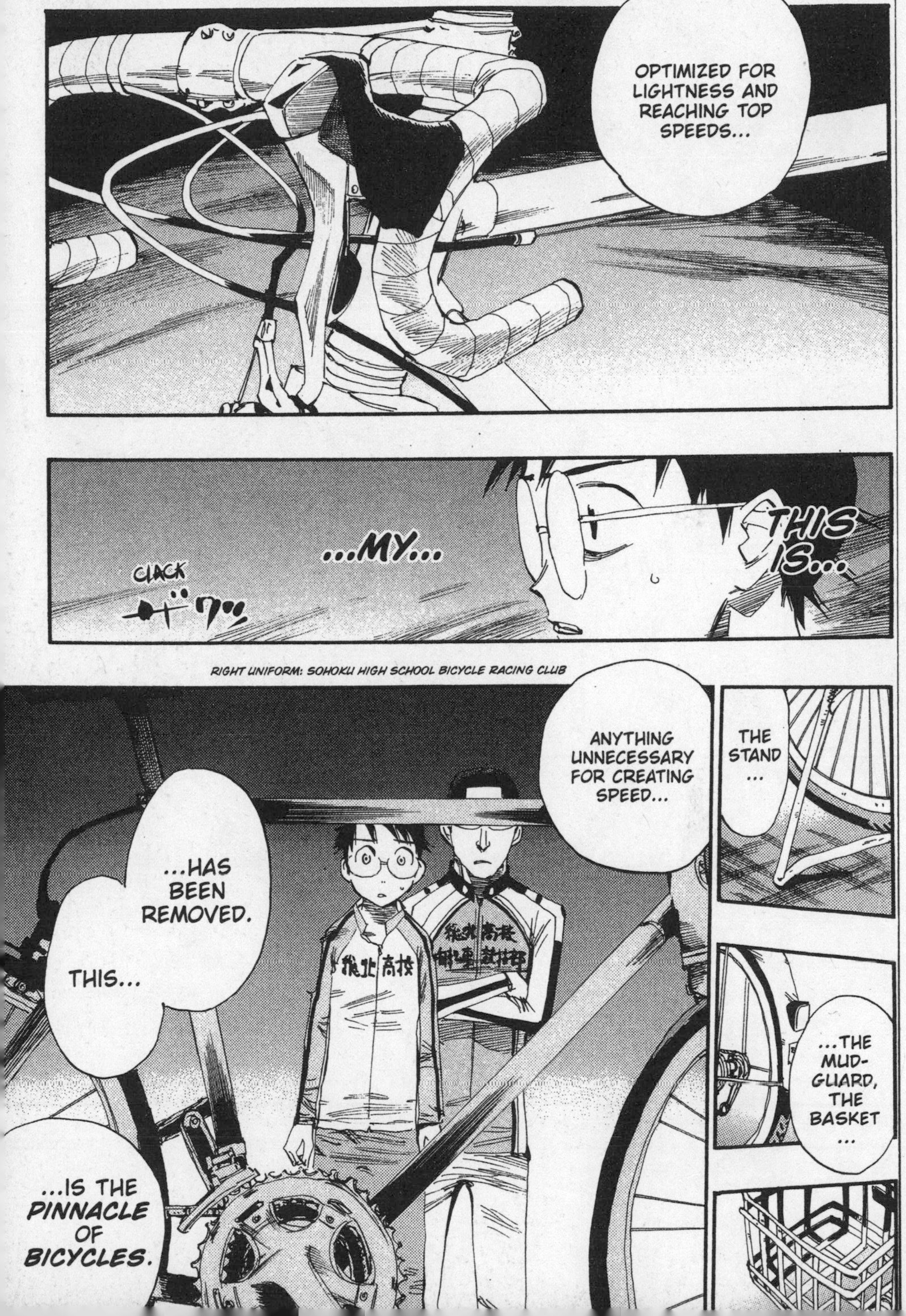
OPTIMIZED FOR LIGHTNESS AND REACHING TOP SPEEDS...
THIS IS...
...MY...
CLACK
RIGHT UNIFORM: SOHOKU HIGH SCHOOL BICYCLE RACING CLUB
THE STAND ...
...THE MUD-GUARD, THE BASKET ...
ANYTHING UNNECESSARY FOR CREATING SPEED...
...HAS BEEN REMOVED.
THIS...
...IS THE PINNACLE OF BICYCLES.

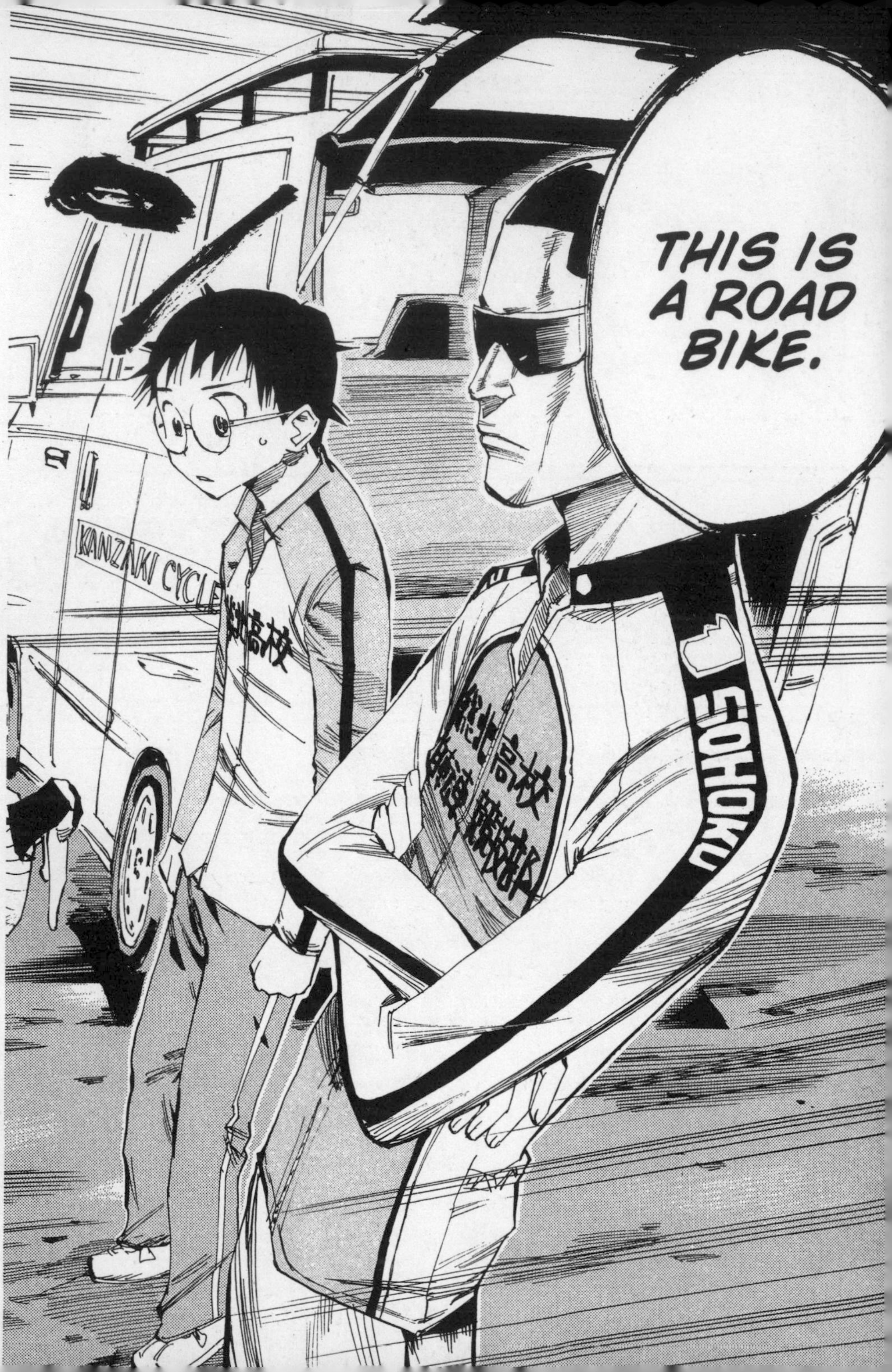
THIS IS A ROAD BIKE.
SOHOKU
KANZAKI CYCLE

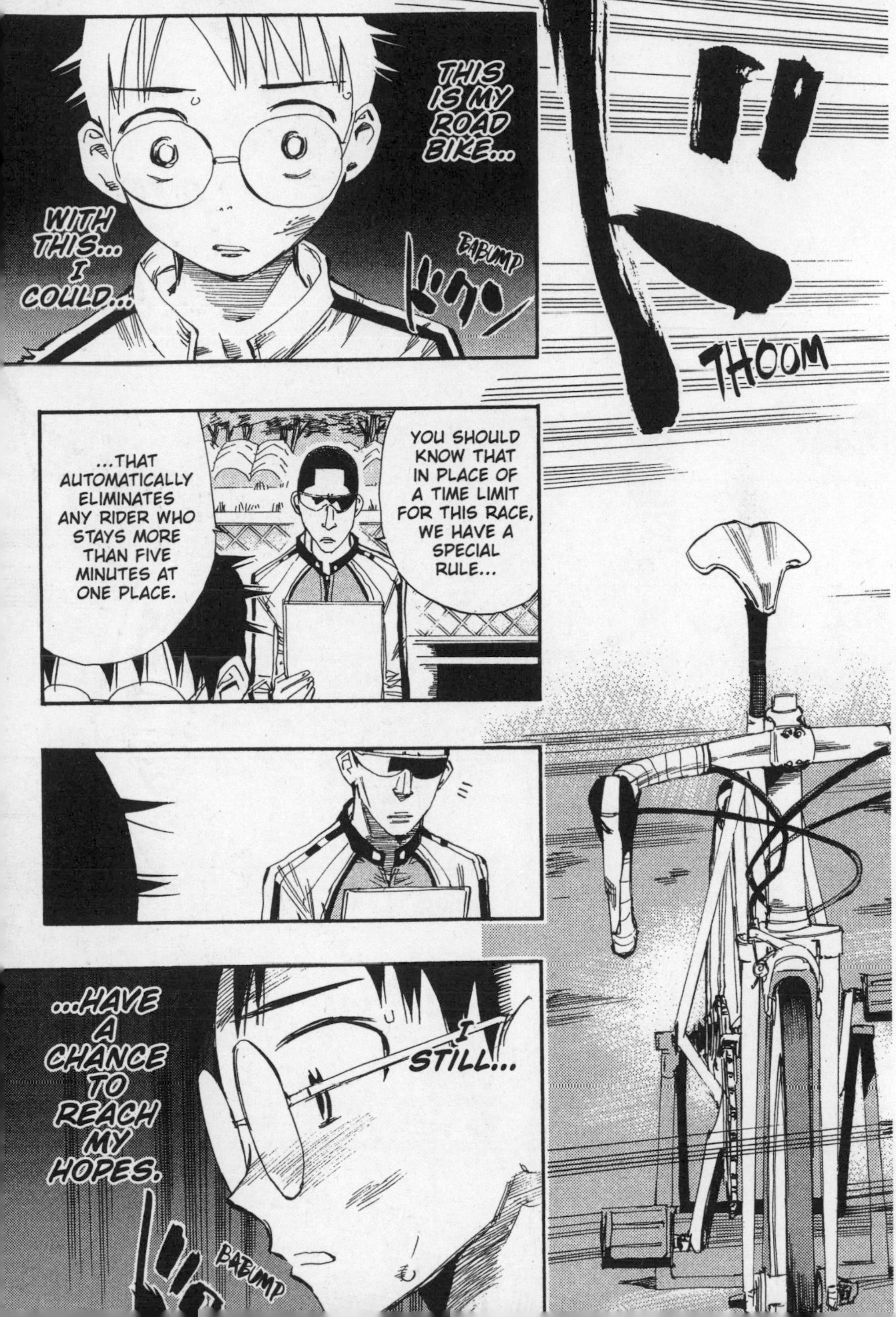
THOOM
THIS IS MY ROAD BIKE...
BABUMP
WITH THIS... I COULD...
YOU SHOULD KNOW THAT IN PLACE OF A TIME LIMIT FOR THIS RACE, WE HAVE A SPECIAL RULE...
...THAT AUTOMATICALLY ELIMINATES ANY RIDER WHO STAYS MORE THAN FIVE MINUTES AT ONE PLACE.
I STILL...
...HAVE A CHANCE TO REACH MY HOPES.
BABUMP

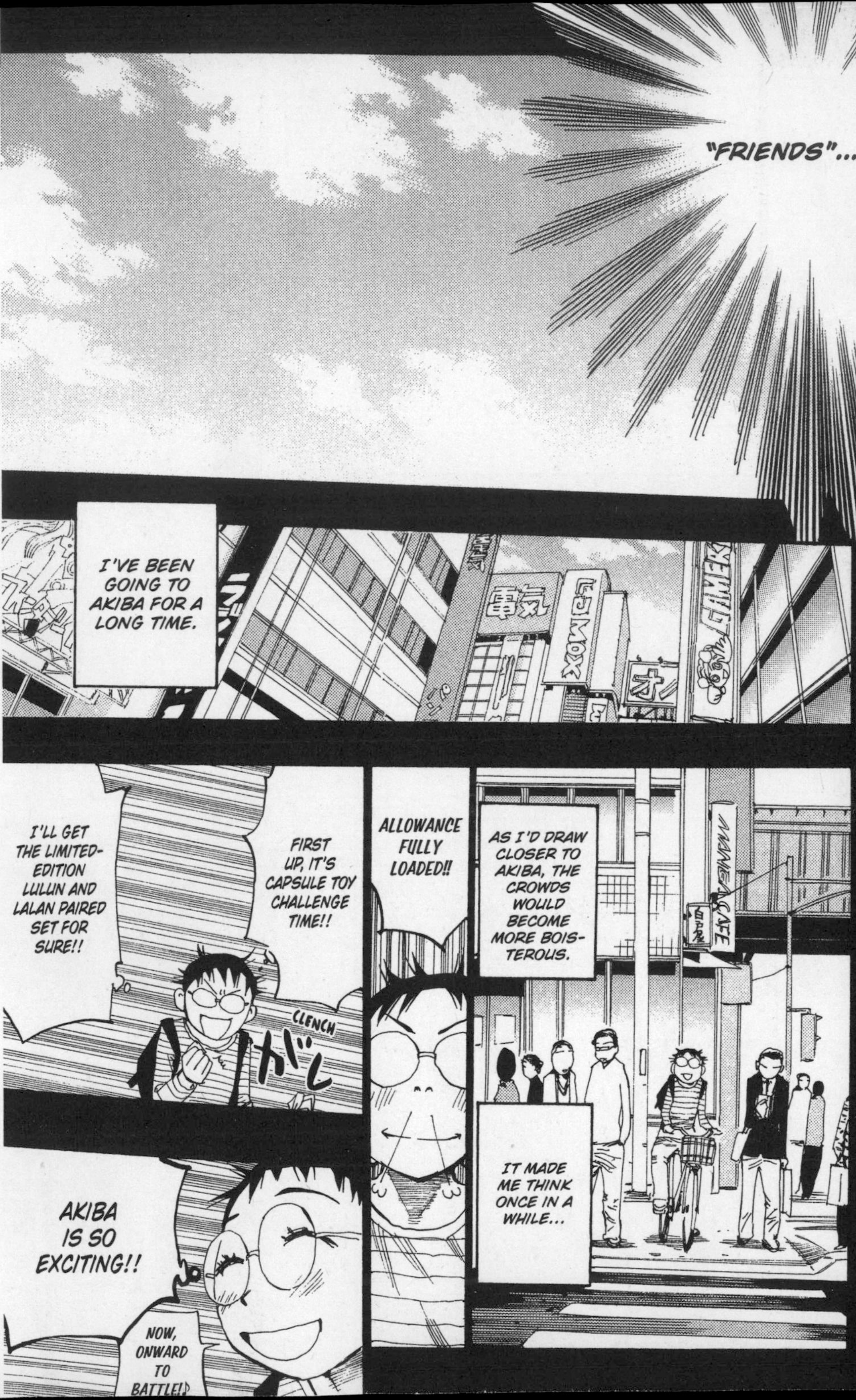
"FRIENDS"...
I'VE BEEN GOING TO AKIBA FOR A LONG TIME.
AS I'D DRAW CLOSER TO AKIBA, THE CROWDS WOULD BECOME MORE BOIS-TEROUS.
IT MADE ME THINK ONCE IN A WHILE...
ALLOWANCE FULLY LOADED!!
FIRST UP, IT'S CAPSULE TOY CHALLENGE TIME!!
I'LL GET THE LIMITED-EDITION LULUN AND LALAN PAIRED SET FOR SURE!!
CLENCH
AKIBA IS SO EXCITING!!
NOW, ONWARD TO BATTLE!!

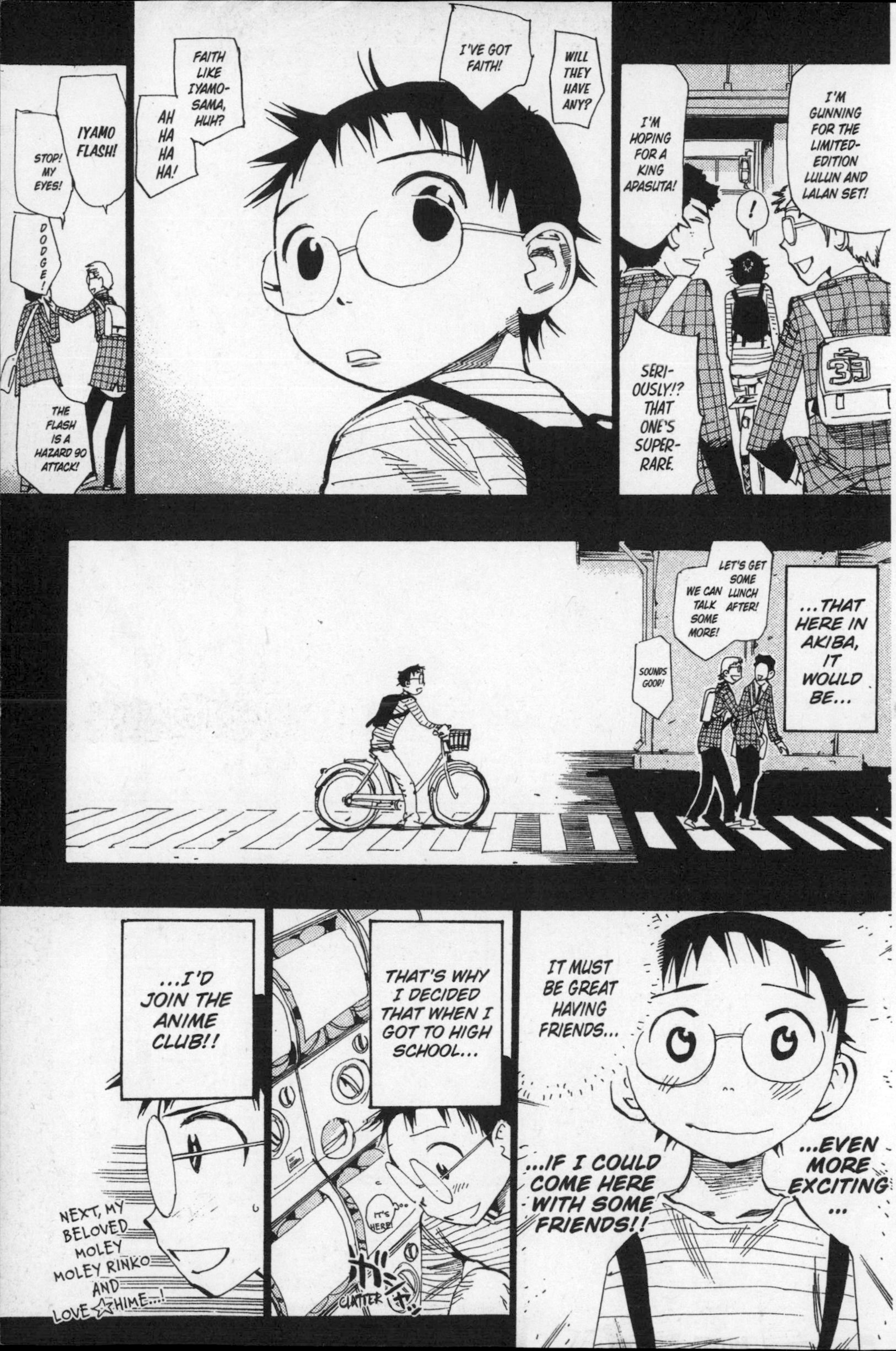
I'M GUNNING FOR THE LIMITED-EDITION LULUN AND LALAN SET!
I'M HOPING FOR A KING APASUTA!
!
SERIOUSLY!? THAT ONE'S SUPER-RARE.
WILL THEY HAVE ANY?
I'VE GOT FAITH!
FAITH LIKE IYAMO-SAMA, HUH?
AH HA HA HA!
IYAMO FLASH!
STOP! MY EYES!
DODGE!
THE FLASH IS A HAZARD 90 ATTACK!
...THAT HERE IN AKIBA, IT WOULD BE...
LET'S GET SOME LUNCH AFTER!
WE CAN TALK SOME MORE!
SOUNDS GOOD!
IT MUST BE GREAT HAVING FRIENDS...
...EVEN MORE EXCITING...
...IF I COULD COME HERE WITH SOME FRIENDS!!
THAT'S WHY I DECIDED THAT WHEN I GOT TO HIGH SCHOOL...
IT'S HERE!
CLATTER
...I'D JOIN THE ANIME CLUB!!
NEXT, MY BELOVED MOLEY MOLEY RINKO AND LOVE☆HIME...!

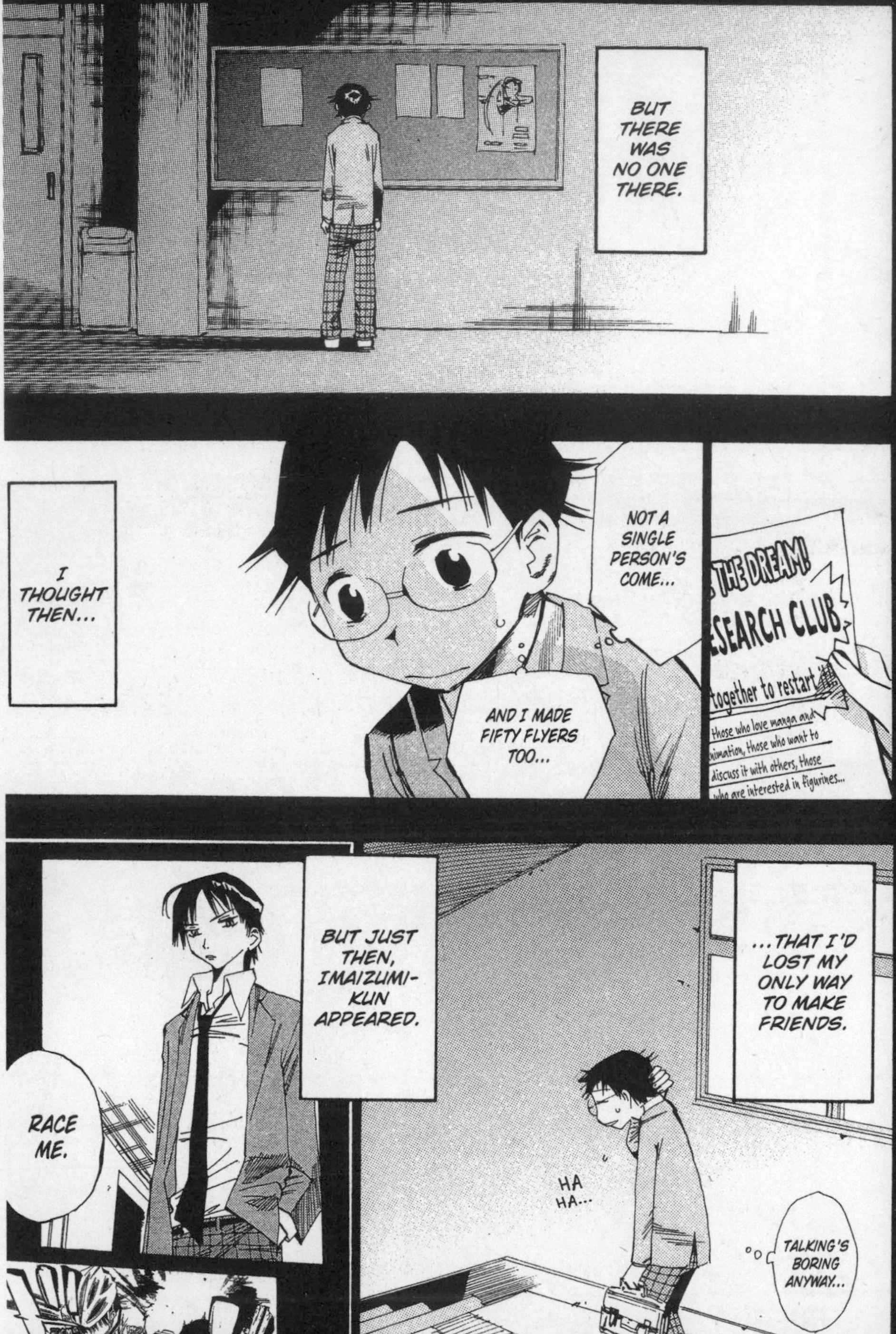
BUT THERE WAS NO ONE THERE.
THE DREAM!
ESEARCH CLUB
together to restart
Those who love manga and
nimation, Those who want to
discuss it with others, Those
who are interested in figurines...
NOT A SINGLE PERSON'S COME...
AND I MADE FIFTY FLYERS TOO...
I THOUGHT THEN...
...THAT I'D LOST MY ONLY WAY TO MAKE FRIENDS.
HA HA...
TALKING'S BORING ANYWAY...
BUT JUST THEN, IMAIZUMI-KUN APPEARED.
RACE ME.

BOTH KAN-ZAKI-SAN...

...AND NARUKO-KUN TOLD ME...

...THAT I...

...ALREADY HAD A TOOL...

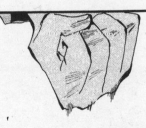

...THAT COULD LEAD ME TO MY FRIENDS.

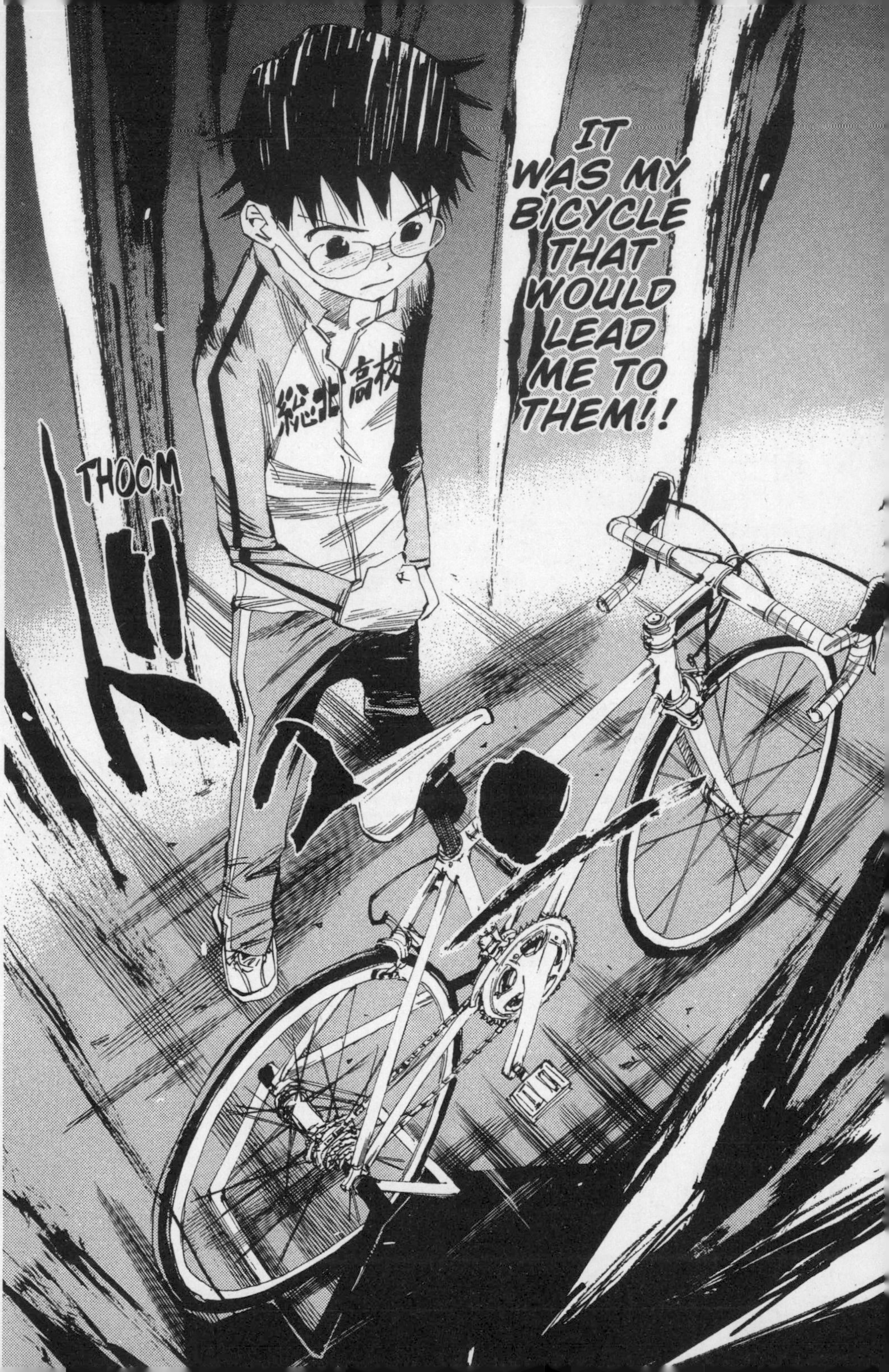
IT WAS MY BICYCLE THAT WOULD LEAD ME TO THEM!!
THOOM
総北高校

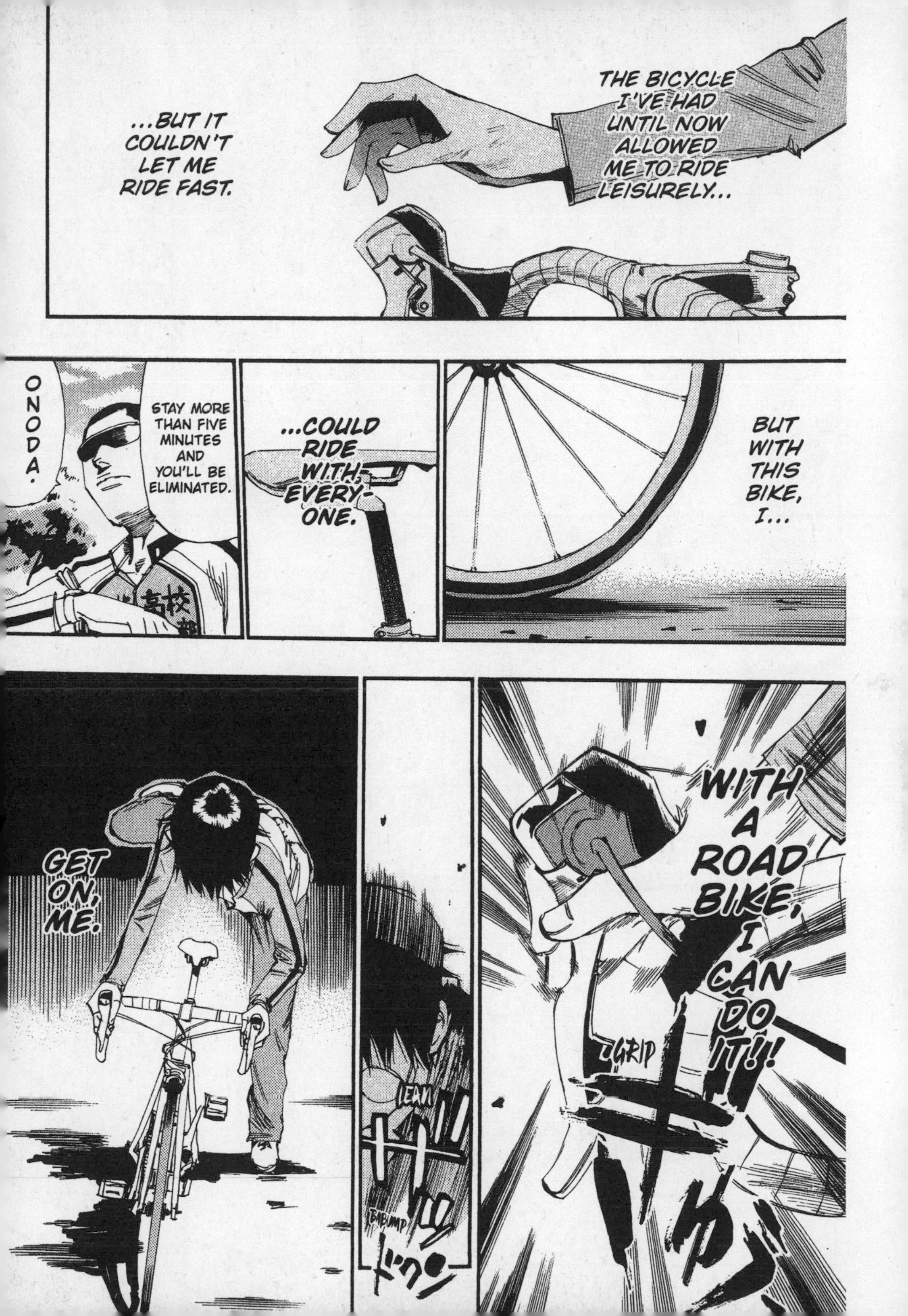
THE BICYCLE I'VE HAD UNTIL NOW ALLOWED ME TO RIDE LEISURELY...
...BUT IT COULDN'T LET ME RIDE FAST.
BUT WITH THIS BIKE, I...
...COULD RIDE WITH EVERY-ONE.
ONODA.
STAY MORE THAN FIVE MINUTES AND YOU'LL BE ELIMINATED.
WITH A ROAD BIKE, I CAN DO IT!!!
GRIP
LEAN
BABUMP
GET ON, ME.

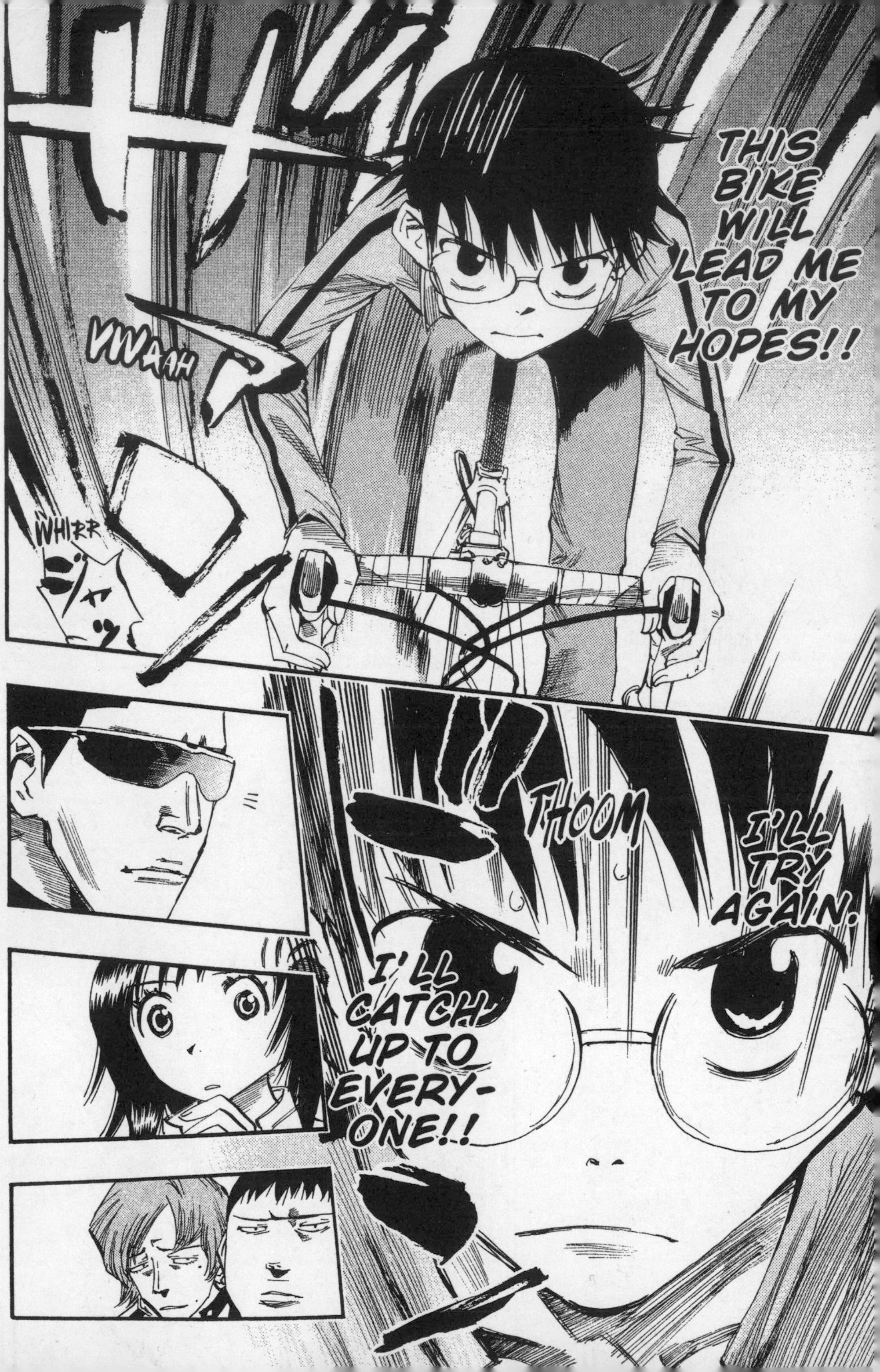
THIS BIKE WILL LEAD ME TO MY HOPES!!
VWAAH
WHIRR
ジャッ
THOOM
I'LL TRY AGAIN.
I'LL CATCH UP TO EVERY-ONE!!

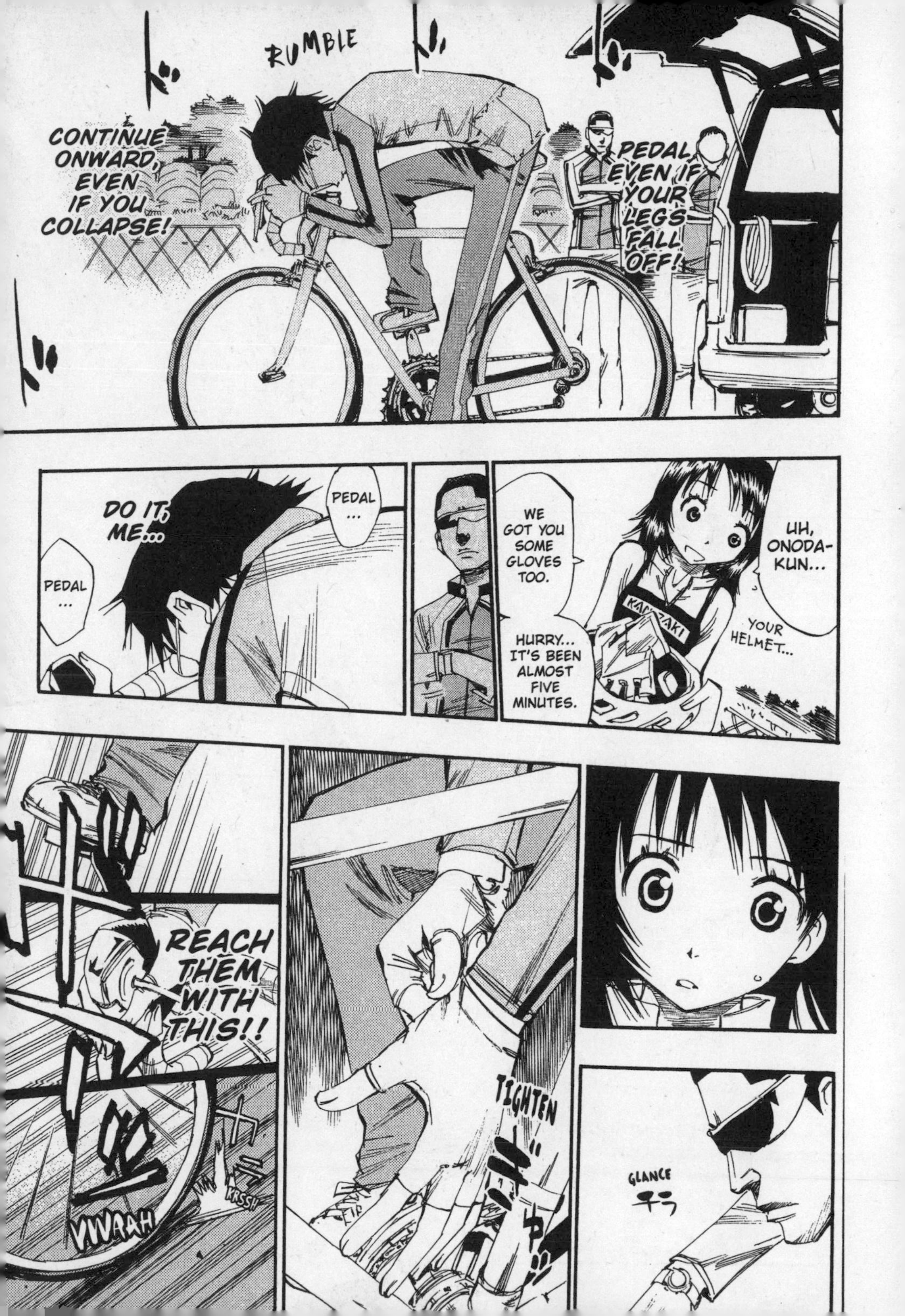
RUMBLE
PEDAL EVEN IF YOUR LEGS FALL OFF!
CONTINUE ONWARD, EVEN IF YOU COLLAPSE!
UH, ONODA-KUN...
YOUR HELMET...
WE GOT YOU SOME GLOVES TOO.
HURRY... IT'S BEEN ALMOST FIVE MINUTES.
PEDAL ...
DO IT, ME...
PEDAL ...
GLANCE
TIGHTEN
REACH THEM WITH THIS!!
KRSSH
VWAAH

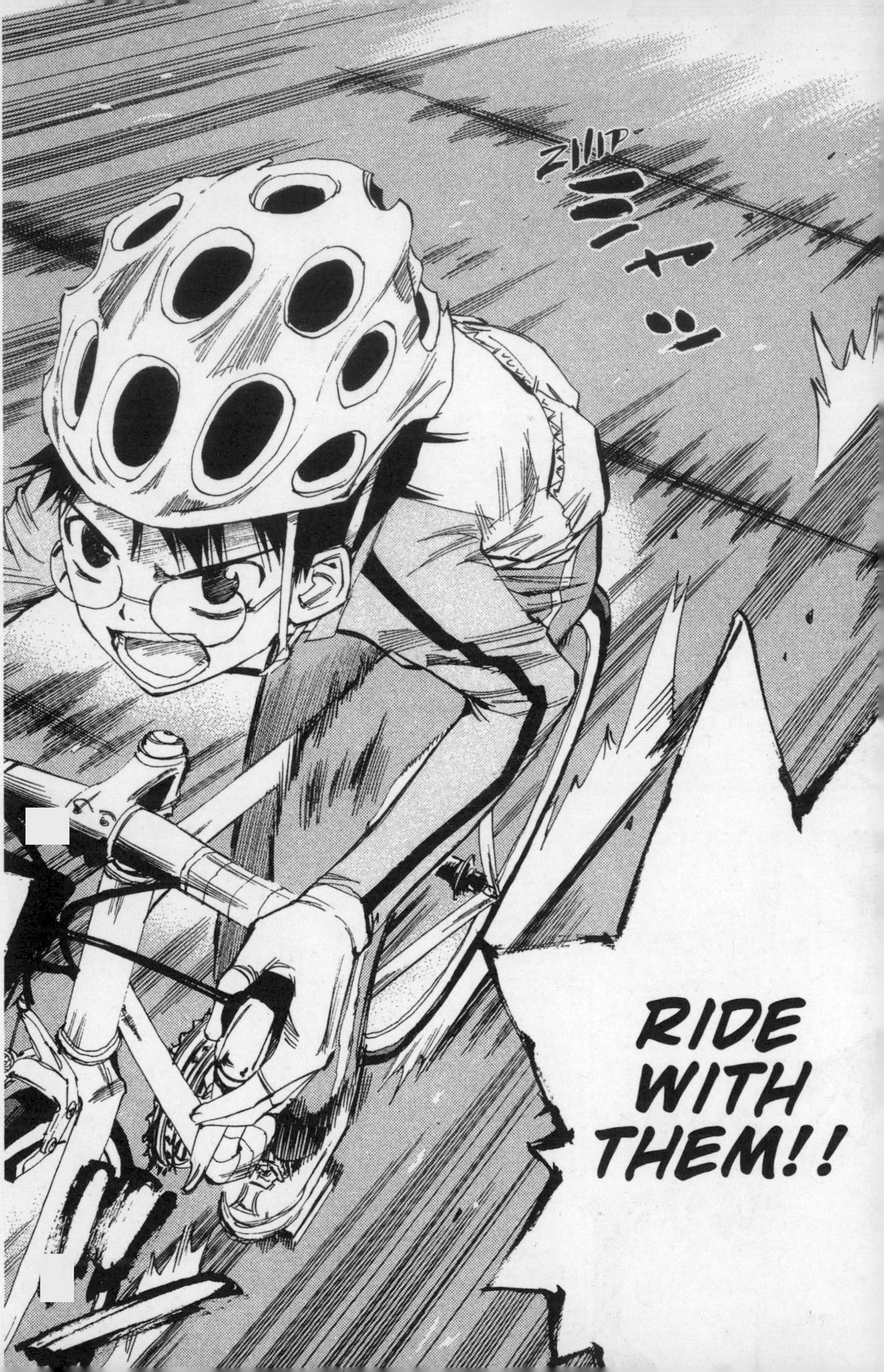
ZIIIP
ジャーッ
RIDE WITH THEM!!

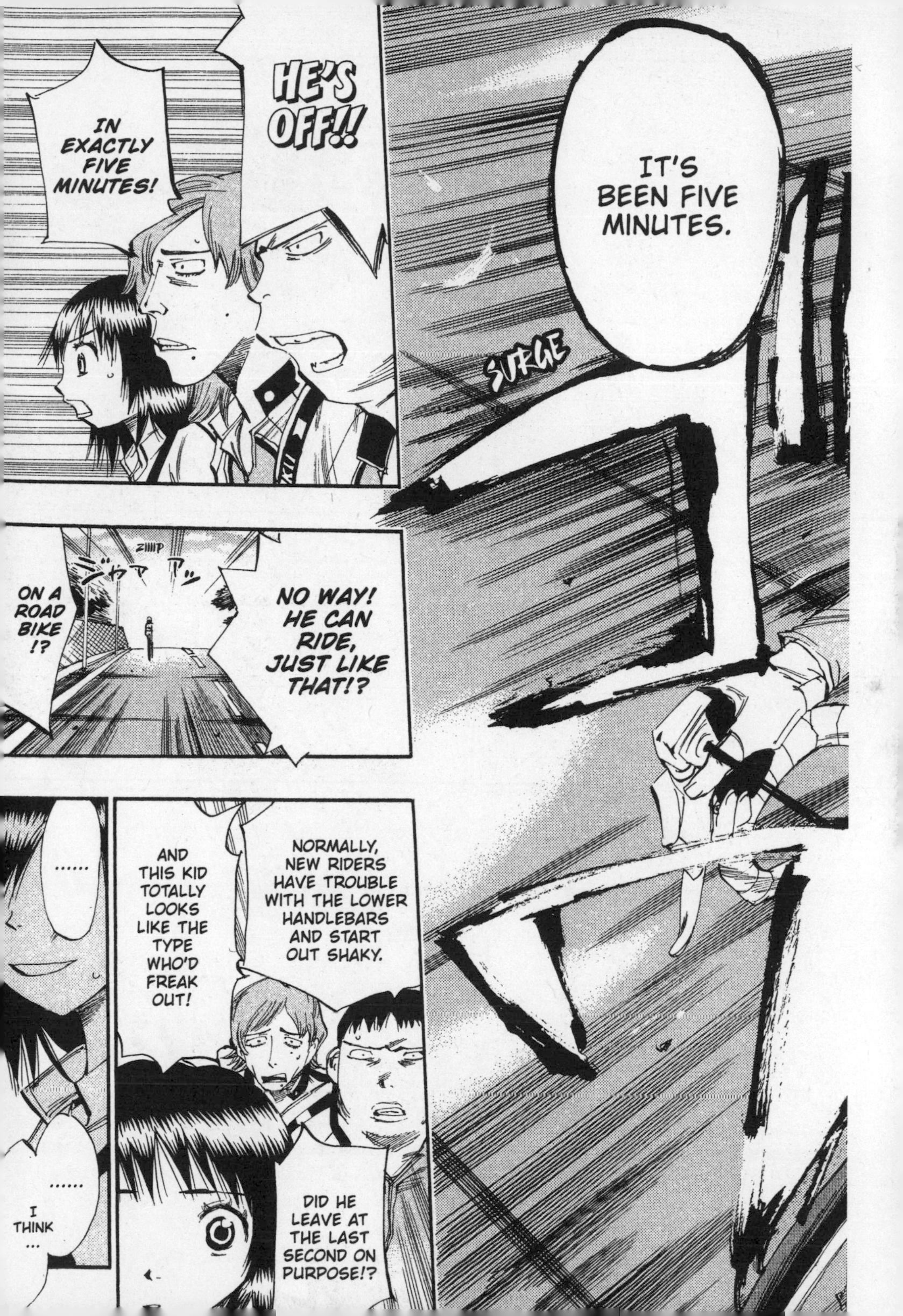
IT'S BEEN FIVE MINUTES.
SURGE
HE'S OFF!!
IN EXACTLY FIVE MINUTES!
ZIIIP
NO WAY! HE CAN RIDE, JUST LIKE THAT!?
ON A ROAD BIKE!?
NORMALLY, NEW RIDERS HAVE TROUBLE WITH THE LOWER HANDLEBARS AND START OUT SHAKY.
AND THIS KID TOTALLY LOOKS LIKE THE TYPE WHO'D FREAK OUT!
DID HE LEAVE AT THE LAST SECOND ON PURPOSE!?
......
...... I THINK...

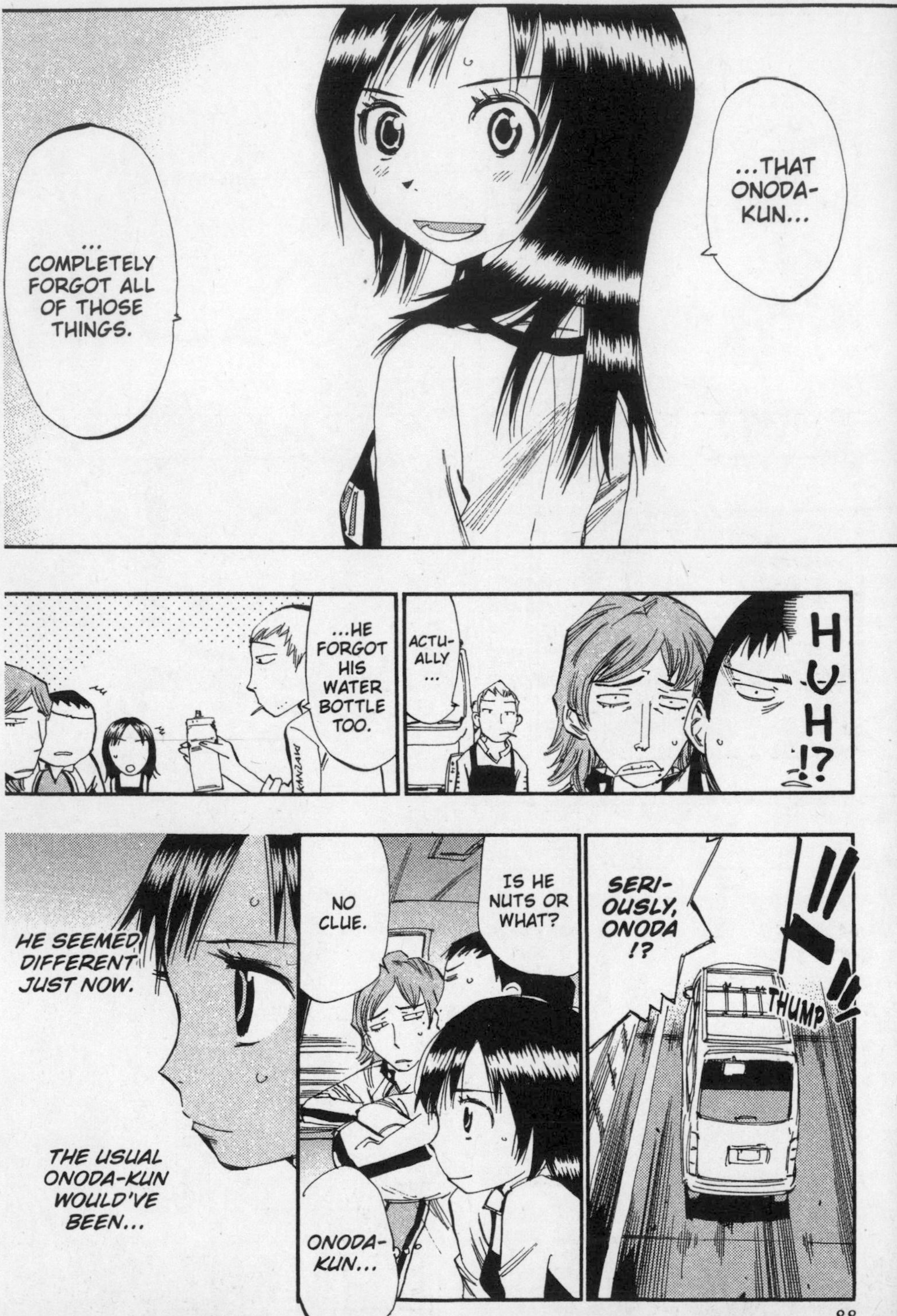
...THAT ONODA-KUN...
... COMPLETELY FORGOT ALL OF THOSE THINGS.
HUH!?
ACTU-ALLY...
...HE FORGOT HIS WATER BOTTLE TOO.
SERI-OUSLY, ONODA!?
THUMP
IS HE NUTS OR WHAT?
NO CLUE.
ONODA-KUN...
HE SEEMED DIFFERENT JUST NOW.
THE USUAL ONODA-KUN WOULD'VE BEEN...

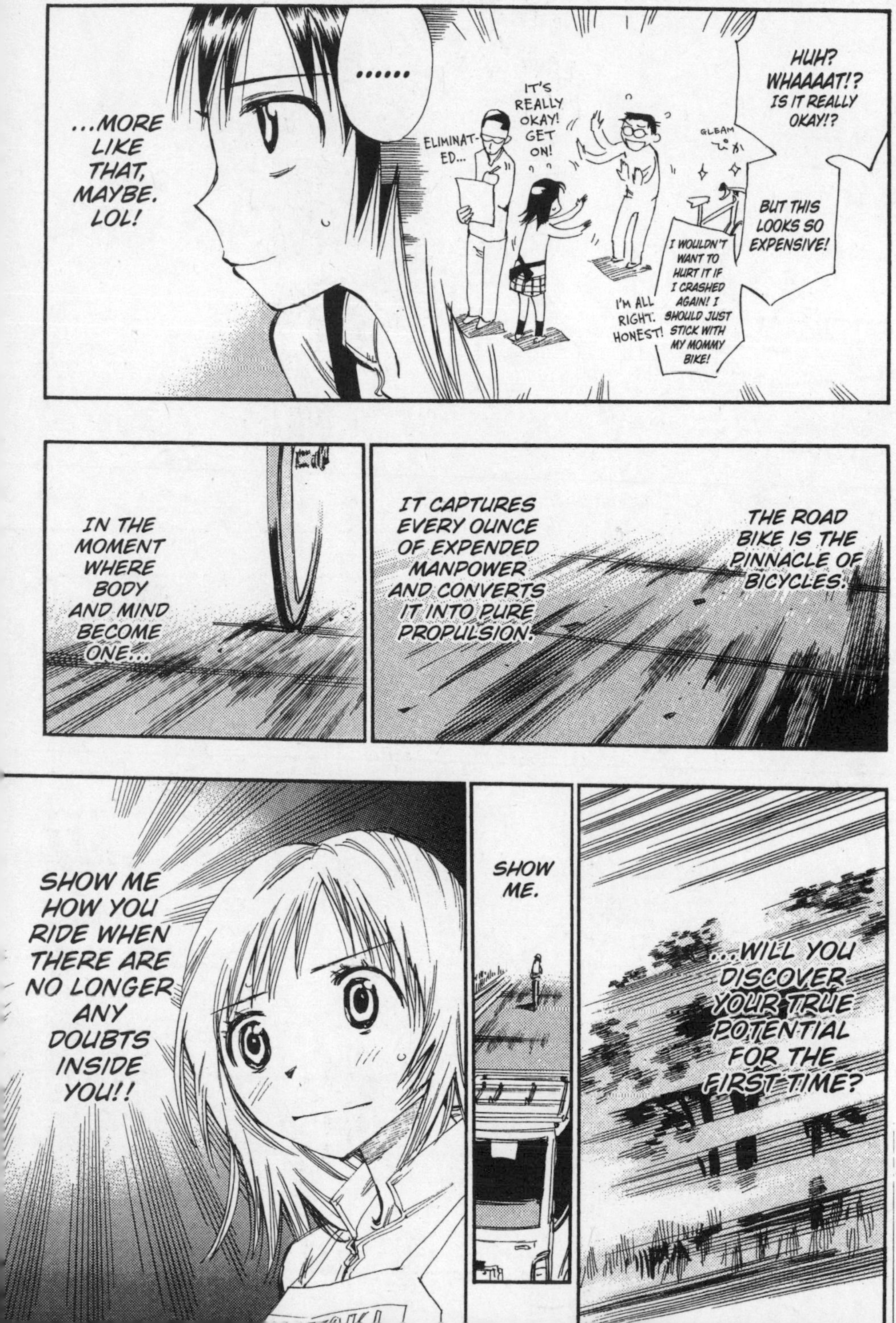
HUH? WHAAAAT!? IS IT REALLY OKAY!?
BUT THIS LOOKS SO EXPENSIVE!
I WOULDN'T WANT TO HURT IT IF I CRASHED AGAIN! I SHOULD JUST STICK WITH MY MOMMY BIKE!
GLEAM
I'M ALL RIGHT. HONEST!
IT'S REALLY OKAY! GET ON!
ELIMINATED...
......
...MORE LIKE THAT, MAYBE. LOL!
THE ROAD BIKE IS THE PINNACLE OF BICYCLES.
IT CAPTURES EVERY OUNCE OF EXPENDED MANPOWER AND CONVERTS IT INTO PURE PROPULSION.
IN THE MOMENT WHERE BODY AND MIND BECOME ONE...
...WILL YOU DISCOVER YOUR TRUE POTENTIAL FOR THE FIRST TIME?
SHOW ME.
SHOW ME HOW YOU RIDE WHEN THERE ARE NO LONGER ANY DOUBTS INSIDE YOU!!

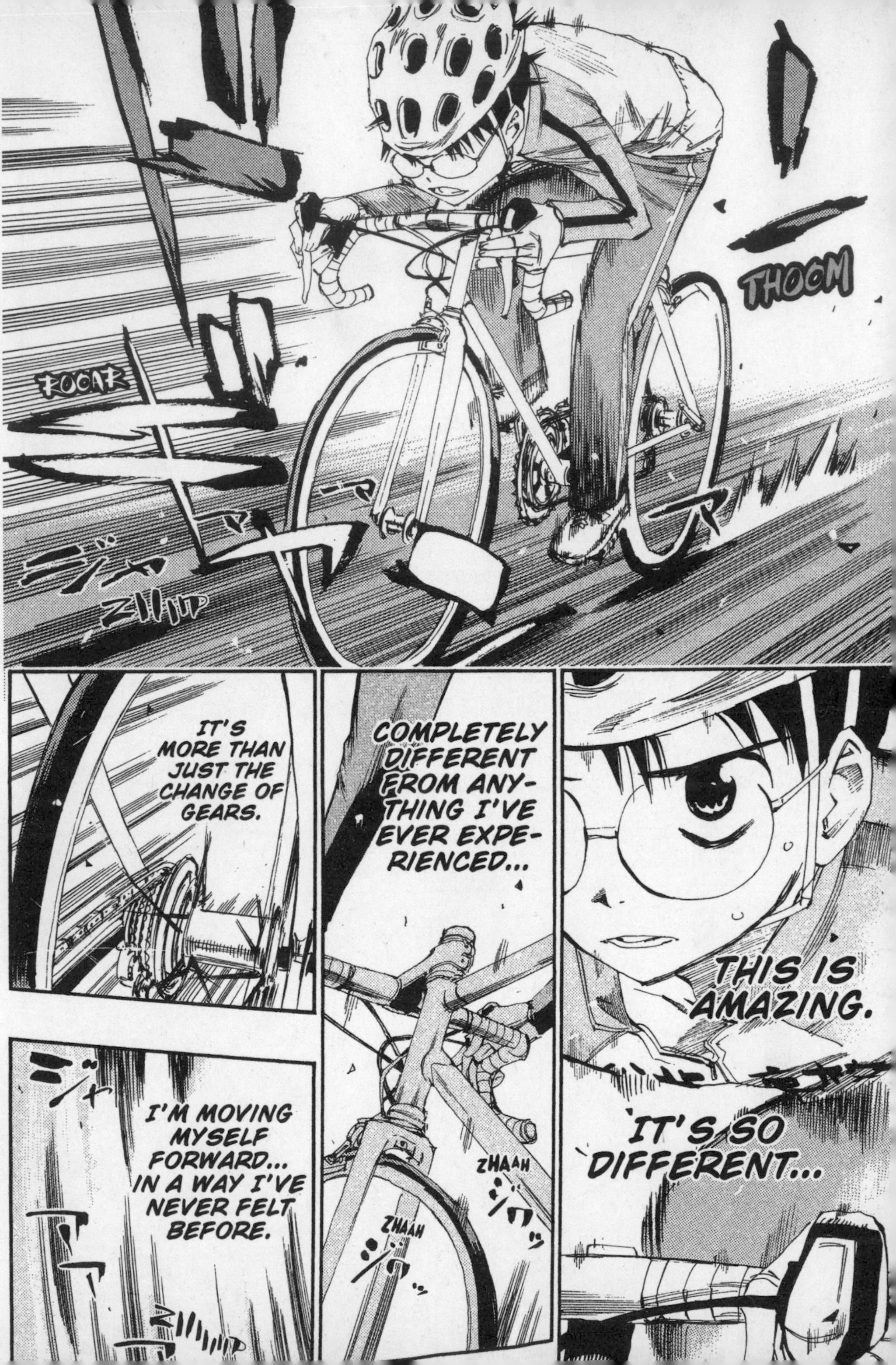
THOOM
ROOAR
ZIIIP
THIS IS AMAZING.
IT'S SO DIFFERENT...
COMPLETELY DIFFERENT FROM ANYTHING I'VE EVER EXPERIENCED...
ZHAAH
ZHAAH
IT'S MORE THAN JUST THE CHANGE OF GEARS.
I'M MOVING MYSELF FORWARD... IN A WAY I'VE NEVER FELT BEFORE.
ZIIIP

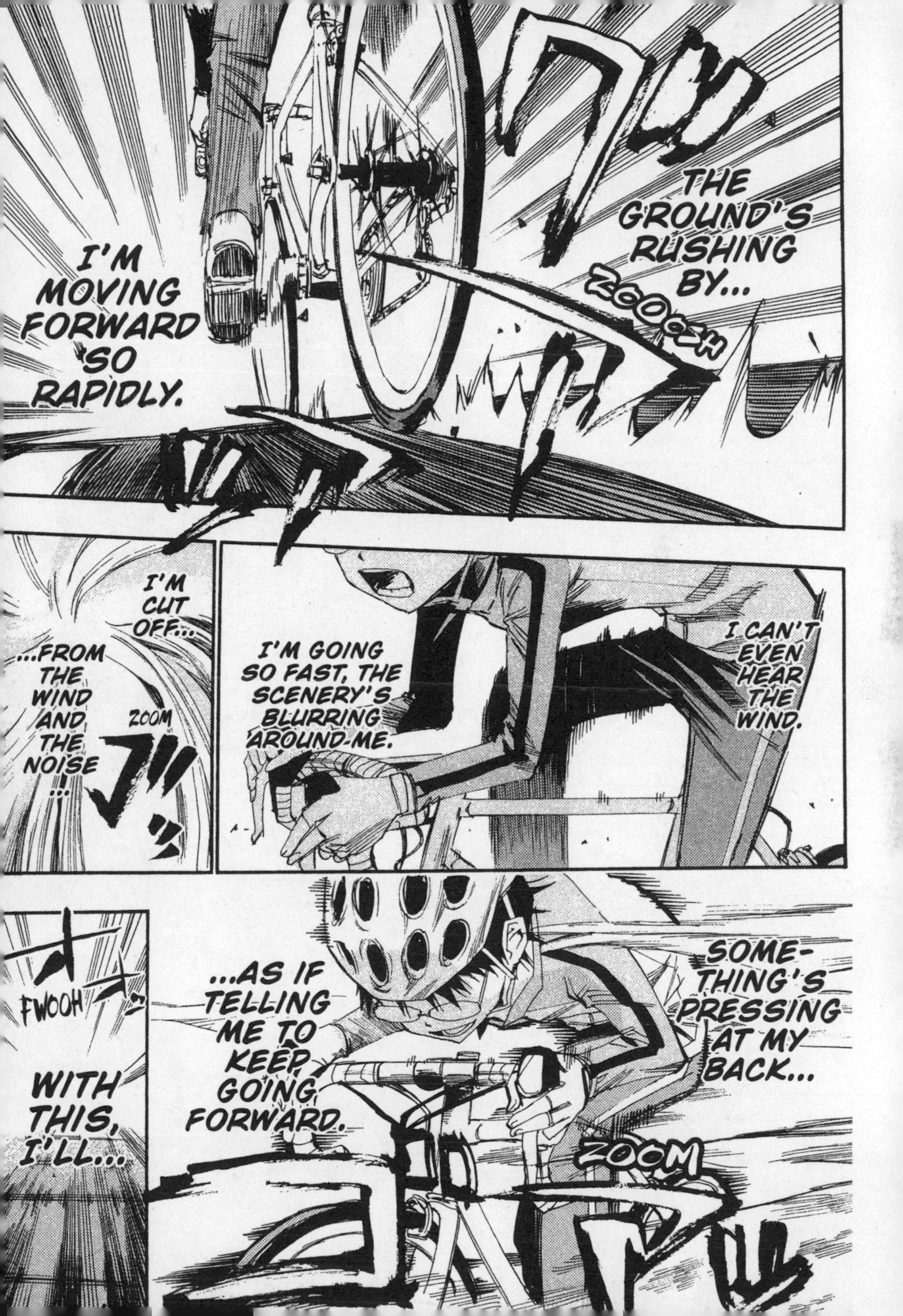
THE GROUND'S RUSHING BY...
ZOOOOSH
I'M MOVING FORWARD SO RAPIDLY.
I CAN'T EVEN HEAR THE WIND.
I'M GOING SO FAST, THE SCENERY'S BLURRING AROUND ME.
I'M CUT OFF...
...FROM THE WIND AND THE NOISE...
ZOOM
SOMETHING'S PRESSING AT MY BACK...
...AS IF TELLING ME TO KEEP GOING FORWARD.
ZOOM
FWOOH
WITH THIS, I'LL...

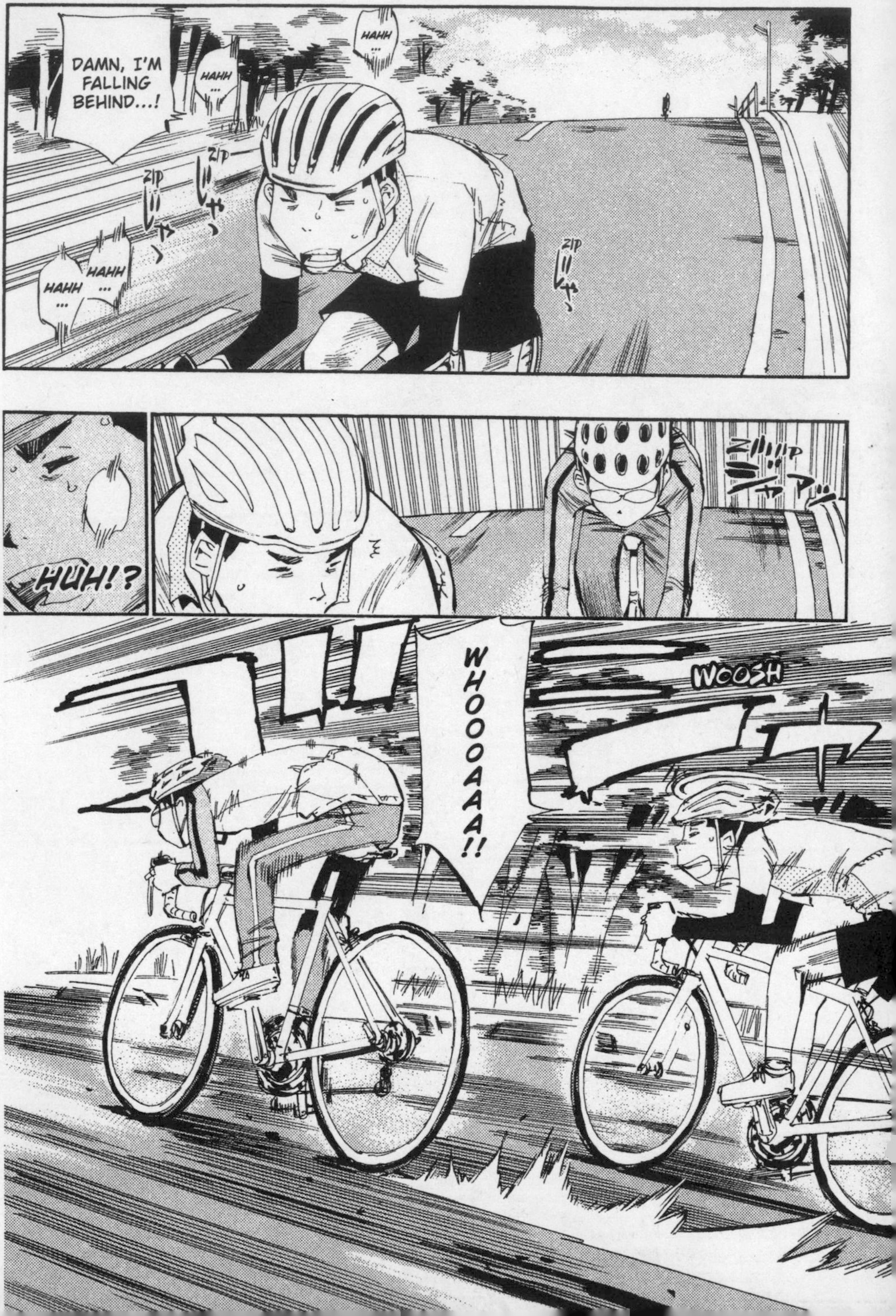
ZIP
HAHH...
ZIP
HAHH...
ZIP
DAMN, I'M FALLING BEHIND...!
HAHH...
HAHH...
ZIIIIP
HUH!?
WOOSH
WHOOOAAAA!!

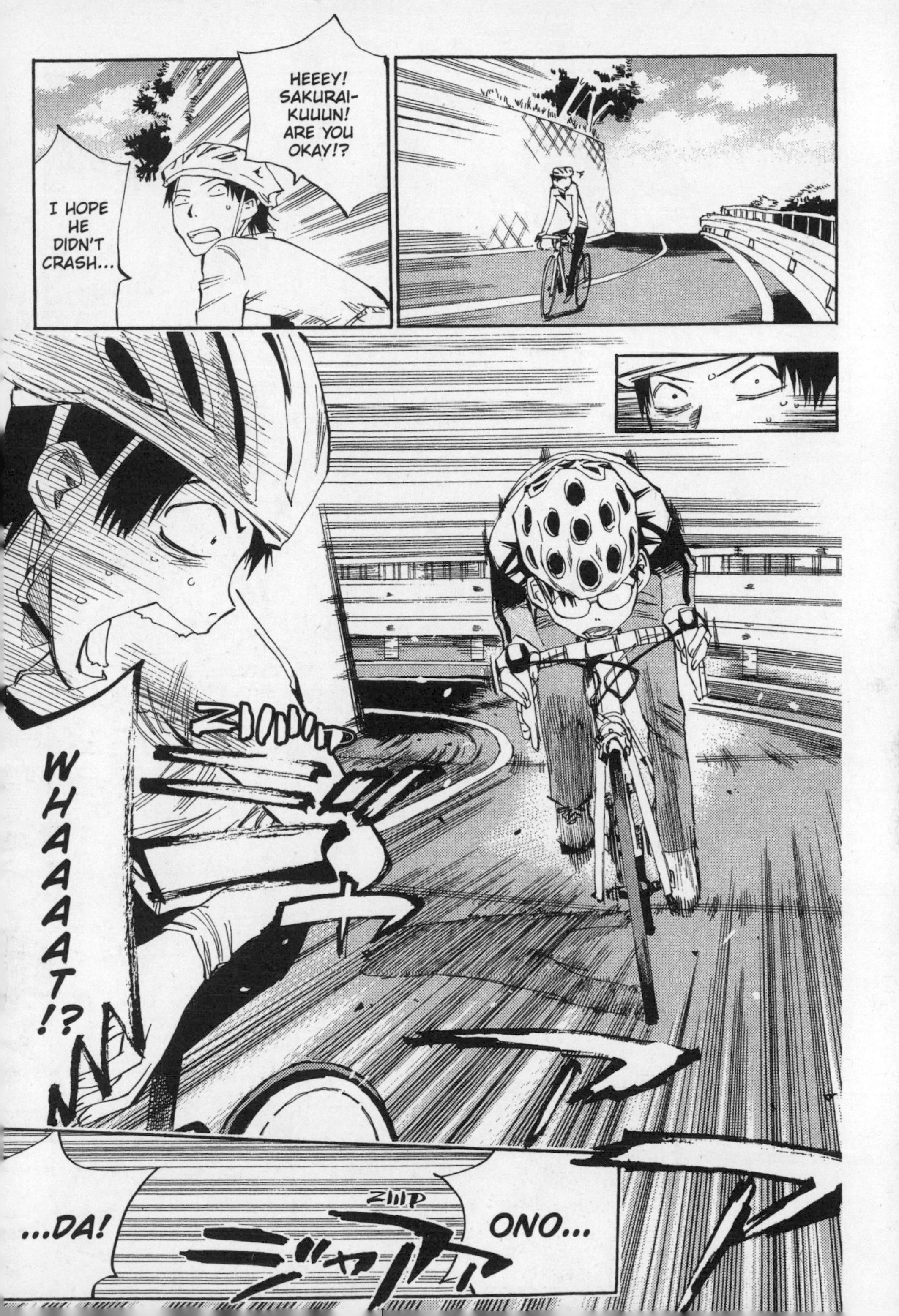
HEEEY! SAKURAI-KUUUN! ARE YOU OKAY!?
I HOPE HE DIDN'T CRASH...
ZIIIIIIP
WHAAAAAT!?
ONO...
ZIIIP
...DA!

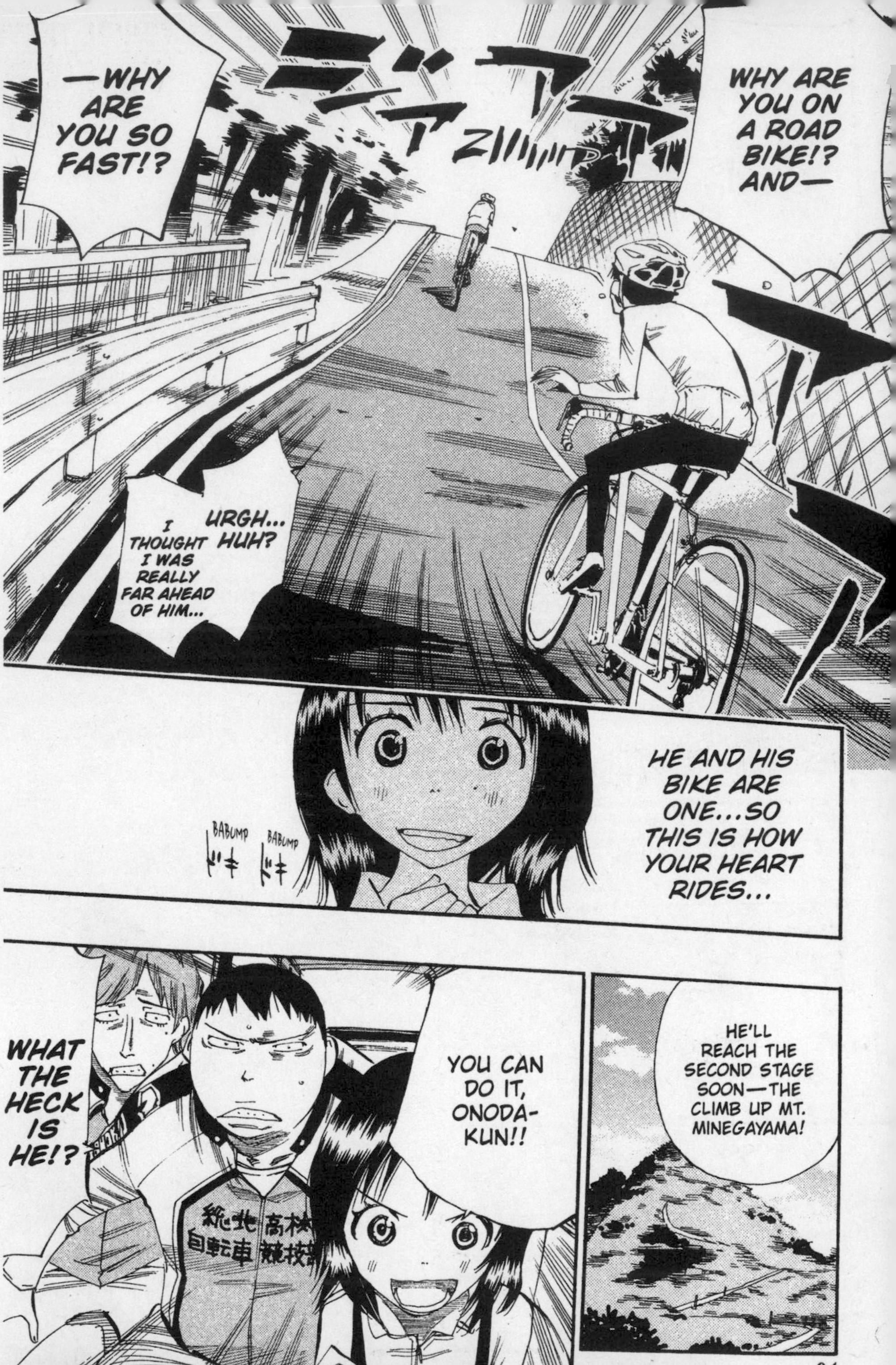
WHY ARE YOU ON A ROAD BIKE!? AND—
—WHY ARE YOU SO FAST!?
ZIIIII
URGH... HUH?
I THOUGHT I WAS REALLY FAR AHEAD OF HIM...
HE AND HIS BIKE ARE ONE...SO THIS IS HOW YOUR HEART RIDES...
BABUMP BABUMP
HE'LL REACH THE SECOND STAGE SOON—THE CLIMB UP MT. MINEGAYAMA!
YOU CAN DO IT, ONODA-KUN!!
WHAT THE HECK IS HE!?

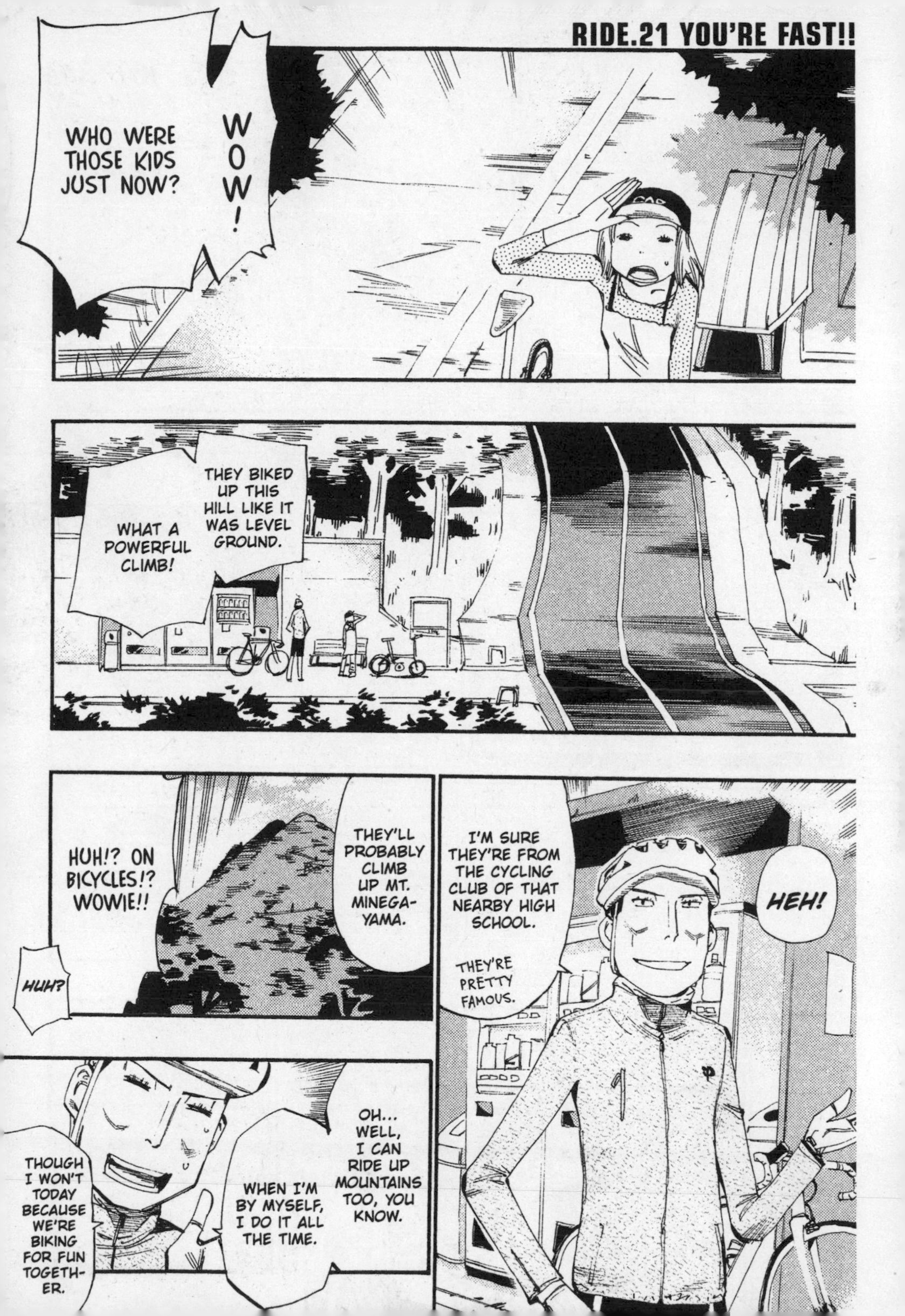
WOW!
WHO WERE THOSE KIDS JUST NOW?
THEY BIKED UP THIS HILL LIKE IT WAS LEVEL GROUND.
WHAT A POWERFUL CLIMB!
HEH!
I'M SURE THEY'RE FROM THE CYCLING CLUB OF THAT NEARBY HIGH SCHOOL.
THEY'RE PRETTY FAMOUS.
THEY'LL PROBABLY CLIMB UP MT. MINEGA-YAMA.
HUH!? ON BICYCLES!? WOWIE!!
HUH?
OH... WELL, I CAN RIDE UP MOUNTAINS TOO, YOU KNOW.
WHEN I'M BY MYSELF, I DO IT ALL THE TIME.
THOUGH I WON'T TODAY BECAUSE WE'RE BIKING FOR FUN TOGETH-ER.

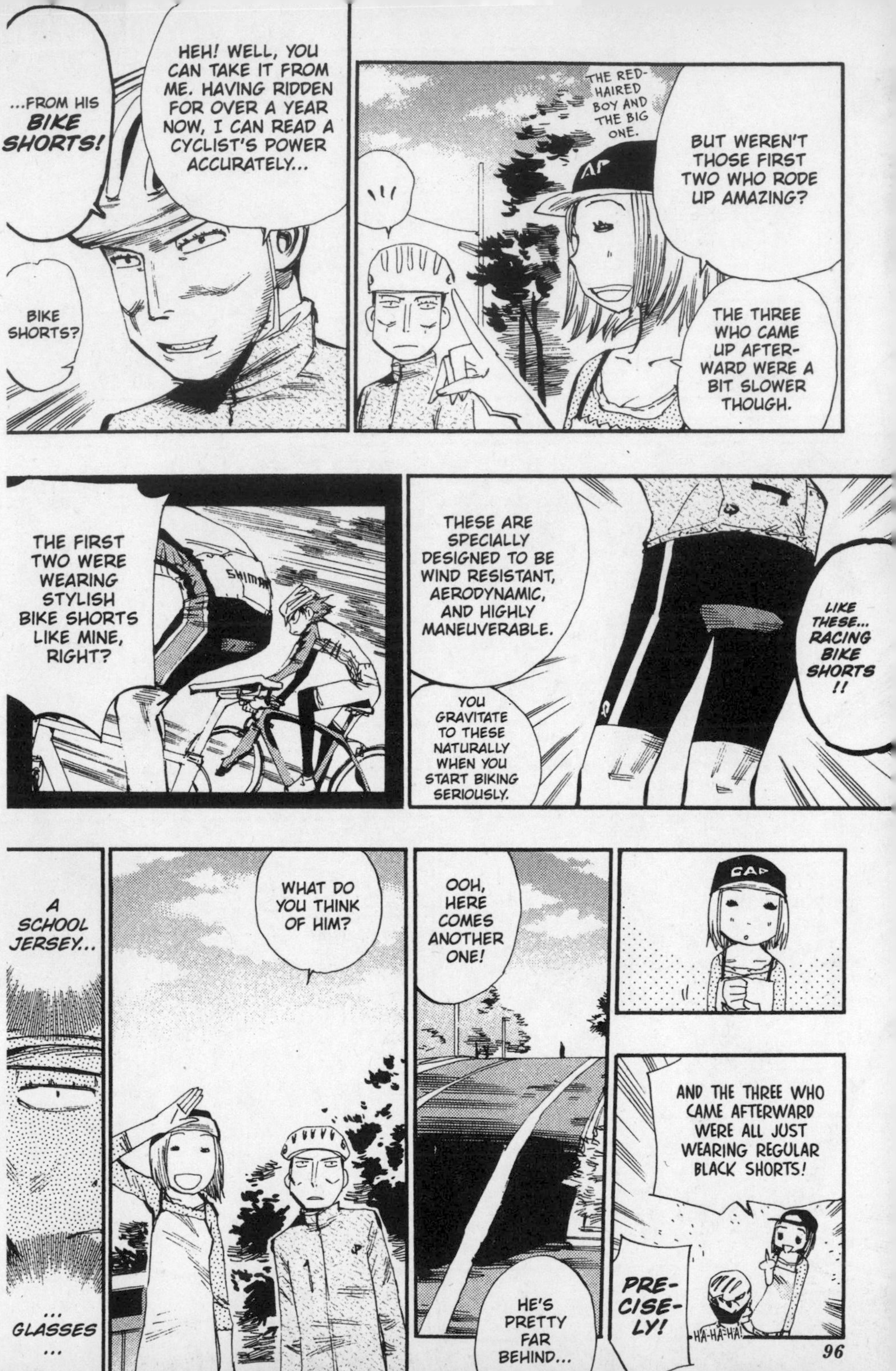
BUT WEREN'T THOSE FIRST TWO WHO RODE UP AMAZING?
THE RED-HAIRED BOY AND THE BIG ONE.
THE THREE WHO CAME UP AFTERWARD WERE A BIT SLOWER THOUGH.
HEH! WELL, YOU CAN TAKE IT FROM ME. HAVING RIDDEN FOR OVER A YEAR NOW, I CAN READ A CYCLIST'S POWER ACCURATELY...
...FROM HIS BIKE SHORTS!
BIKE SHORTS?
LIKE THESE... RACING BIKE SHORTS!!
THESE ARE SPECIALLY DESIGNED TO BE WIND RESISTANT, AERODYNAMIC, AND HIGHLY MANEUVERABLE.
YOU GRAVITATE TO THESE NATURALLY WHEN YOU START BIKING SERIOUSLY.
THE FIRST TWO WERE WEARING STYLISH BIKE SHORTS LIKE MINE, RIGHT?
AND THE THREE WHO CAME AFTERWARD WERE ALL JUST WEARING REGULAR BLACK SHORTS!
PRE-CISE-LY!
HA-HA-HA!
OOH, HERE COMES ANOTHER ONE!
HE'S PRETTY FAR BEHIND...
WHAT DO YOU THINK OF HIM?
A SCHOOL JERSEY...
...GLASSES...

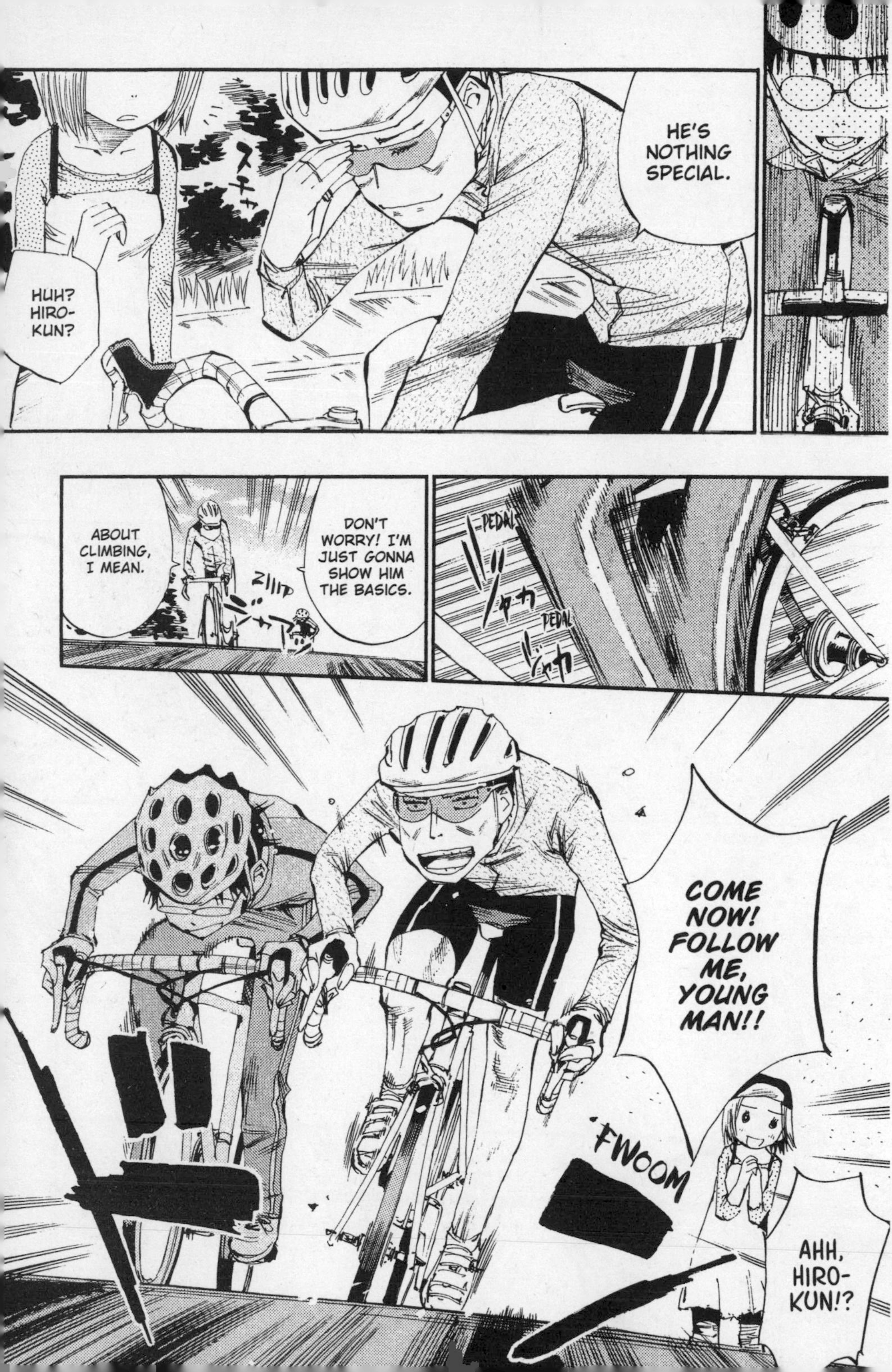
HE'S NOTHING SPECIAL.
HUH? HIRO-KUN?
PEDAL
PEDAL
DON'T WORRY! I'M JUST GONNA SHOW HIM THE BASICS.
ABOUT CLIMBING, I MEAN.
ZIIIP
COME NOW! FOLLOW ME, YOUNG MAN!!
FWOOM
AHH, HIRO-KUN!?

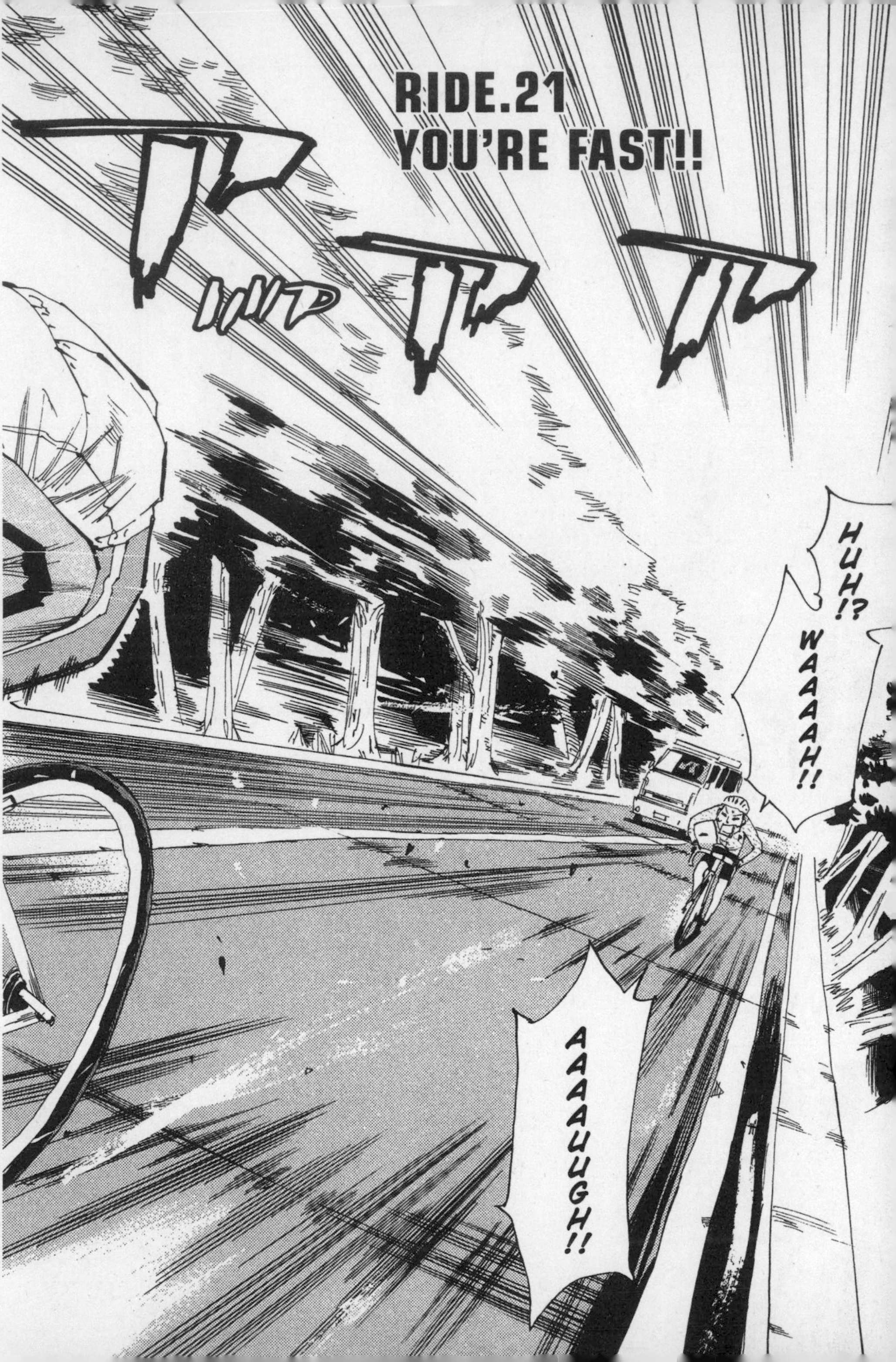
RIDE.21
YOU'RE FAST!!
HUH!? WAAAAAH!!
AAAAAUGH!!

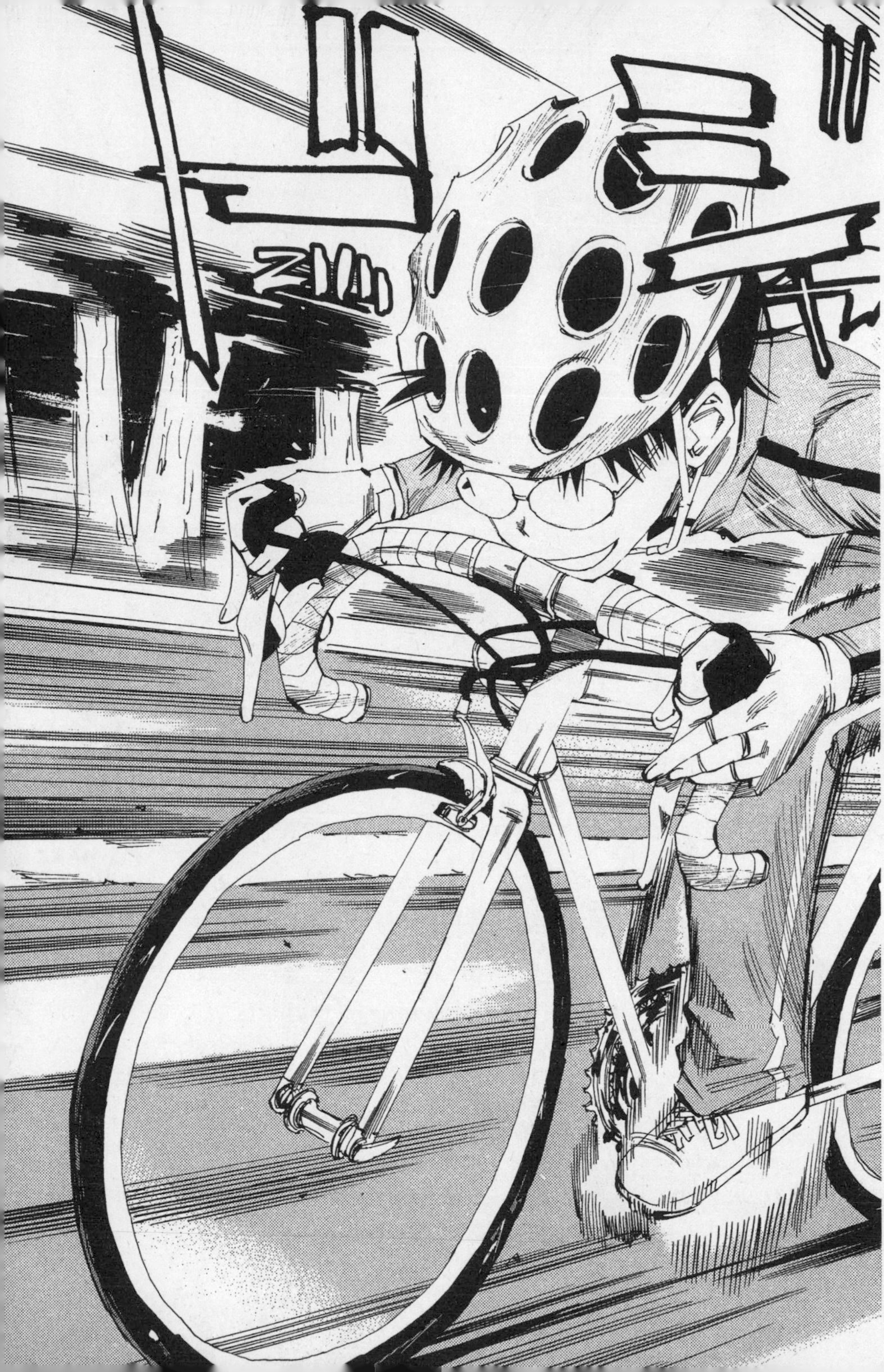

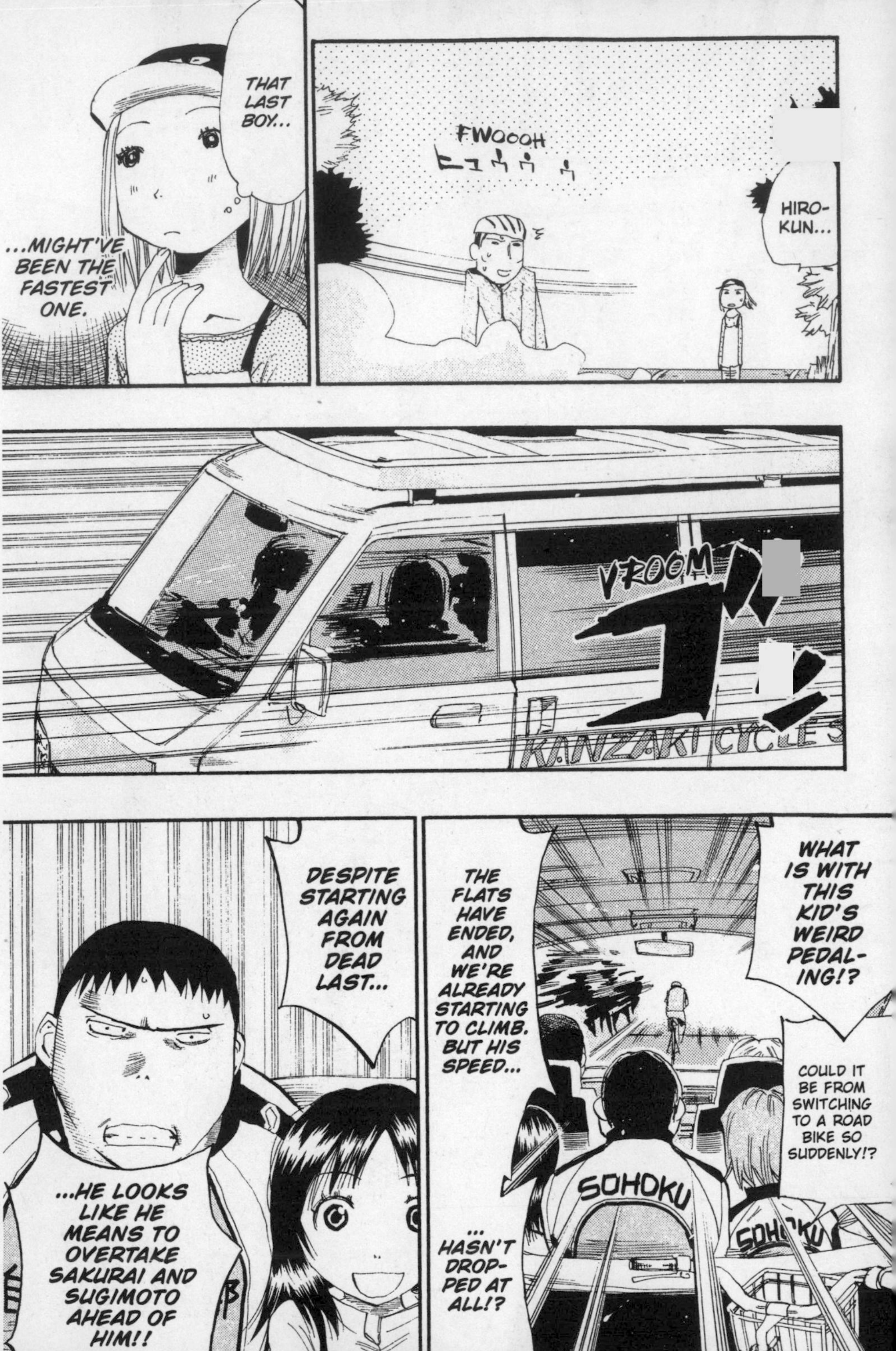
FWOOOH
HIRO-KUN...
THAT LAST BOY...
...MIGHT'VE BEEN THE FASTEST ONE.
VROOM
KANZAKI CYCLE
WHAT IS WITH THIS KID'S WEIRD PEDALING!?
THE FLATS HAVE ENDED, AND WE'RE ALREADY STARTING TO CLIMB. BUT HIS SPEED...
COULD IT BE FROM SWITCHING TO A ROAD BIKE SO SUDDENLY!?
SOHOKU
...HASN'T DROPPED AT ALL!?
DESPITE STARTING AGAIN FROM DEAD LAST...
...HE LOOKS LIKE HE MEANS TO OVERTAKE SAKURAI AND SUGIMOTO AHEAD OF HIM!!

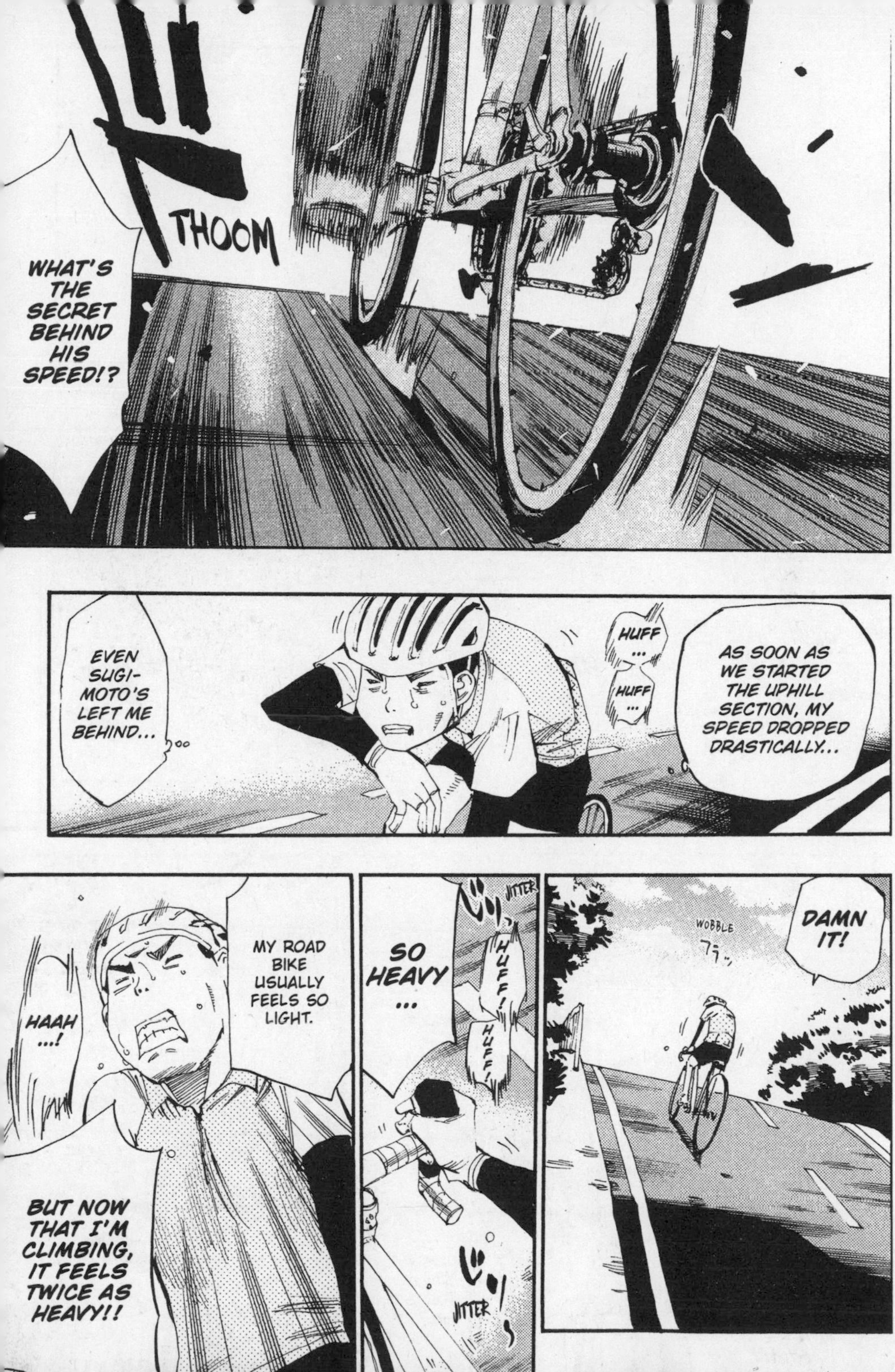
THOOM
WHAT'S THE SECRET BEHIND HIS SPEED!?
AS SOON AS WE STARTED THE UPHILL SECTION, MY SPEED DROPPED DRASTICALLY...
HUFF... HUFF...
EVEN SUGI-MOTO'S LEFT ME BEHIND...
DAMN IT!
WOBBLE
JITTER
HUFF! HUFF!
SO HEAVY...
JITTER
MY ROAD BIKE USUALLY FEELS SO LIGHT.
HAAH...!
BUT NOW THAT I'M CLIMBING, IT FEELS TWICE AS HEAVY!!

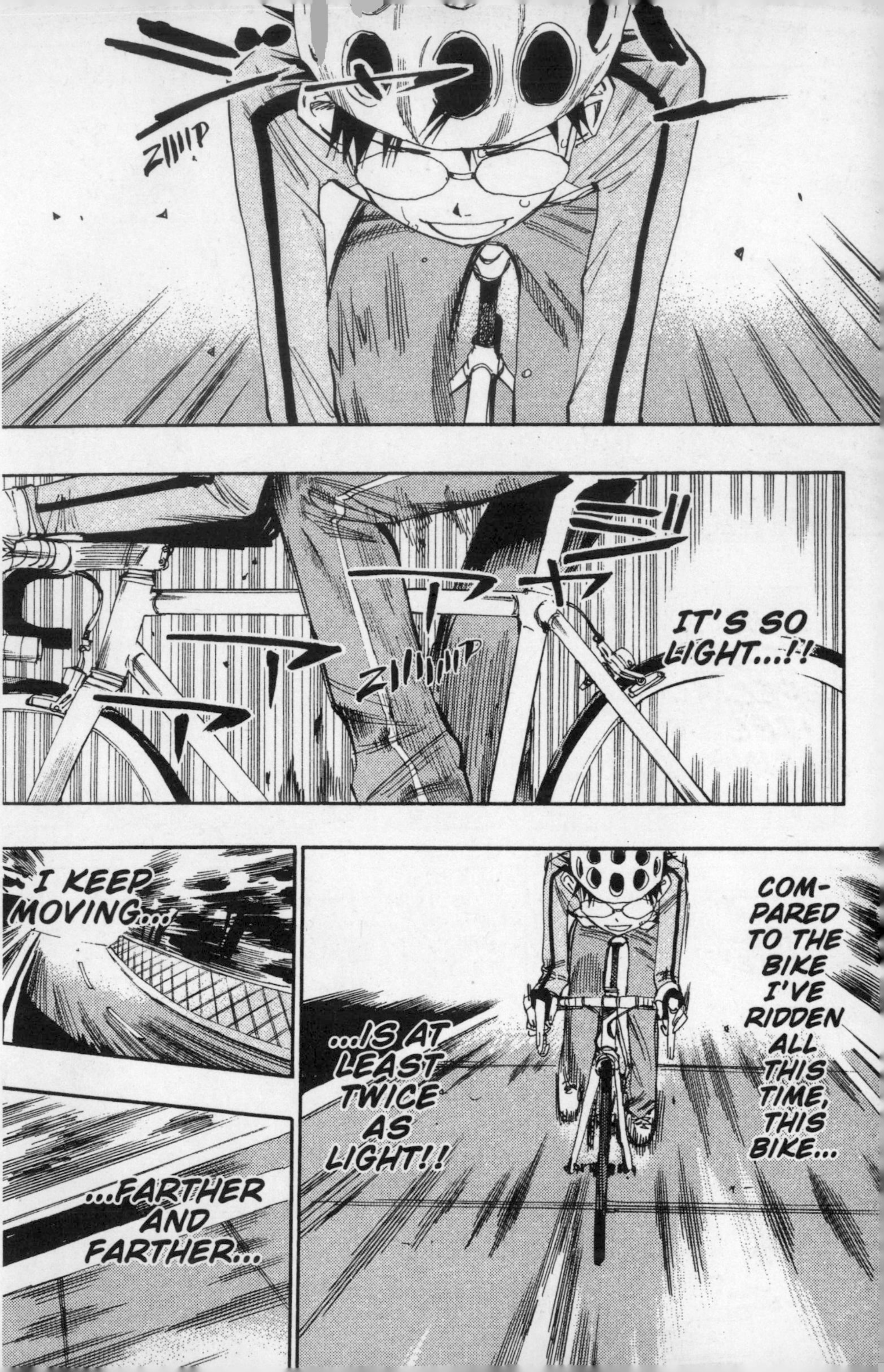
ZIIIIP
IT'S SO LIGHT...!!
ZIIIIIIIP
COMPARED TO THE BIKE I'VE RIDDEN ALL THIS TIME, THIS BIKE...
...IS AT LEAST TWICE AS LIGHT!!
I KEEP MOVING...
...FARTHER AND FARTHER...

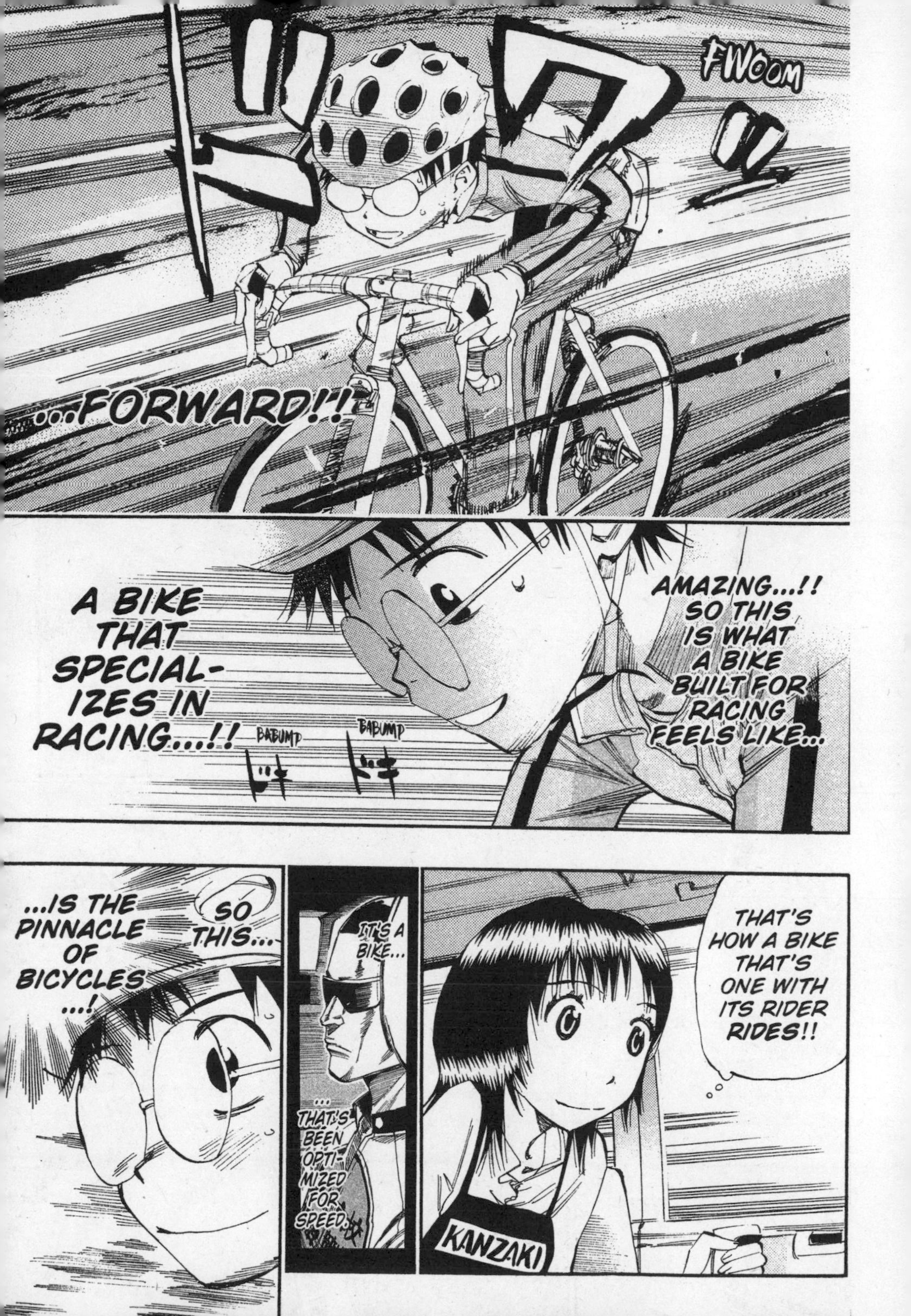
FWOOM
...FORWARD!!
AMAZING...!! SO THIS IS WHAT A BIKE BUILT FOR RACING FEELS LIKE...
A BIKE THAT SPECIAL-IZES IN RACING...!!
BABUMP
BABUMP
THAT'S HOW A BIKE THAT'S ONE WITH ITS RIDER RIDES!!
IT'S A BIKE...
...THAT'S BEEN OPTI-MIZED FOR SPEED.
KANZAKI
SO THIS...
...IS THE PINNACLE OF BICYCLES...!

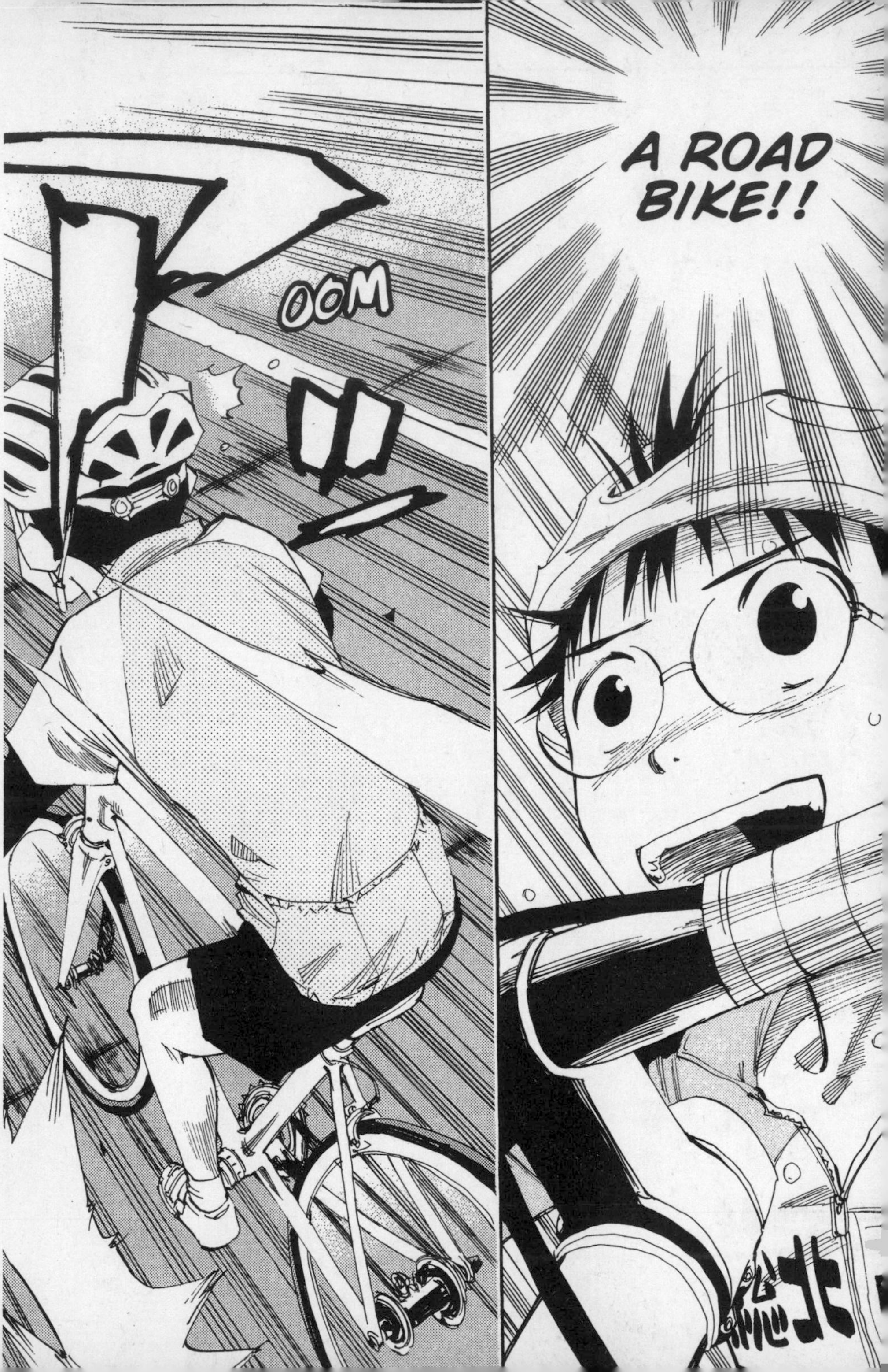
A ROAD BIKE!!
OOM

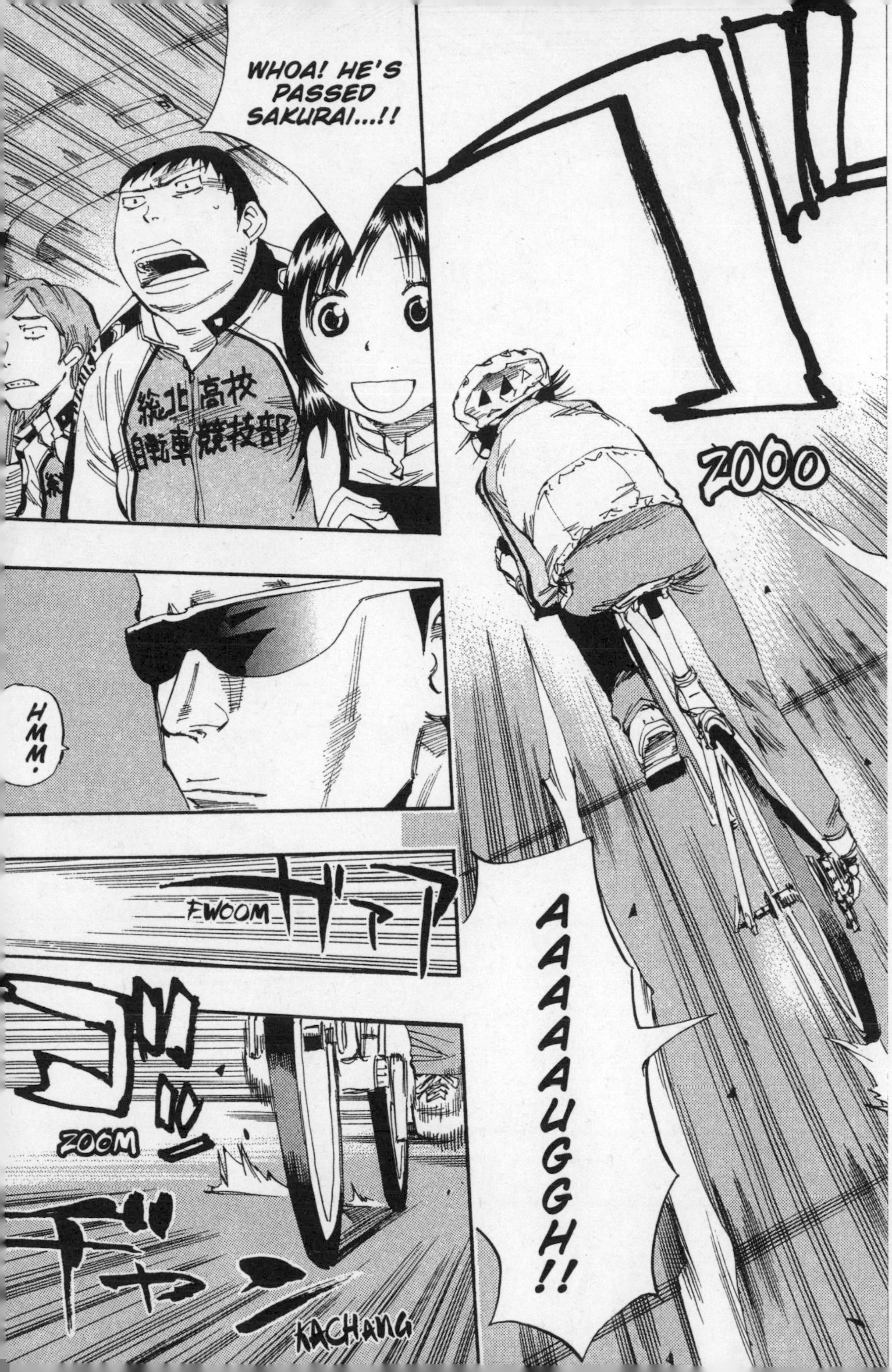
ZOOO
AAAAAAUGGGH!!
WHOA! HE'S PASSED SAKURAI...!!
総北高校
自転車競技部
HMM.
FWOOM
ZOOM
KACHANG

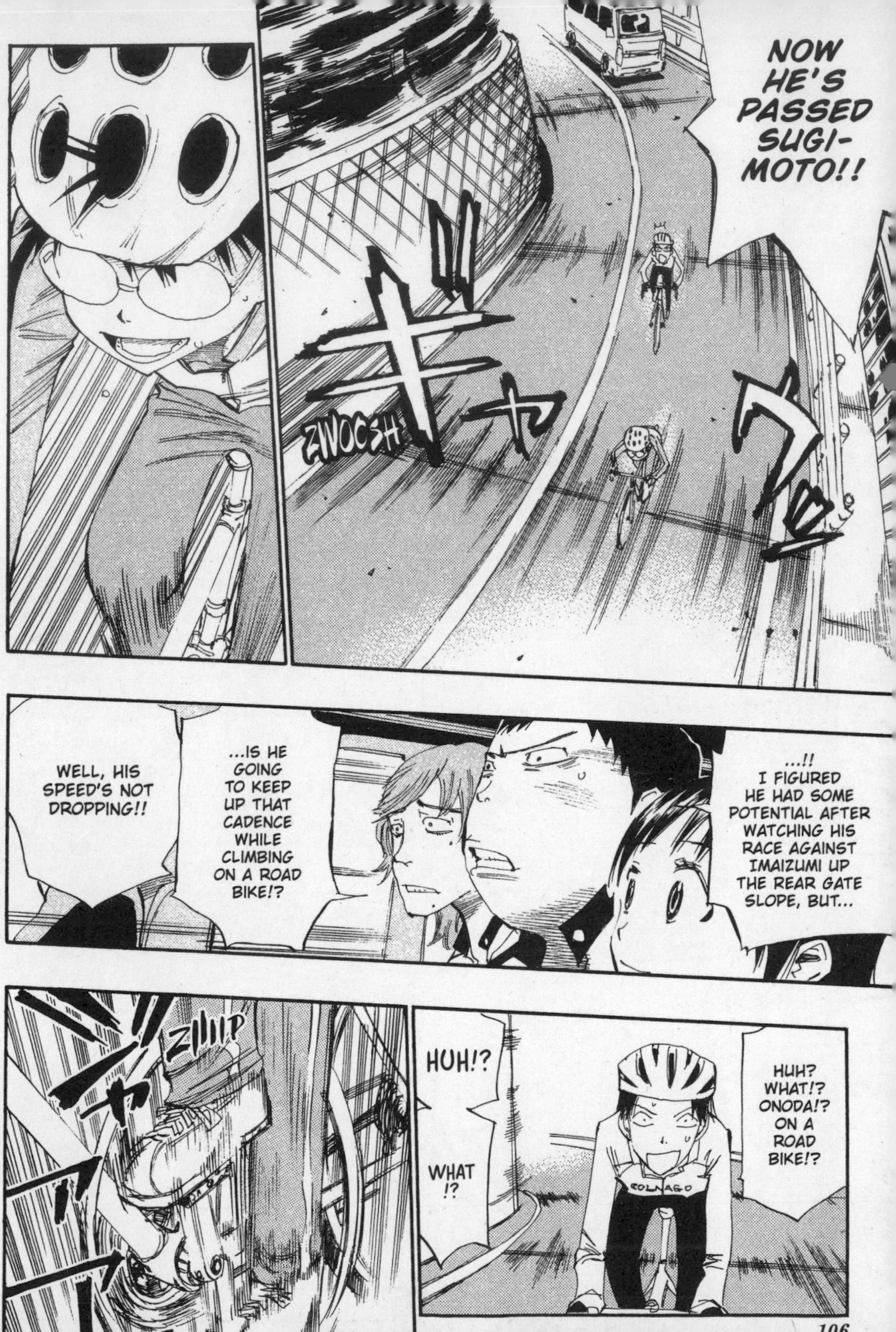
NOW HE'S PASSED SUGI-MOTO!!
ZWOOSH
...!! I FIGURED HE HAD SOME POTENTIAL AFTER WATCHING HIS RACE AGAINST IMAIZUMI UP THE REAR GATE SLOPE, BUT...
...IS HE GOING TO KEEP UP THAT CADENCE WHILE CLIMBING ON A ROAD BIKE!?
WELL, HIS SPEED'S NOT DROPPING!!
HUH? WHAT!? ONODA!? ON A ROAD BIKE!?
COLNAGO
HUH!?
WHAT !?
ZIIIIP

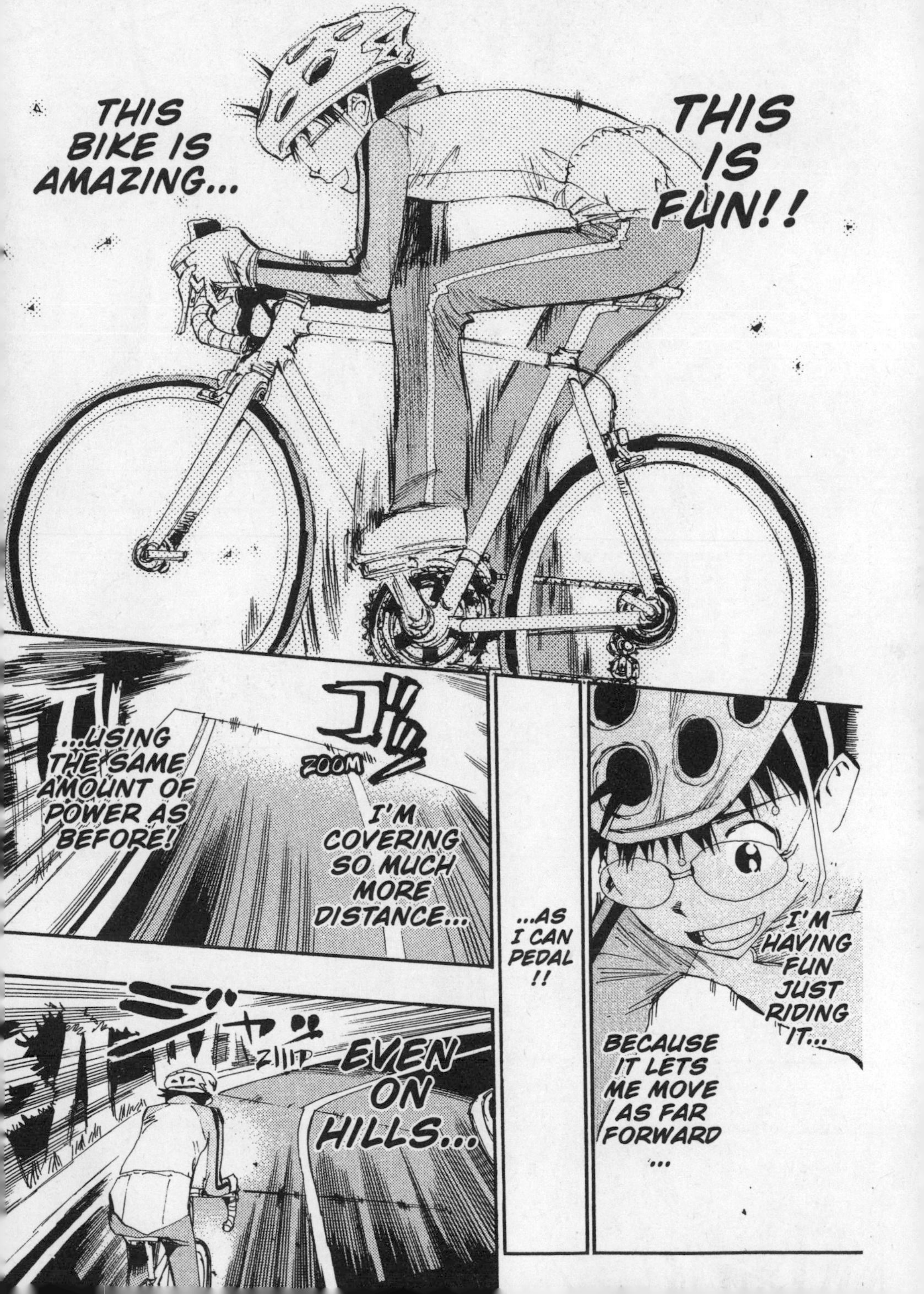
THIS IS FUN!!
THIS BIKE IS AMAZING...
I'M HAVING FUN JUST RIDING IT...
BECAUSE IT LETS ME MOVE AS FAR FORWARD ...
...AS I CAN PEDAL!!
ZOOM
I'M COVERING SO MUCH MORE DISTANCE...
...USING THE SAME AMOUNT OF POWER AS BEFORE!
ZIIIP
EVEN ON HILLS...

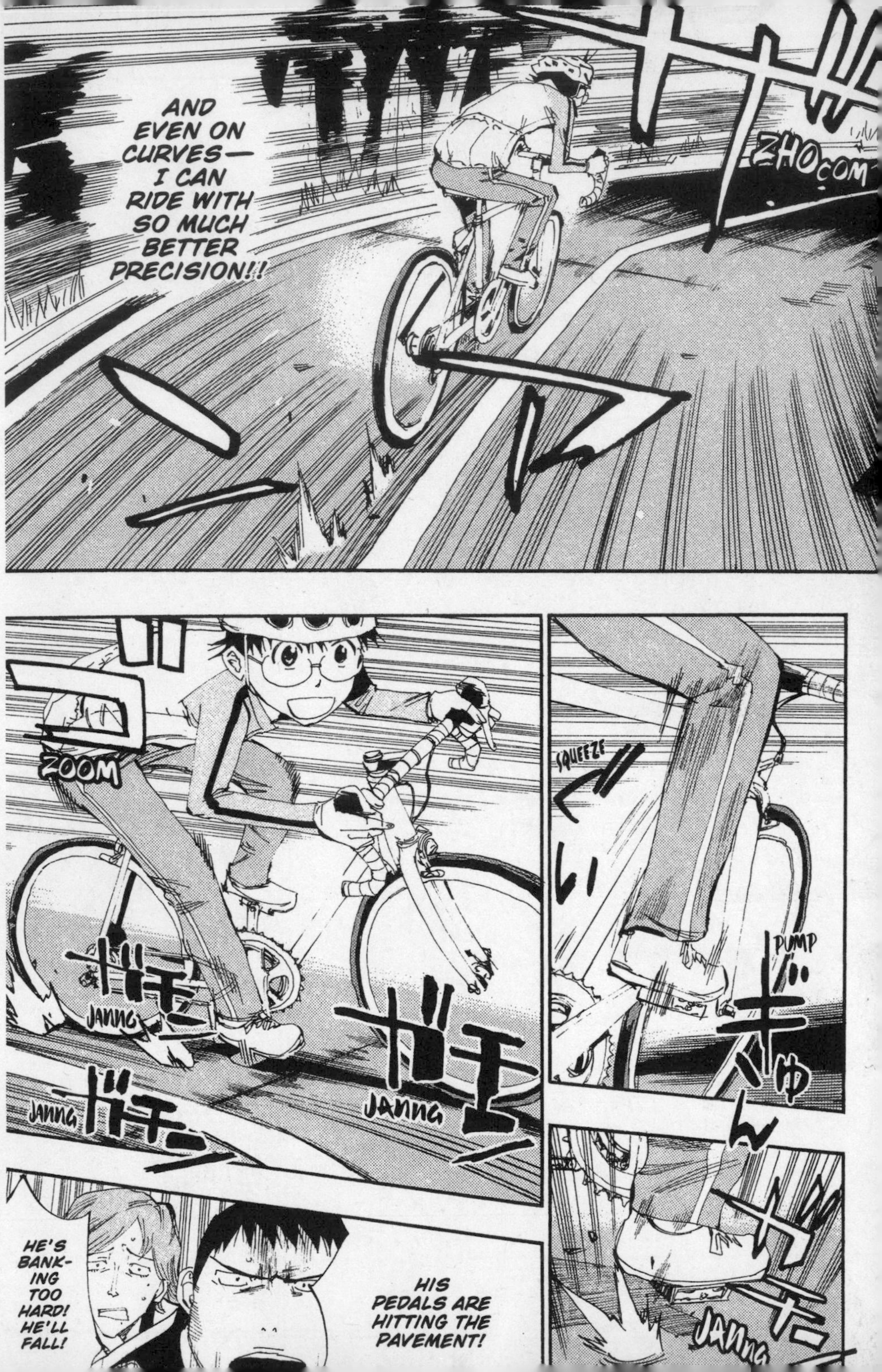
AND EVEN ON CURVES— I CAN RIDE WITH SO MUCH BETTER PRECISION!!
ZHOOOM
SQUEEZE
PUMP
JANNG
ZOOM
JANNG
JANNG
JANNG
HIS PEDALS ARE HITTING THE PAVEMENT!
HE'S BANKING TOO HARD! HE'LL FALL!

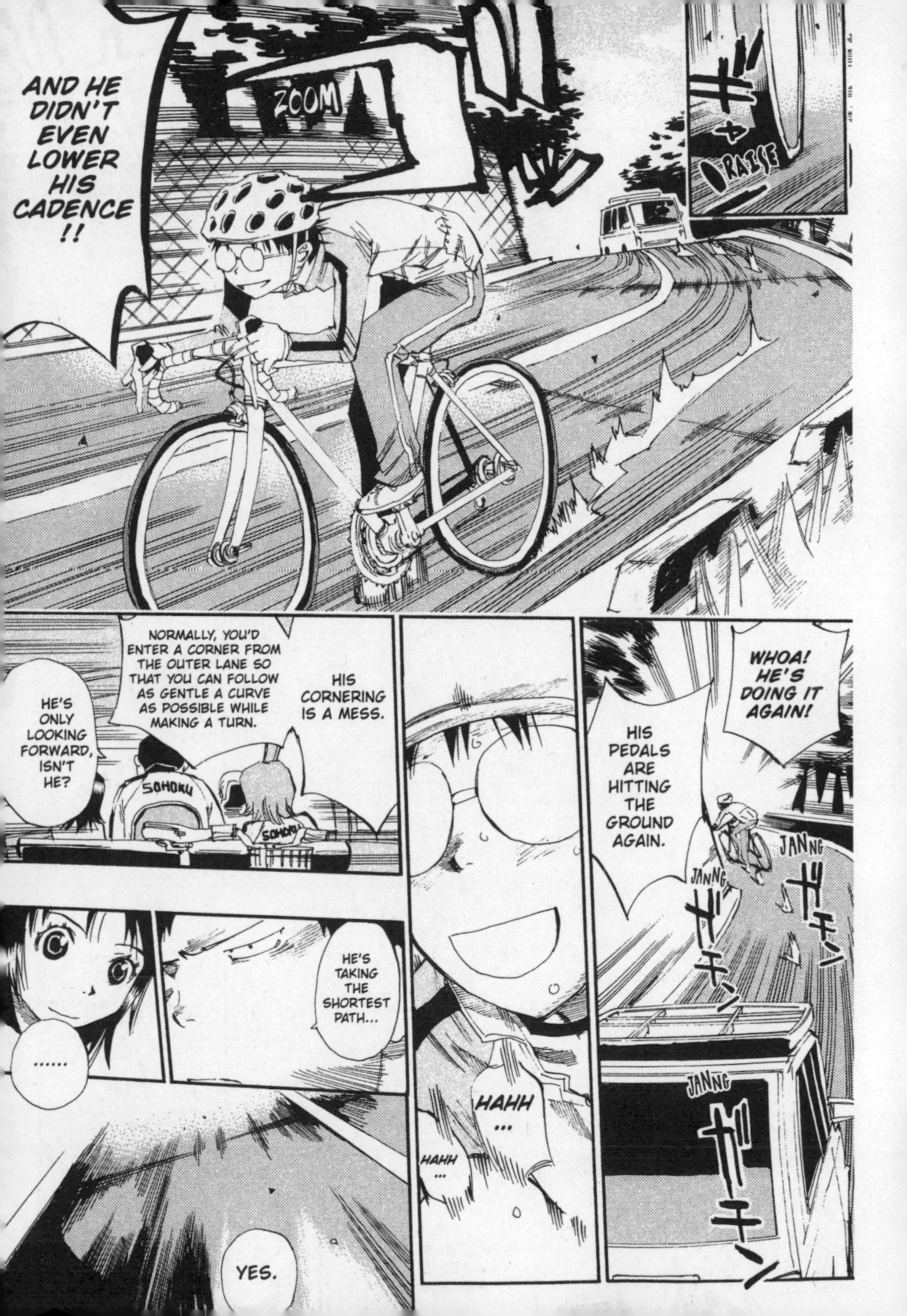
RAISE
ZOOM
AND HE DIDN'T EVEN LOWER HIS CADENCE!!
WHOA! HE'S DOING IT AGAIN!
HIS PEDALS ARE HITTING THE GROUND AGAIN.
JANNG
JANNG
JANNG
HAHH...
HAHH...
HIS CORNERING IS A MESS.
NORMALLY, YOU'D ENTER A CORNER FROM THE OUTER LANE SO THAT YOU CAN FOLLOW AS GENTLE A CURVE AS POSSIBLE WHILE MAKING A TURN.
HE'S ONLY LOOKING FORWARD, ISN'T HE?
SOHOKU
SOHOKU
HE'S TAKING THE SHORTEST PATH...
......
YES.

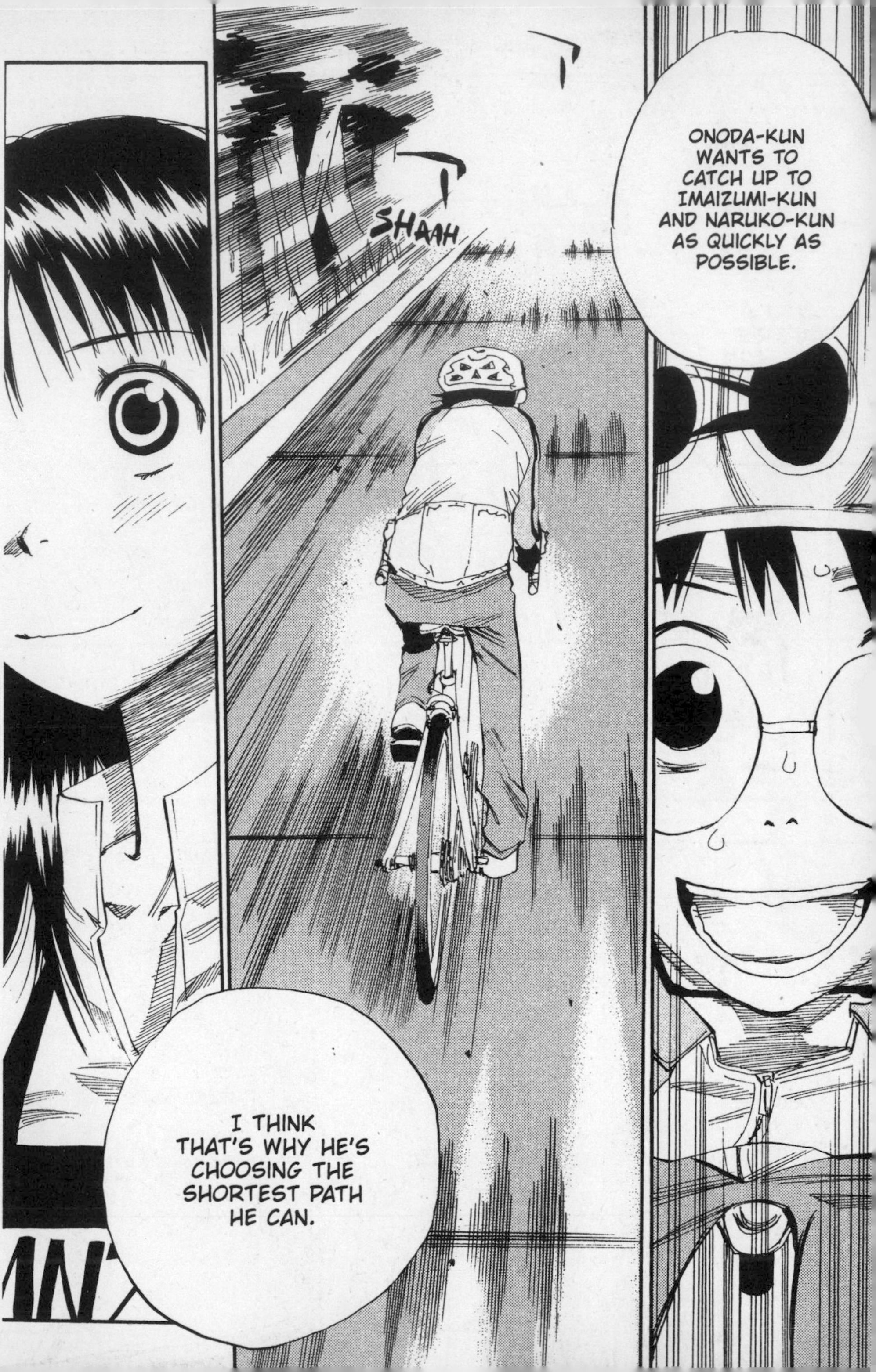
ONODA-KUN WANTS TO CATCH UP TO IMAIZUMI-KUN AND NARUKO-KUN AS QUICKLY AS POSSIBLE.
SHAAH
I THINK THAT'S WHY HE'S CHOOSING THE SHORTEST PATH HE CAN.

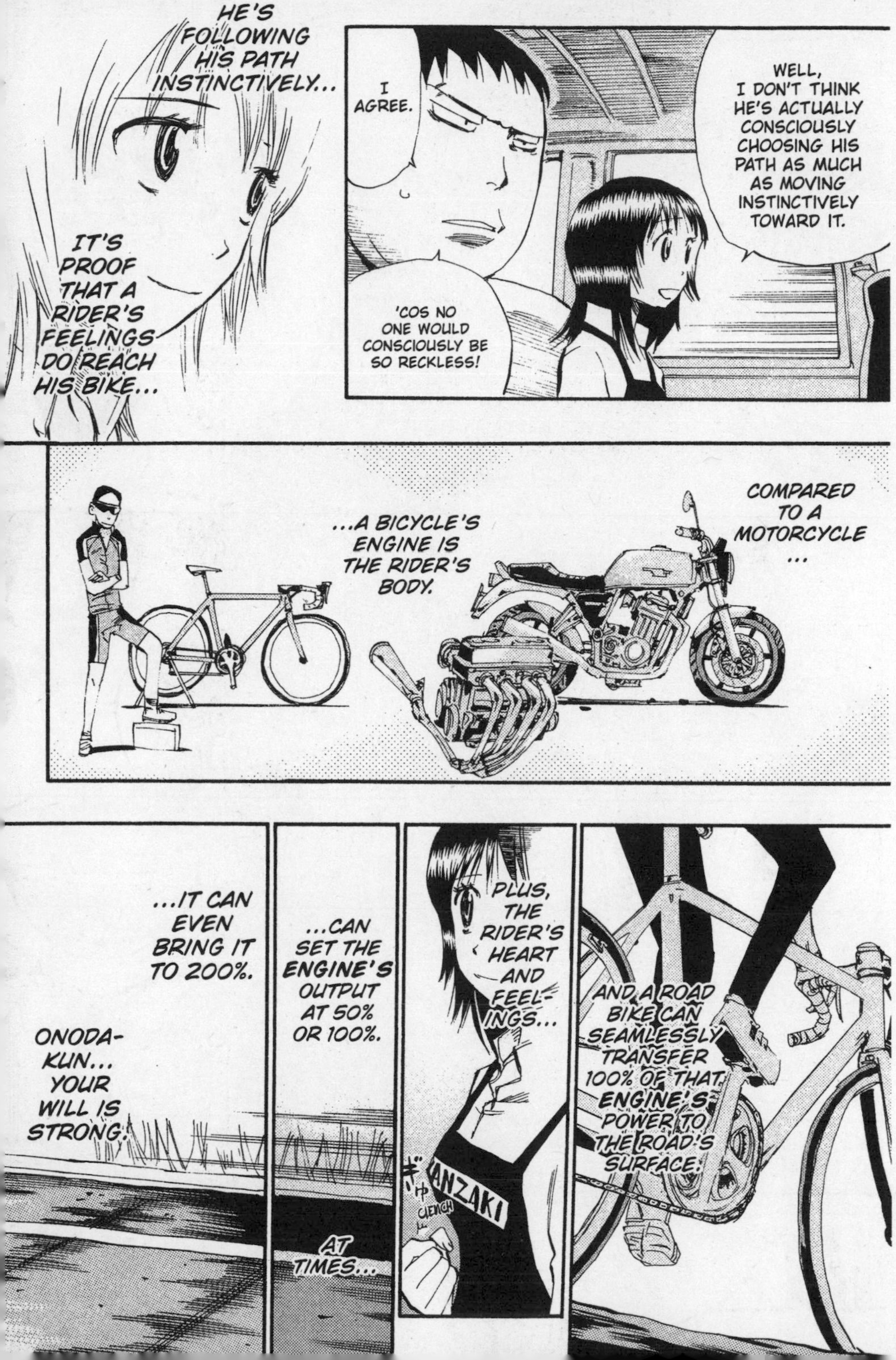
WELL, I DON'T THINK HE'S ACTUALLY CONSCIOUSLY CHOOSING HIS PATH AS MUCH AS MOVING INSTINCTIVELY TOWARD IT.
I AGREE.
'COS NO ONE WOULD CONSCIOUSLY BE SO RECKLESS!
HE'S FOLLOWING HIS PATH INSTINCTIVELY...
IT'S PROOF THAT A RIDER'S FEELINGS DO REACH HIS BIKE...
COMPARED TO A MOTORCYCLE...
...A BICYCLE'S ENGINE IS THE RIDER'S BODY.
AND A ROAD BIKE CAN SEAMLESSLY TRANSFER 100% OF THAT ENGINE'S POWER TO THE ROAD'S SURFACE.
PLUS, THE RIDER'S HEART AND FEELINGS...
ANZAKI
CLENCH
...CAN SET THE ENGINE'S OUTPUT AT 50% OR 100%.
AT TIMES...
...IT CAN EVEN BRING IT TO 200%.
ONODA-KUN... YOUR WILL IS STRONG.

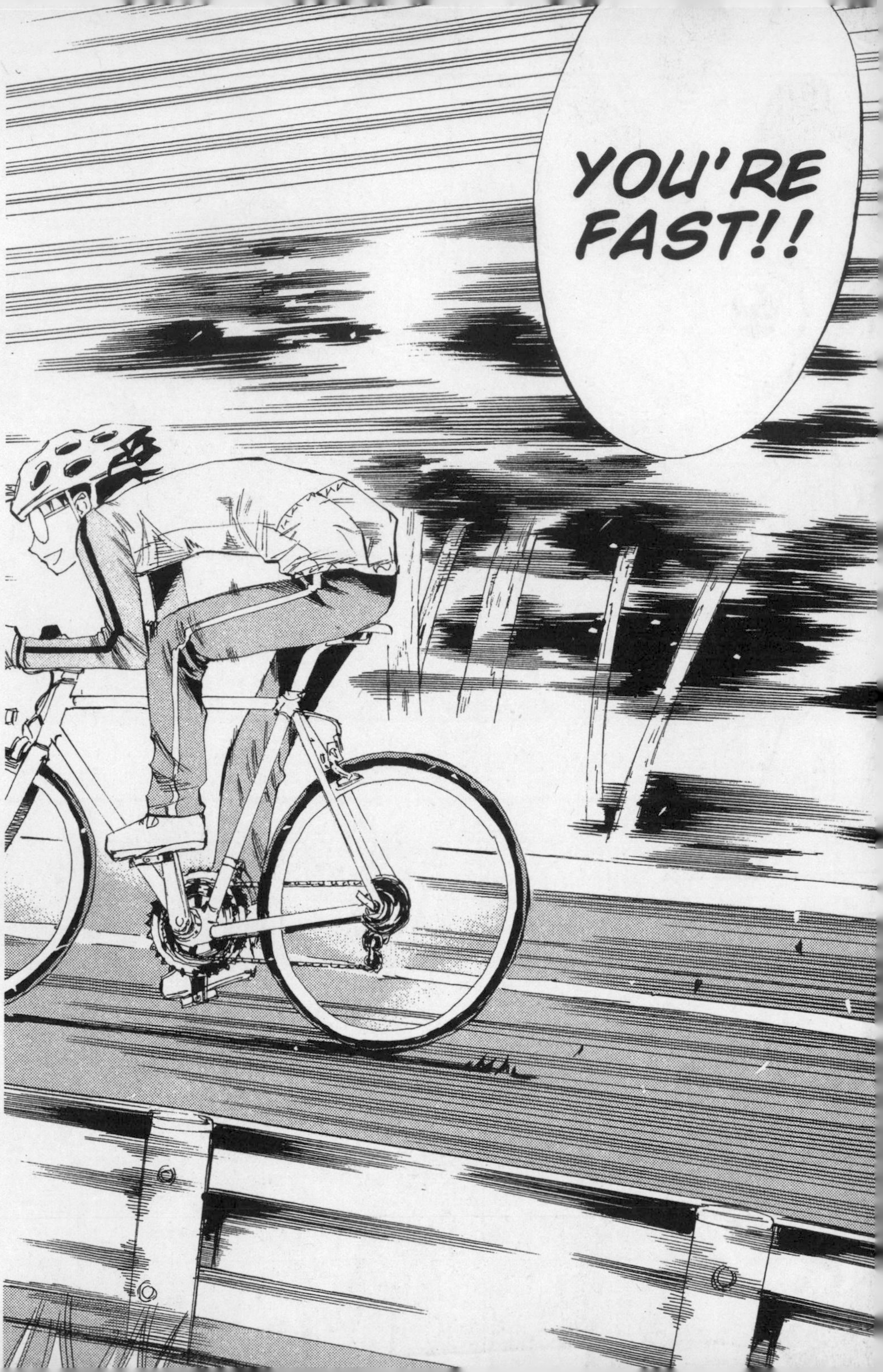
YOU'RE FAST!!

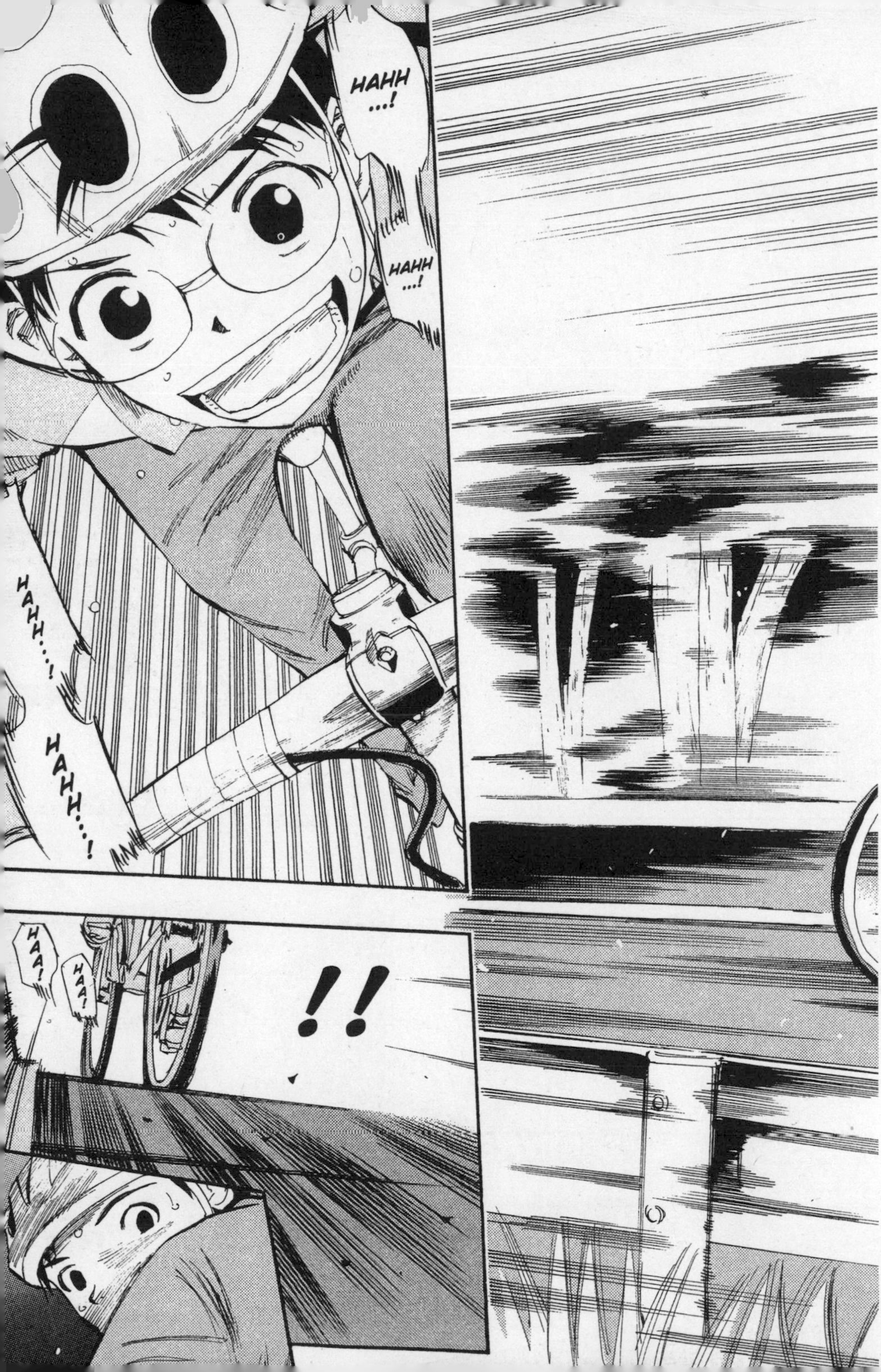
HAHH ...!
HAHH ...!
HAHH...!
HAHH...!
HAA!
HAA!
!!

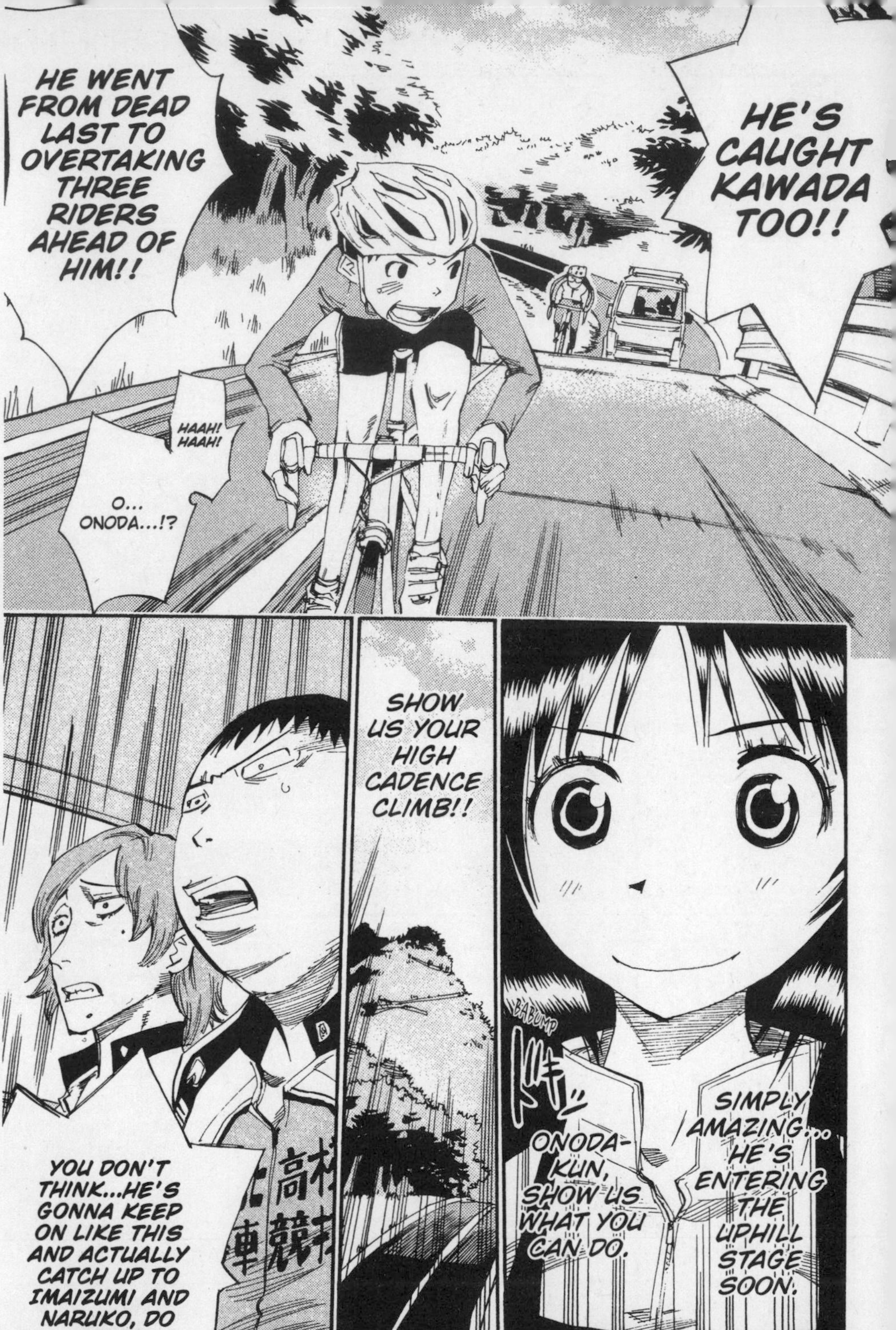
HE'S CAUGHT KAWADA TOO!!
HE WENT FROM DEAD LAST TO OVERTAKING THREE RIDERS AHEAD OF HIM!!
HAAH! HAAH!
O... ONODA...!?
BABUMP
SIMPLY AMAZING... HE'S ENTERING THE UPHILL STAGE SOON.
ONODA-KUN, SHOW US WHAT YOU CAN DO.
SHOW US YOUR HIGH CADENCE CLIMB!!
YOU DON'T THINK...HE'S GONNA KEEP ON LIKE THIS AND ACTUALLY CATCH UP TO IMAIZUMI AND NARUKO, DO YOU!?

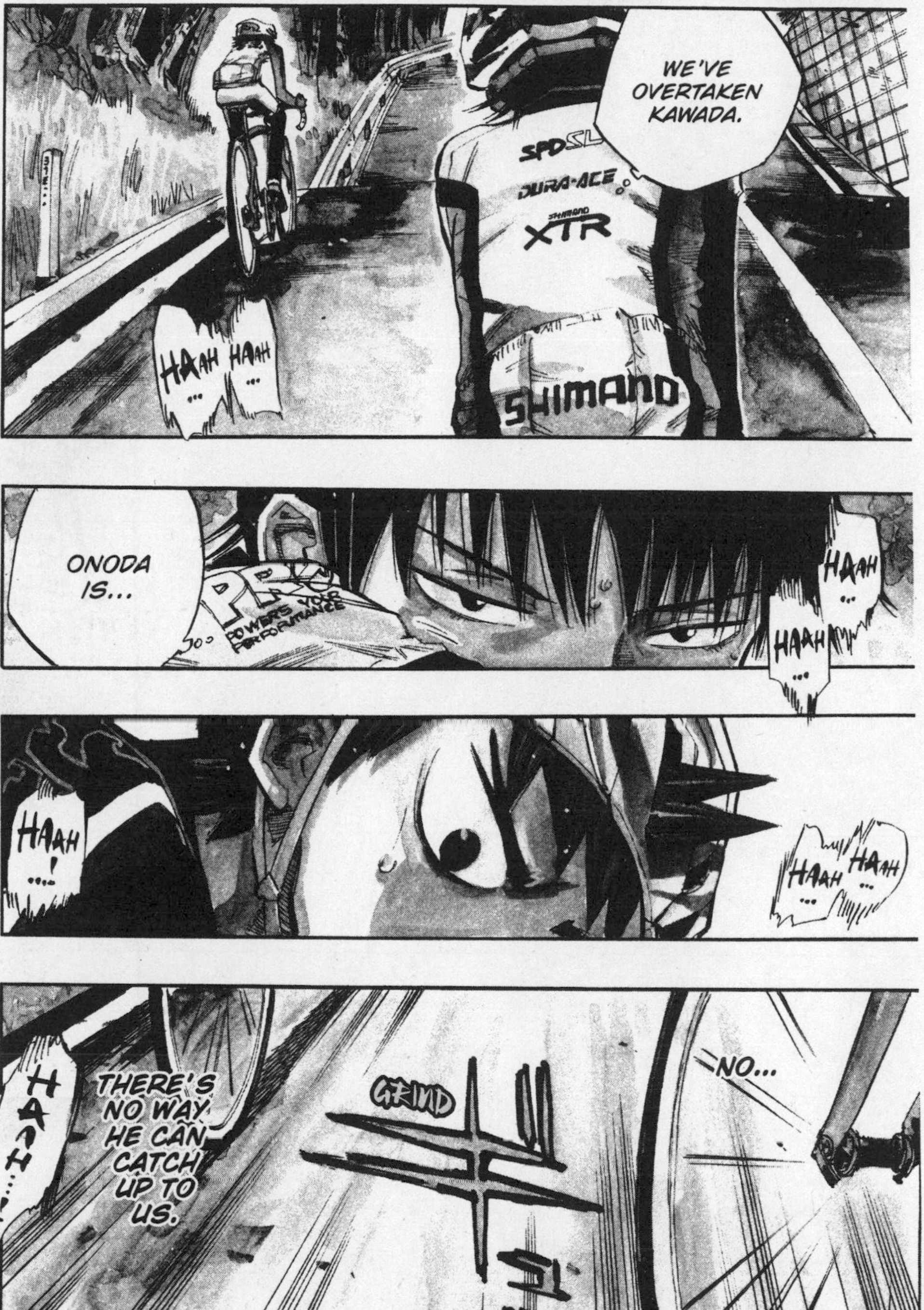
WE'VE OVERTAKEN KAWADA.
DURA-ACE
XTR
SHIMANO
HAAH HAAH...
HAAH... HAAH...
ONODA IS...
HAAH HAAH...
HAAH...!
NO...
GRIND
THERE'S NO WAY HE CAN CATCH UP TO US.
HAAH...!!

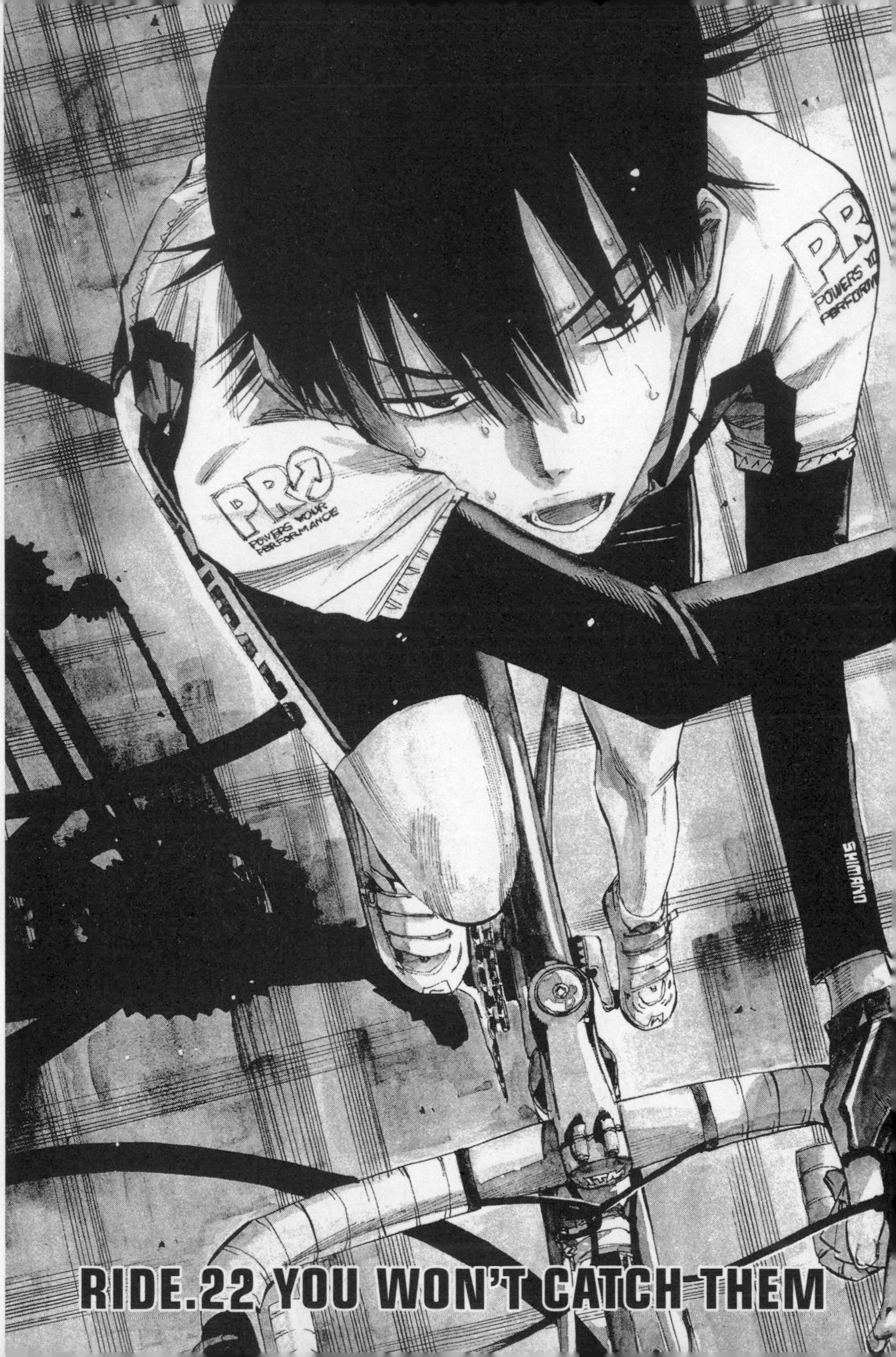
PRO POWERS YOUR PERFORMANCE
SHIMANO

RIDE.22 YOU WON'T CATCH THEM

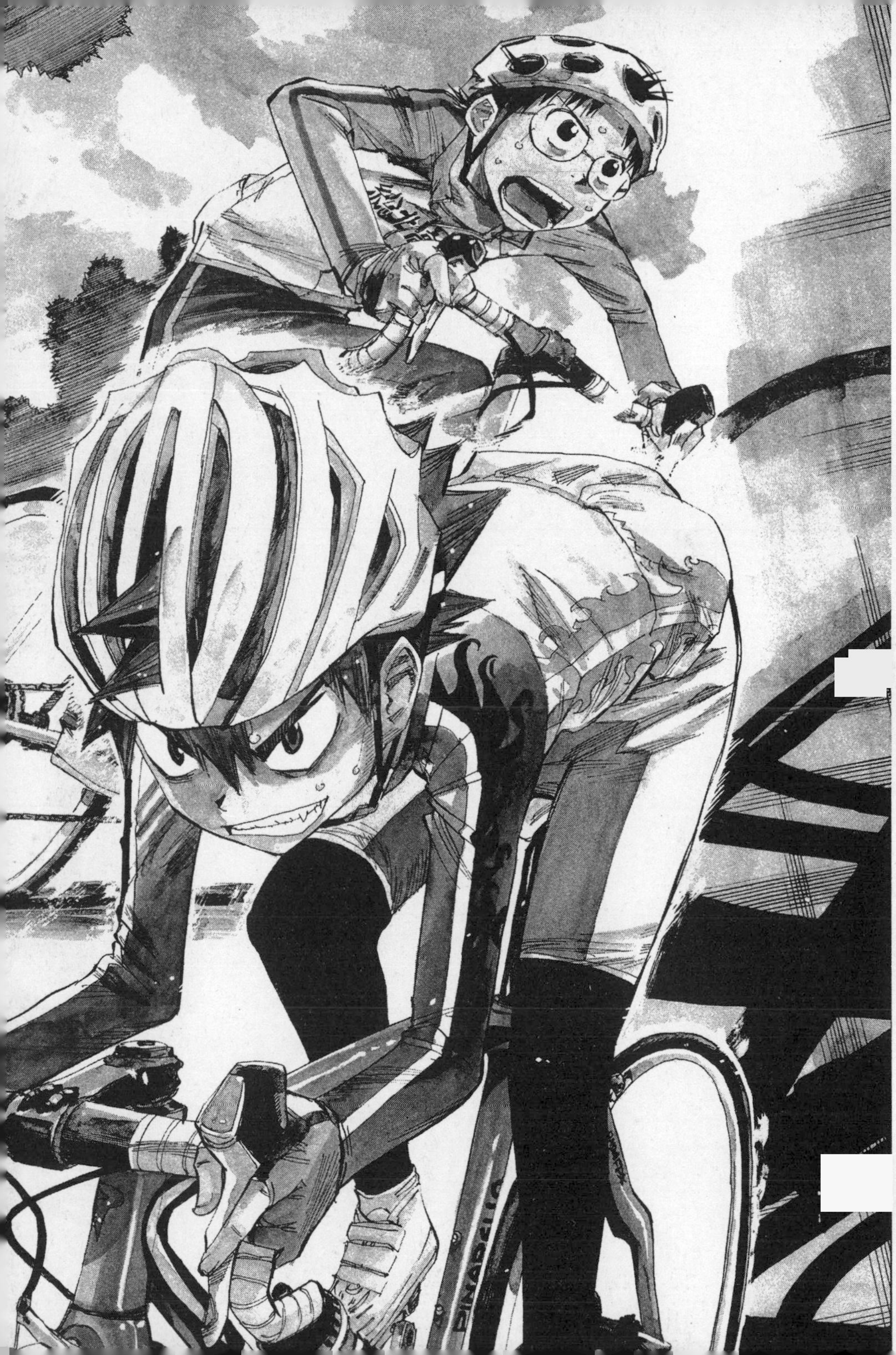
PINARELLO

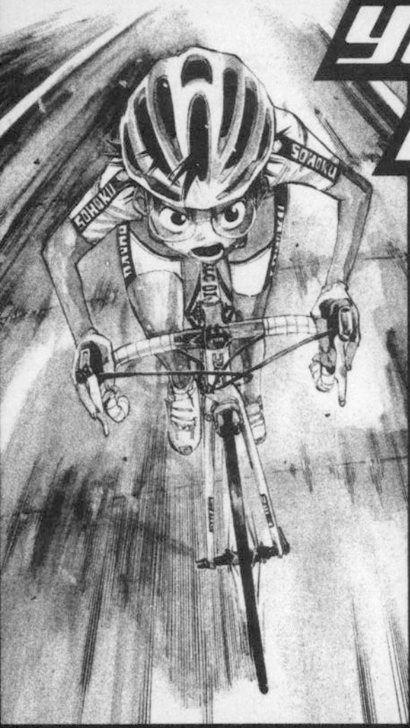

YOWAMUSHI PEDAL 2

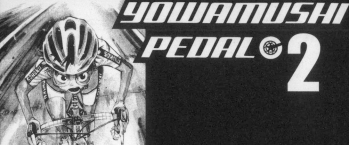

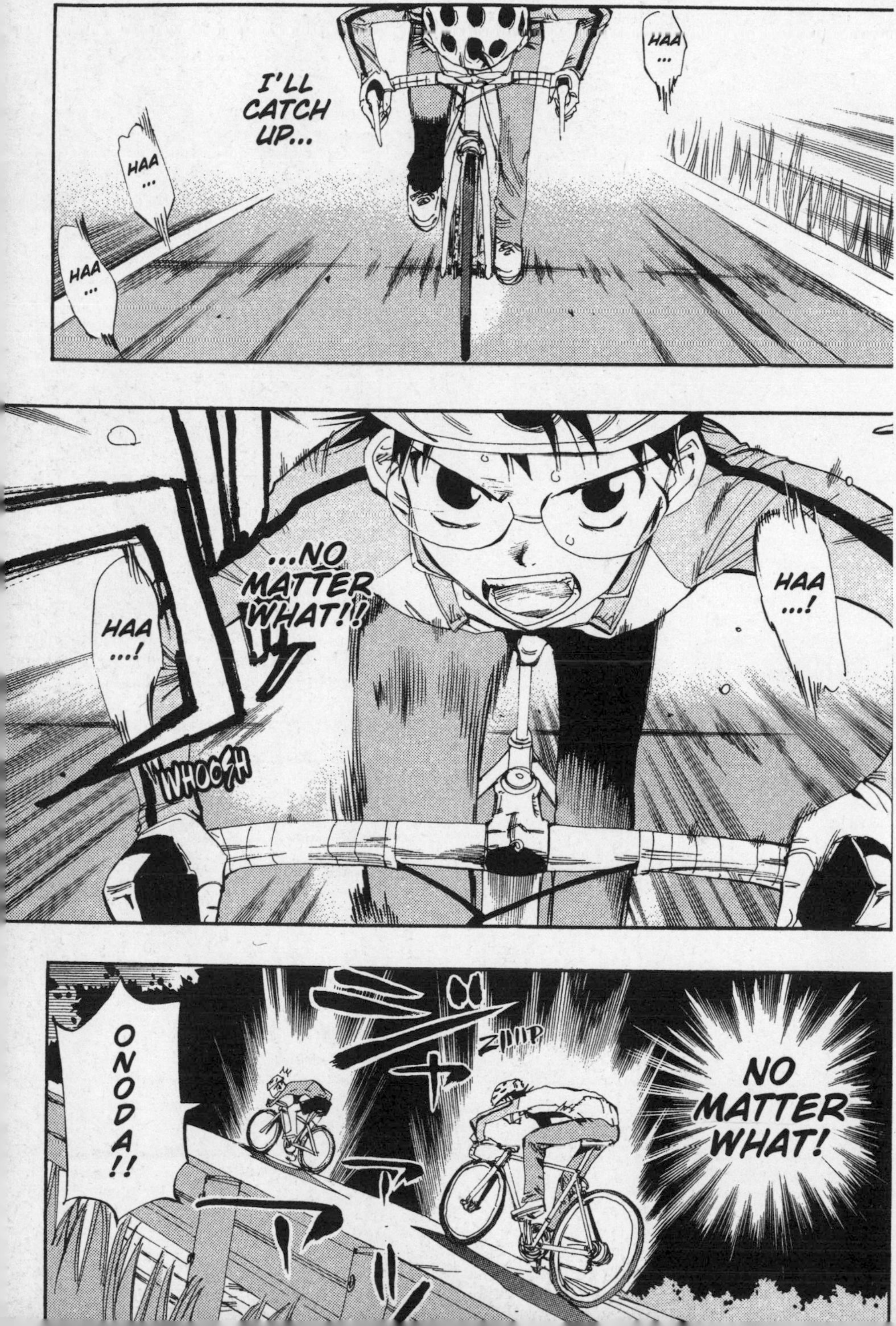
HAA...
I'LL CATCH UP...
HAA...
HAA...
HAA...!
...NO MATTER WHAT!!
HAA...!
WHOOSH
NO MATTER WHAT!
ZIIIP
ONODA!!

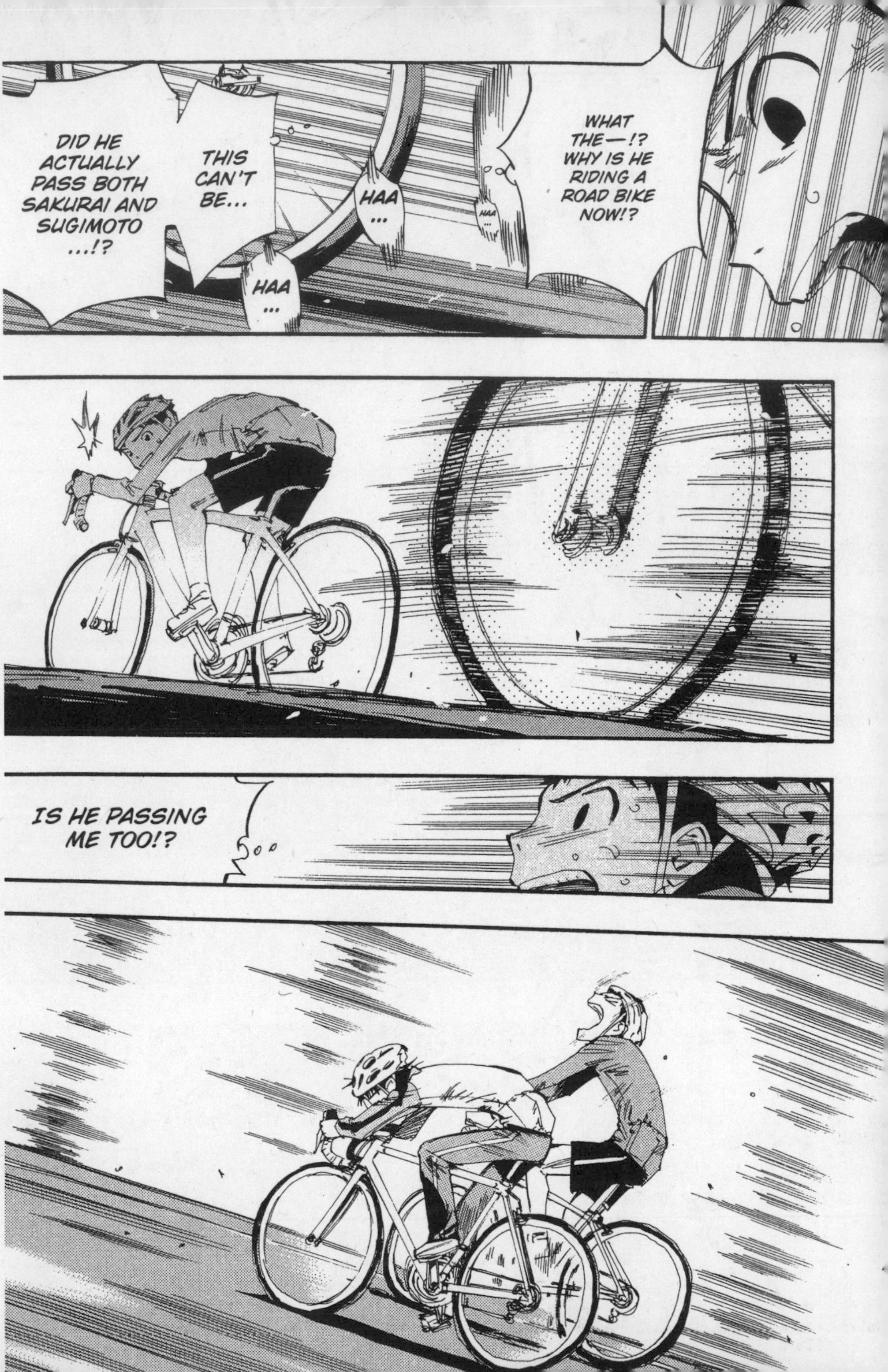
WHAT THE—!? WHY IS HE RIDING A ROAD BIKE NOW!?
HAA ...
HAA ...
THIS CAN'T BE...
HAA ...
DID HE ACTUALLY PASS BOTH SAKURAI AND SUGIMOTO ...!?
IS HE PASSING ME TOO!?

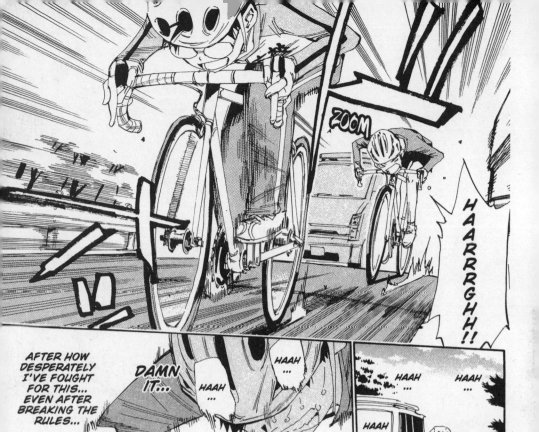

ZOOM
HAARRRGHH!!
HAAH...
HAAH...
HAAH...
HAAH...
DAMN IT...
HAAH...
AFTER HOW DESPERATELY I'VE FOUGHT FOR THIS... EVEN AFTER BREAKING THE RULES...
HAAH...
I WAS IN THIRD PLACE...
HAAH...
HAAH...
WHAT THE HECK!? HOW IS THIS THE SAME GUY FROM BEFORE!? WAS HE FAKING US OUT!?
HAAH...
DAMN IT...
AT LEAST LOOK AT ME WHEN YOU'RE PASSING ME!

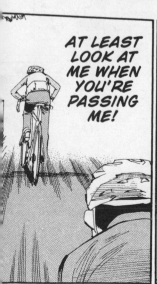

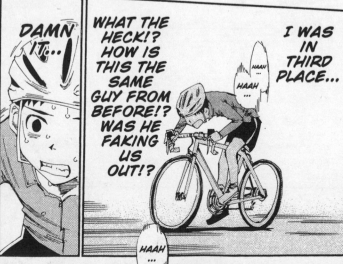

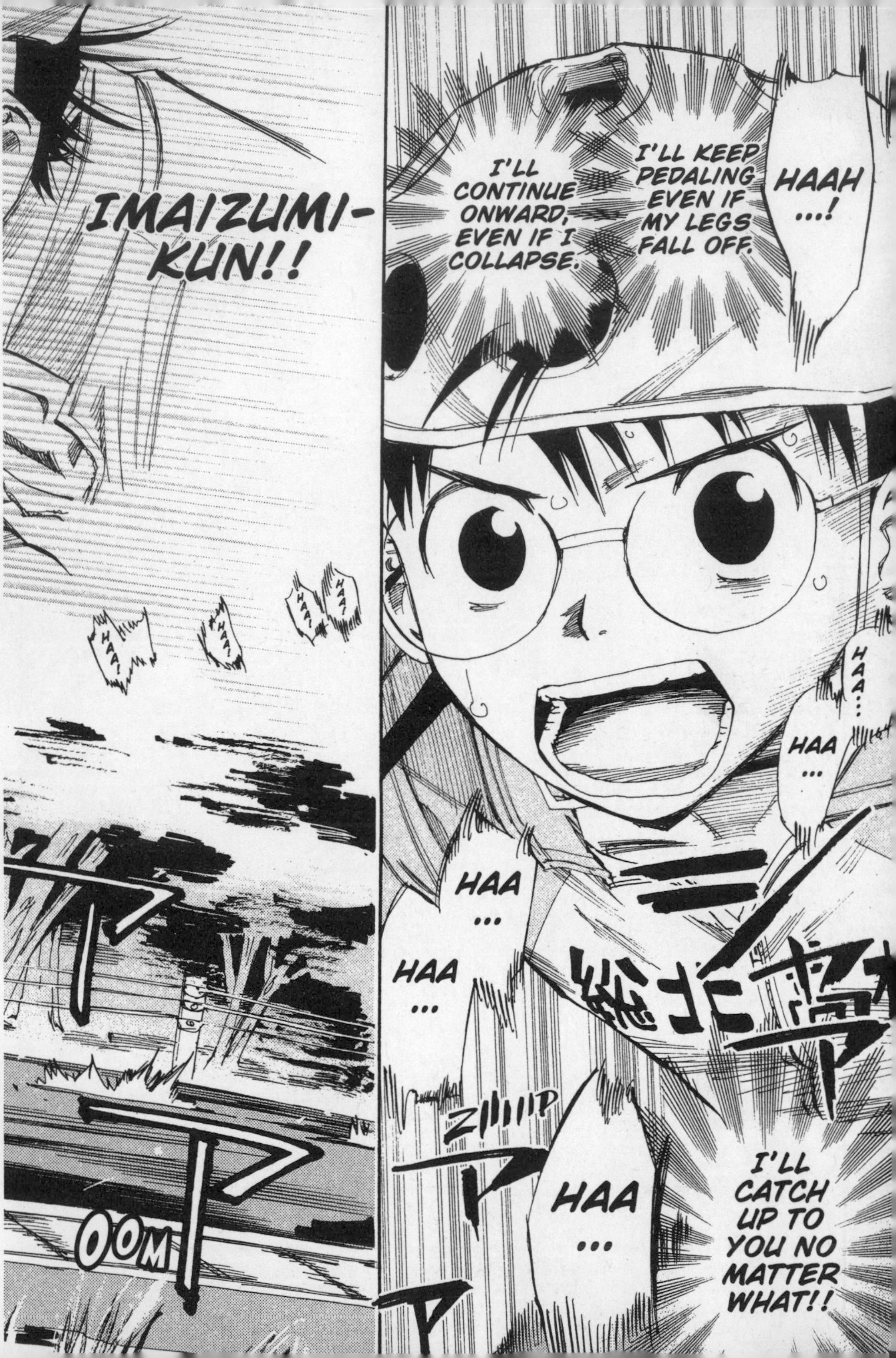
HAAH ...!
I'LL KEEP PEDALING EVEN IF MY LEGS FALL OFF.
I'LL CONTINUE ONWARD, EVEN IF I COLLAPSE.
HAA...
HAA ...
HAA ...
HAA ...
HAA ...
ZIIIIP
I'LL CATCH UP TO YOU NO MATTER WHAT!!
IMAIZUMI-KUN!!
HAA! HAA!
HAA! HAA!
HAA! HAA!
OOM

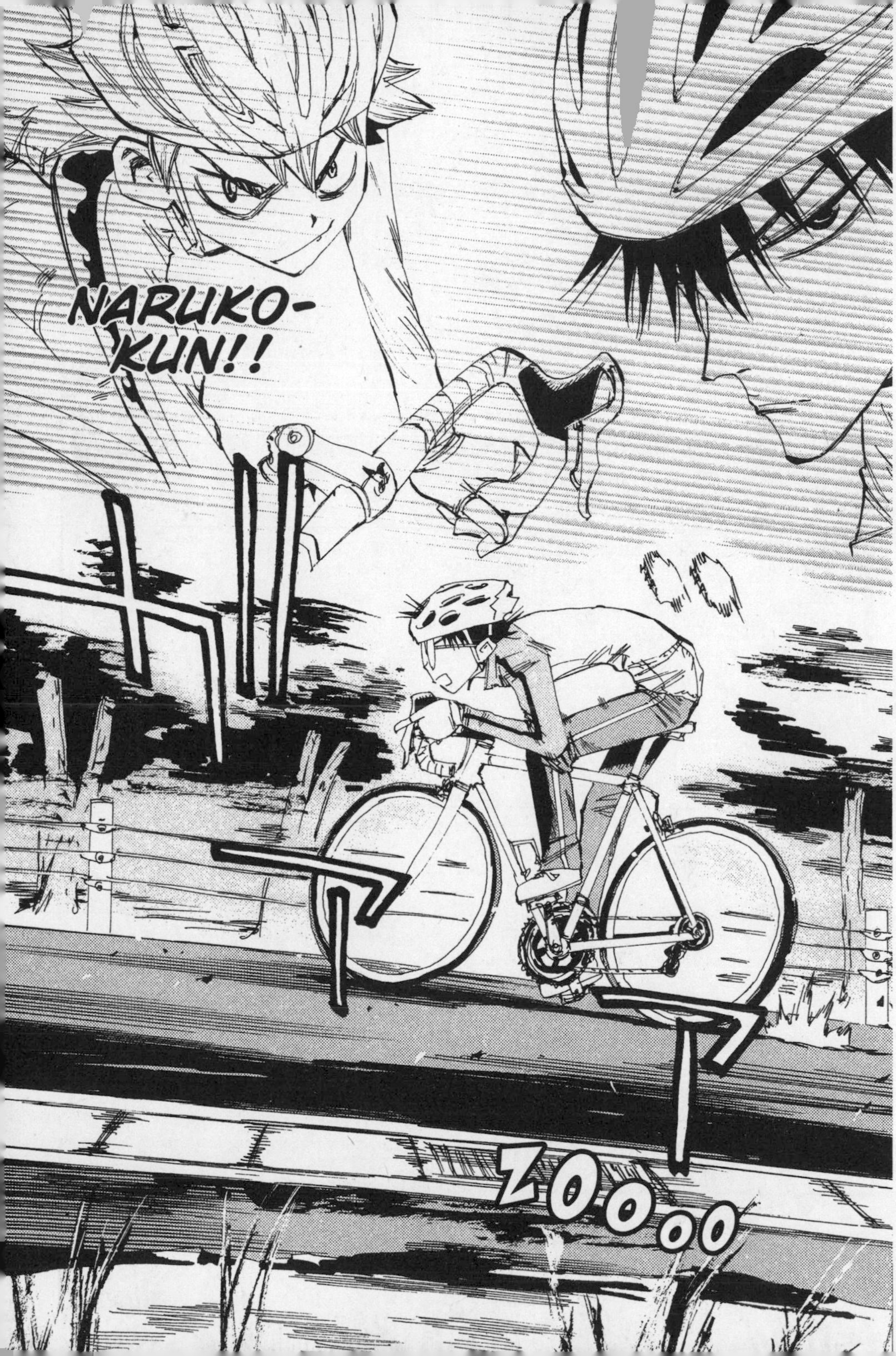
NARUKO-KUN!!
ZOOOO

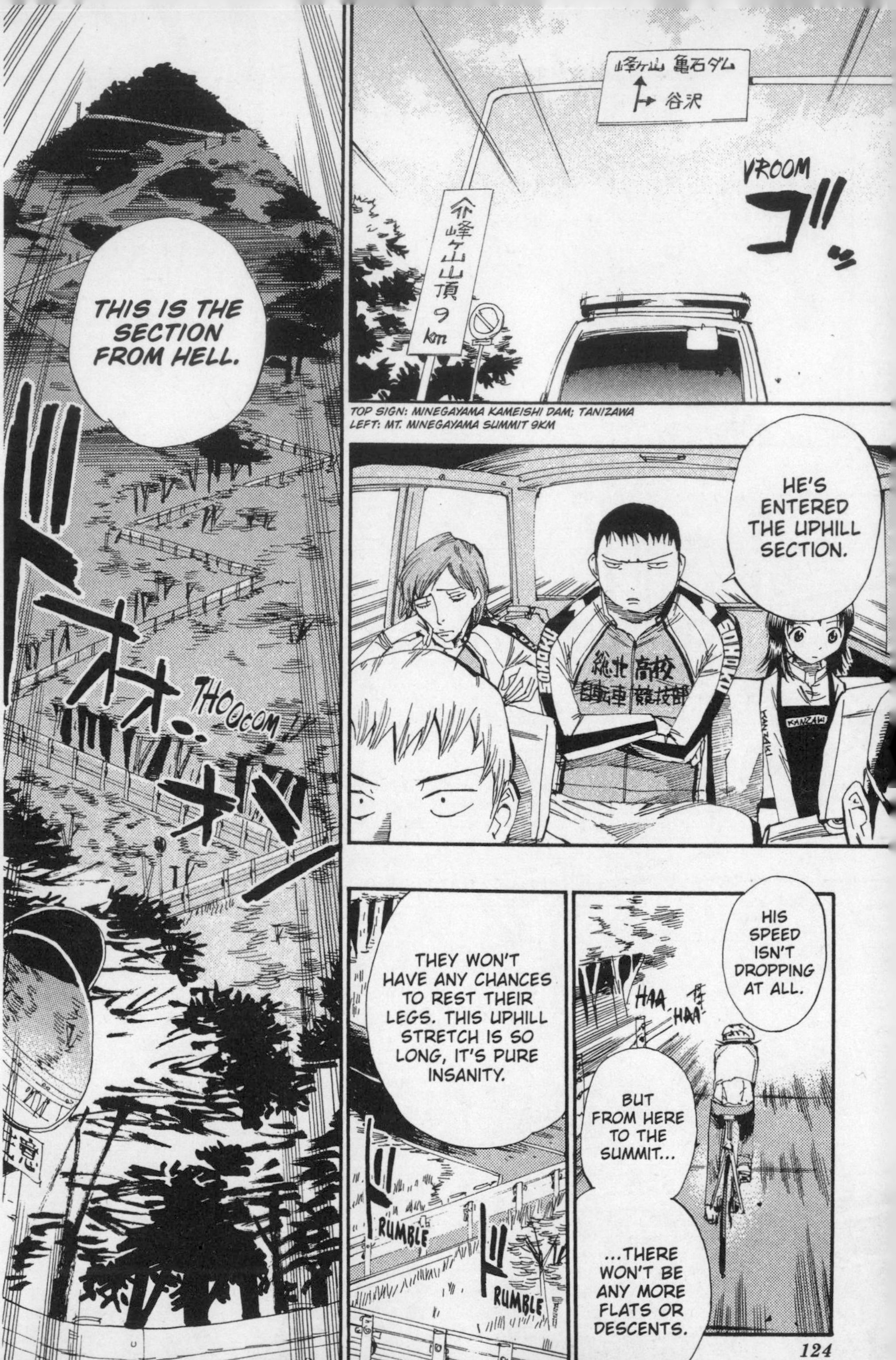

峰ヶ山 亀石ダム
谷沢
峰ヶ山山頂 9km
VROOM
TOP SIGN: MINEGAYAMA KAMEISHI DAM; TANIZAWA
LEFT: MT. MINEGAYAMA SUMMIT 9KM
HE'S ENTERED THE UPHILL SECTION.
総北高校 自転車競技部
SOHOKU
HIS SPEED ISN'T DROPPING AT ALL.
HAA HAA
BUT FROM HERE TO THE SUMMIT...
...THERE WON'T BE ANY MORE FLATS OR DESCENTS.
THEY WON'T HAVE ANY CHANCES TO REST THEIR LEGS. THIS UPHILL STRETCH IS SO LONG, IT'S PURE INSANITY.
RUMBLE
RUMBLE
THIS IS THE SECTION FROM HELL.
THOOOOM

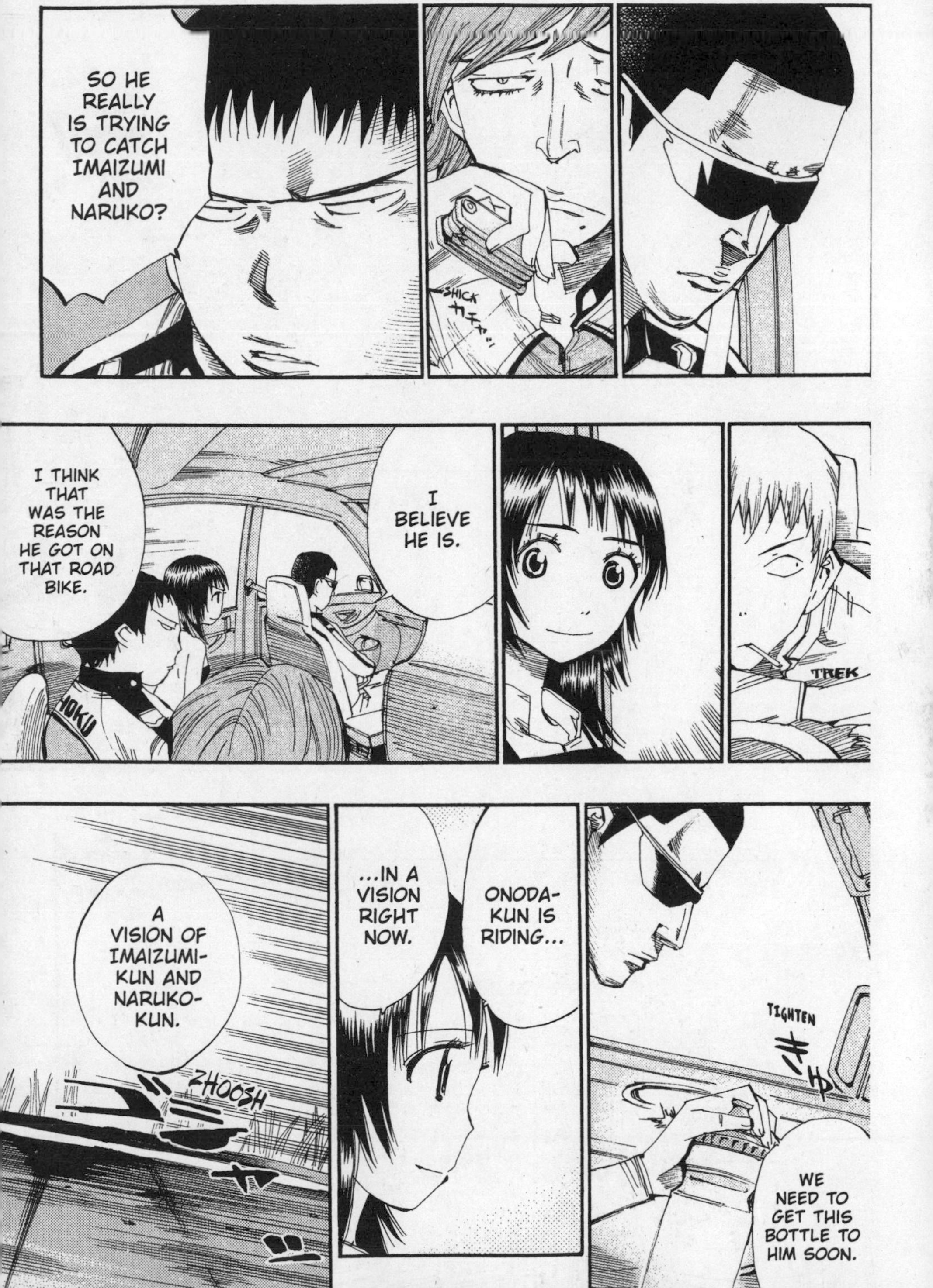
SHICK
SO HE REALLY IS TRYING TO CATCH IMAIZUMI AND NARUKO?
TREK
I BELIEVE HE IS.
I THINK THAT WAS THE REASON HE GOT ON THAT ROAD BIKE.
TIGHTEN
WE NEED TO GET THIS BOTTLE TO HIM SOON.
ONODA-KUN IS RIDING...
...IN A VISION RIGHT NOW.
A VISION OF IMAIZUMI-KUN AND NARUKO-KUN.
ZHOOSH

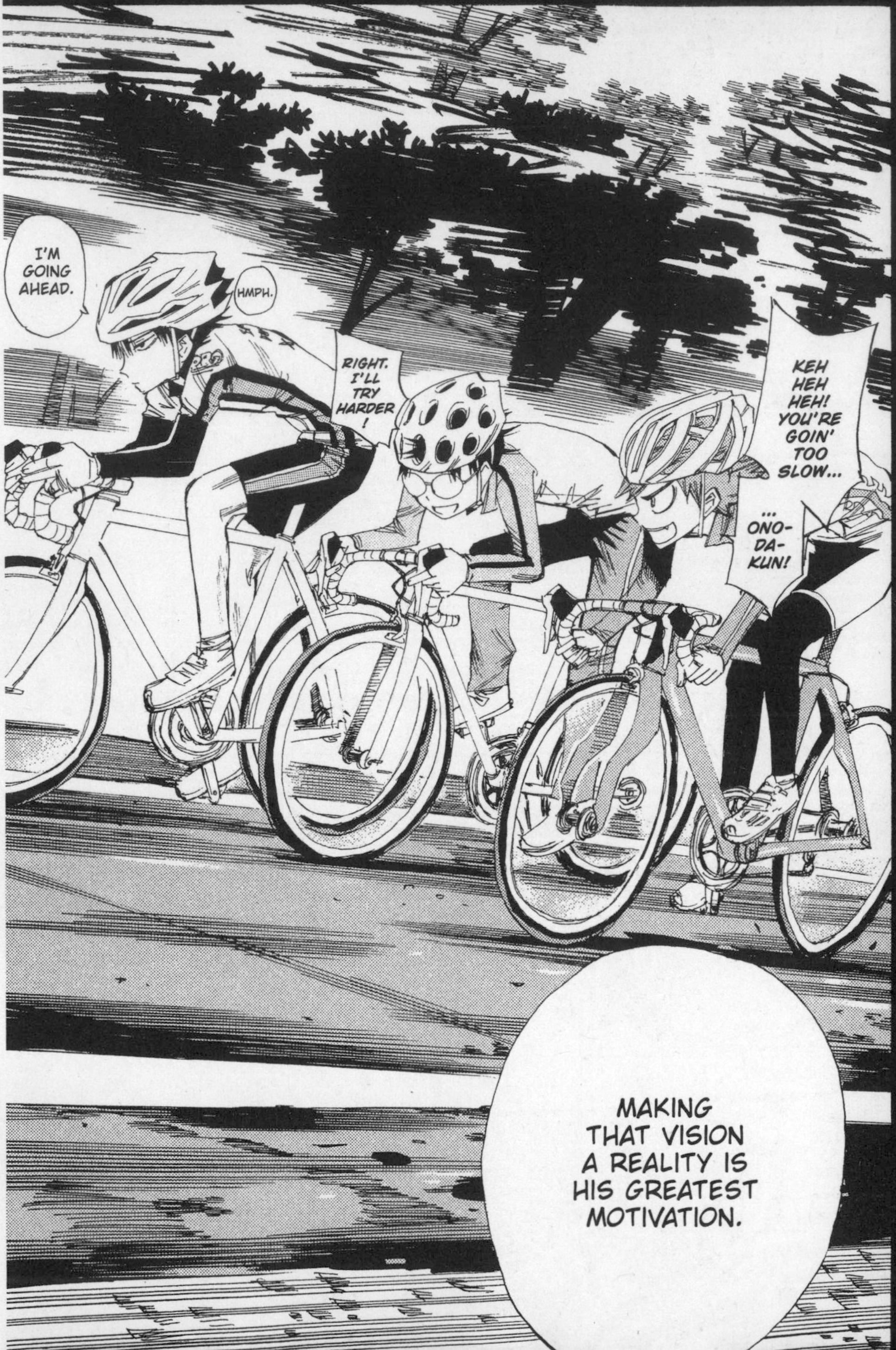
KEH HEH HEH! YOU'RE GOIN' TOO SLOW...
...ONO-DA-KUN!
RIGHT. I'LL TRY HARDER!
HMPH.
I'M GOING AHEAD.
MAKING THAT VISION A REALITY IS HIS GREATEST MOTIVATION.

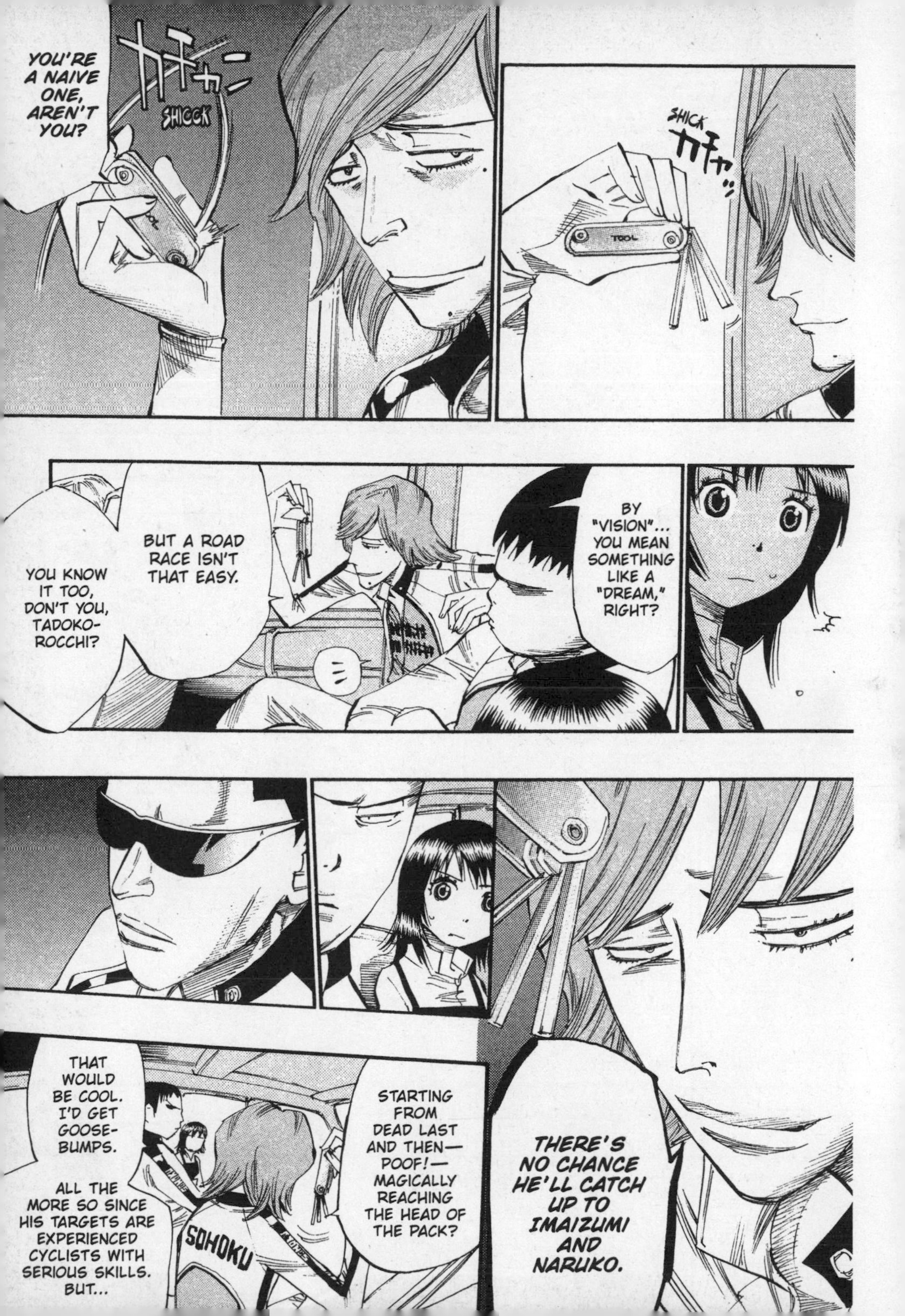
SHICK
YOU'RE A NAIVE ONE, AREN'T YOU?
SHICCK
BY "VISION"... YOU MEAN SOMETHING LIKE A "DREAM," RIGHT?
BUT A ROAD RACE ISN'T THAT EASY.
YOU KNOW IT TOO, DON'T YOU, TADOKOROCCHI?
STARTING FROM DEAD LAST AND THEN—POOF!—MAGICALLY REACHING THE HEAD OF THE PACK?
THAT WOULD BE COOL. I'D GET GOOSE-BUMPS.
ALL THE MORE SO SINCE HIS TARGETS ARE EXPERIENCED CYCLISTS WITH SERIOUS SKILLS. BUT...
THERE'S NO CHANCE HE'LL CATCH UP TO IMAIZUMI AND NARUKO.
SOHOKU

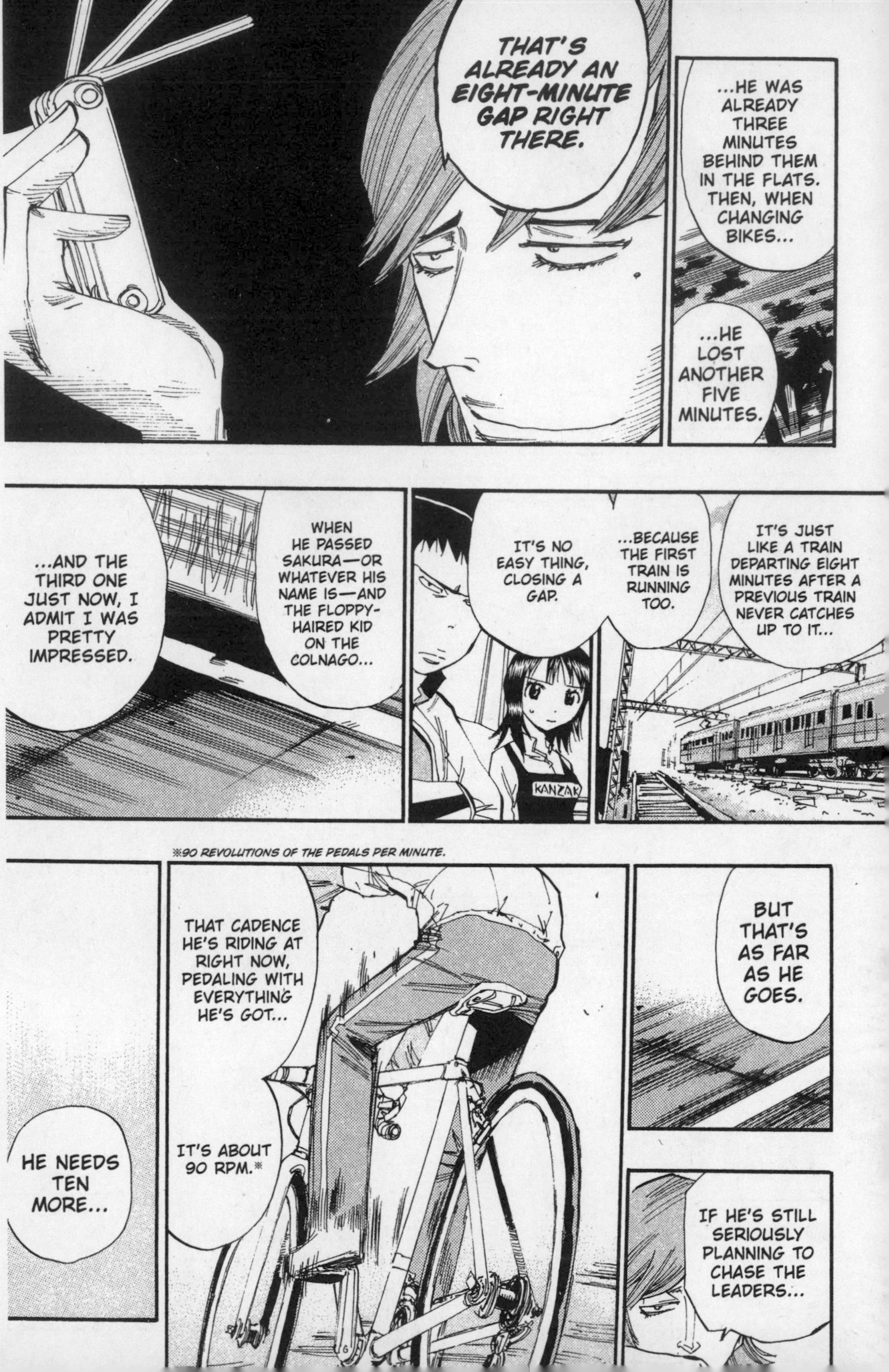
...HE WAS ALREADY THREE MINUTES BEHIND THEM IN THE FLATS. THEN, WHEN CHANGING BIKES...
...HE LOST ANOTHER FIVE MINUTES.
THAT'S ALREADY AN EIGHT-MINUTE GAP RIGHT THERE.
IT'S JUST LIKE A TRAIN DEPARTING EIGHT MINUTES AFTER A PREVIOUS TRAIN NEVER CATCHES UP TO IT...
...BECAUSE THE FIRST TRAIN IS RUNNING TOO.
IT'S NO EASY THING, CLOSING A GAP.
KANZAK
WHEN HE PASSED SAKURA—OR WHATEVER HIS NAME IS—AND THE FLOPPY-HAIRED KID ON THE COLNAGO...
...AND THE THIRD ONE JUST NOW, I ADMIT I WAS PRETTY IMPRESSED.
BUT THAT'S AS FAR AS HE GOES.
IF HE'S STILL SERIOUSLY PLANNING TO CHASE THE LEADERS...
THAT CADENCE HE'S RIDING AT RIGHT NOW, PEDALING WITH EVERYTHING HE'S GOT...
IT'S ABOUT 90 RPM.※
HE NEEDS TEN MORE...

※90 REVOLUTIONS OF THE PEDALS PER MINUTE.

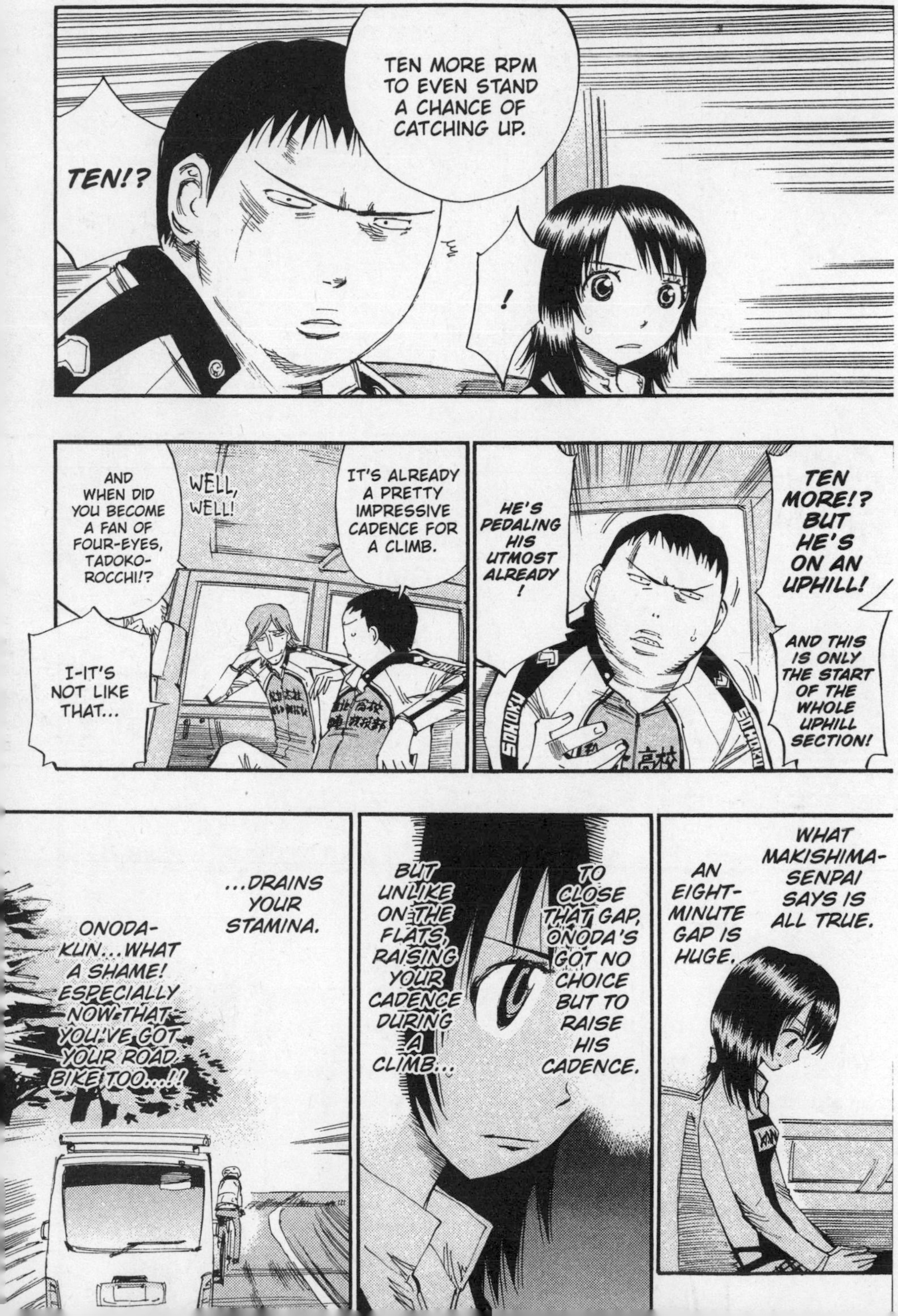
TEN MORE RPM TO EVEN STAND A CHANCE OF CATCHING UP.
!
TEN!?
TEN MORE!? BUT HE'S ON AN UPHILL!
HE'S PEDALING HIS UTMOST ALREADY!
AND THIS IS ONLY THE START OF THE WHOLE UPHILL SECTION!
IT'S ALREADY A PRETTY IMPRESSIVE CADENCE FOR A CLIMB.
WELL, WELL!
AND WHEN DID YOU BECOME A FAN OF FOUR-EYES, TADOKOROCCHI!?
I-IT'S NOT LIKE THAT...
WHAT MAKISHIMA-SENPAI SAYS IS ALL TRUE.
AN EIGHT-MINUTE GAP IS HUGE.
TO CLOSE THAT GAP, ONODA'S GOT NO CHOICE BUT TO RAISE HIS CADENCE.
BUT UNLIKE ON THE FLATS, RAISING YOUR CADENCE DURING A CLIMB...
...DRAINS YOUR STAMINA.
ONODA-KUN...WHAT A SHAME! ESPECIALLY NOW THAT YOU'VE GOT YOUR ROAD BIKE TOO...!!

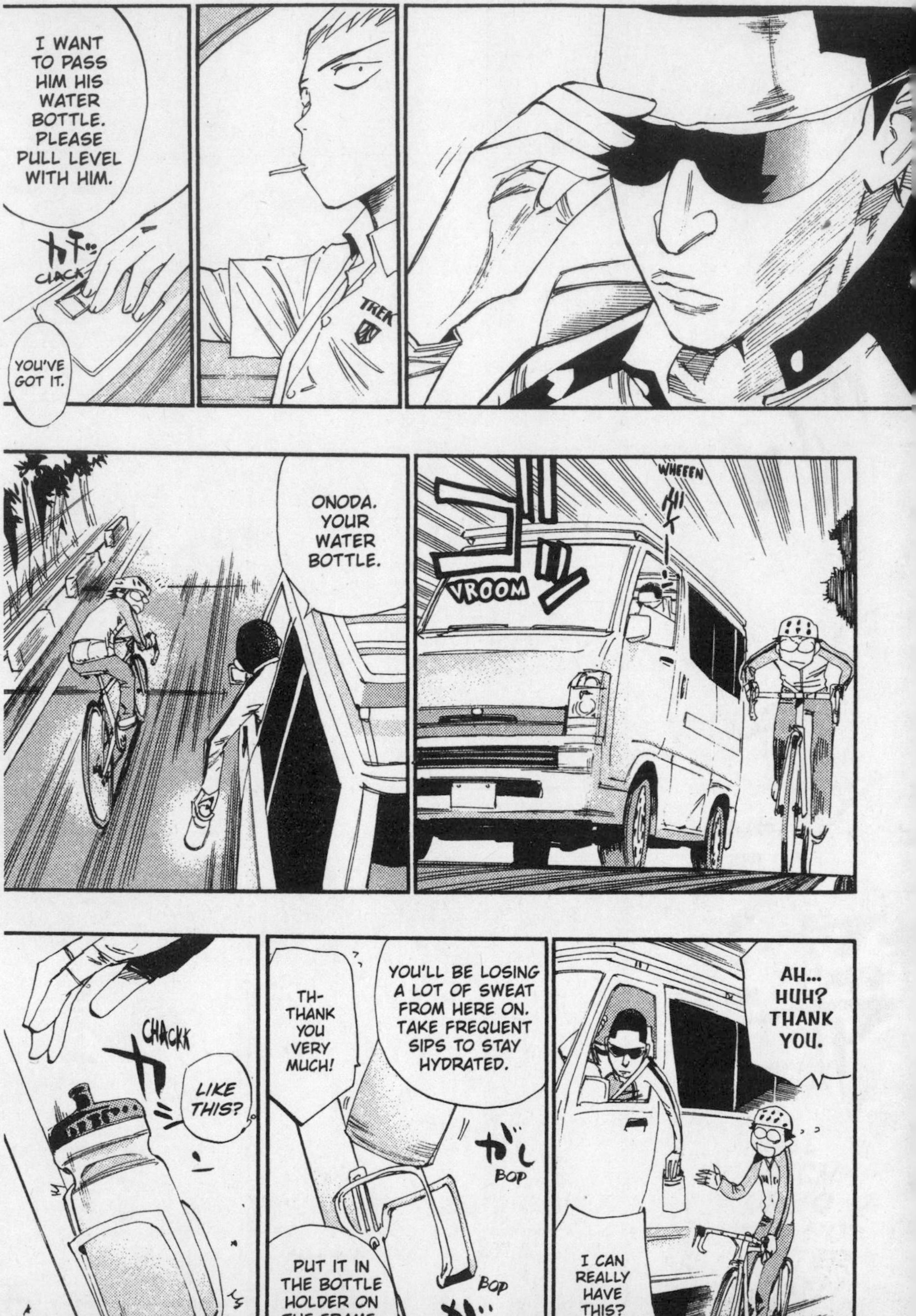
I WANT TO PASS HIM HIS WATER BOTTLE. PLEASE PULL LEVEL WITH HIM.
CLACK
YOU'VE GOT IT.
WHEEEN
VROOM
ONODA. YOUR WATER BOTTLE.
AH... HUH? THANK YOU.
I CAN REALLY HAVE THIS?
YOU'LL BE LOSING A LOT OF SWEAT FROM HERE ON. TAKE FREQUENT SIPS TO STAY HYDRATED.
TH-THANK YOU VERY MUCH!
BOP
PUT IT IN THE BOTTLE HOLDER ON THE FRAME.
BOP
CHACKK
LIKE THIS?

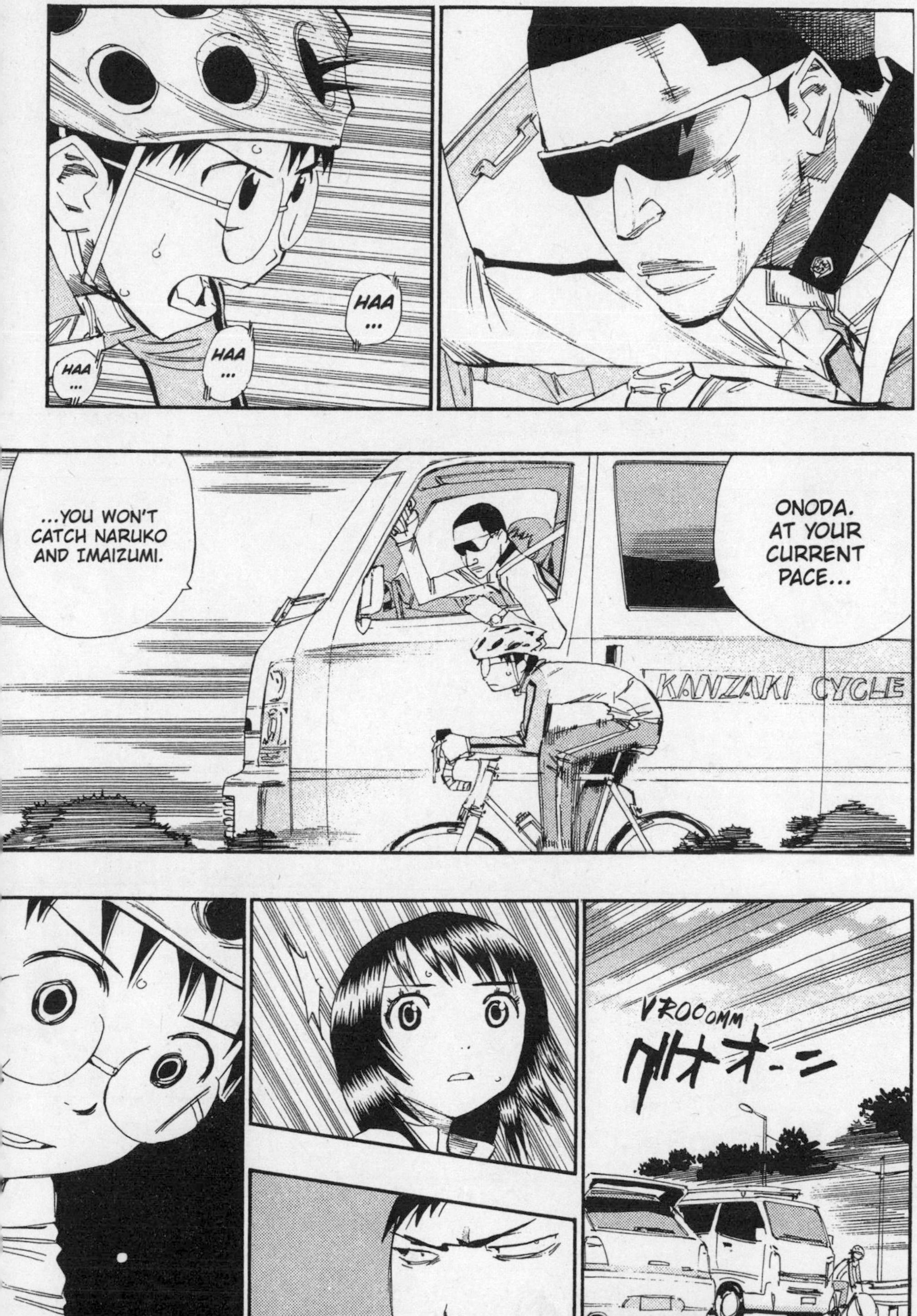
HAA ...
HAA ...
HAA ...
ONODA. AT YOUR CURRENT PACE...
...YOU WON'T CATCH NARUKO AND IMAIZUMI.
KANZAKI CYCLE
VROOOMM
グオオーン

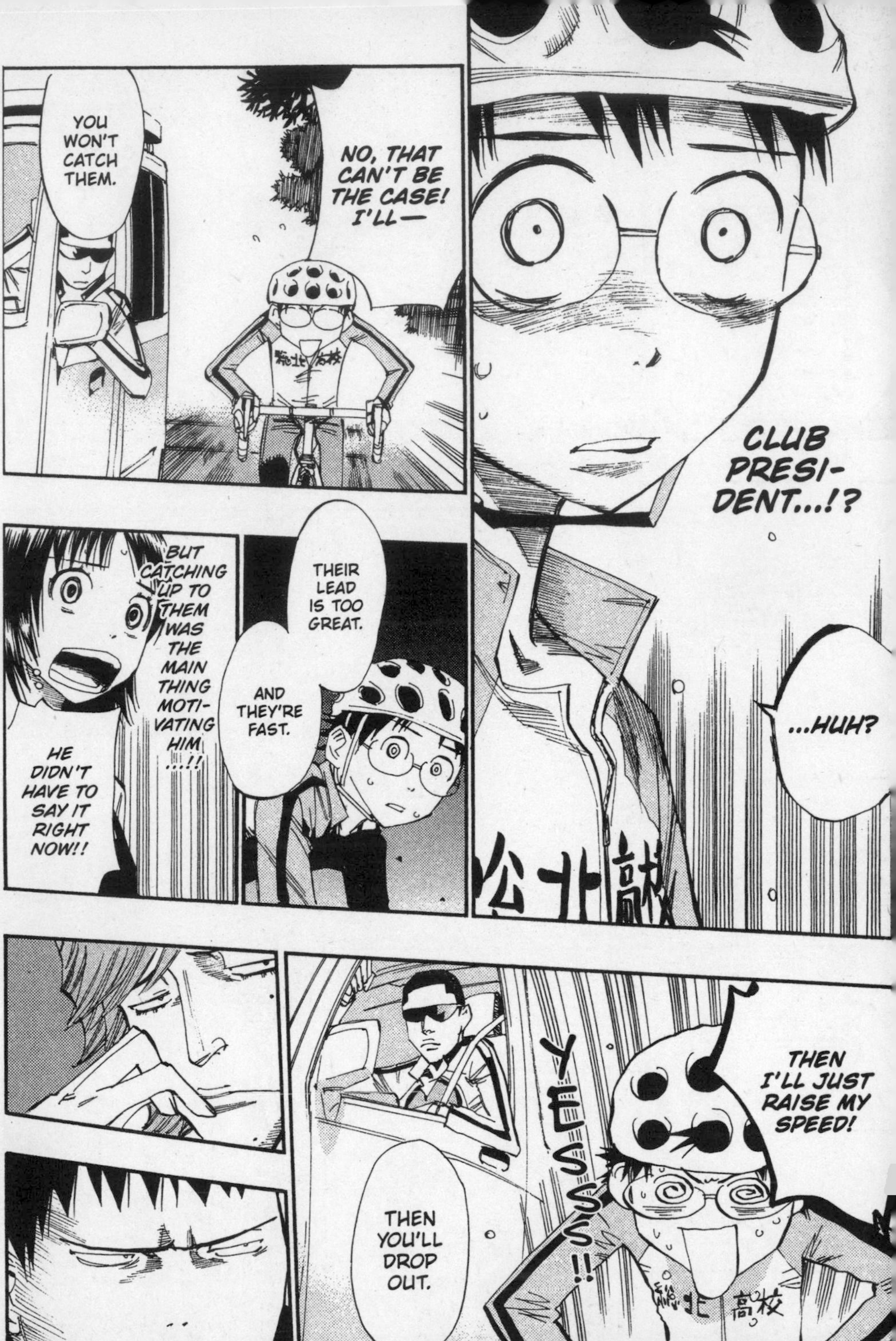
CLUB PRESI-DENT...!?
...HUH?
NO, THAT CAN'T BE THE CASE! I'LL—
YOU WON'T CATCH THEM.
THEIR LEAD IS TOO GREAT.
AND THEY'RE FAST.
BUT CATCHING UP TO THEM WAS THE MAIN THING MOTI-VATING HIM...!!
HE DIDN'T HAVE TO SAY IT RIGHT NOW!!
THEN I'LL JUST RAISE MY SPEED!
YESSS!!
THEN YOU'LL DROP OUT.

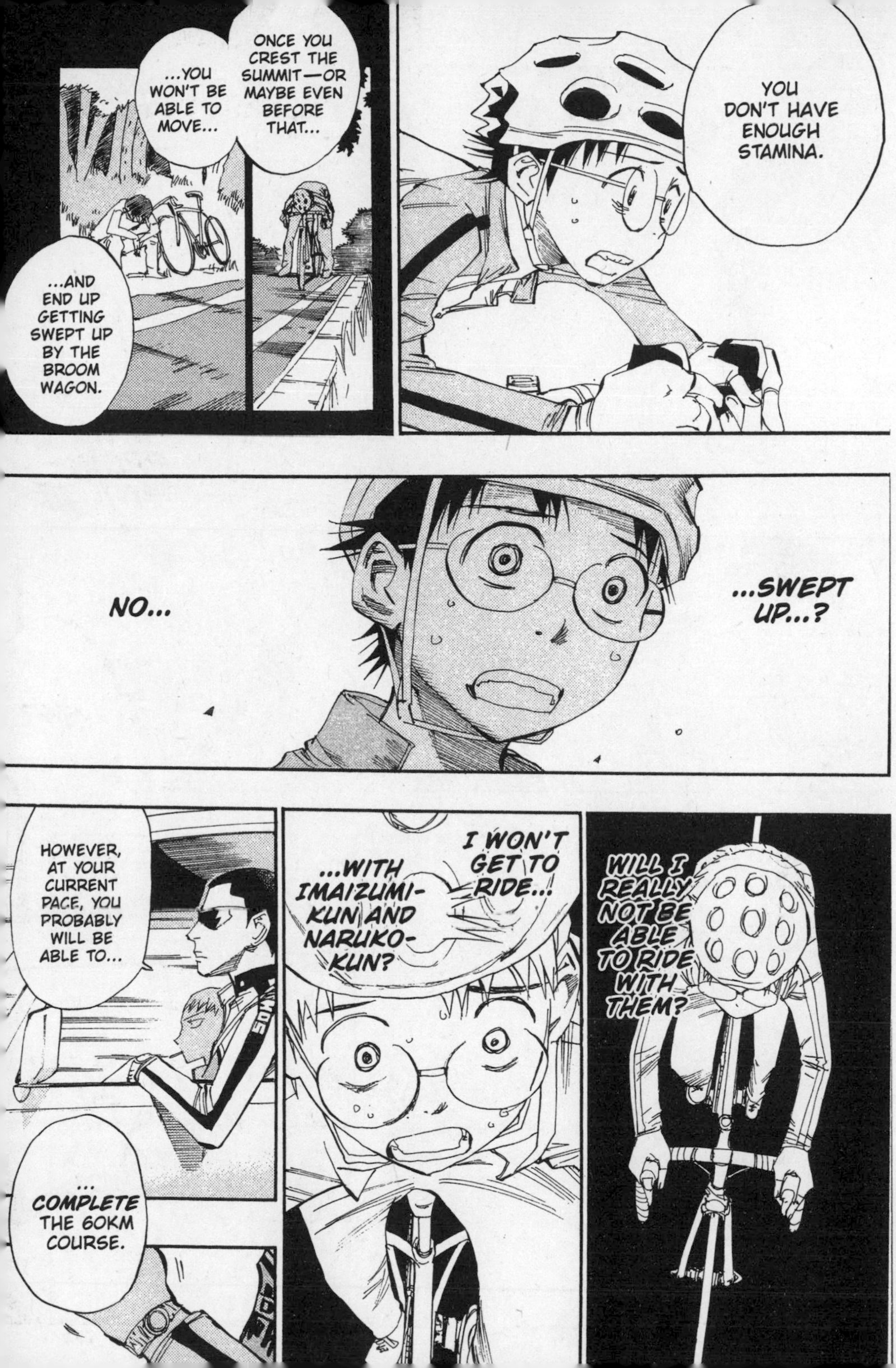
YOU DON'T HAVE ENOUGH STAMINA.
ONCE YOU CREST THE SUMMIT—OR MAYBE EVEN BEFORE THAT...
...YOU WON'T BE ABLE TO MOVE...
...AND END UP GETTING SWEPT UP BY THE BROOM WAGON.
...SWEPT UP...?
NO...
WILL I REALLY NOT BE ABLE TO RIDE WITH THEM?
I WON'T GET TO RIDE...
...WITH IMAIZUMI-KUN AND NARUKO-KUN?
HOWEVER, AT YOUR CURRENT PACE, YOU PROBABLY WILL BE ABLE TO...
...COMPLETE THE 60KM COURSE.

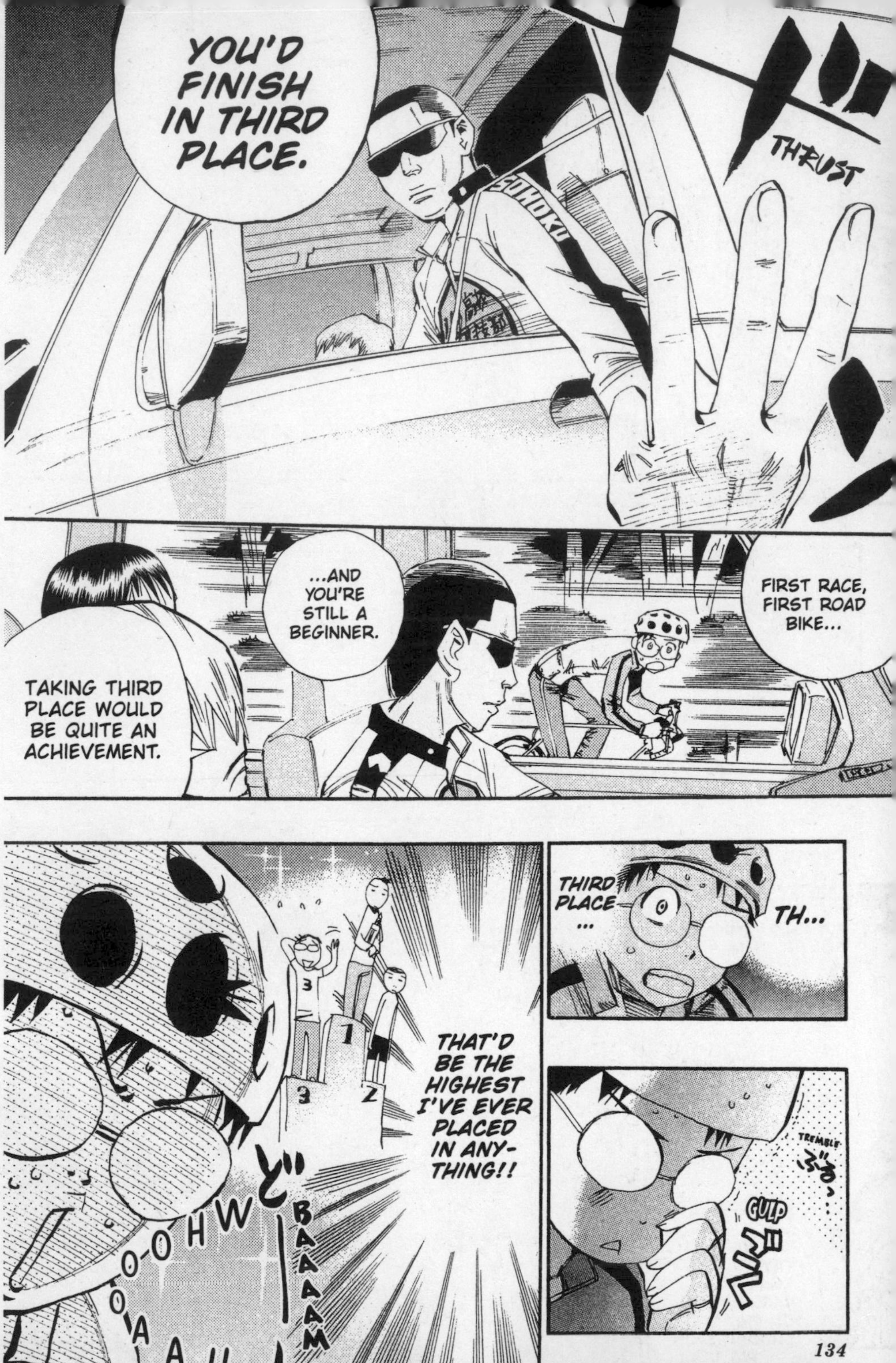
THRUST
YOU'D FINISH IN THIRD PLACE.
FIRST RACE, FIRST ROAD BIKE...
...AND YOU'RE STILL A BEGINNER.
TAKING THIRD PLACE WOULD BE QUITE AN ACHIEVEMENT.
TH...
THIRD PLACE...
TREMBLE
GULP
THAT'D BE THE HIGHEST I'VE EVER PLACED IN ANYTHING!!
BAAAAAAM
WHOO-OOAAA

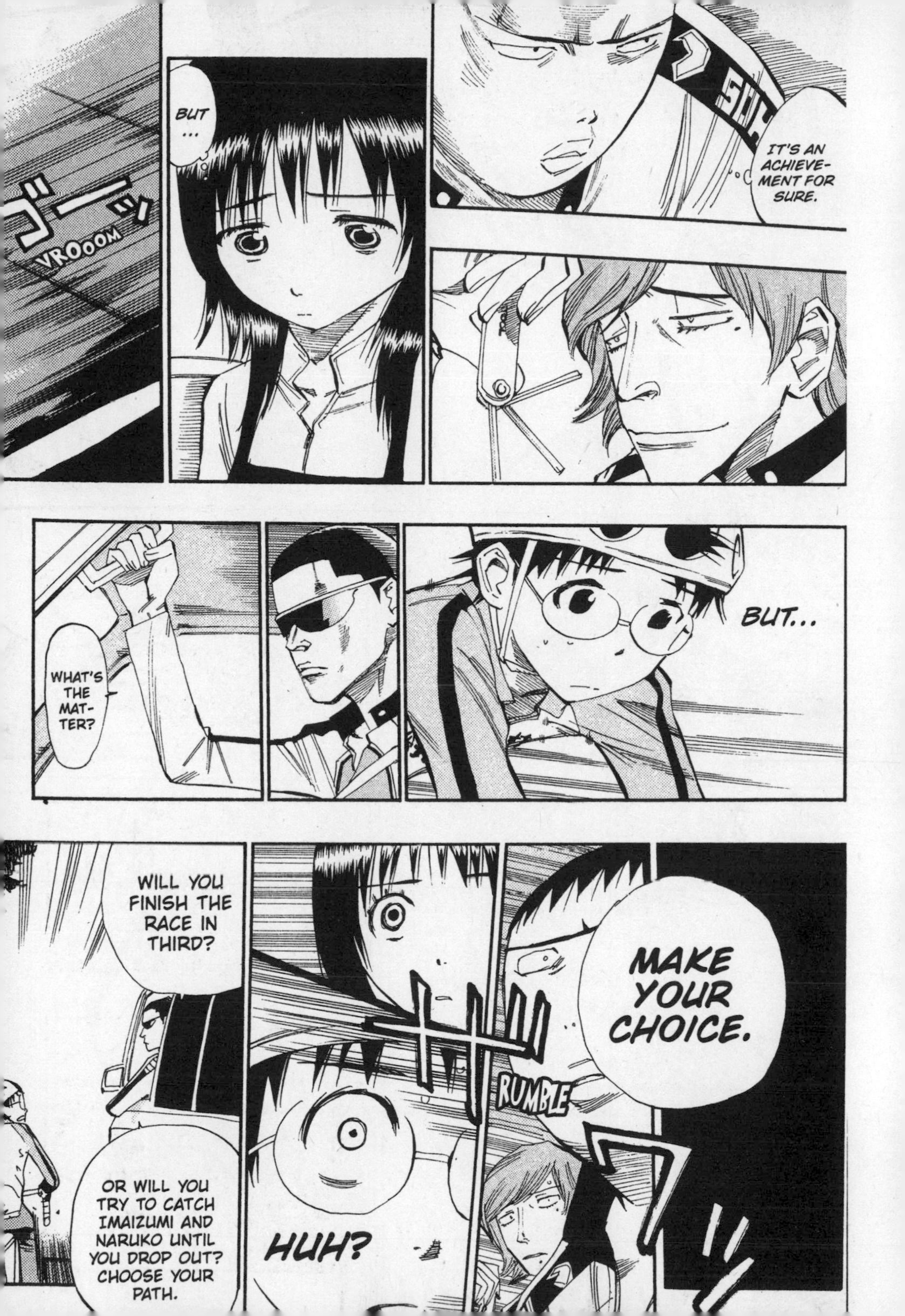
IT'S AN ACHIEVEMENT FOR SURE.
BUT ...
VROOOM
BUT...
WHAT'S THE MATTER?
MAKE YOUR CHOICE.
RUMBLE
HUH?
WILL YOU FINISH THE RACE IN THIRD?
OR WILL YOU TRY TO CATCH IMAIZUMI AND NARUKO UNTIL YOU DROP OUT? CHOOSE YOUR PATH.

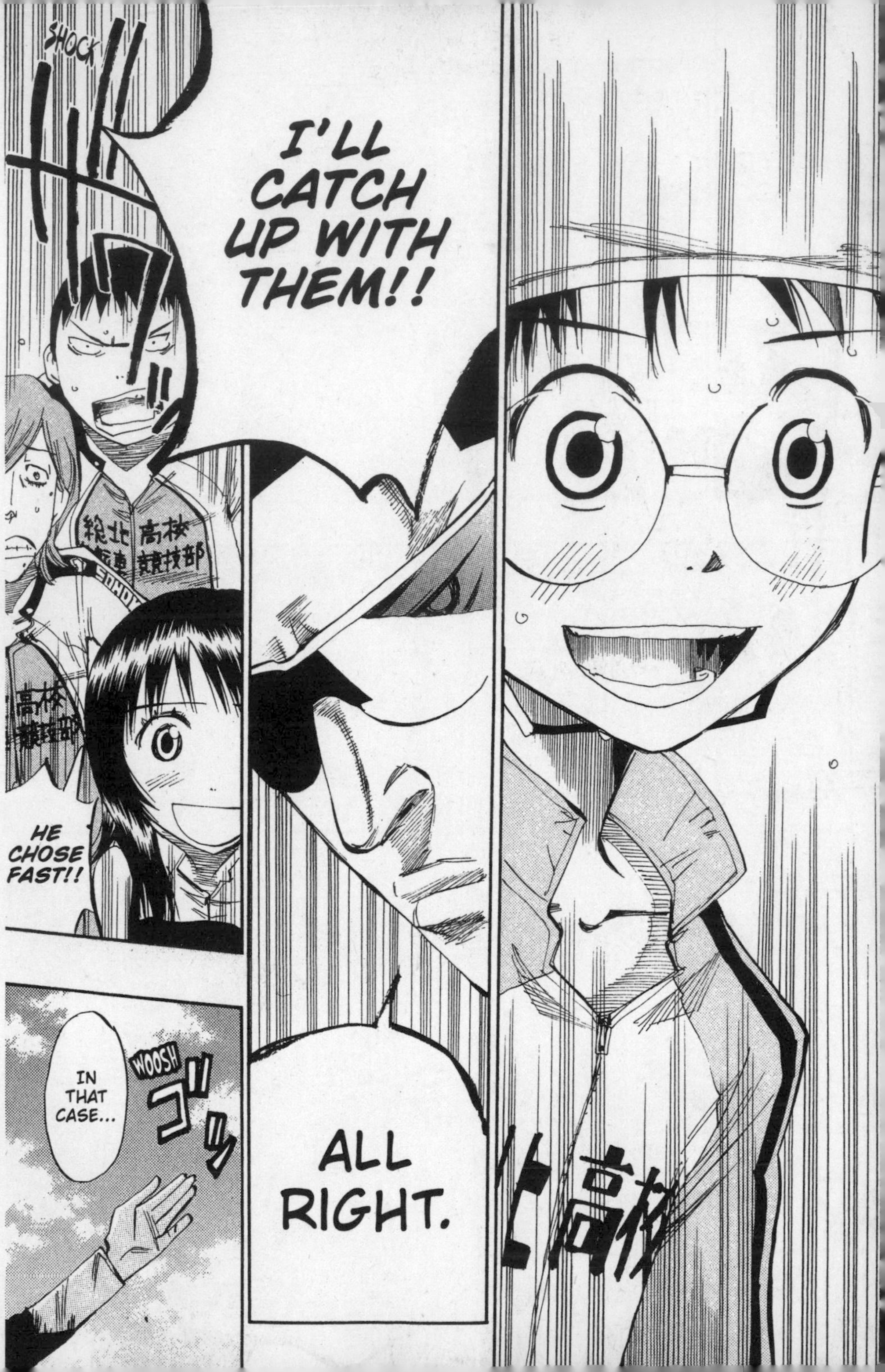
I'LL CATCH UP WITH THEM!!
ALL RIGHT.
SHOCK
HE CHOSE FAST!!
IN THAT CASE...
WOOSH

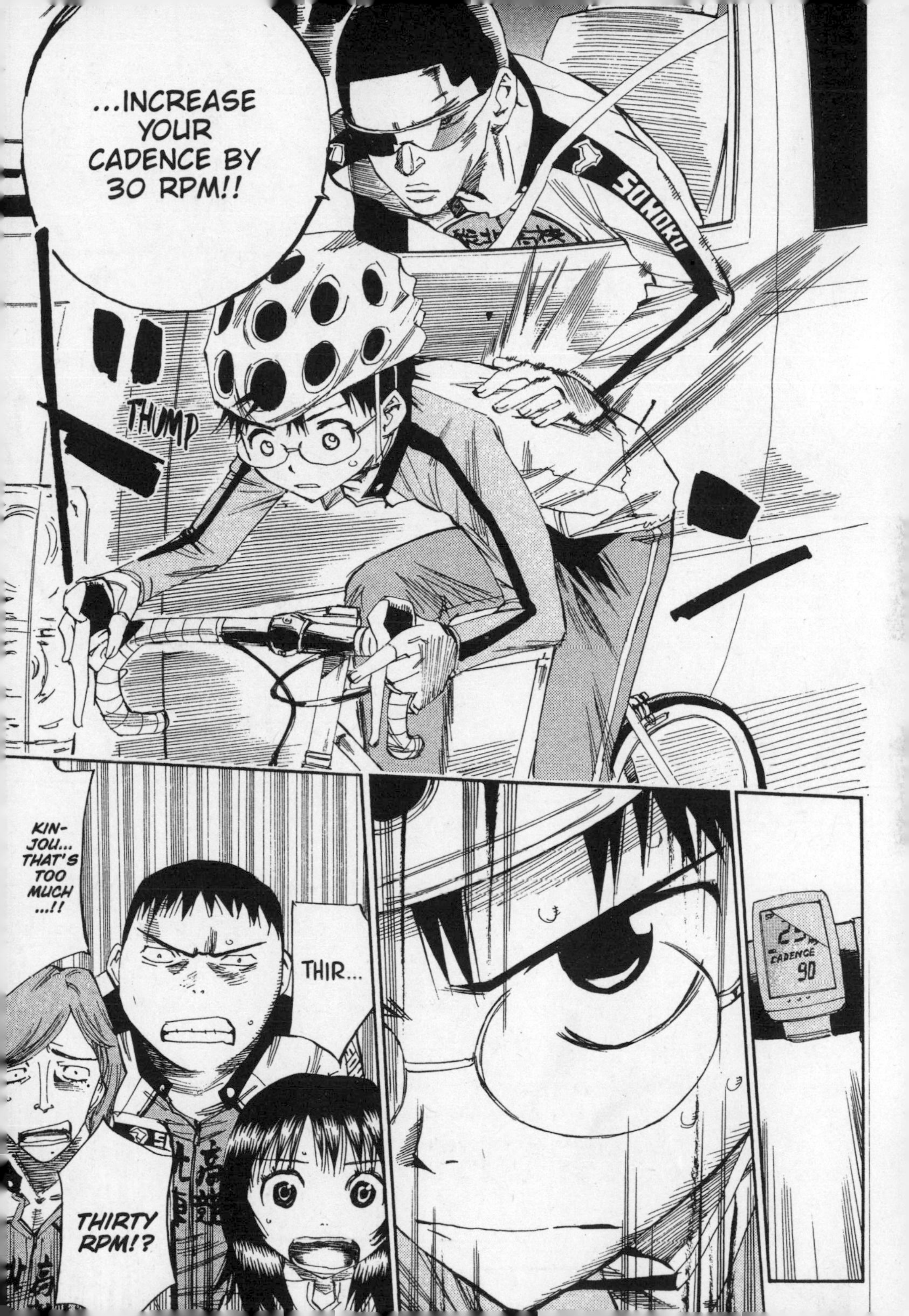
...INCREASE YOUR CADENCE BY 30 RPM!!
SOHOKU
THUMP
CADENCE
90
THIR...
KIN-JOU... THAT'S TOO MUCH...!!
THIRTY RPM!?

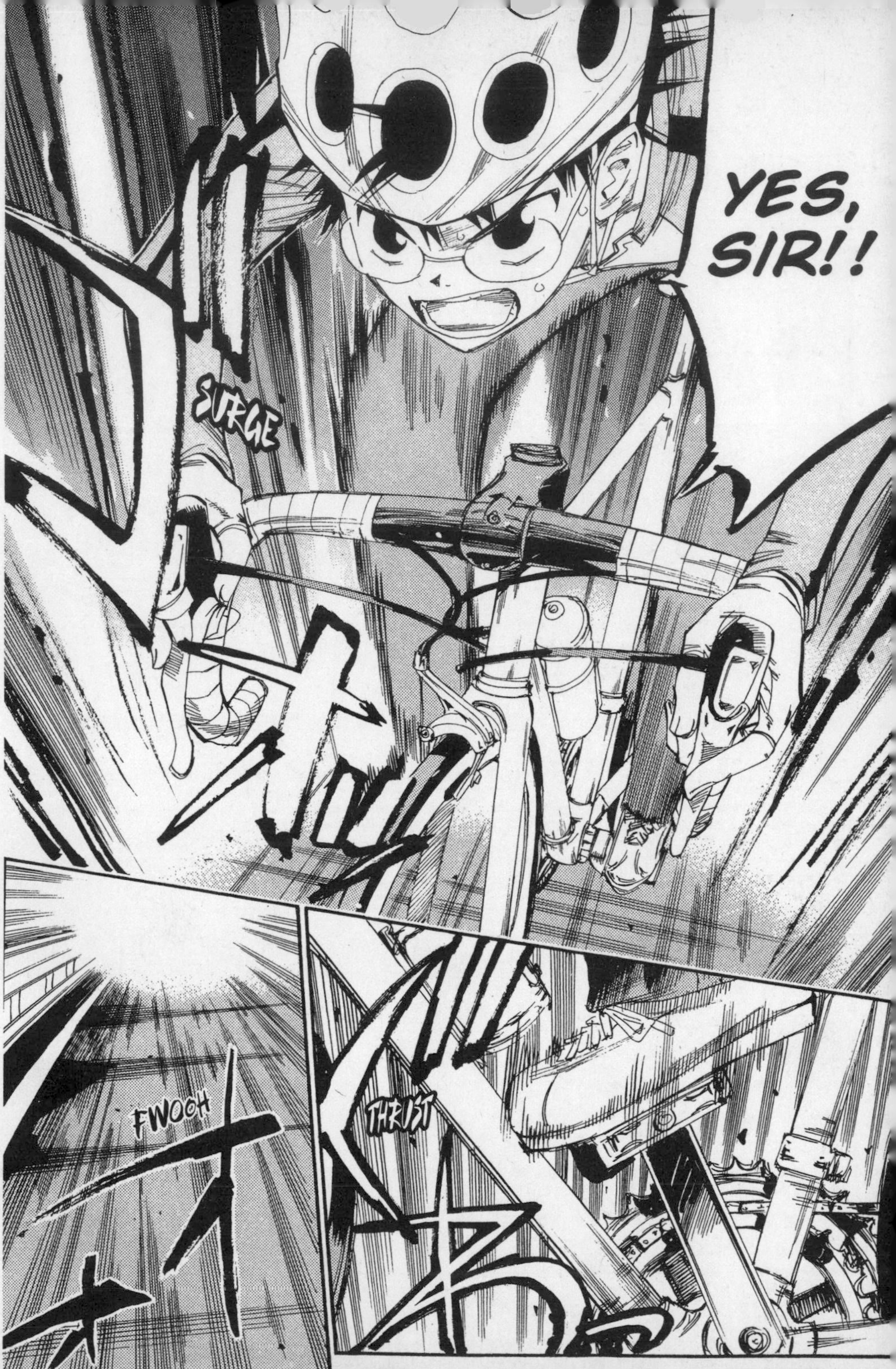
YES, SIR!!
SURGE
THRUST
FWOOH

RIDE.23 TESTING ONE ANOTHER

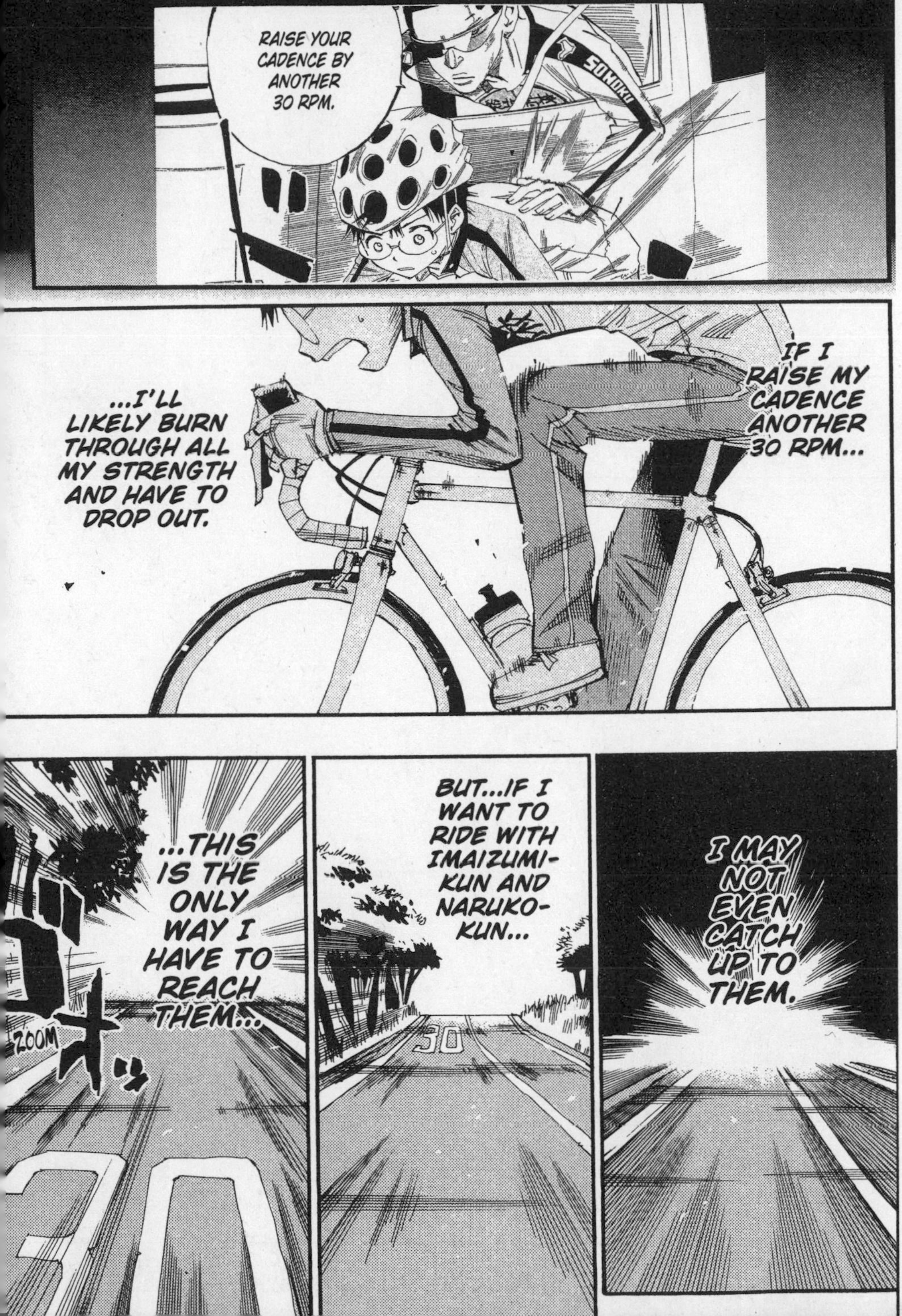
RAISE YOUR CADENCE BY ANOTHER 30 RPM.
IF I RAISE MY CADENCE ANOTHER 30 RPM...
...I'LL LIKELY BURN THROUGH ALL MY STRENGTH AND HAVE TO DROP OUT.
I MAY NOT EVEN CATCH UP TO THEM.
BUT...IF I WANT TO RIDE WITH IMAIZUMI-KUN AND NARUKO-KUN...
...THIS IS THE ONLY WAY I HAVE TO REACH THEM...
ZOOM

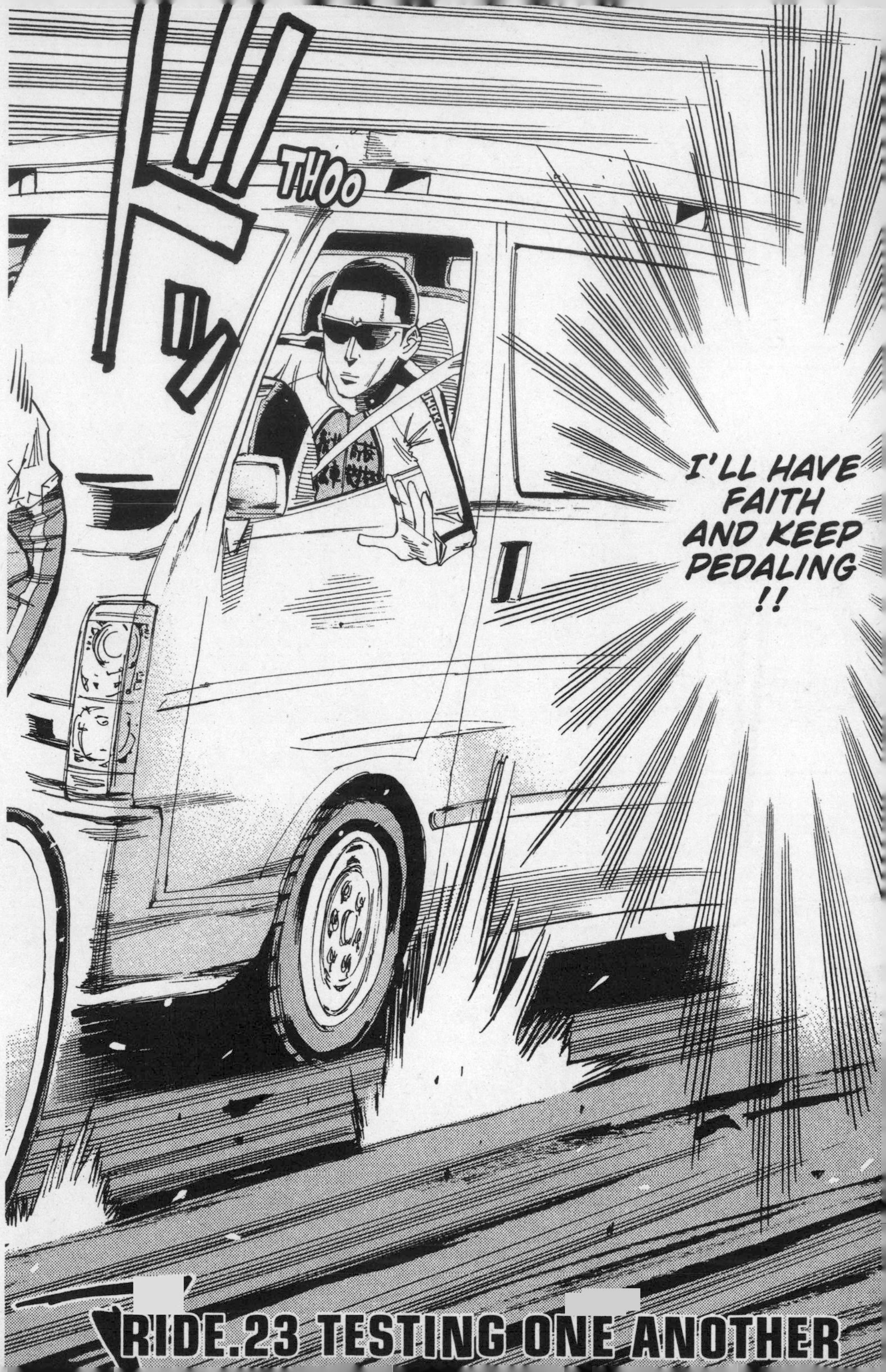
ドッ
THOO
I'LL HAVE FAITH AND KEEP PEDALING!!

RIDE.23 TESTING ONE ANOTHER

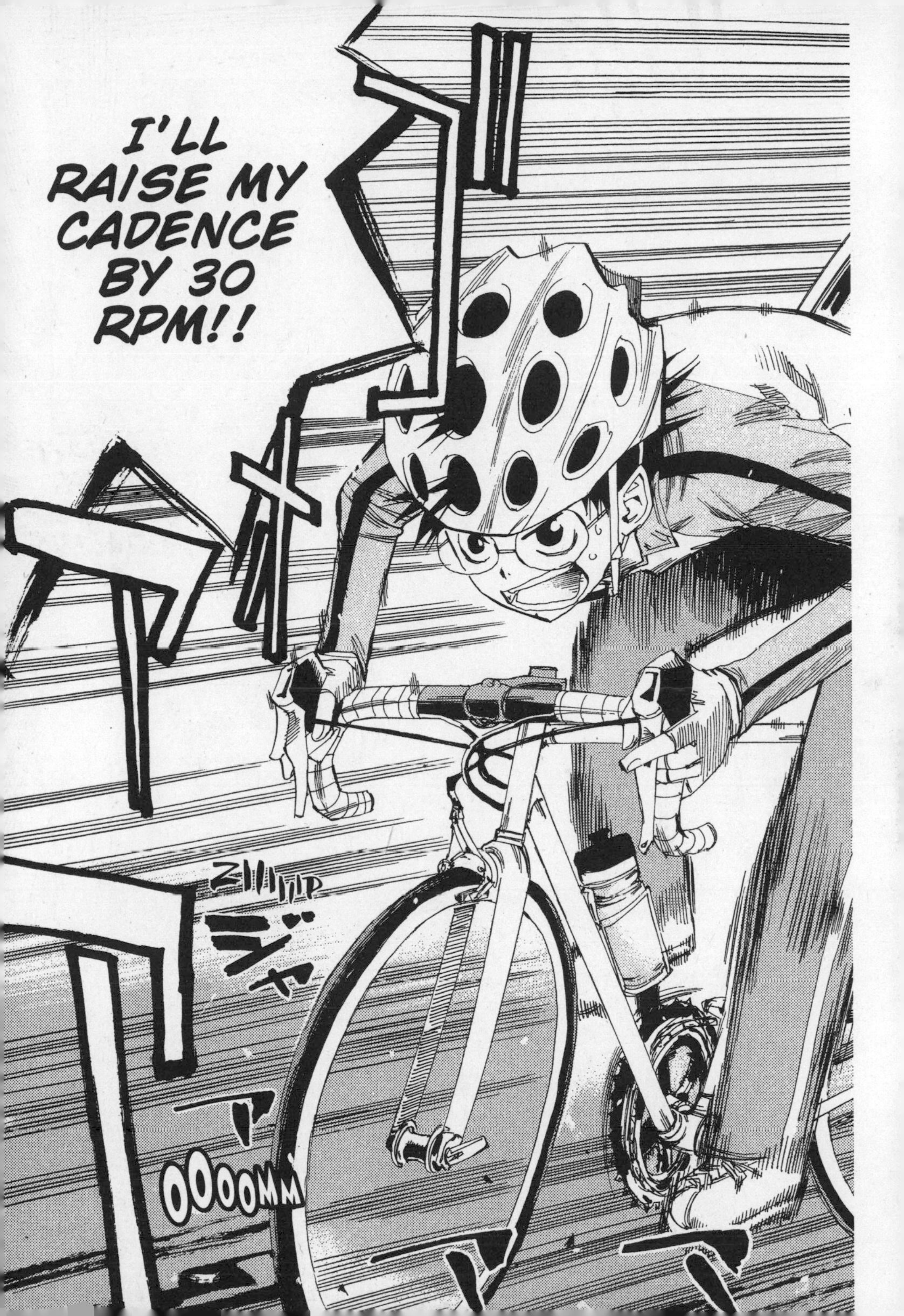
I'LL RAISE MY CADENCE BY 30 RPM!!
ZIIIIIP
ジャ
OOOOMM
ア

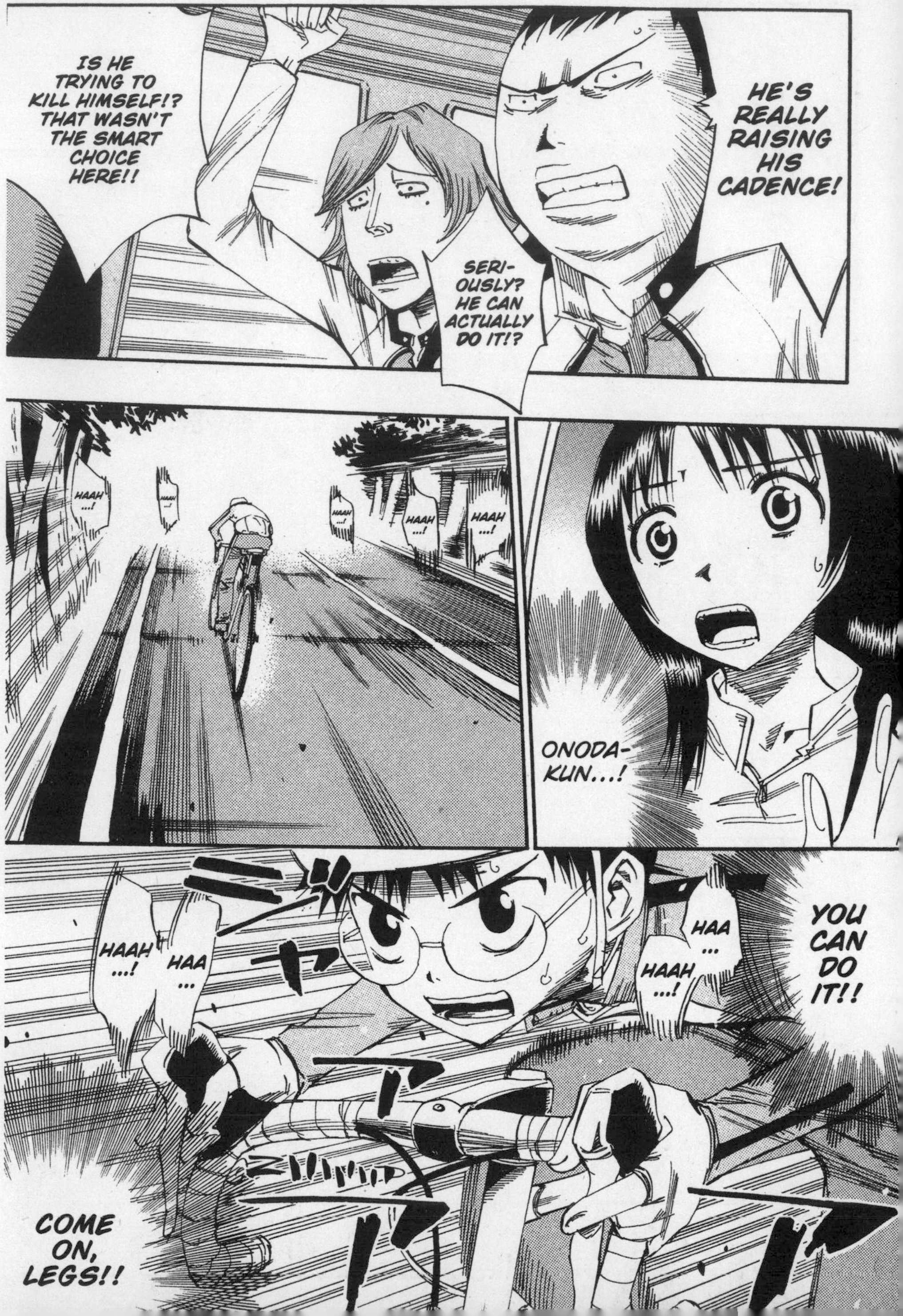
HE'S REALLY RAISING HIS CADENCE!
IS HE TRYING TO KILL HIMSELF!? THAT WASN'T THE SMART CHOICE HERE!!
SERI-OUSLY? HE CAN ACTUALLY DO IT!?
ONODA-KUN...!
HAAH ...!
HAAH ...!
HAAH ...!
HAAH ...!
HAAH ...!
YOU CAN DO IT!!
HAA ...
HAAH ...!
HAA ...
HAAH ...!
COME ON, LEGS!!

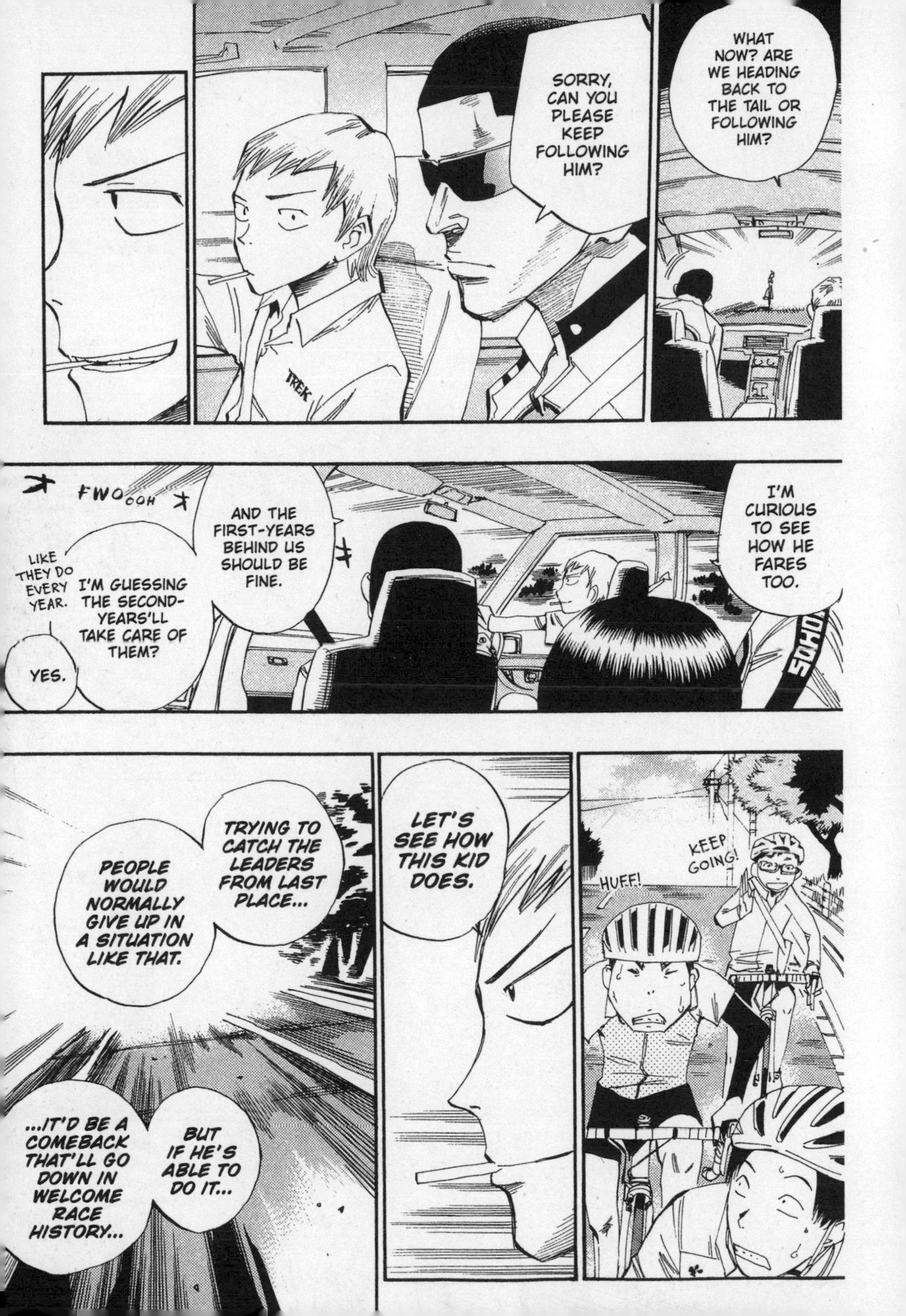
WHAT NOW? ARE WE HEADING BACK TO THE TAIL OR FOLLOWING HIM?
SORRY, CAN YOU PLEASE KEEP FOLLOWING HIM?
TREK
I'M CURIOUS TO SEE HOW HE FARES TOO.
AND THE FIRST-YEARS BEHIND US SHOULD BE FINE.
FWOOOH
I'M GUESSING THE SECOND-YEARS'LL TAKE CARE OF THEM?
LIKE THEY DO EVERY YEAR.
YES.
KEEP GOING!
HUFF!
LET'S SEE HOW THIS KID DOES.
TRYING TO CATCH THE LEADERS FROM LAST PLACE...
PEOPLE WOULD NORMALLY GIVE UP IN A SITUATION LIKE THAT.
BUT IF HE'S ABLE TO DO IT...
...IT'D BE A COMEBACK THAT'LL GO DOWN IN WELCOME RACE HISTORY...

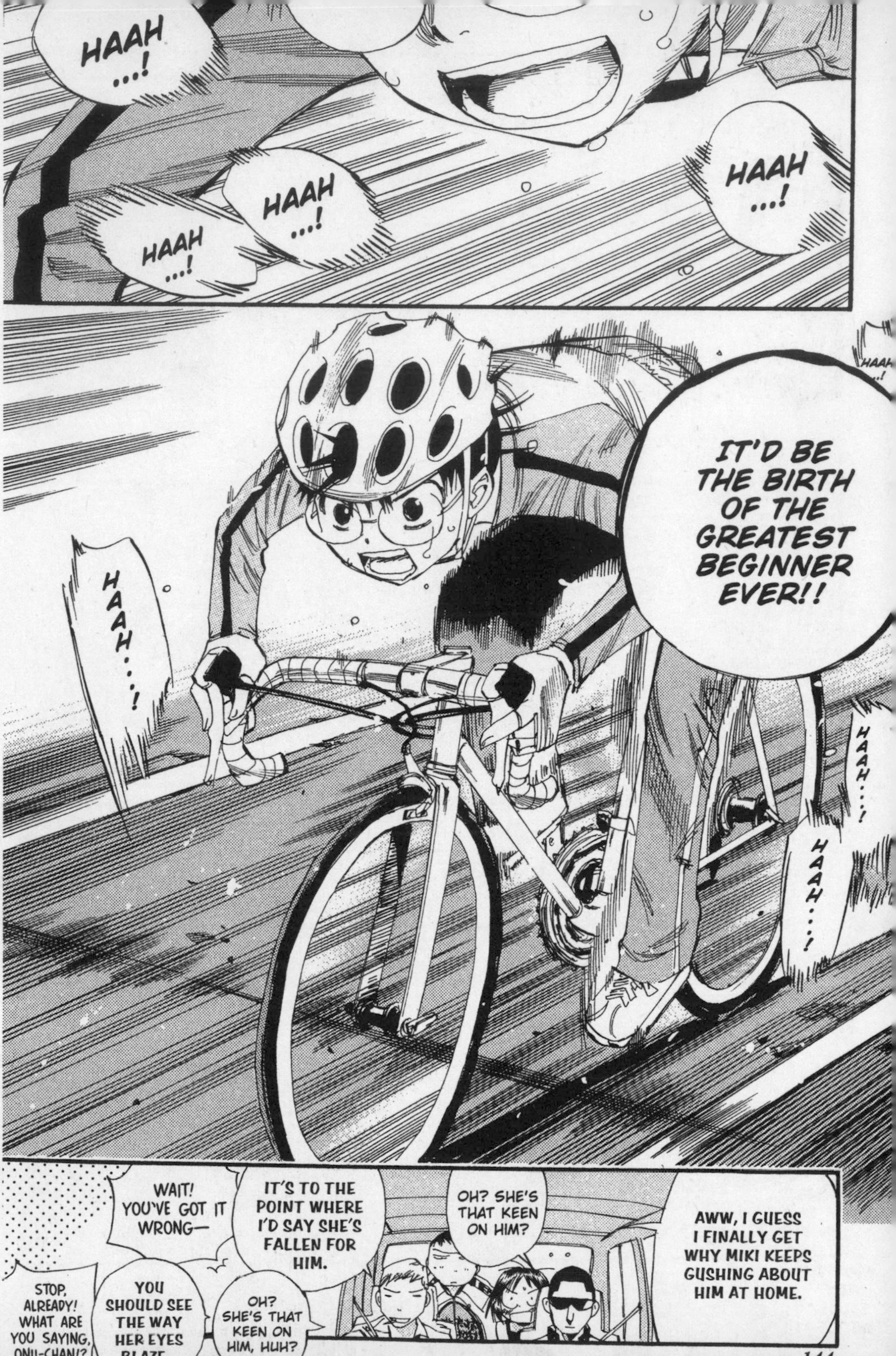
HAAH ...!
HAAH ...!
HAAH ...!
HAAH ...!
HAAH ...!
IT'D BE THE BIRTH OF THE GREATEST BEGINNER EVER!!
HAAH...!
HAAH...!
HAAH...!
AWW, I GUESS I FINALLY GET WHY MIKI KEEPS GUSHING ABOUT HIM AT HOME.
OH? SHE'S THAT KEEN ON HIM?
IT'S TO THE POINT WHERE I'D SAY SHE'S FALLEN FOR HIM.
WAIT! YOU'VE GOT IT WRONG—
OH? SHE'S THAT KEEN ON HIM, HUH?
YOU SHOULD SEE THE WAY HER EYES BLAZE...
STOP, ALREADY! WHAT ARE YOU SAYING, ONII-CHAN!?

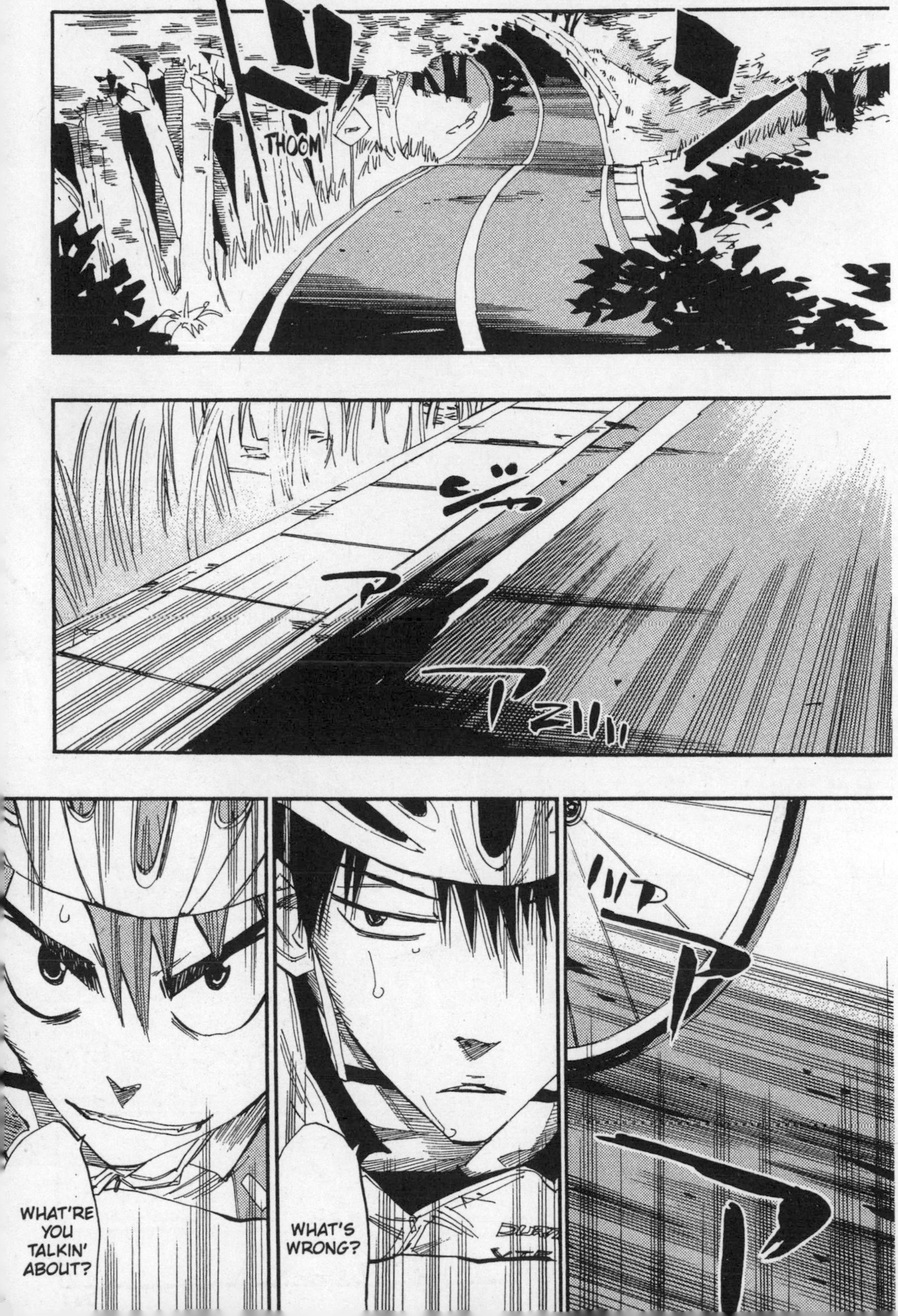
THOOM
WHAT'S WRONG?
WHAT'RE YOU TALKIN' ABOUT?

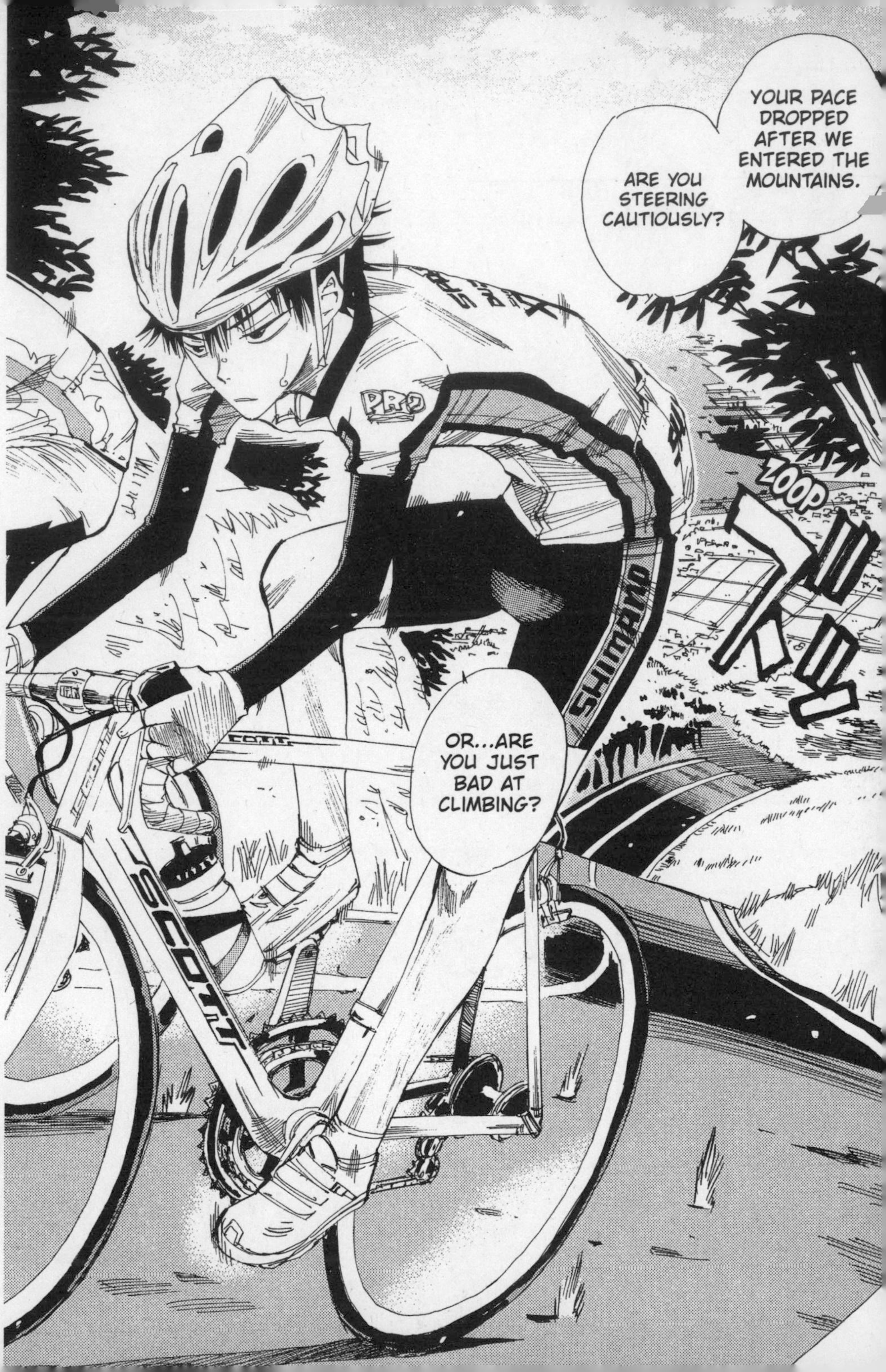
YOUR PACE DROPPED AFTER WE ENTERED THE MOUNTAINS.
ARE YOU STEERING CAUTIOUSLY?
ZOOP
OR...ARE YOU JUST BAD AT CLIMBING?

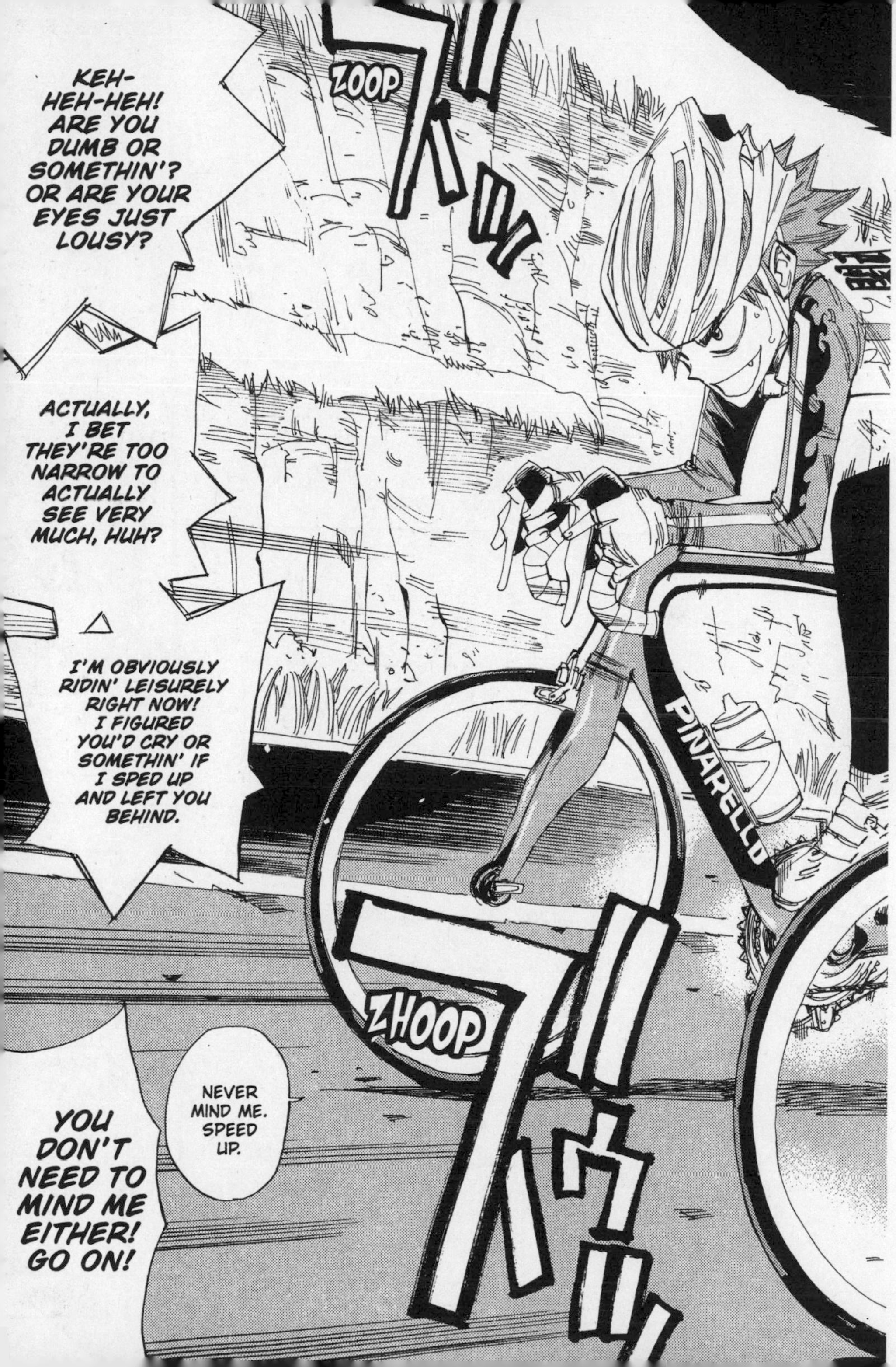
ZOOP
KEH-HEH-HEH! ARE YOU DUMB OR SOMETHIN'? OR ARE YOUR EYES JUST LOUSY?
ACTUALLY, I BET THEY'RE TOO NARROW TO ACTUALLY SEE VERY MUCH, HUH?
I'M OBVIOUSLY RIDIN' LEISURELY RIGHT NOW! I FIGURED YOU'D CRY OR SOMETHIN' IF I SPED UP AND LEFT YOU BEHIND.
PINARELLO
ZHOOP
NEVER MIND ME. SPEED UP.
YOU DON'T NEED TO MIND ME EITHER! GO ON!

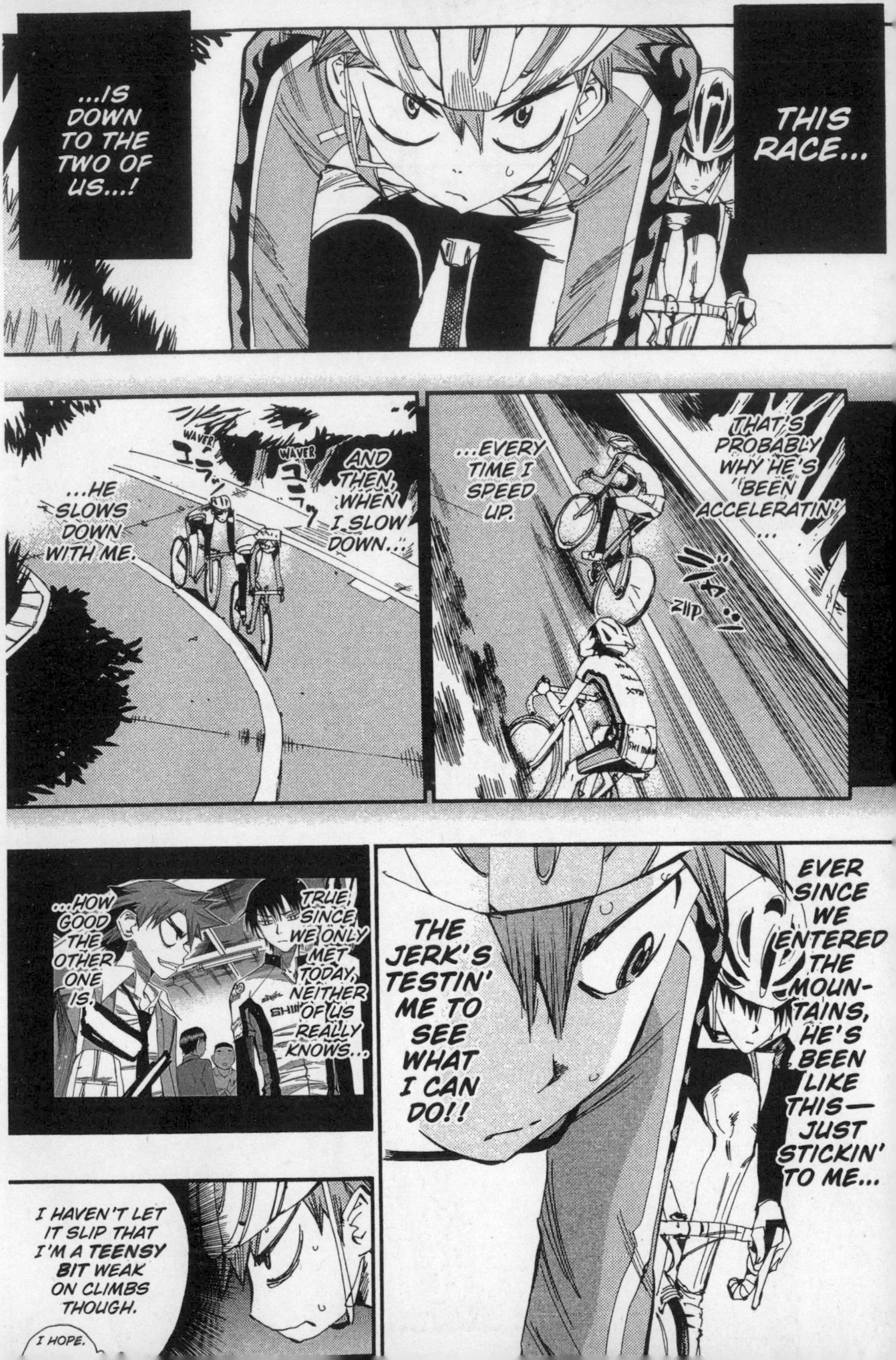
THIS RACE...
...IS DOWN TO THE TWO OF US...!
THAT'S PROBABLY WHY HE'S BEEN ACCELERATIN'...
...EVERY TIME I SPEED UP.
ZIIP
AND THEN, WHEN I SLOW DOWN...
...HE SLOWS DOWN WITH ME.
WAVER
WAVER
EVER SINCE WE ENTERED THE MOUN-TAINS, HE'S BEEN LIKE THIS— JUST STICKIN' TO ME...
THE JERK'S TESTIN' ME TO SEE WHAT I CAN DO!!
TRUE, SINCE WE ONLY MET TODAY, NEITHER OF US REALLY KNOWS...
...HOW GOOD THE OTHER ONE IS.
I HAVEN'T LET IT SLIP THAT I'M A TEENSY BIT WEAK ON CLIMBS THOUGH.
I HOPE.

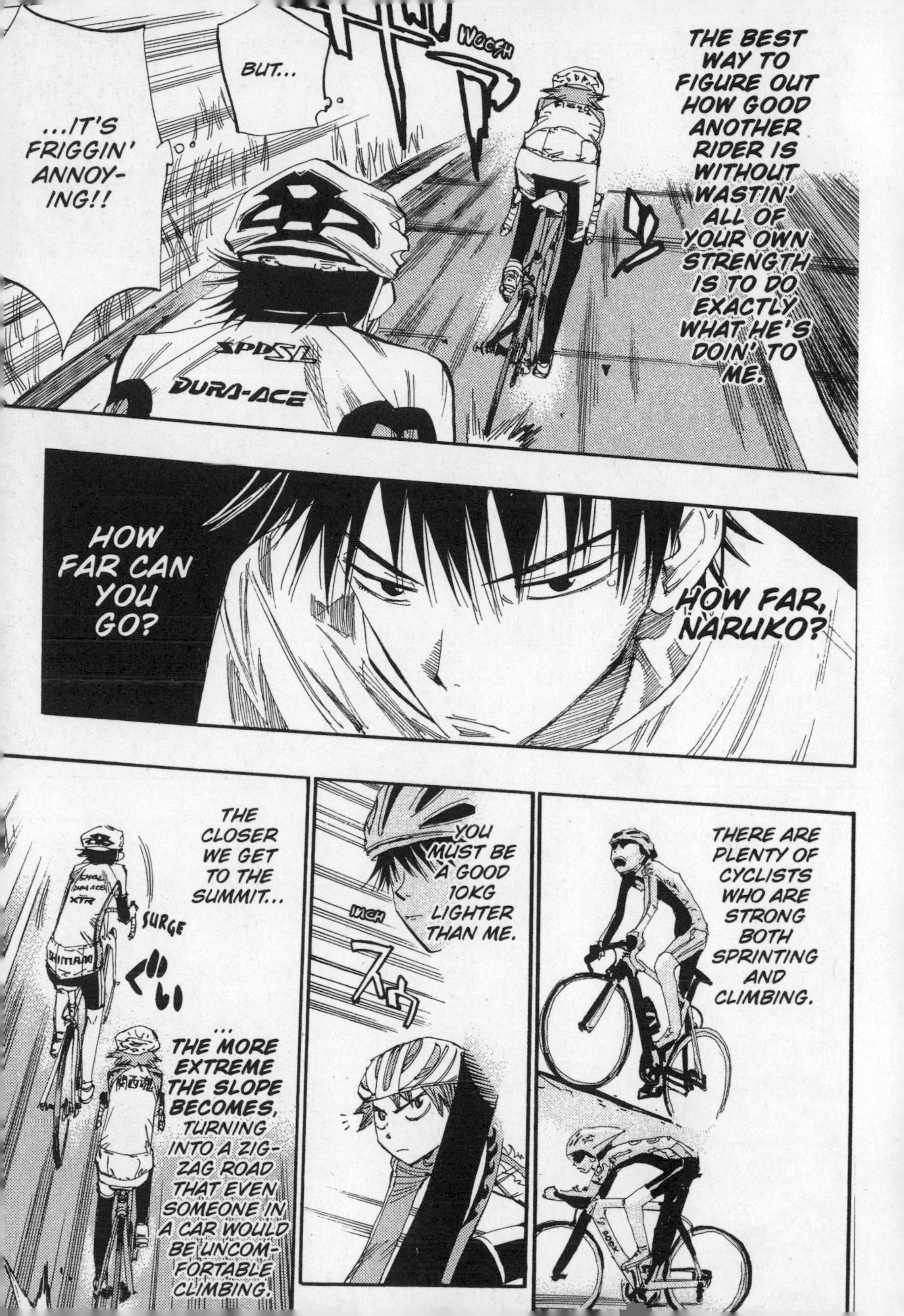
THE BEST WAY TO FIGURE OUT HOW GOOD ANOTHER RIDER IS WITHOUT WASTIN' ALL OF YOUR OWN STRENGTH IS TO DO EXACTLY WHAT HE'S DOIN' TO ME.
WOOSH
BUT...
...IT'S FRIGGIN' ANNOY-ING!!
SPDSL
DURA-ACE
HOW FAR, NARUKO?
HOW FAR CAN YOU GO?
THERE ARE PLENTY OF CYCLISTS WHO ARE STRONG BOTH SPRINTING AND CLIMBING.
YOU MUST BE A GOOD 10KG LIGHTER THAN ME.
INCH
THE CLOSER WE GET TO THE SUMMIT...
SURGE
...THE MORE EXTREME THE SLOPE BECOMES, TURNING INTO A ZIG-ZAG ROAD THAT EVEN SOMEONE IN A CAR WOULD BE UNCOM-FORTABLE CLIMBING.

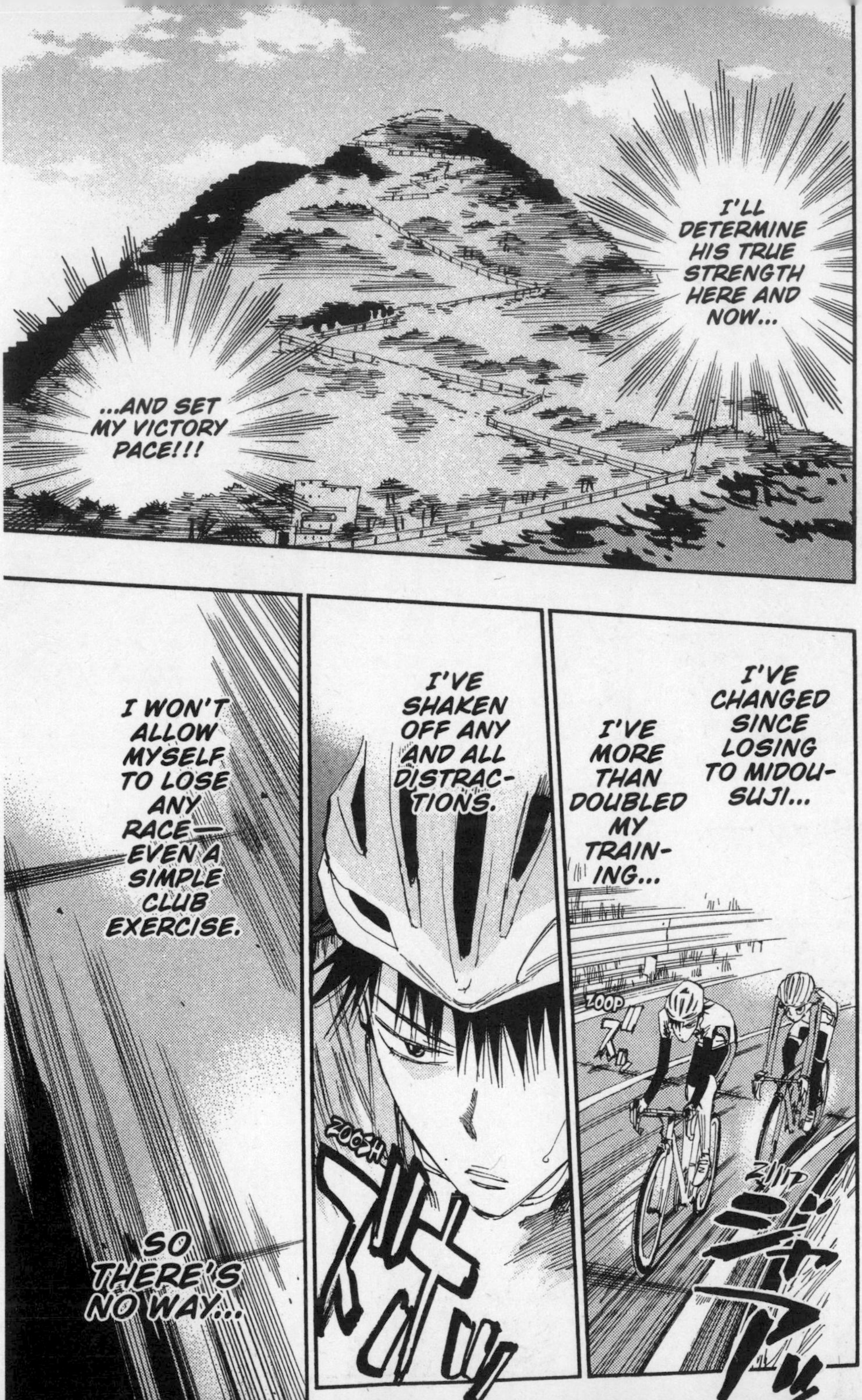

I'LL DETERMINE HIS TRUE STRENGTH HERE AND NOW...
...AND SET MY VICTORY PACE!!!
I'VE CHANGED SINCE LOSING TO MIDOU-SUJI...
I'VE MORE THAN DOUBLED MY TRAIN-ING...
ZOOP
ZIIIP
I'VE SHAKEN OFF ANY AND ALL DISTRAC-TIONS.
ZOOSH
I WON'T ALLOW MYSELF TO LOSE ANY RACE—EVEN A SIMPLE CLUB EXERCISE.
SO THERE'S NO WAY...

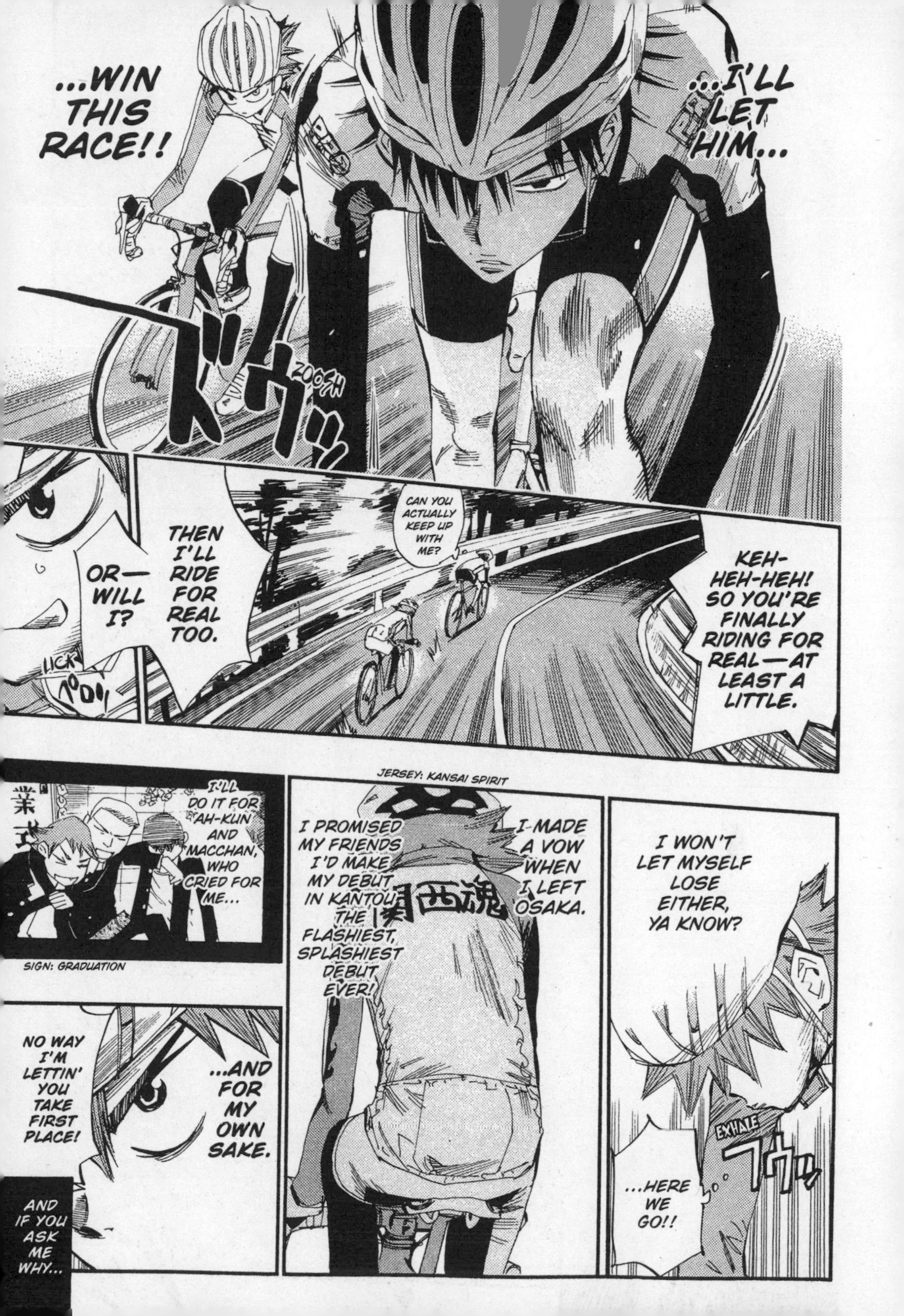
...I'LL LET HIM...
...WIN THIS RACE!!
ZOOSH
KEH-HEH-HEH! SO YOU'RE FINALLY RIDING FOR REAL—AT LEAST A LITTLE.
CAN YOU ACTUALLY KEEP UP WITH ME?
THEN I'LL RIDE FOR REAL TOO.
OR— WILL I?
LICK
I WON'T LET MYSELF LOSE EITHER, YA KNOW?
EXHALE
...HERE WE GO!!
JERSEY: KANSAI SPIRIT
I MADE A VOW WHEN I LEFT OSAKA.
I PROMISED MY FRIENDS I'D MAKE MY DEBUT IN KANTOU THE FLASHIEST, SPLASHIEST DEBUT EVER!
I'LL DO IT FOR AH-KUN AND MACCHAN, WHO CRIED FOR ME...
SIGN: GRADUATION
...AND FOR MY OWN SAKE.
NO WAY I'M LETTIN' YOU TAKE FIRST PLACE!
AND IF YOU ASK ME WHY...

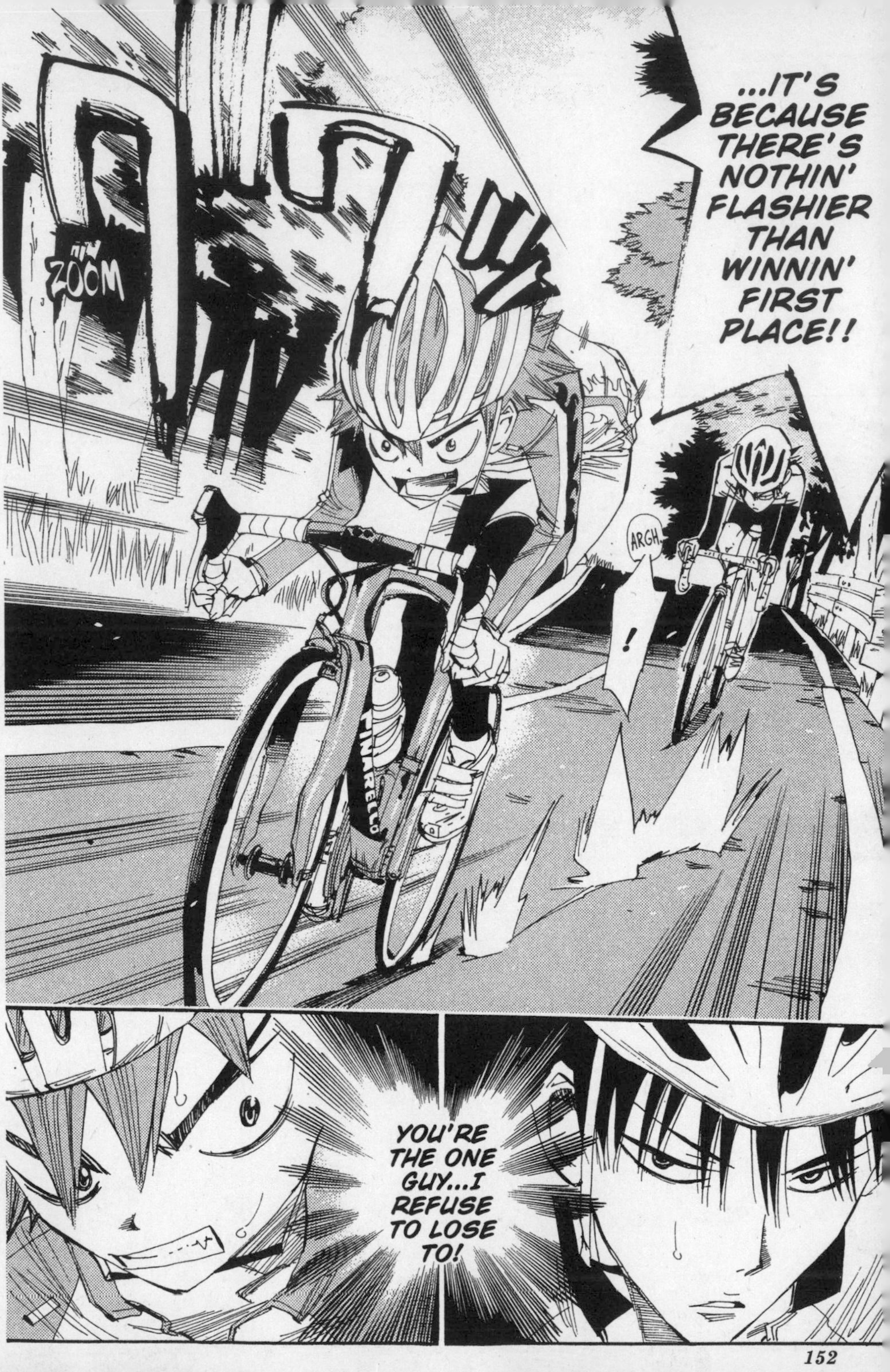
...IT'S BECAUSE THERE'S NOTHIN' FLASHIER THAN WINNIN' FIRST PLACE!!
ZOOM
ARGH.
!
YOU'RE THE ONE GUY...I REFUSE TO LOSE TO!

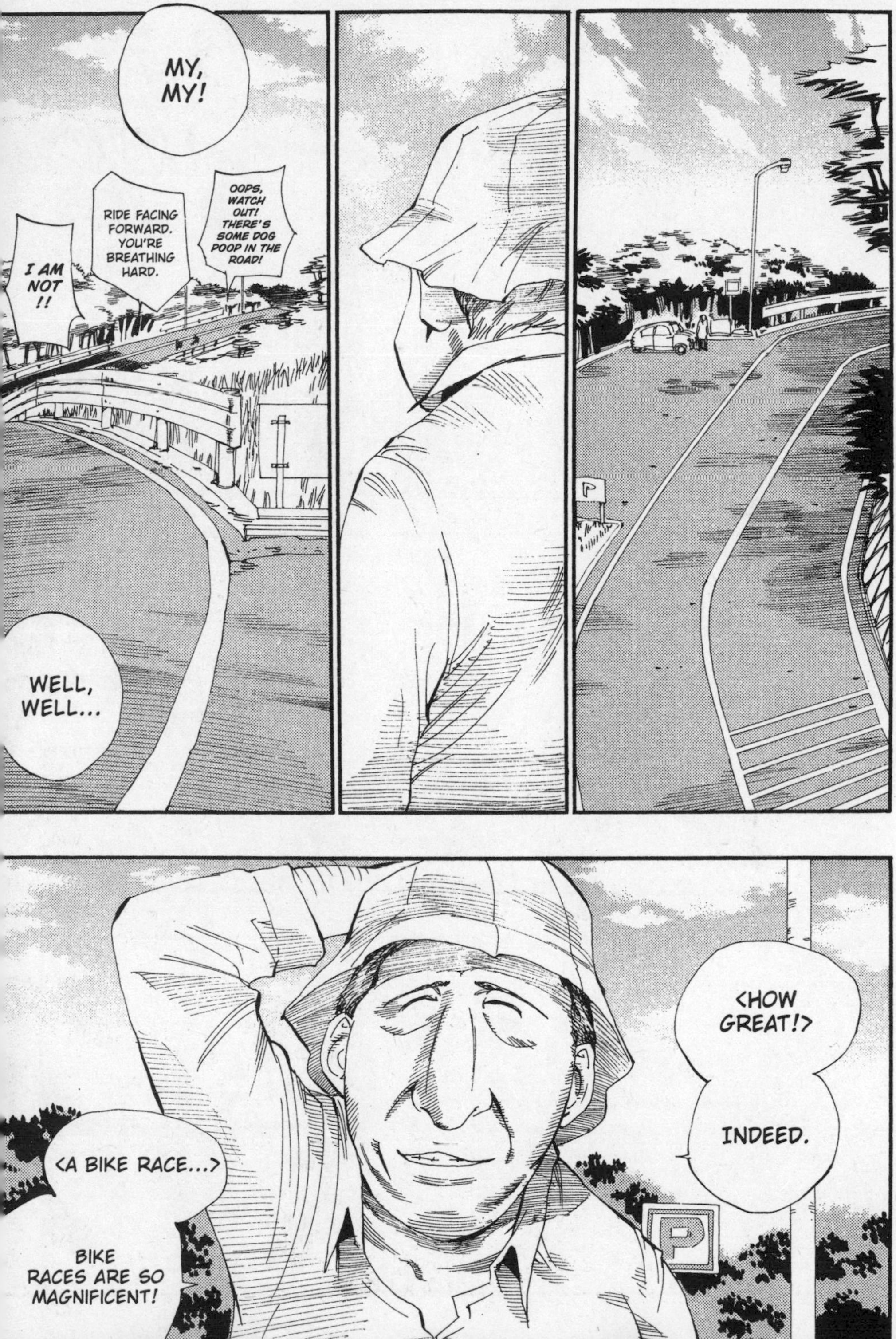
MY, MY!
OOPS, WATCH OUT! THERE'S SOME DOG POOP IN THE ROAD!
RIDE FACING FORWARD. YOU'RE BREATHING HARD.
I AM NOT !!
WELL, WELL...
<HOW GREAT!>
INDEED.
<A BIKE RACE...>
BIKE RACES ARE SO MAGNIFICENT!

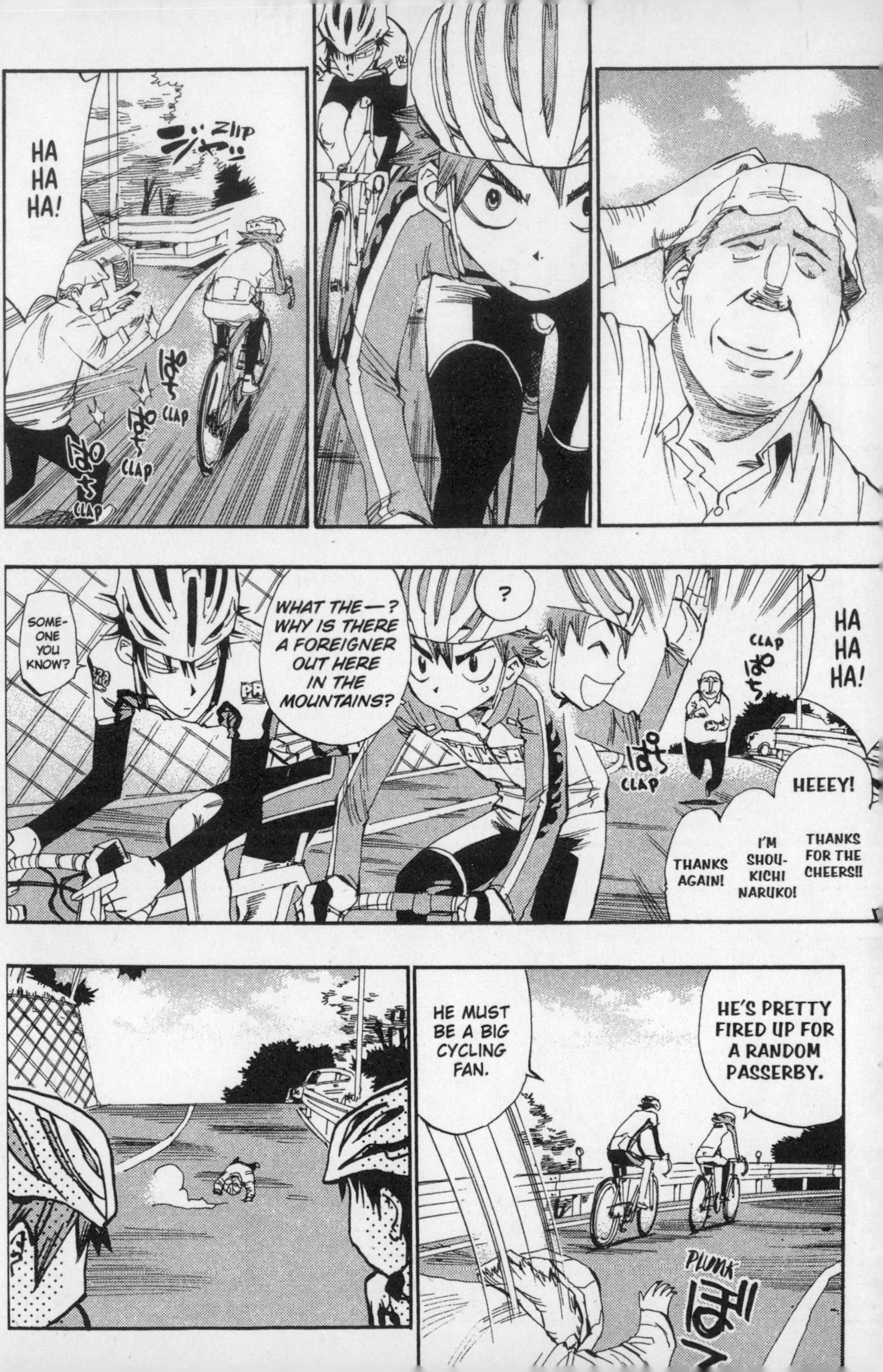
HA HA HA!
ZIIP
CLAP
CLAP
CLAP
HA HA HA!
CLAP
CLAP
HEEEY!
THANKS FOR THE CHEERS!!
I'M SHOU-KICHI NARUKO!
THANKS AGAIN!
?
WHAT THE—? WHY IS THERE A FOREIGNER OUT HERE IN THE MOUNTAINS?
SOME-ONE YOU KNOW?
HE'S PRETTY FIRED UP FOR A RANDOM PASSERBY.
HE MUST BE A BIG CYCLING FAN.
PLUNK

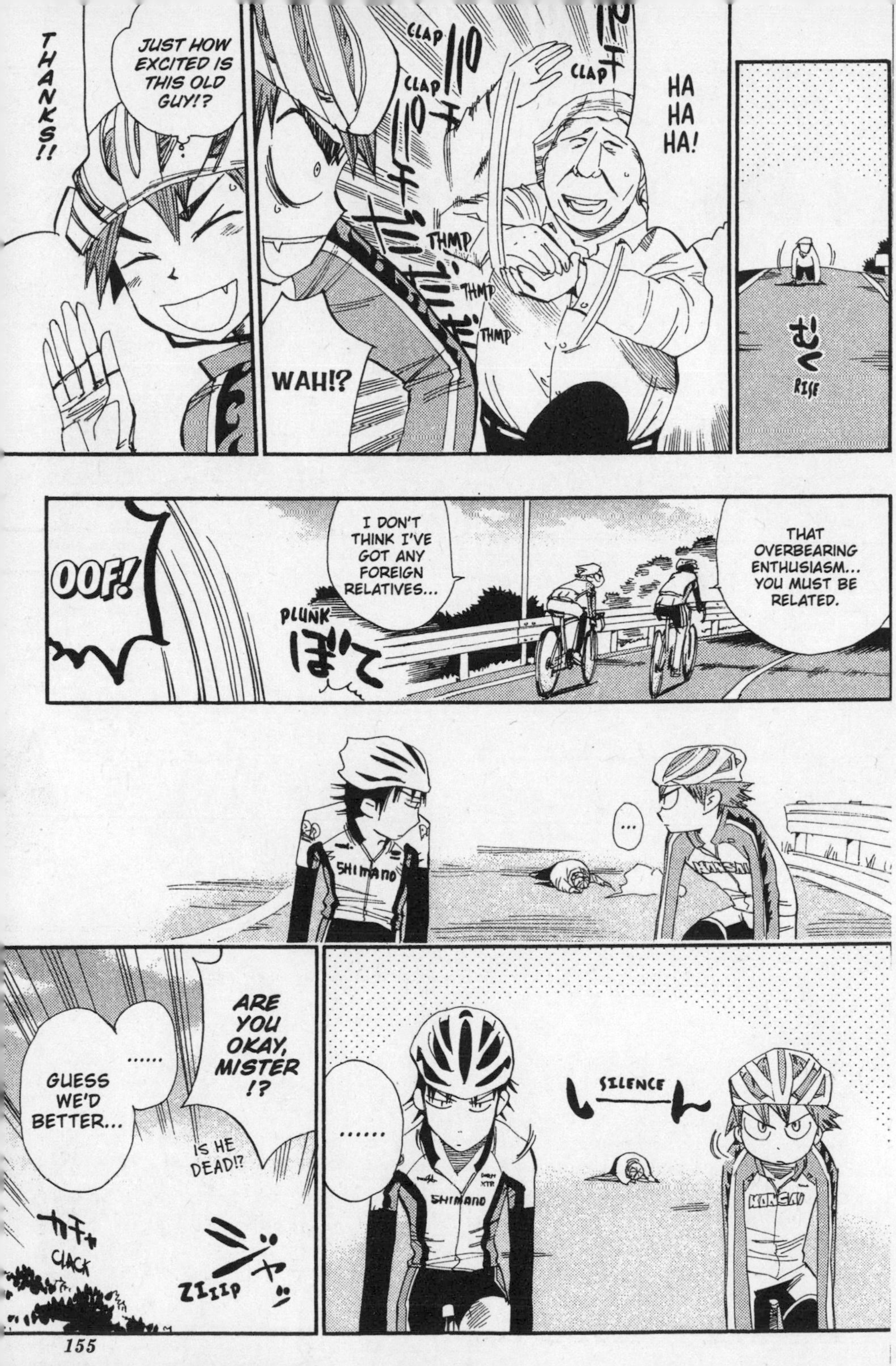

むく
RISE
HA HA HA!
CLAP
CLAP
CLAP
THMP
THMP
THMP
WAH!?
JUST HOW EXCITED IS THIS OLD GUY!?
THANKS!!
THAT OVERBEARING ENTHUSIASM... YOU MUST BE RELATED.
I DON'T THINK I'VE GOT ANY FOREIGN RELATIVES...
PLUNK
ぽて
OOF!
...
SILENCE
......
ARE YOU OKAY, MISTER!?
IS HE DEAD!?
......
GUESS WE'D BETTER...
CLACK
ZIIIP

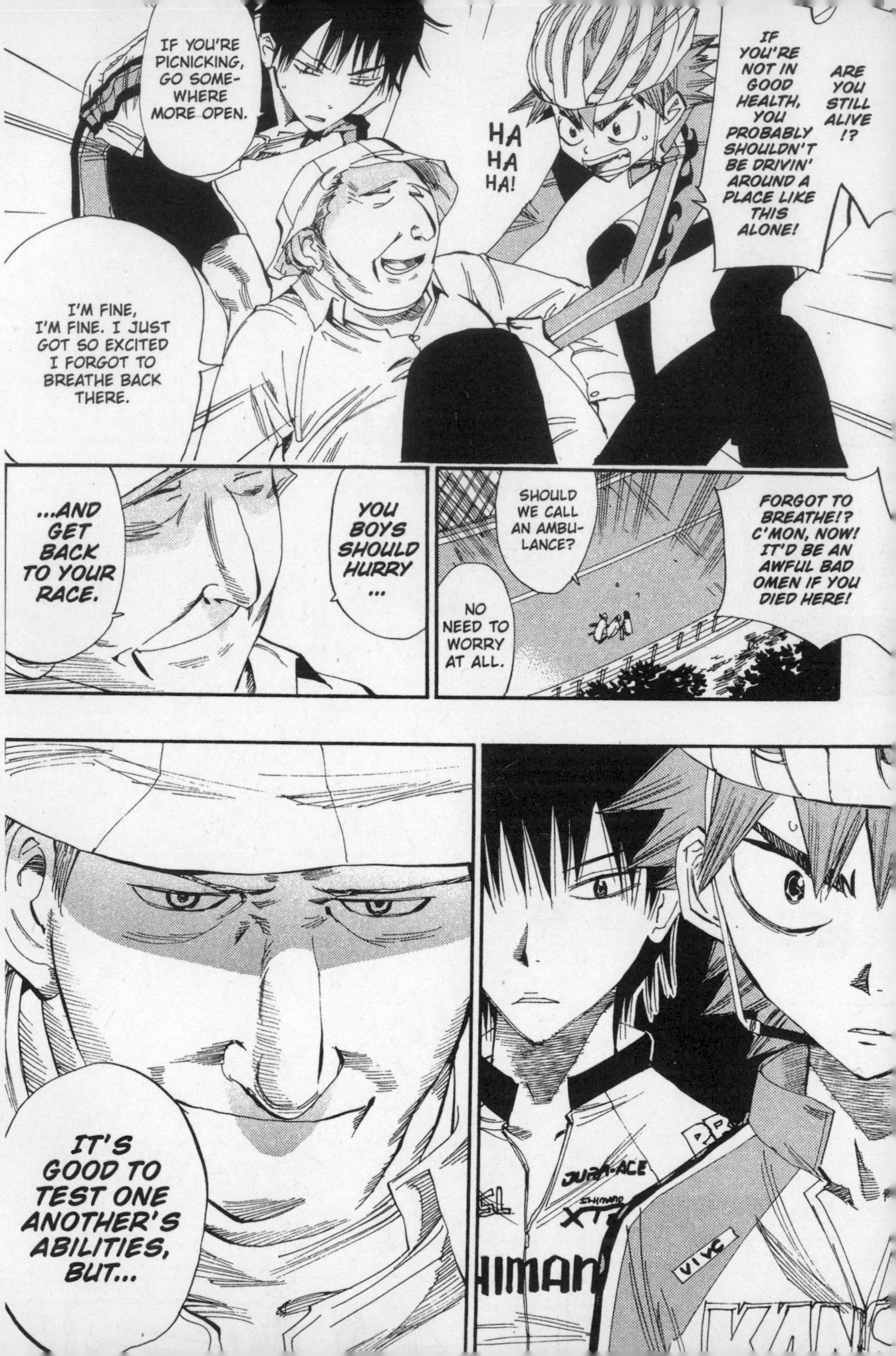
ARE YOU STILL ALIVE!?
IF YOU'RE NOT IN GOOD HEALTH, YOU PROBABLY SHOULDN'T BE DRIVIN' AROUND A PLACE LIKE THIS ALONE!
HA HA HA HA!
IF YOU'RE PICNICKING, GO SOME-WHERE MORE OPEN.
I'M FINE, I'M FINE. I JUST GOT SO EXCITED I FORGOT TO BREATHE BACK THERE.
FORGOT TO BREATHE!? C'MON, NOW! IT'D BE AN AWFUL BAD OMEN IF YOU DIED HERE!
SHOULD WE CALL AN AMBU-LANCE?
NO NEED TO WORRY AT ALL.
YOU BOYS SHOULD HURRY...
...AND GET BACK TO YOUR RACE.
IT'S GOOD TO TEST ONE ANOTHER'S ABILITIES, BUT...

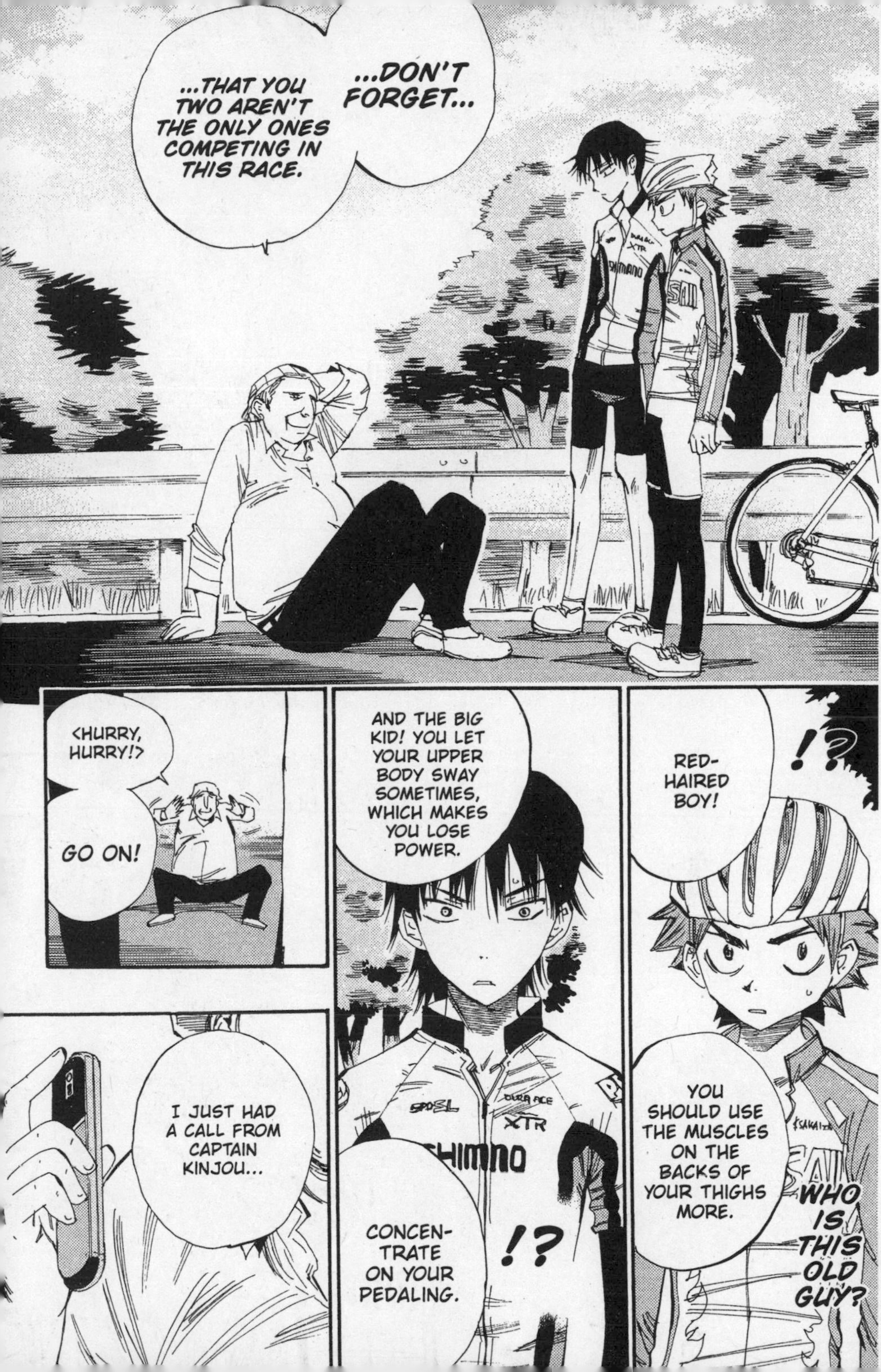
...DON'T FORGET...
...THAT YOU TWO AREN'T THE ONLY ONES COMPETING IN THIS RACE.
RED-HAIRED BOY!
!?
YOU SHOULD USE THE MUSCLES ON THE BACKS OF YOUR THIGHS MORE.
WHO IS THIS OLD GUY?
AND THE BIG KID! YOU LET YOUR UPPER BODY SWAY SOMETIMES, WHICH MAKES YOU LOSE POWER.
CONCEN-TRATE ON YOUR PEDALING.
!?
<HURRY, HURRY!>
GO ON!
I JUST HAD A CALL FROM CAPTAIN KINJOU...

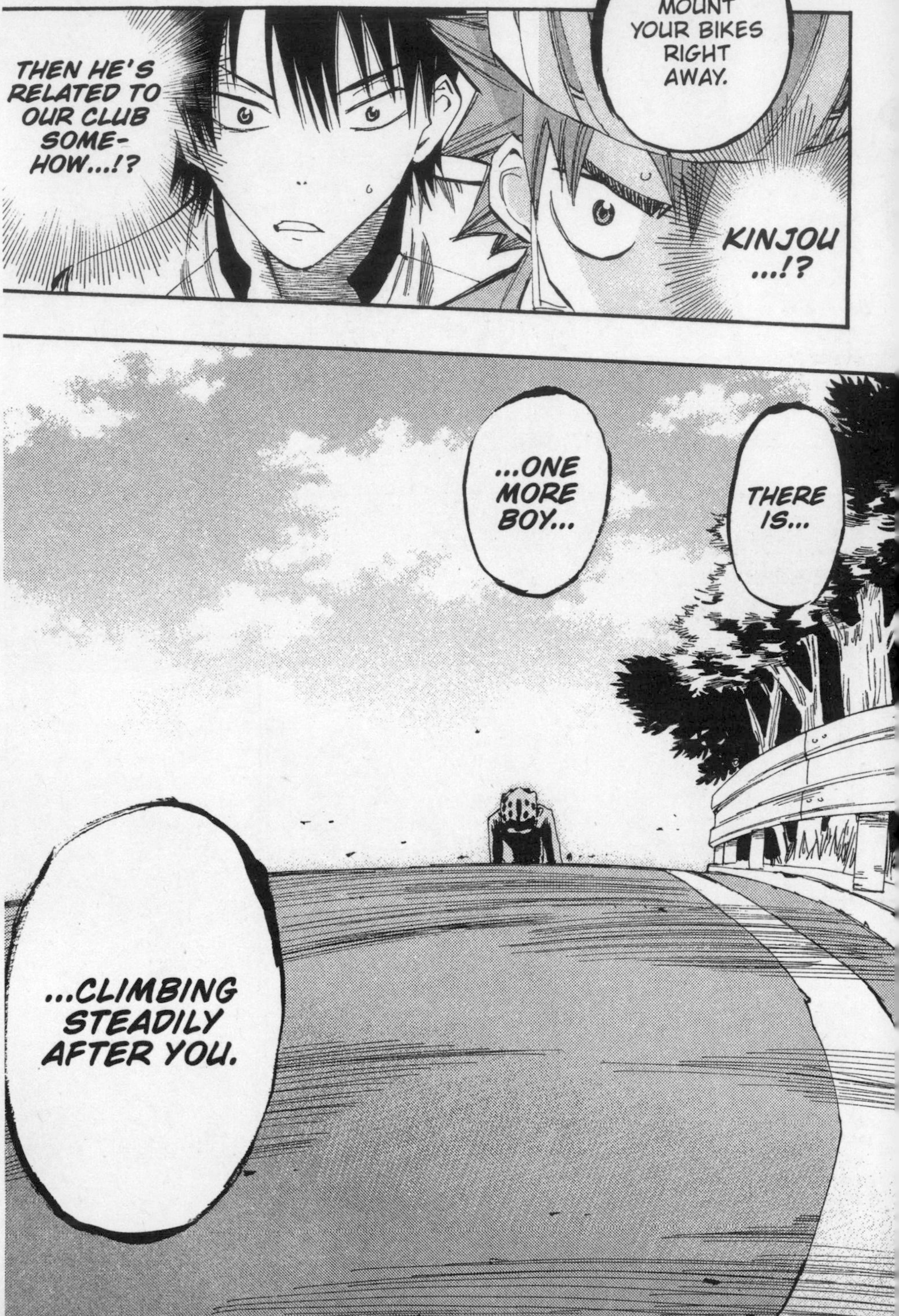
MOUNT YOUR BIKES RIGHT AWAY.
KINJOU ...!?
THEN HE'S RELATED TO OUR CLUB SOME-HOW...!?
THERE IS...
...ONE MORE BOY...
...CLIMBING STEADILY AFTER YOU.

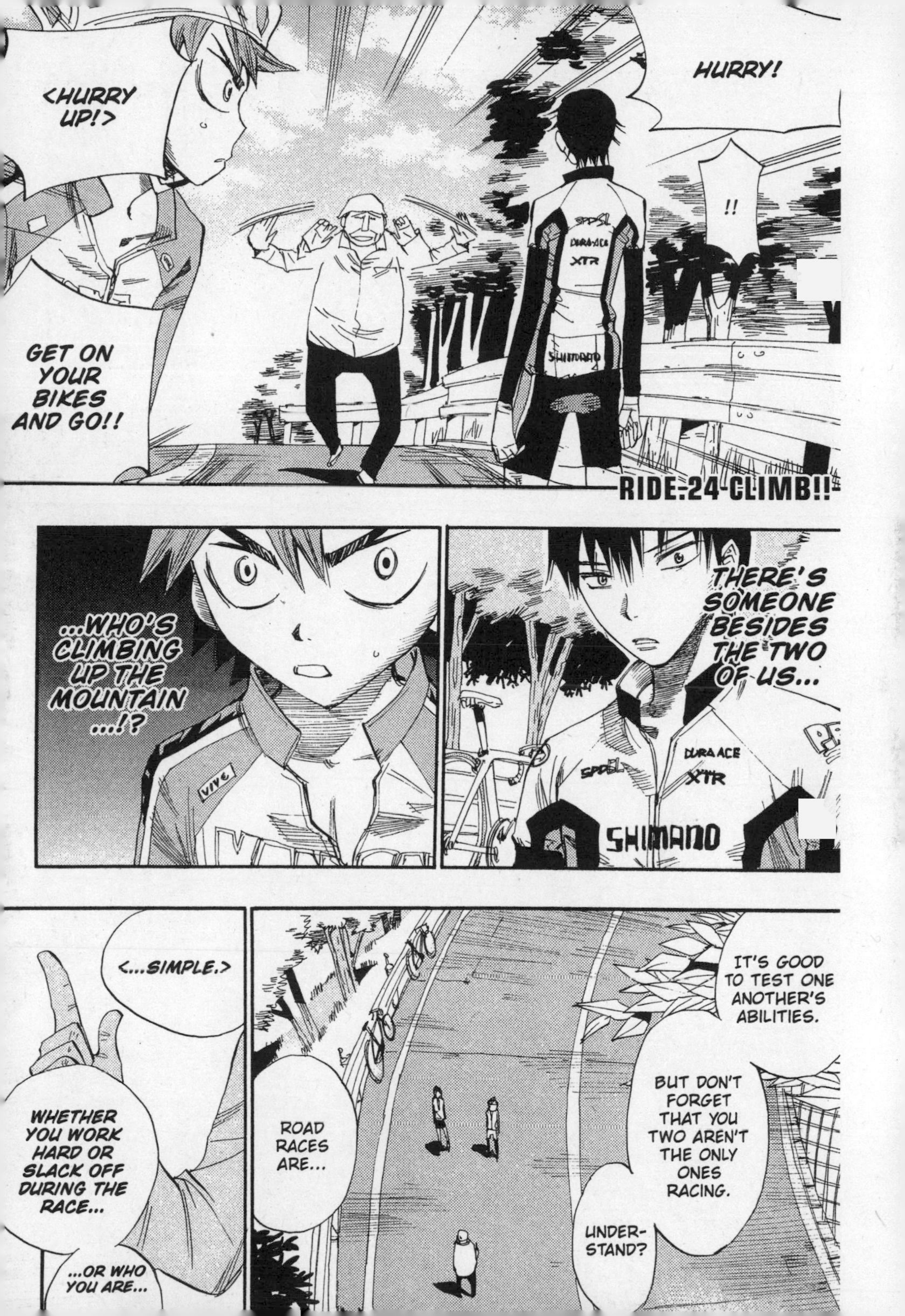
HURRY!
!!
<HURRY UP!>
GET ON YOUR BIKES AND GO!!
RIDE.24 CLIMB!!
THERE'S SOMEONE BESIDES THE TWO OF US...
...WHO'S CLIMBING UP THE MOUNTAIN ...!?
IT'S GOOD TO TEST ONE ANOTHER'S ABILITIES.
BUT DON'T FORGET THAT YOU TWO AREN'T THE ONLY ONES RACING.
UNDER-STAND?
ROAD RACES ARE...
<...SIMPLE.>
WHETHER YOU WORK HARD OR SLACK OFF DURING THE RACE...
...OR WHO YOU ARE...

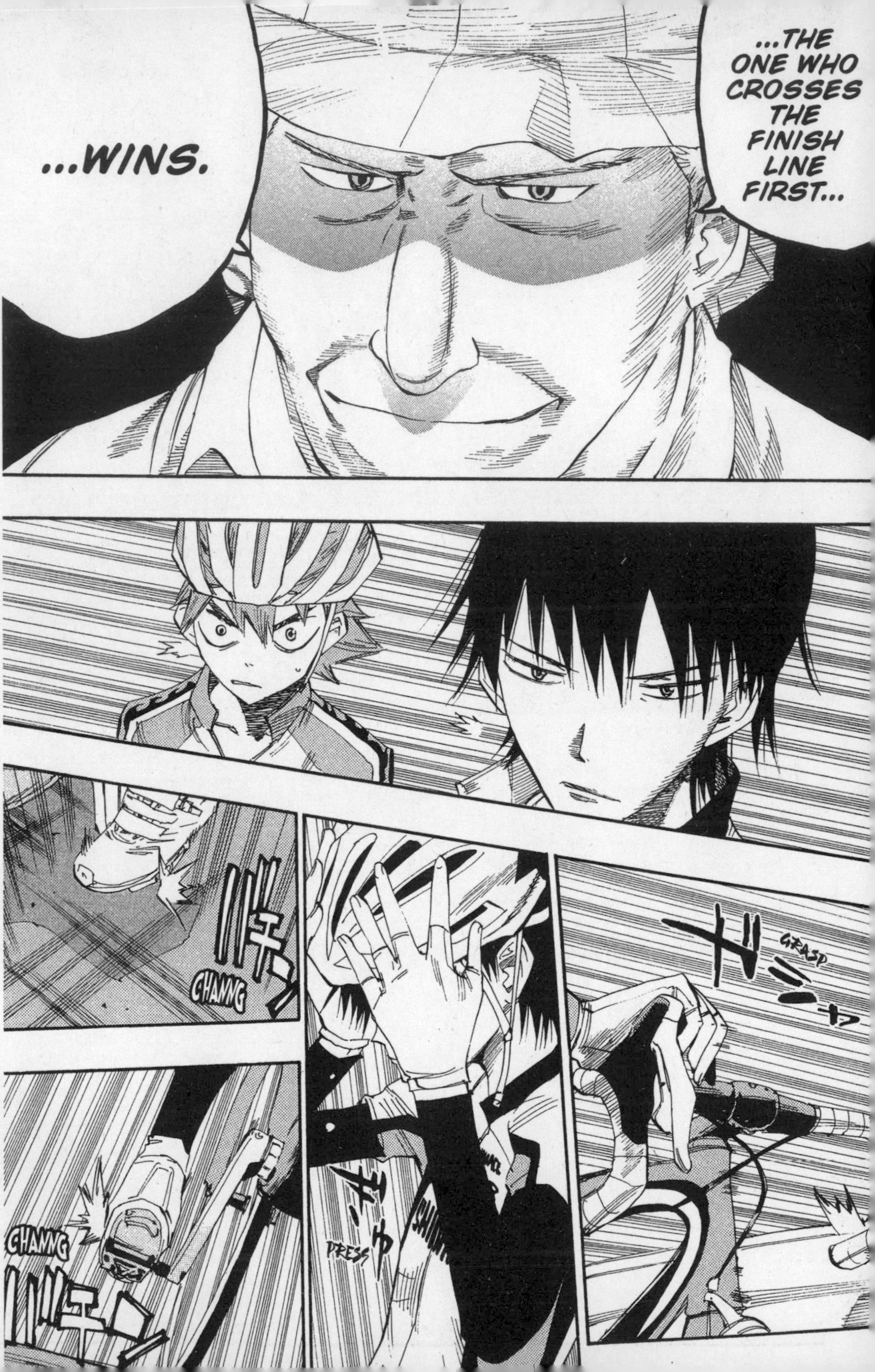
...THE ONE WHO CROSSES THE FINISH LINE FIRST...
...WINS.
GRASP
PRESS
CHANNG
CHANNG

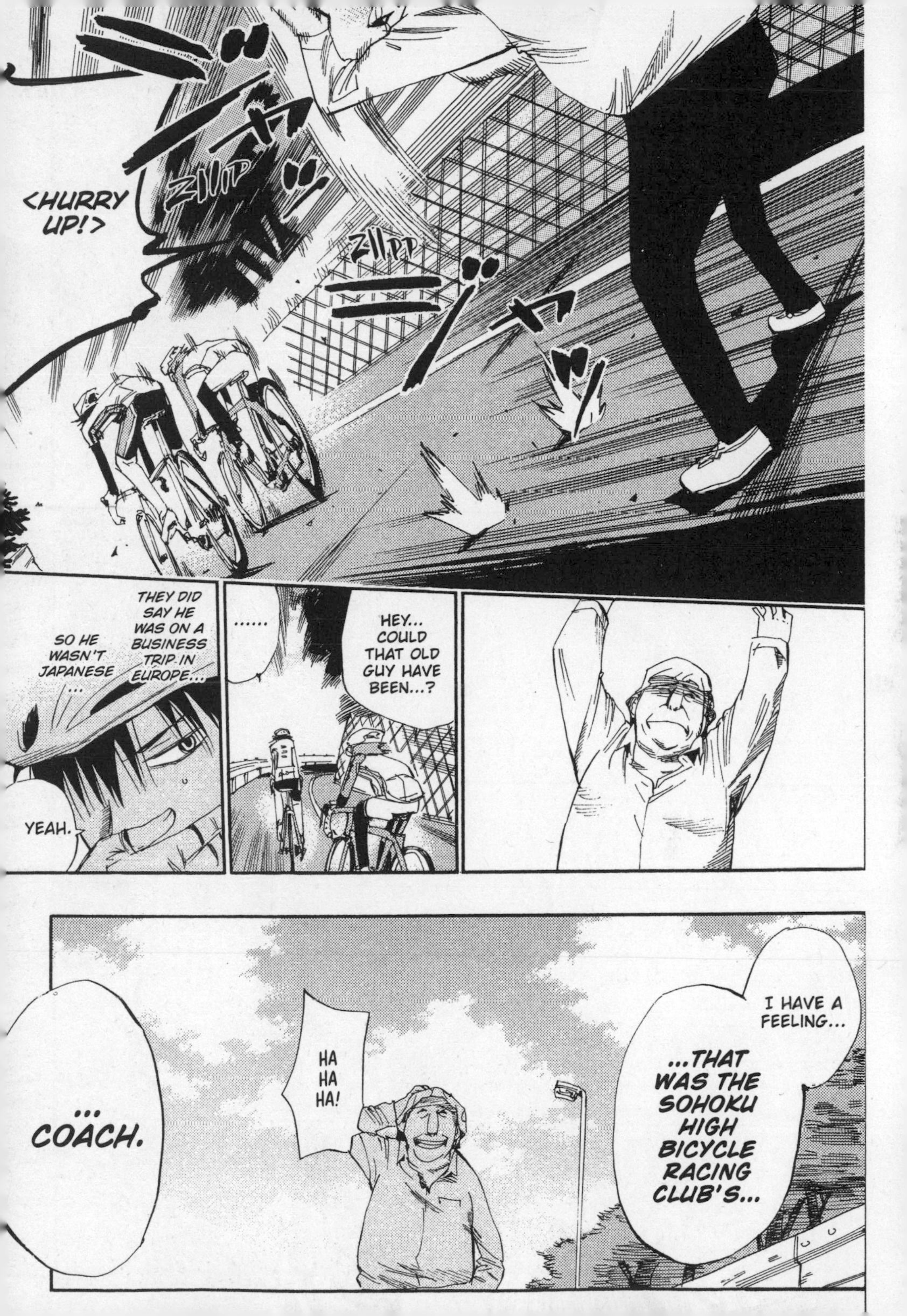
ZIIID
ZIIPP
<HURRY UP!>
HEY... COULD THAT OLD GUY HAVE BEEN...?
......
THEY DID SAY HE WAS ON A BUSINESS TRIP IN EUROPE...
SO HE WASN'T JAPANESE...
YEAH.
I HAVE A FEELING...
...THAT WAS THE SOHOKU HIGH BICYCLE RACING CLUB'S...
HA HA HA!
...COACH.

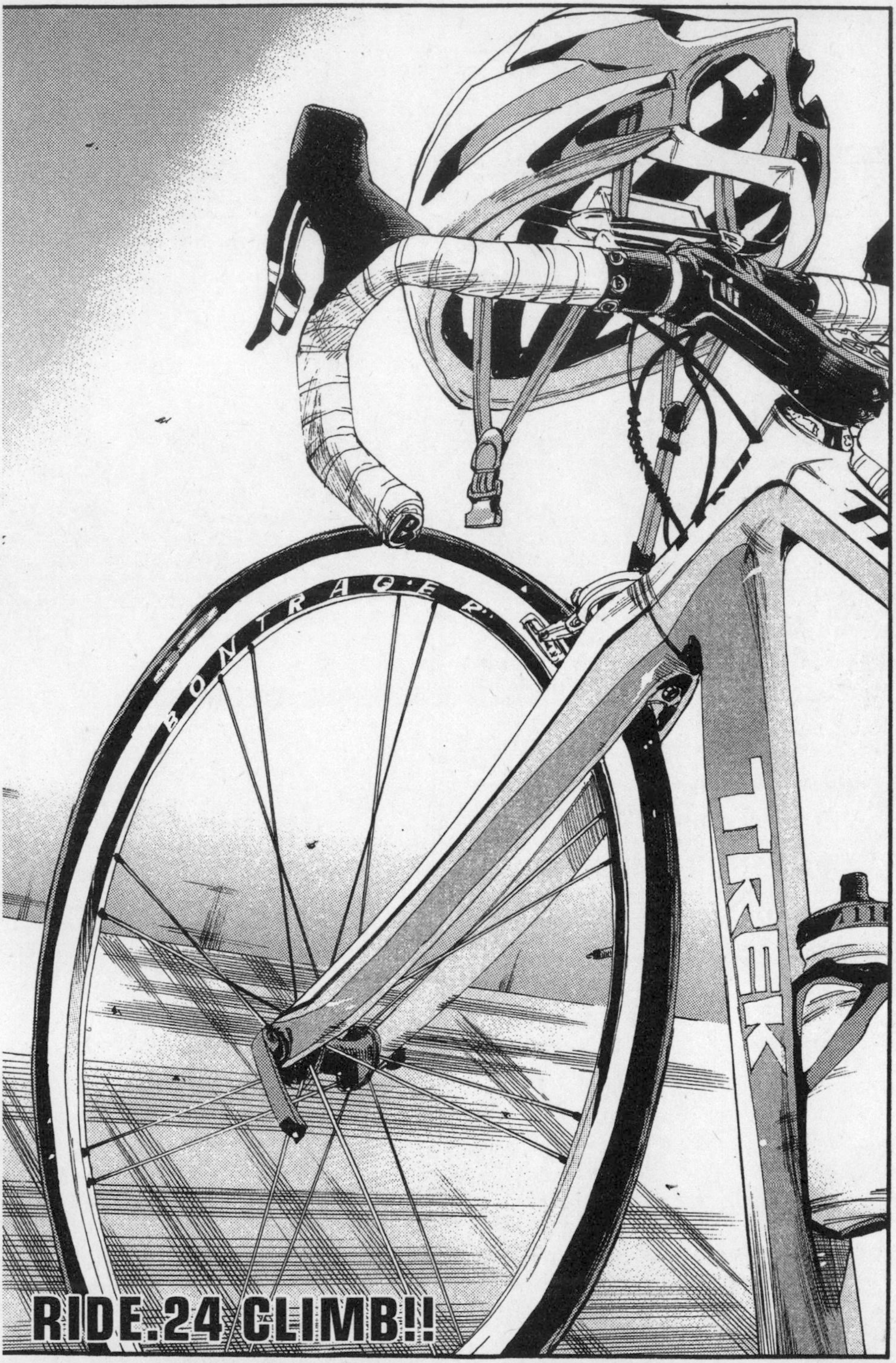
BONTRAGER
TREK

RIDE.24 CLIMB!!

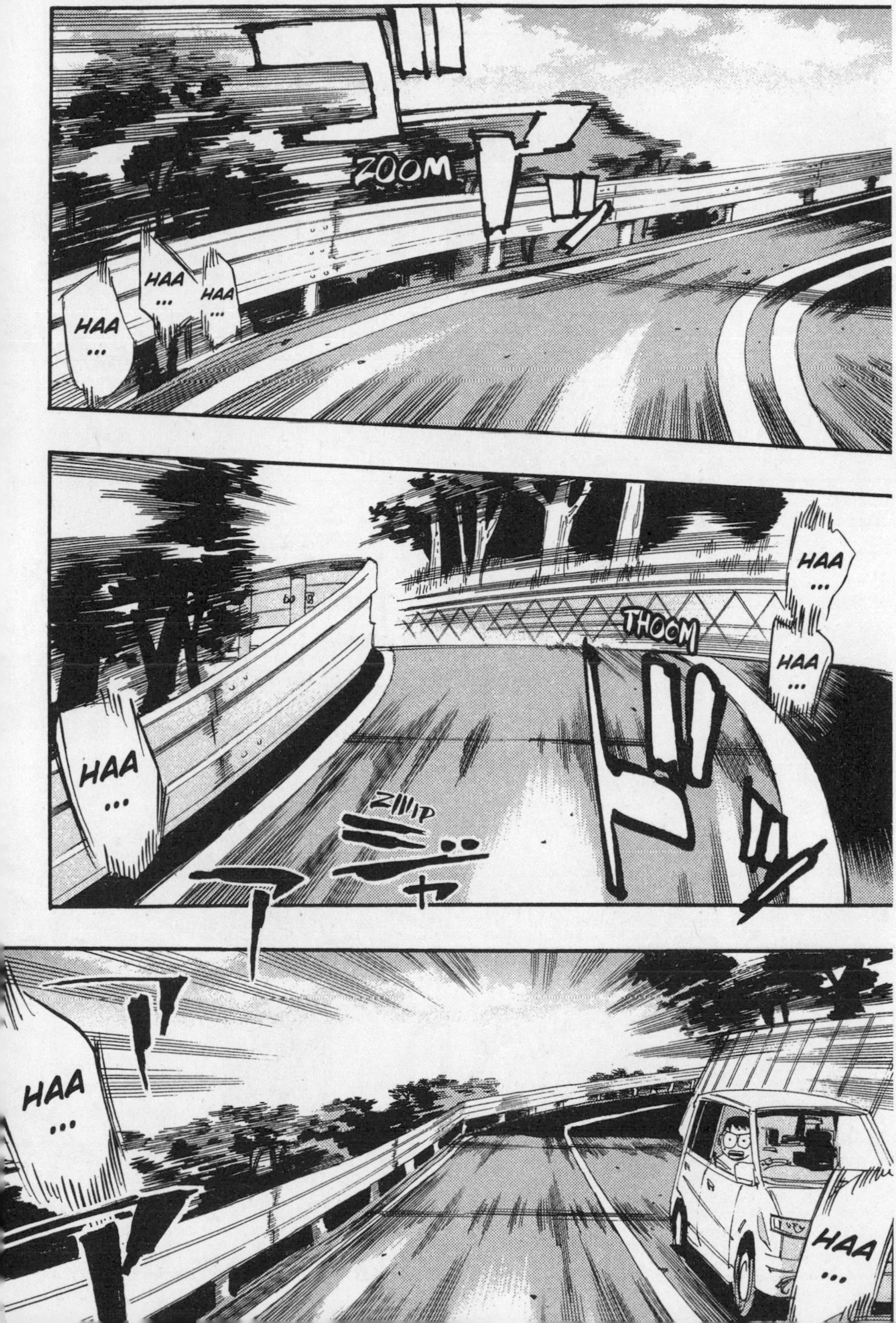
ZOOM
HAA ...
HAA ...
HAA ...
HAA ...
THOOM
HAA ...
HAA ...
ZIIIP
HAA ...
HAA ...

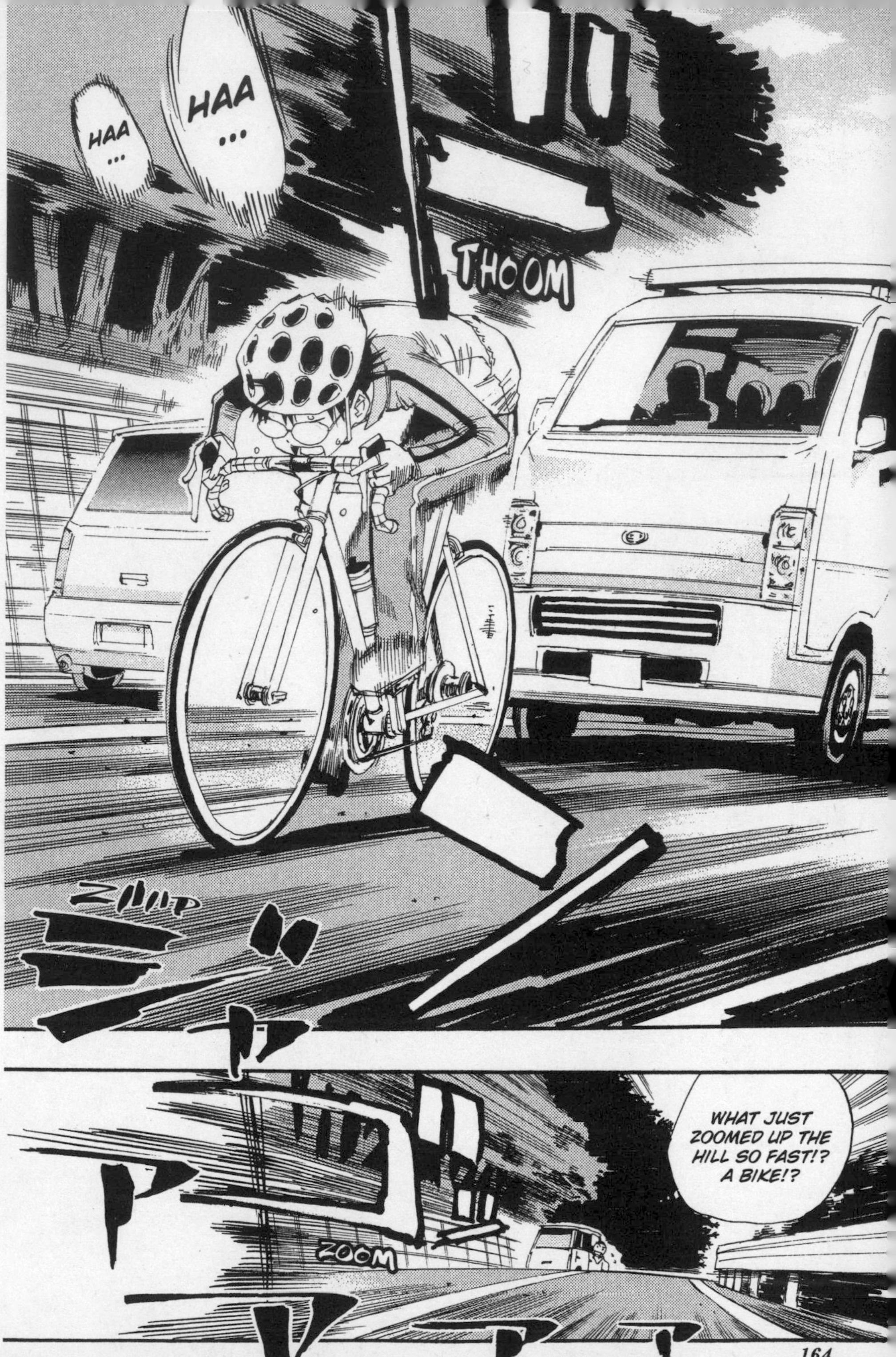
HAA ...
HAA ...
THOOM
ZWIP
WHAT JUST ZOOMED UP THE HILL SO FAST!? A BIKE!?
ZOOM

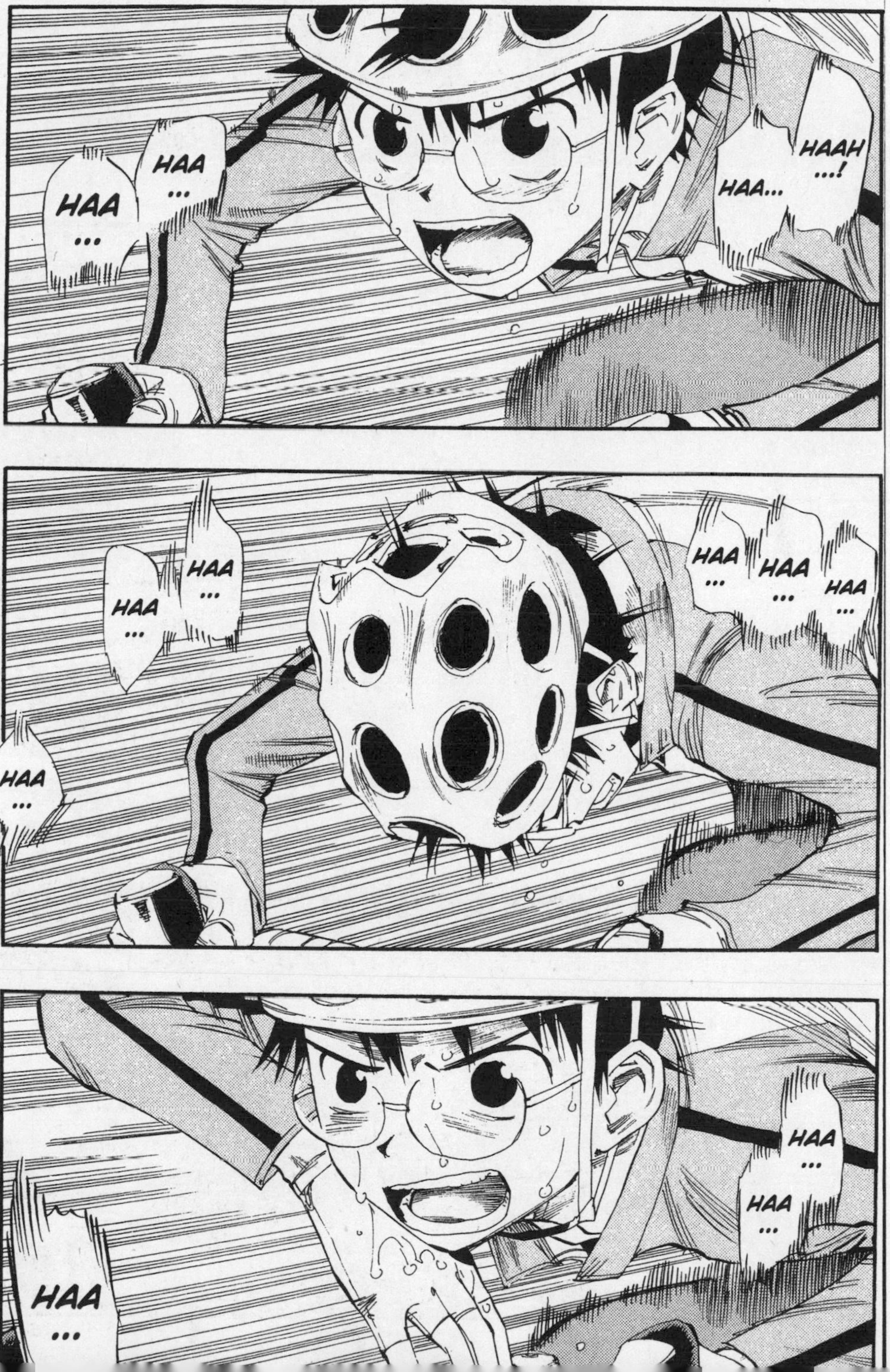
HAAH...!
HAA...
HAA...
HAA...
HAA...
HAA...
HAA...
HAA...
HAA...
HAA...
HAA...
HAA...
HAA...

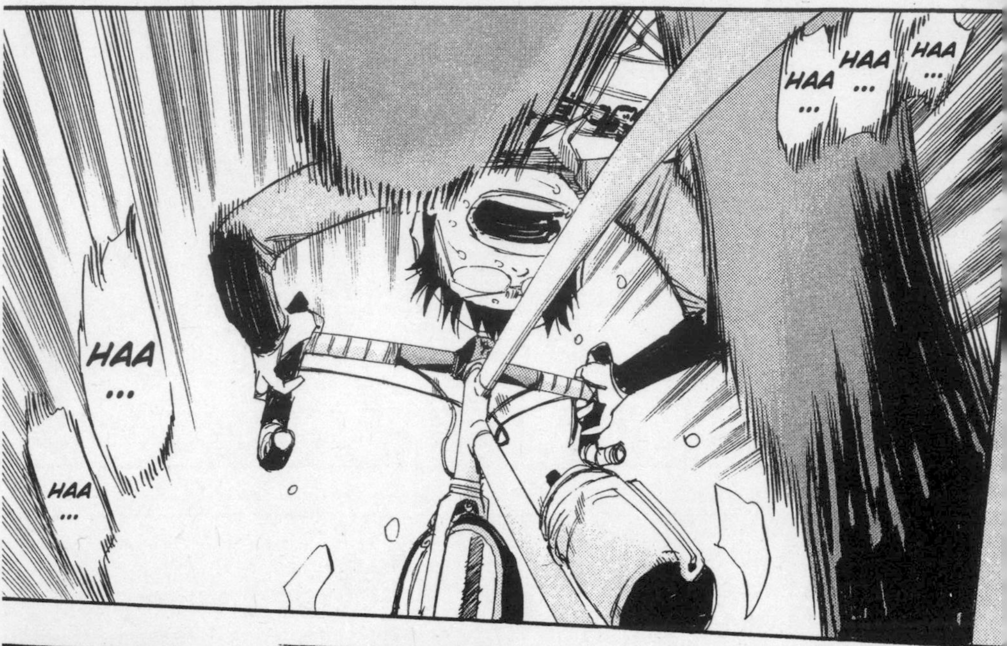
HAA...
HAA...
HAA...
HAA...
HAA...
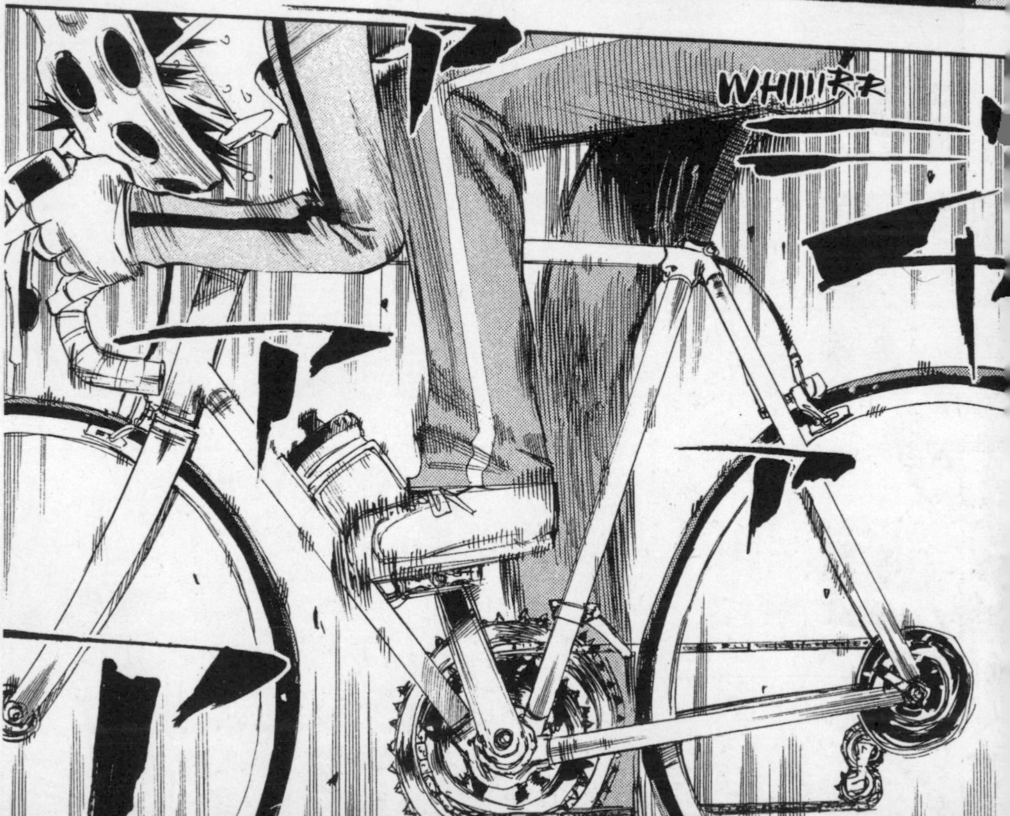
WHIIIIRR

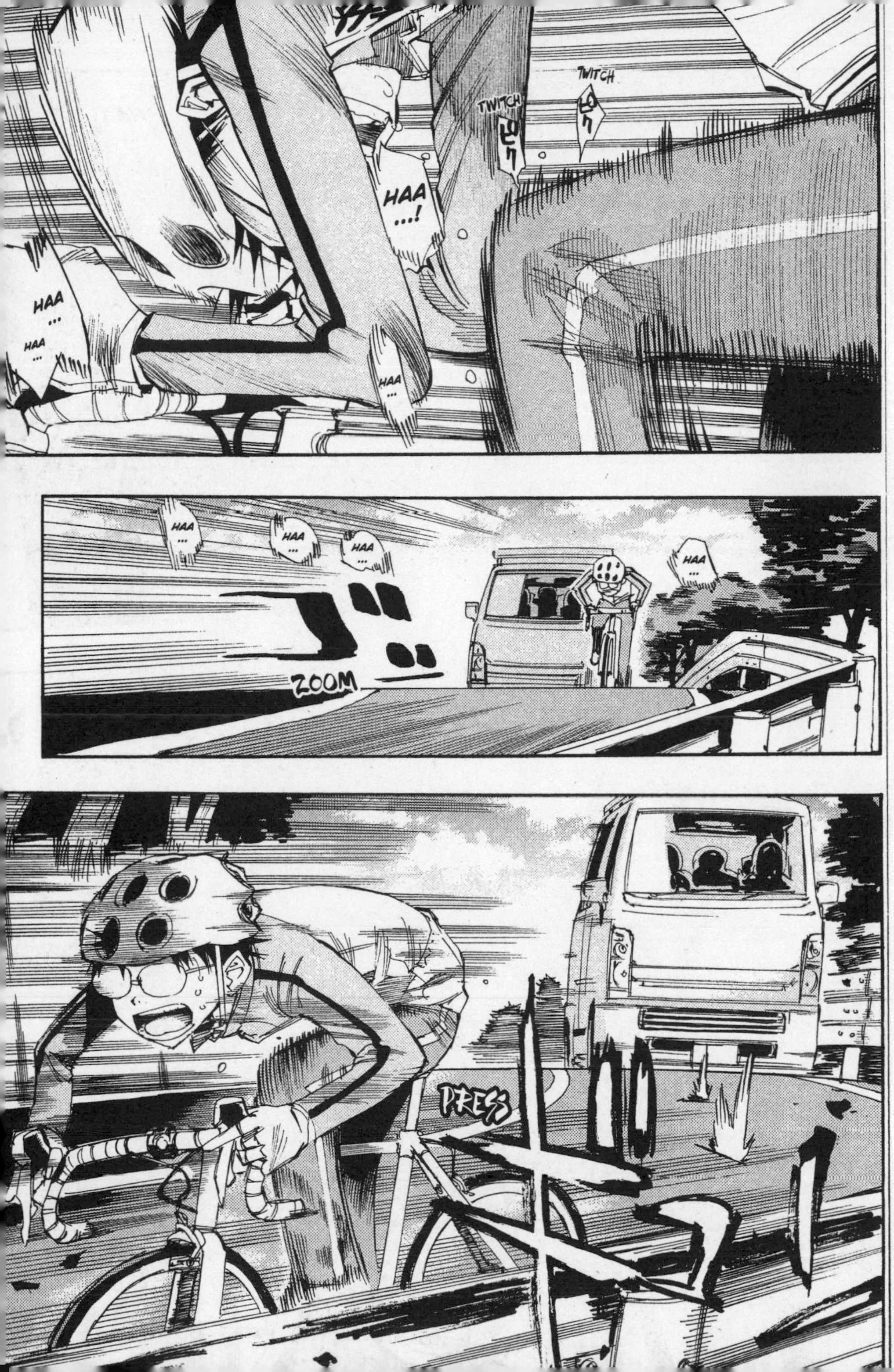
TWITCH
TWITCH
HAA ...!
HAA ...
HAA ...
HAA ...
HAA ...
HAA ...
HAA ...
HAA ...
ZOOM
PRESS

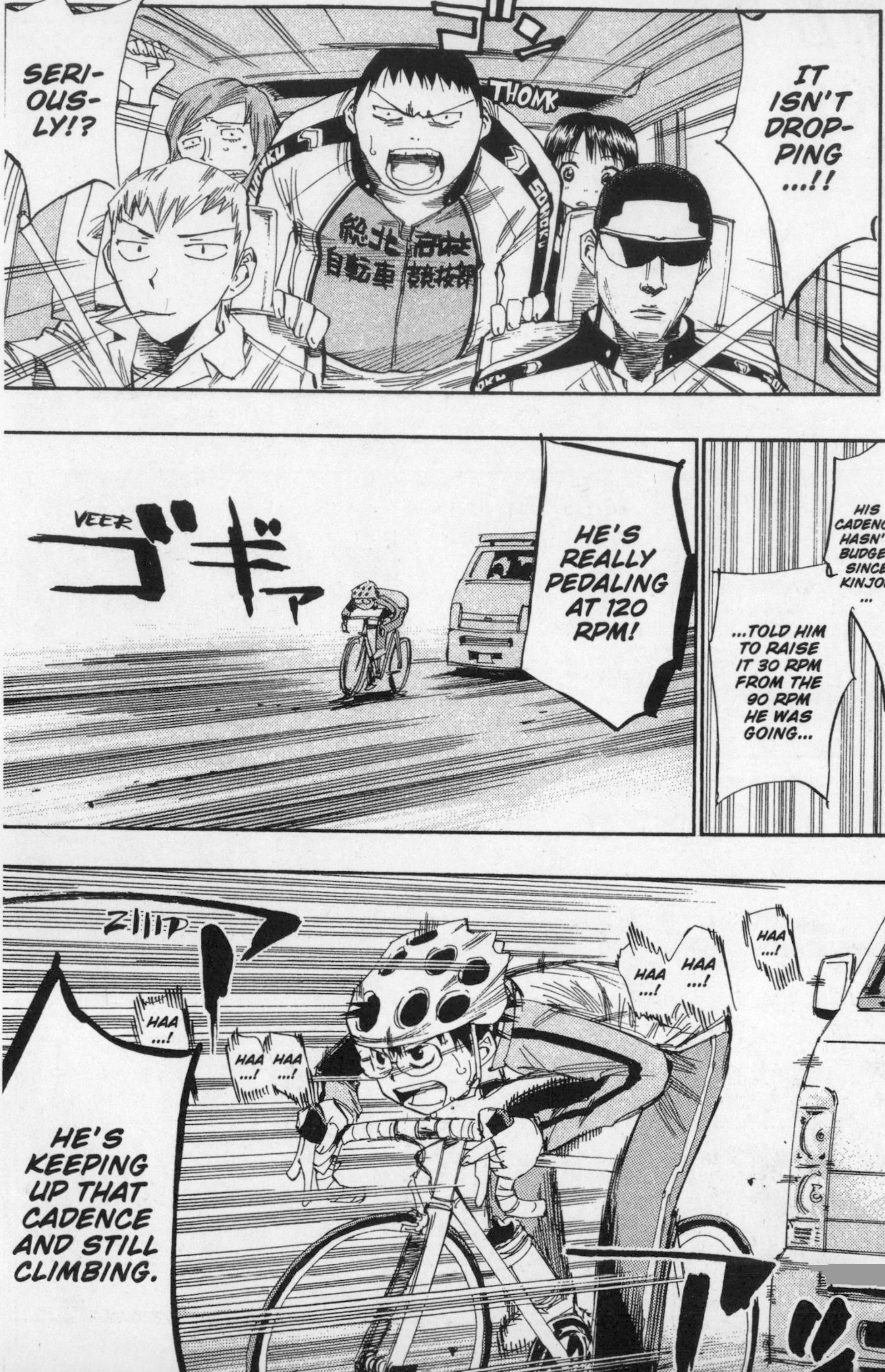

IT ISN'T DROPPING ...!!
THONK
SERIOUSLY!?
HIS CADENCE HASN'T BUDGED SINCE KINJOU ...
...TOLD HIM TO RAISE IT 30 RPM FROM THE 90 RPM HE WAS GOING...
HE'S REALLY PEDALING AT 120 RPM!
VEER
HAA ...!
HAA ...!
HAA ...!
ZIIIP
HAA ...!
HAA ...!
HAA ...!
HE'S KEEPING UP THAT CADENCE AND STILL CLIMBING.

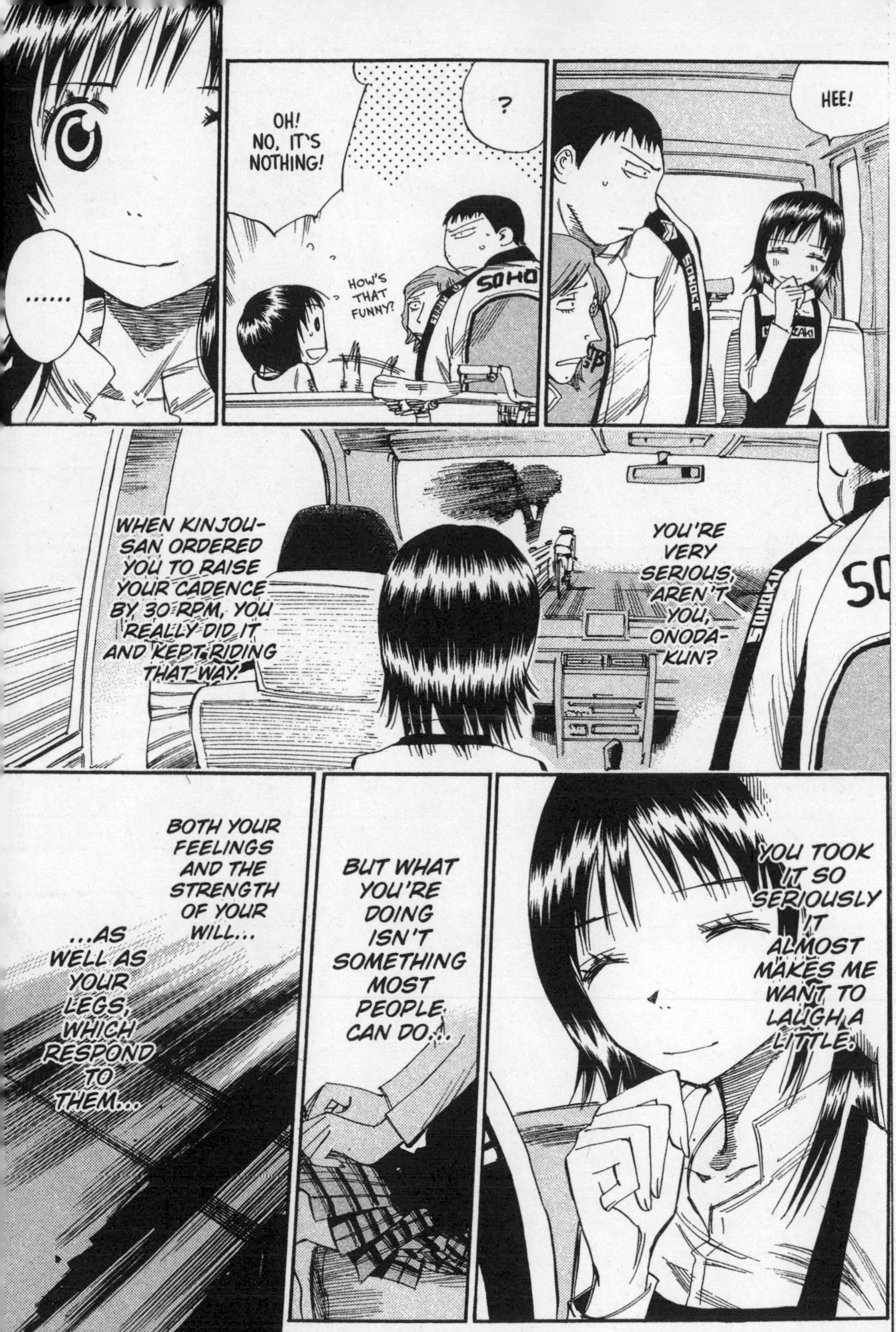
HEE!
?
OH! NO, IT'S NOTHING!
HOW'S THAT FUNNY?
......
YOU'RE VERY SERIOUS, AREN'T YOU, ONODA-KUN?
WHEN KINJOU-SAN ORDERED YOU TO RAISE YOUR CADENCE BY 30 RPM, YOU REALLY DID IT AND KEPT RIDING THAT WAY.
YOU TOOK IT SO SERIOUSLY IT ALMOST MAKES ME WANT TO LAUGH A LITTLE.
BUT WHAT YOU'RE DOING ISN'T SOMETHING MOST PEOPLE CAN DO...
BOTH YOUR FEELINGS AND THE STRENGTH OF YOUR WILL...
...AS WELL AS YOUR LEGS, WHICH RESPOND TO THEM...

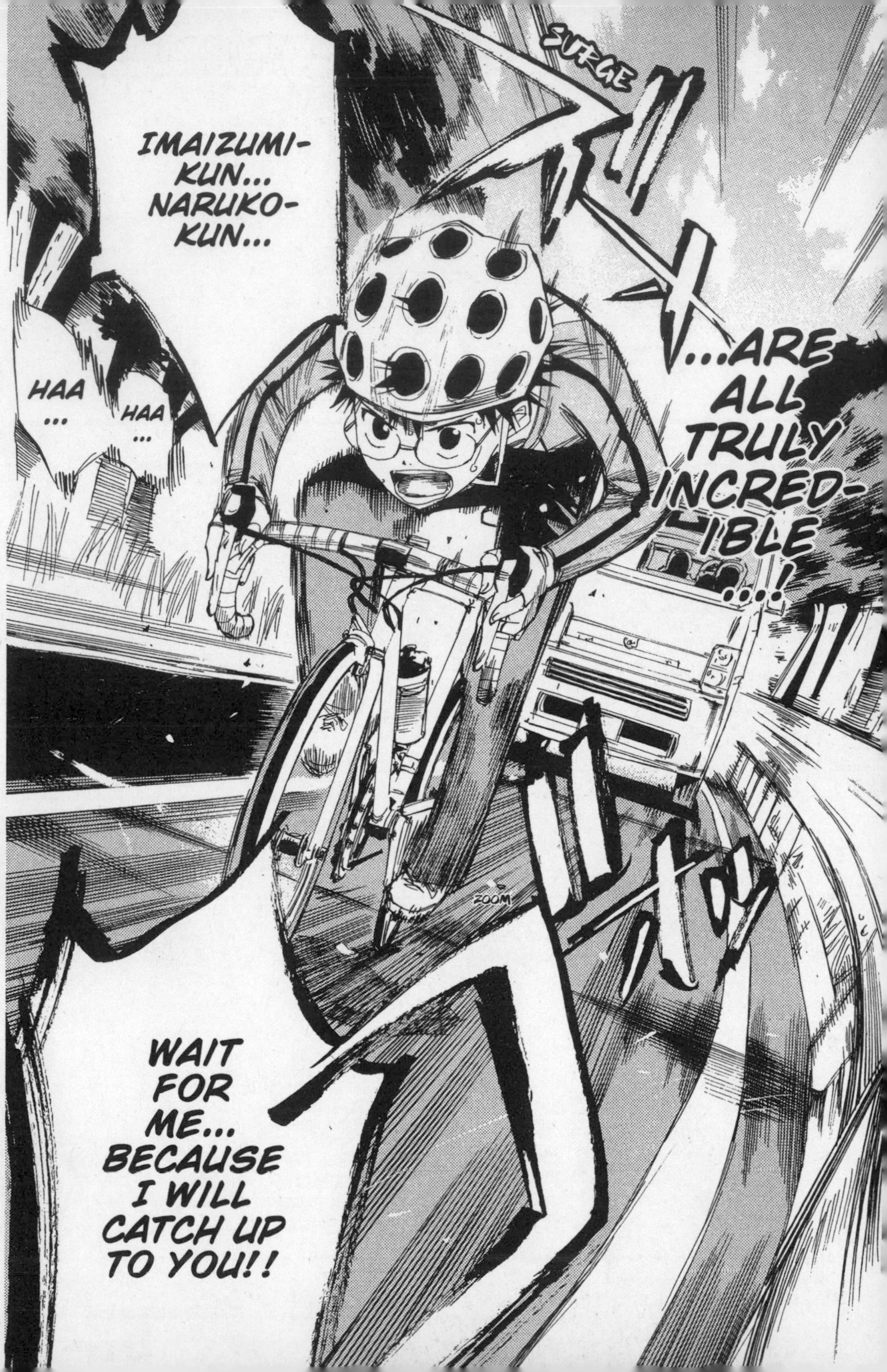
SURGE
IMAIZUMI-KUN... NARUKO-KUN...
...ARE ALL TRULY INCRED-IBLE...!
HAA...
HAA...
ZOOM
WAIT FOR ME... BECAUSE I WILL CATCH UP TO YOU!!

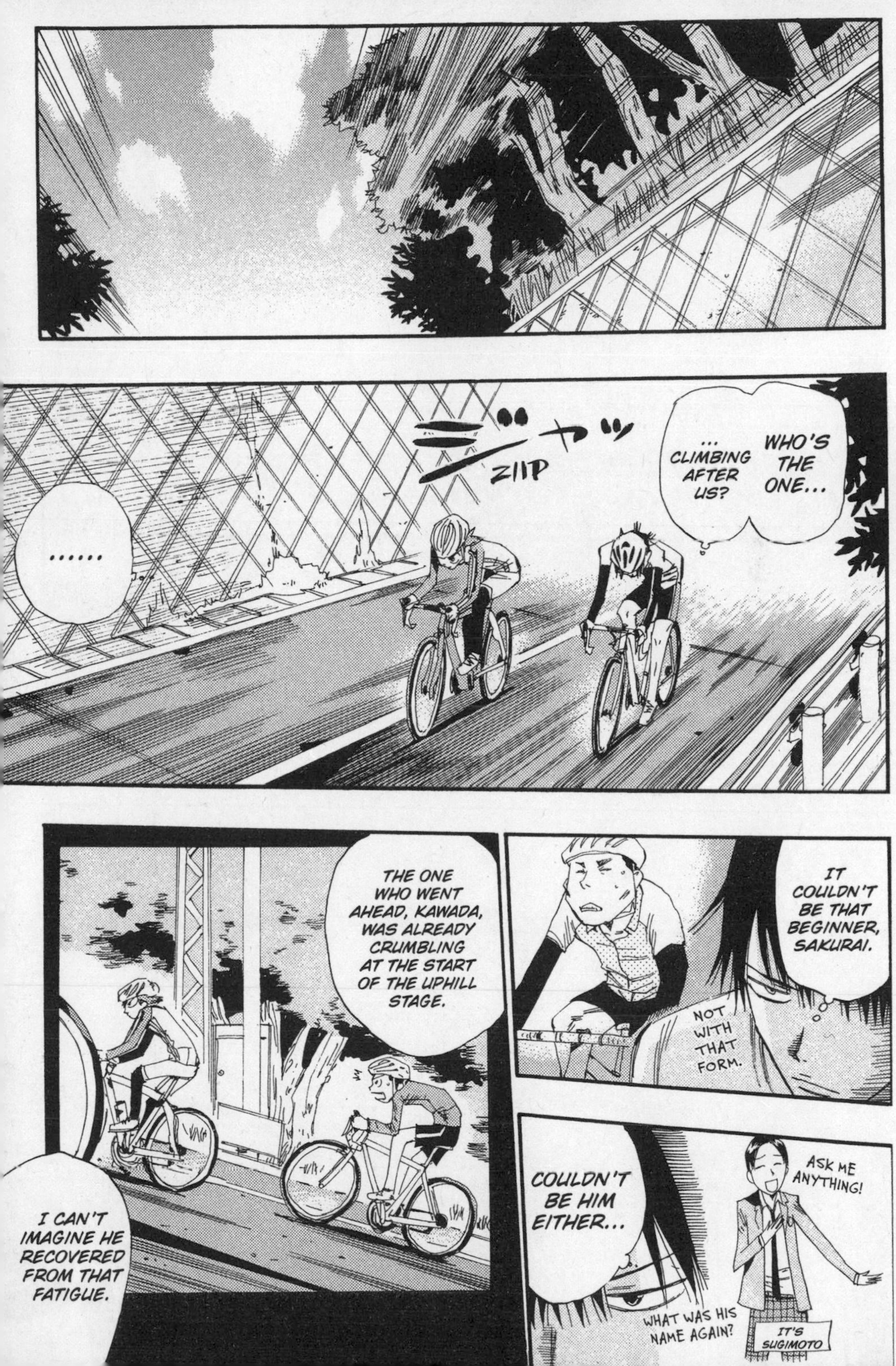
WHO'S THE ONE...
...CLIMBING AFTER US?
ZIIP
......
IT COULDN'T BE THAT BEGINNER, SAKURAI.
NOT WITH THAT FORM.
ASK ME ANYTHING!
COULDN'T BE HIM EITHER...
WHAT WAS HIS NAME AGAIN?
IT'S SUGIMOTO
THE ONE WHO WENT AHEAD, KAWADA, WAS ALREADY CRUMBLING AT THE START OF THE UPHILL STAGE.
I CAN'T IMAGINE HE RECOVERED FROM THAT FATIGUE.

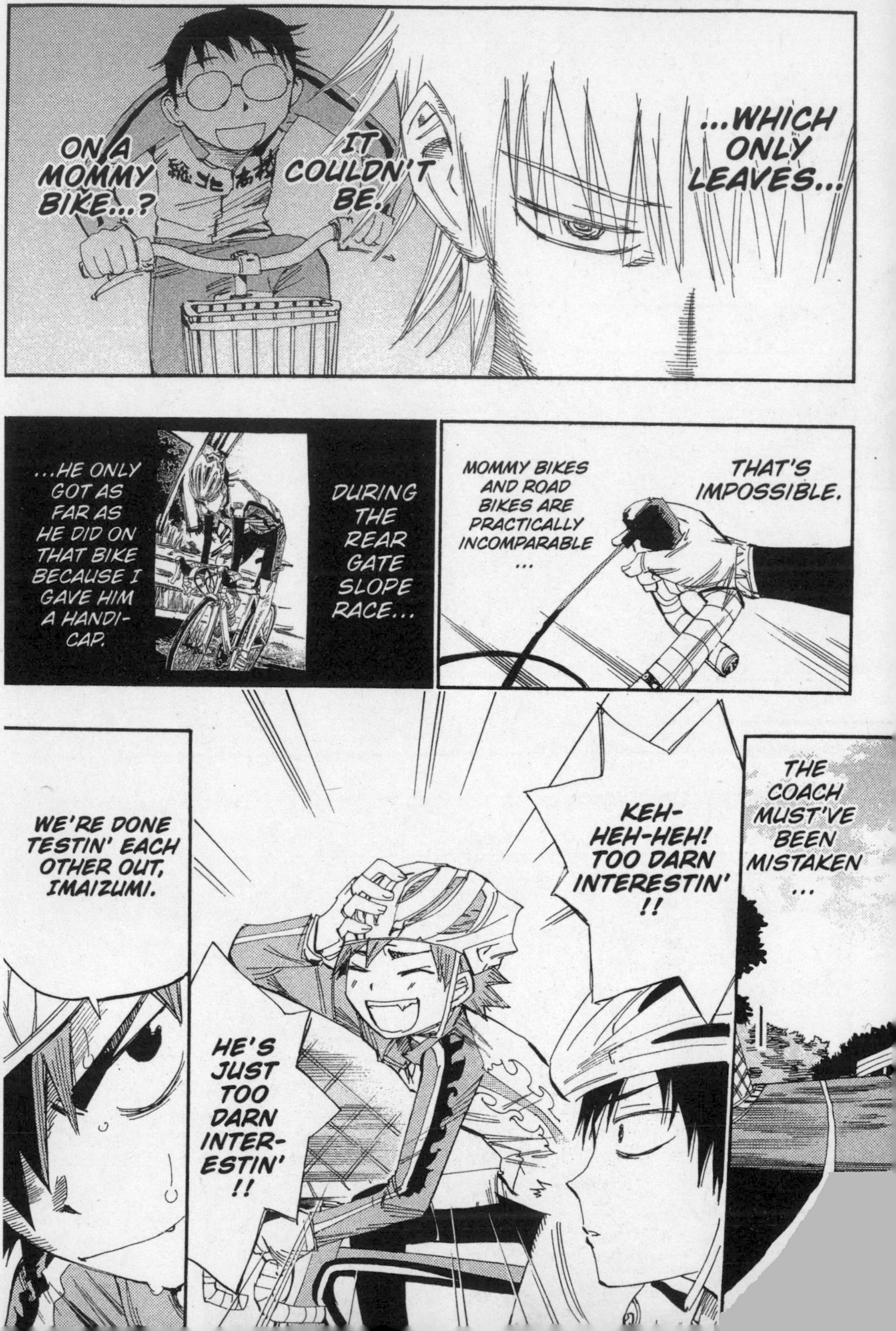
...WHICH ONLY LEAVES...
IT COULDN'T BE.
ON A MOMMY BIKE...?
THAT'S IMPOSSIBLE.
MOMMY BIKES AND ROAD BIKES ARE PRACTICALLY INCOMPARABLE ...
DURING THE REAR GATE SLOPE RACE...
...HE ONLY GOT AS FAR AS HE DID ON THAT BIKE BECAUSE I GAVE HIM A HANDI-CAP.
THE COACH MUST'VE BEEN MISTAKEN ...
KEH-HEH-HEH! TOO DARN INTERESTIN' !!
WE'RE DONE TESTIN' EACH OTHER OUT, IMAIZUMI.
HE'S JUST TOO DARN INTER-ESTIN' !!

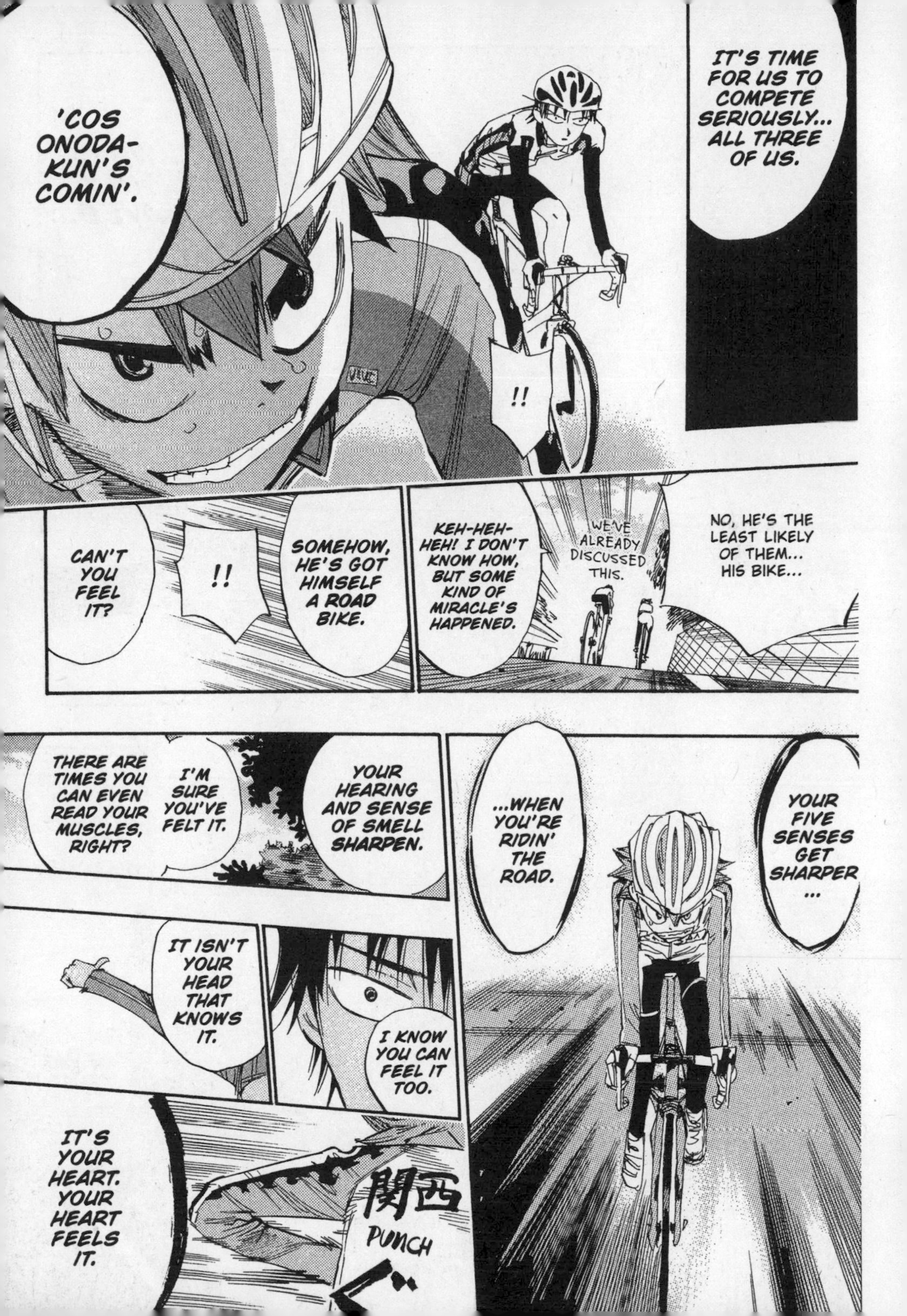
IT'S TIME FOR US TO COMPETE SERIOUSLY... ALL THREE OF US.
!!
'COS ONODA-KUN'S COMIN'.
NO, HE'S THE LEAST LIKELY OF THEM... HIS BIKE...
WE'VE ALREADY DISCUSSED THIS.
KEH-HEH-HEH! I DON'T KNOW HOW, BUT SOME KIND OF MIRACLE'S HAPPENED.
SOMEHOW, HE'S GOT HIMSELF A ROAD BIKE.
!!
CAN'T YOU FEEL IT?
YOUR FIVE SENSES GET SHARPER ...
...WHEN YOU'RE RIDIN' THE ROAD.
YOUR HEARING AND SENSE OF SMELL SHARPEN.
I'M SURE YOU'VE FELT IT.
THERE ARE TIMES YOU CAN EVEN READ YOUR MUSCLES, RIGHT?
I KNOW YOU CAN FEEL IT TOO.
IT ISN'T YOUR HEAD THAT KNOWS IT.
IT'S YOUR HEART. YOUR HEART FEELS IT.
関西
PUNCH

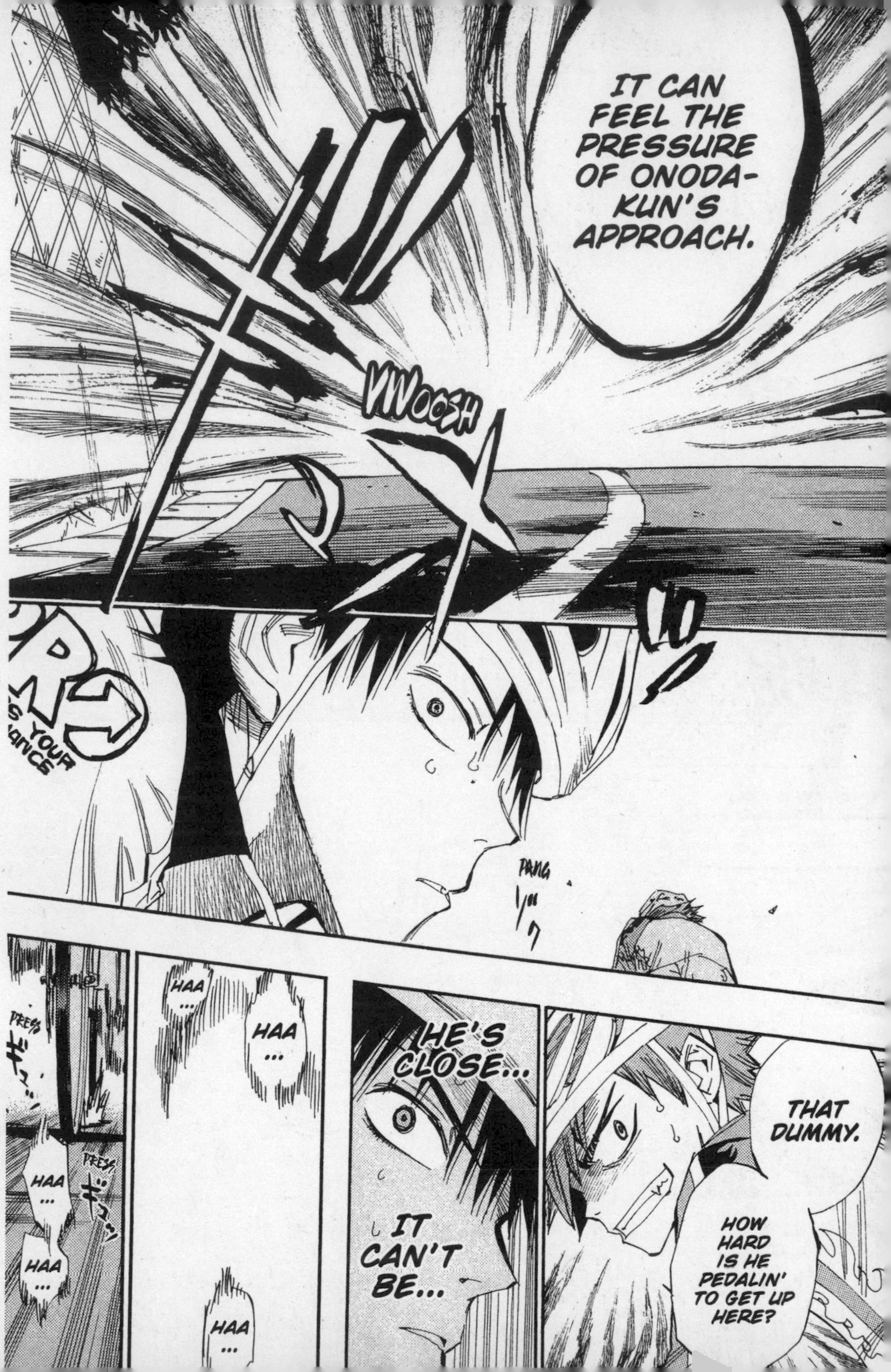
IT CAN FEEL THE PRESSURE OF ONODA-KUN'S APPROACH.
VVVOOSH
PANG
THAT DUMMY.
HOW HARD IS HE PEDALIN' TO GET UP HERE?
HE'S CLOSE...
IT CAN'T BE...
HAA ...
HAA ...
HAA ...
PRESS
PRESS
HAA ...
HAA ...

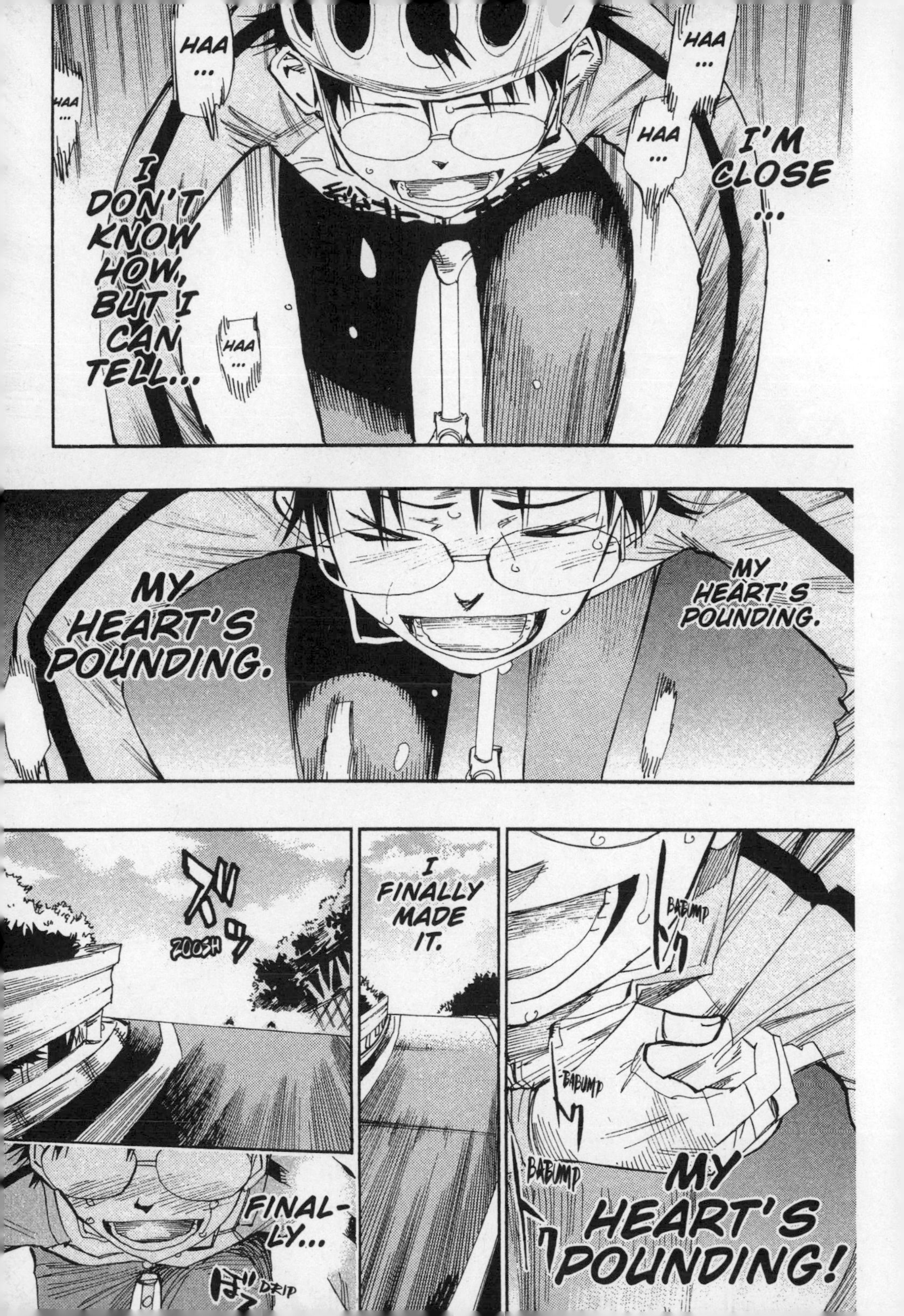
HAA ...
HAA ...
I'M CLOSE ...
HAA ...
HAA ...
I DON'T KNOW HOW, BUT I CAN TELL...
HAA ...
MY HEART'S POUNDING.
MY HEART'S POUNDING.
BABUMP
BABUMP
BABUMP
MY HEART'S POUNDING!
I FINALLY MADE IT.
ZOOSH
FINAL-LY...
DRIP

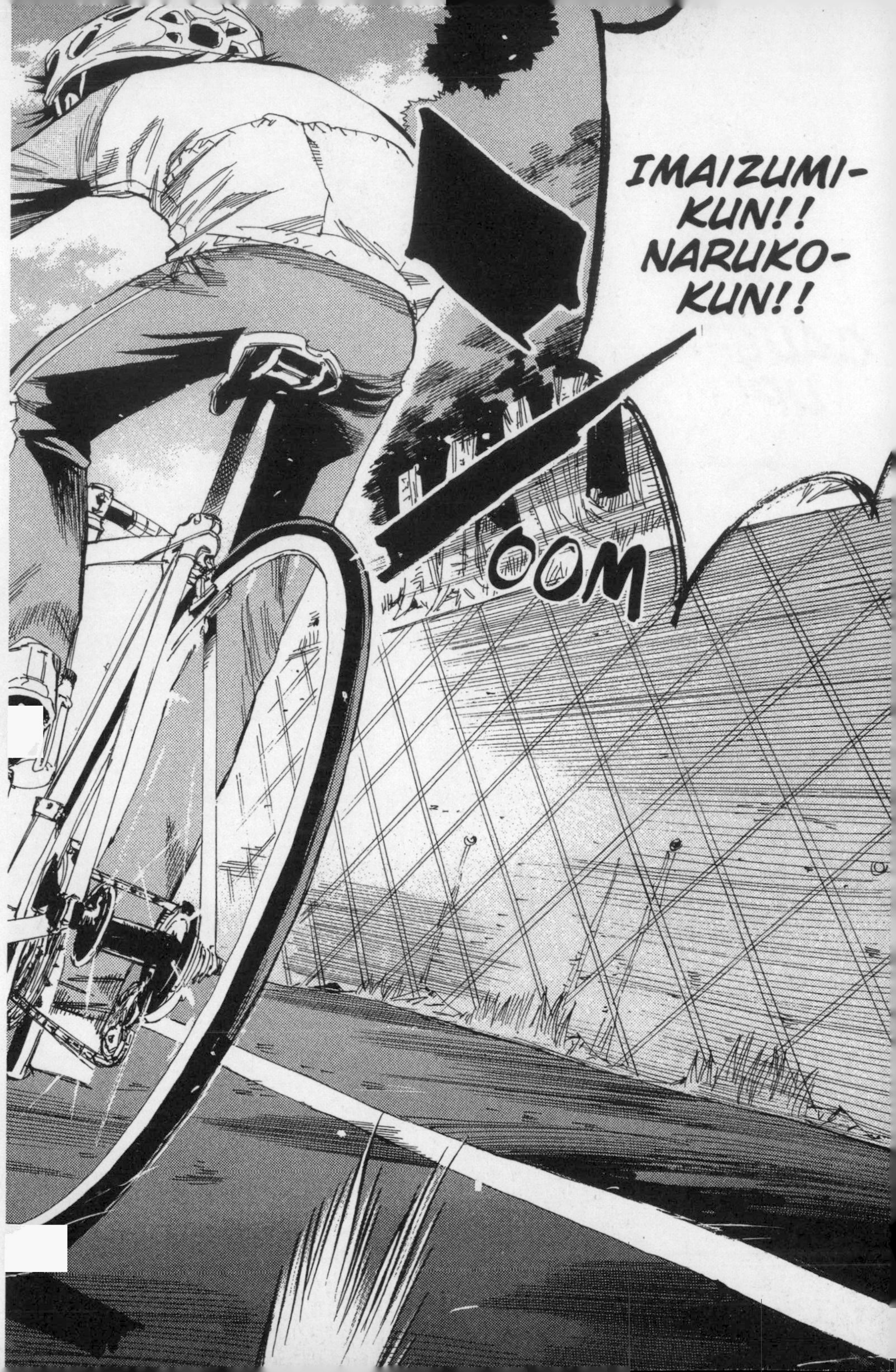
IMAIZUMI-KUN!! NARUKO-KUN!!
OOM

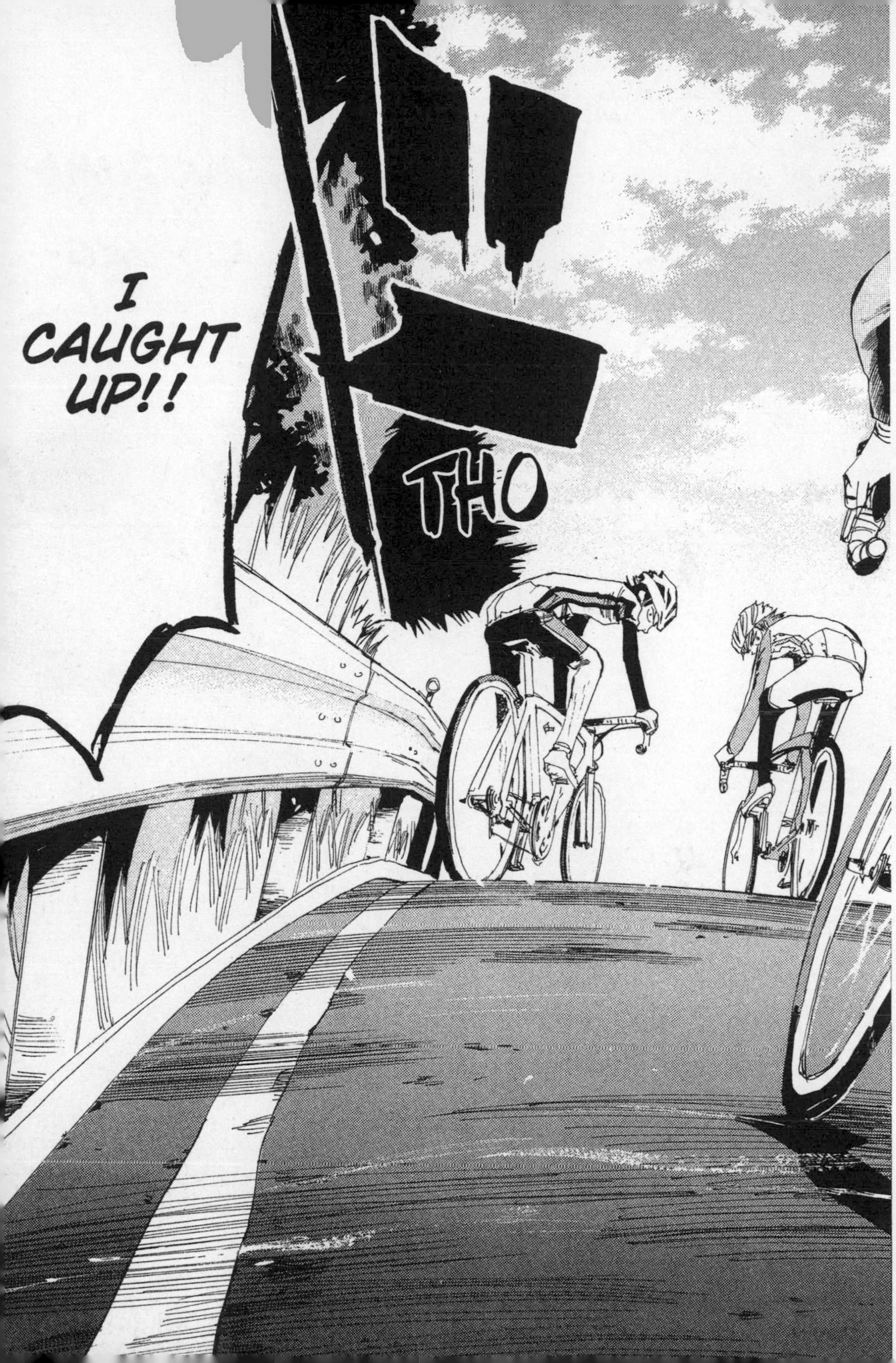
I CAUGHT UP!!
THO

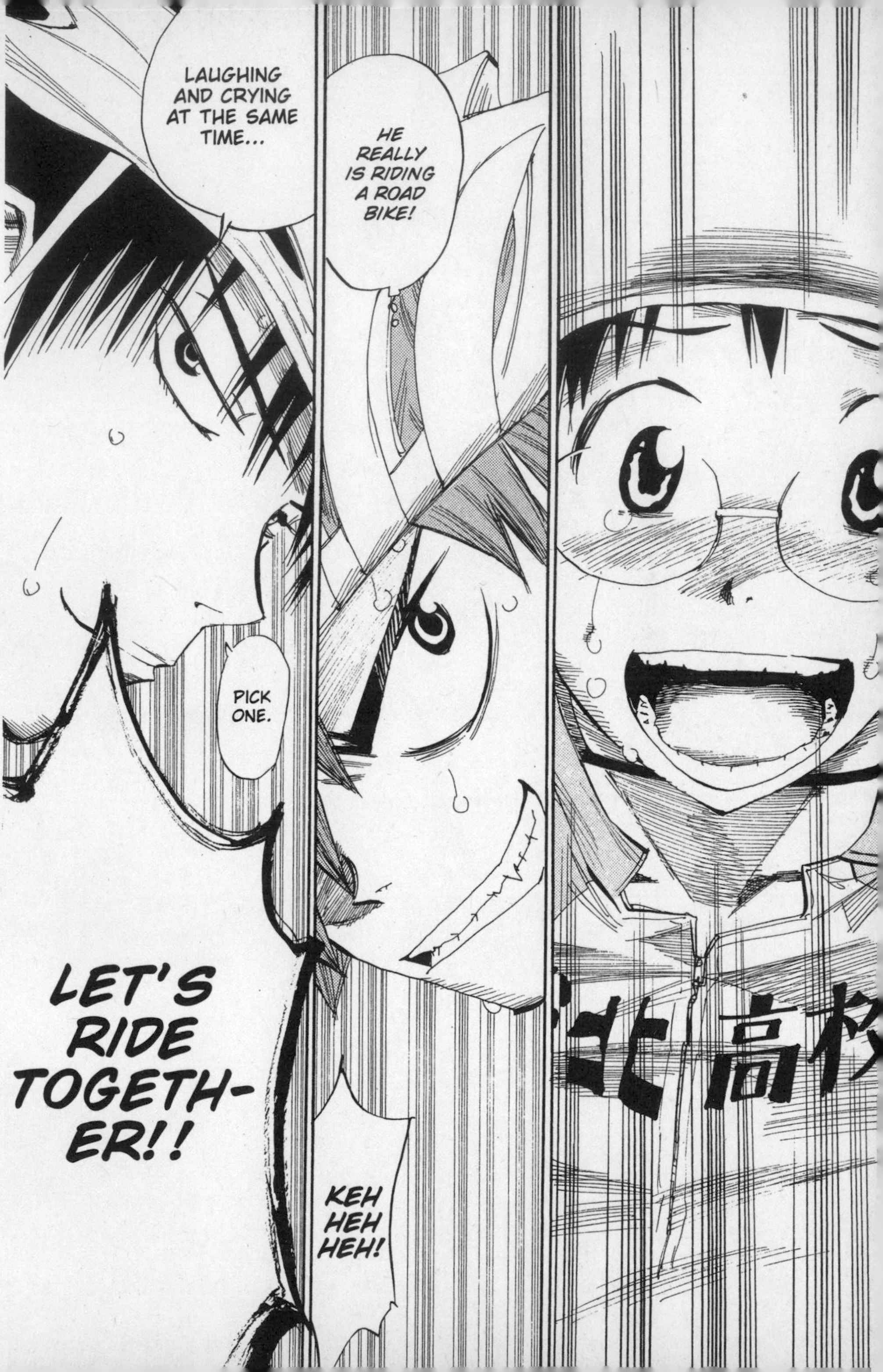
北高校
HE REALLY IS RIDING A ROAD BIKE!
KEH HEH HEH!
LAUGHING AND CRYING AT THE SAME TIME...
PICK ONE.
LET'S RIDE TOGETH-ER!!

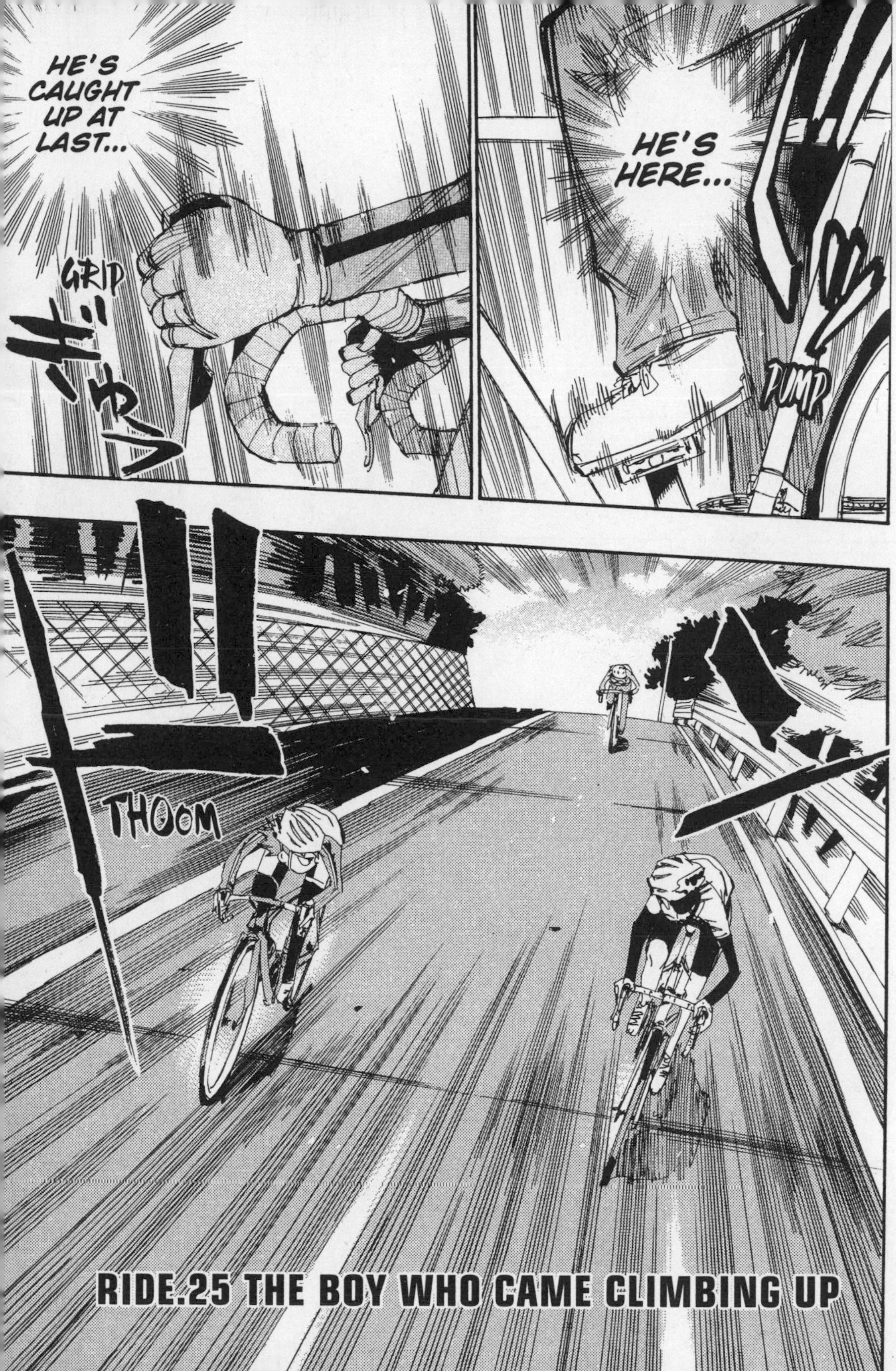
HE'S HERE...
PUMP
HE'S CAUGHT UP AT LAST...
GRIP
ぎゅっ
THOOM
RIDE.25 THE BOY WHO CAME CLIMBING UP

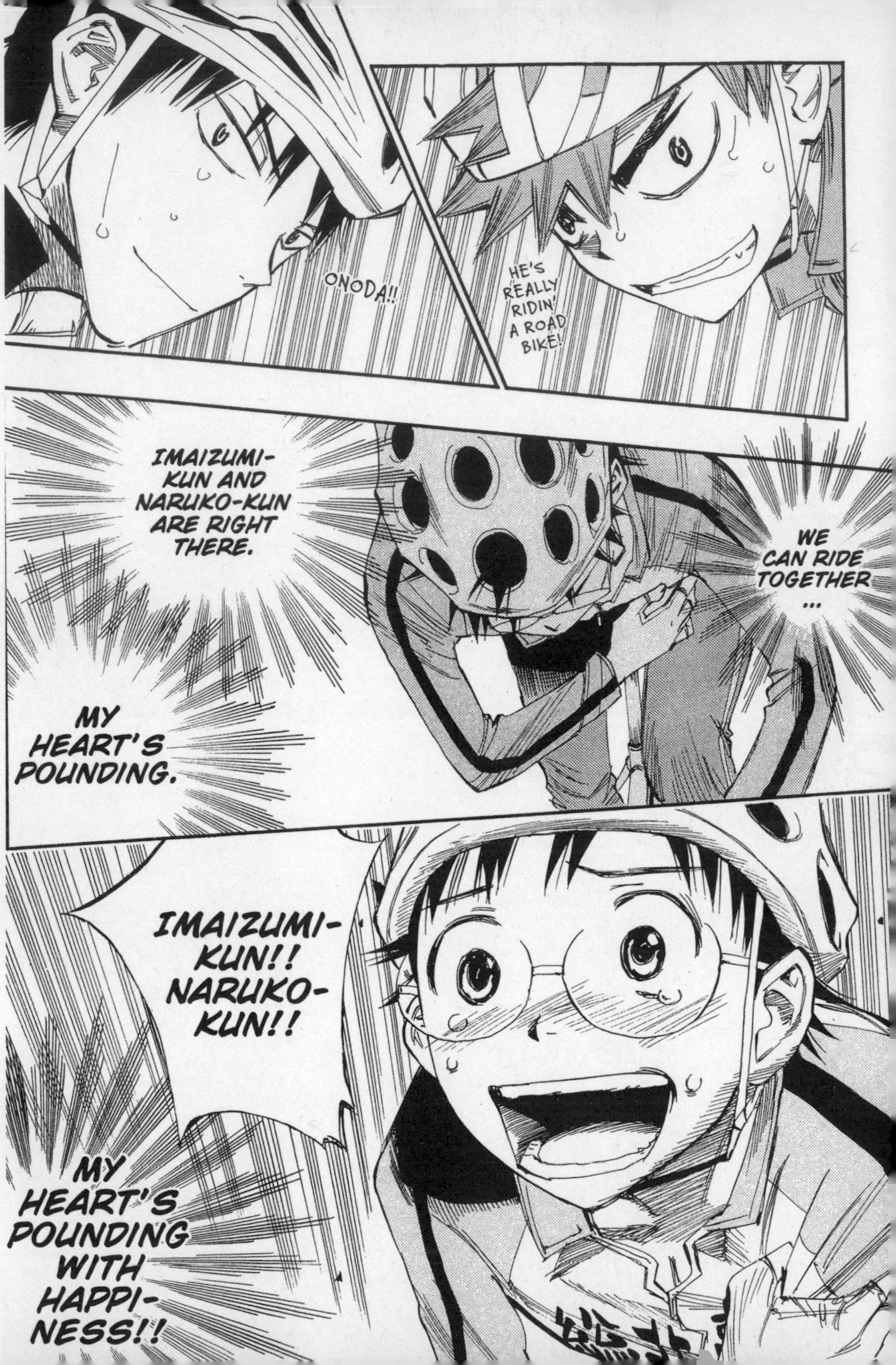
HE'S REALLY RIDIN' A ROAD BIKE!
ONODA!!
IMAIZUMI-KUN AND NARUKO-KUN ARE RIGHT THERE.
WE CAN RIDE TOGETHER...
MY HEART'S POUNDING.
IMAIZUMI-KUN!! NARUKO-KUN!!
MY HEART'S POUNDING WITH HAPPINESS!!

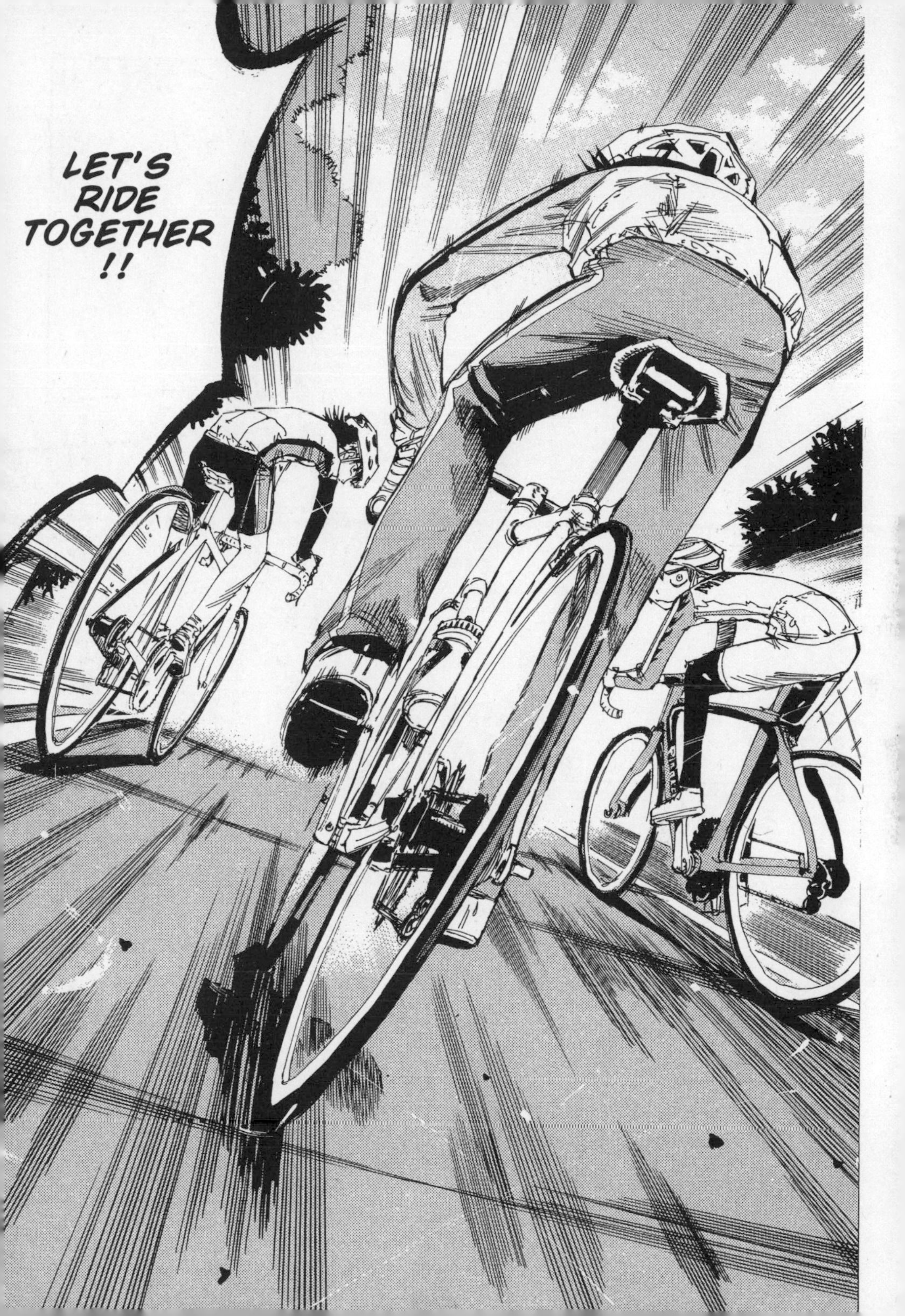
LET'S RIDE TOGETHER !!

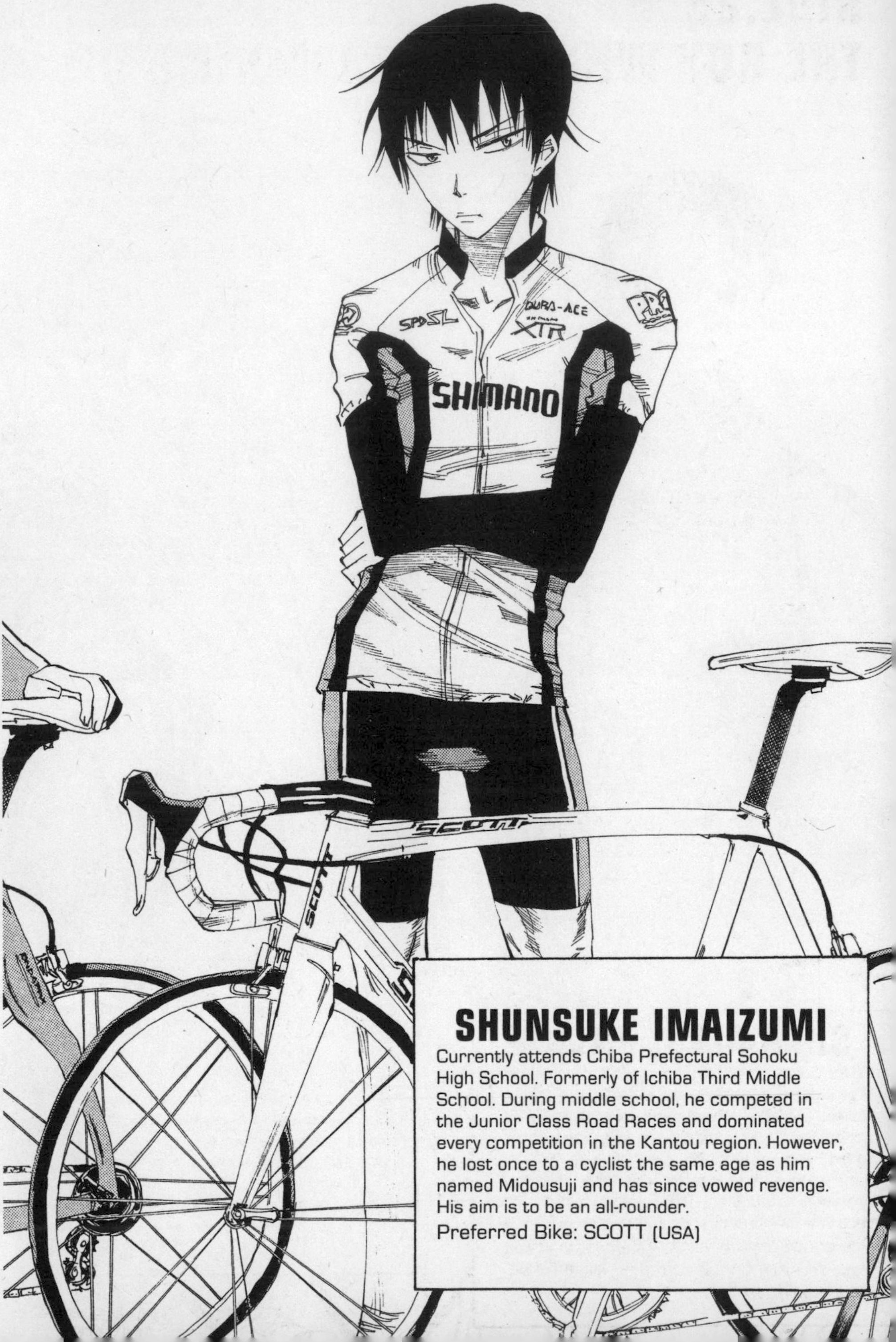
SPD SL
DURA-ACE
XTR
SHIMANO
SCOTT
SCOTT

SHUNSUKE IMAIZUMI

Currently attends Chiba Prefectural Sohoku High School. Formerly of Ichiba Third Middle School. During middle school, he competed in the Junior Class Road Races and dominated every competition in the Kantou region. However, he lost once to a cyclist the same age as him named Midousuji and has since vowed revenge. His aim is to be an all-rounder.

Preferred Bike: SCOTT (USA)

RIDE.25
THE BOY WHO CAME CLIMBING UP

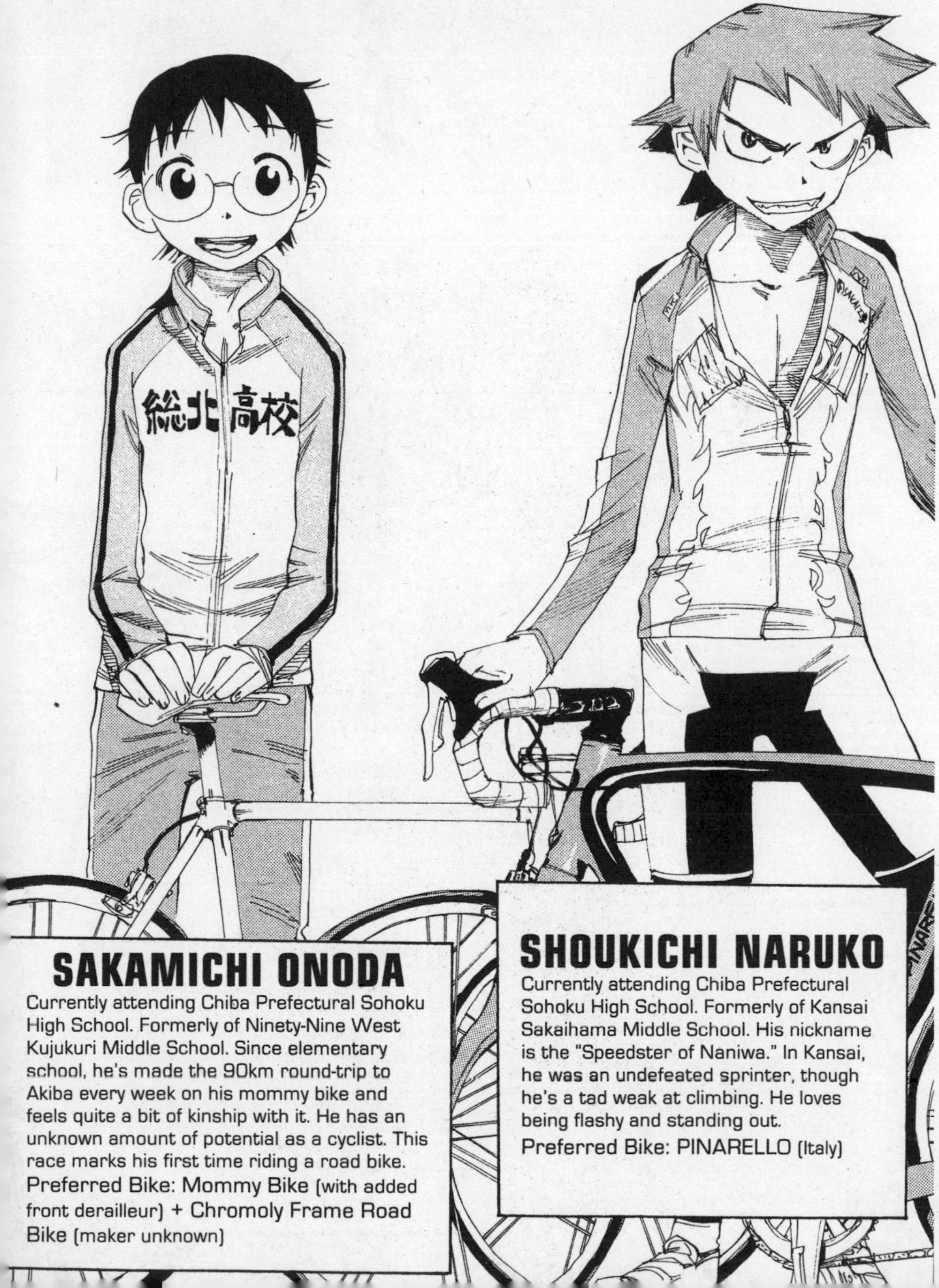
総北高校

SAKAMICHI ONODA

Currently attending Chiba Prefectural Sohoku High School. Formerly of Ninety-Nine West Kujukuri Middle School. Since elementary school, he's made the 90km round-trip to Akiba every week on his mommy bike and feels quite a bit of kinship with it. He has an unknown amount of potential as a cyclist. This race marks his first time riding a road bike.

Preferred Bike: Mommy Bike (with added front derailleur) + Chromoly Frame Road Bike (maker unknown)

SHOUKICHI NARUKO

Currently attending Chiba Prefectural Sohoku High School. Formerly of Kansai Sakaihama Middle School. His nickname is the "Speedster of Naniwa." In Kansai, he was an undefeated sprinter, though he's a tad weak at climbing. He loves being flashy and standing out.

Preferred Bike: PINARELLO (Italy)

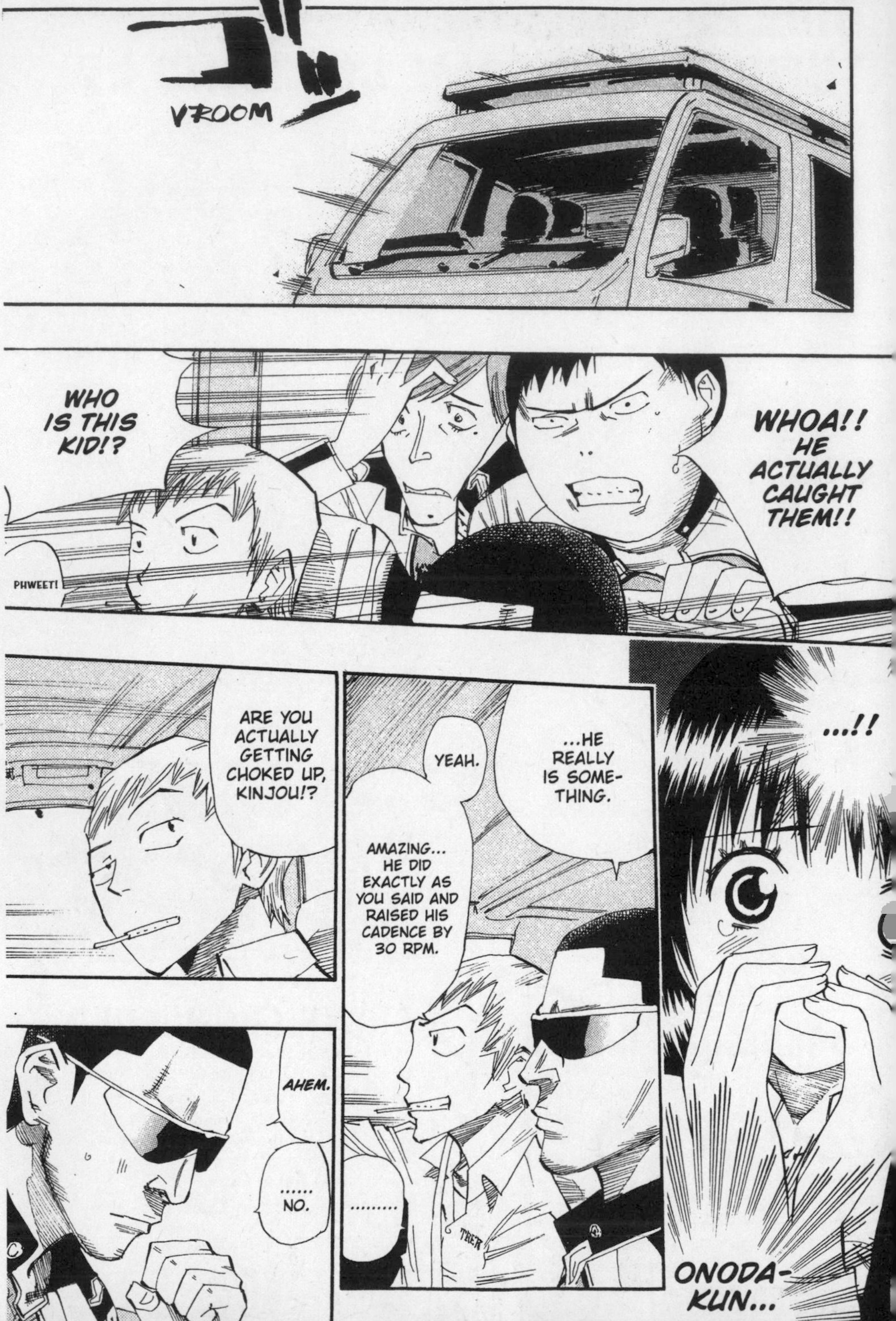
VROOM
WHOA!! HE ACTUALLY CAUGHT THEM!!
WHO IS THIS KID!?
PHWEET!
...!!
ONODA-KUN...
...HE REALLY IS SOME-THING.
YEAH.
AMAZING... HE DID EXACTLY AS YOU SAID AND RAISED HIS CADENCE BY 30 RPM.
ARE YOU ACTUALLY GETTING CHOKED UP, KINJOU!?
....
AHEM.
...... NO.

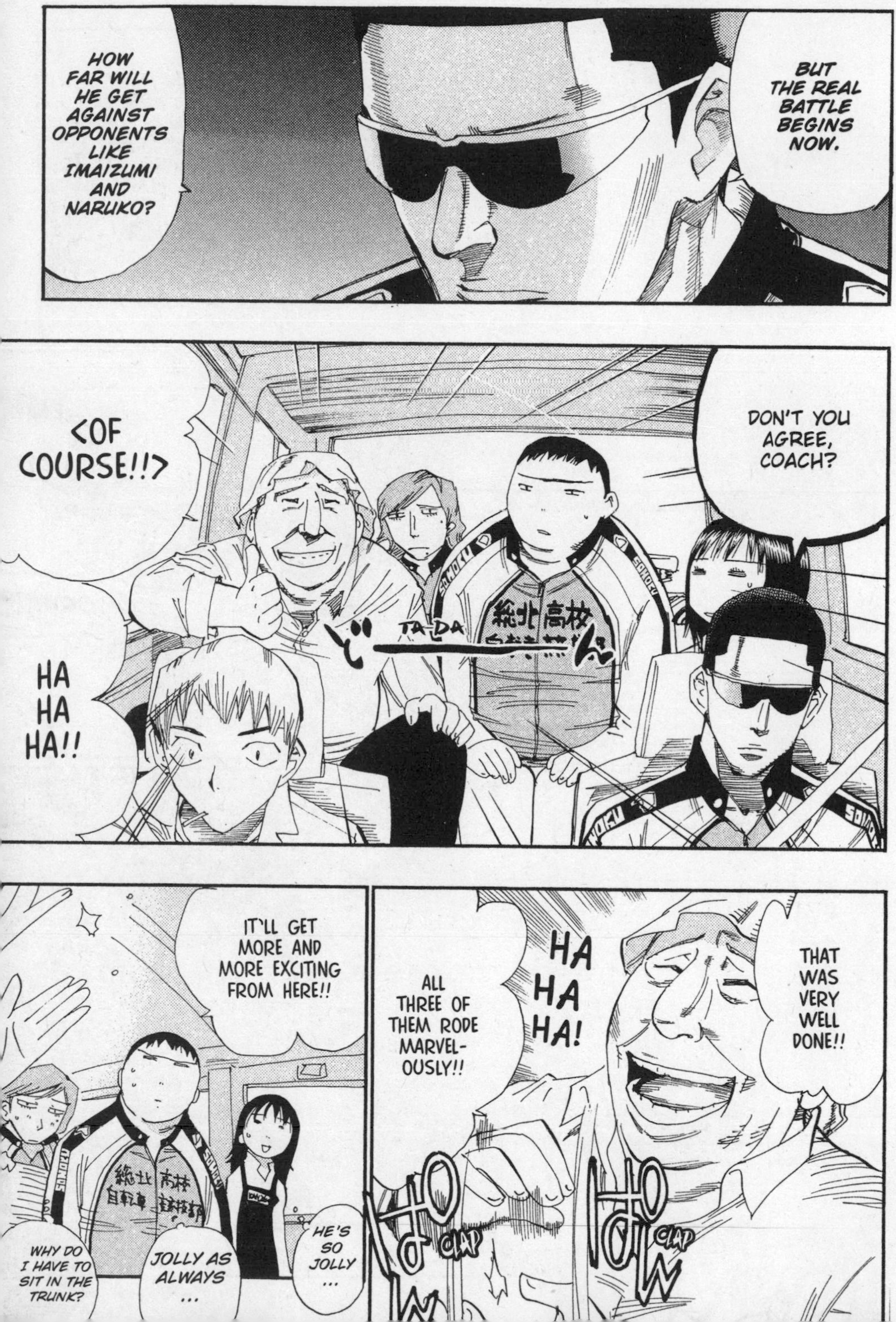
BUT THE REAL BATTLE BEGINS NOW.
HOW FAR WILL HE GET AGAINST OPPONENTS LIKE IMAIZUMI AND NARUKO?
DON'T YOU AGREE, COACH?
TA-DA
<OF COURSE!!>
HA HA HA!!
THAT WAS VERY WELL DONE!!
HA HA HA!
ALL THREE OF THEM RODE MARVEL-OUSLY!!
CLAP
CLAP
IT'LL GET MORE AND MORE EXCITING FROM HERE!!
HE'S SO JOLLY ...
JOLLY AS ALWAYS ...
WHY DO I HAVE TO SIT IN THE TRUNK?

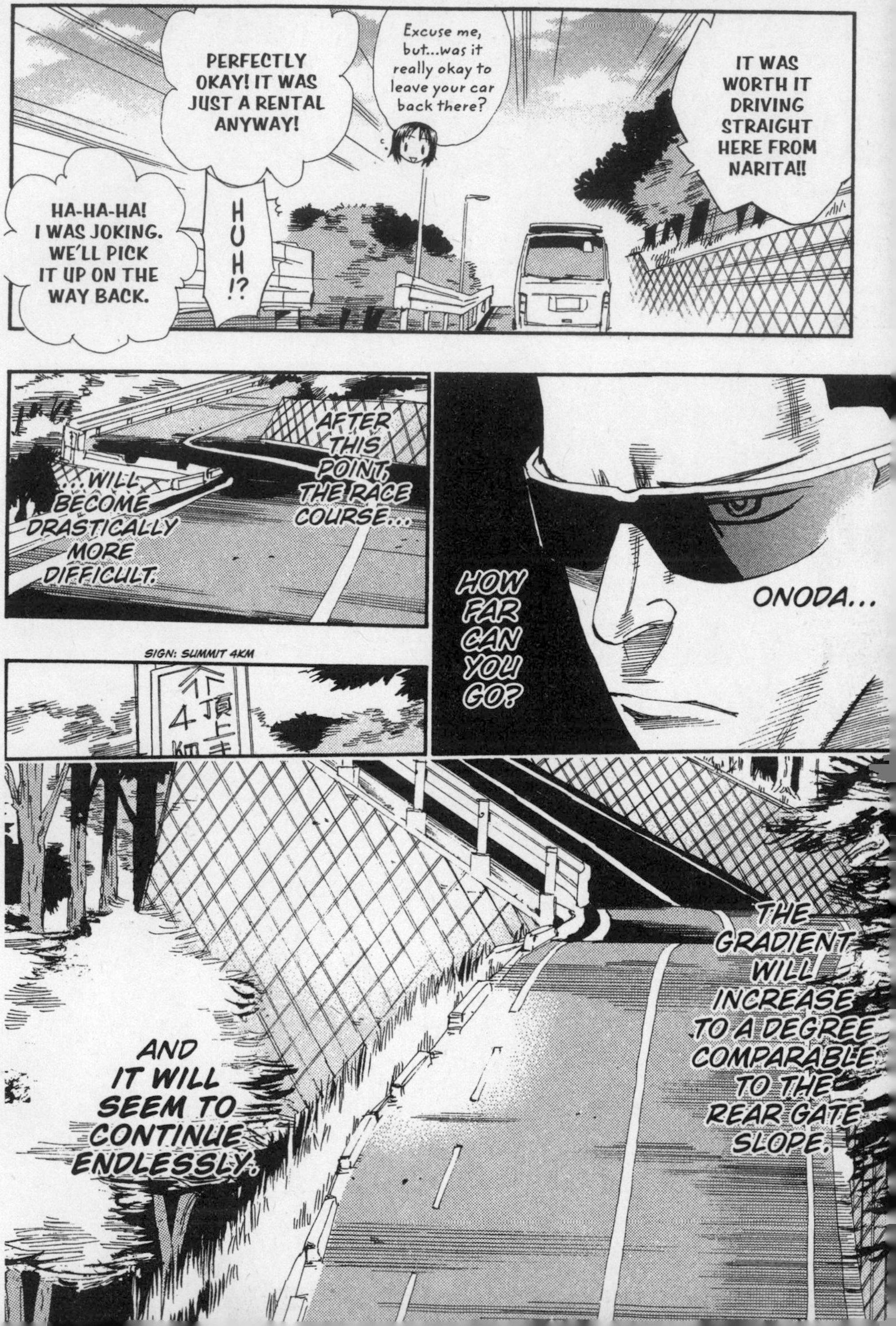
IT WAS WORTH IT DRIVING STRAIGHT HERE FROM NARITA!!
Excuse me, but...was it really okay to leave your car back there?
PERFECTLY OKAY! IT WAS JUST A RENTAL ANYWAY!
HUH!?
HA-HA-HA! I WAS JOKING. WE'LL PICK IT UP ON THE WAY BACK.
ONODA...
HOW FAR CAN YOU GO?
AFTER THIS POINT, THE RACE COURSE...
...WILL BECOME DRASTICALLY MORE DIFFICULT.
SIGN: SUMMIT 4KM
THE GRADIENT WILL INCREASE TO A DEGREE COMPARABLE TO THE REAR GATE SLOPE.
AND IT WILL SEEM TO CONTINUE ENDLESSLY.

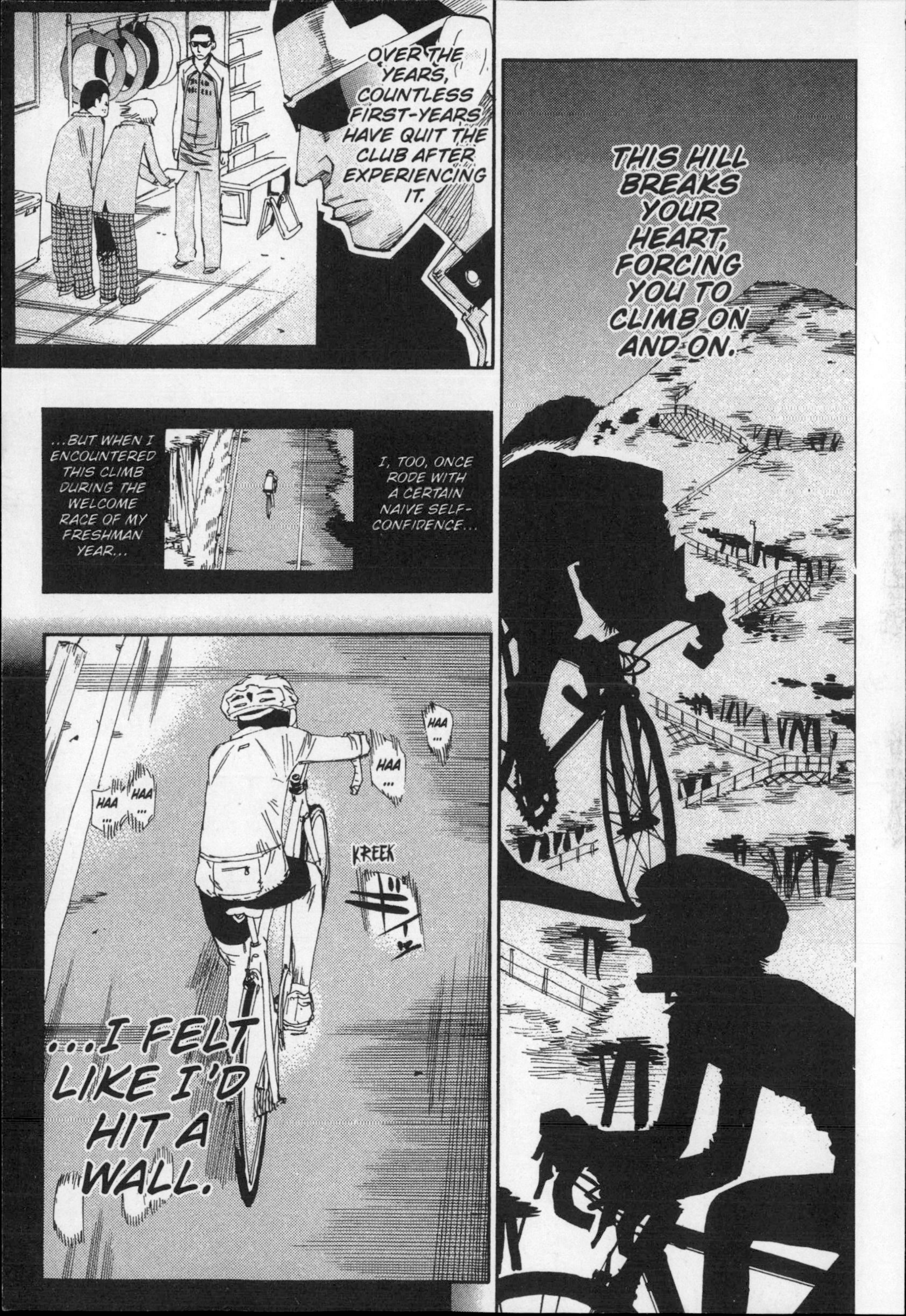
THIS HILL BREAKS YOUR HEART, FORCING YOU TO CLIMB ON AND ON.
OVER THE YEARS, COUNTLESS FIRST-YEARS HAVE QUIT THE CLUB AFTER EXPERIENCING IT.
I, TOO, ONCE RODE WITH A CERTAIN NAIVE SELF-CONFIDENCE...
...BUT WHEN I ENCOUNTERED THIS CLIMB DURING THE WELCOME RACE OF MY FRESHMAN YEAR...
HAA...
HAA...
HAA...
HAA...
KREEK
...I FELT LIKE I'D HIT A WALL.

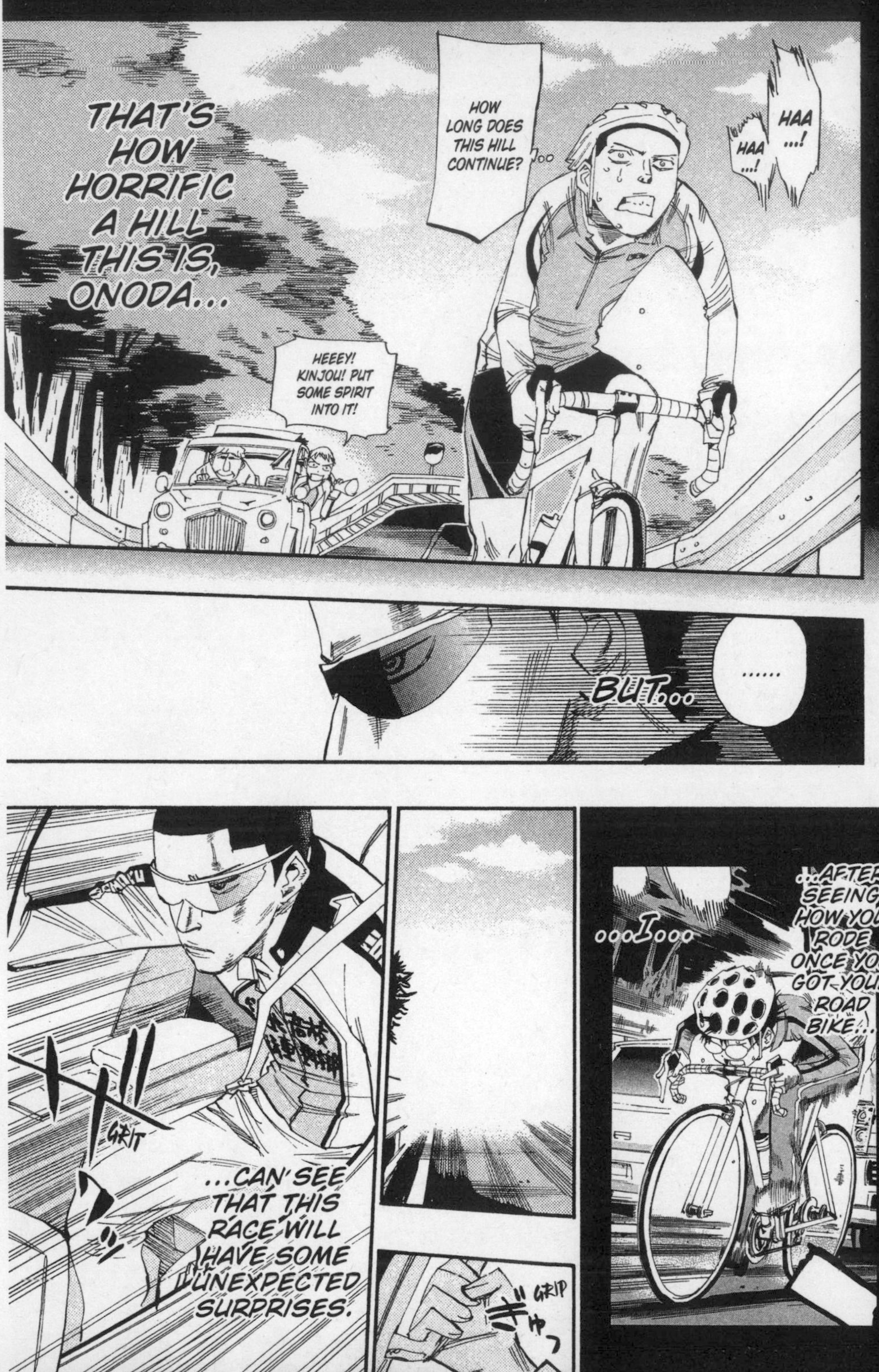
HAA ...!
HAA ...!
HOW LONG DOES THIS HILL CONTINUE?
THAT'S HOW HORRIFIC A HILL THIS IS, ONODA...
HEEEY! KINJOU! PUT SOME SPIRIT INTO IT!
......
BUT...
...AFTER SEEING HOW YOU RODE ONCE YOU GOT YOUR ROAD BIKE...
...I...
GRIP
GRIT
...CAN SEE THAT THIS RACE WILL HAVE SOME UNEXPECTED SURPRISES.

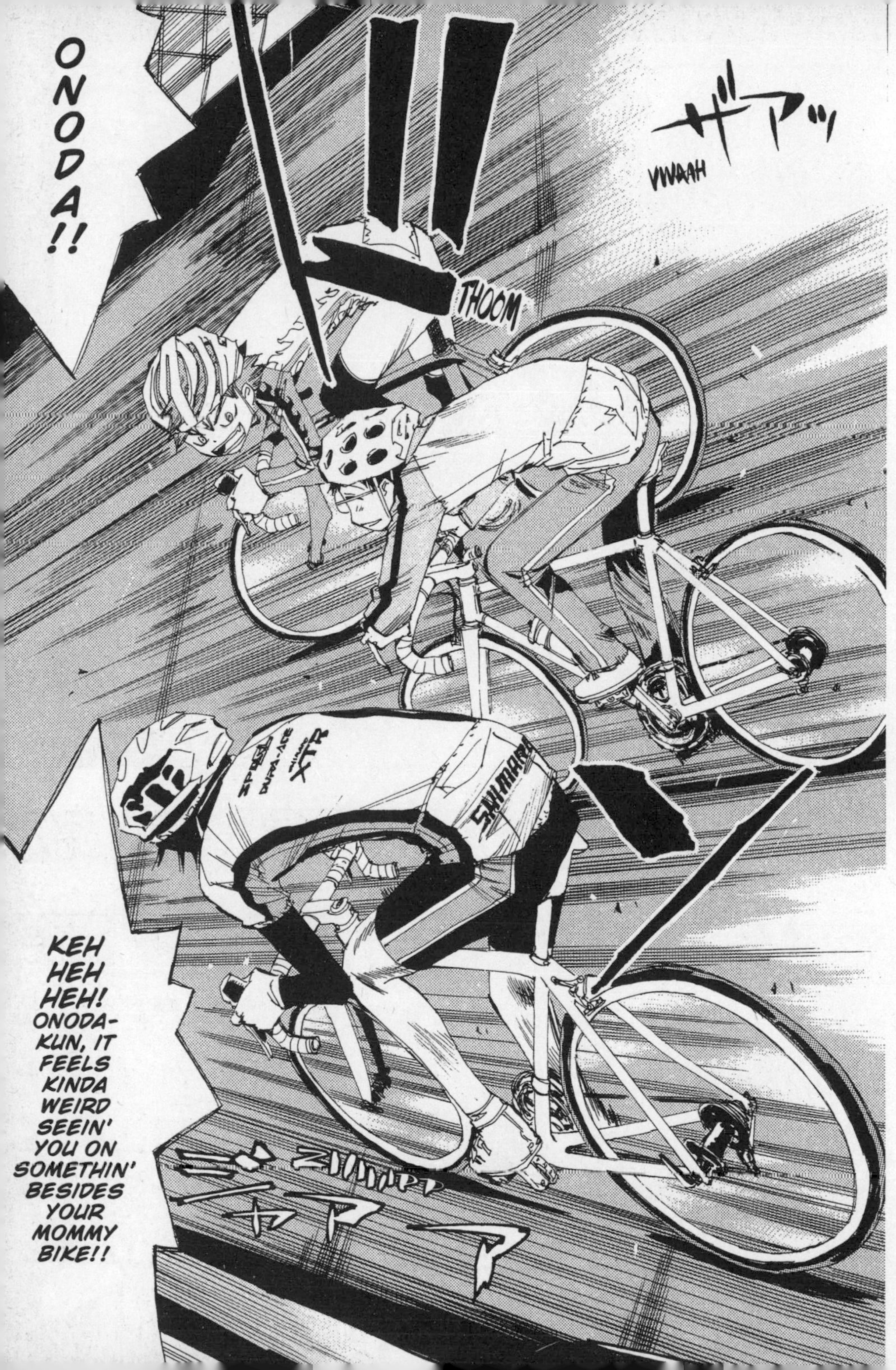
ザアッ
VWAAH
ONODA!!
THOOM
KEH HEH HEH! ONODA-KUN, IT FEELS KINDA WEIRD SEEIN' YOU ON SOMETHIN' BESIDES YOUR MOMMY BIKE!!
ジャアーア

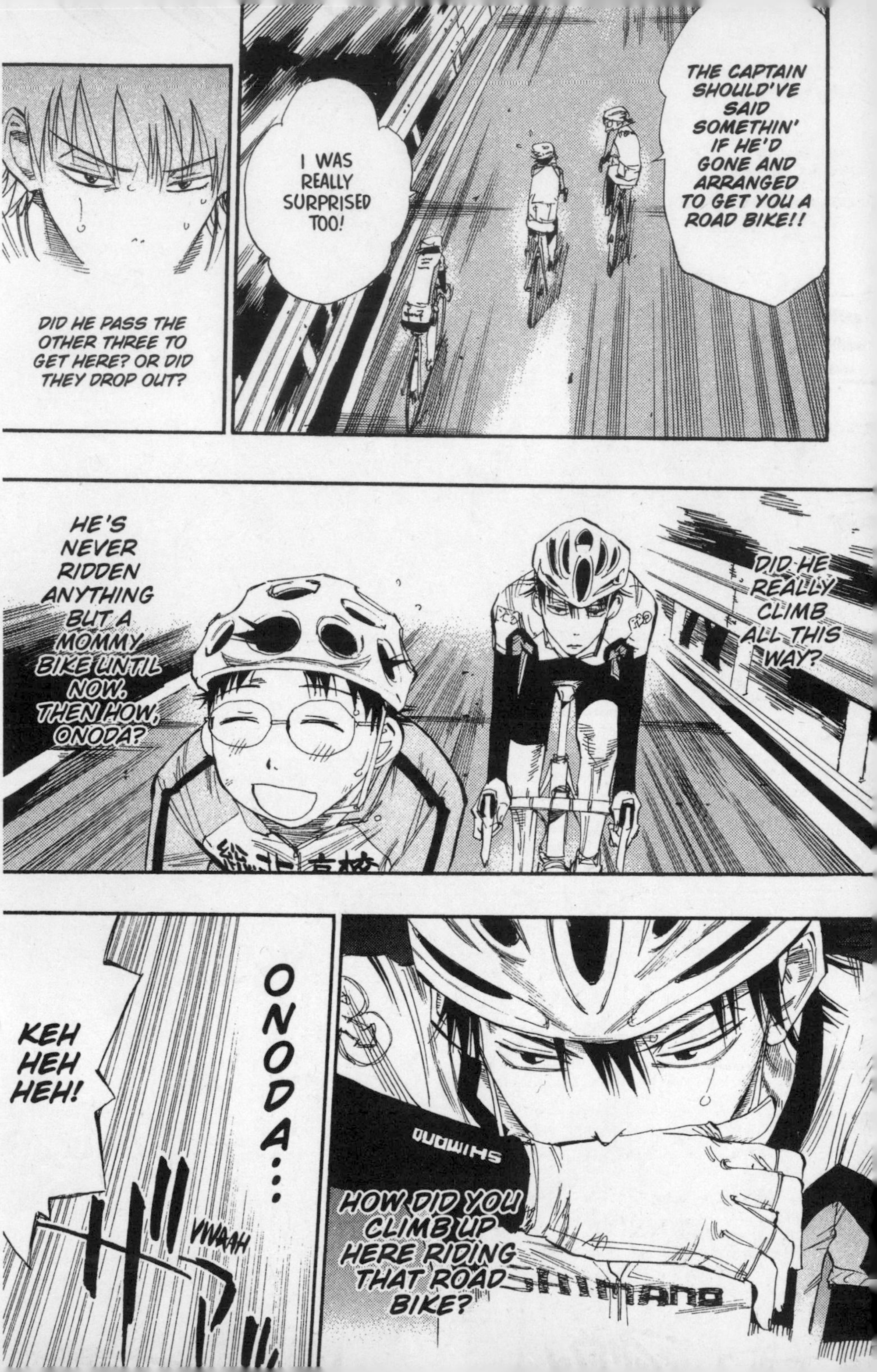
THE CAPTAIN SHOULD'VE SAID SOMETHIN' IF HE'D GONE AND ARRANGED TO GET YOU A ROAD BIKE!!
I WAS REALLY SURPRISED TOO!
DID HE PASS THE OTHER THREE TO GET HERE? OR DID THEY DROP OUT?
DID HE REALLY CLIMB ALL THIS WAY?
HE'S NEVER RIDDEN ANYTHING BUT A MOMMY BIKE UNTIL NOW. THEN HOW, ONODA?
HOW DID YOU CLIMB UP HERE RIDING THAT ROAD BIKE?
ONODA...
KEH HEH HEH!
VWAAH

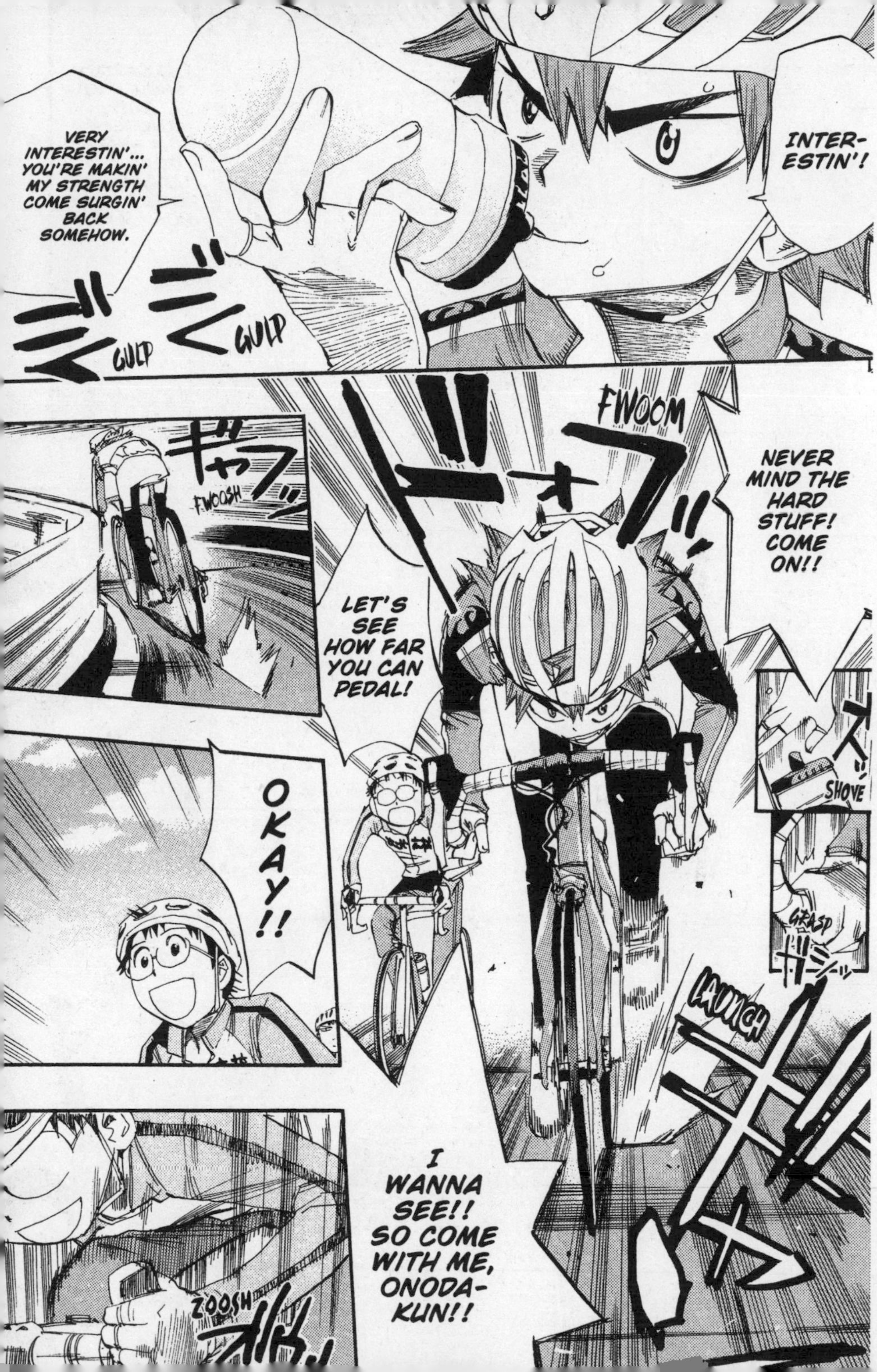
INTER-ESTIN'!
VERY INTERESTIN'... YOU'RE MAKIN' MY STRENGTH COME SURGIN' BACK SOMEHOW.
GULP
GULP
FWOOM
NEVER MIND THE HARD STUFF! COME ON!!
LET'S SEE HOW FAR YOU CAN PEDAL!
SHOVE
GRASP
FWOOSH
OKAY!!
LAUNCH
I WANNA SEE!! SO COME WITH ME, ONODA-KUN!!
ZOOSH

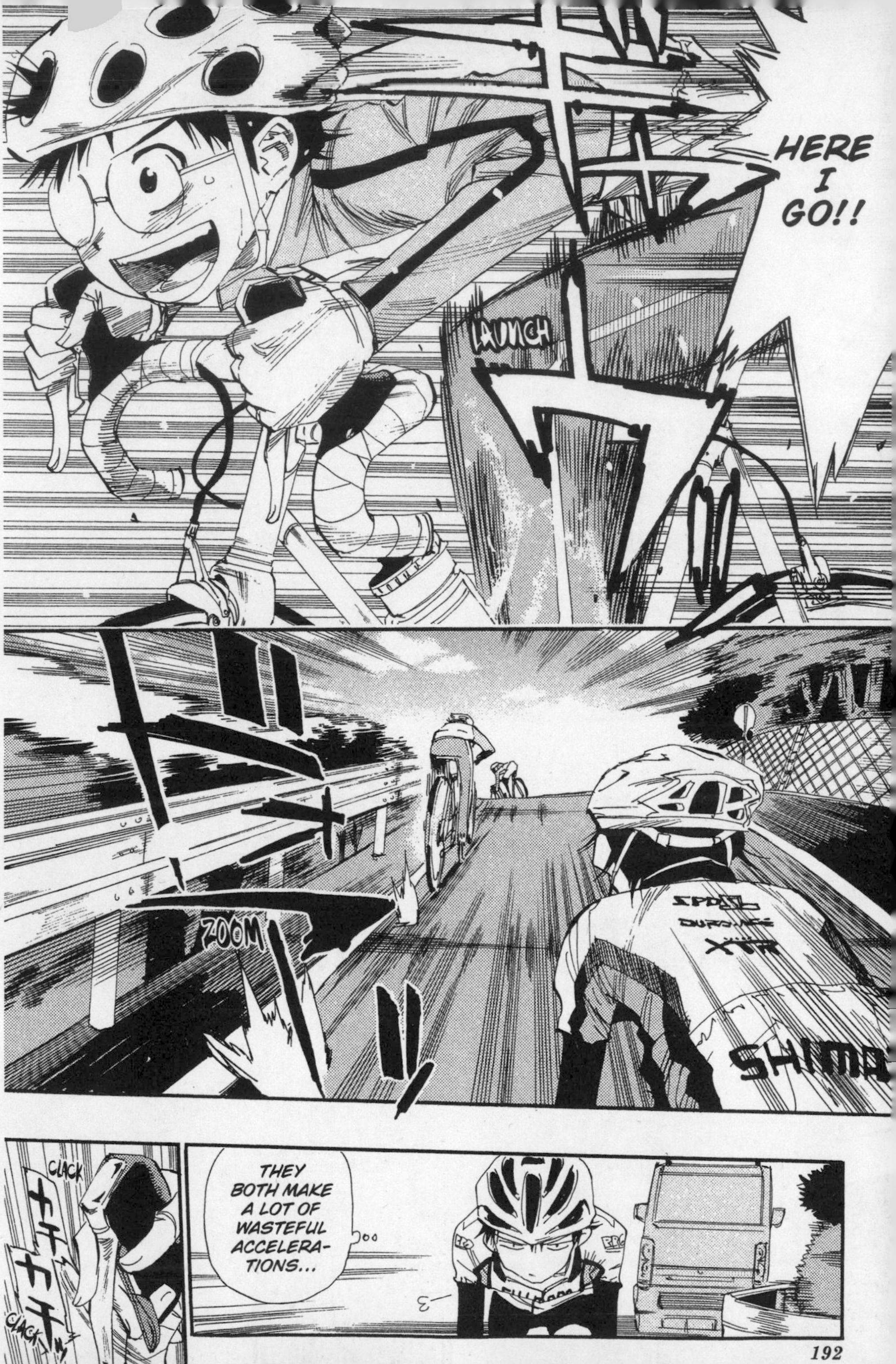
HERE I GO!!
LAUNCH
ZOOM
THEY BOTH MAKE A LOT OF WASTEFUL ACCELERA-TIONS...
CLACK
CLACK

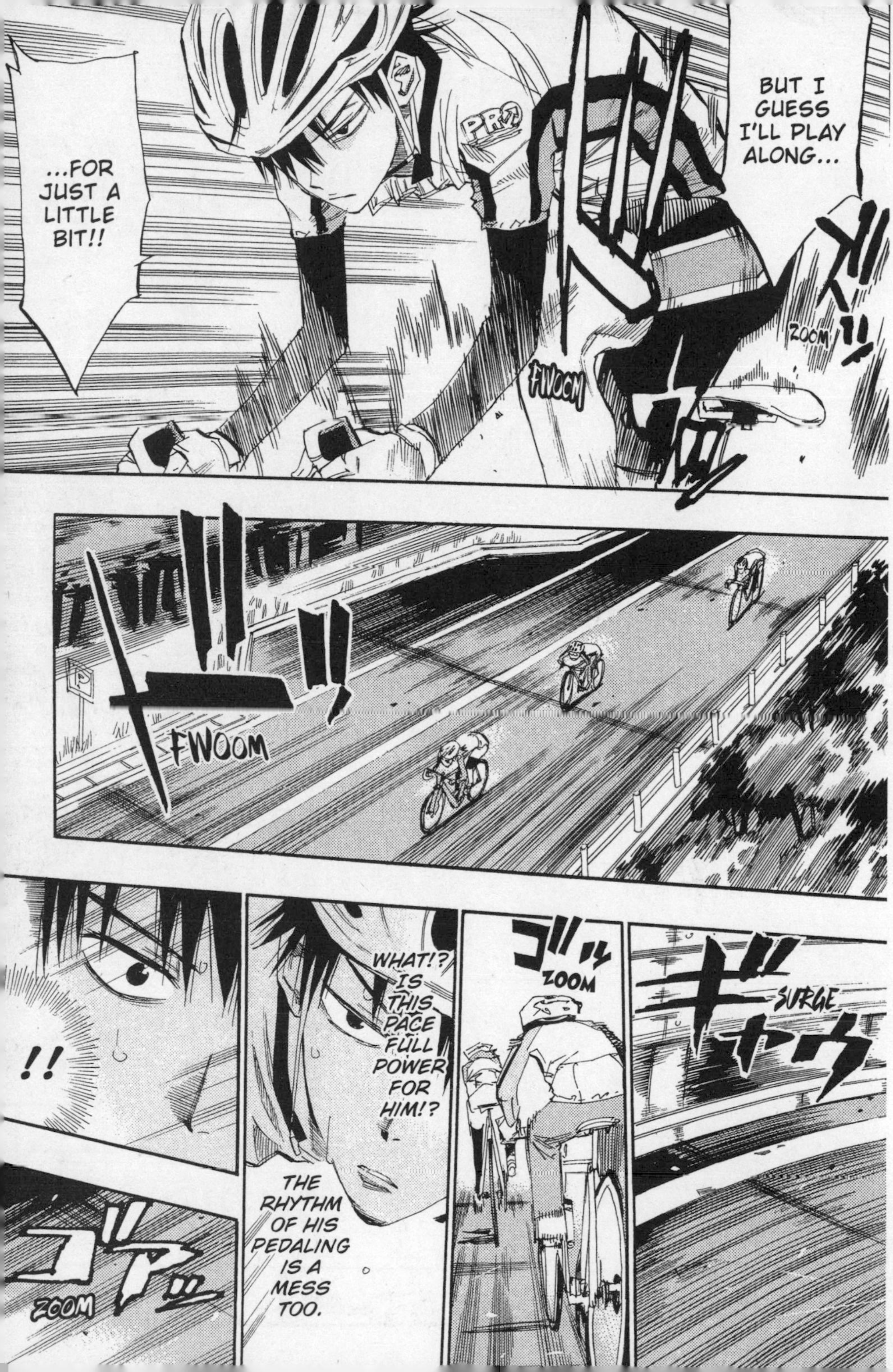
BUT I GUESS I'LL PLAY ALONG...
...FOR JUST A LITTLE BIT!!
ZOOM
FWOOM
FWOOM
SURGE
ZOOM
WHAT!? IS THIS PACE FULL POWER FOR HIM!?
THE RHYTHM OF HIS PEDALING IS A MESS TOO.
!!
ZOOM

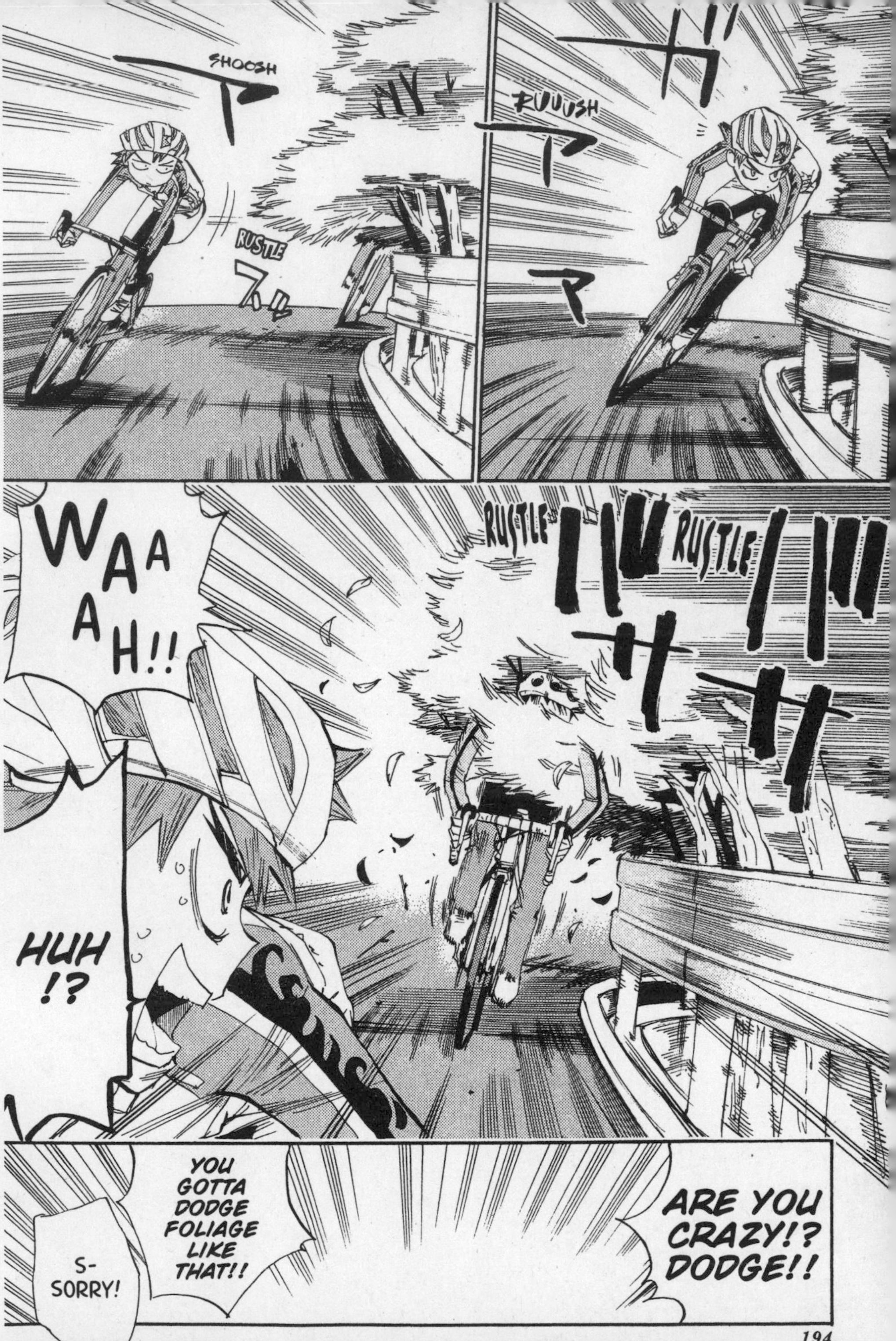
RUUUSH
SHOOSH
RUSTLE
RUSTLE
RUSTLE
WAAAAH!!
HUH!?
ARE YOU CRAZY!? DODGE!!
YOU GOTTA DODGE FOLIAGE LIKE THAT!!
S-SORRY!

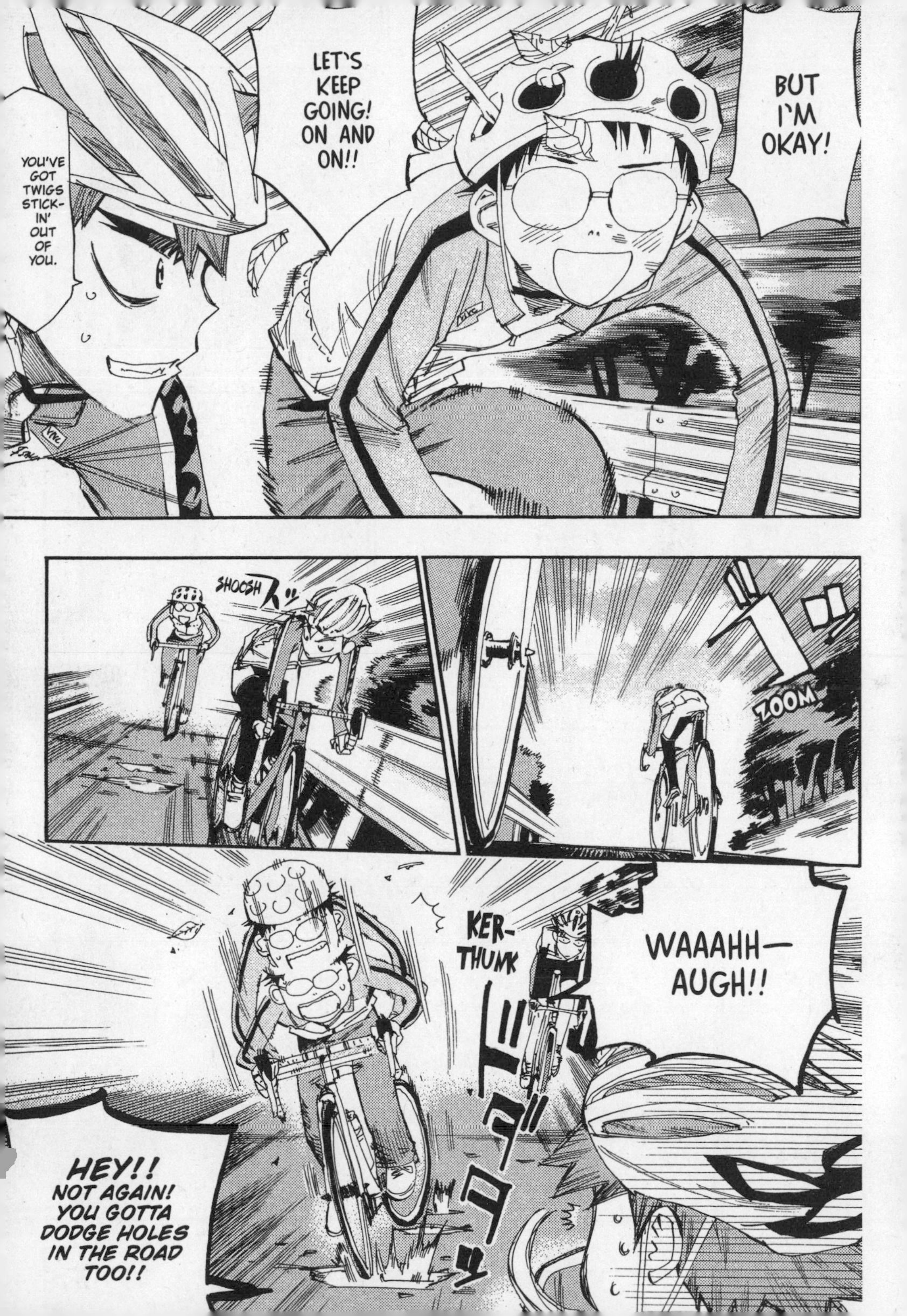
BUT I'M OKAY!
LET'S KEEP GOING! ON AND ON!!
YOU'VE GOT TWIGS STICK-IN' OUT OF YOU.
ZOOM
SHOOSH
WAAAHH—AUGH!!
KER-THUMK
HEY!! NOT AGAIN! YOU GOTTA DODGE HOLES IN THE ROAD TOO!!

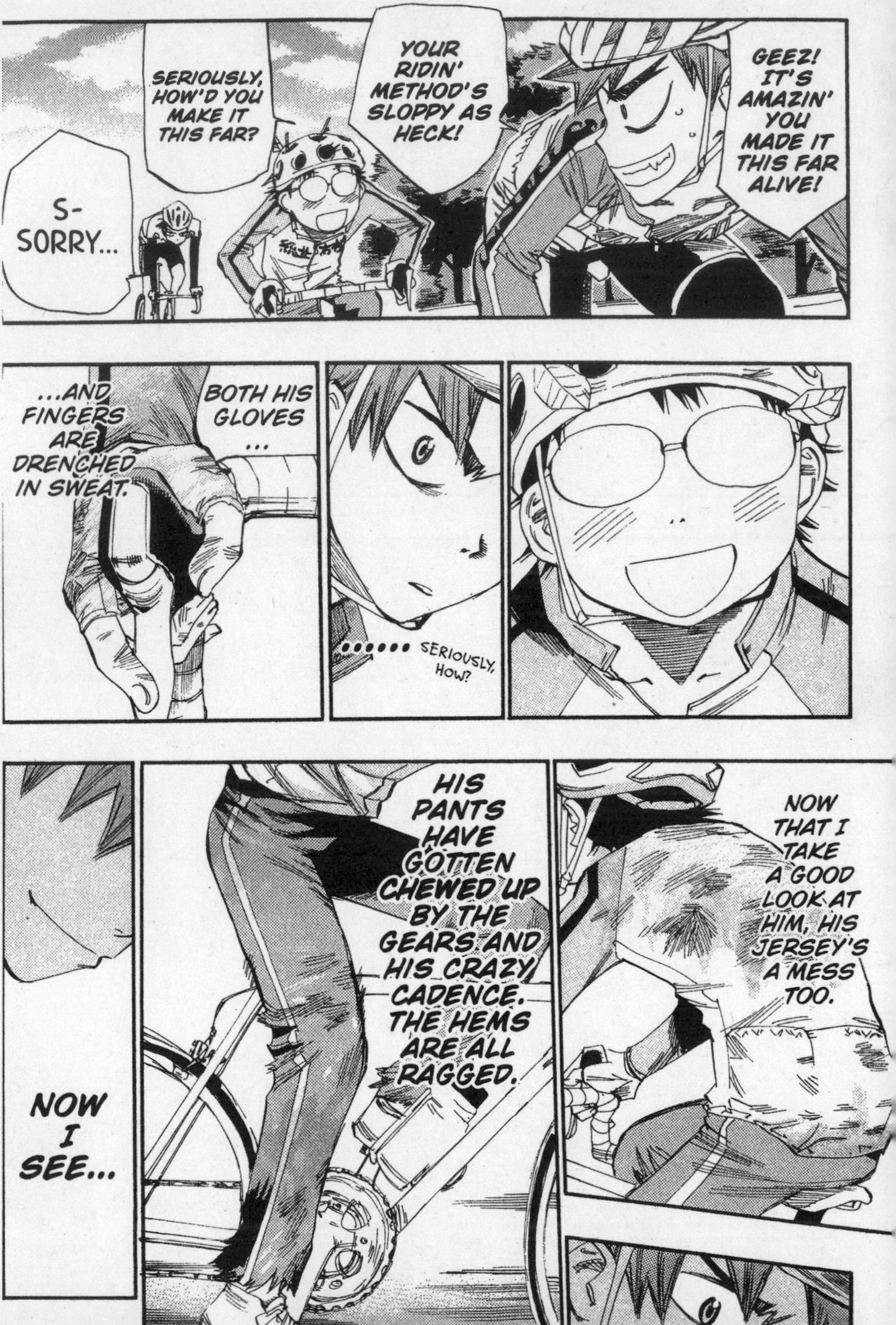
GEEZ! IT'S AMAZIN' YOU MADE IT THIS FAR ALIVE!
YOUR RIDIN' METHOD'S SLOPPY AS HECK!
SERIOUSLY, HOW'D YOU MAKE IT THIS FAR?
S-SORRY...
......SERIOUSLY, HOW?
BOTH HIS GLOVES ...
...AND FINGERS ARE DRENCHED IN SWEAT.
NOW THAT I TAKE A GOOD LOOK AT HIM, HIS JERSEY'S A MESS TOO.
HIS PANTS HAVE GOTTEN CHEWED UP BY THE GEARS AND HIS CRAZY CADENCE. THE HEMS ARE ALL RAGGED.
NOW I SEE...

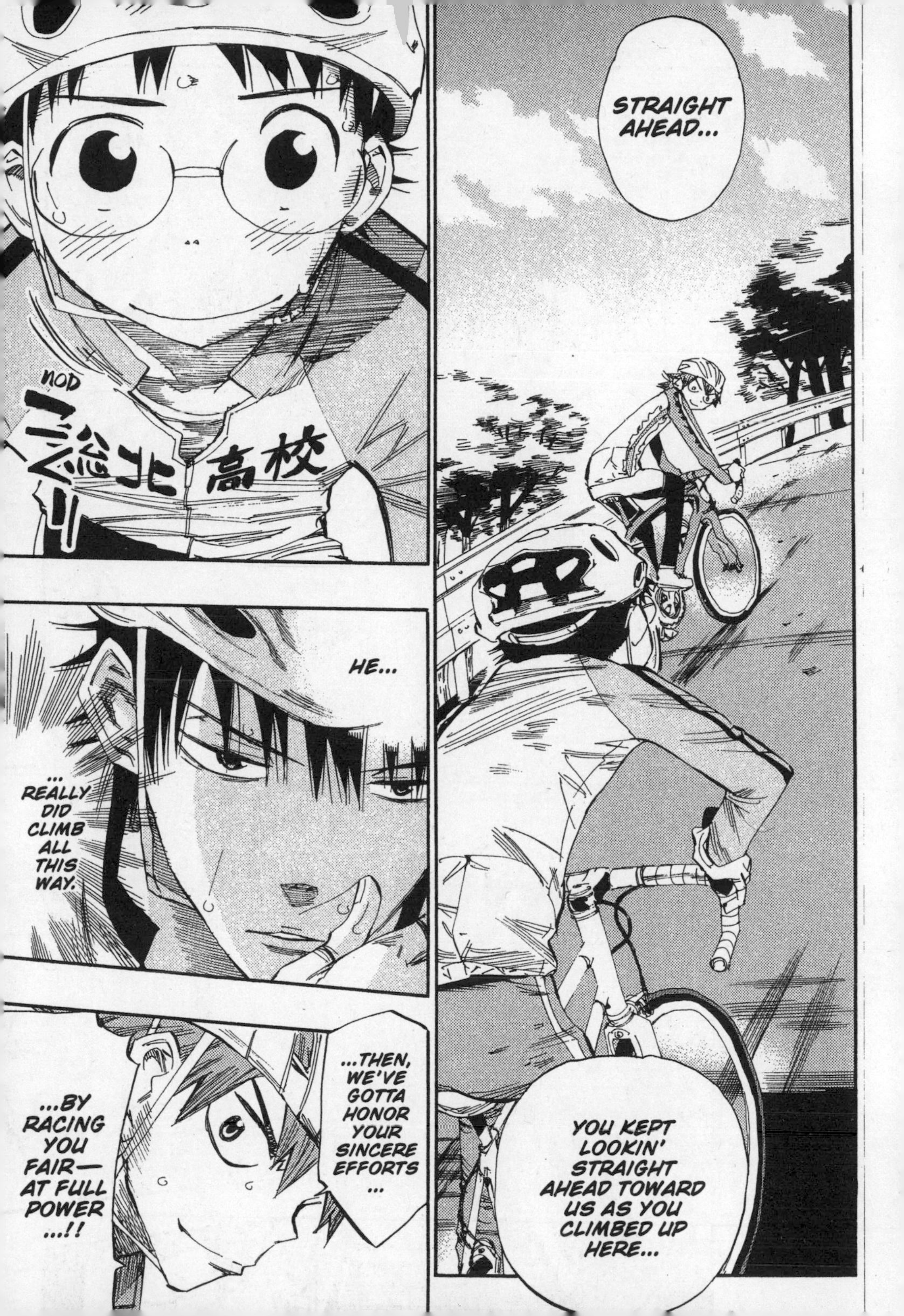
STRAIGHT AHEAD...
YOU KEPT LOOKIN' STRAIGHT AHEAD TOWARD US AS YOU CLIMBED UP HERE...
NOD
総北高校
HE...
...REALLY DID CLIMB ALL THIS WAY.
...THEN, WE'VE GOTTA HONOR YOUR SINCERE EFFORTS...
...BY RACING YOU FAIR—AT FULL POWER...!!

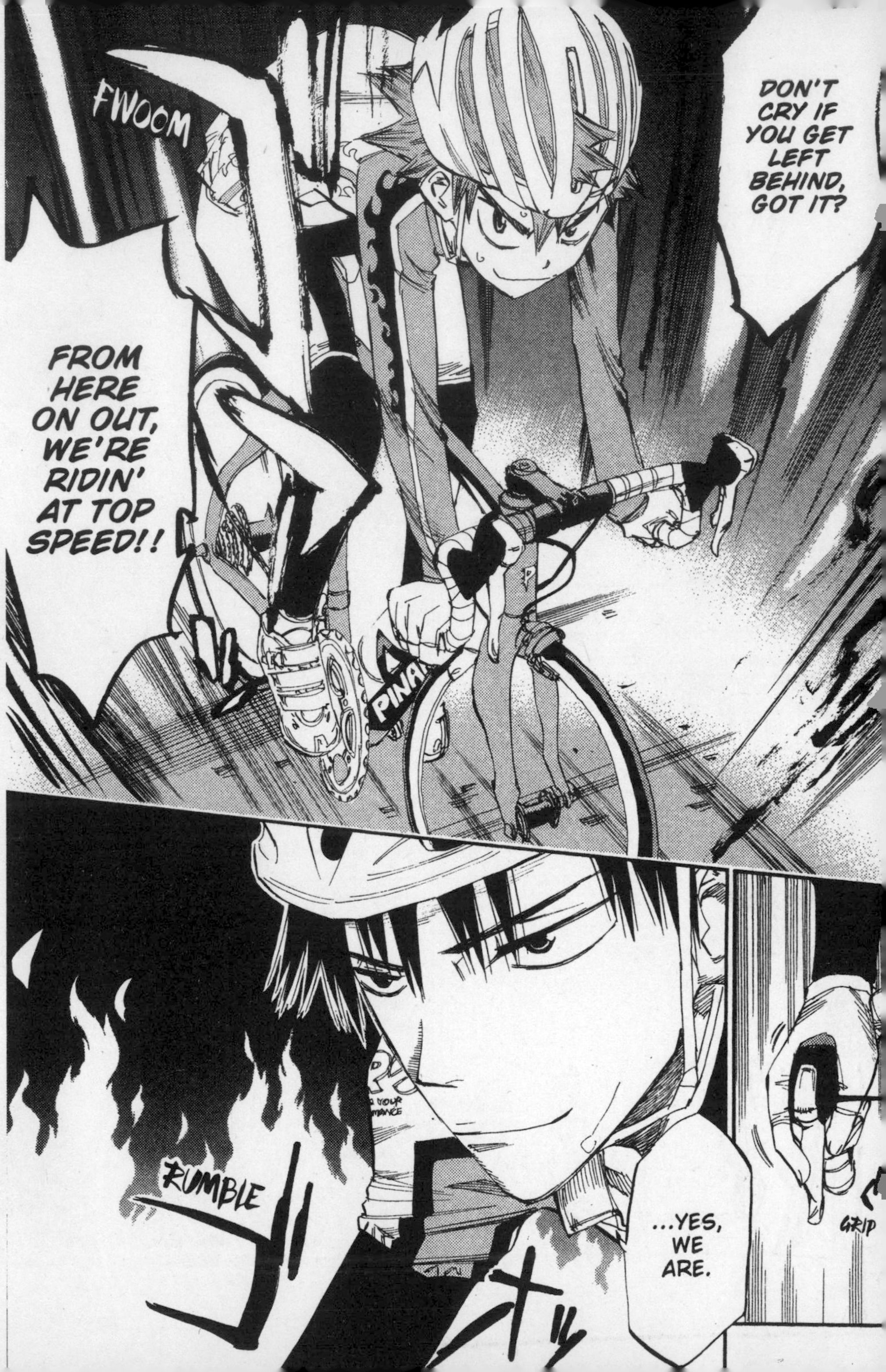
DON'T CRY IF YOU GET LEFT BEHIND, GOT IT?
FWOOM
FROM HERE ON OUT, WE'RE RIDIN' AT TOP SPEED!!
GRIP
...YES, WE ARE.
RUMBLE

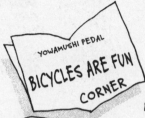

SAKAMICHI'S BIKE
YOWAMUSHI PEDAL
BICYCLES ARE FUN CORNER
LET'S EXPLAIN SOME STUFF
ABOUT SAKAMICHI-KUN'S FRONT DERAILLEUR
(FRONT DERAILLEUR = GEAR SHIFTER)
WA TA NA BE
SAKAMICHI-KUN'S BIKE HAS A DOUBLE CHAINRING AND A FRONT DERAILLEUR THAT WERE ADDED FOR HIM BY THE KANZAKI BIKE SHOP.
IT'S SCREWED TO THE FRAME LIKE SO.
THIS IS THE FRONT DERAILLEUR.
IT MOVES THE CHAIN LEFT AND RIGHT SO THAT IT SWITCHES BETWEEN THE INNER AND OUTER CHAINRINGS.
TWO GEAR CHAINRINGS, AS USED BY ROAD BIKES.
THOUGH I DREW IT THIS WAY IN THE MANGA, YOU CAN'T ACTUALLY SHIFT GEARS WITH THIS SETUP.
IF YOU TRIED TO SHIFT FROM THE INNER SMALL TO OUTER LARGE CHAINRING HERE...
...THE CHAIN WOULDN'T BE LONG ENOUGH TO ACCOMMODATE THE OUTER CHAINRING, AND YOU COULDN'T SWITCH GEARS.
THAT'S WHY, IN REALITY, YOU'D HAVE THIS:
THIS
THIS IS CALLED A "TENSIONER" AND IT ADJUSTS THE TENSION OF THE CHAIN FOR US.
OF COURSE, IN ROAD BIKES AND MTBs, TENSION PULLEYS COME BUILT-IN AS PART OF THE DRIVETRAIN SYSTEM.
RIGHT HERE.
▼THE CHAIN'S TENSION ADJUSTS AUTOMATICALLY BASED ON WHAT GEAR YOU SHIFT INTO.
▼WHEN YOU CHANGE GEARS, THIS IS WHAT HAPPENS:
※ I LEFT THIS EXPLANATION OUT OF THE MANGA TO PREVENT CONFUSION/GETTING TOO OVERLY TECHNICAL. LOL

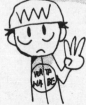

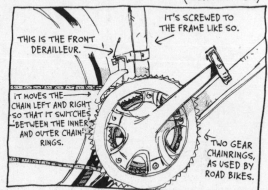

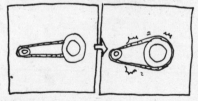

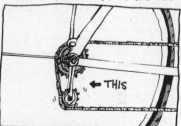

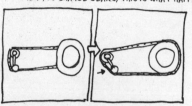

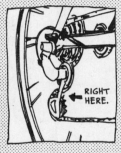

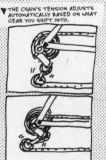

LET'S EXPLAIN SOME STUFF 2

ABOUT ROAD BIKES

YOWAMUSHI PEDAL
BICYCLES ARE FUN
CORNER
3.5

SO LET'S EXPLAIN A BIT ABOUT THESE "ROAD BIKES" I'VE MENTIONED THROUGHOUT THE MANGA AS PART OF THE SCENE-SETTING. ROAD BIKES ARE DIFFERENT FROM REGULAR, RECREATIONAL BICYCLES, AND ARE USED PROFESSIONALLY IN COMPETITIONS! (THAT'S WHY THEY DON'T HAVE BASKETS OR KICKSTANDS.)

BOY

① WEIGHT

MOST ROAD BIKES WEIGH 8-9KG/18-20LBS, AND LIGHTER ONES WEIGH 6-7KG/13-15LBS. IN HUMAN TERMS, THAT'S ABOUT HOW MUCH A ONE- OR TWO-YEAR-OLD WOULD WEIGH. MOMMY BIKES ARE GENERALLY 15-20KG/33-44LBS, SO YOU COULD SAY THEY'RE ABOUT TWICE AS HEAVY AS ROAD BIKES.

JOSHI
LIGHT ENOUGH FOR LADIES TO LIFT EASILY!

IN GENERAL, THE LIGHTER A ROAD BIKE IS, THE PRICIER IT IS.

② FRAME MATERIAL

ALTHOUGH BICYCLE FRAMES ARE MADE OF ALL KINDS OF MATERIALS, MOST USE ONE OF THESE THREE MATERIALS: CHROMOLY, ALUMINUM, OR CARBON.

CHROMOLY —LIGHTER→ ALUMINUM —LIGHTER→ CARBON

STEEL
HEAVY, BUT HAS A UNIQUE FLEXIBILITY THAT MAKES FOR VERY COMFORTABLE RIDING. IN THE MANGA, THIS IS SAKAMICHI-KUN'S FAVORITE FRAME MATERIAL! ALL BICYCLES USED STEEL FRAMES IN THE PAST, AND MOMMY BIKES STILL TEND TO USE THEM TODAY.

FORMERLY THE MOST POPULAR FRAME MATERIAL FOR ROAD BIKES, IT'S VERY LIGHT BUT RIGID. ALUMINUM TUBES ARE EVEN WIDER THAN CHROMOLY ONES.

CHROMOLY
ALUMINUM

THINNER TUBES LOOK COOLER.

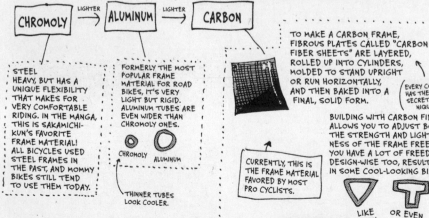

TO MAKE A CARBON FRAME, FIBROUS PLATES CALLED "CARBON FIBER SHEETS" ARE LAYERED, ROLLED UP INTO CYLINDERS, MOLDED TO STAND UPRIGHT OR RUN HORIZONTALLY, AND THEN BAKED INTO A FINAL, SOLID FORM.

(EVERY COMPANY HAS THEIR OWN SECRET TECHNIQUES.)

BUILDING WITH CARBON FIBER ALLOWS YOU TO ADJUST BOTH THE STRENGTH AND LIGHTNESS OF THE FRAME FREELY. YOU HAVE A LOT OF FREEDOM DESIGN-WISE TOO, RESULTING IN SOME COOL-LOOKING BIKES!!

CURRENTLY, THIS IS THE FRAME MATERIAL FAVORED BY MOST PRO CYCLISTS.

LIKE THIS!
OR EVEN THIS!

YOU CAN MAKE TUBE SHAPES!

BUT IT'S REALLY EXPENSIVE...

※ INCIDENTALLY, YOURS TRULY'S TREK ROAD BIKE HAS AN ALUMINUM FRAME.

③ BIKE BRANDS

UNLIKE WITH CAR AND MOTORCYCLE MANUFACTURERS, BICYCLE MANUFACTURERS DON'T ACTUALLY MAKE ANYTHING BESIDES THE FRAME OF THE BIKE.

MOST BIKE MANUFACTURING IS CENTERED IN EUROPE, NORTH AMERICA, JAPAN, AND TAIWAN.

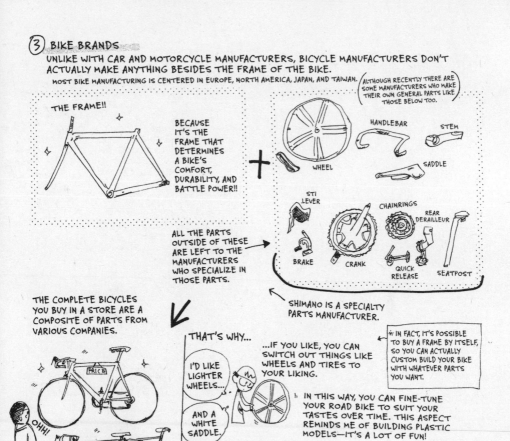

(ALTHOUGH RECENTLY THERE ARE SOME MANUFACTURERS WHO MAKE THEIR OWN GENERAL PARTS LIKE THOSE BELOW TOO.)

THE FRAME!!

BECAUSE IT'S THE FRAME THAT DETERMINES A BIKE'S COMFORT, DURABILITY, AND BATTLE POWER!!

WHEEL
HANDLEBAR
STEM
SADDLE
STI LEVER
CHAINRINGS
REAR DERAILLEUR
BRAKE
CRANK
QUICK RELEASE
SEATPOST

ALL THE PARTS OUTSIDE OF THESE ARE LEFT TO THE MANUFACTURERS WHO SPECIALIZE IN THOSE PARTS.

SHIMANO IS A SPECIALTY PARTS MANUFACTURER.

THE COMPLETE BICYCLES YOU BUY IN A STORE ARE A COMPOSITE OF PARTS FROM VARIOUS COMPANIES.

PRICE
OHH!

THAT'S WHY...

I'D LIKE LIGHTER WHEELS...
AND A WHITE SADDLE.

...IF YOU LIKE, YOU CAN SWITCH OUT THINGS LIKE WHEELS AND TIRES TO YOUR LIKING.

※ IN FACT, IT'S POSSIBLE TO BUY A FRAME BY ITSELF, SO YOU CAN ACTUALLY CUSTOM BUILD YOUR BIKE WITH WHATEVER PARTS YOU WANT.

IN THIS WAY, YOU CAN FINE-TUNE YOUR ROAD BIKE TO SUIT YOUR TASTES OVER TIME. THIS ASPECT REMINDS ME OF BUILDING PLASTIC MODELS—IT'S A LOT OF FUN!

④ YOUR DREAM MACHINE

AN F1 RACECAR COSTS MILLIONS OF DOLLARS AND IS IMPOSSIBLE FOR A FAN TO BUY...BUT WITH BICYCLES, AS LONG AS YOU HAVE THE MONEY, YOU CAN OWN THE **EXACT SAME ROAD BIKE AS YOUR FAVORITE PRO!!** AND YOU CAN RIDE IT TOO—THE VERY SAME BIKE THE PROS ARE RIDING IN THE TOUR DE FRANCE!!

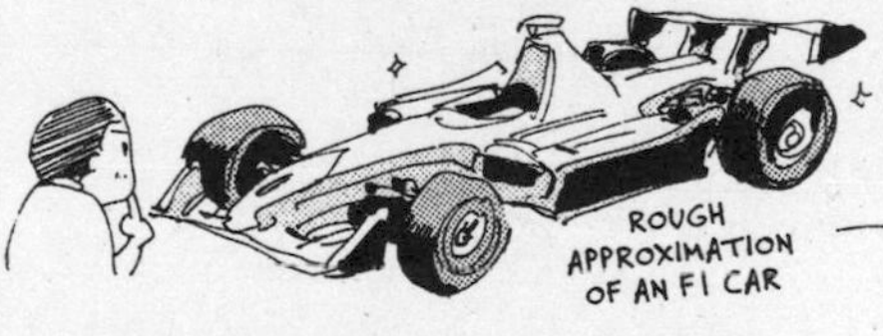

ROUGH APPROXIMATION OF AN F1 CAR

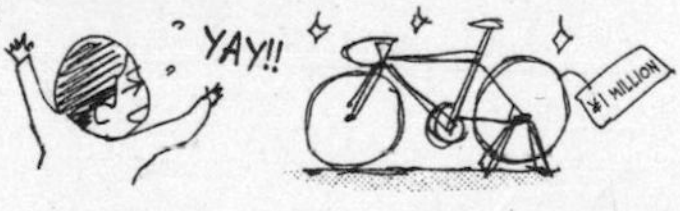

YAY!!
¥1 MILLION

HOWEVER—WHILE AN F1 CAR COMES WITH AN ENGINE, A BICYCLE DOES NOT. THEREFORE, YOU MUST BUILD UP **YOUR LEGS** IN ORDER TO ACHIEVE COMPARABLE SPEEDS WITH A PRO!!

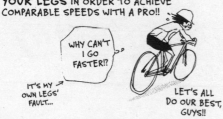

WHY CAN'T I GO FASTER!?

IT'S MY OWN LEGS' FAULT...

LET'S ALL DO OUR BEST, GUYS!!

ROAD BIKES ARE FUN IN ALL SORTS OF WAYS! ROAD BIKES ARE BEAUTIFUL EVEN IF YOU DECORATE THEM WITH STUFF! FOR THOSE WITH AN INTEREST IN THEM, EVEN DOING RESEARCH ON ROAD BIKES IS FUN! FOR THOSE READY TO RIDE A ROAD BIKE, REMEMBER TO **OBEY ALL TRAFFIC LAWS!!** IT'LL BE MORE FUN THAT WAY, TRUST ME! **NEVER IGNORE TRAFFIC LIGHTS OR RIDE AGAINST ONCOMING TRAFFIC!!** INCIDENTALLY, WHEN I WAS INTERVIEWING FUMIYUKI BEPPU-SAN, HE SAID THAT WHENEVER HE SEES A BICYCLIST IGNORING TRAFFIC LIGHTS, HE'LL CHASE THEM DOWN AND CHEW THEM OUT. AND REMEMBER, NONE OF US CAN POSSIBLY OUTRIDE HIM, SO YOU WILL GET CHEWED OUT...

YOWAMUSHI PEDAL

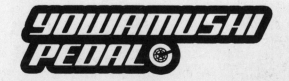

RIDE.26 SPRINT CLIMB!!

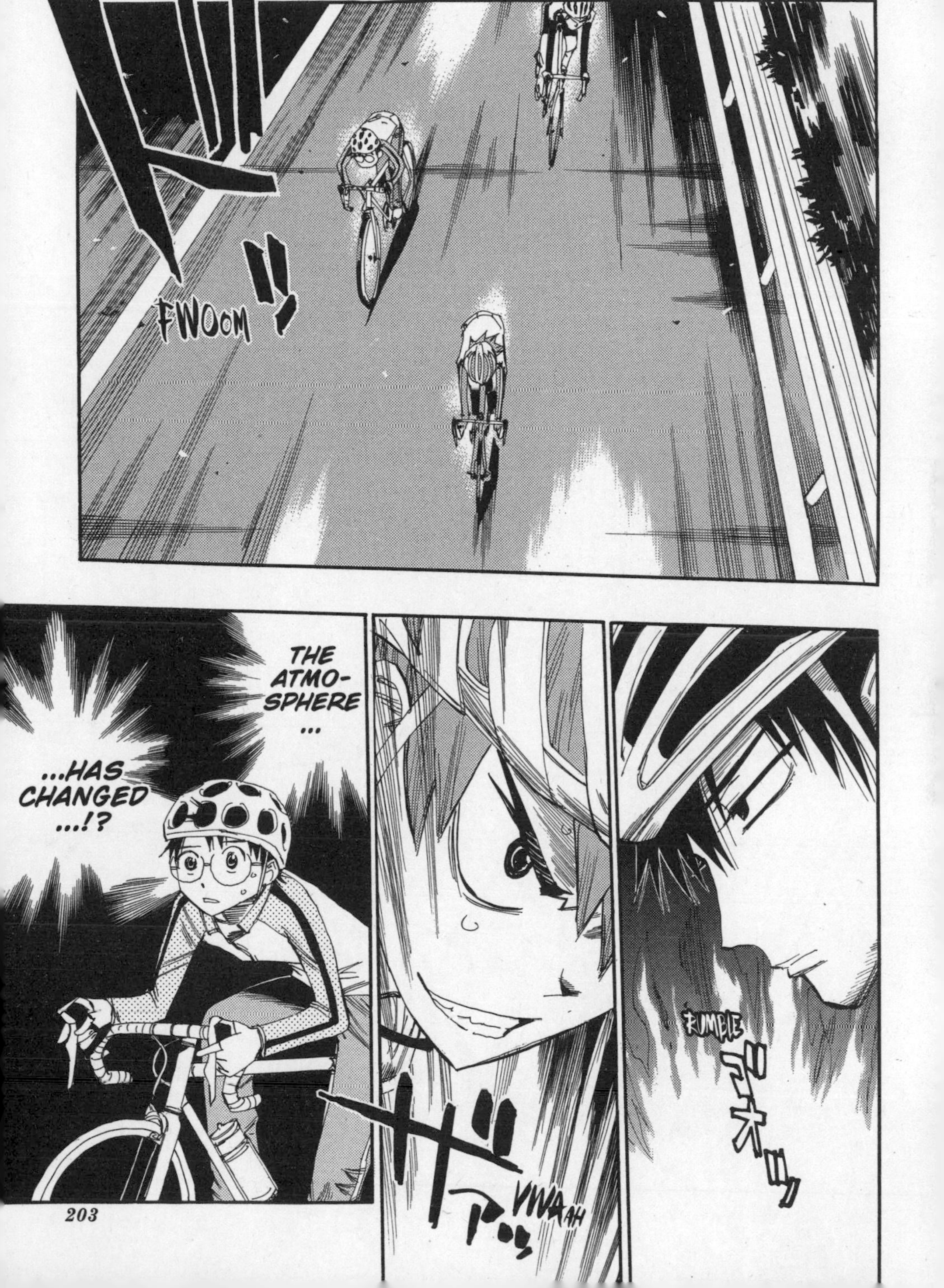
FWOOM
RUMBLE
VWAAH
THE ATMOSPHERE...
...HAS CHANGED...!?

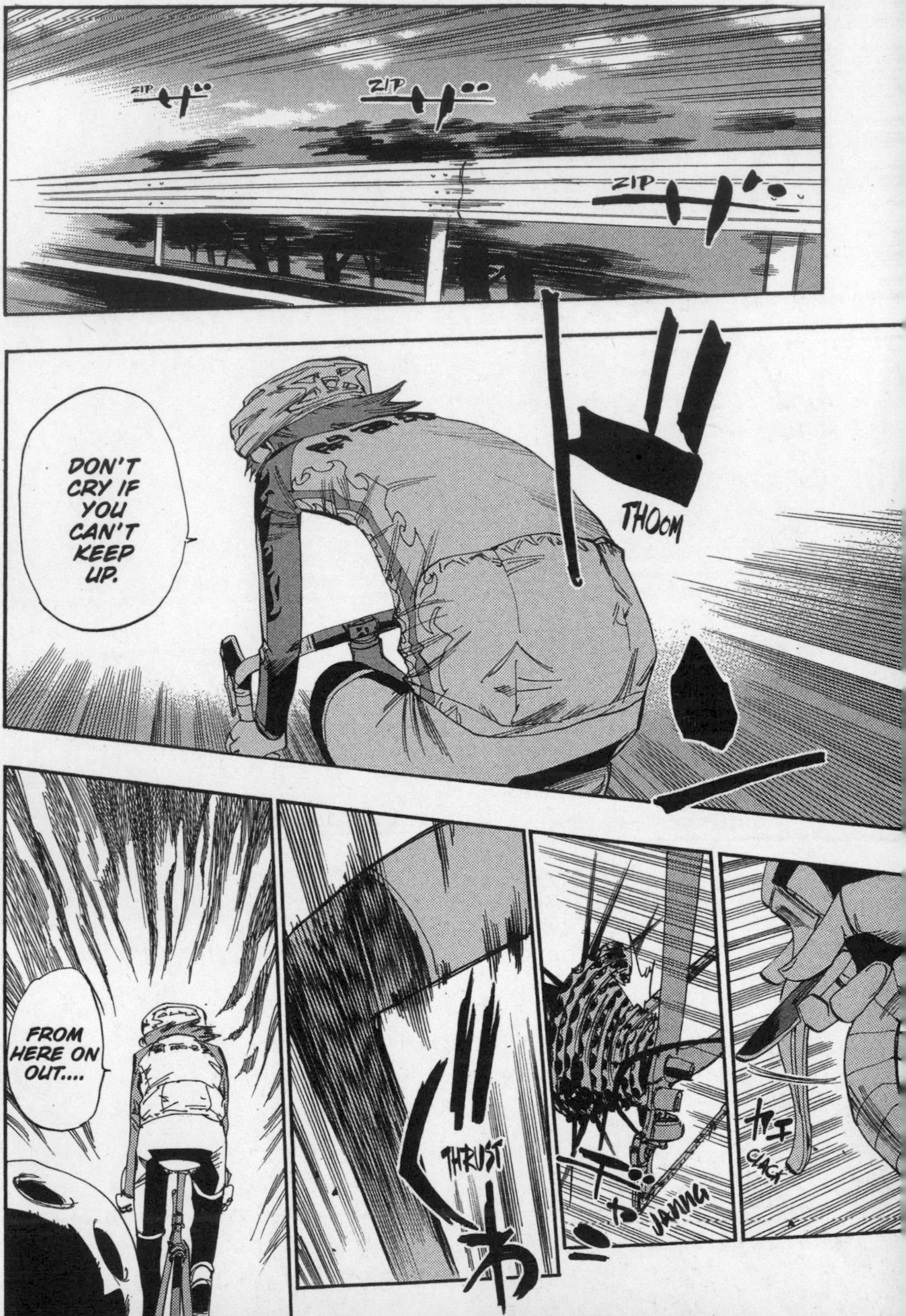
ZIP
ZIP
ZIP
THOOM
DON'T CRY IF YOU CAN'T KEEP UP.
CLACK
JANNG
THRUST
FROM HERE ON OUT....

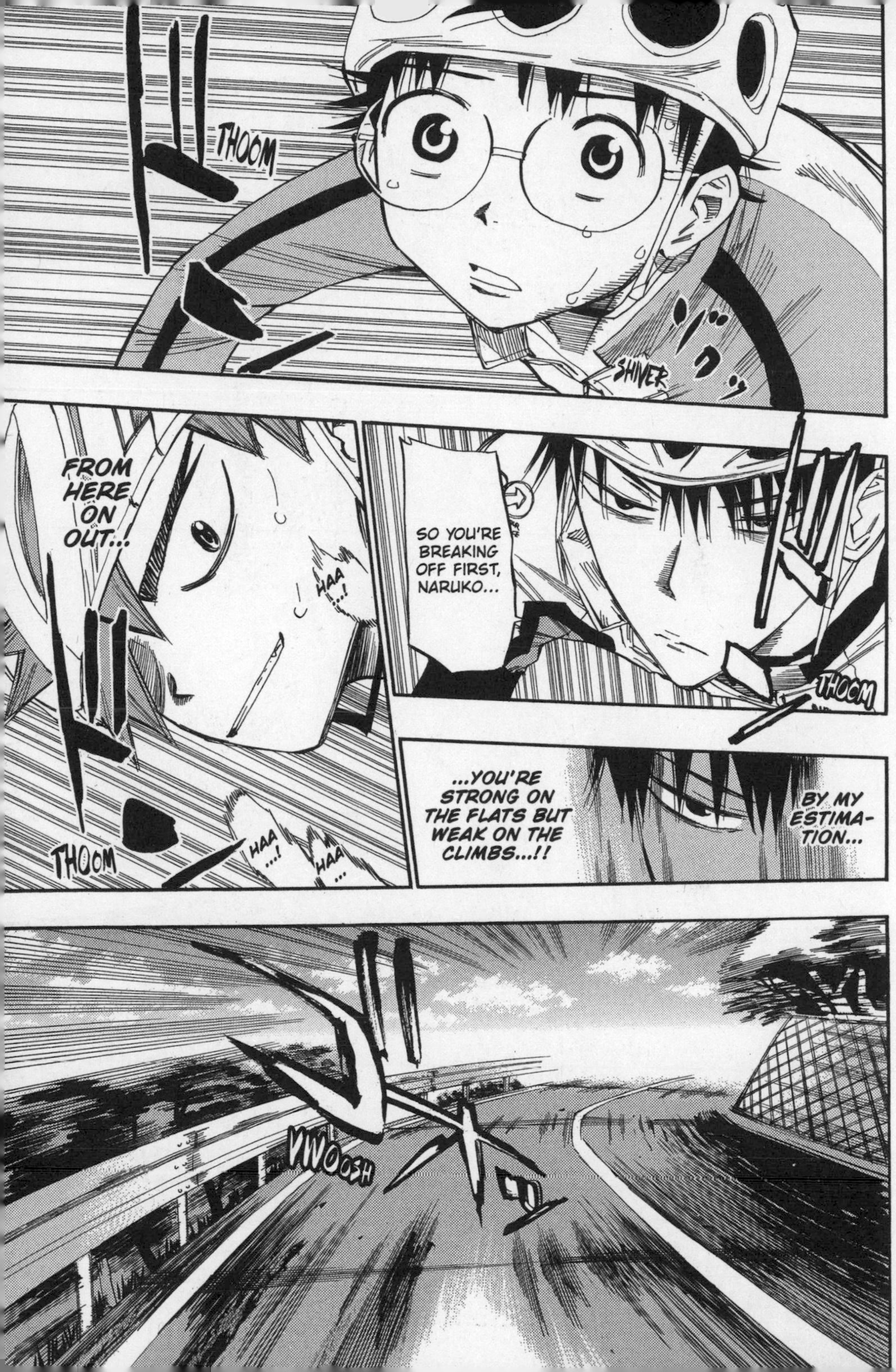
THOOM
SHIVER
SO YOU'RE BREAKING OFF FIRST, NARUKO...
THOOM
BY MY ESTIMATION...
...YOU'RE STRONG ON THE FLATS BUT WEAK ON THE CLIMBS...!!
FROM HERE ON OUT...
HAA...!
HAA...!
HAA...
THOOM
VWOOSH

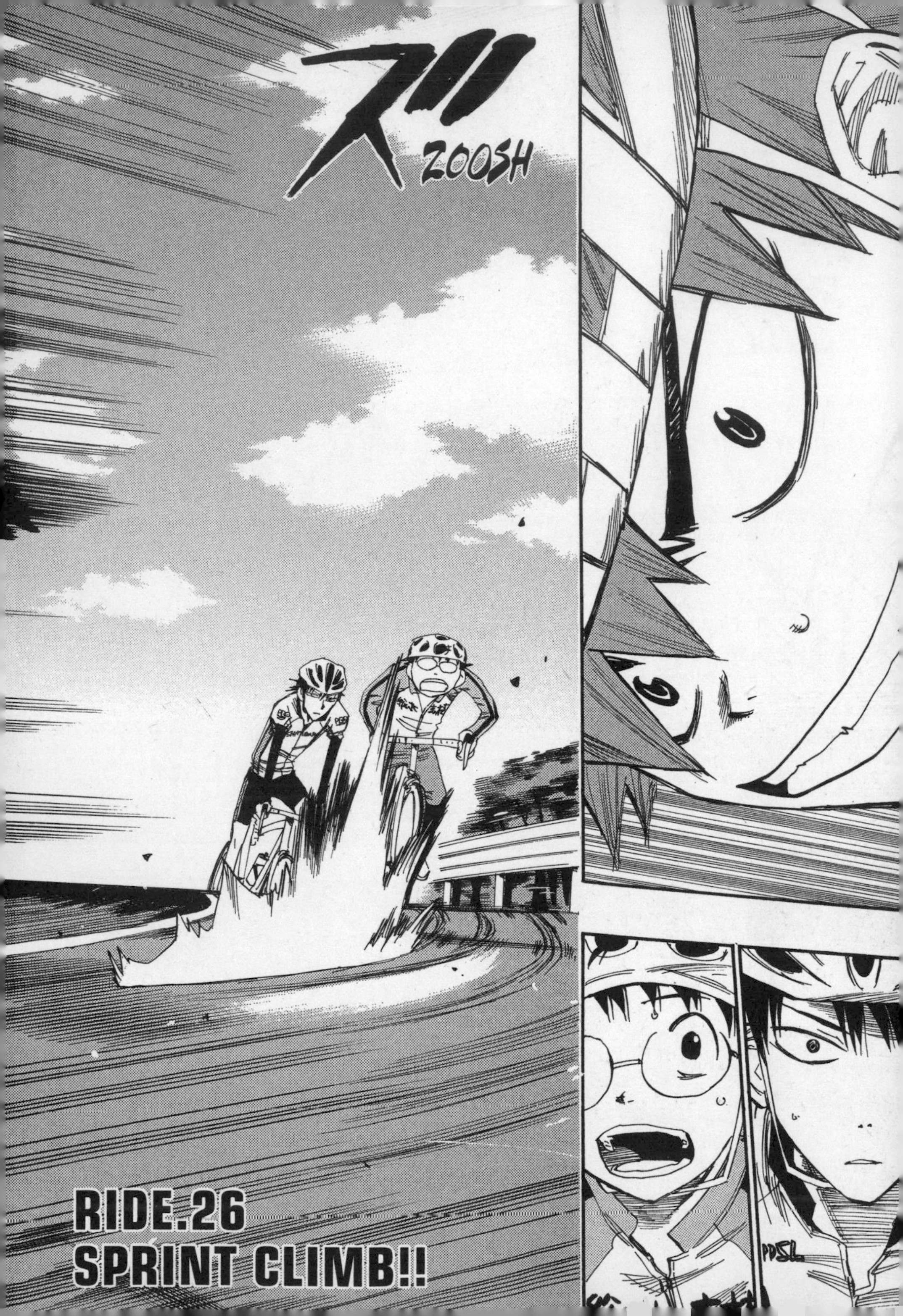
PDSL
ZOOSH
RIDE.26
SPRINT CLIMB!!

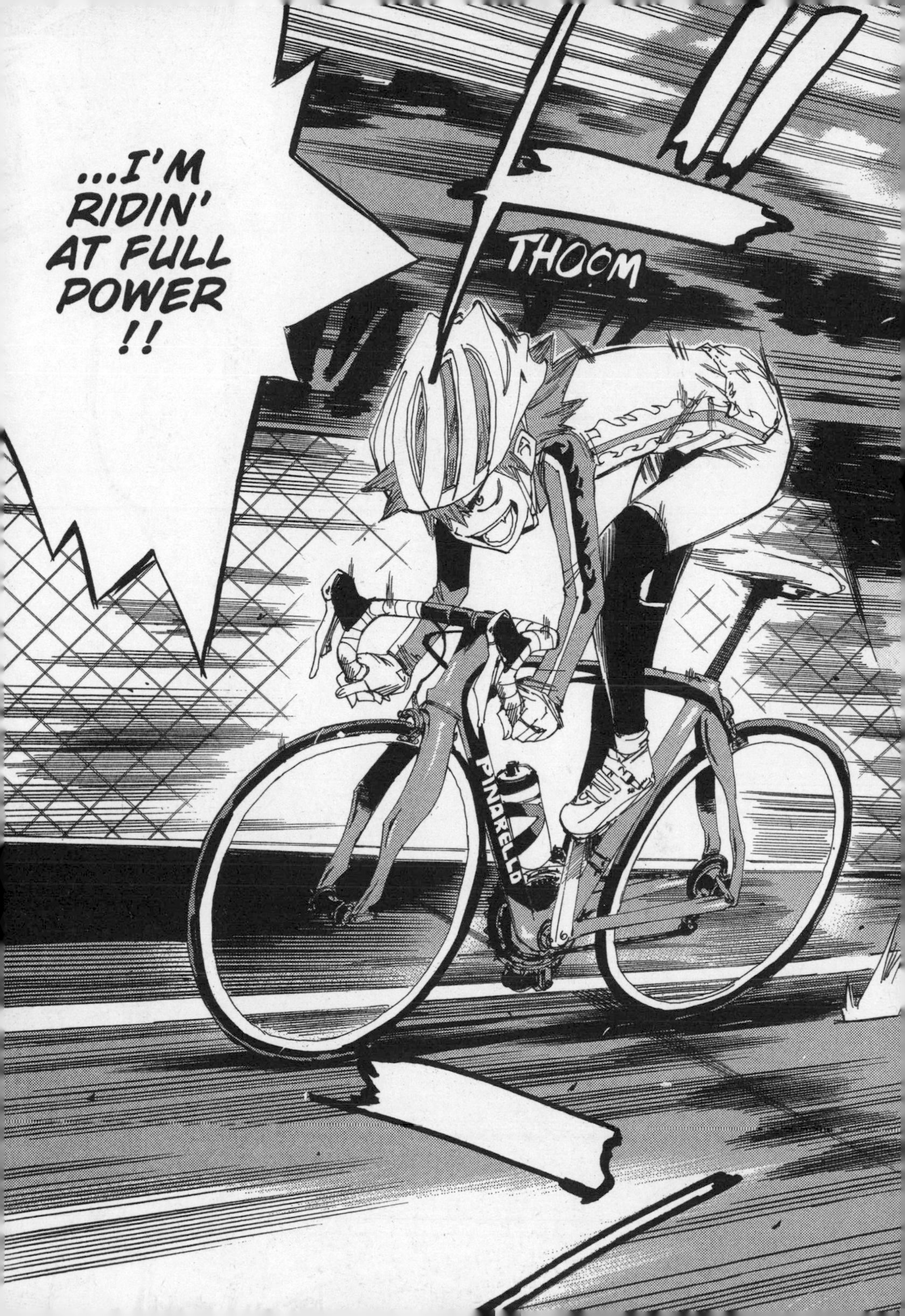
...I'M RIDIN' AT FULL POWER !!
THOOM
PINARELLO

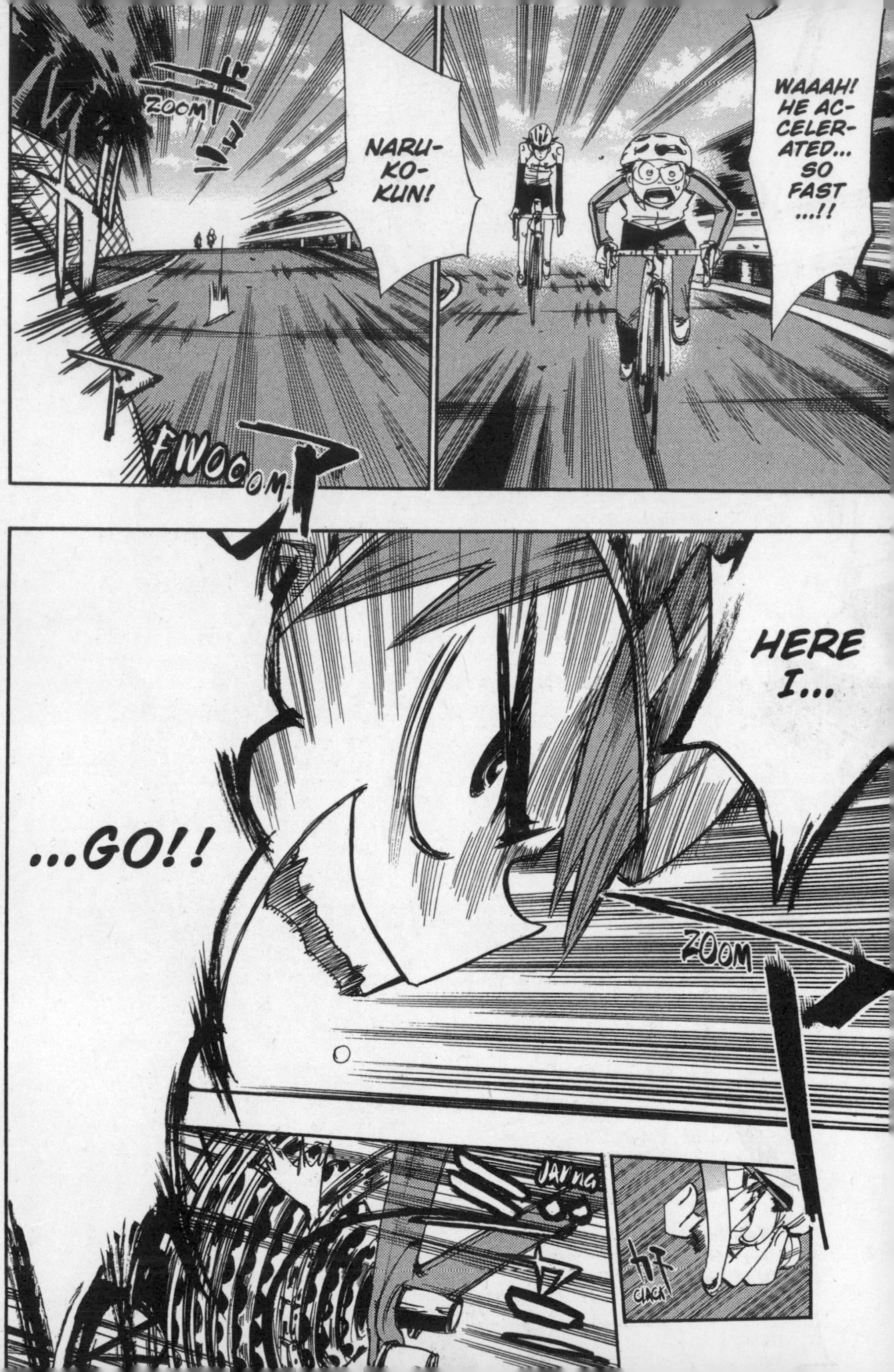
WAAAH! HE ACCELERATED... SO FAST...!!
NARUKO-KUN!
ZOOM
FWOOOM
HERE I...
...GO!!
ZOOM
CLACK
JANG

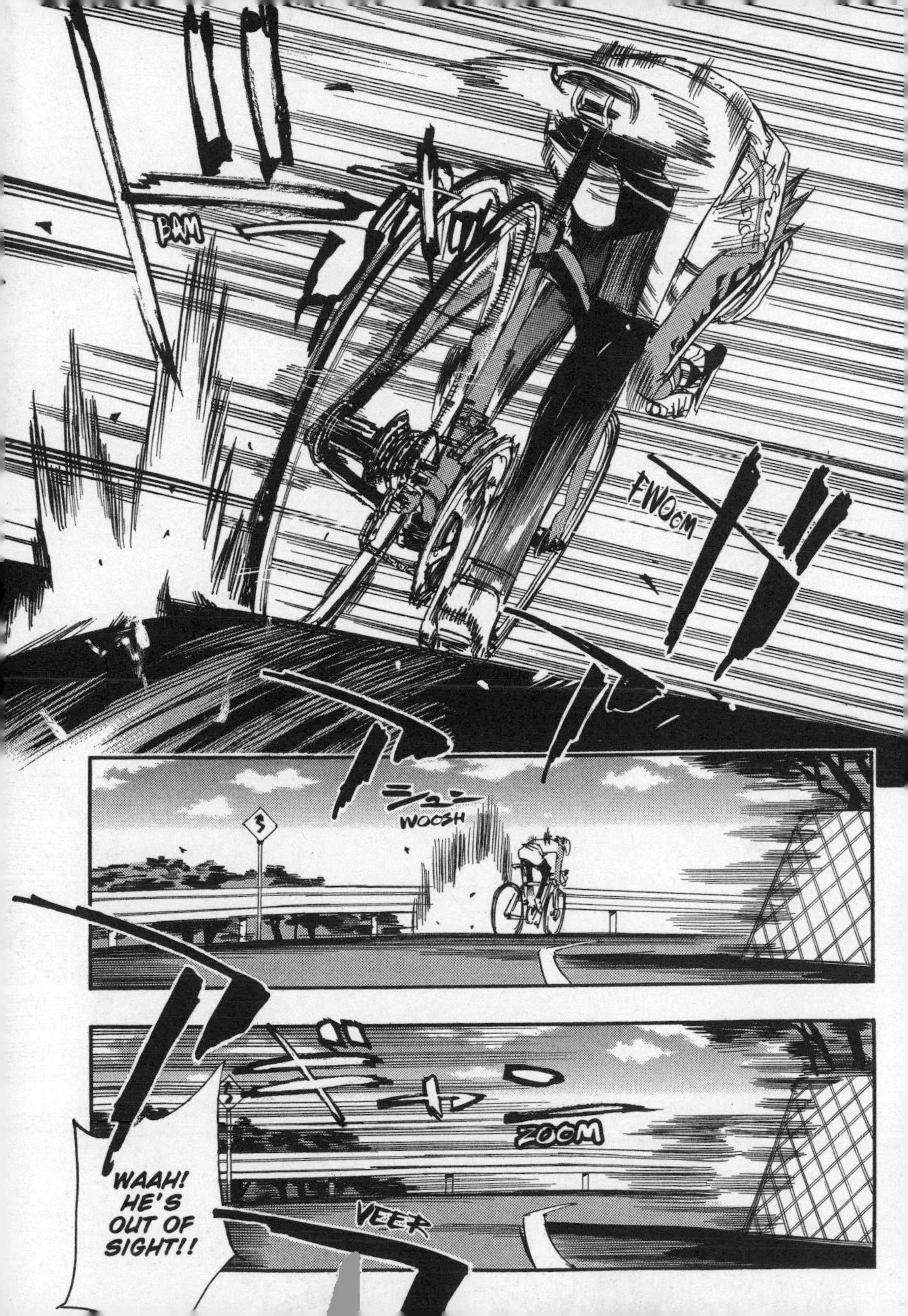
BAM
FWOOM
シュー
WOOSH
ZOOM
VEER
WAAH! HE'S OUT OF SIGHT!!

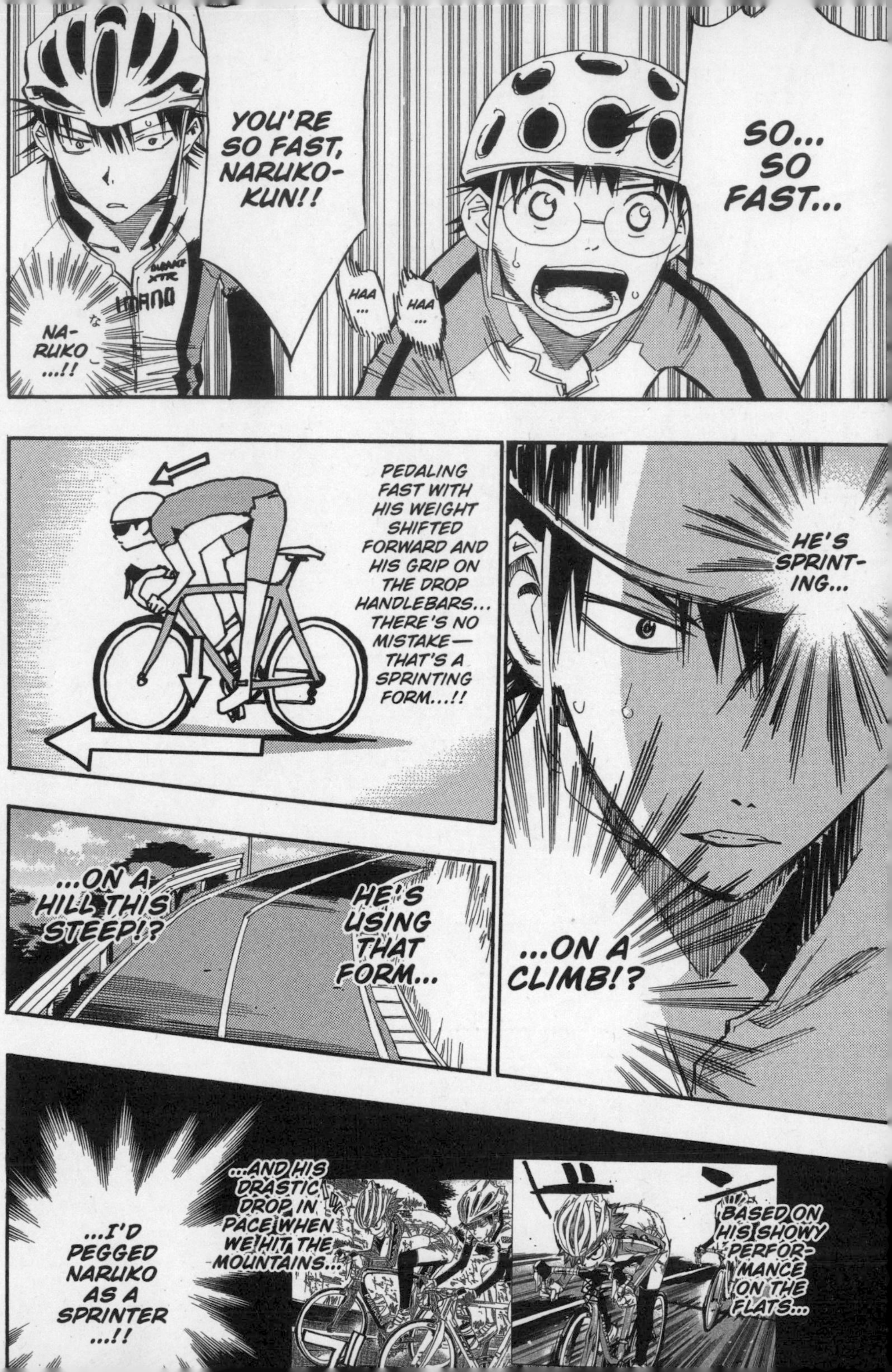
SO... SO FAST...
HAA ...
HAA ...
YOU'RE SO FAST, NARUKO-KUN!!
NA- RUKO ...!!
な
HE'S SPRINT- ING...
...ON A CLIMB!?
PEDALING FAST WITH HIS WEIGHT SHIFTED FORWARD AND HIS GRIP ON THE DROP HANDLEBARS... THERE'S NO MISTAKE— THAT'S A SPRINTING FORM...!!
HE'S USING THAT FORM...
...ON A HILL THIS STEEP!?
BASED ON HIS SHOWY PERFOR- MANCE ON THE FLATS...
...AND HIS DRASTIC DROP IN PACE WHEN WE HIT THE MOUNTAINS...
...I'D PEGGED NARUKO AS A SPRINTER ...!!

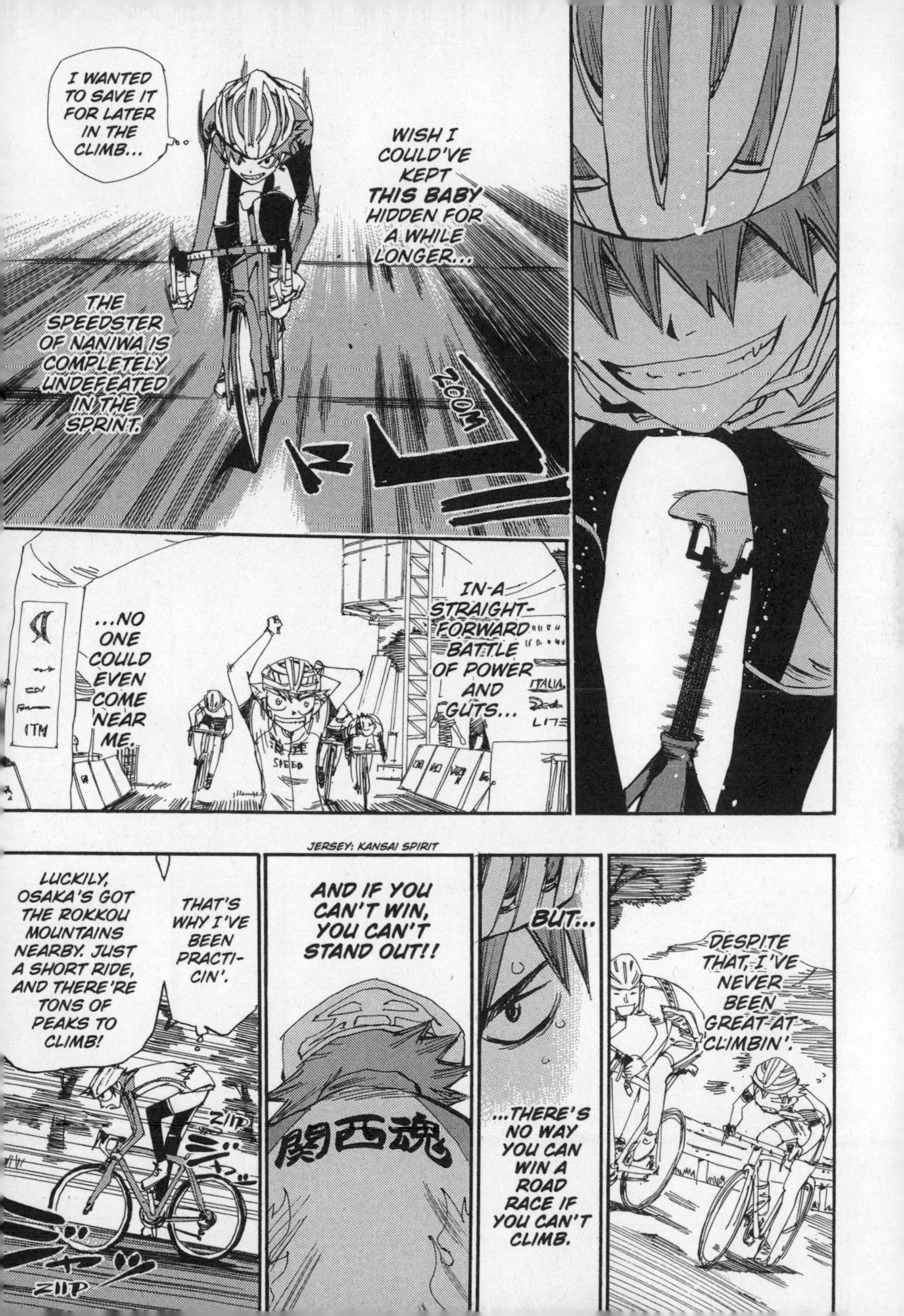
WISH I COULD'VE KEPT THIS BABY HIDDEN FOR A WHILE LONGER...
I WANTED TO SAVE IT FOR LATER IN THE CLIMB...
THE SPEEDSTER OF NANIWA IS COMPLETELY UNDEFEATED IN THE SPRINT.
ZOOM
IN A STRAIGHT-FORWARD BATTLE OF POWER AND GUTS...
...NO ONE COULD EVEN COME NEAR ME.
ITALIA
LITE
ITM
SPEED
DESPITE THAT, I'VE NEVER BEEN GREAT AT CLIMBIN'.
BUT...
...THERE'S NO WAY YOU CAN WIN A ROAD RACE IF YOU CAN'T CLIMB.
AND IF YOU CAN'T WIN, YOU CAN'T STAND OUT!!
関西魂
JERSEY: KANSAI SPIRIT
THAT'S WHY I'VE BEEN PRACTICIN'.
LUCKILY, OSAKA'S GOT THE ROKKOU MOUNTAINS NEARBY. JUST A SHORT RIDE, AND THERE'RE TONS OF PEAKS TO CLIMB!
ZIP
ZIP

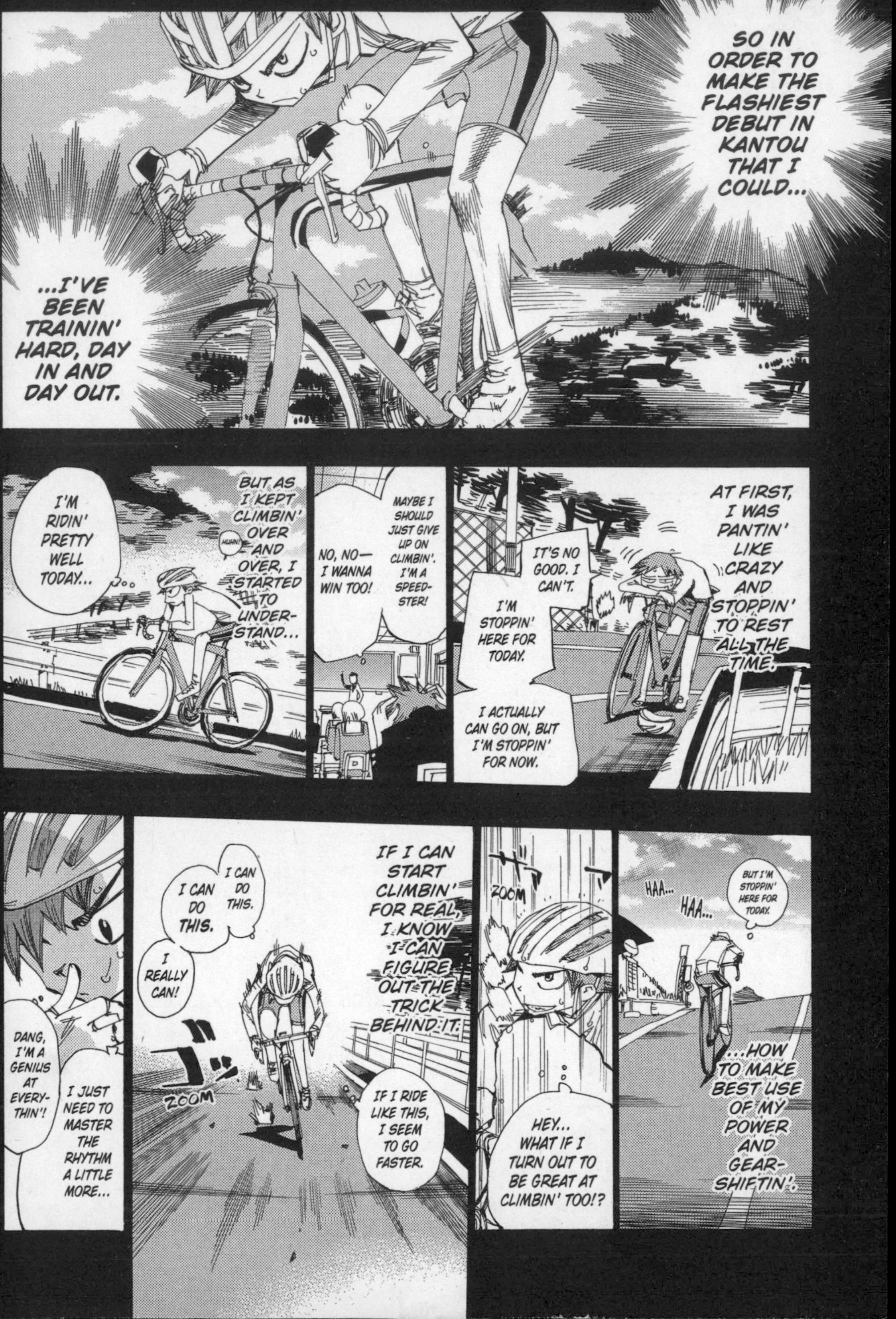
SO IN ORDER TO MAKE THE FLASHIEST DEBUT IN KANTOU THAT I COULD...
...I'VE BEEN TRAININ' HARD, DAY IN AND DAY OUT.
AT FIRST, I WAS PANTIN' LIKE CRAZY AND STOPPIN' TO REST ALL THE TIME.
IT'S NO GOOD. I CAN'T.
I'M STOPPIN' HERE FOR TODAY.
I ACTUALLY CAN GO ON, BUT I'M STOPPIN' FOR NOW.
MAYBE I SHOULD JUST GIVE UP ON CLIMBIN'. I'M A SPEEDSTER!
NO, NO— I WANNA WIN TOO!
BUT AS I KEPT CLIMBIN' OVER AND OVER, I STARTED TO UNDERSTAND...
I'M RIDIN' PRETTY WELL TODAY...
HAA...
HAA...
BUT I'M STOPPIN' HERE FOR TODAY.
...HOW TO MAKE BEST USE OF MY POWER AND GEAR-SHIFTIN'.
ZOOM
HEY... WHAT IF I TURN OUT TO BE GREAT AT CLIMBIN' TOO!?
IF I CAN START CLIMBIN' FOR REAL, I KNOW I CAN FIGURE OUT THE TRICK BEHIND IT.
I CAN DO THIS.
I CAN DO THIS.
I REALLY CAN!
ZOOM
IF I RIDE LIKE THIS, I SEEM TO GO FASTER.
DANG, I'M A GENIUS AT EVERYTHIN'!
I JUST NEED TO MASTER THE RHYTHM A LITTLE MORE...

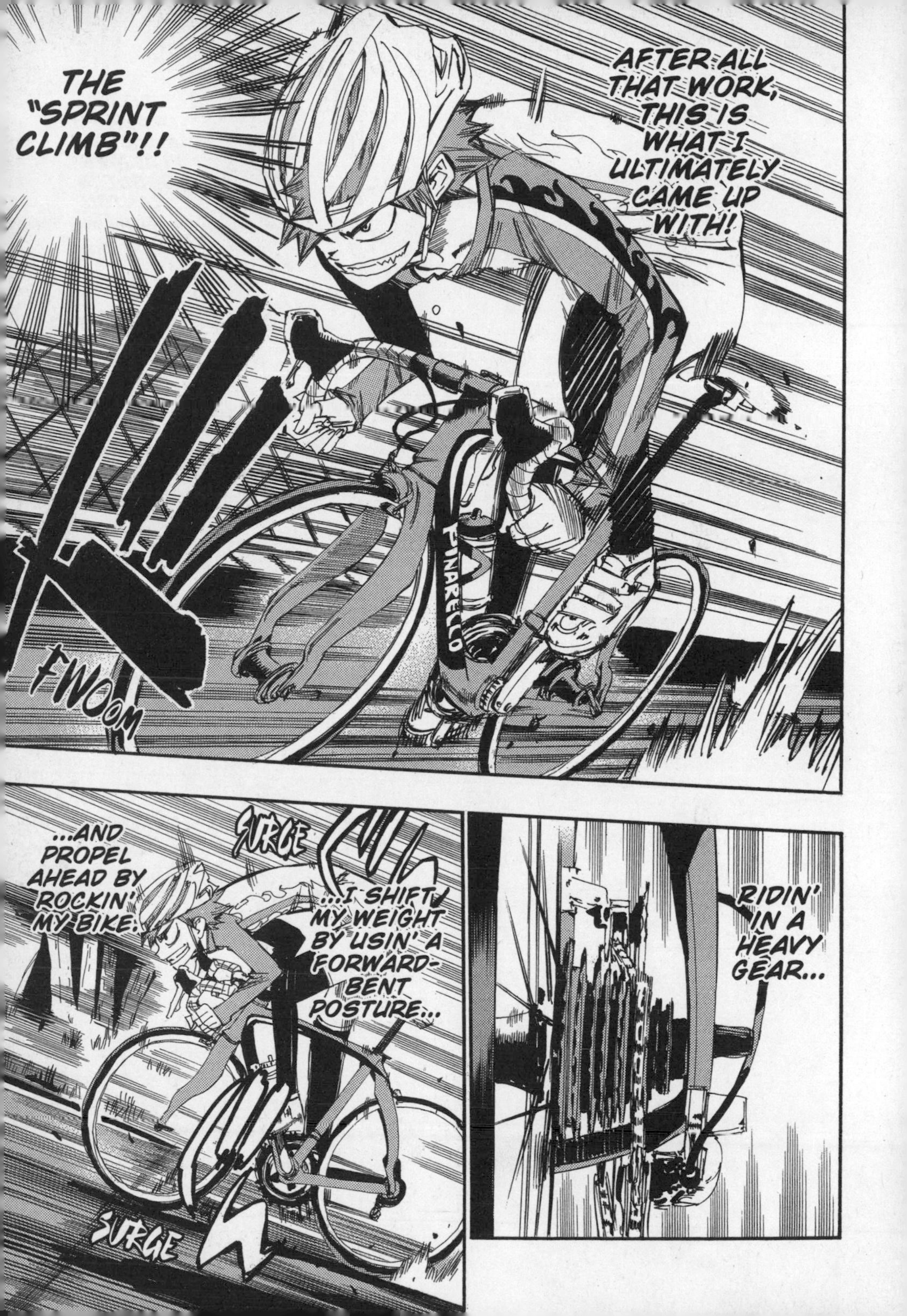
AFTER ALL THAT WORK, THIS IS WHAT I ULTIMATELY CAME UP WITH!
THE "SPRINT CLIMB"!!
FWOOM
RIDIN' IN A HEAVY GEAR...
SURGE
...I SHIFT MY WEIGHT BY USIN' A FORWARD-BENT POSTURE...
...AND PROPEL AHEAD BY ROCKIN' MY BIKE.
SURGE

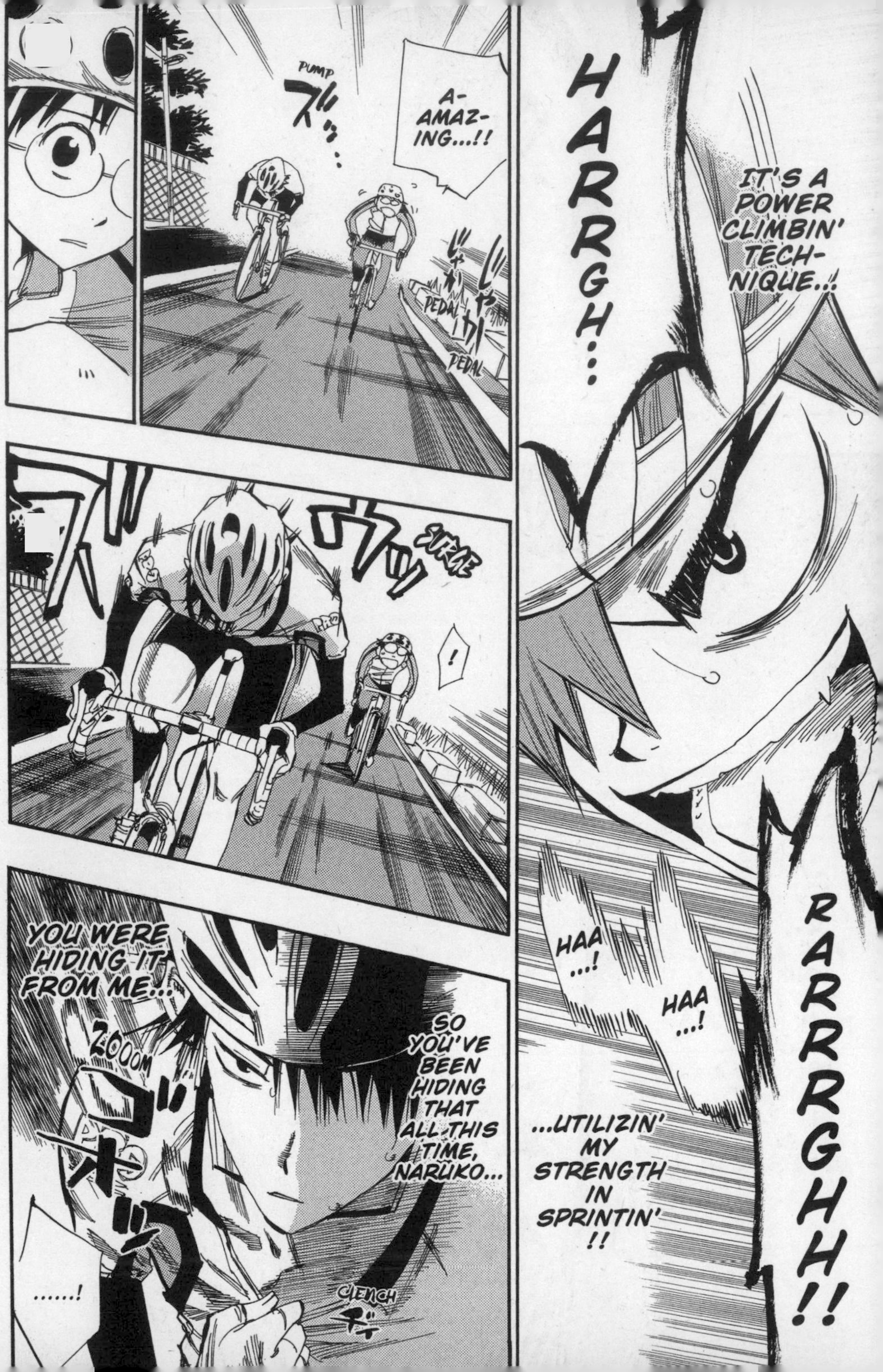
IT'S A POWER CLIMBIN' TECH-NIQUE...
HARRGH...
RARRRGHH!!
HAA...!
HAA...!
...UTILIZIN' MY STRENGTH IN SPRINTIN'!!
A-AMAZ-ING...!!
PUMP
PEDAL
PEDAL
SURGE
!
SO YOU'VE BEEN HIDING THAT ALL THIS TIME, NARUKO...
YOU WERE HIDING IT FROM ME...
ZOOOM
CLENCH
......!

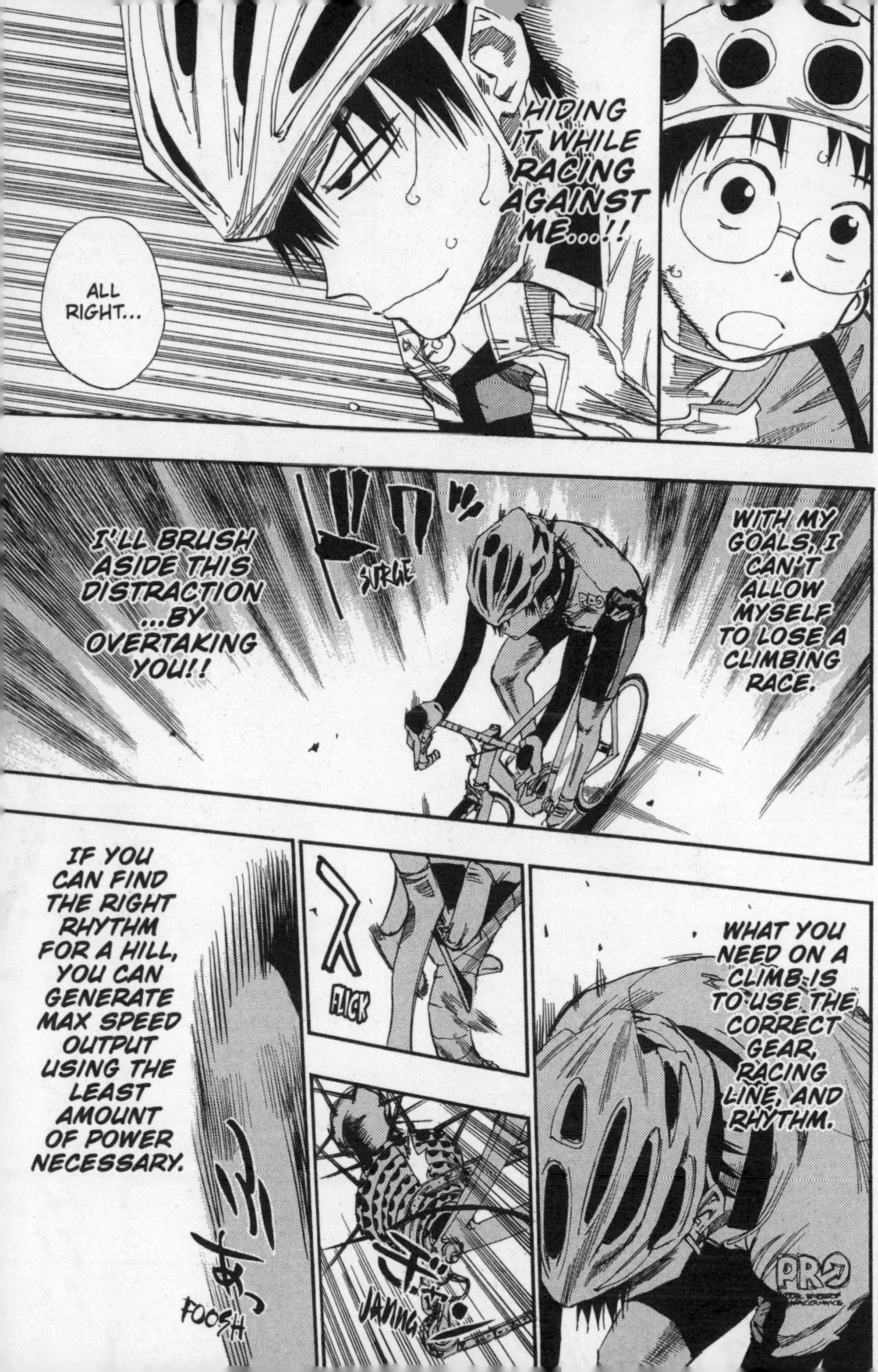
HIDING IT WHILE RACING AGAINST ME...!!
ALL RIGHT...
WITH MY GOALS, I CAN'T ALLOW MYSELF TO LOSE A CLIMBING RACE.
SURGE
I'LL BRUSH ASIDE THIS DISTRACTION ...BY OVERTAKING YOU!!
WHAT YOU NEED ON A CLIMB IS TO USE THE CORRECT GEAR, RACING LINE, AND RHYTHM.
FLICK
JANNG
IF YOU CAN FIND THE RIGHT RHYTHM FOR A HILL, YOU CAN GENERATE MAX SPEED OUTPUT USING THE LEAST AMOUNT OF POWER NECESSARY.
FOOSH

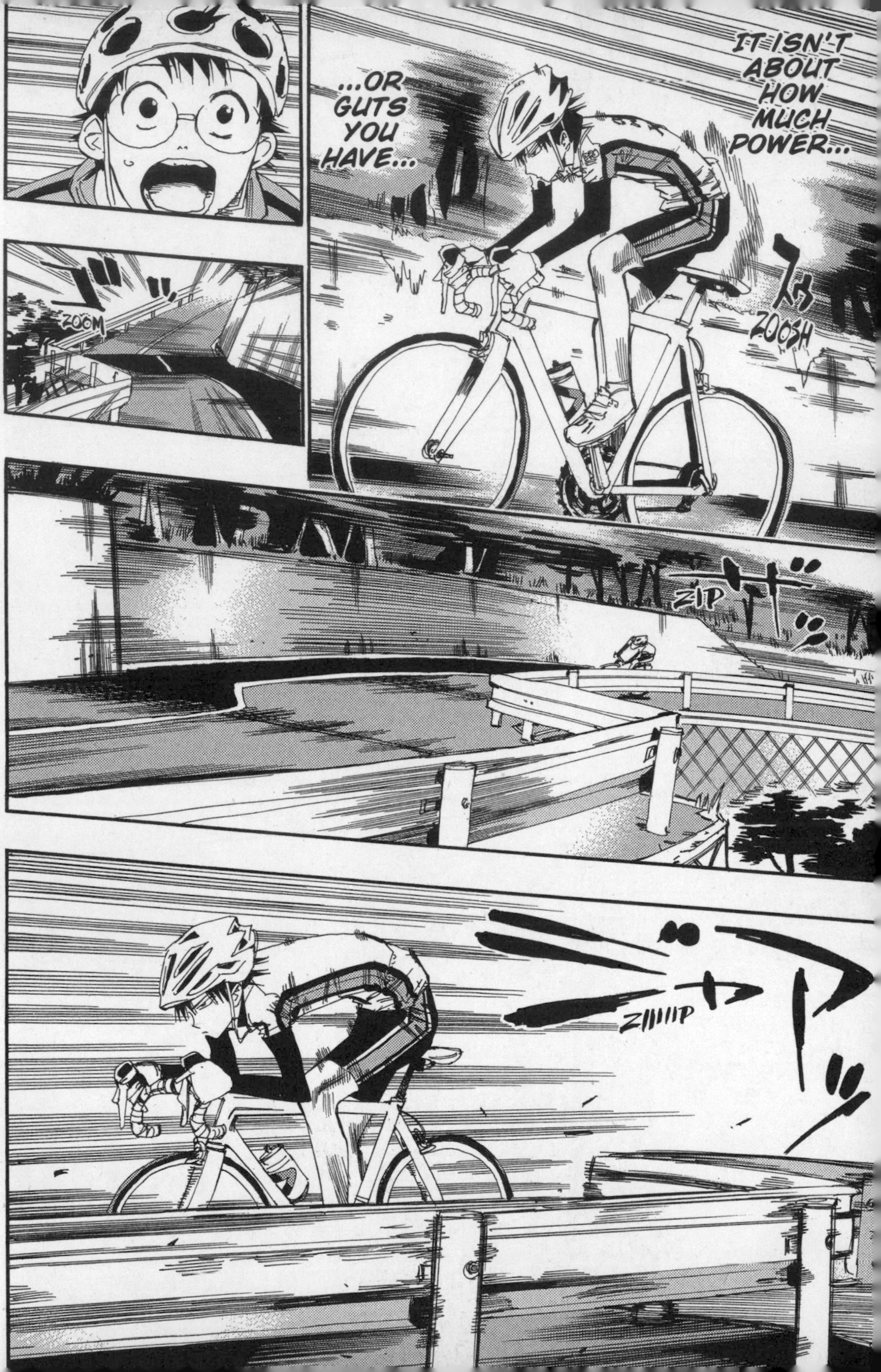
IT ISN'T ABOUT HOW MUCH POWER...
...OR GUTS YOU HAVE...
ZOOSH
ZOOM
ZIP
ZIIIIIP

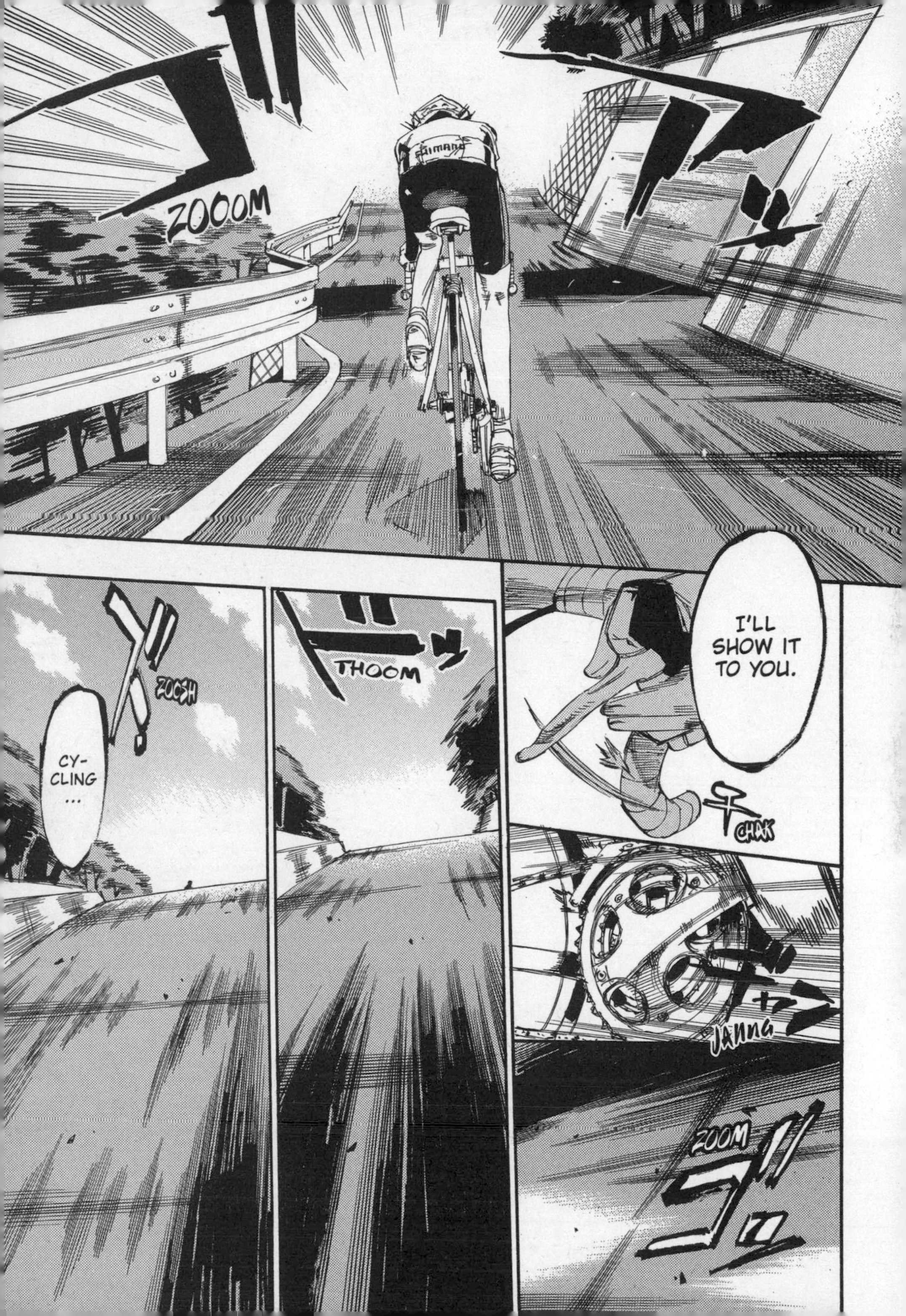
ZOOOM
I'LL SHOW IT TO YOU.
CHAK
JANNG
ZOOM
THOOM
ZOOSH
CY-CLING ...

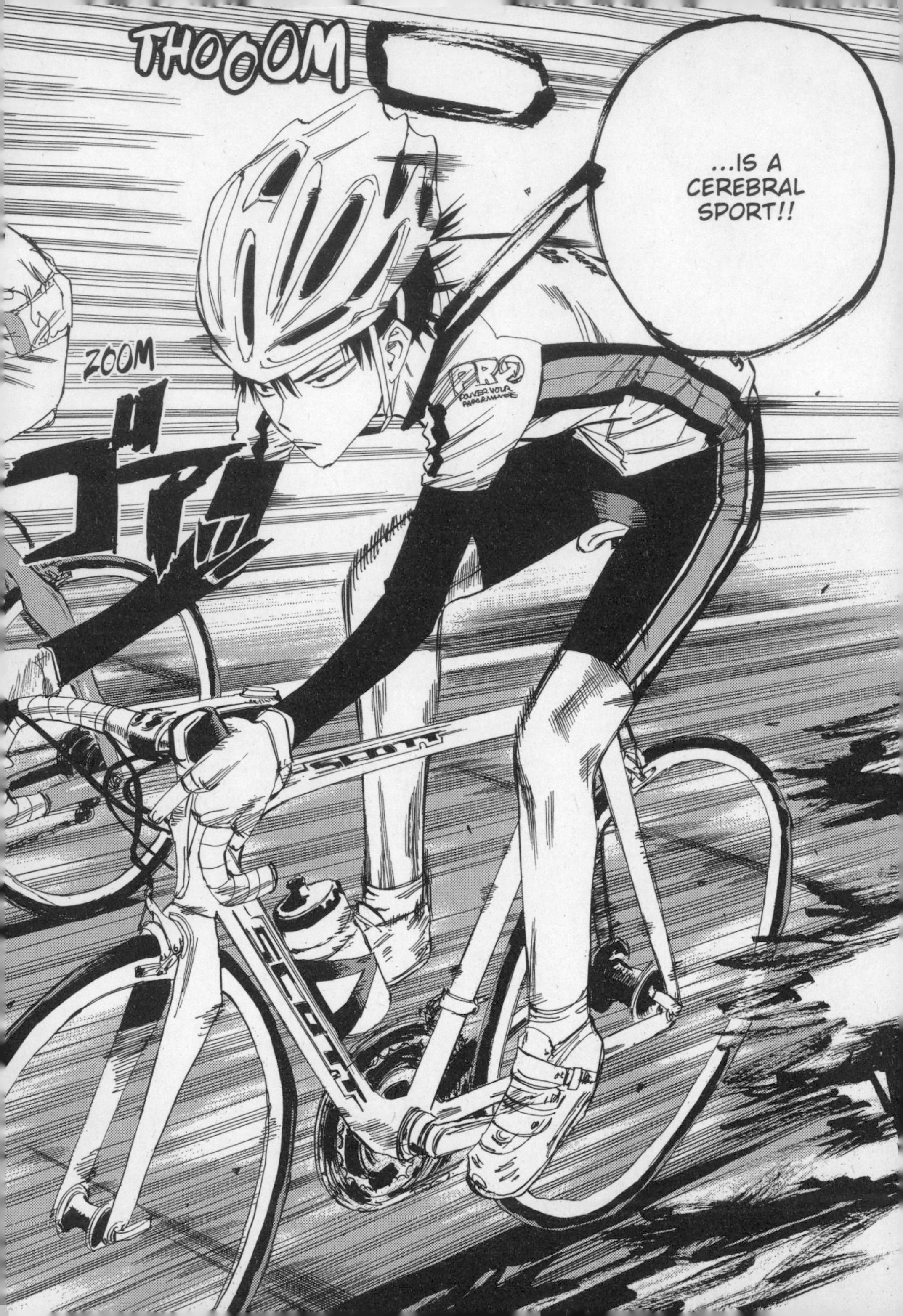
THOOOM
...IS A CEREBRAL SPORT!!
ZOOM
PRO POWER YOUR PERFORMANCE
SCOTT

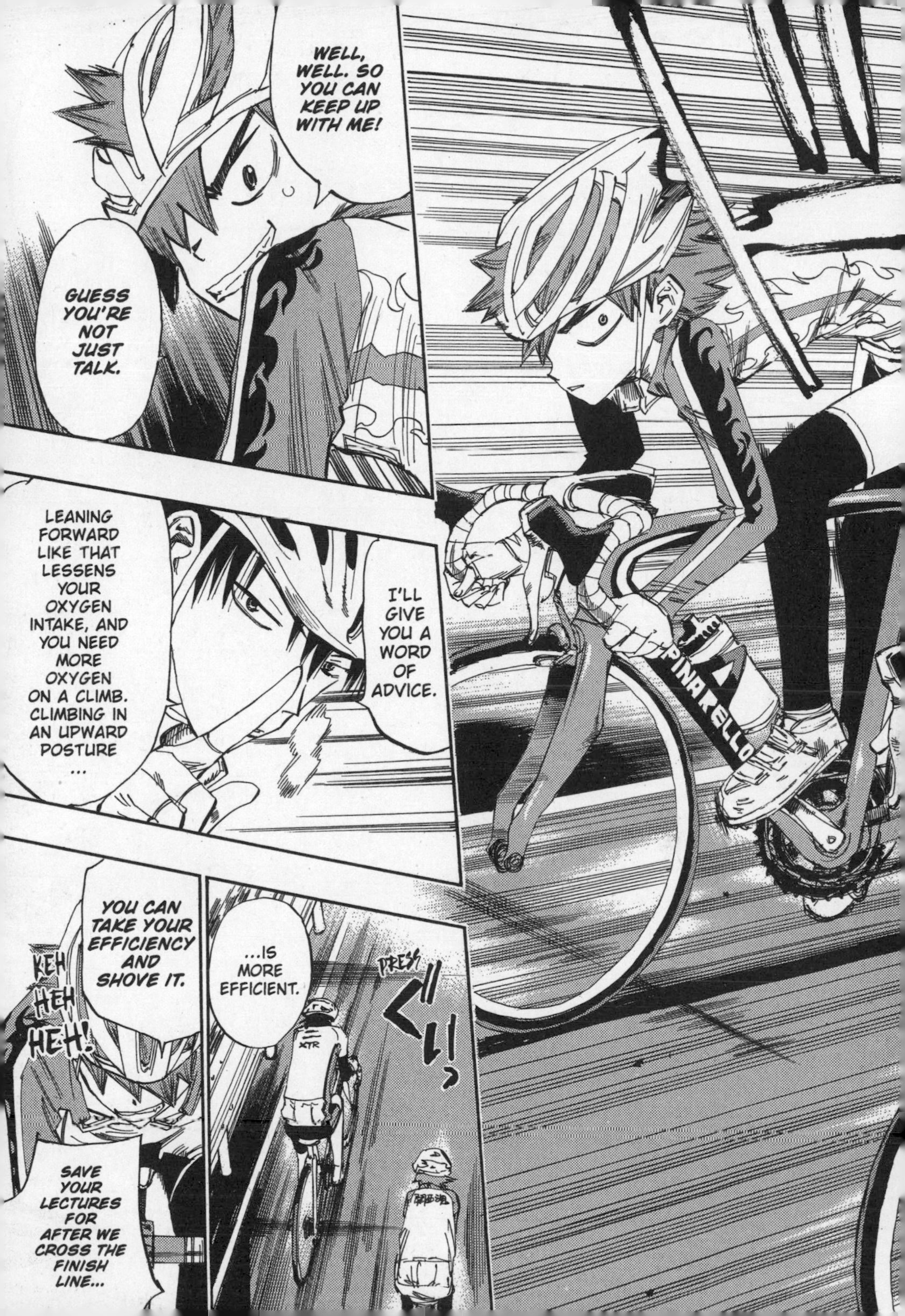

WELL, WELL. SO YOU CAN KEEP UP WITH ME!
GUESS YOU'RE NOT JUST TALK.
I'LL GIVE YOU A WORD OF ADVICE.
LEANING FORWARD LIKE THAT LESSENS YOUR OXYGEN INTAKE, AND YOU NEED MORE OXYGEN ON A CLIMB. CLIMBING IN AN UPWARD POSTURE ...
...IS MORE EFFICIENT.
PRESS
YOU CAN TAKE YOUR EFFICIENCY AND SHOVE IT.
KEH HEH HEH!
SAVE YOUR LECTURES FOR AFTER WE CROSS THE FINISH LINE...

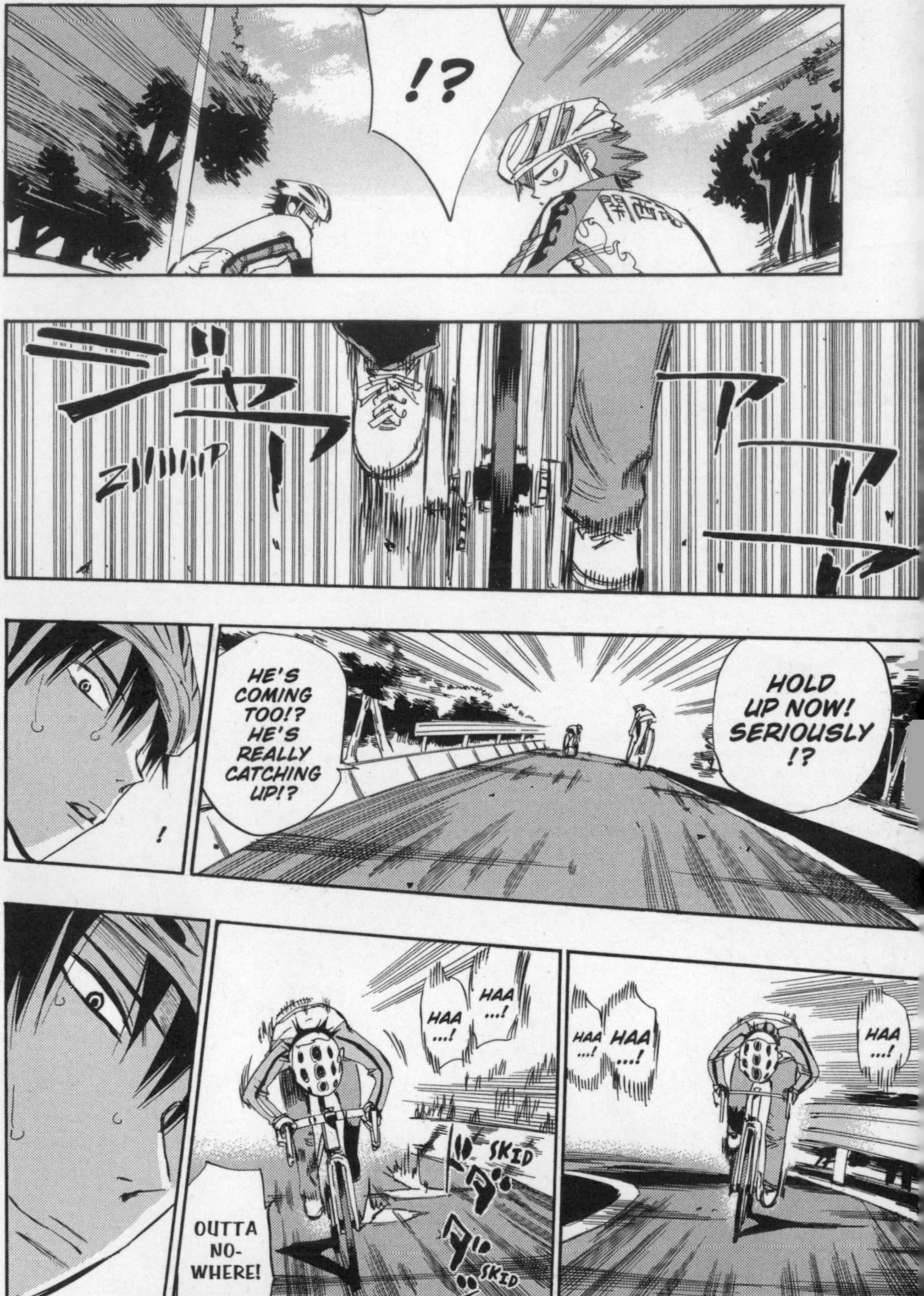
!?
ジャアアア
ZIIIIIIIP
HOLD UP NOW! SERIOUSLY!?
HE'S COMING TOO!? HE'S REALLY CATCHING UP!?
!
HAA...!
HAA...!
HAA...!
HAA...!
HAA...!
SKID
SKID
OUTTA NO-WHERE!

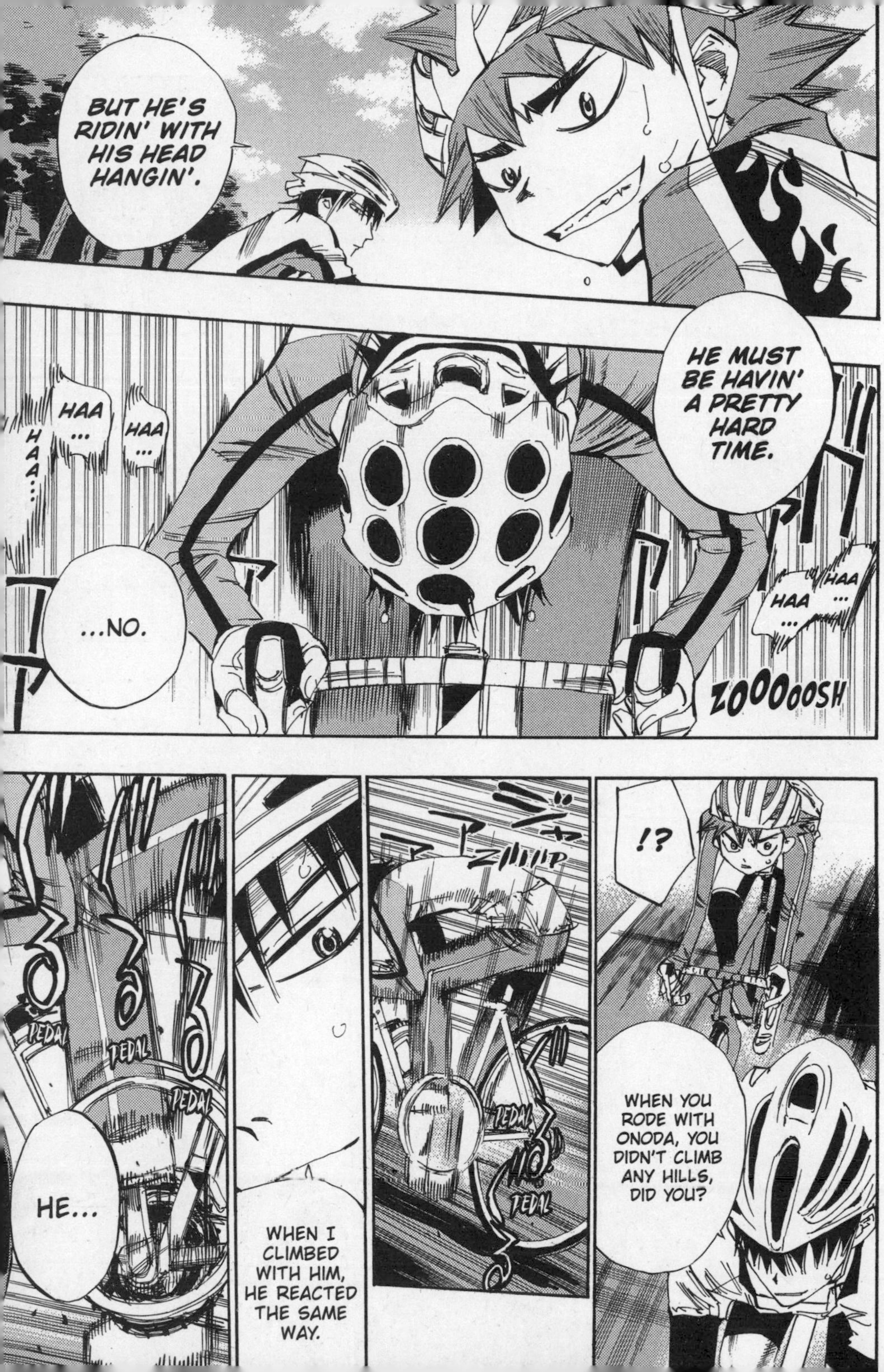
BUT HE'S RIDIN' WITH HIS HEAD HANGIN'.
HE MUST BE HAVIN' A PRETTY HARD TIME.
HAA...
HAA...
ZOOOoOSH
...NO.
HAA...
HAA...
HAA...
!?
WHEN YOU RODE WITH ONODA, YOU DIDN'T CLIMB ANY HILLS, DID YOU?
ZIIIIP
PEDAL
PEDAL
WHEN I CLIMBED WITH HIM, HE REACTED THE SAME WAY.
PEDAL
PEDAL
PEDAL
HE...

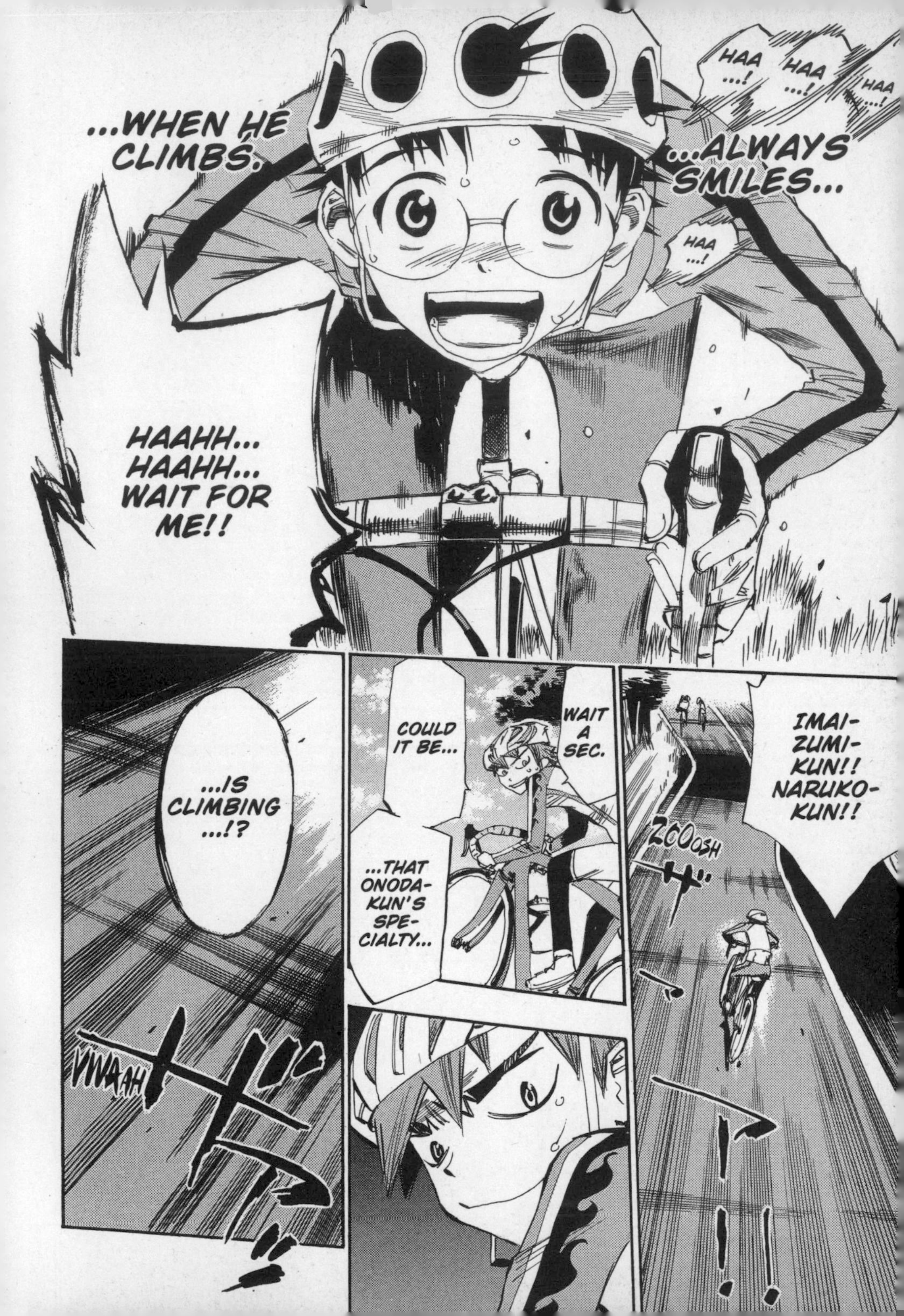
HAA ...!
HAA ...!
HAA ...!
...ALWAYS SMILES...
...WHEN HE CLIMBS.
HAA ...!
HAAHH... HAAHH... WAIT FOR ME!!
IMAI-ZUMI-KUN!! NARUKO-KUN!!
ZOOOSH
WAIT A SEC.
COULD IT BE...
...THAT ONODA-KUN'S SPE-CIALTY...
!!
...IS CLIMBING ...!?
VWAAH

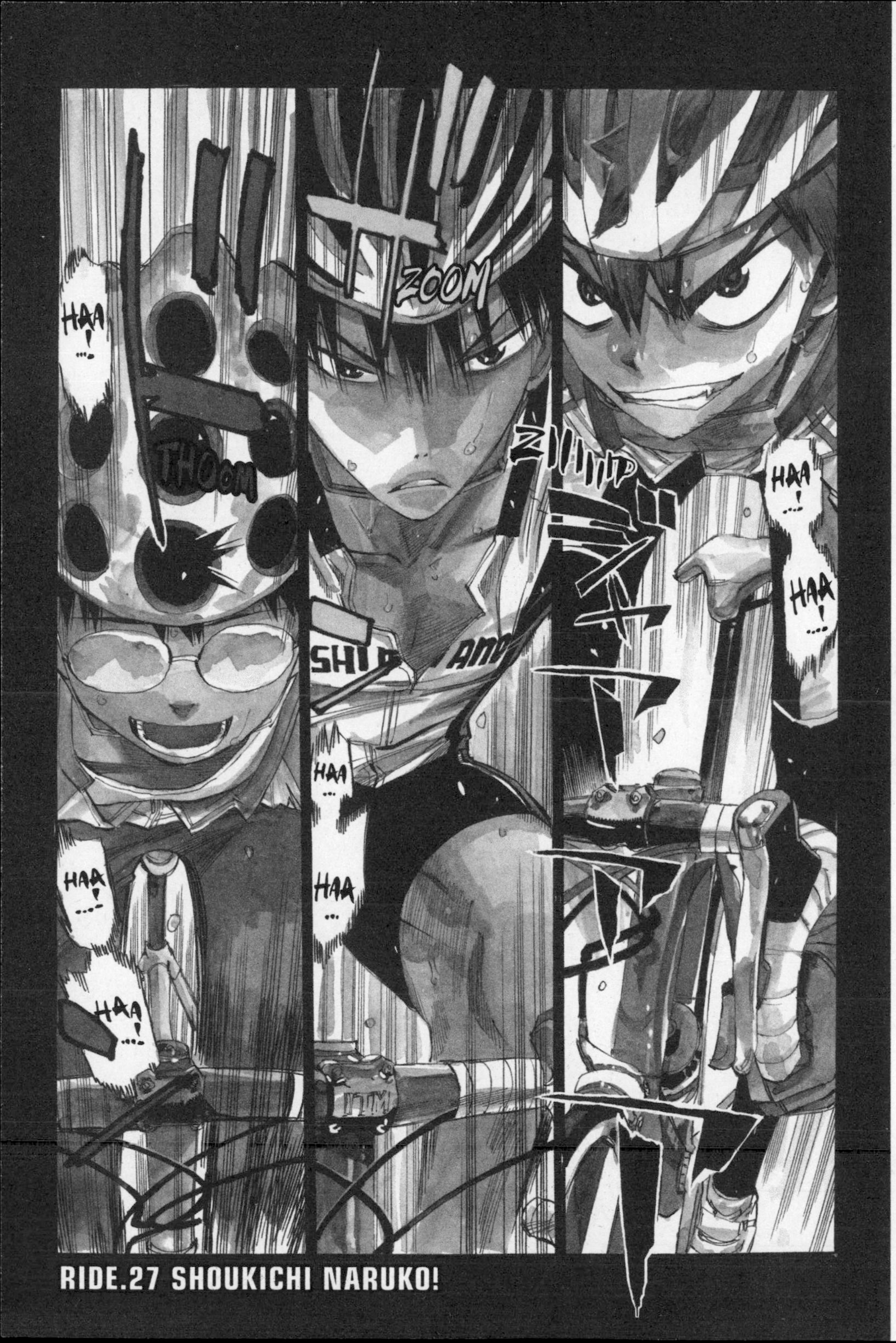
ZIIIIIP
HAA!...
HAA!...
ZOOM
HAA...
HAA...
HAA!...
THOOM
HAA!...
HAA!...

RIDE.27 SHOUKICHI NARUKO!

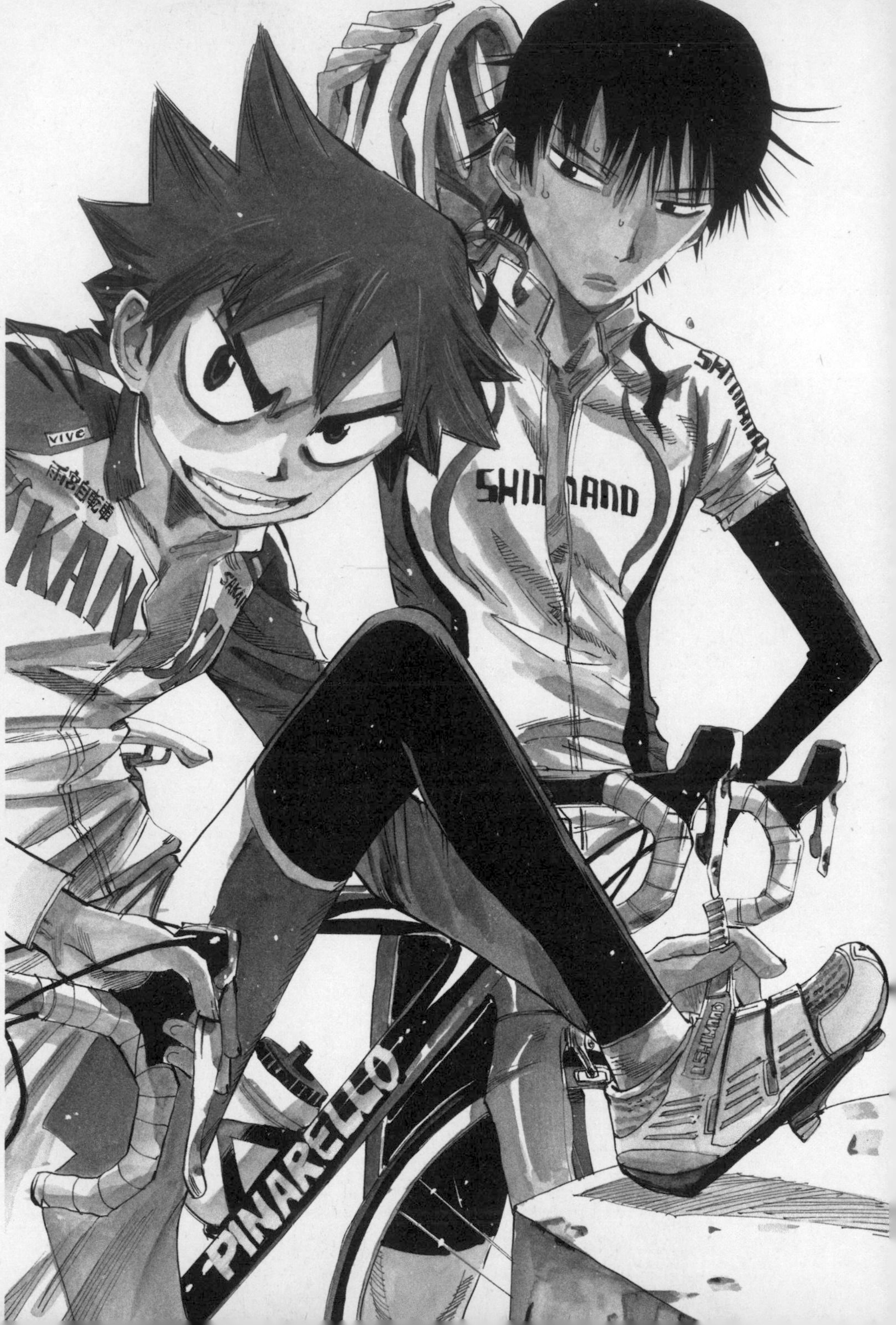
SHIMANO
PINARELLO

RIDE.27
SHOUKICHI NARUKO!

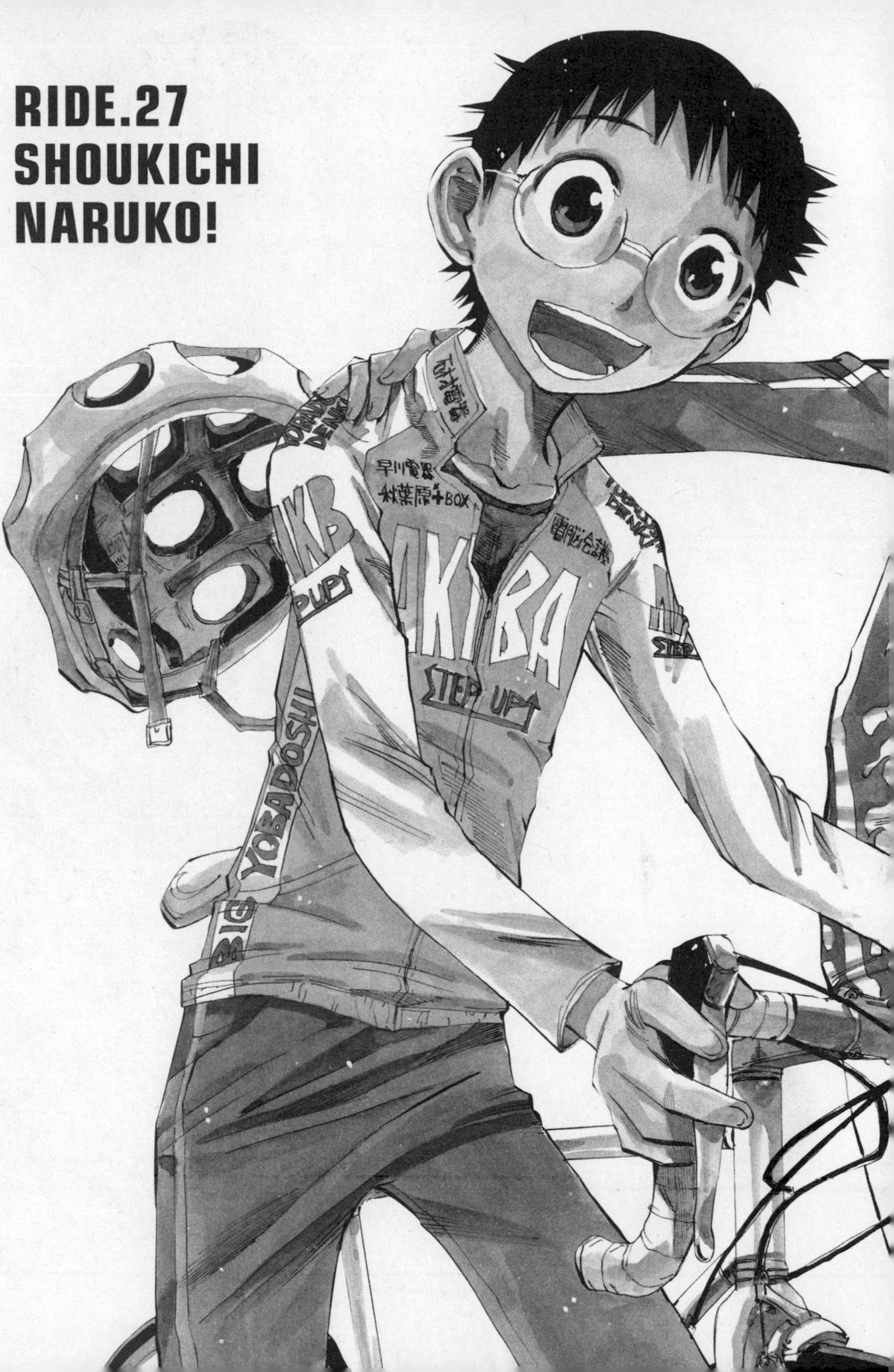
STEP UP
YOBADOSHI
BIG

YOWAMUSHI
PEDAL 2

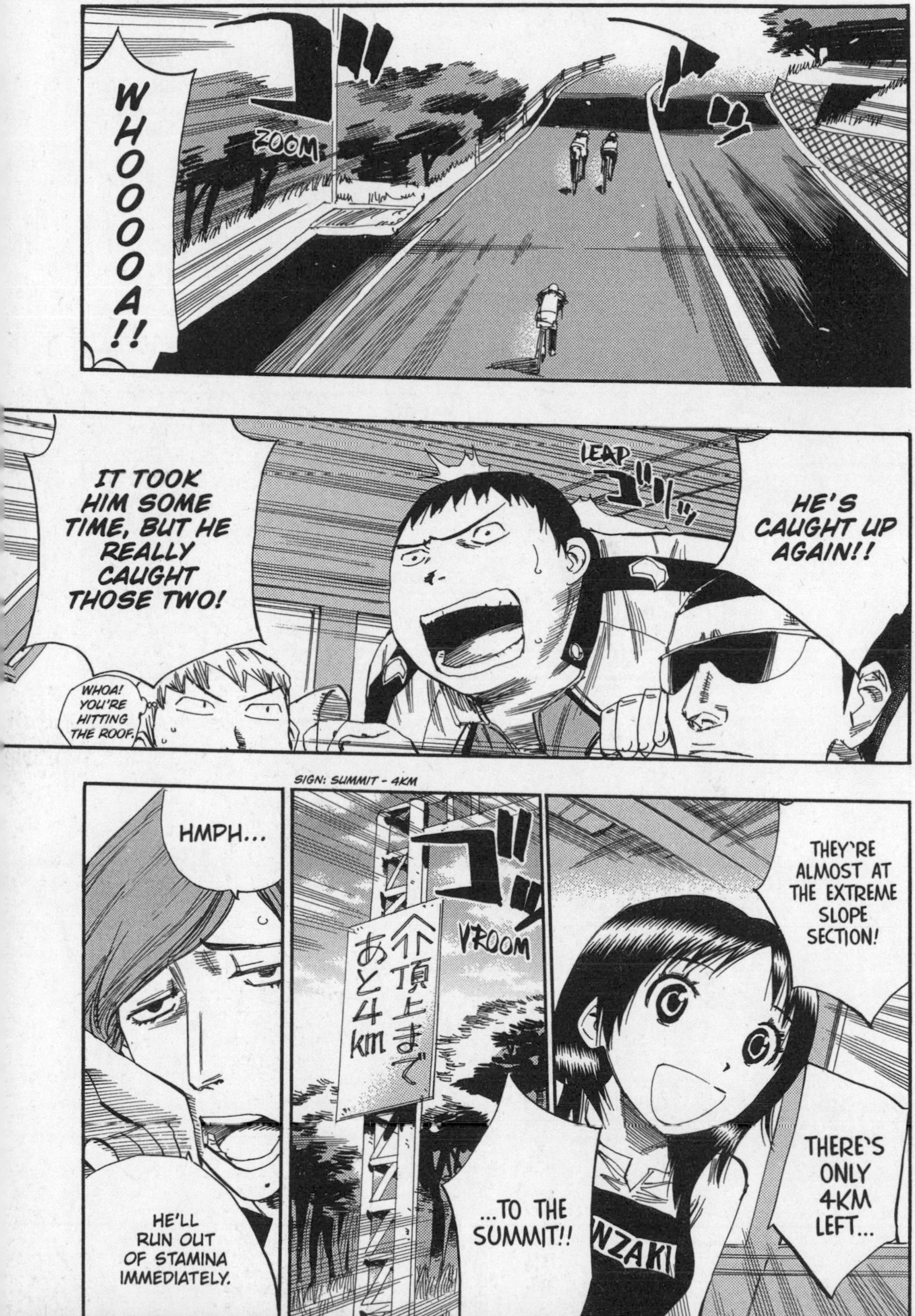

WHOOOOOA!!
ZOOM
HE'S CAUGHT UP AGAIN!!
LEAP
IT TOOK HIM SOME TIME, BUT HE REALLY CAUGHT THOSE TWO!
WHOA! YOU'RE HITTING THE ROOF.
THEY'RE ALMOST AT THE EXTREME SLOPE SECTION!
THERE'S ONLY 4KM LEFT...
...TO THE SUMMIT!!
SIGN: SUMMIT - 4KM
頂上まで あと4km
VROOM
HMPH...
HE'LL RUN OUT OF STAMINA IMMEDIATELY.

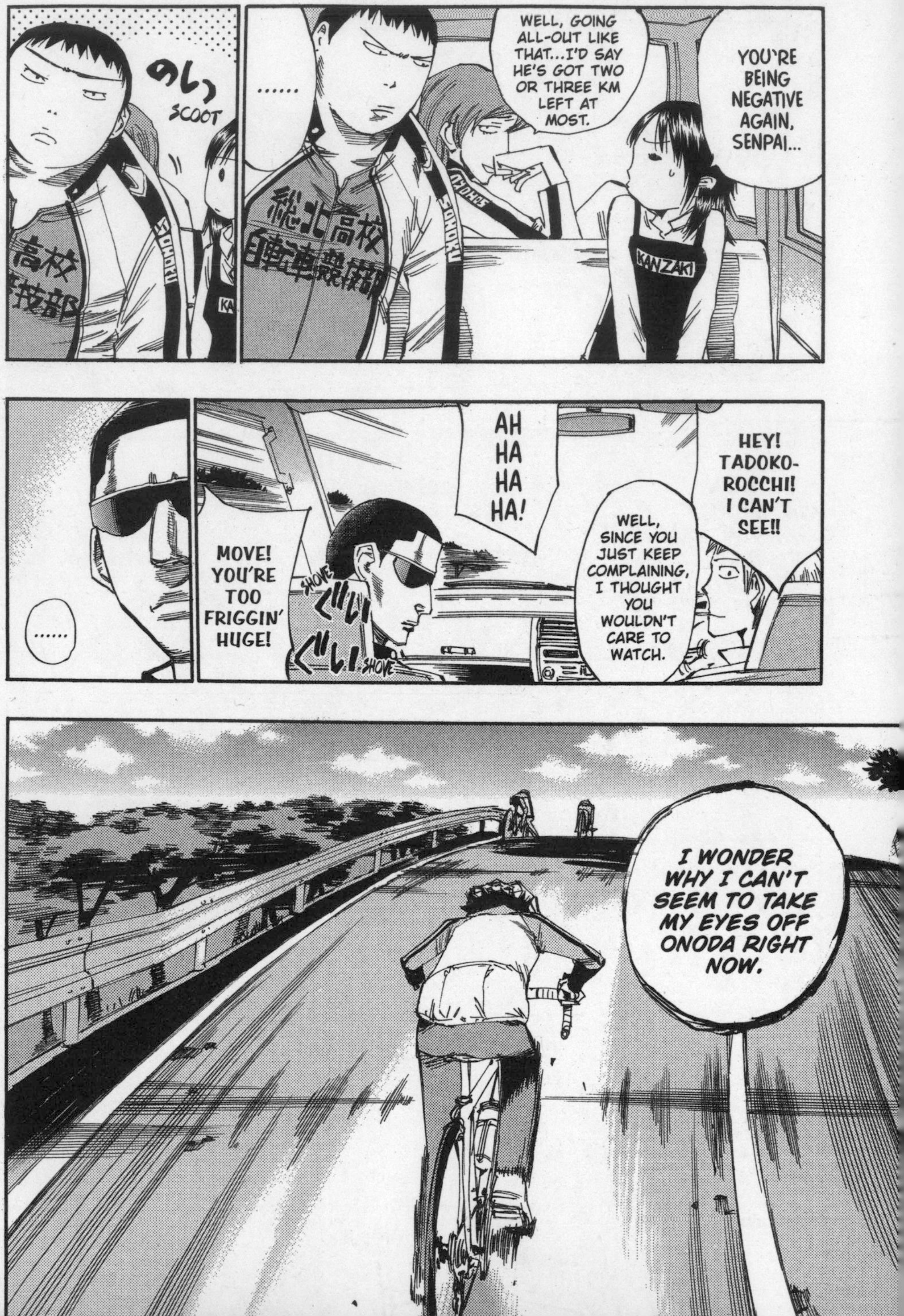
WELL, GOING ALL-OUT LIKE THAT...I'D SAY HE'S GOT TWO OR THREE KM LEFT AT MOST.
YOU'RE BEING NEGATIVE AGAIN, SENPAI...
......
のしっ
SCOOT
HEY! TADOKO-ROCCHI! I CAN'T SEE!!
AH HA HA HA!
WELL, SINCE YOU JUST KEEP COMPLAINING, I THOUGHT YOU WOULDN'T CARE TO WATCH.
MOVE! YOU'RE TOO FRIGGIN' HUGE!
ぐいぐい SHOVE SHOVE
......
I WONDER WHY I CAN'T SEEM TO TAKE MY EYES OFF ONODA RIGHT NOW.

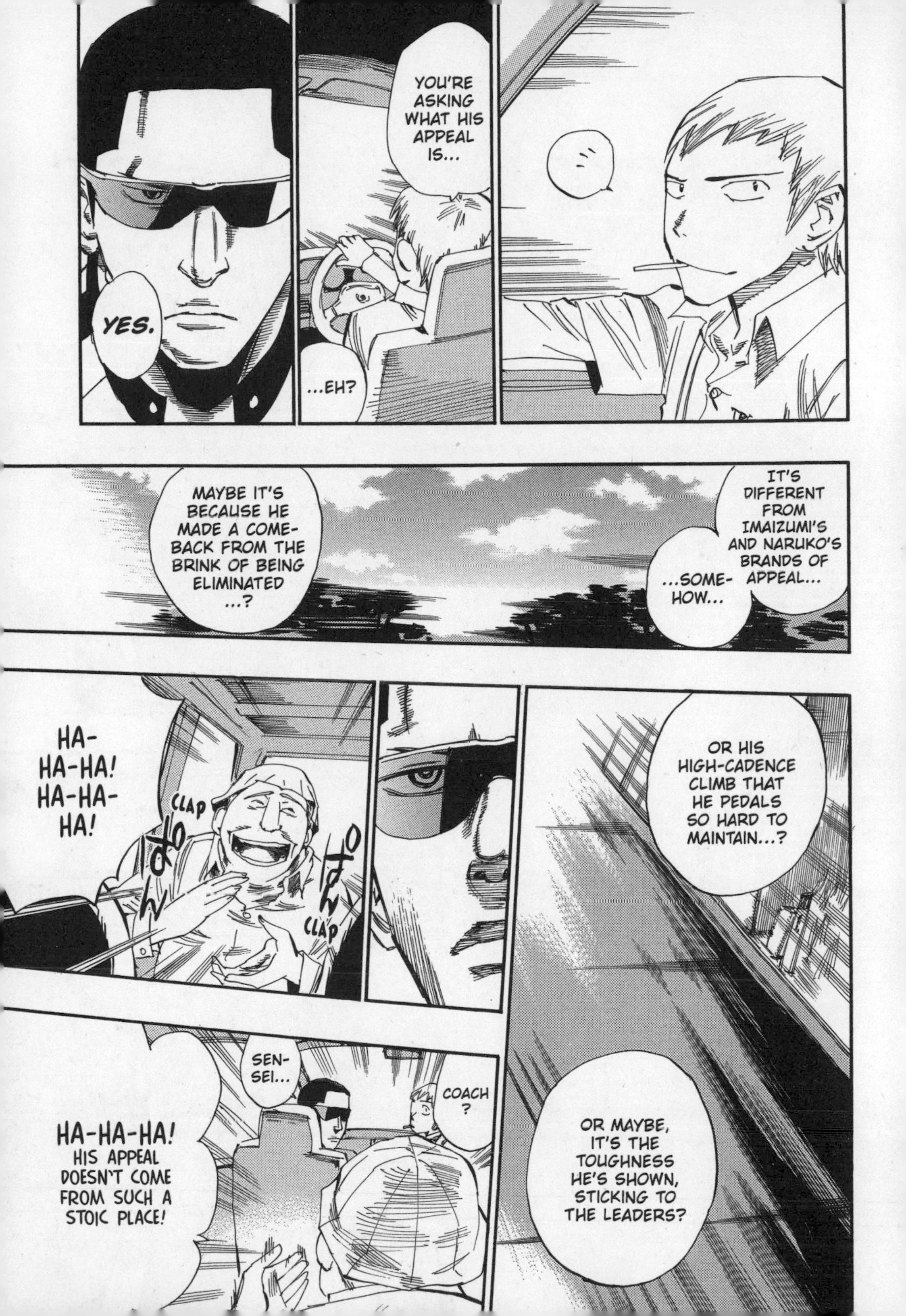
...
YOU'RE ASKING WHAT HIS APPEAL IS...
...EH?
YES.
IT'S DIFFERENT FROM IMAIZUMI'S AND NARUKO'S BRANDS OF APPEAL...
...SOMEHOW...
MAYBE IT'S BECAUSE HE MADE A COME-BACK FROM THE BRINK OF BEING ELIMINATED ...?
OR HIS HIGH-CADENCE CLIMB THAT HE PEDALS SO HARD TO MAINTAIN...?
OR MAYBE, IT'S THE TOUGHNESS HE'S SHOWN, STICKING TO THE LEADERS?
HA-HA-HA! HA-HA-HA!
CLAP
CLAP
COACH?
SEN-SEI...
HA-HA-HA! HIS APPEAL DOESN'T COME FROM SUCH A STOIC PLACE!

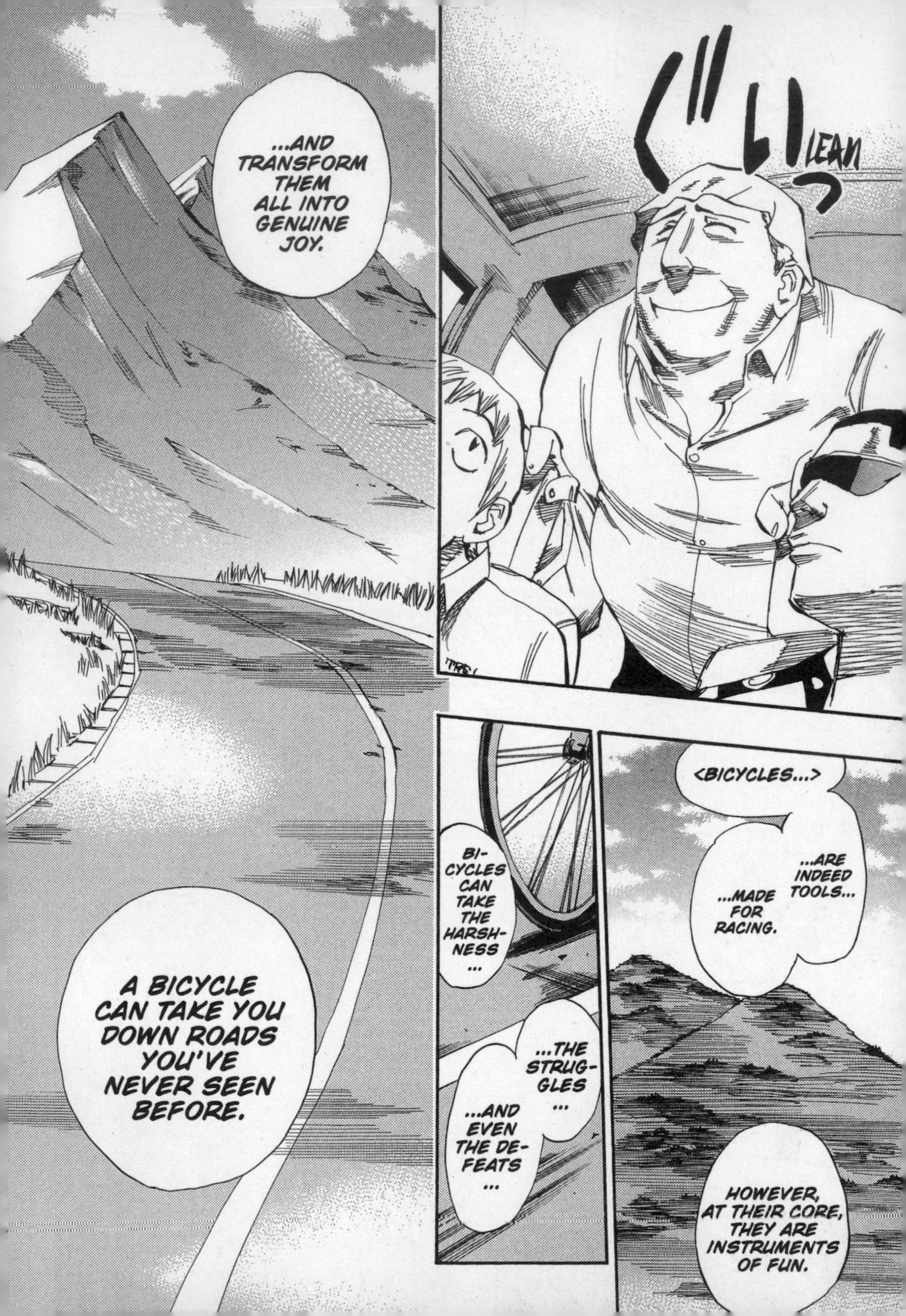
LEAN
<BICYCLES...>
...ARE INDEED TOOLS...
...MADE FOR RACING.
HOWEVER, AT THEIR CORE, THEY ARE INSTRUMENTS OF FUN.
BI-CYCLES CAN TAKE THE HARSH-NESS...
...THE STRUG-GLES...
...AND EVEN THE DE-FEATS...
...AND TRANSFORM THEM ALL INTO GENUINE JOY.
A BICYCLE CAN TAKE YOU DOWN ROADS YOU'VE NEVER SEEN BEFORE.

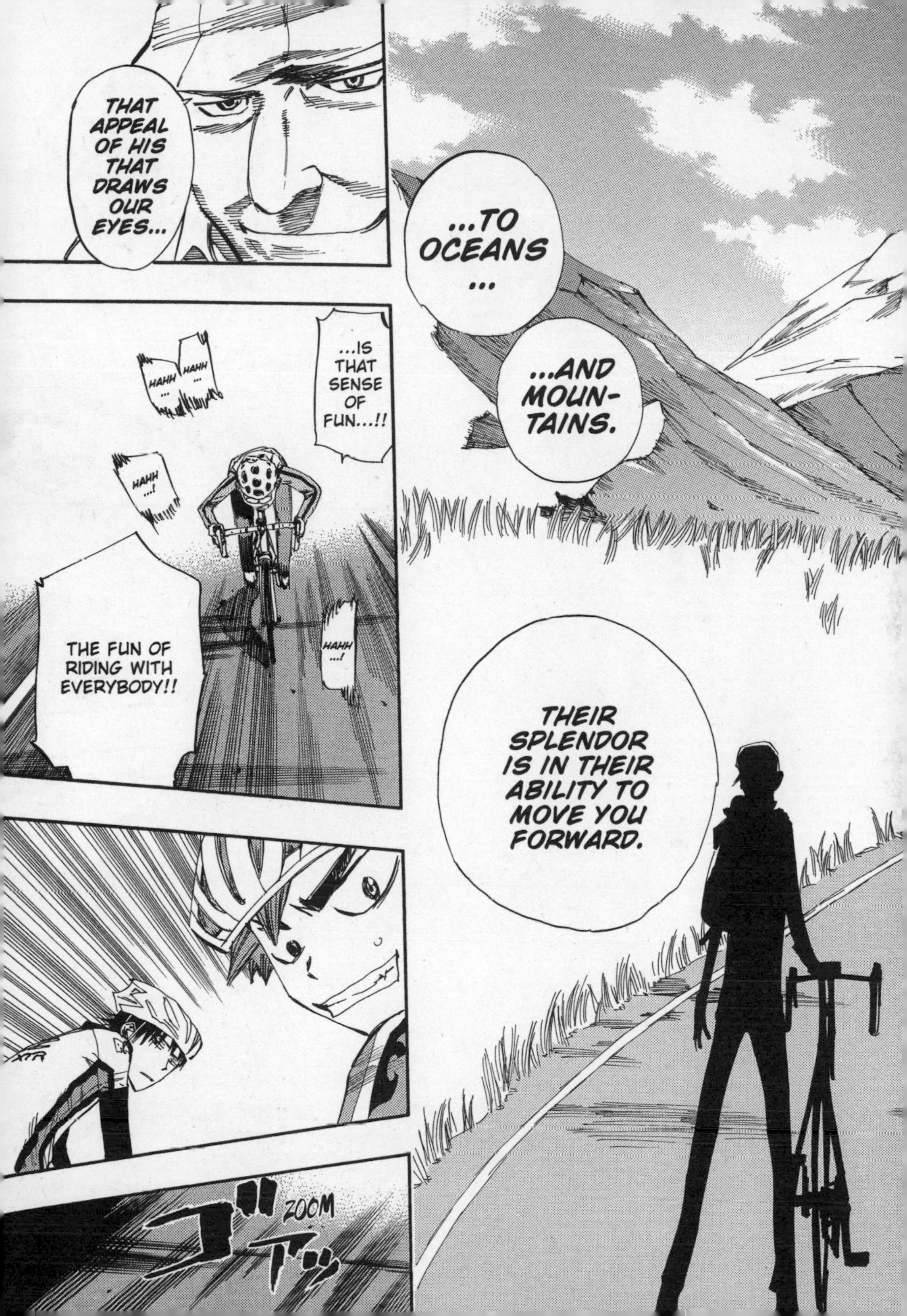
...TO OCEANS ...
...AND MOUN-TAINS.
THEIR SPLENDOR IS IN THEIR ABILITY TO MOVE YOU FORWARD.
THAT APPEAL OF HIS THAT DRAWS OUR EYES...
...IS THAT SENSE OF FUN...!!
HAHH ...
HAHH ...
HAHH ...!
THE FUN OF RIDING WITH EVERYBODY!!
HAHH ...!
ZOOM

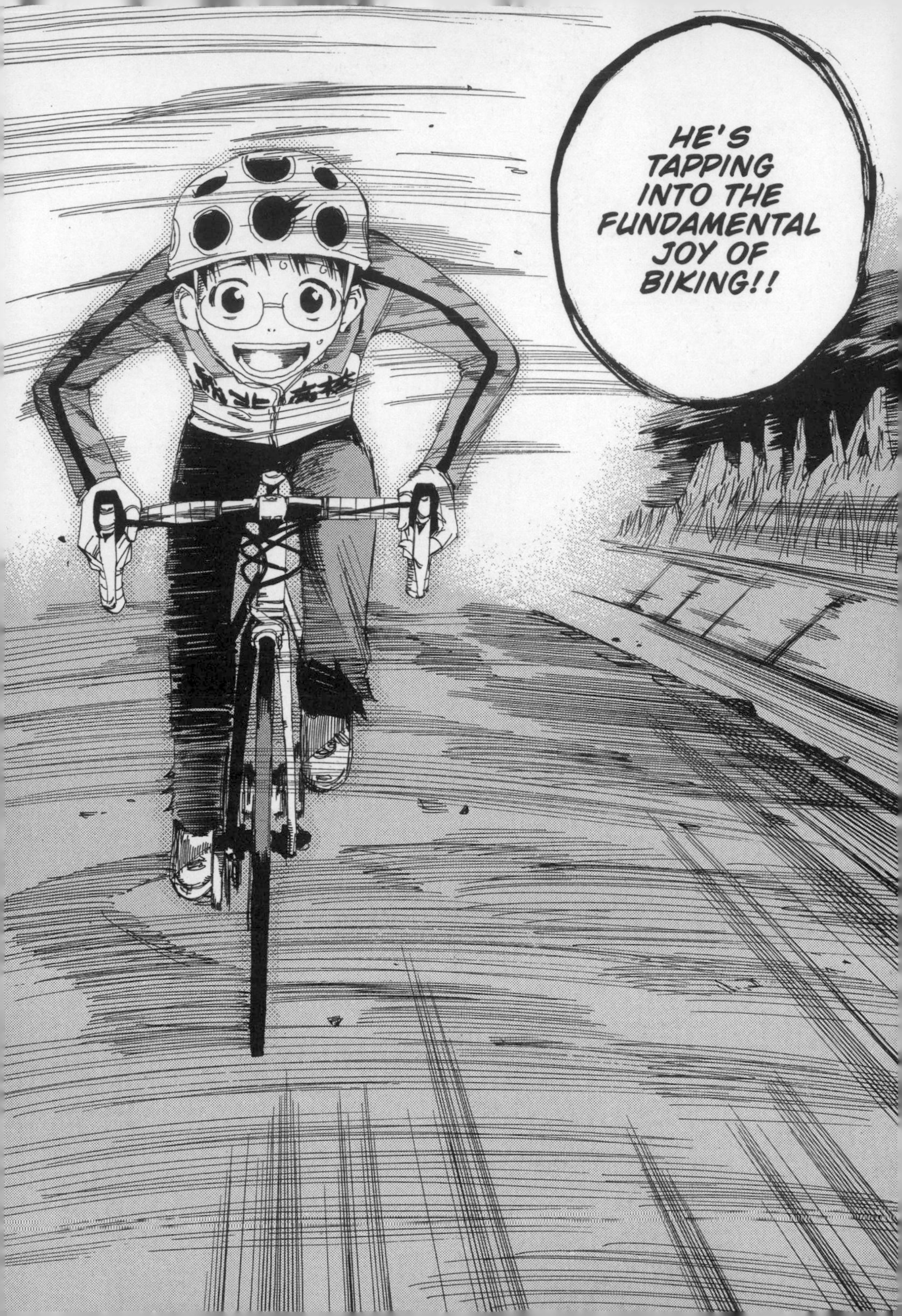
HE'S TAPPING INTO THE FUNDAMENTAL JOY OF BIKING!!

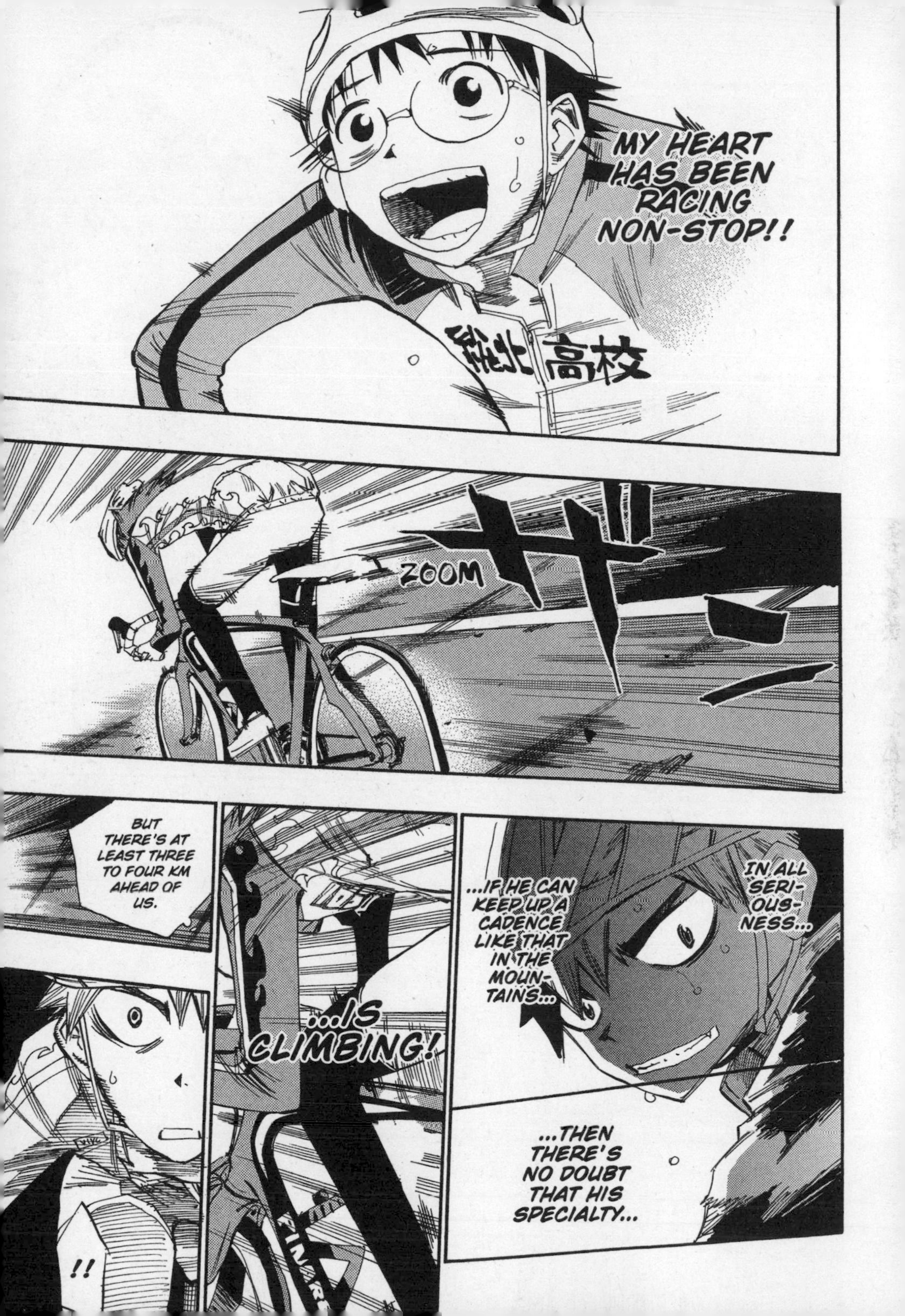
MY HEART HAS BEEN RACING NON-STOP!!
ZOOM
IN ALL SERI-OUS-NESS...
...IF HE CAN KEEP UP A CADENCE LIKE THAT IN THE MOUN-TAINS...
...THEN THERE'S NO DOUBT THAT HIS SPECIALTY...
...IS CLIMBING!
BUT THERE'S AT LEAST THREE TO FOUR KM AHEAD OF US.
!!

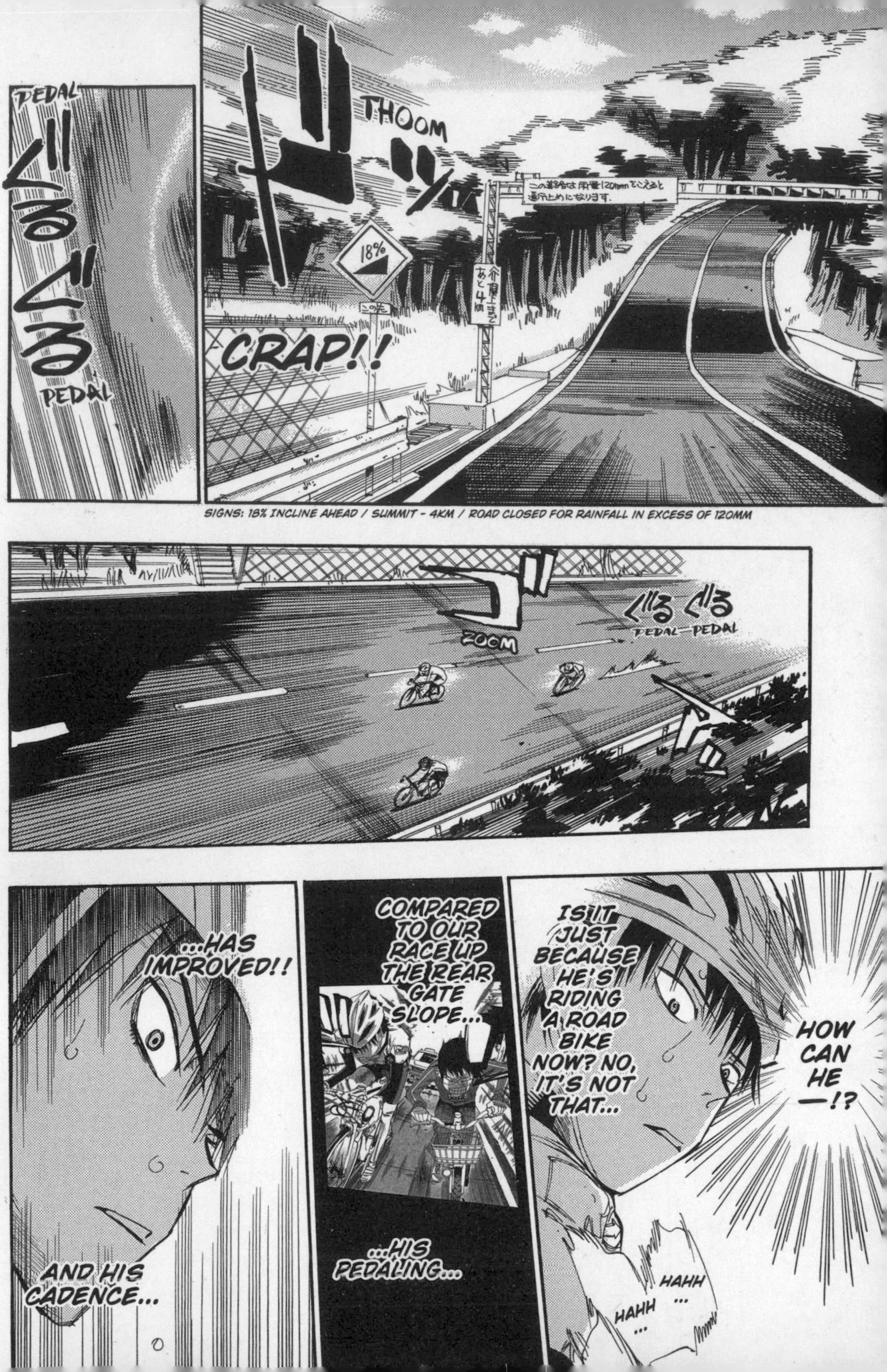
THOOM
CRAP!!
18%
この道路は雨量120mmをこえると通行止めになります。
PEDAL
ぐるぐる
PEDAL
SIGNS: 18% INCLINE AHEAD / SUMMIT - 4KM / ROAD CLOSED FOR RAINFALL IN EXCESS OF 120MM
ZOOM
ぐる ぐる
PEDAL—PEDAL
HOW CAN HE—!?
IS IT JUST BECAUSE HE'S RIDING A ROAD BIKE NOW? NO, IT'S NOT THAT...
HAHH... HAHH...
COMPARED TO OUR RACE UP THE REAR GATE SLOPE...
...HIS PEDALING...
...HAS IMPROVED!!
AND HIS CADENCE...

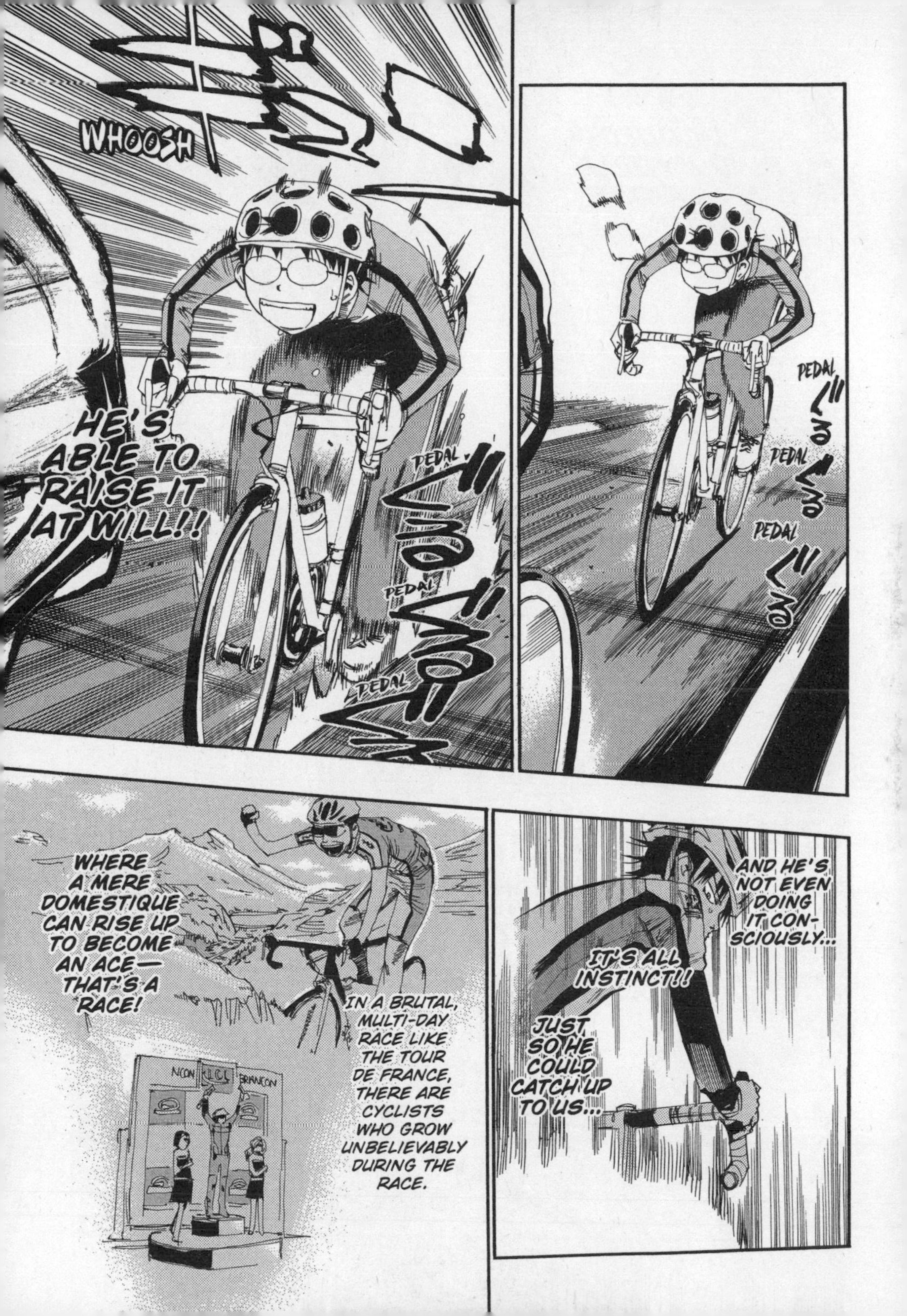
PEDAL
PEDAL
PEDAL
WHOOSH
HE'S ABLE TO RAISE IT AT WILL!!
PEDAL
PEDAL
PEDAL
AND HE'S NOT EVEN DOING IT CONSCIOUSLY...
IT'S ALL INSTINCT!!
JUST SO HE COULD CATCH UP TO US...
IN A BRUTAL, MULTI-DAY RACE LIKE THE TOUR DE FRANCE, THERE ARE CYCLISTS WHO GROW UNBELIEVABLY DURING THE RACE.
WHERE A MERE DOMESTIQUE CAN RISE UP TO BECOME AN ACE—THAT'S A RACE!

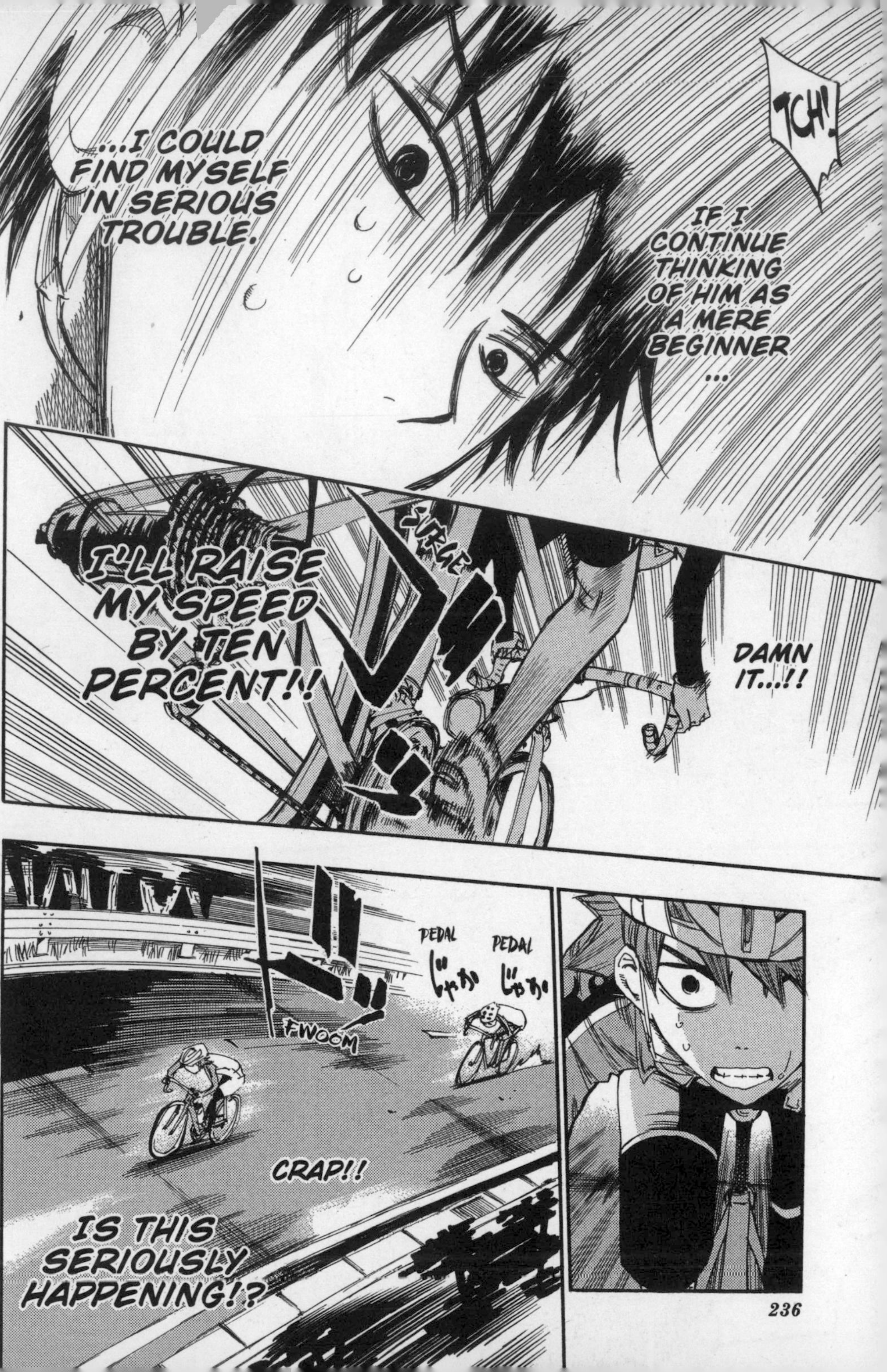
TCH!
IF I CONTINUE THINKING OF HIM AS A MERE BEGINNER ...
...I COULD FIND MYSELF IN SERIOUS TROUBLE.
DAMN IT...!!
SURGE
I'LL RAISE MY SPEED BY TEN PERCENT!!
PEDAL
PEDAL
FWOOM
CRAP!!
IS THIS SERIOUSLY HAPPENING!?

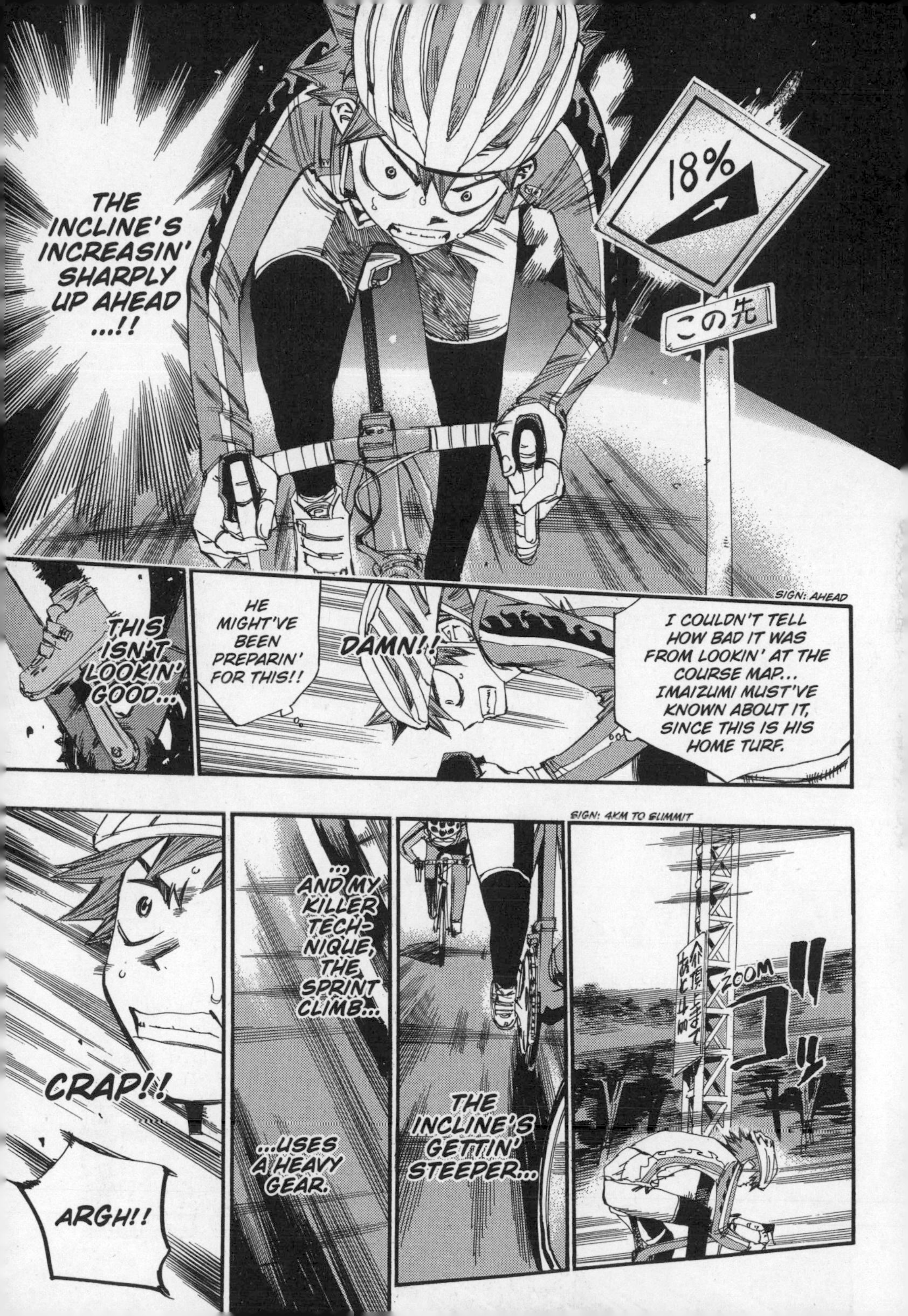
18%
この先
THE INCLINE'S INCREASIN' SHARPLY UP AHEAD ...!!
SIGN: AHEAD
I COULDN'T TELL HOW BAD IT WAS FROM LOOKIN' AT THE COURSE MAP... IMAIZUMI MUST'VE KNOWN ABOUT IT, SINCE THIS IS HIS HOME TURF.
DAMN!!
HE MIGHT'VE BEEN PREPARIN' FOR THIS!!
THIS ISN'T LOOKIN' GOOD...
SIGN: 4KM TO SUMMIT
ZOOM
THE INCLINE'S GETTIN' STEEPER...
...AND MY KILLER TECH-NIQUE, THE SPRINT CLIMB...
...USES A HEAVY GEAR.
CRAP!!
ARGH!!

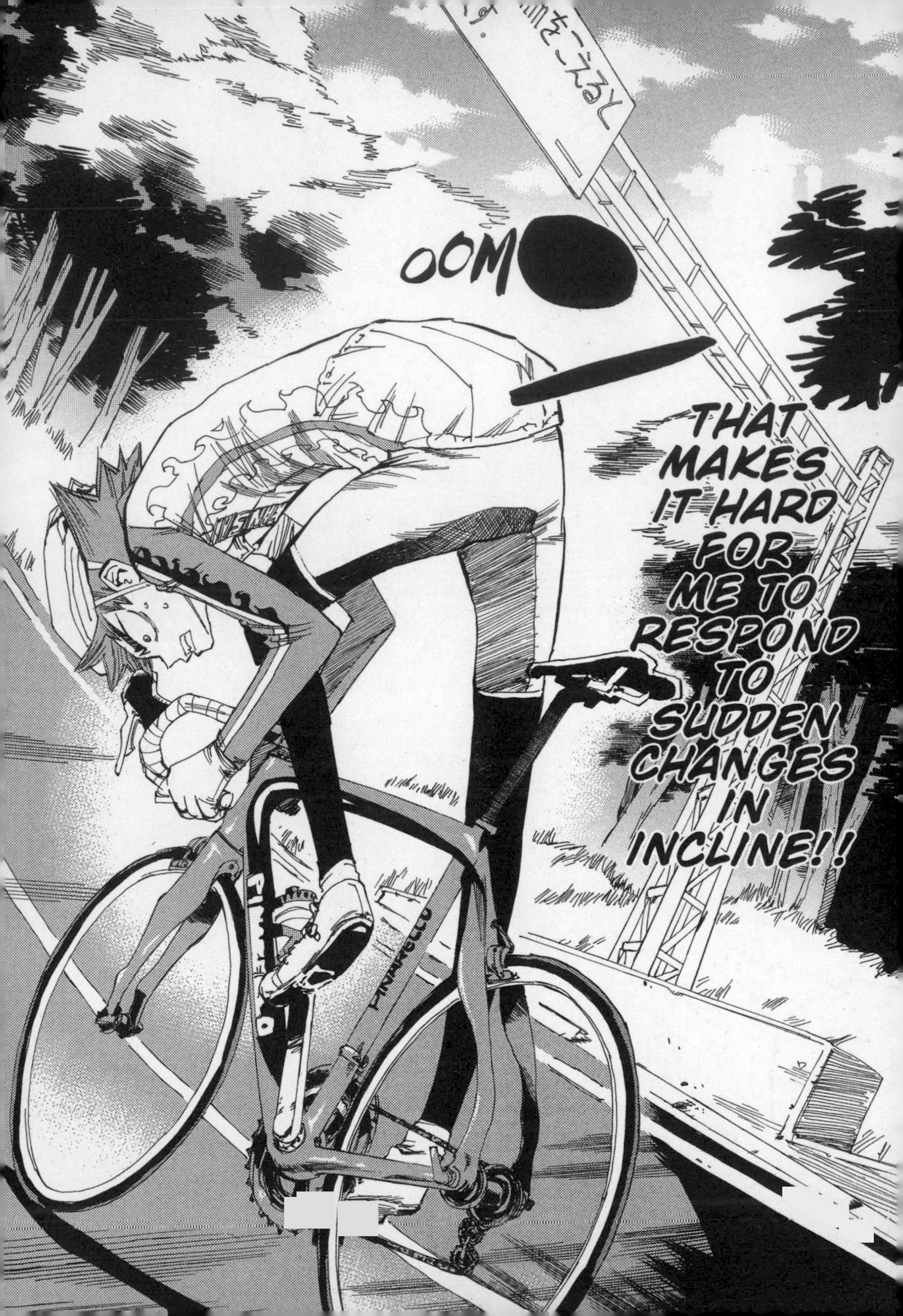
OOM
THAT MAKES IT HARD FOR ME TO RESPOND TO SUDDEN CHANGES IN INCLINE!!

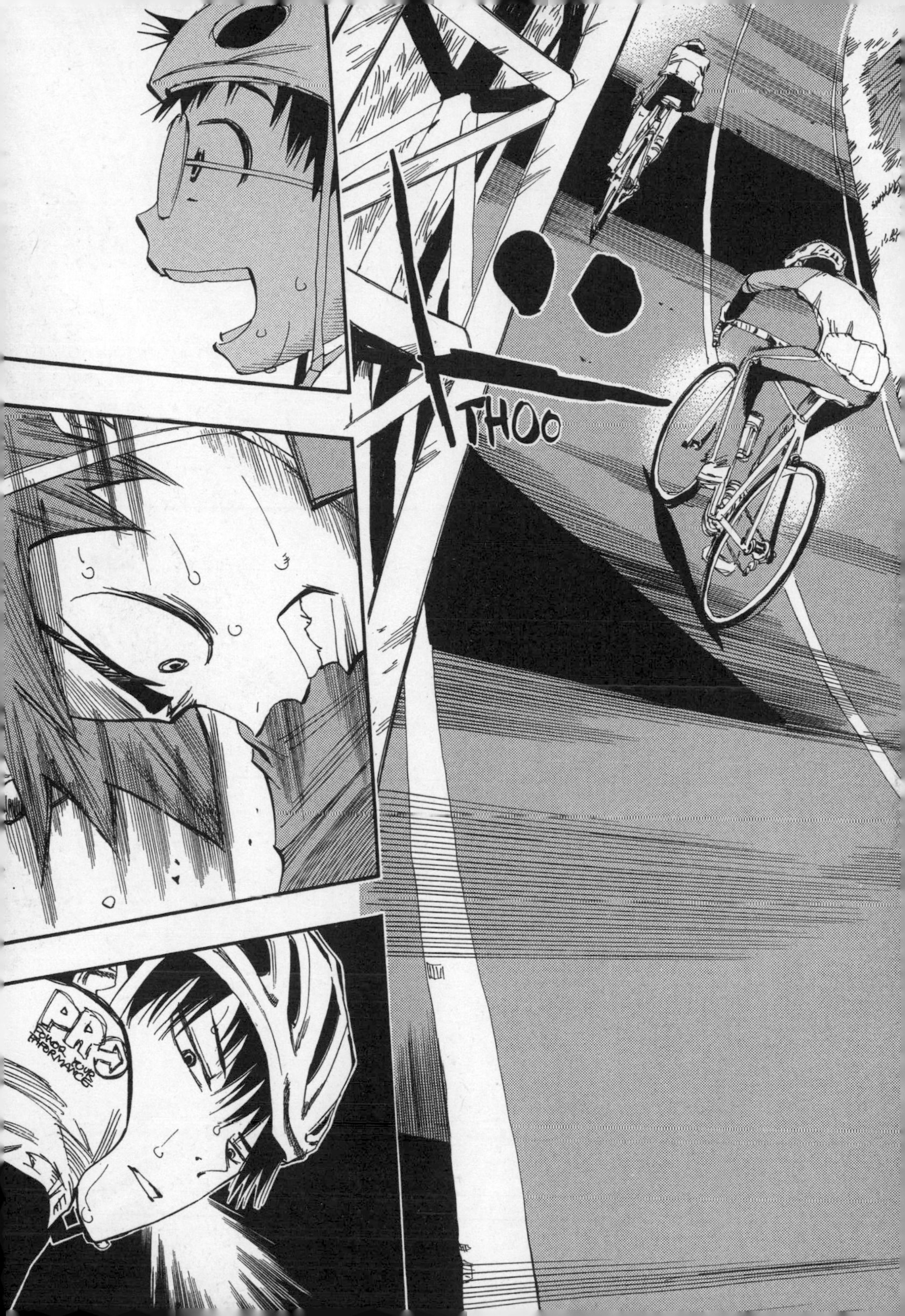
THOO

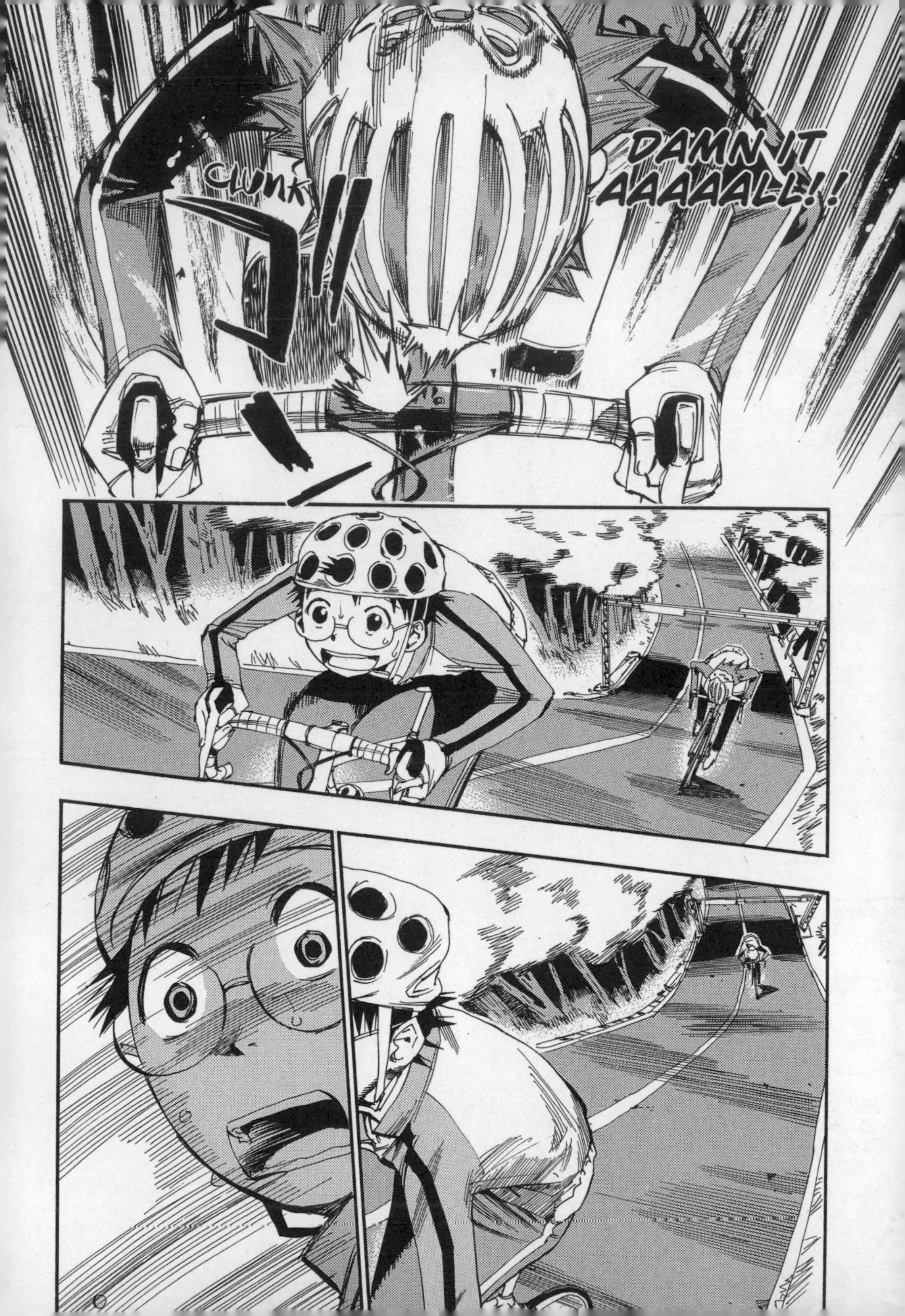
DAMN IT AAAAALL!!
CLUNK

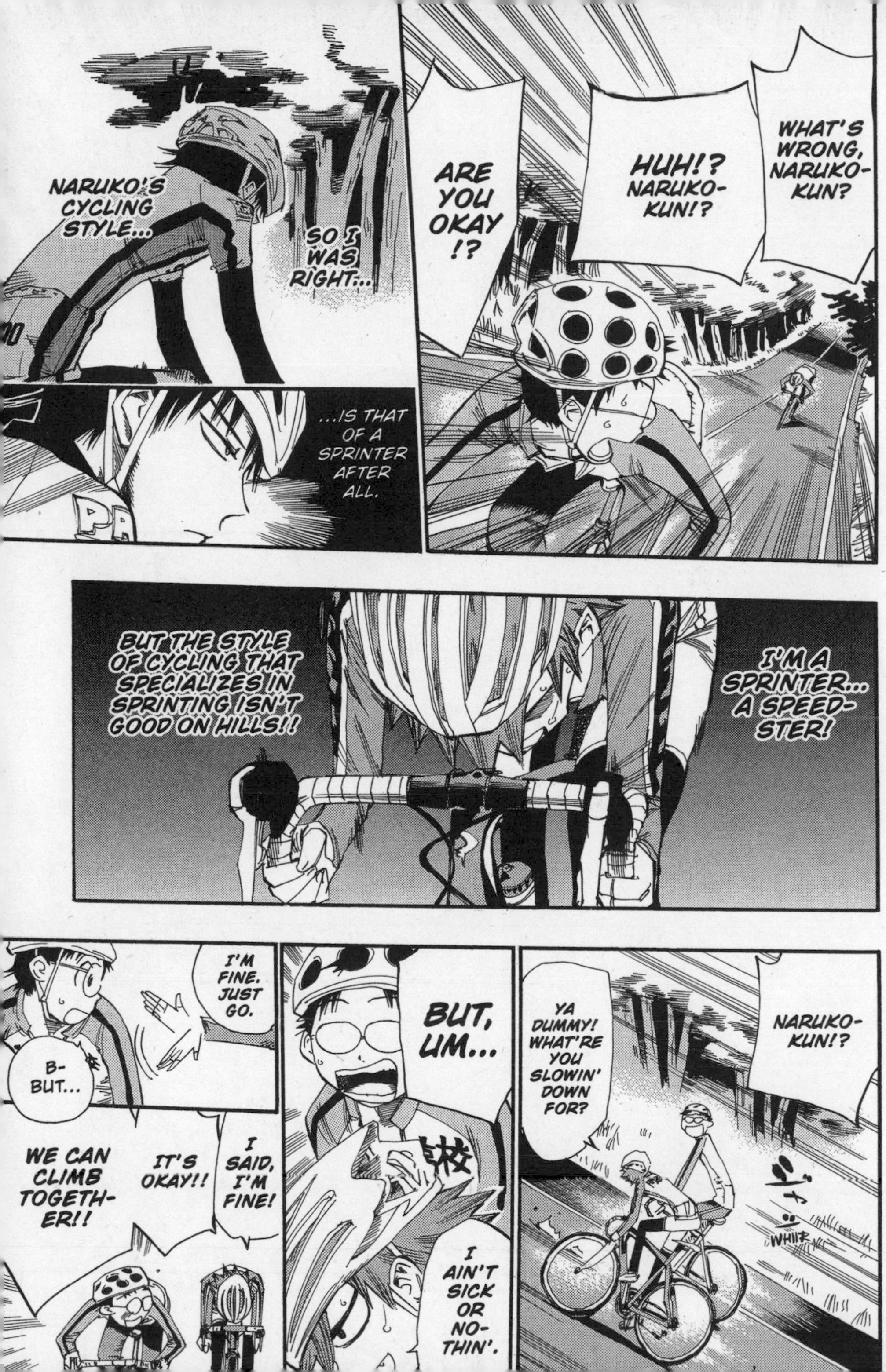
WHAT'S WRONG, NARUKO-KUN?
HUH!? NARUKO-KUN!?
ARE YOU OKAY!?
SO I WAS RIGHT...
NARUKO'S CYCLING STYLE...
...IS THAT OF A SPRINTER AFTER ALL.
I'M A SPRINTER... A SPEEDSTER!
BUT THE STYLE OF CYCLING THAT SPECIALIZES IN SPRINTING ISN'T GOOD ON HILLS!!
NARUKO-KUN!?
YA DUMMY! WHAT'RE YOU SLOWIN' DOWN FOR?
WHIIR
BUT, UM...
I AIN'T SICK OR NOTHIN'.
I'M FINE. JUST GO.
B-BUT...
I SAID, I'M FINE!
IT'S OKAY!!
WE CAN CLIMB TOGETHER!!

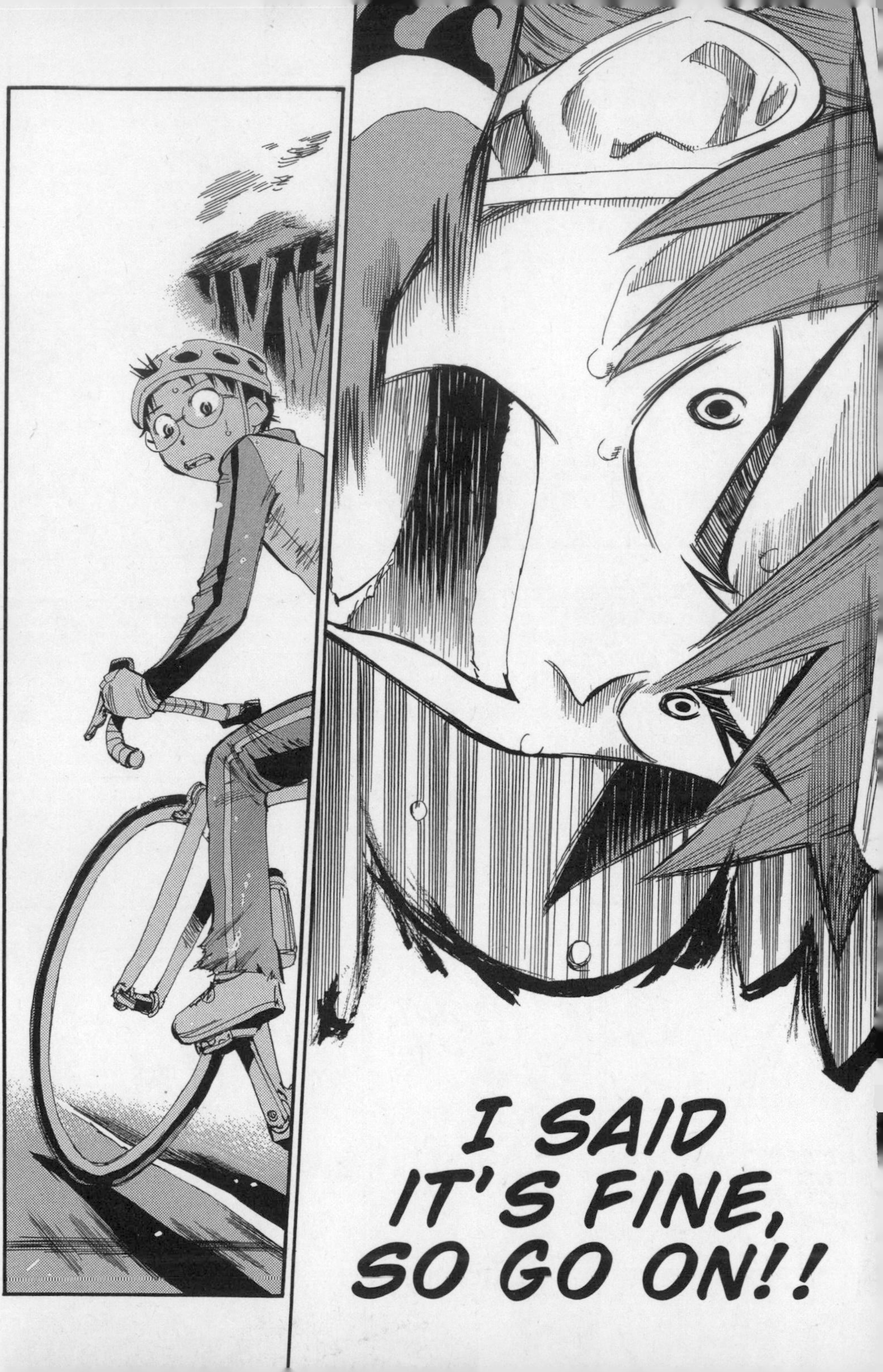
I SAID IT'S FINE, SO GO ON!!

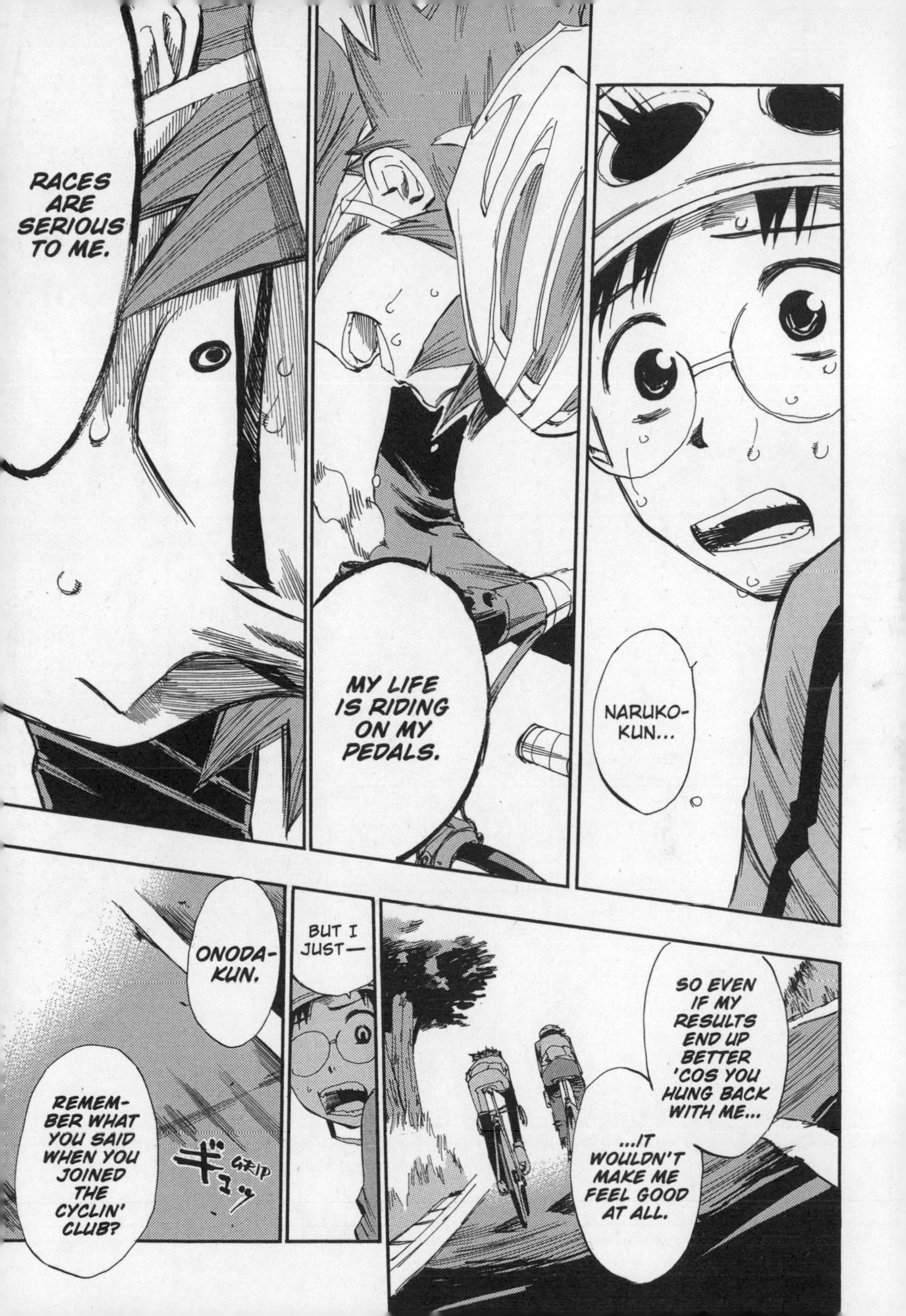
NARUKO-KUN...
MY LIFE IS RIDING ON MY PEDALS.
RACES ARE SERIOUS TO ME.
SO EVEN IF MY RESULTS END UP BETTER 'COS YOU HUNG BACK WITH ME...
...IT WOULDN'T MAKE ME FEEL GOOD AT ALL.
BUT I JUST—
ONODA-KUN.
REMEMBER WHAT YOU SAID WHEN YOU JOINED THE CYCLIN' CLUB?
GRIP

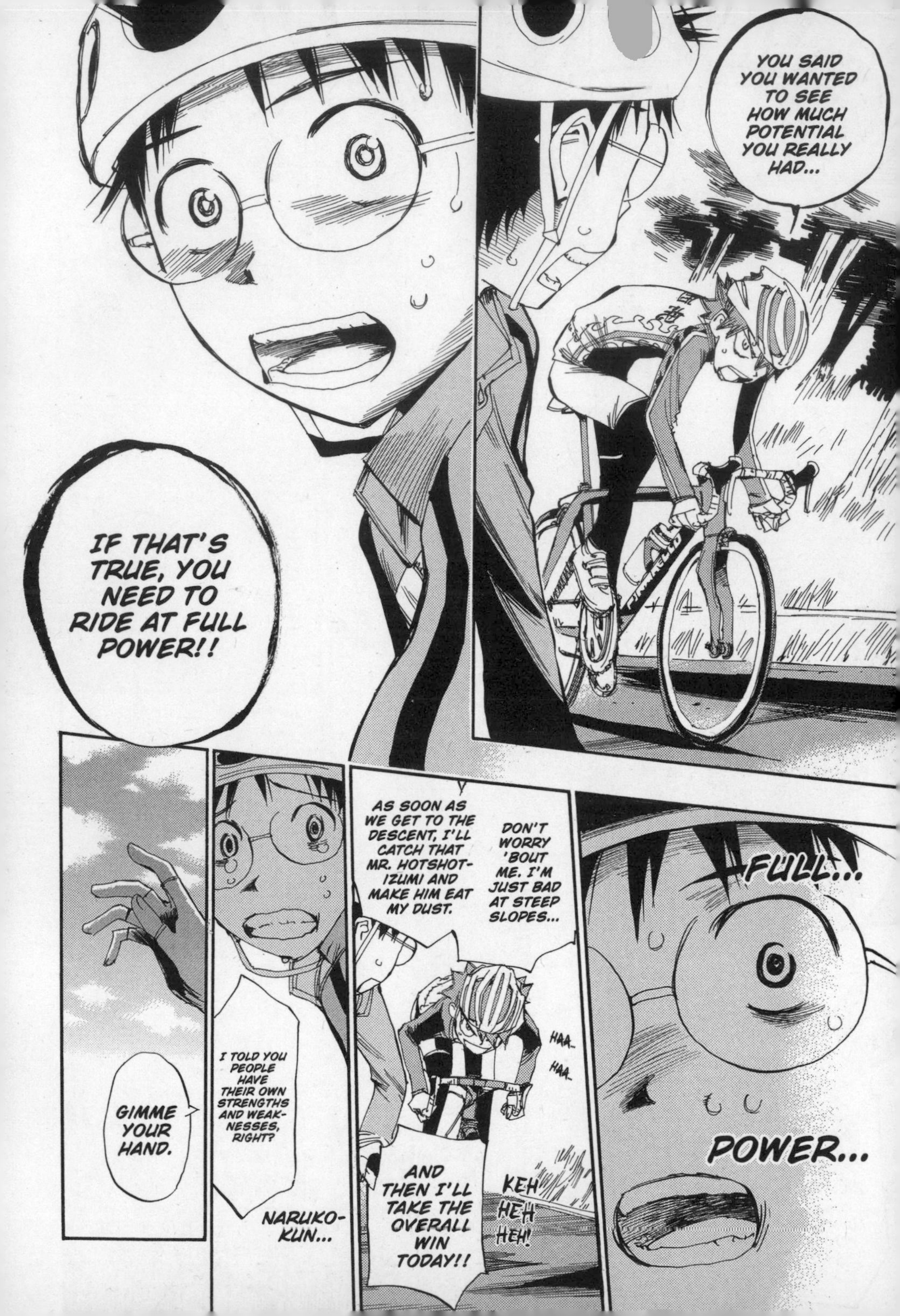
YOU SAID YOU WANTED TO SEE HOW MUCH POTENTIAL YOU REALLY HAD...
IF THAT'S TRUE, YOU NEED TO RIDE AT FULL POWER!!
FULL...
POWER...
DON'T WORRY 'BOUT ME. I'M JUST BAD AT STEEP SLOPES...
AS SOON AS WE GET TO THE DESCENT, I'LL CATCH THAT MR. HOTSHOT-IZUMI AND MAKE HIM EAT MY DUST.
HAA..
HAA..
KEH HEH HEH!
AND THEN I'LL TAKE THE OVERALL WIN TODAY!!
I TOLD YOU PEOPLE HAVE THEIR OWN STRENGTHS AND WEAK-NESSES, RIGHT?
NARUKO-KUN...
GIMME YOUR HAND.

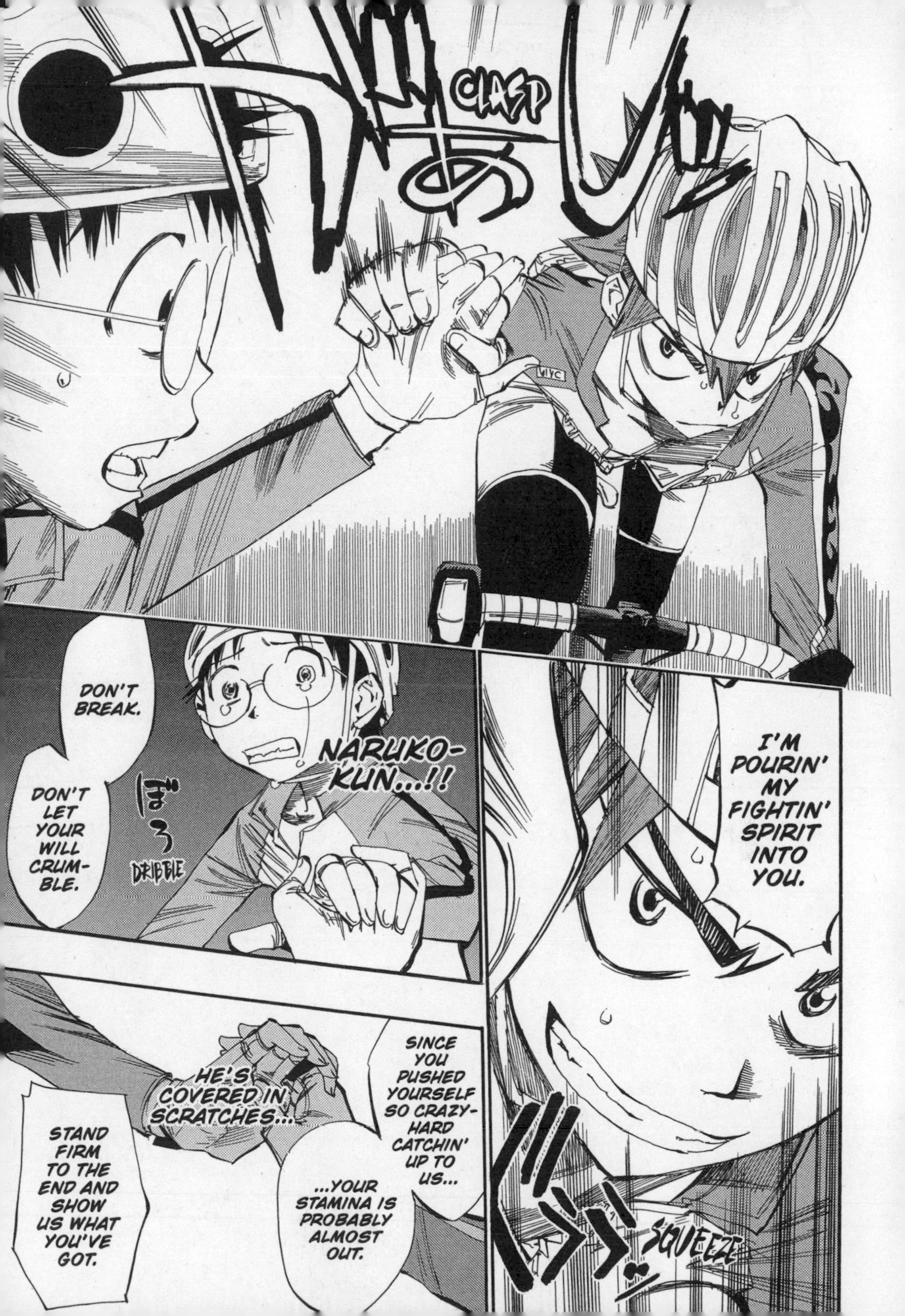
CLASP
I'M POURIN' MY FIGHTIN' SPIRIT INTO YOU.
SQUEEZE
NARUKO-KUN...!!
DRIBBLE
DON'T BREAK.
DON'T LET YOUR WILL CRUMBLE.
SINCE YOU PUSHED YOURSELF SO CRAZY-HARD CATCHIN' UP TO US...
...YOUR STAMINA IS PROBABLY ALMOST OUT.
HE'S COVERED IN SCRATCHES...
STAND FIRM TO THE END AND SHOW US WHAT YOU'VE GOT.

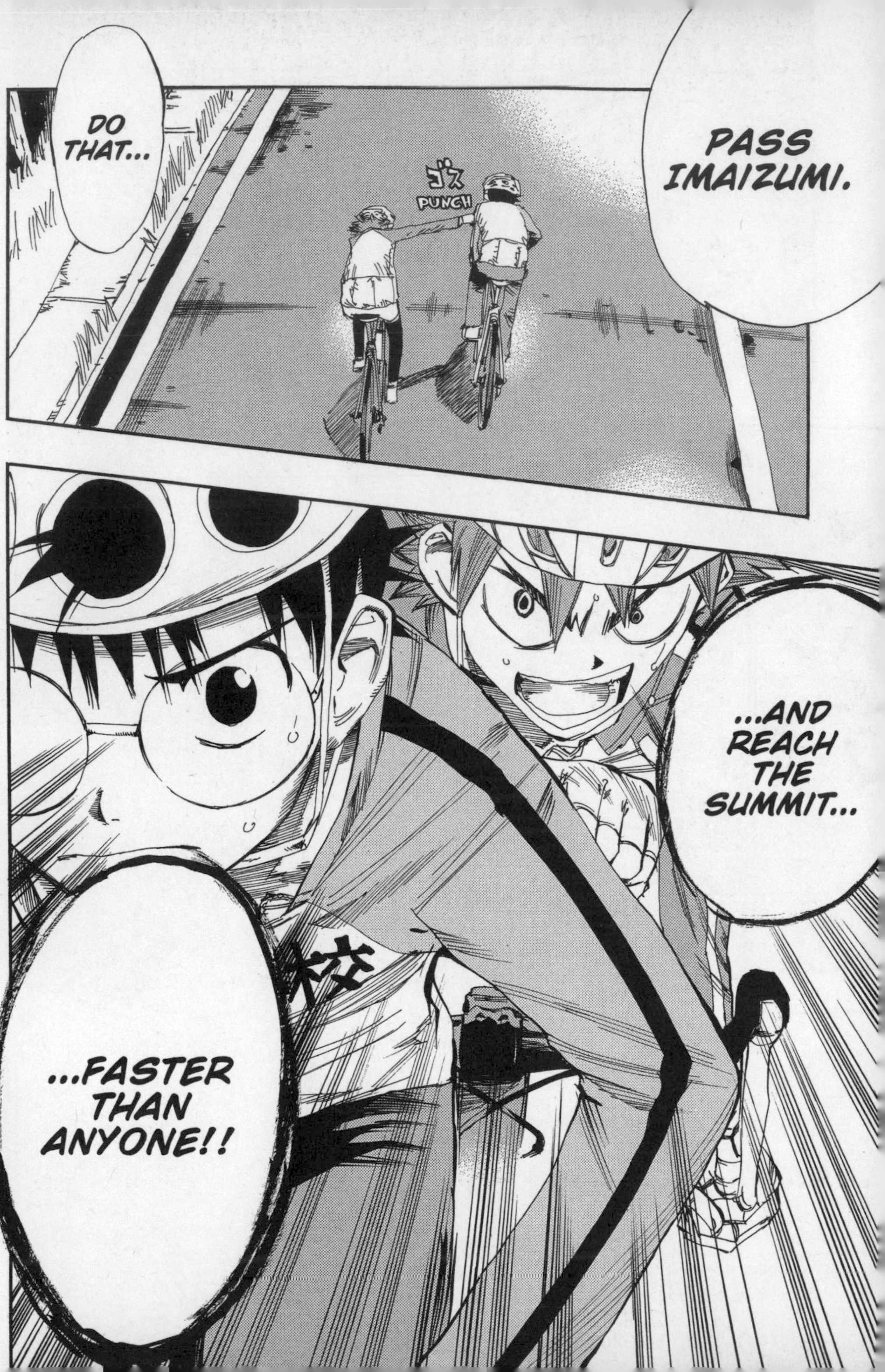
PASS IMAIZUMI.
ゴス
PUNCH
DO THAT...
...AND REACH THE SUMMIT...
...FASTER THAN ANYONE!!

RIDE.28 FASTER THAN ANYONE

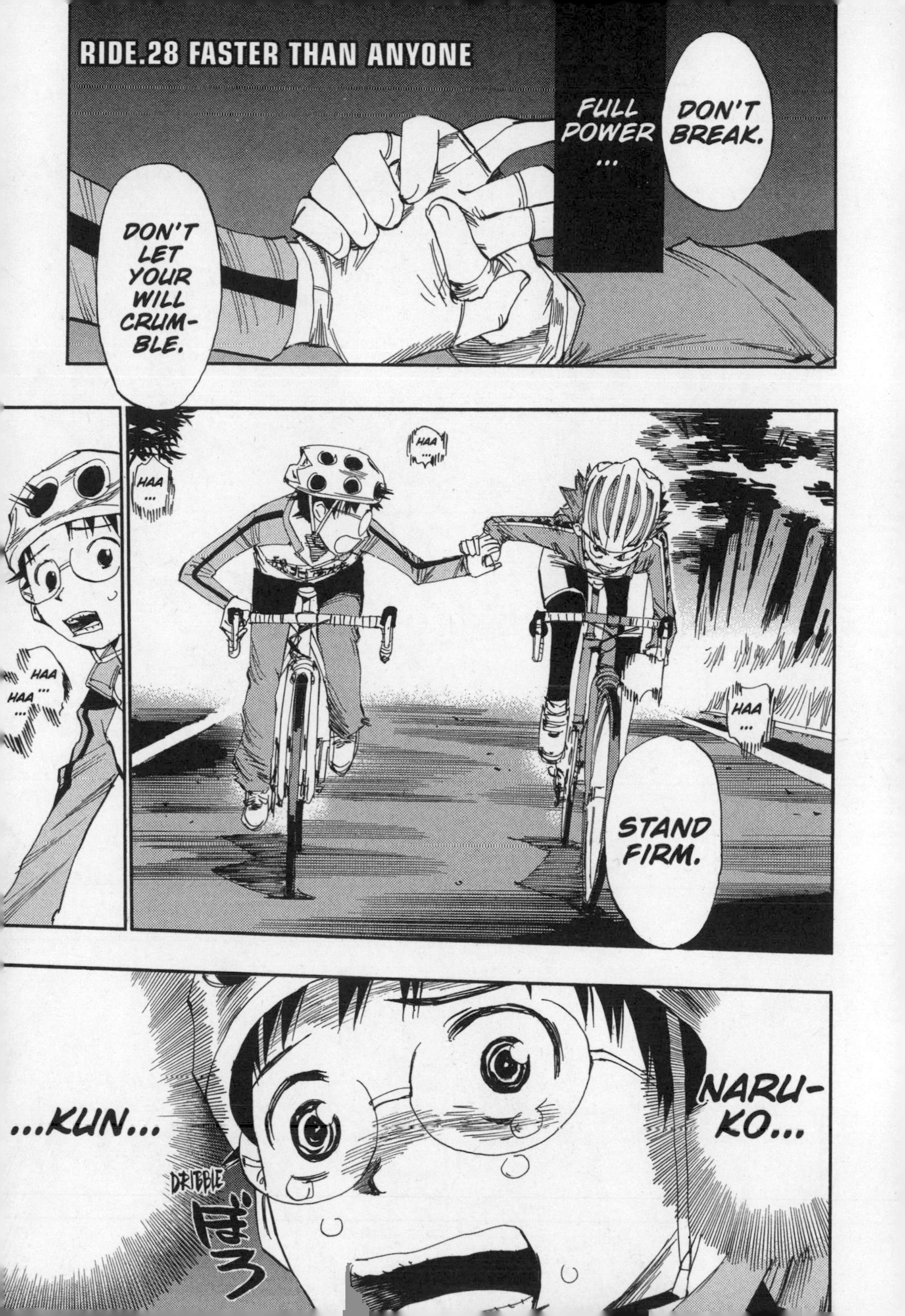
DON'T BREAK.
FULL POWER ...
DON'T LET YOUR WILL CRUMBLE.
HAA ...
HAA ...
HAA ...
STAND FIRM.
HAA ...
HAA ...
HAA ...
NARUKO...
...KUN...
DRIBBLE
ぼろ

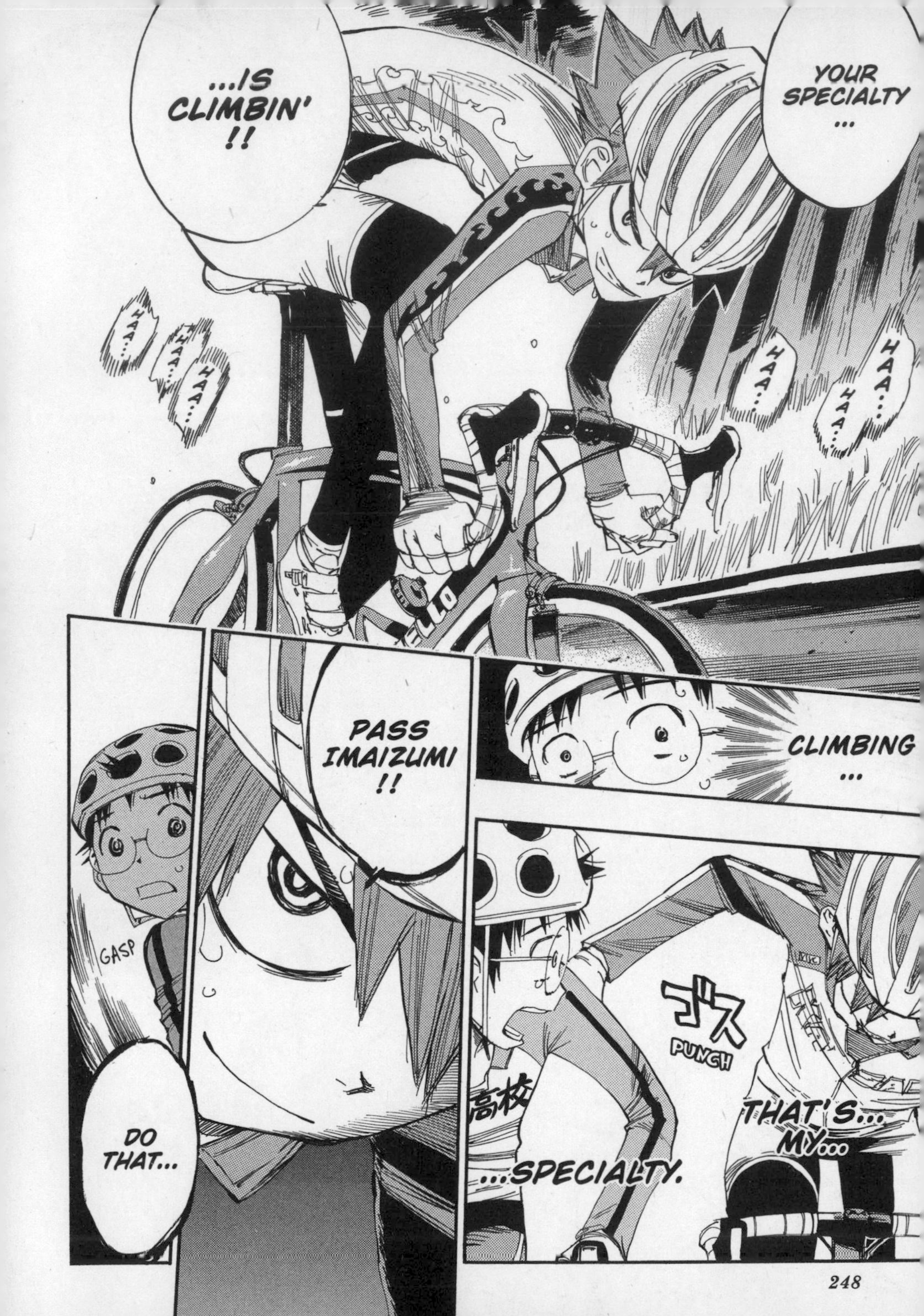
YOUR SPECIALTY ...
...IS CLIMBIN' !!
HAA... HAA... HAA...
HAA... HAA... HAA...
CLIMBING ...
ゴス
PUNCH
高校
THAT'S... MY...
...SPECIALTY.
PASS IMAIZUMI !!
DO THAT...
GASP

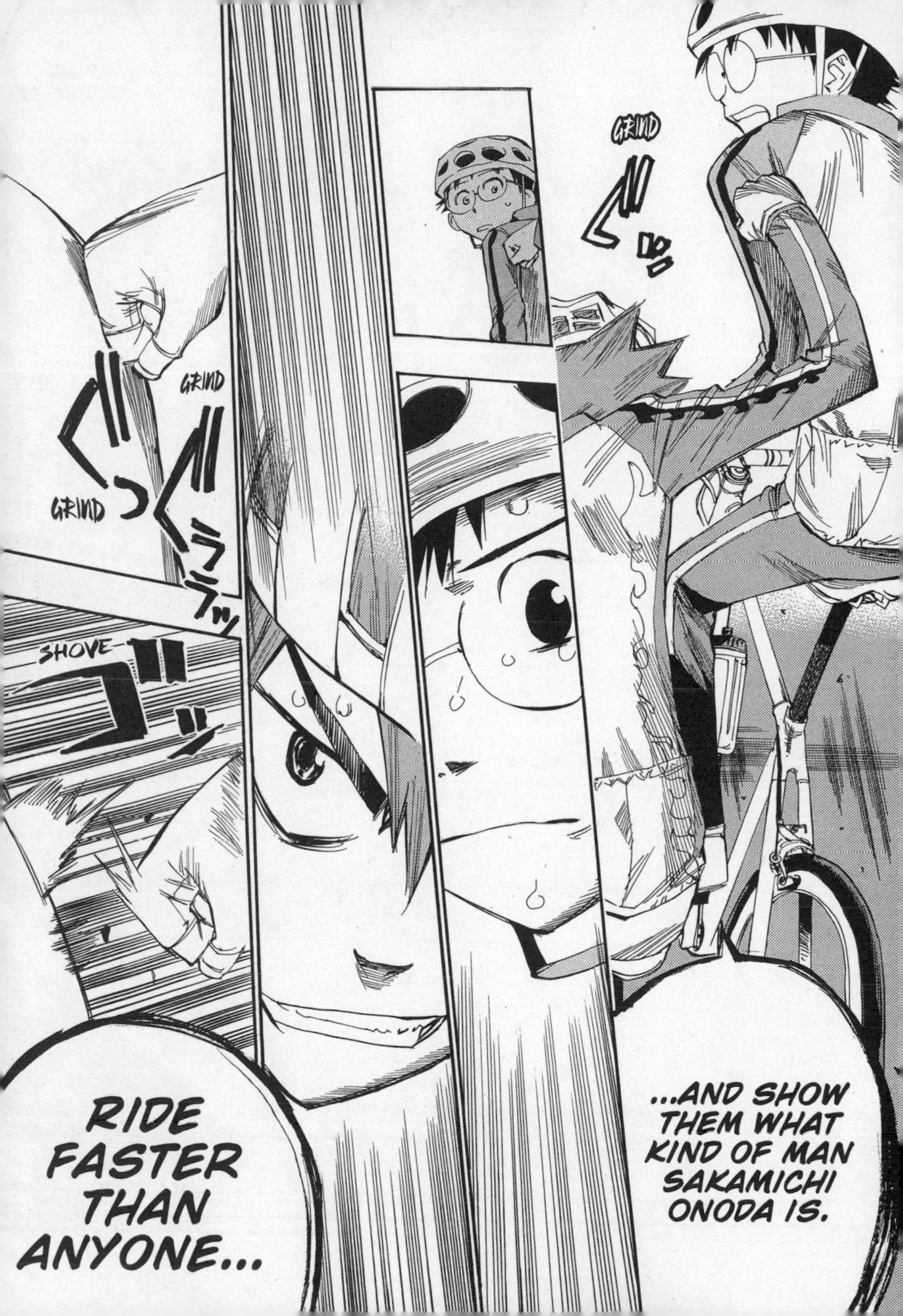
GRIND
GRIND
GRIND
SHOVE
...AND SHOW THEM WHAT KIND OF MAN SAKAMICHI ONODA IS.
RIDE FASTER THAN ANYONE...

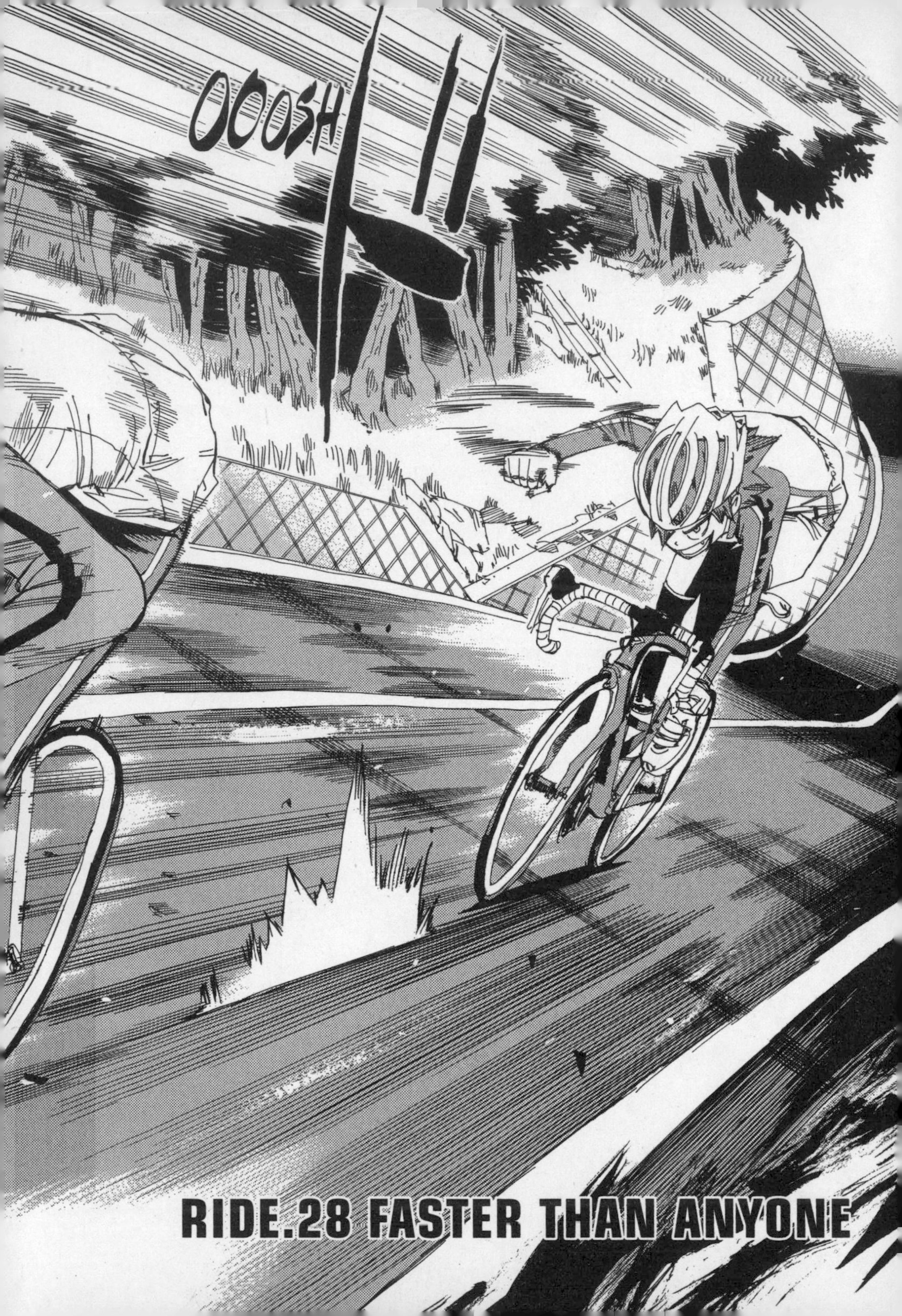
OOOSH
RIDE.28 FASTER THAN ANYONE

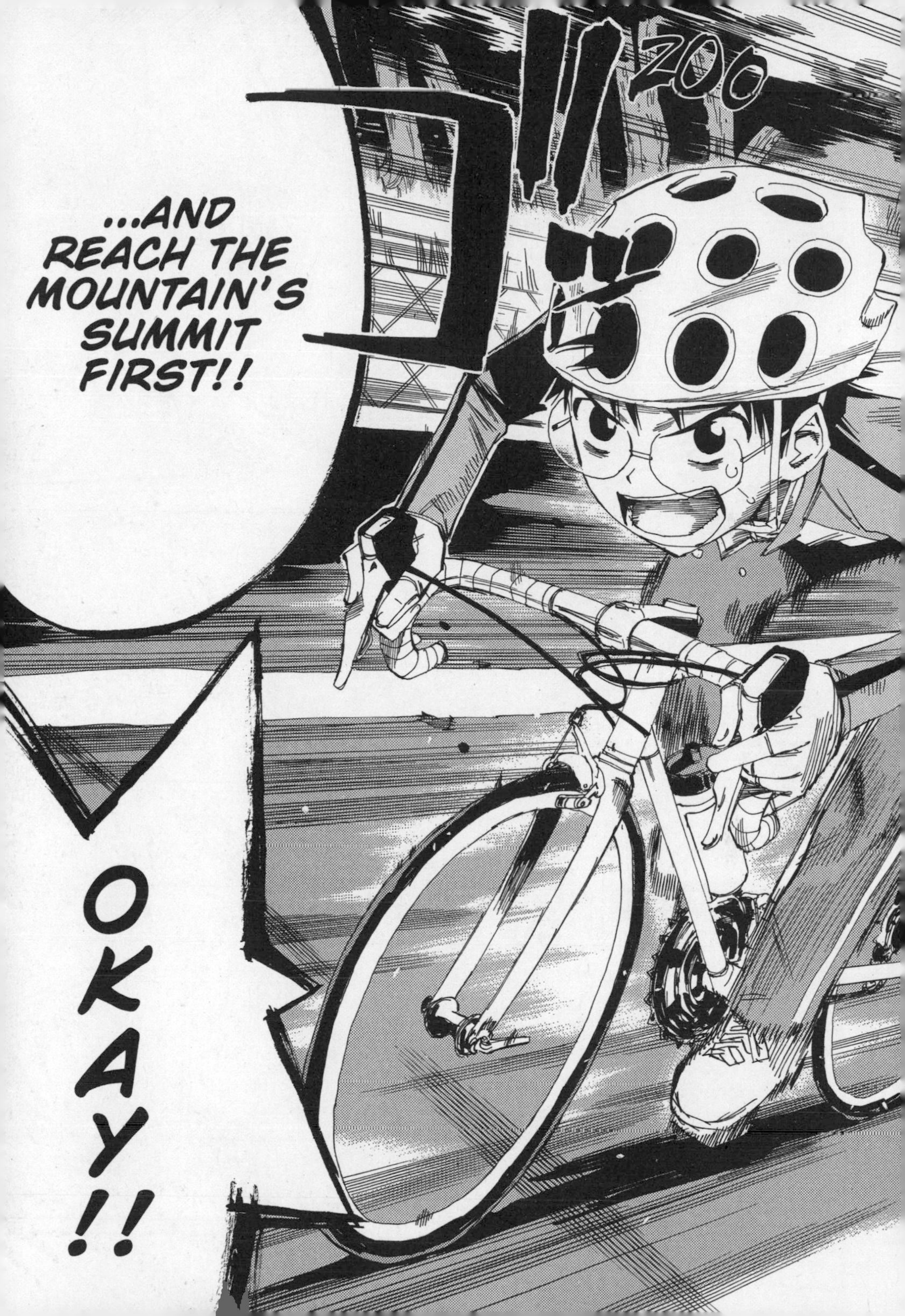
ZOO
...AND REACH THE MOUNTAIN'S SUMMIT FIRST!!
OKAY!!

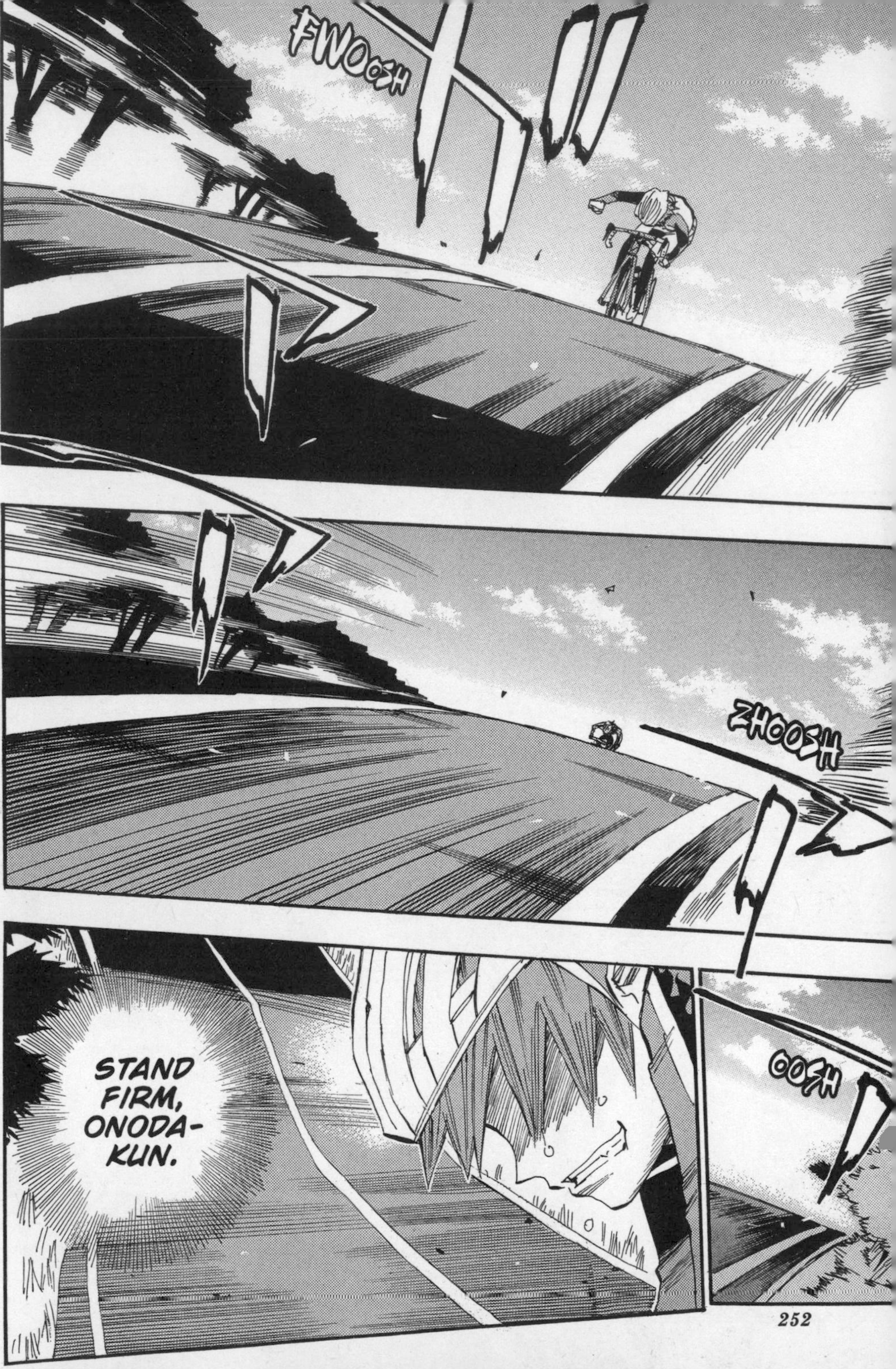
FWOOSH
ZHOOSH
OOSH
STAND FIRM, ONODA-KUN.

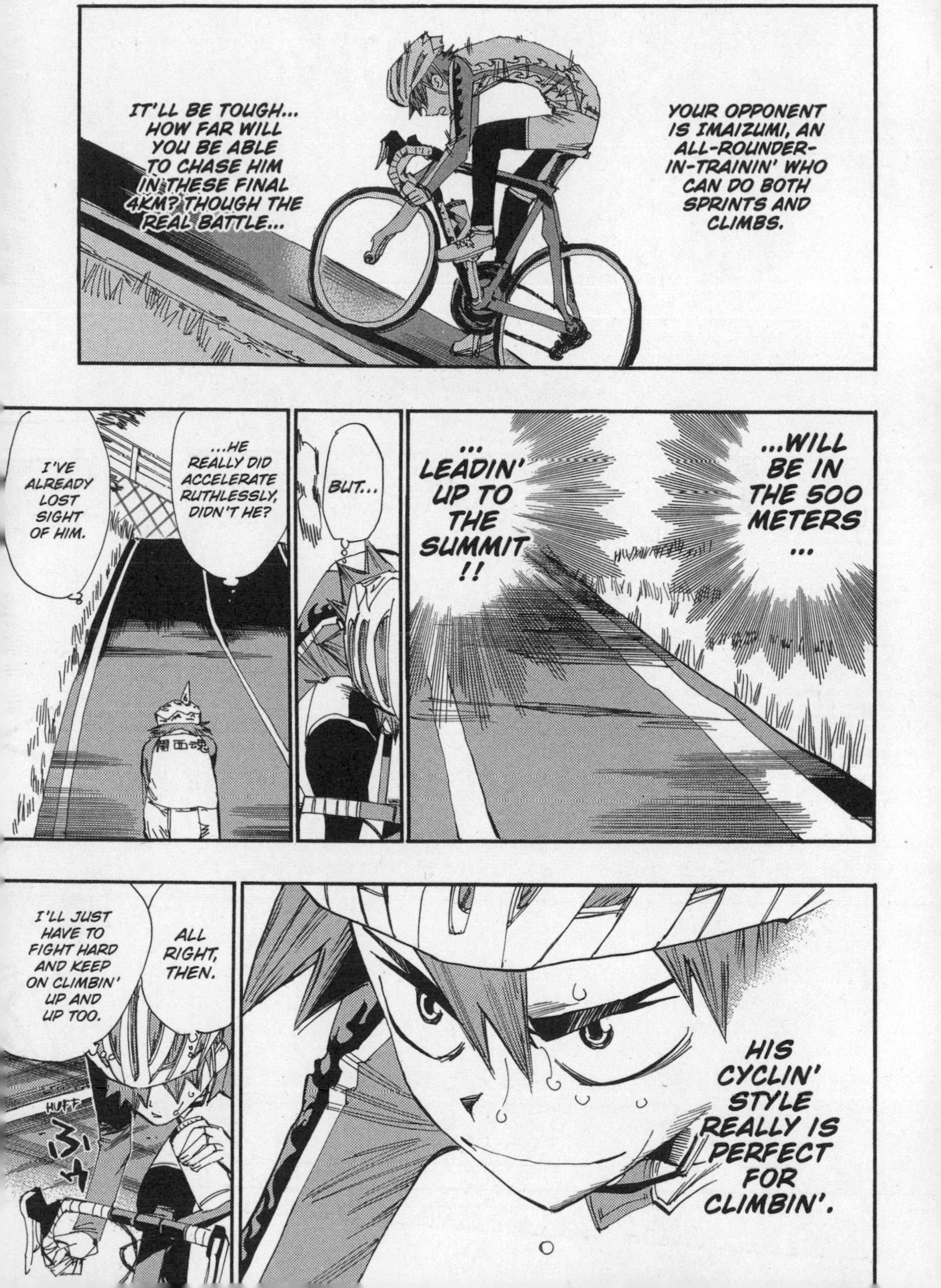

YOUR OPPONENT IS IMAIZUMI, AN ALL-ROUNDER-IN-TRAININ' WHO CAN DO BOTH SPRINTS AND CLIMBS.
IT'LL BE TOUGH... HOW FAR WILL YOU BE ABLE TO CHASE HIM IN THESE FINAL 4KM? THOUGH THE REAL BATTLE...
...WILL BE IN THE 500 METERS...
...LEADIN' UP TO THE SUMMIT!!
BUT...
...HE REALLY DID ACCELERATE RUTHLESSLY, DIDN'T HE?
I'VE ALREADY LOST SIGHT OF HIM.
関西魂
HIS CYCLIN' STYLE REALLY IS PERFECT FOR CLIMBIN'.
ALL RIGHT, THEN.
I'LL JUST HAVE TO FIGHT HARD AND KEEP ON CLIMBIN' UP AND UP TOO.
HUFF

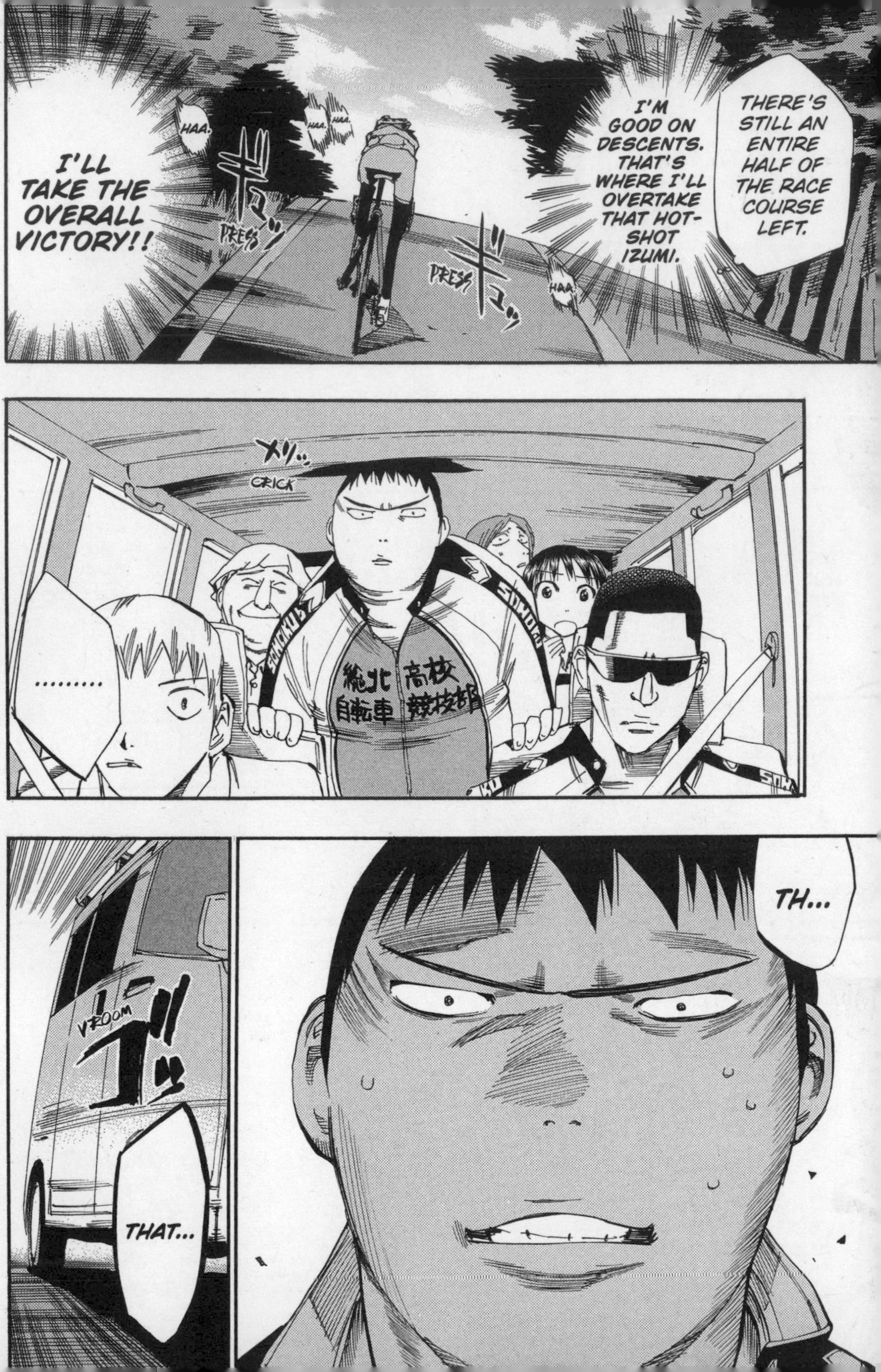
THERE'S STILL AN ENTIRE HALF OF THE RACE COURSE LEFT.
I'M GOOD ON DESCENTS. THAT'S WHERE I'LL OVERTAKE THAT HOT-SHOT IZUMI.
HAA.
PRESS
HAA. HAA.
HAA.
PRESS
I'LL TAKE THE OVERALL VICTORY!!
CRICK
総北高校
自転車競技部
....
TH...
VROOM
THAT...

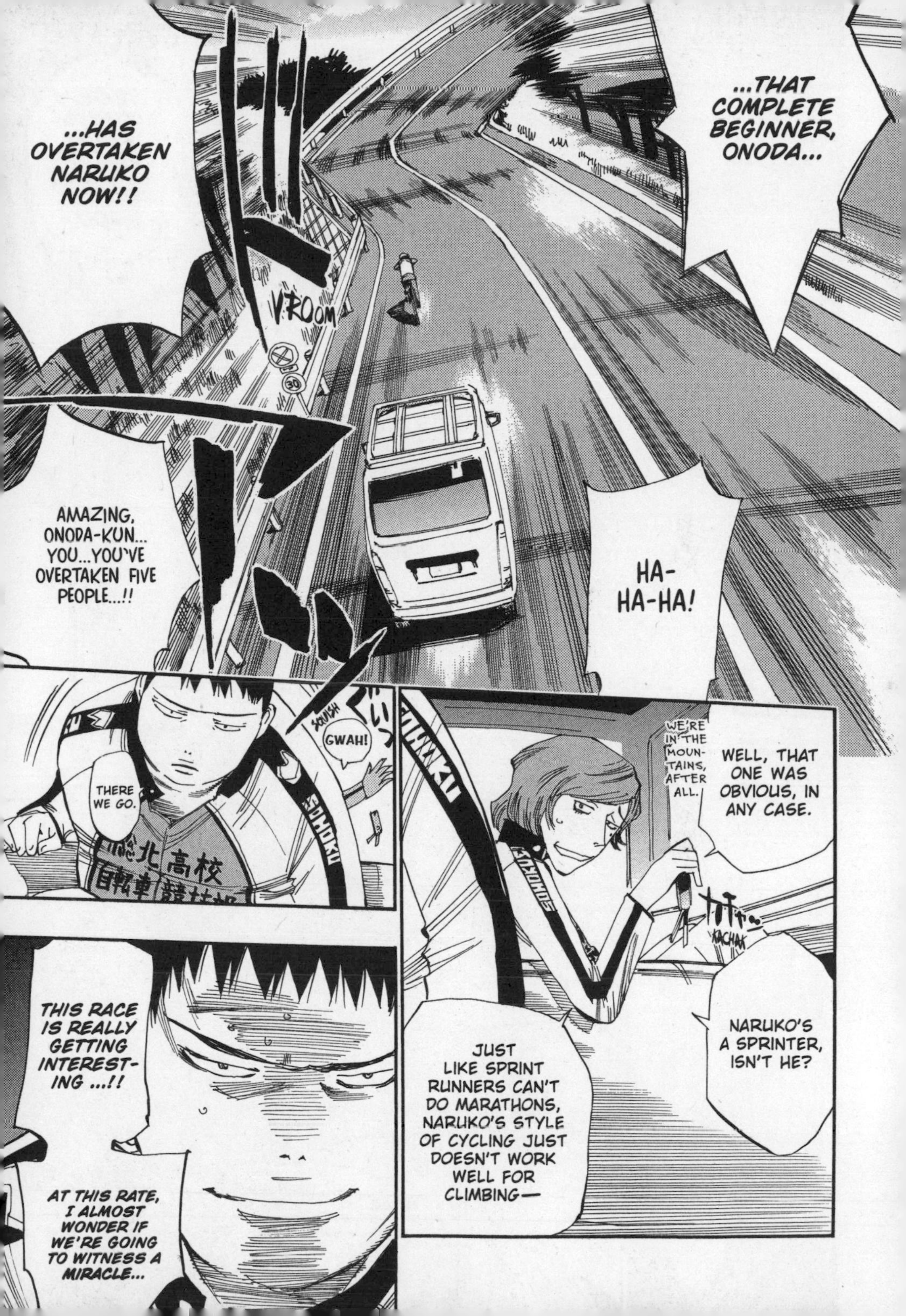
...THAT COMPLETE BEGINNER, ONODA...
...HAS OVERTAKEN NARUKO NOW!!
VROOM
HA-HA-HA!
AMAZING, ONODA-KUN... YOU...YOU'VE OVERTAKEN FIVE PEOPLE...!!
WELL, THAT ONE WAS OBVIOUS, IN ANY CASE.
WE'RE IN THE MOUNTAINS, AFTER ALL.
KACHAK
NARUKO'S A SPRINTER, ISN'T HE?
JUST LIKE SPRINT RUNNERS CAN'T DO MARATHONS, NARUKO'S STYLE OF CYCLING JUST DOESN'T WORK WELL FOR CLIMBING—
SQUISH
GWAH!
THERE WE GO.
THIS RACE IS REALLY GETTING INTERESTING ...!!
AT THIS RATE, I ALMOST WONDER IF WE'RE GOING TO WITNESS A MIRACLE...

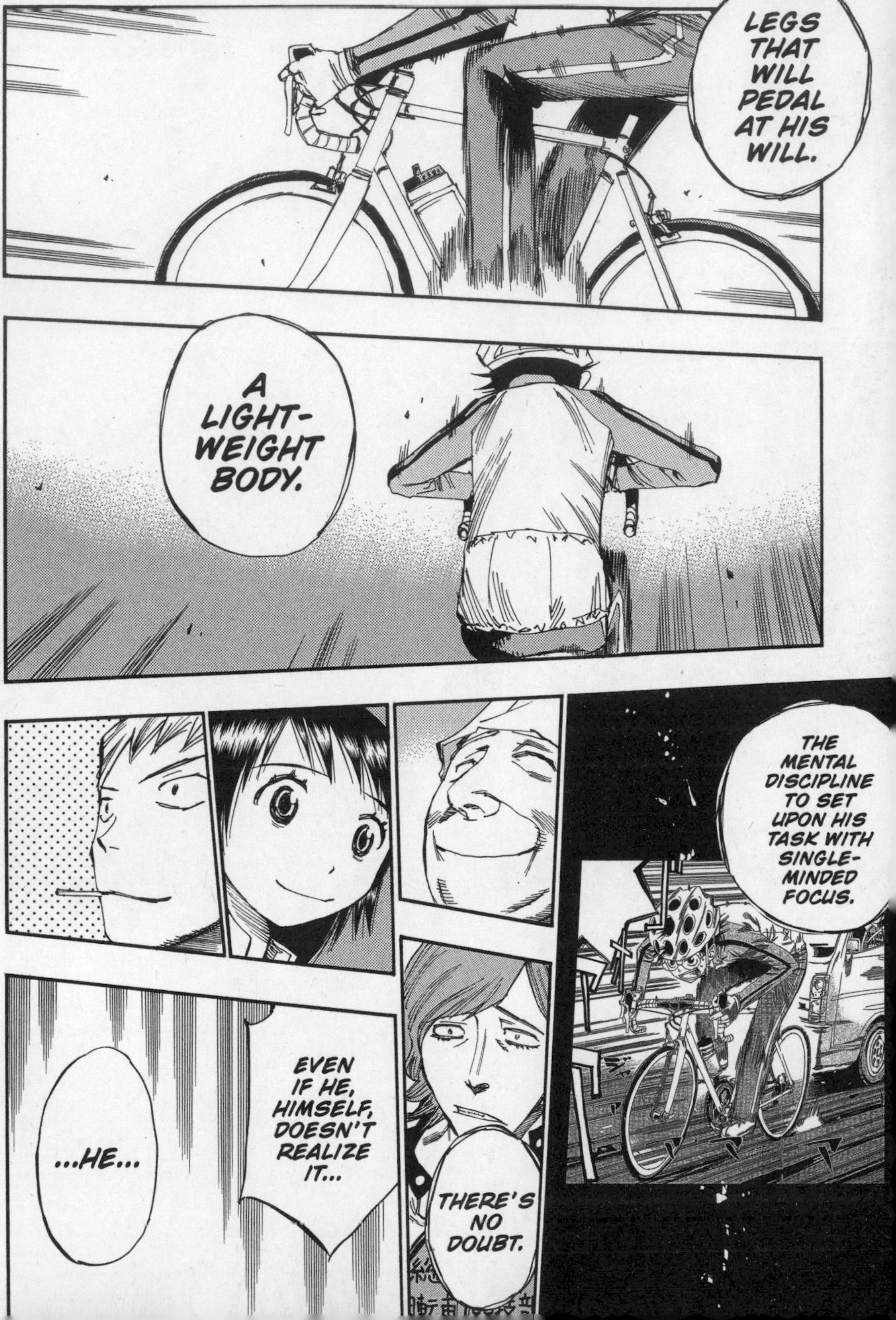
LEGS THAT WILL PEDAL AT HIS WILL.
A LIGHT-WEIGHT BODY.
THE MENTAL DISCIPLINE TO SET UPON HIS TASK WITH SINGLE-MINDED FOCUS.
THERE'S NO DOUBT.
EVEN IF HE, HIMSELF, DOESN'T REALIZE IT...
...HE...

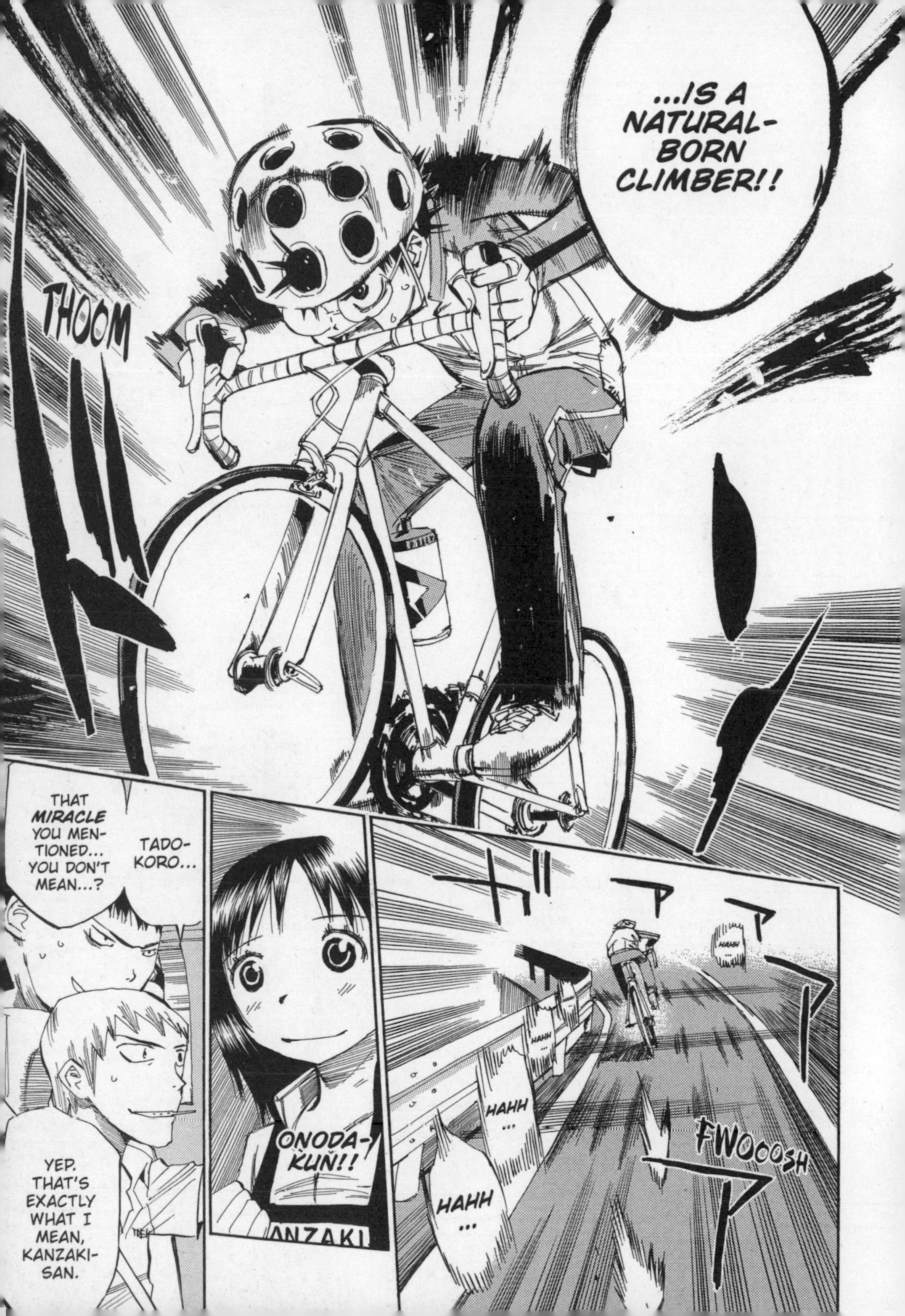
...IS A NATURAL-BORN CLIMBER!!
THOOM
HAHH...
HAHH...
HAHH...
HAHH...
FWOOOSH
ONODA-KUN!!
TADO-KORO...
THAT MIRACLE YOU MENTIONED... YOU DON'T MEAN...?
YEP. THAT'S EXACTLY WHAT I MEAN, KANZAKI-SAN.

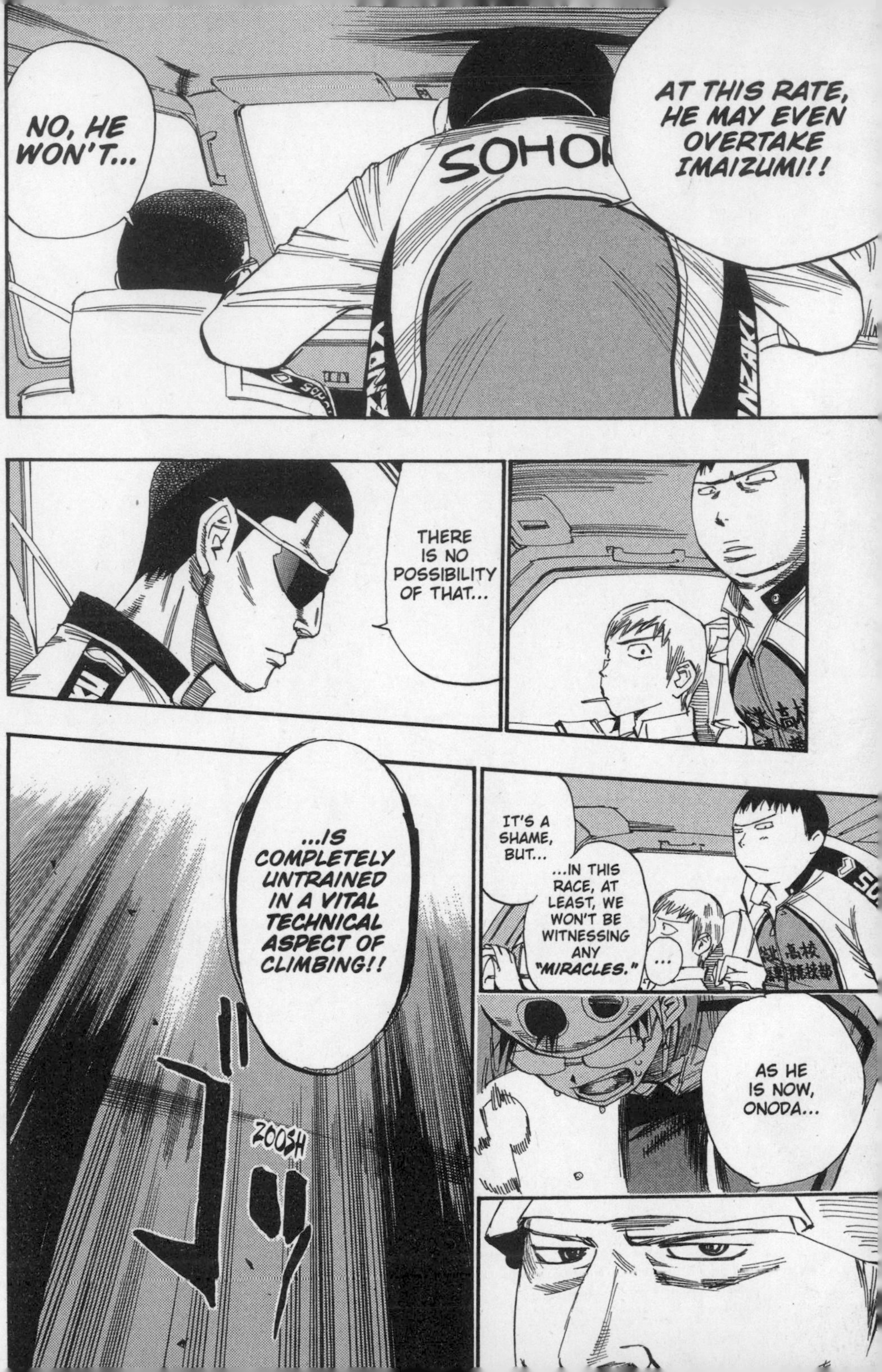
AT THIS RATE, HE MAY EVEN OVERTAKE IMAIZUMI!!
NO, HE WON'T...
THERE IS NO POSSIBILITY OF THAT...
IT'S A SHAME, BUT...
...IN THIS RACE, AT LEAST, WE WON'T BE WITNESSING ANY "MIRACLES."
...
AS HE IS NOW, ONODA...
...IS COMPLETELY UNTRAINED IN A VITAL TECHNICAL ASPECT OF CLIMBING!!
ZOOSH

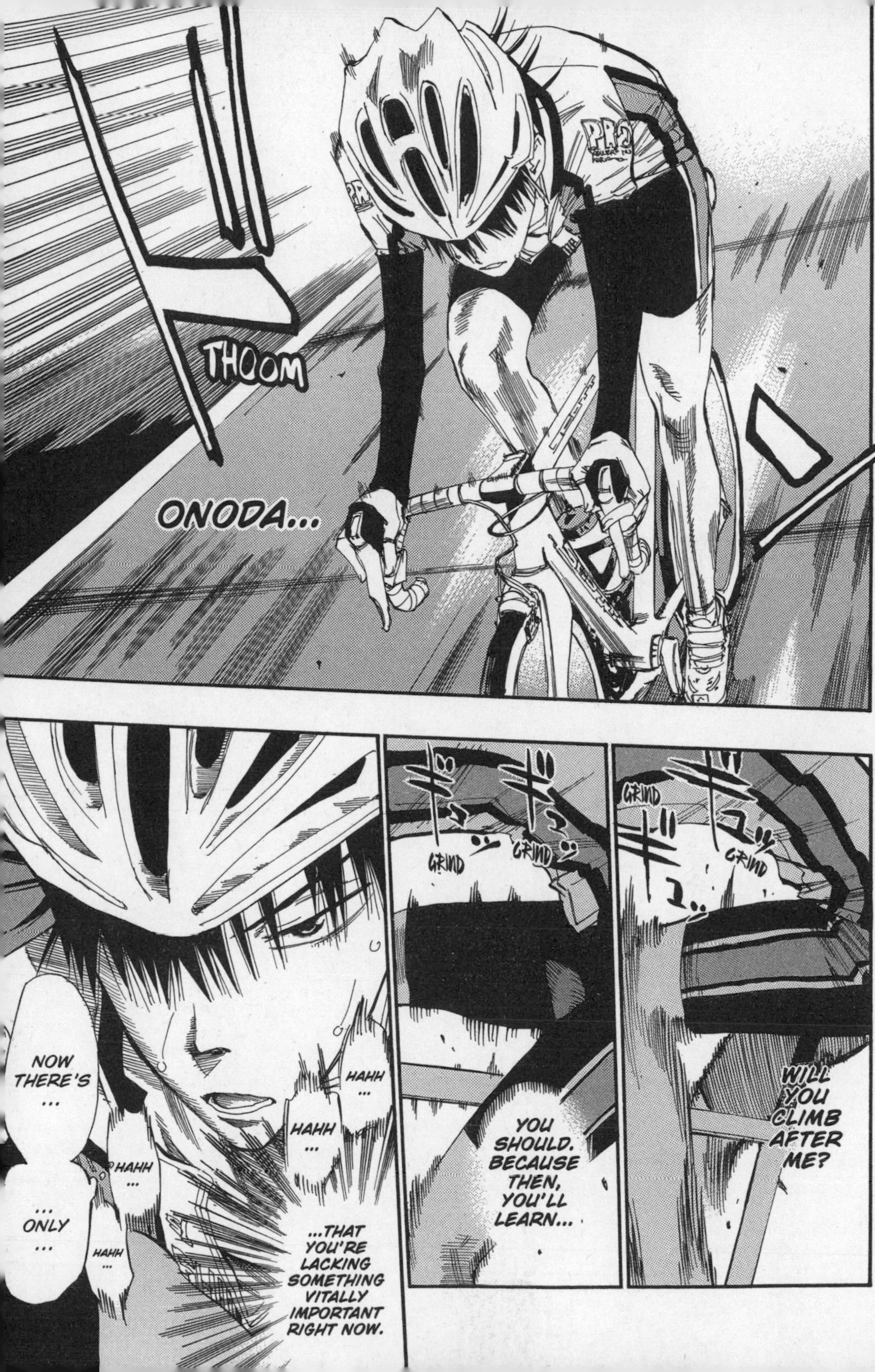
THOOM
ONODA...
GRIND
GRIND
WILL YOU CLIMB AFTER ME?
GRIND
GRIND
YOU SHOULD. BECAUSE THEN, YOU'LL LEARN...
...THAT YOU'RE LACKING SOMETHING VITALLY IMPORTANT RIGHT NOW.
HAHH ...
HAHH ...
HAHH ...
HAHH ...
NOW THERE'S ...
... ONLY ...

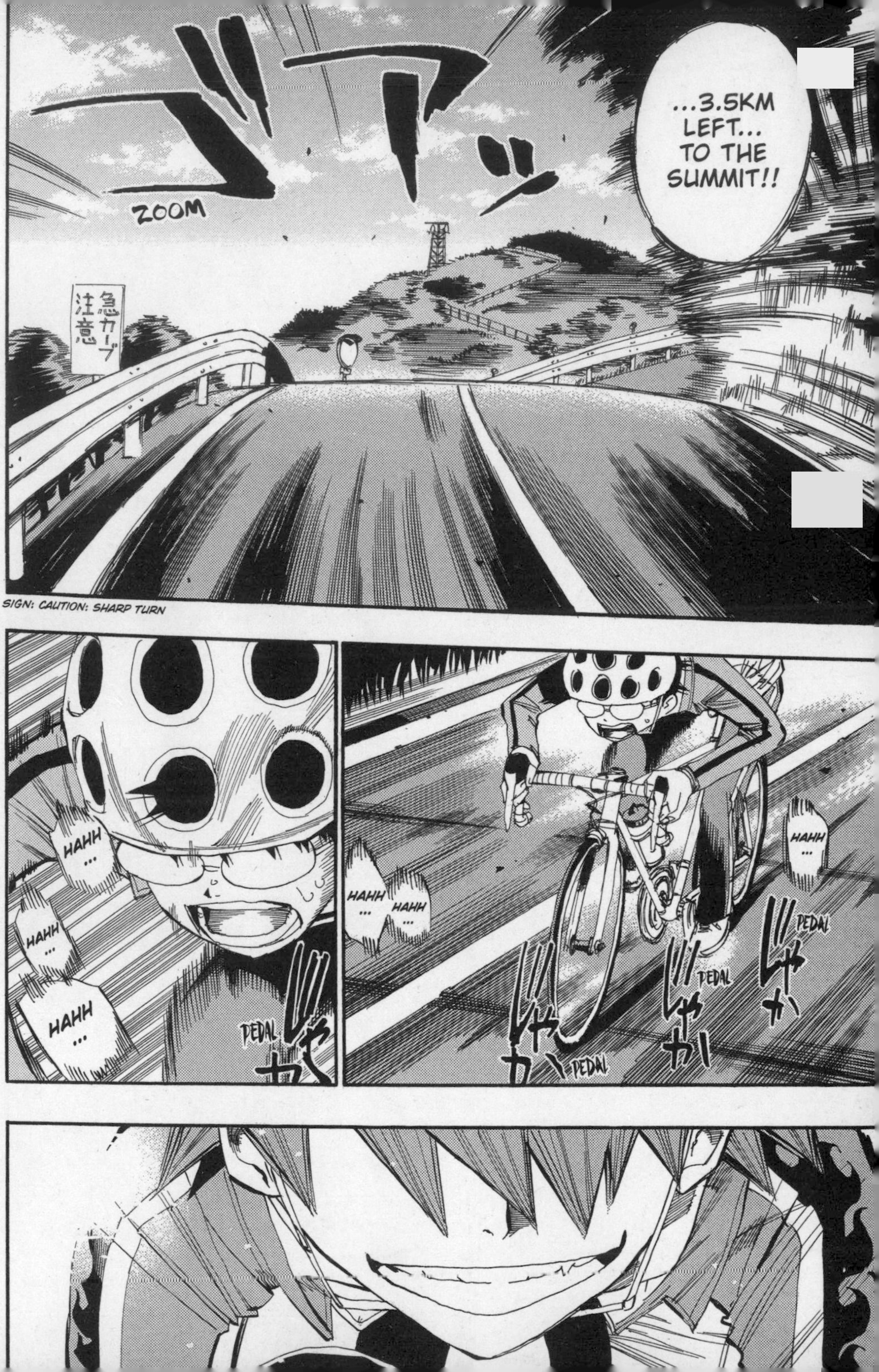

...3.5KM LEFT... TO THE SUMMIT!!
ZOOM
急カーブ注意
SIGN: CAUTION: SHARP TURN
HAHH ...
PEDAL
PEDAL
PEDAL
HAHH ...
HAHH ...
HAHH ...
HAHH ...
HAHH ...
PEDAL

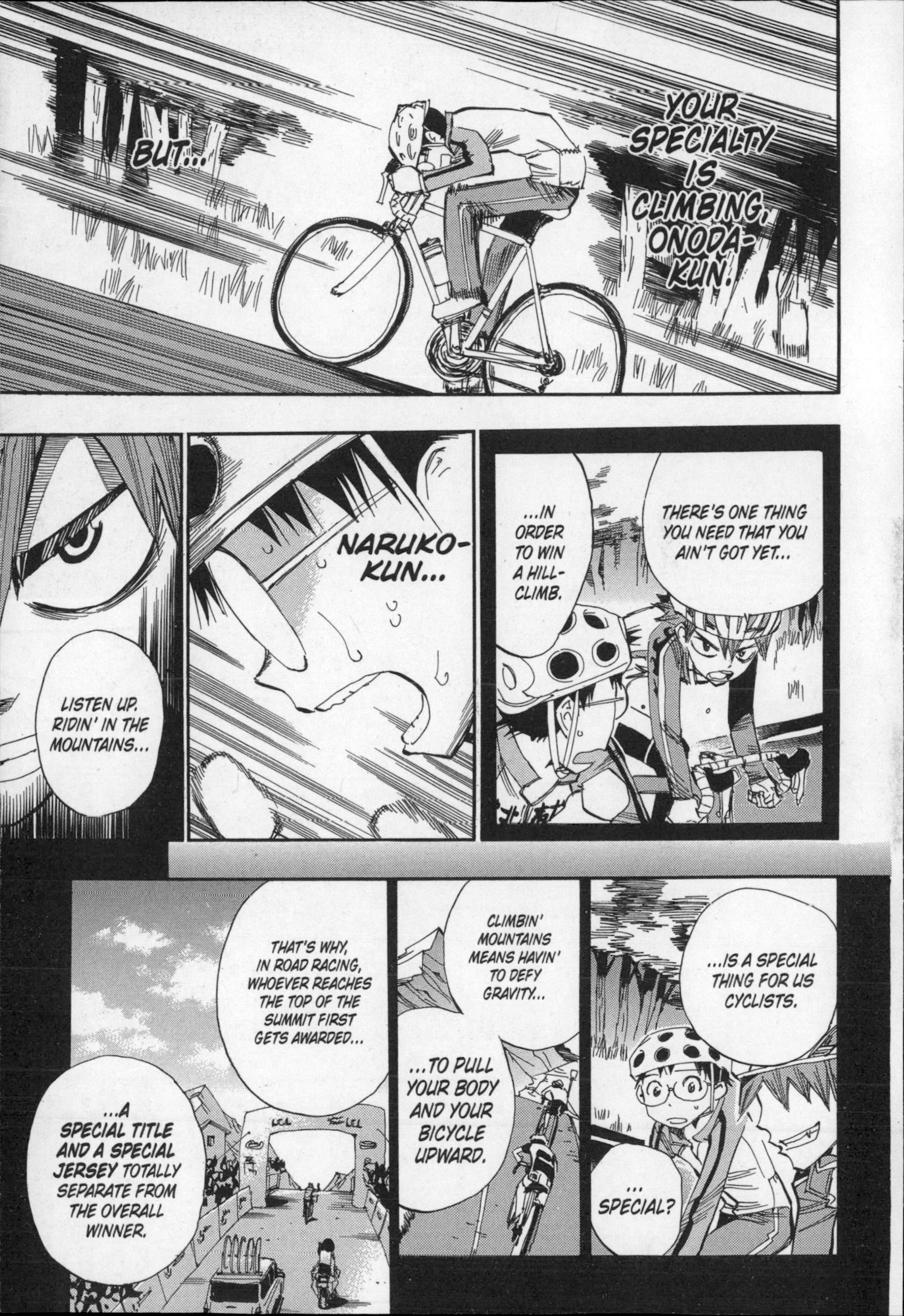
YOUR SPECIALTY IS CLIMBING, ONODA-KUN.
BUT...
THERE'S ONE THING YOU NEED THAT YOU AIN'T GOT YET...
...IN ORDER TO WIN A HILL-CLIMB.
NARUKO-KUN...
LISTEN UP. RIDIN' IN THE MOUNTAINS...
...IS A SPECIAL THING FOR US CYCLISTS.
...SPECIAL?
CLIMBIN' MOUNTAINS MEANS HAVIN' TO DEFY GRAVITY...
...TO PULL YOUR BODY AND YOUR BICYCLE UPWARD.
THAT'S WHY, IN ROAD RACING, WHOEVER REACHES THE TOP OF THE SUMMIT FIRST GETS AWARDED...
...A SPECIAL TITLE AND A SPECIAL JERSEY TOTALLY SEPARATE FROM THE OVERALL WINNER.

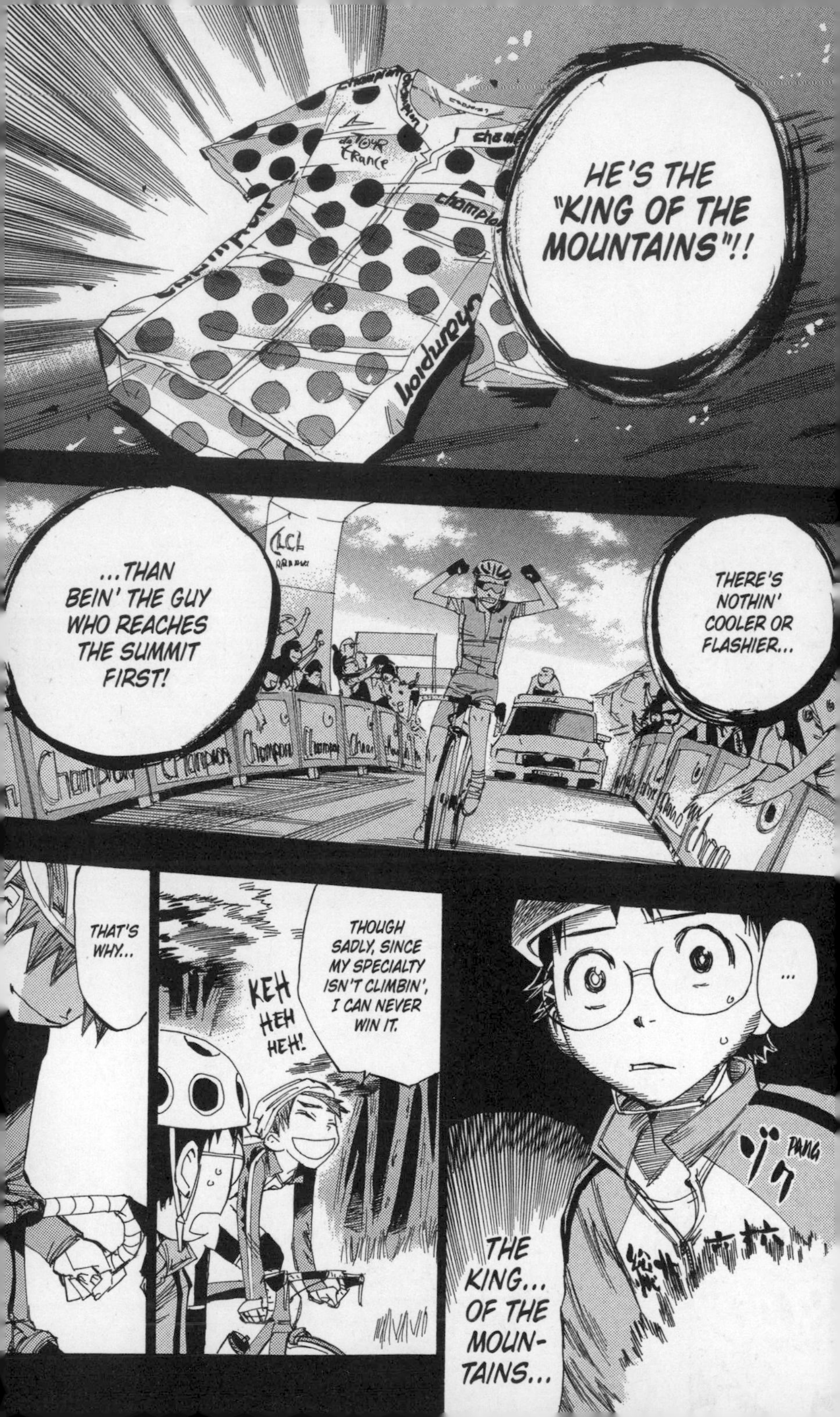
HE'S THE "KING OF THE MOUNTAINS"!!
THERE'S NOTHIN' COOLER OR FLASHIER...
...THAN BEIN' THE GUY WHO REACHES THE SUMMIT FIRST!
...
PANG
THE KING... OF THE MOUN-TAINS...
THOUGH SADLY, SINCE MY SPECIALTY ISN'T CLIMBIN', I CAN NEVER WIN IT.
KEH HEH HEH!
THAT'S WHY...

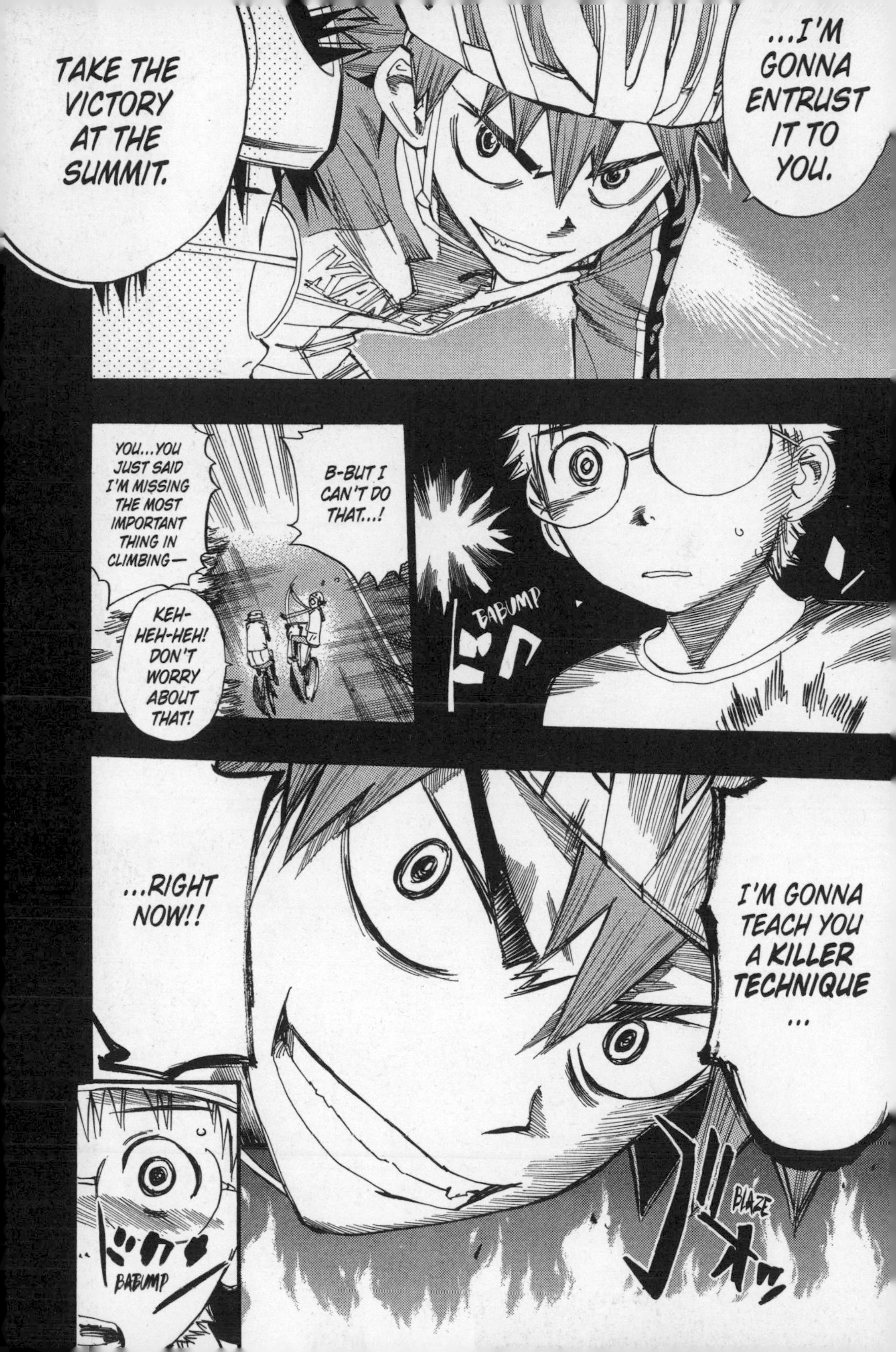
...I'M GONNA ENTRUST IT TO YOU.
TAKE THE VICTORY AT THE SUMMIT.
BABUMP
B-BUT I CAN'T DO THAT...!
YOU...YOU JUST SAID I'M MISSING THE MOST IMPORTANT THING IN CLIMBING—
KEH-HEH-HEH! DON'T WORRY ABOUT THAT!
I'M GONNA TEACH YOU A KILLER TECHNIQUE ...
...RIGHT NOW!!
BLAZE
BABUMP

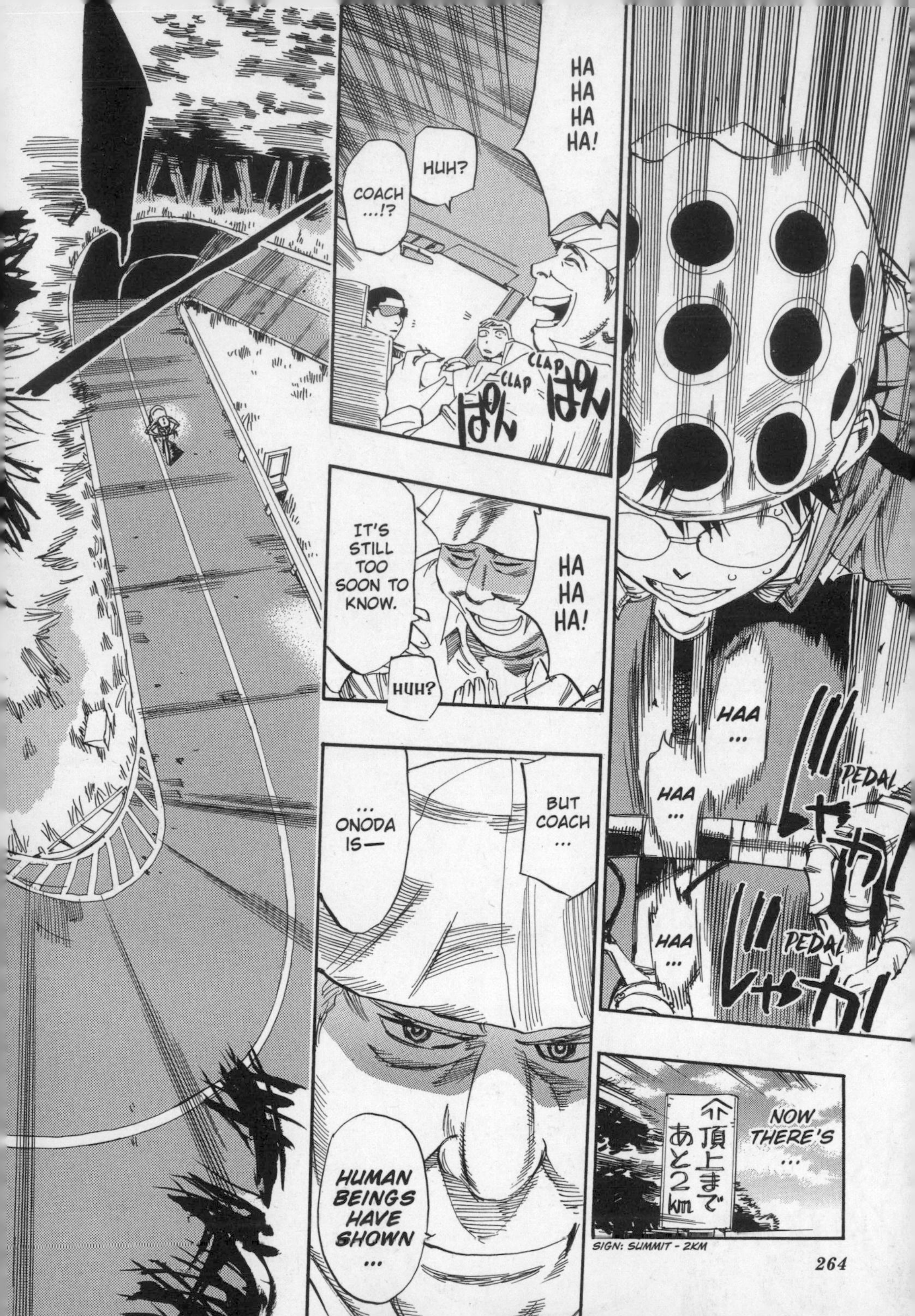
HAA …
HAA …
HAA …
PEDAL
じゃかっ
PEDAL
じゃかっ
HA HA HA HA!
HUH?
COACH …!?
CLAP
ぱん
CLAP
ぱん
IT'S STILL TOO SOON TO KNOW.
HA HA HA!
HUH?
BUT COACH …
… ONODA IS—
HUMAN BEINGS HAVE SHOWN …
頂上まで あと2km
NOW THERE'S …
SIGN: SUMMIT - 2KM

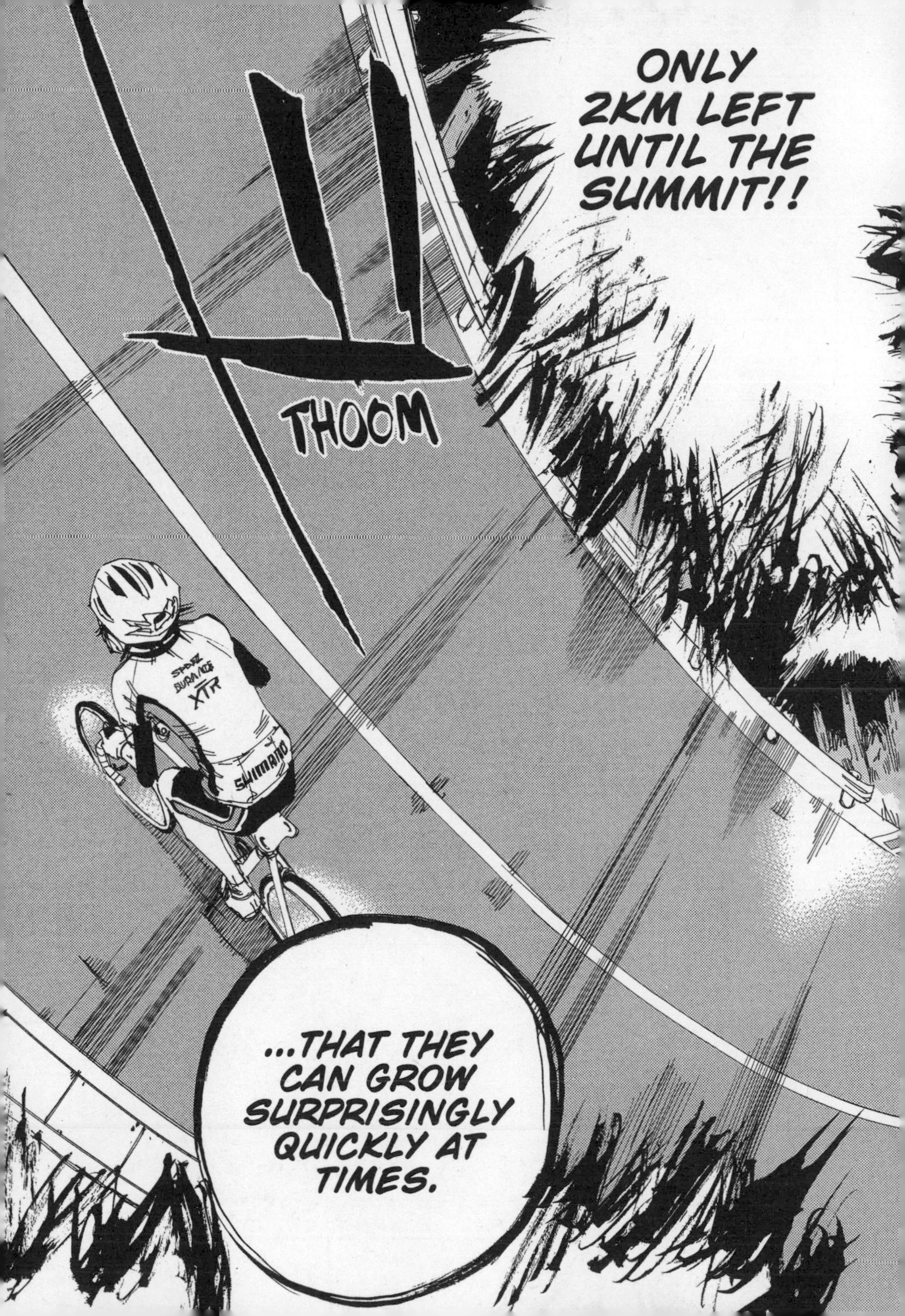
ONLY 2KM LEFT UNTIL THE SUMMIT!!
THOOM
...THAT THEY CAN GROW SURPRISINGLY QUICKLY AT TIMES.

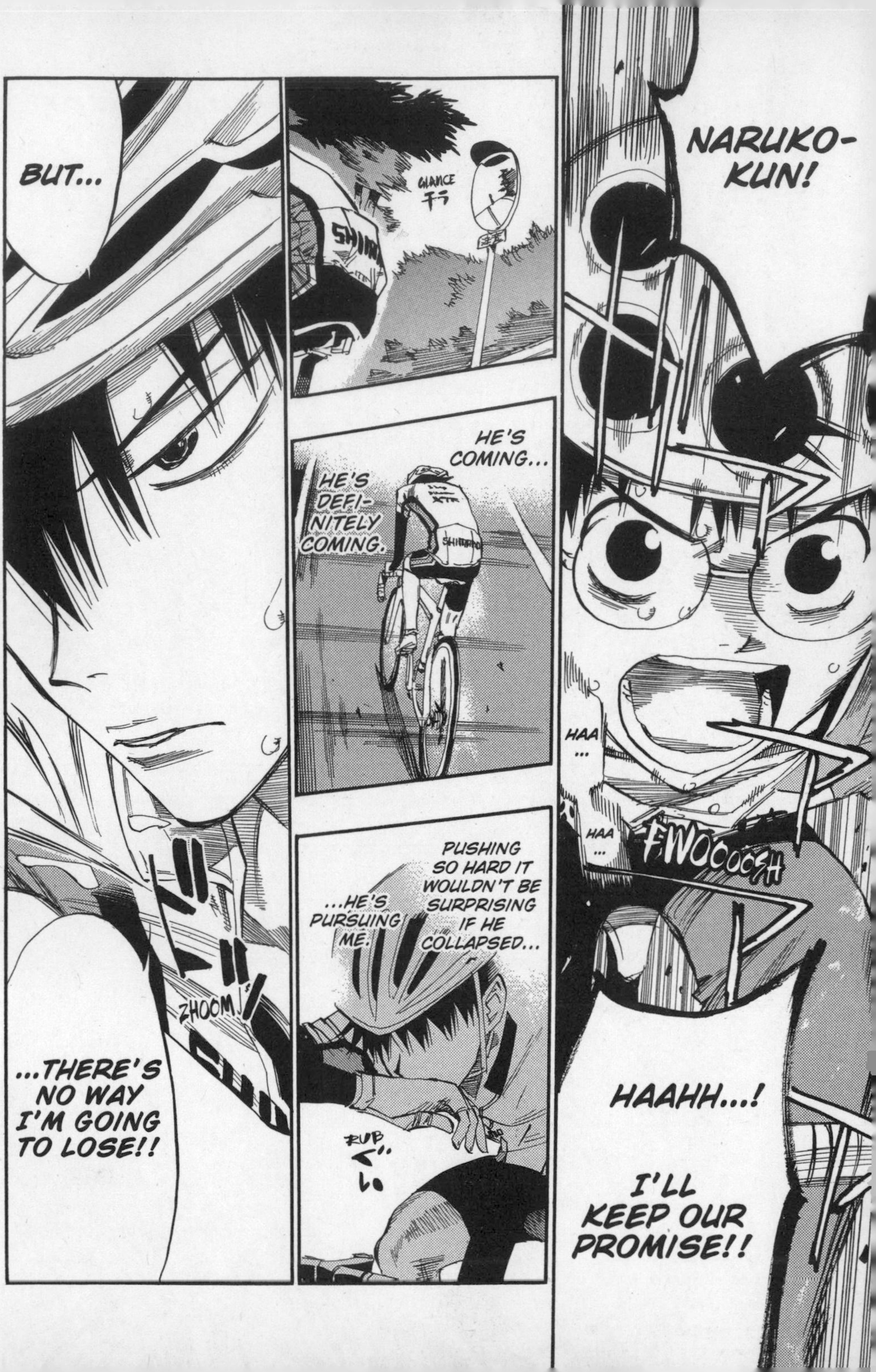
NARUKO-KUN!
HAA...
HAA...
FWOOOOSH
HAAHH...!
I'LL KEEP OUR PROMISE!!
GLANCE
HE'S COMING...
HE'S DEFINITELY COMING.
PUSHING SO HARD IT WOULDN'T BE SURPRISING IF HE COLLAPSED...
...HE'S PURSUING ME.
RUB
BUT...
ZHOOM
...THERE'S NO WAY I'M GOING TO LOSE!!

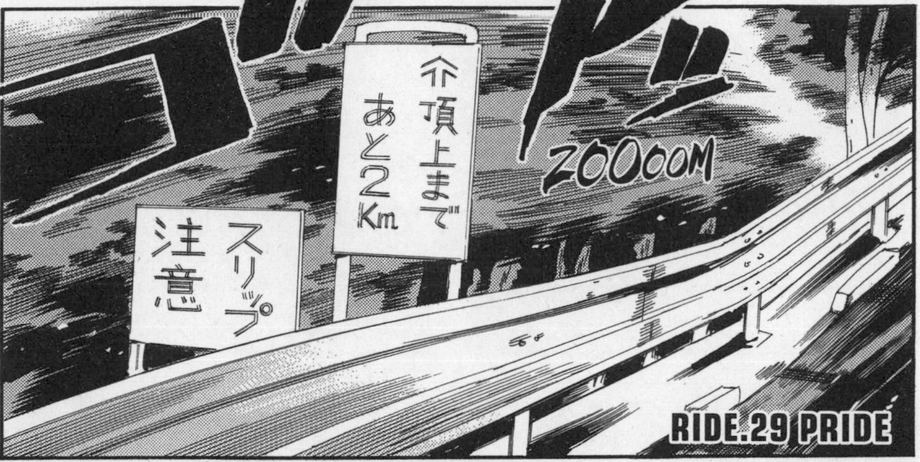
スリップ注意
あと2Km
ZOOOOM
RIDE.29 PRIDE

SIGNS: CAUTION: SLIPPERY ROAD, 2KM TO SUMMIT

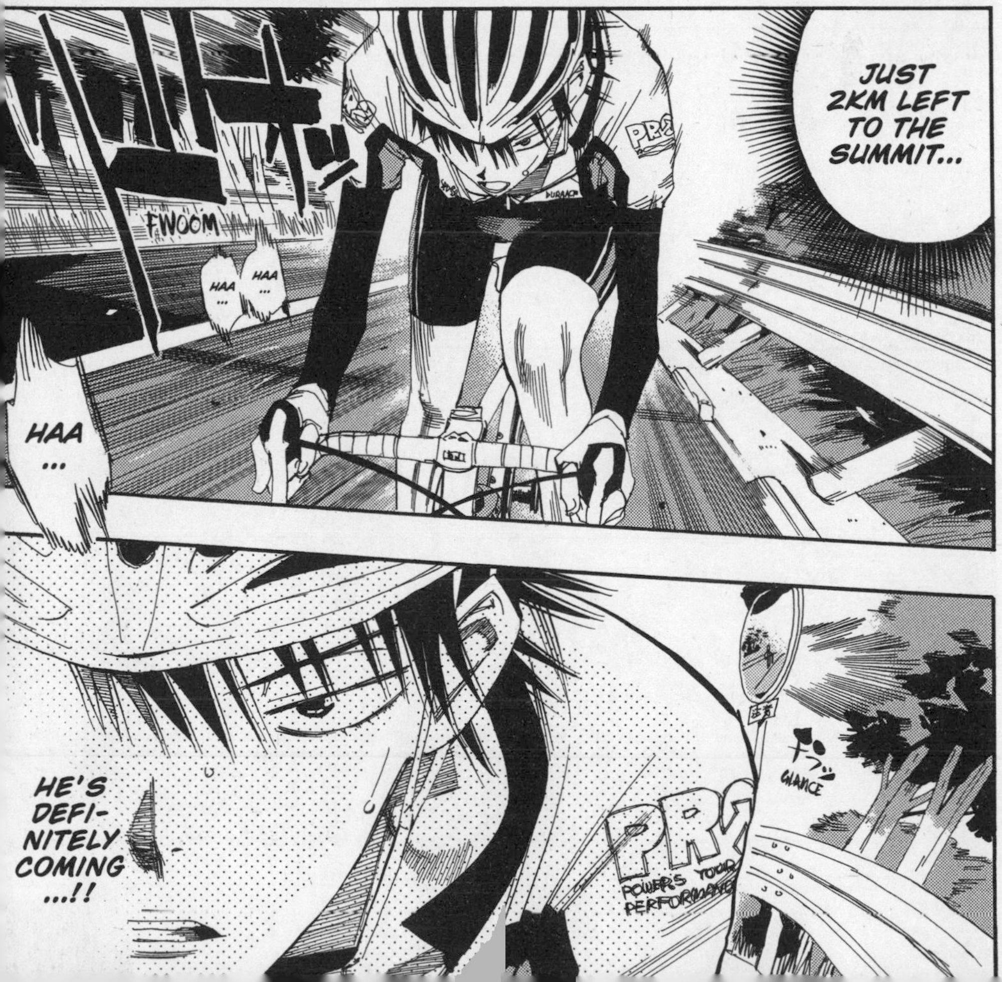
JUST 2KM LEFT TO THE SUMMIT...
FWOOM
HAA...
HAA...
HAA...
GLANCE
HE'S DEFINITELY COMING...!!

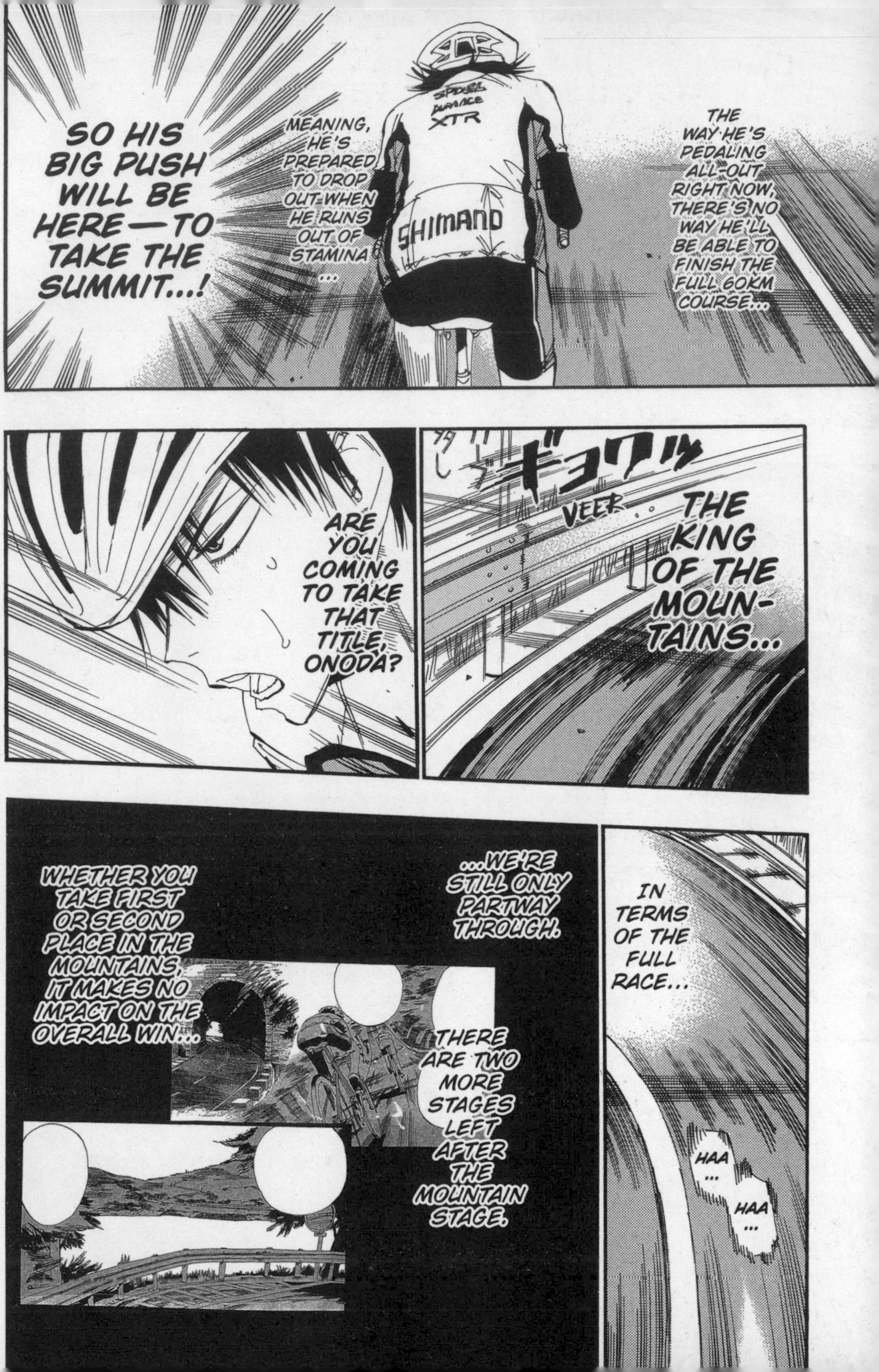
THE WAY HE'S PEDALING ALL-OUT RIGHT NOW, THERE'S NO WAY HE'LL BE ABLE TO FINISH THE FULL 60KM COURSE...
MEANING, HE'S PREPARED TO DROP OUT WHEN HE RUNS OUT OF STAMINA...
SO HIS BIG PUSH WILL BE HERE—TO TAKE THE SUMMIT...!
SHIMANO
VEER
THE KING OF THE MOUNTAINS...
ARE YOU COMING TO TAKE THAT TITLE, ONODA?
IN TERMS OF THE FULL RACE...
HAA... HAA...
...WE'RE STILL ONLY PARTWAY THROUGH.
WHETHER YOU TAKE FIRST OR SECOND PLACE IN THE MOUNTAINS, IT MAKES NO IMPACT ON THE OVERALL WIN...
THERE ARE TWO MORE STAGES LEFT AFTER THE MOUNTAIN STAGE.

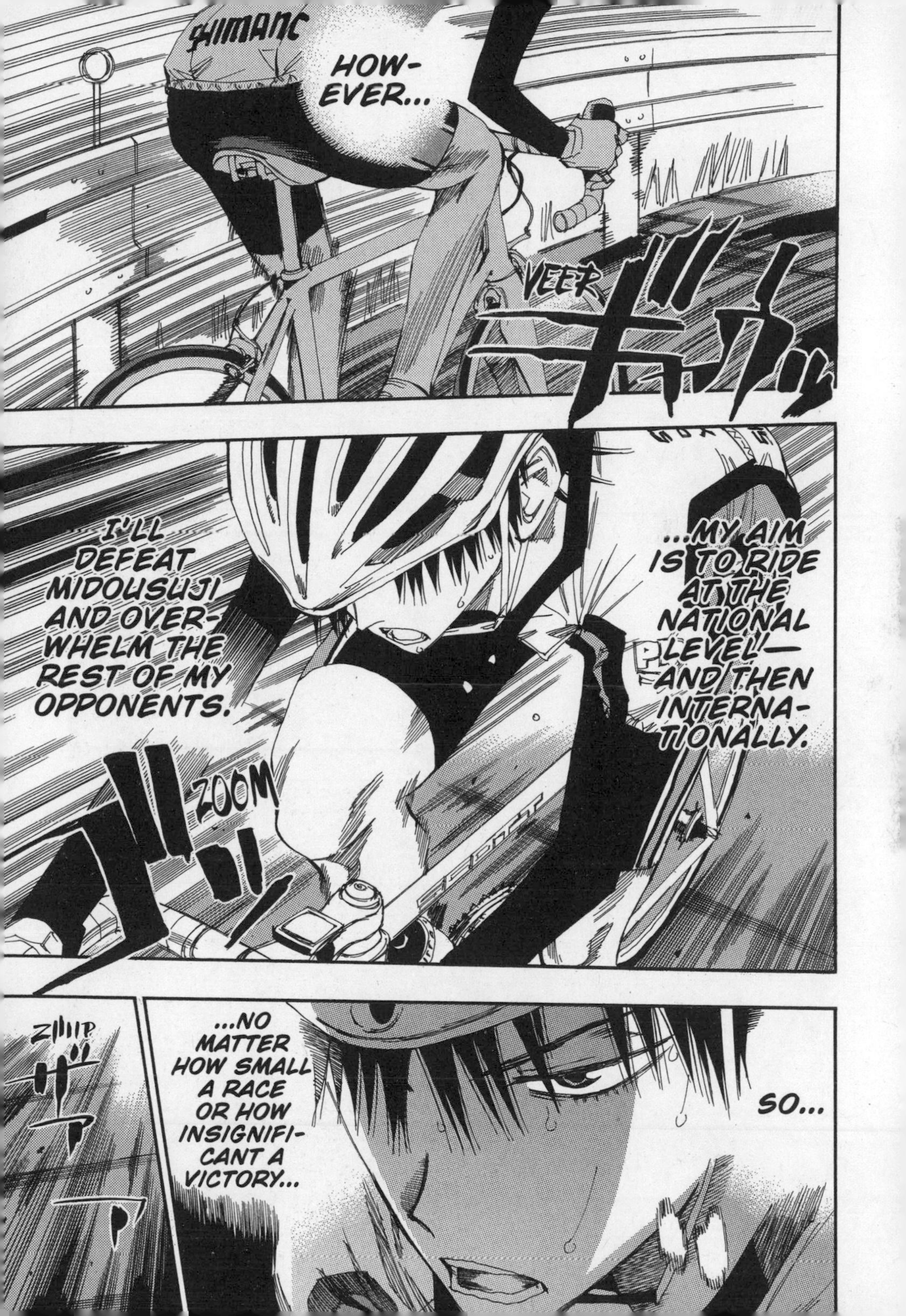
SHIMANO
HOW-EVER...
VEER
...MY AIM IS TO RIDE AT THE NATIONAL LEVEL—AND THEN INTERNATIONALLY.
I'LL DEFEAT MIDOUSUJI AND OVER-WHELM THE REST OF MY OPPONENTS.
ZOOM
SO...
...NO MATTER HOW SMALL A RACE OR HOW INSIGNIFI-CANT A VICTORY...
ZIIIIP

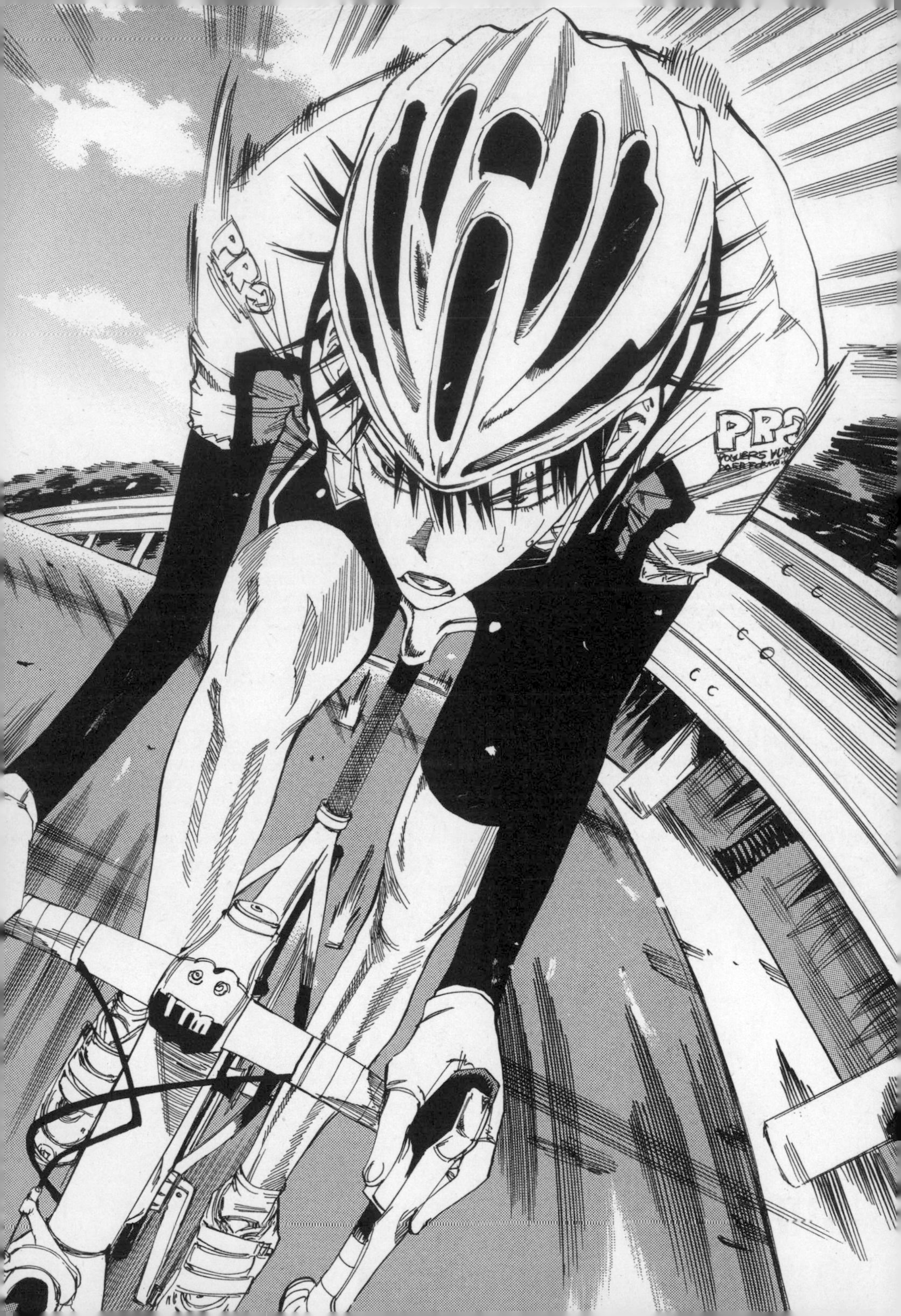

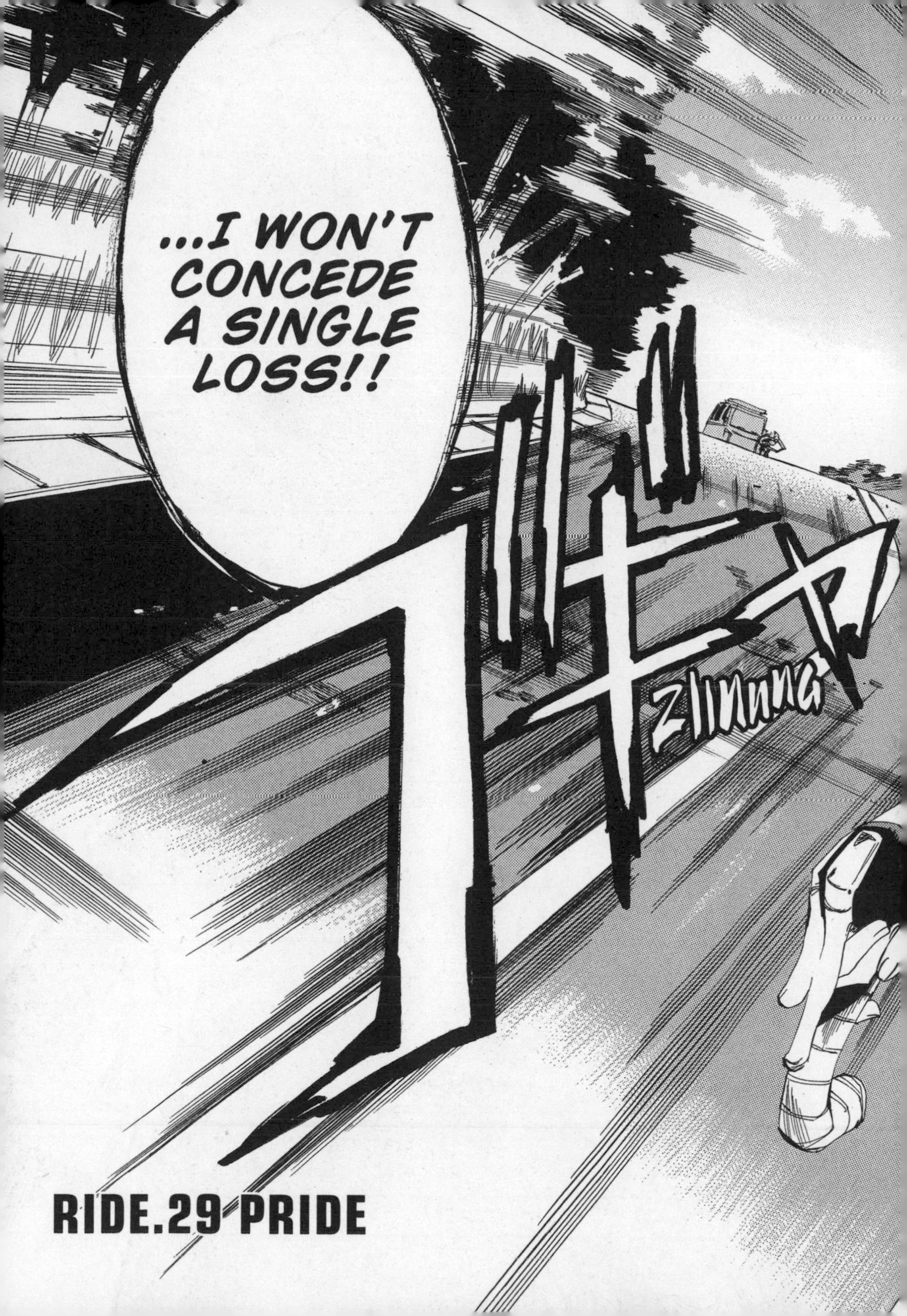
...I WON'T CONCEDE A SINGLE LOSS!!
ZIINNNG
RIDE.29 PRIDE

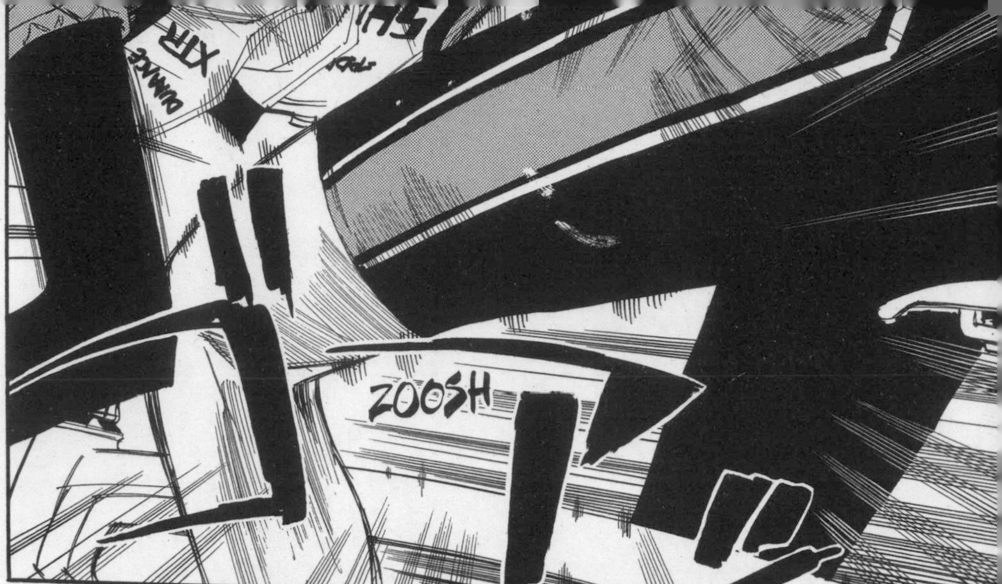
ZOOSH
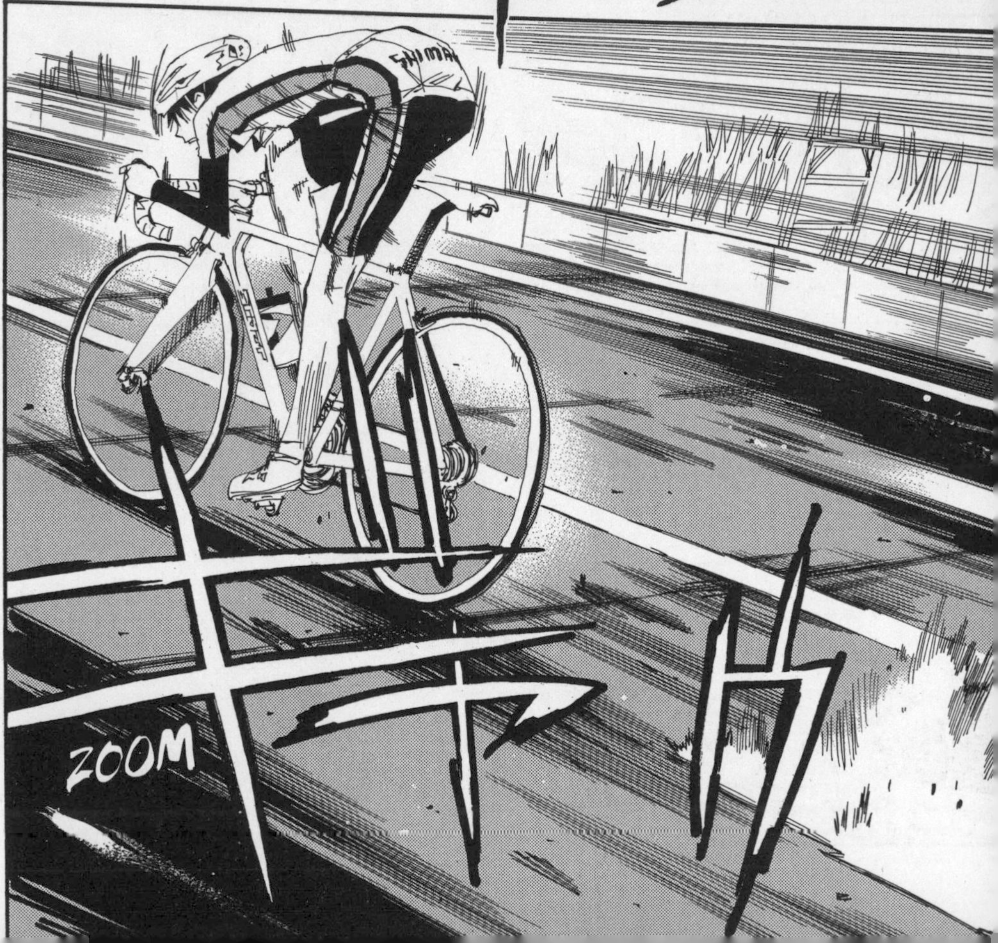
ZOOM

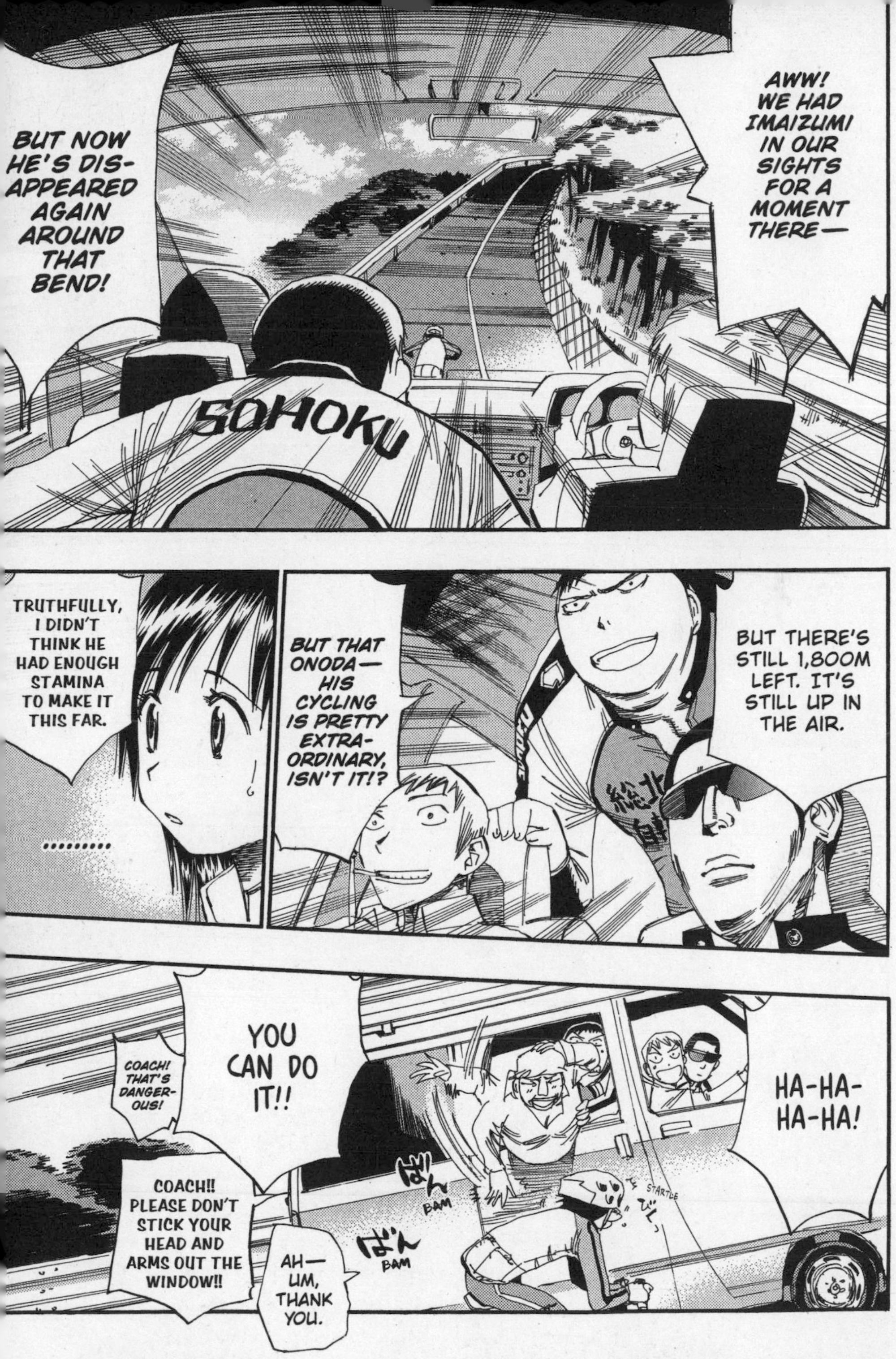
AWW! WE HAD IMAIZUMI IN OUR SIGHTS FOR A MOMENT THERE—
BUT NOW HE'S DIS-APPEARED AGAIN AROUND THAT BEND!
SOHOKU
BUT THERE'S STILL 1,800M LEFT. IT'S STILL UP IN THE AIR.
BUT THAT ONODA—HIS CYCLING IS PRETTY EXTRA-ORDINARY, ISN'T IT!?
TRUTHFULLY, I DIDN'T THINK HE HAD ENOUGH STAMINA TO MAKE IT THIS FAR.
....
HA-HA-HA-HA!
YOU CAN DO IT!!
COACH! THAT'S DANGER-OUS!
STARTLE
ばん BAM
ばん BAM
COACH!! PLEASE DON'T STICK YOUR HEAD AND ARMS OUT THE WINDOW!!
AH—UM, THANK YOU.

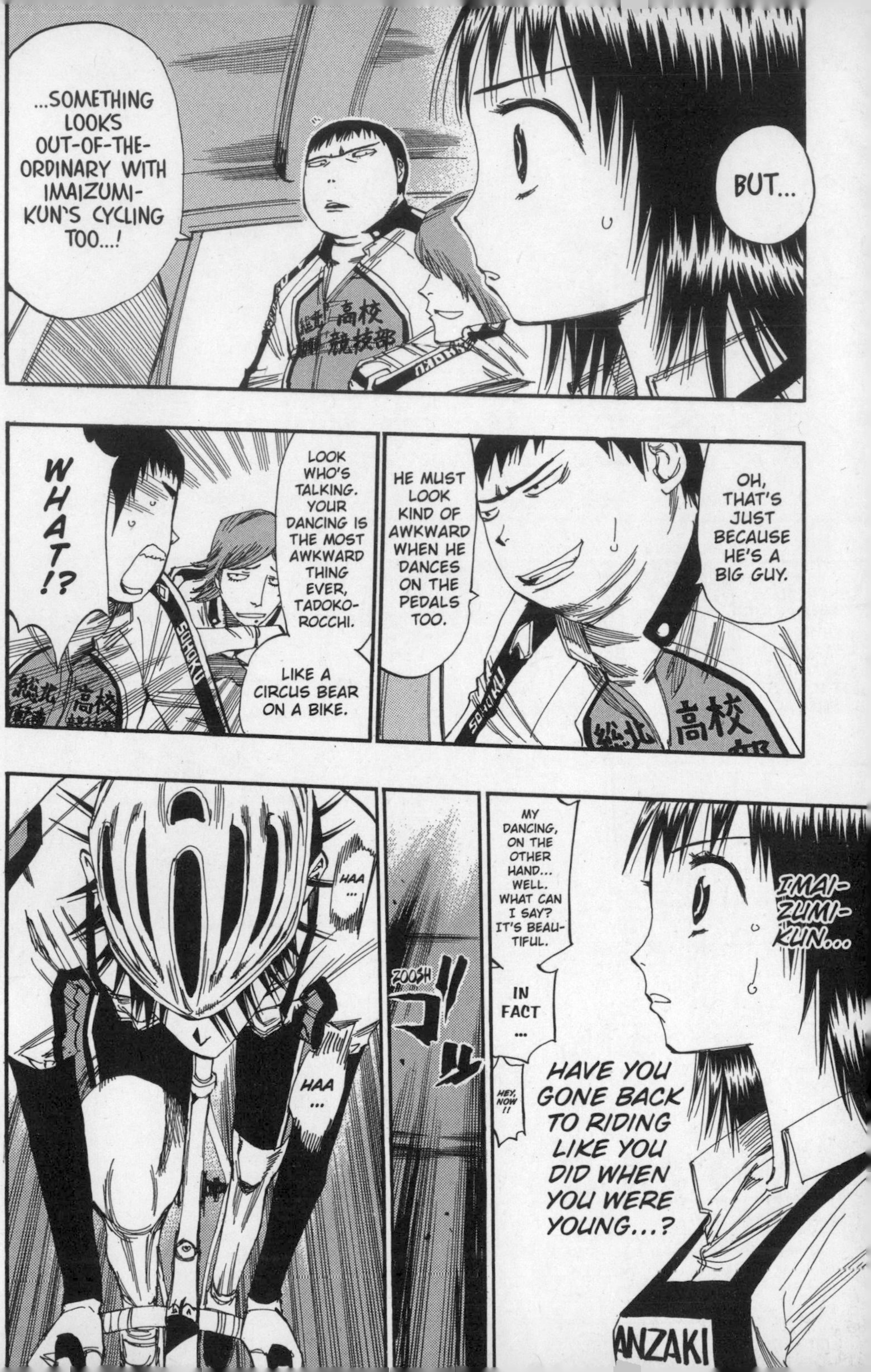
BUT...
...SOMETHING LOOKS OUT-OF-THE-ORDINARY WITH IMAIZUMI-KUN'S CYCLING TOO...!
OH, THAT'S JUST BECAUSE HE'S A BIG GUY.
HE MUST LOOK KIND OF AWKWARD WHEN HE DANCES ON THE PEDALS TOO.
LOOK WHO'S TALKING. YOUR DANCING IS THE MOST AWKWARD THING EVER, TADOKOROCCHI.
LIKE A CIRCUS BEAR ON A BIKE.
WHAT!?
IMAIZUMI-KUN...
HAVE YOU GONE BACK TO RIDING LIKE YOU DID WHEN YOU WERE YOUNG...?
ANZAKI
MY DANCING, ON THE OTHER HAND... WELL. WHAT CAN I SAY? IT'S BEAUTIFUL.
IN FACT...
HEY, NOW!!
ZOOSH
HAA...
HAA...

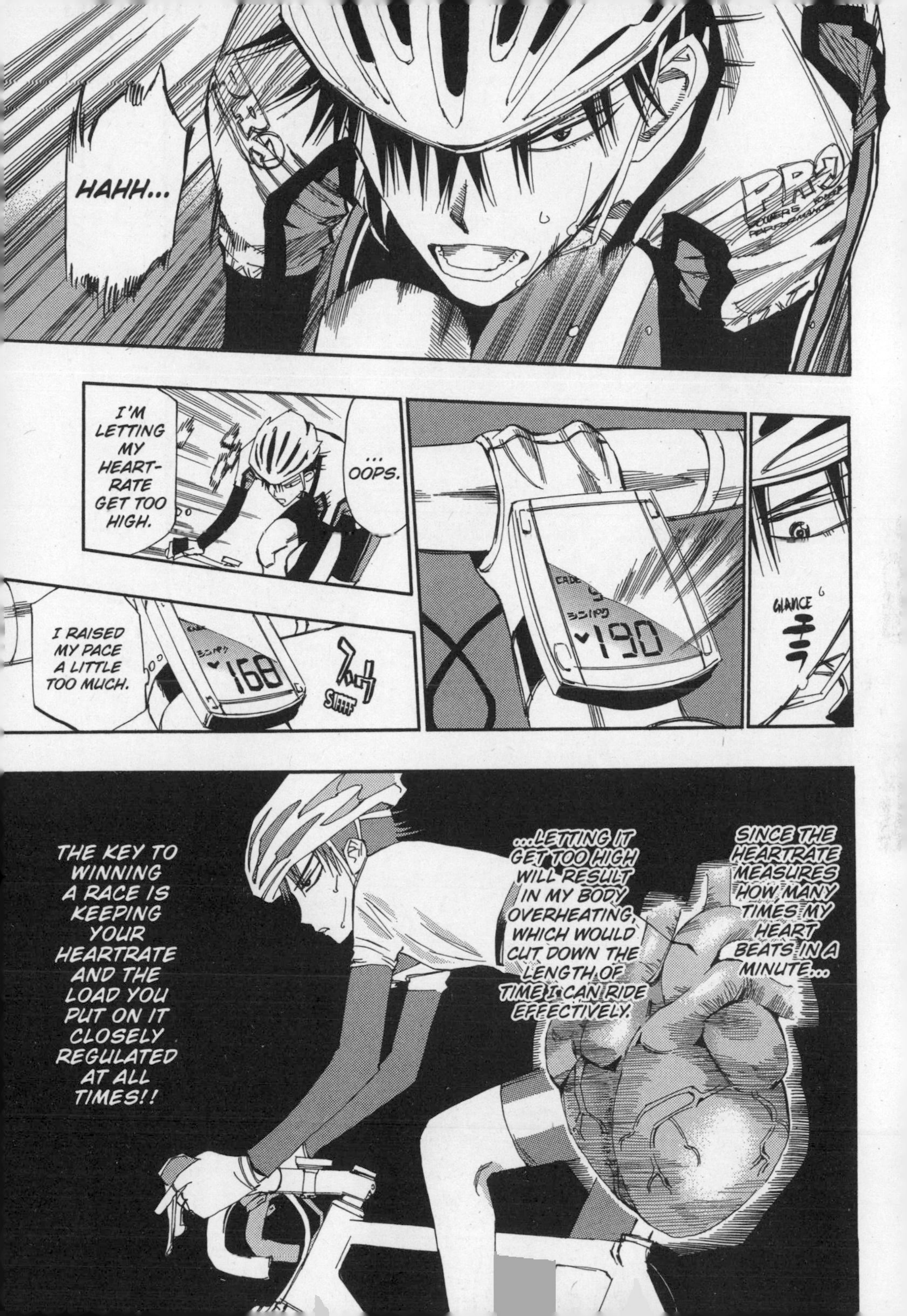
HAHH...
GLANCE
...OOPS.
I'M LETTING MY HEART-RATE GET TOO HIGH.
I RAISED MY PACE A LITTLE TOO MUCH.
SFFFF
SINCE THE HEARTRATE MEASURES HOW MANY TIMES MY HEART BEATS IN A MINUTE...
...LETTING IT GET TOO HIGH WILL RESULT IN MY BODY OVERHEATING, WHICH WOULD CUT DOWN THE LENGTH OF TIME I CAN RIDE EFFECTIVELY.
THE KEY TO WINNING A RACE IS KEEPING YOUR HEARTRATE AND THE LOAD YOU PUT ON IT CLOSELY REGULATED AT ALL TIMES!!

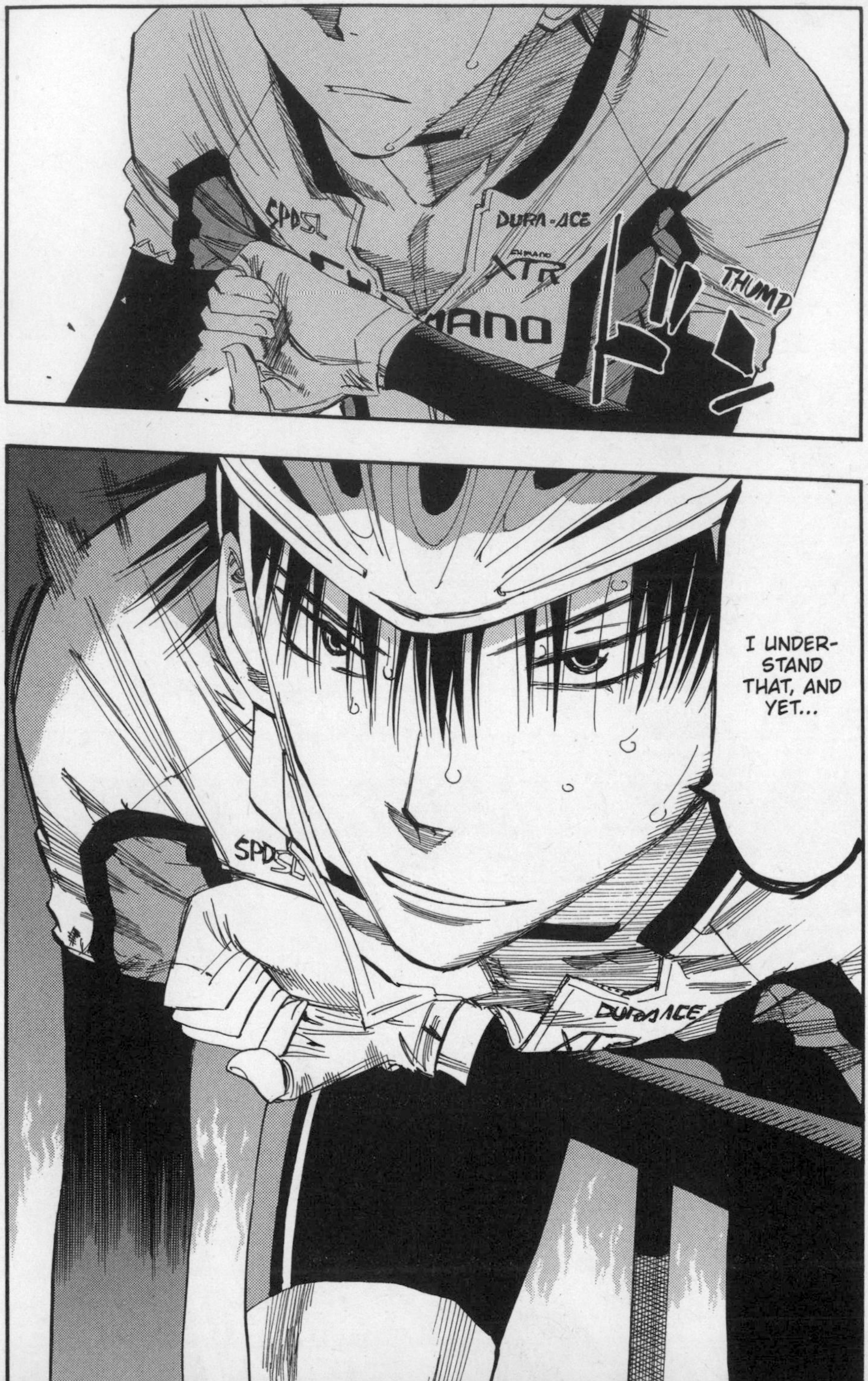
SPD-SL
DURA-ACE
XTR
MANO
THUMP
I UNDER-STAND THAT, AND YET...

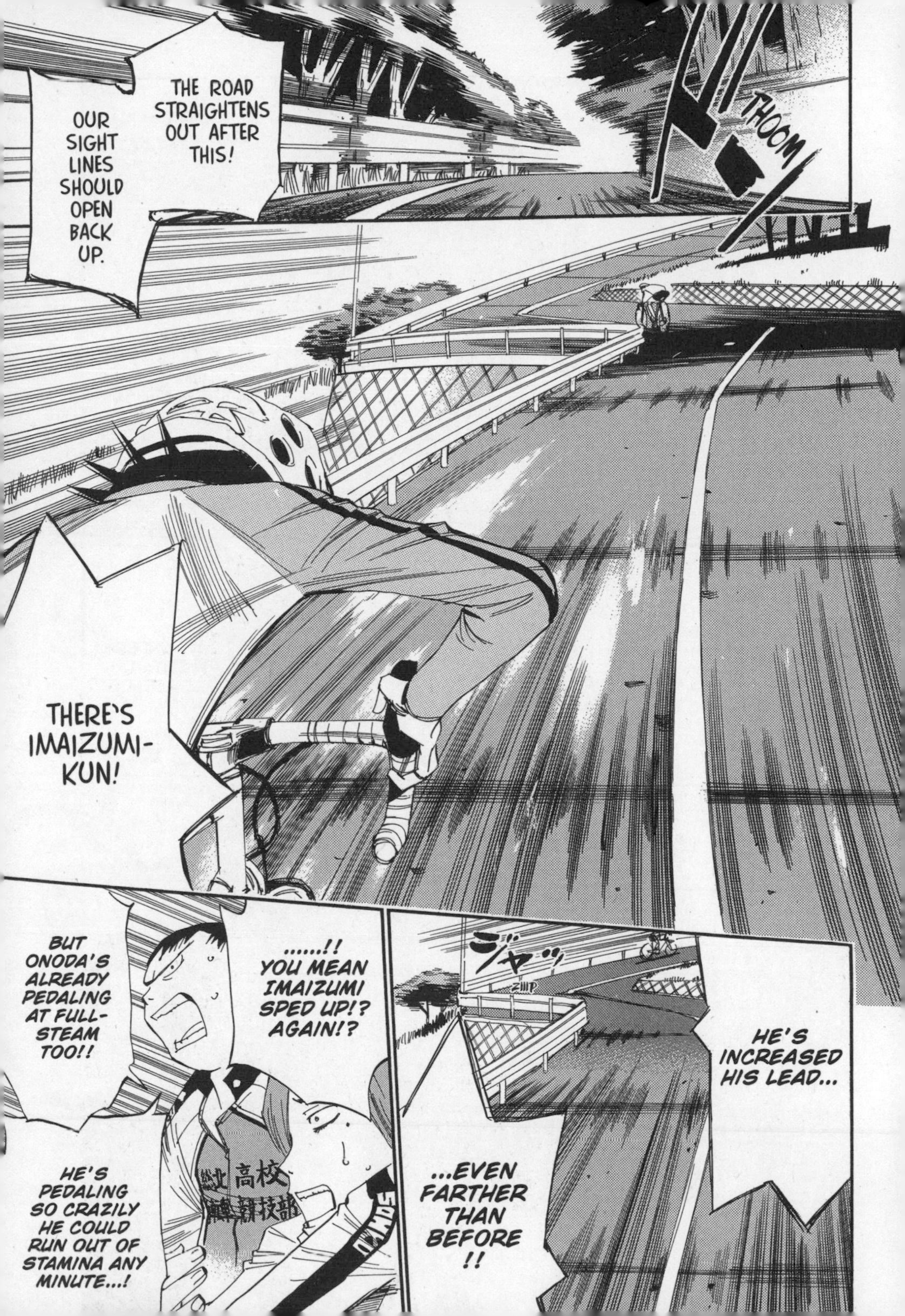
THOOM
THE ROAD STRAIGHTENS OUT AFTER THIS!
OUR SIGHT LINES SHOULD OPEN BACK UP.
THERE'S IMAIZUMI-KUN!
HE'S INCREASED HIS LEAD...
ZIP
...EVEN FARTHER THAN BEFORE!!
......!! YOU MEAN IMAIZUMI SPED UP!? AGAIN!?
BUT ONODA'S ALREADY PEDALING AT FULL-STEAM TOO!!
HE'S PEDALING SO CRAZILY HE COULD RUN OUT OF STAMINA ANY MINUTE...!

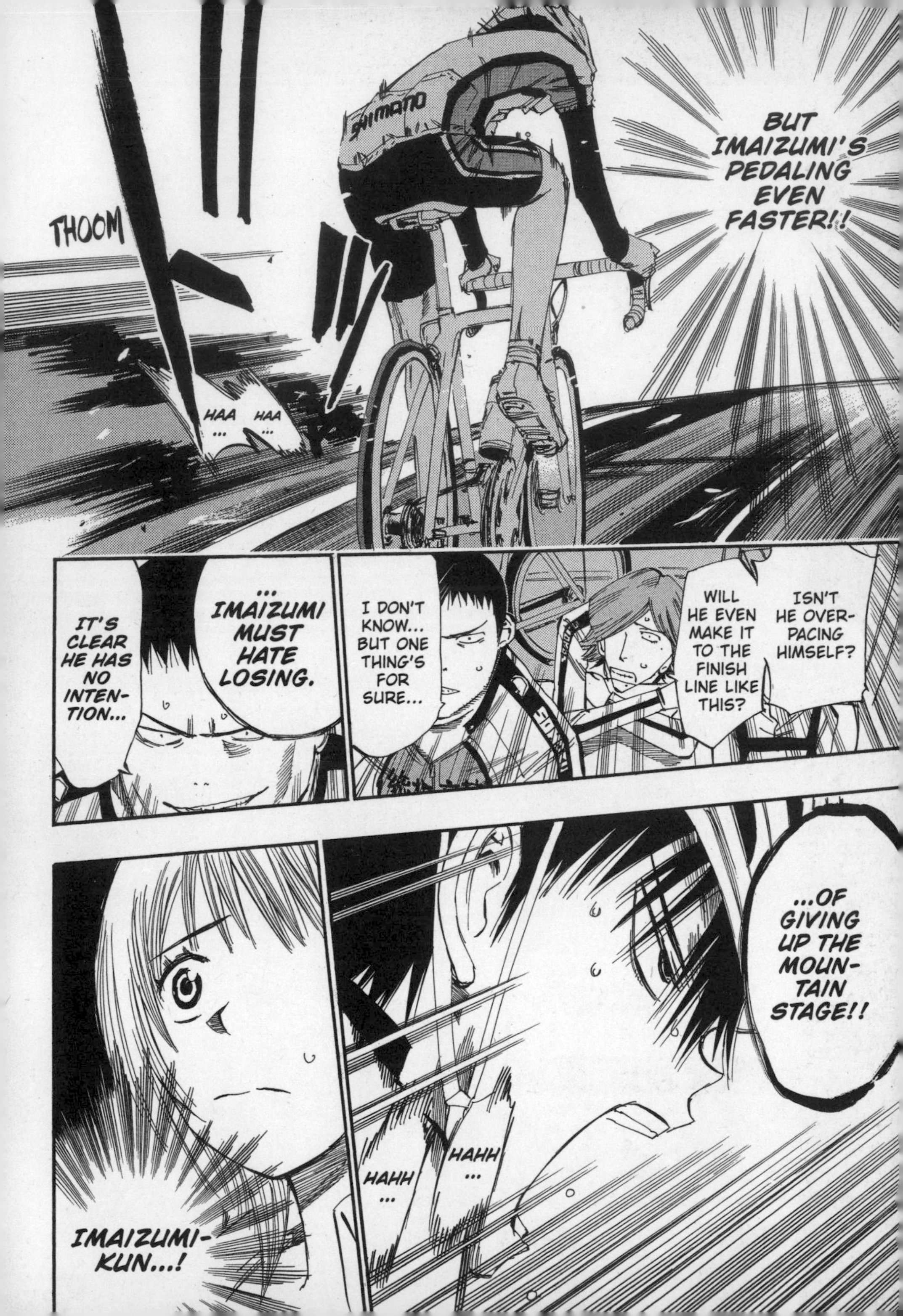
BUT IMAIZUMI'S PEDALING EVEN FASTER!!
THOOM
HAA... HAA...
ISN'T HE OVER-PACING HIMSELF?
WILL HE EVEN MAKE IT TO THE FINISH LINE LIKE THIS?
I DON'T KNOW... BUT ONE THING'S FOR SURE...
...IMAIZUMI MUST HATE LOSING.
IT'S CLEAR HE HAS NO INTENTION...
...OF GIVING UP THE MOUNTAIN STAGE!!
HAHH...
HAHH...
IMAIZUMI-KUN...!

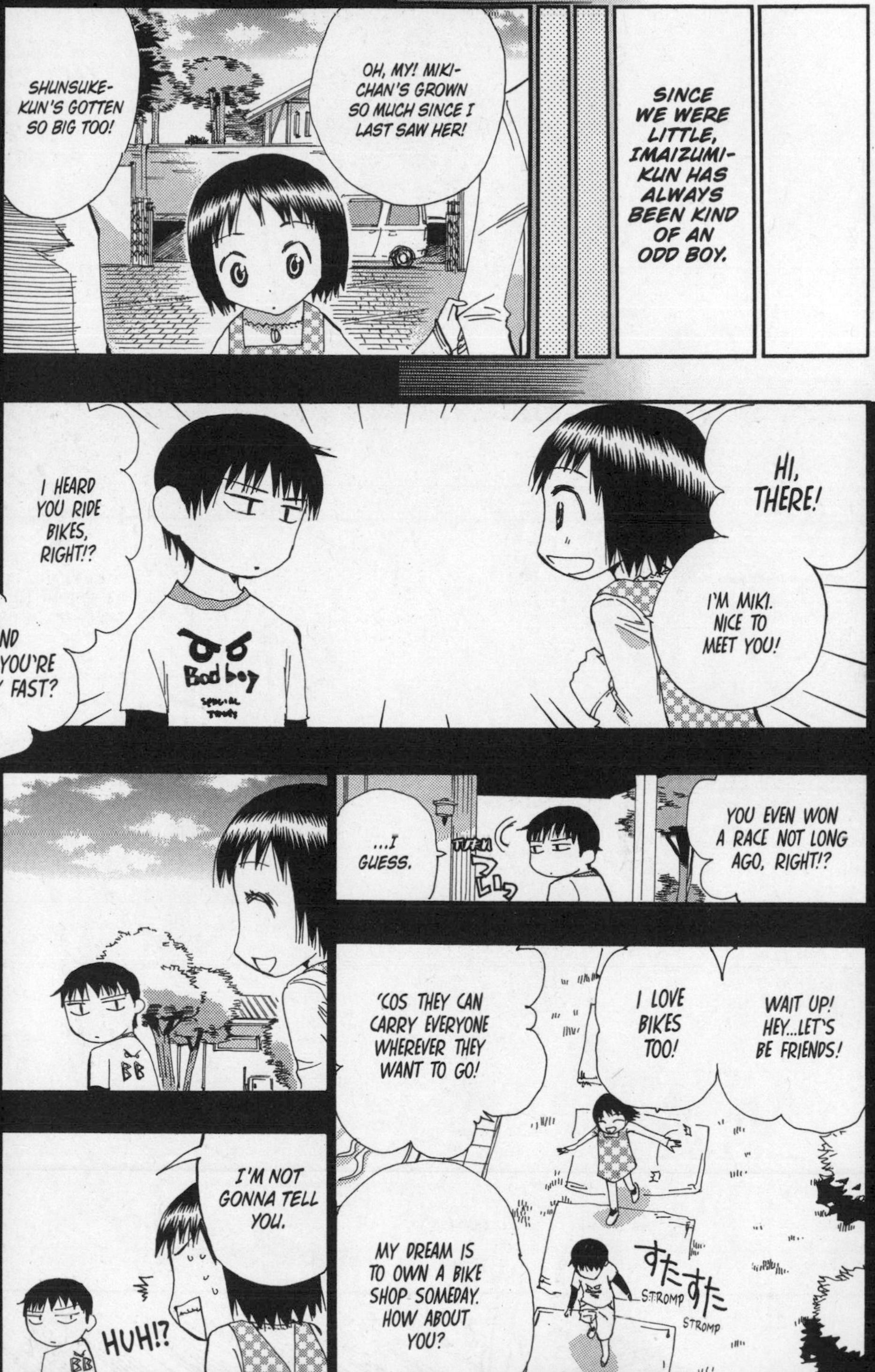
SINCE WE WERE LITTLE, IMAIZUMI-KUN HAS ALWAYS BEEN KIND OF AN ODD BOY.
OH, MY! MIKI-CHAN'S GROWN SO MUCH SINCE I LAST SAW HER!
SHUNSUKE-KUN'S GOTTEN SO BIG TOO!
HI, THERE!
I'M MIKI. NICE TO MEET YOU!
I HEARD YOU RIDE BIKES, RIGHT!?
AND THAT YOU'RE REALLY FAST?
YOU EVEN WON A RACE NOT LONG AGO, RIGHT!?
...I GUESS.
WAIT UP! HEY...LET'S BE FRIENDS!
I LOVE BIKES TOO!
'COS THEY CAN CARRY EVERYONE WHEREVER THEY WANT TO GO!
MY DREAM IS TO OWN A BIKE SHOP SOMEDAY. HOW ABOUT YOU?
すたすた STROMP STROMP
I'M NOT GONNA TELL YOU.
HUH!?

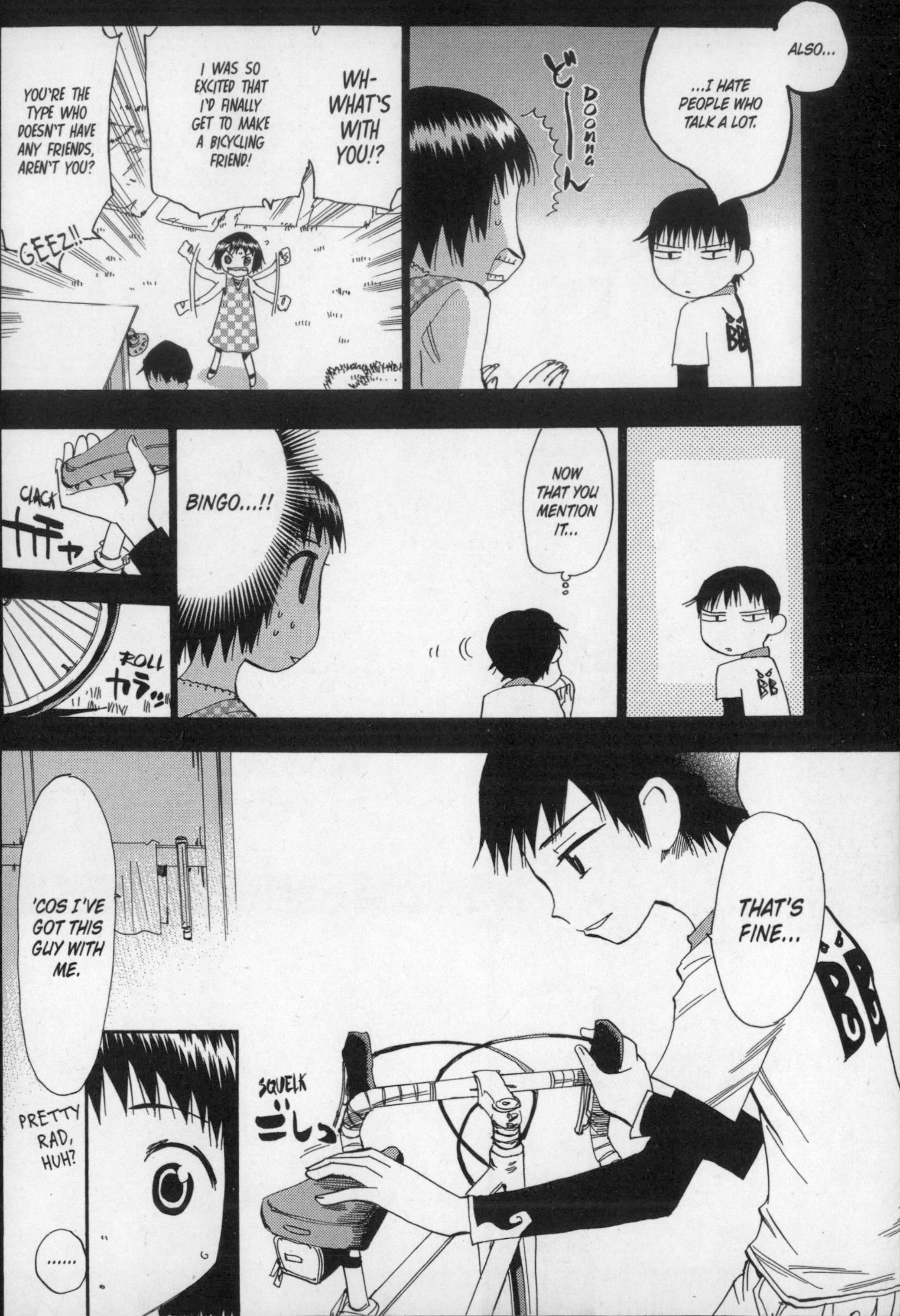
ALSO...
...I HATE PEOPLE WHO TALK A LOT.
DOONNG
どーーん
WH- WHAT'S WITH YOU!?
I WAS SO EXCITED THAT I'D FINALLY GET TO MAKE A BICYCLING FRIEND!
YOU'RE THE TYPE WHO DOESN'T HAVE ANY FRIENDS, AREN'T YOU?
GEEZ!!
NOW THAT YOU MENTION IT...
BINGO...!!
CLACK
カチャ
ROLL
カラ…
THAT'S FINE...
'COS I'VE GOT THIS GUY WITH ME.
SQUELK
ごしっ
PRETTY RAD, HUH?
......

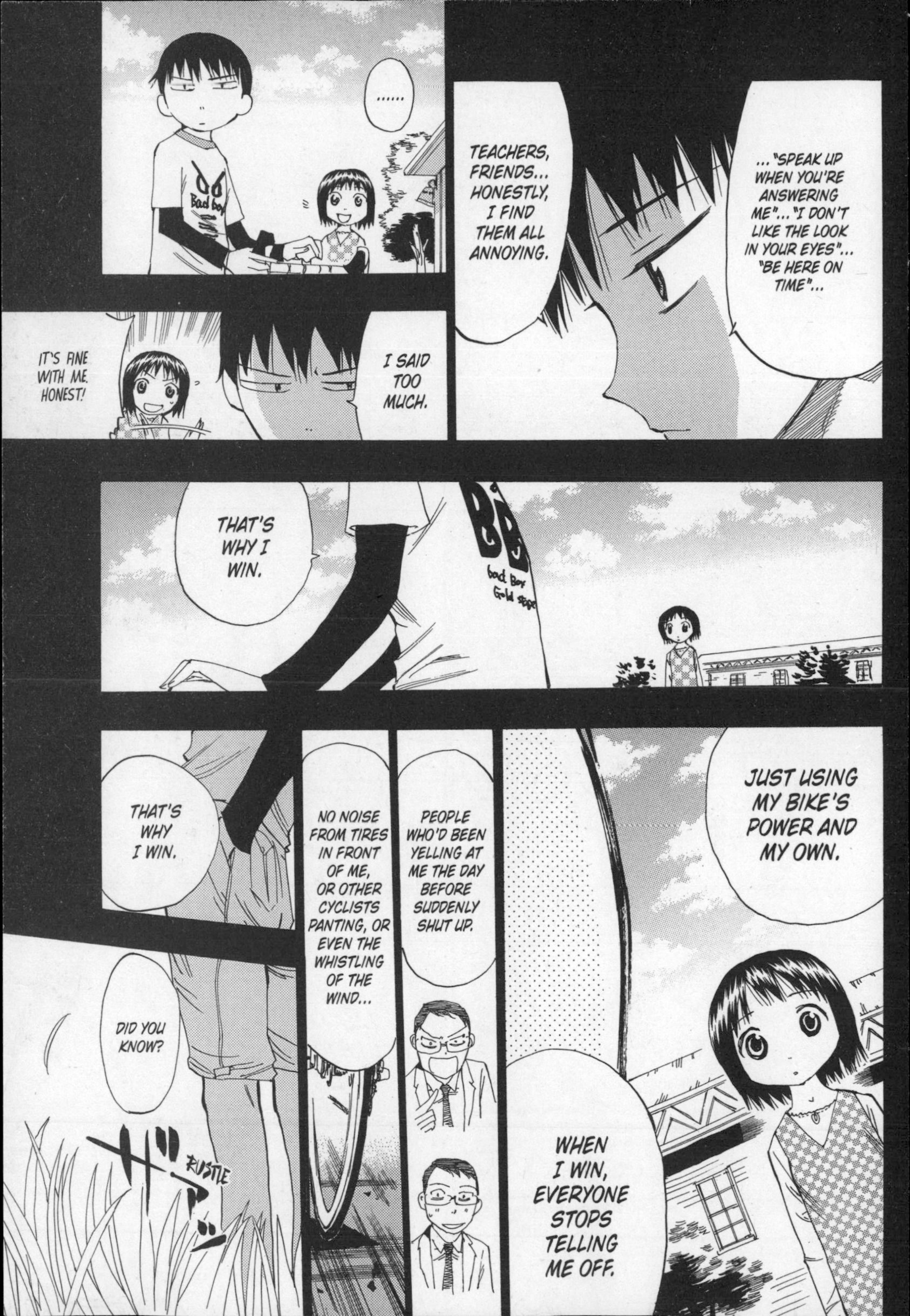
..."SPEAK UP WHEN YOU'RE ANSWERING ME"... "I DON'T LIKE THE LOOK IN YOUR EYES"... "BE HERE ON TIME"...
TEACHERS, FRIENDS... HONESTLY, I FIND THEM ALL ANNOYING.
......
I SAID TOO MUCH.
IT'S FINE WITH ME. HONEST!
THAT'S WHY I WIN.
JUST USING MY BIKE'S POWER AND MY OWN.
WHEN I WIN, EVERYONE STOPS TELLING ME OFF.
PEOPLE WHO'D BEEN YELLING AT ME THE DAY BEFORE SUDDENLY SHUT UP.
NO NOISE FROM TIRES IN FRONT OF ME, OR OTHER CYCLISTS PANTING, OR EVEN THE WHISTLING OF THE WIND...
THAT'S WHY I WIN.
DID YOU KNOW?
RUSTLE

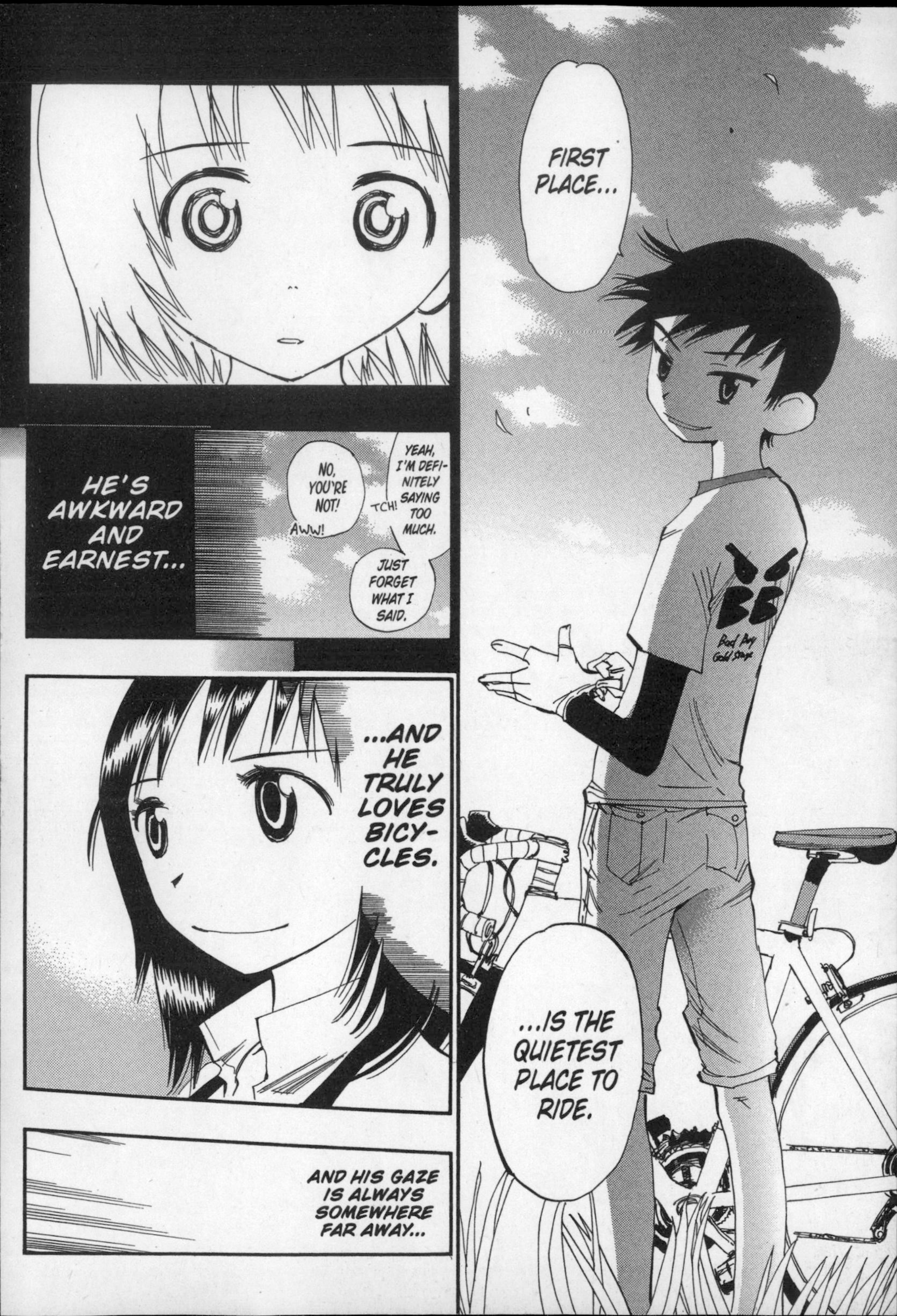
FIRST PLACE...
...IS THE QUIETEST PLACE TO RIDE.
YEAH, I'M DEFI-NITELY SAYING TOO MUCH.
NO, YOU'RE NOT!
TCH!
AWW!
JUST FORGET WHAT I SAID.
HE'S AWKWARD AND EARNEST...
...AND HE TRULY LOVES BICY-CLES.
AND HIS GAZE IS ALWAYS SOMEWHERE FAR AWAY...

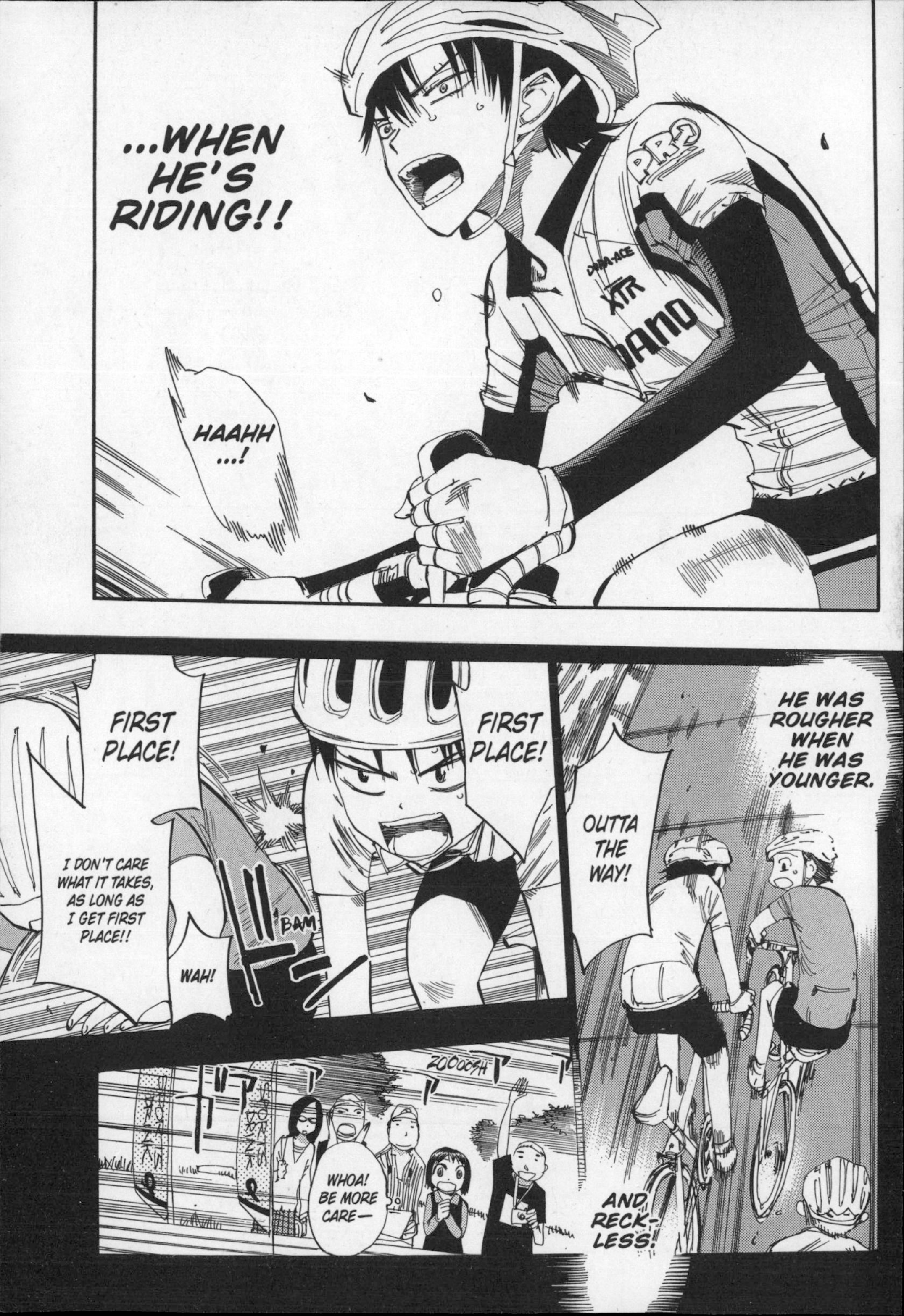
...WHEN HE'S RIDING!!
HAAHH ...!
HE WAS ROUGHER WHEN HE WAS YOUNGER.
OUTTA THE WAY!
AND RECKLESS!
FIRST PLACE!
FIRST PLACE!
I DON'T CARE WHAT IT TAKES, AS LONG AS I GET FIRST PLACE!!
BAM
WAH!
ZOOOOSH
WHOA! BE MORE CARE—

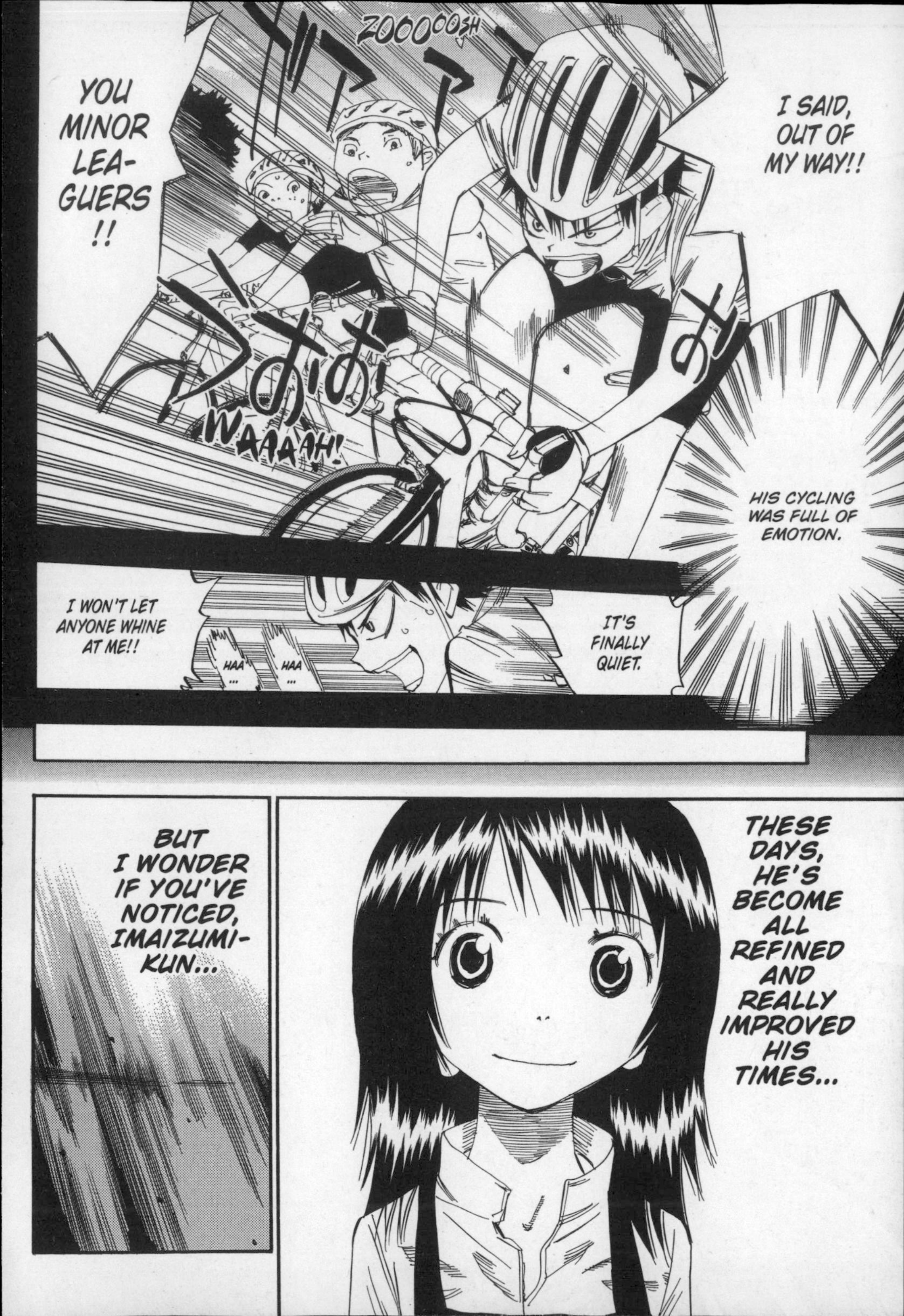
ZOOOOOSH
I SAID, OUT OF MY WAY!!
YOU MINOR LEA-GUERS!!
WAAAAH!
HIS CYCLING WAS FULL OF EMOTION.
IT'S FINALLY QUIET.
I WON'T LET ANYONE WHINE AT ME!!
HAA...
HAA...
THESE DAYS, HE'S BECOME ALL REFINED AND REALLY IMPROVED HIS TIMES...
BUT I WONDER IF YOU'VE NOTICED, IMAIZUMI-KUN...

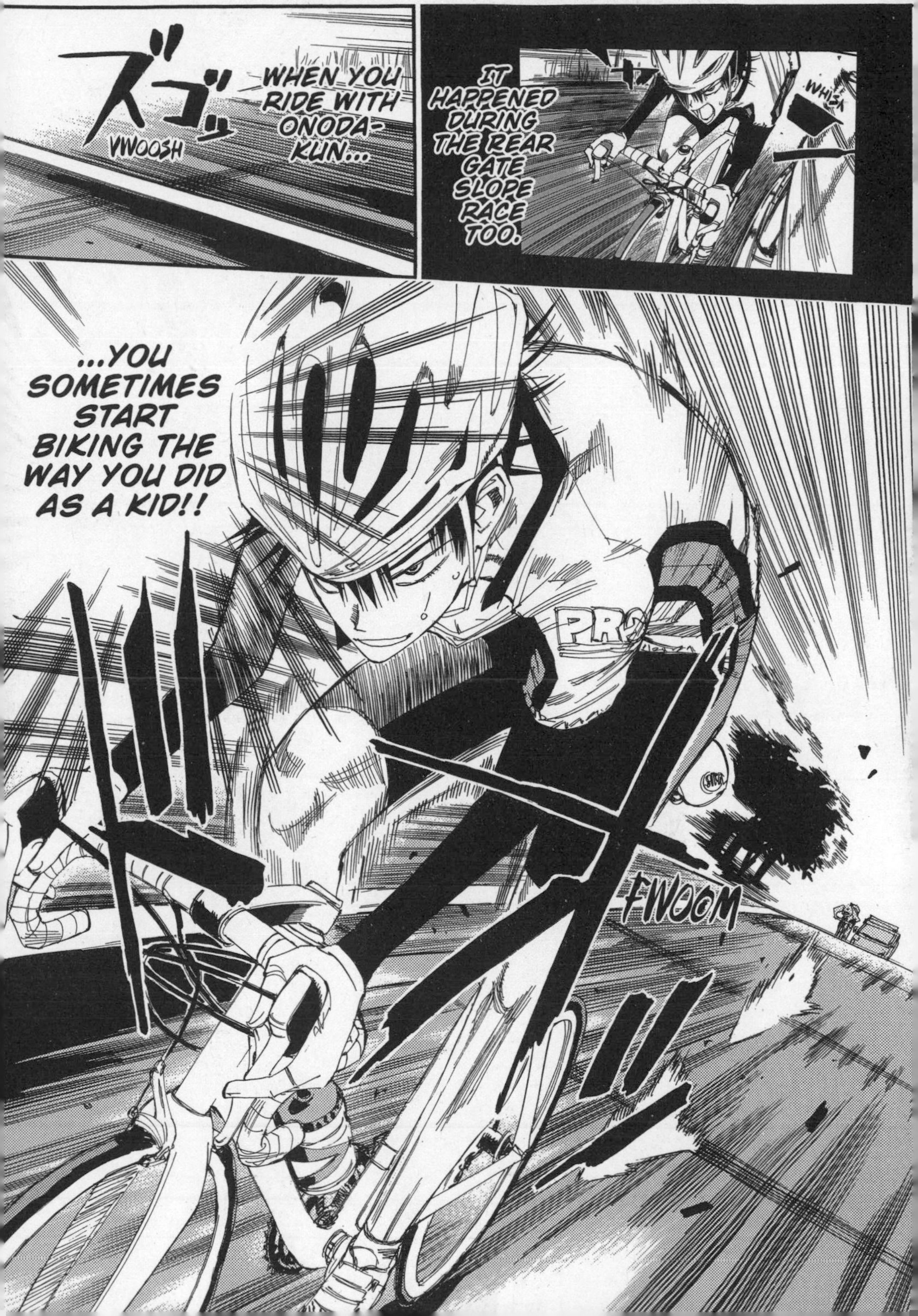
IT HAPPENED DURING THE REAR GATE SLOPE RACE TOO.
WHISK
ズゴッ
VWOOSH
WHEN YOU RIDE WITH ONODA-KUN...
...YOU SOMETIMES START BIKING THE WAY YOU DID AS A KID!!
FWOOM

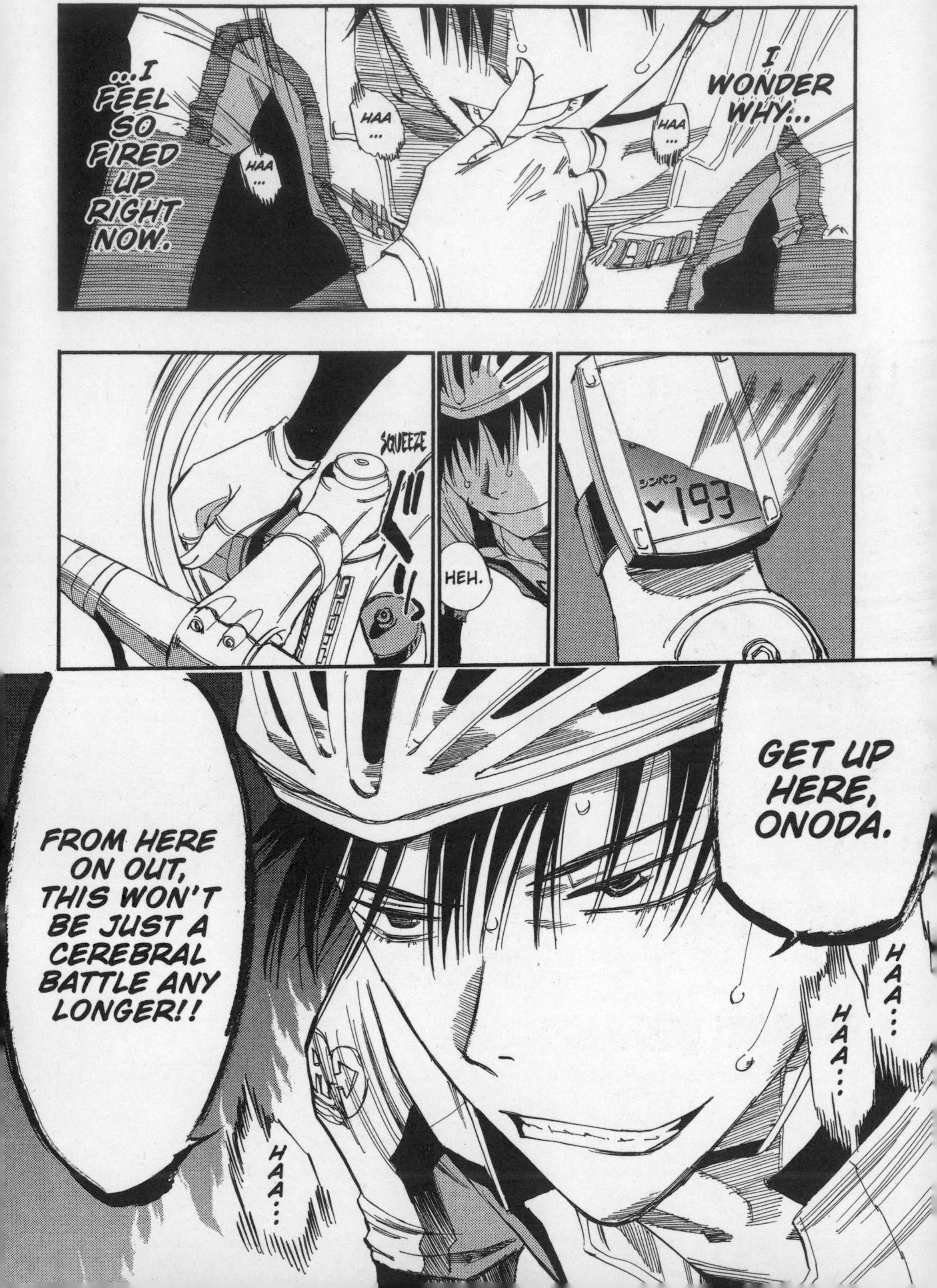
I WONDER WHY...
HAA...
HAA...
HAA...
...I FEEL SO FIRED UP RIGHT NOW.
シンパク
193
HEH.
SQUEEZE
GET UP HERE, ONODA.
HAA...
HAA...
FROM HERE ON OUT, THIS WON'T BE JUST A CEREBRAL BATTLE ANY LONGER!!
HAA...

RIDE.30 THE ONLY THING I CAN DO

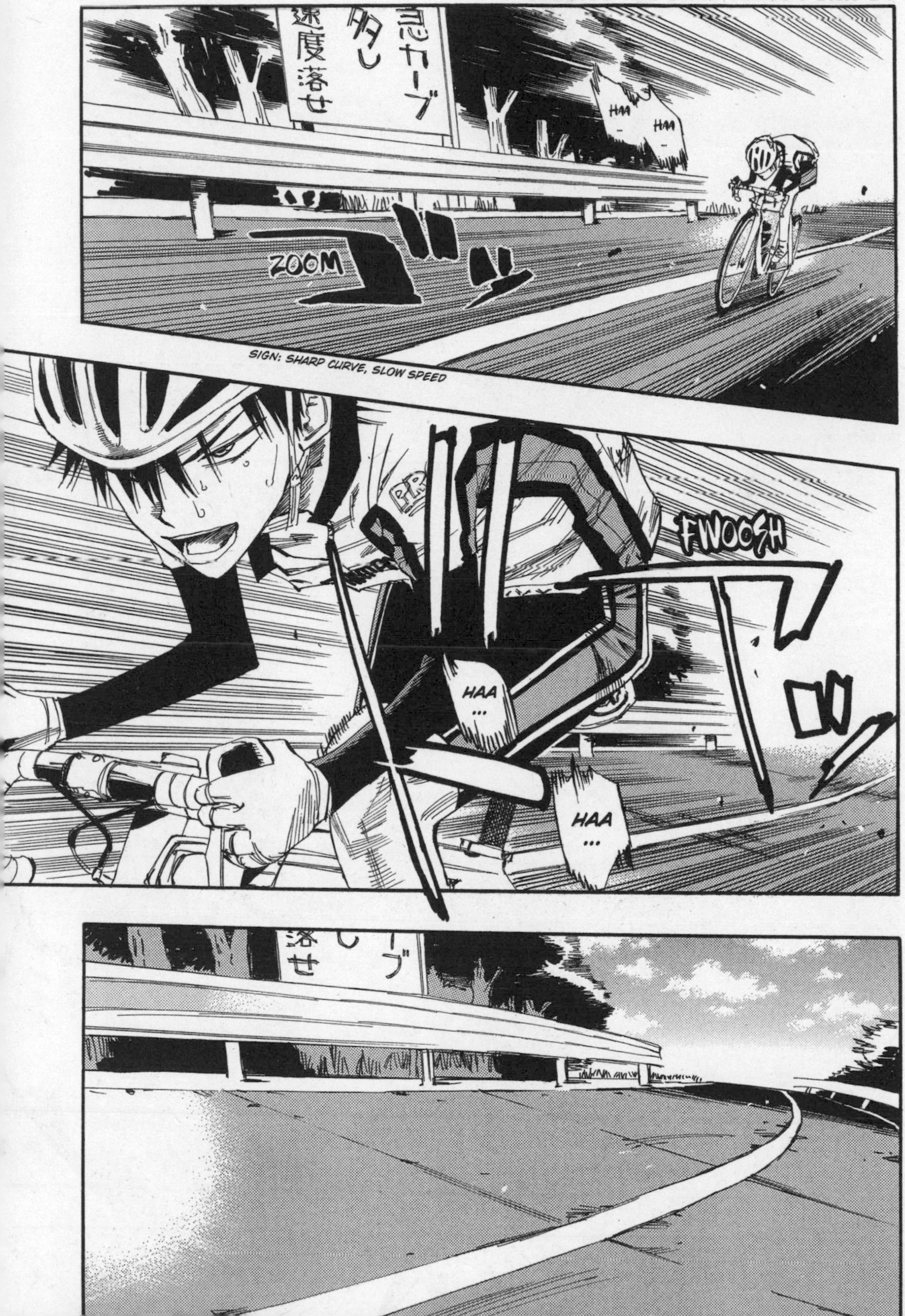
急カーブ多し速度落せ
HAA...
HAA...
ZOOM
ゴッ
SIGN: SHARP CURVE, SLOW SPEED
FWOOSH
HAA...
HAA...

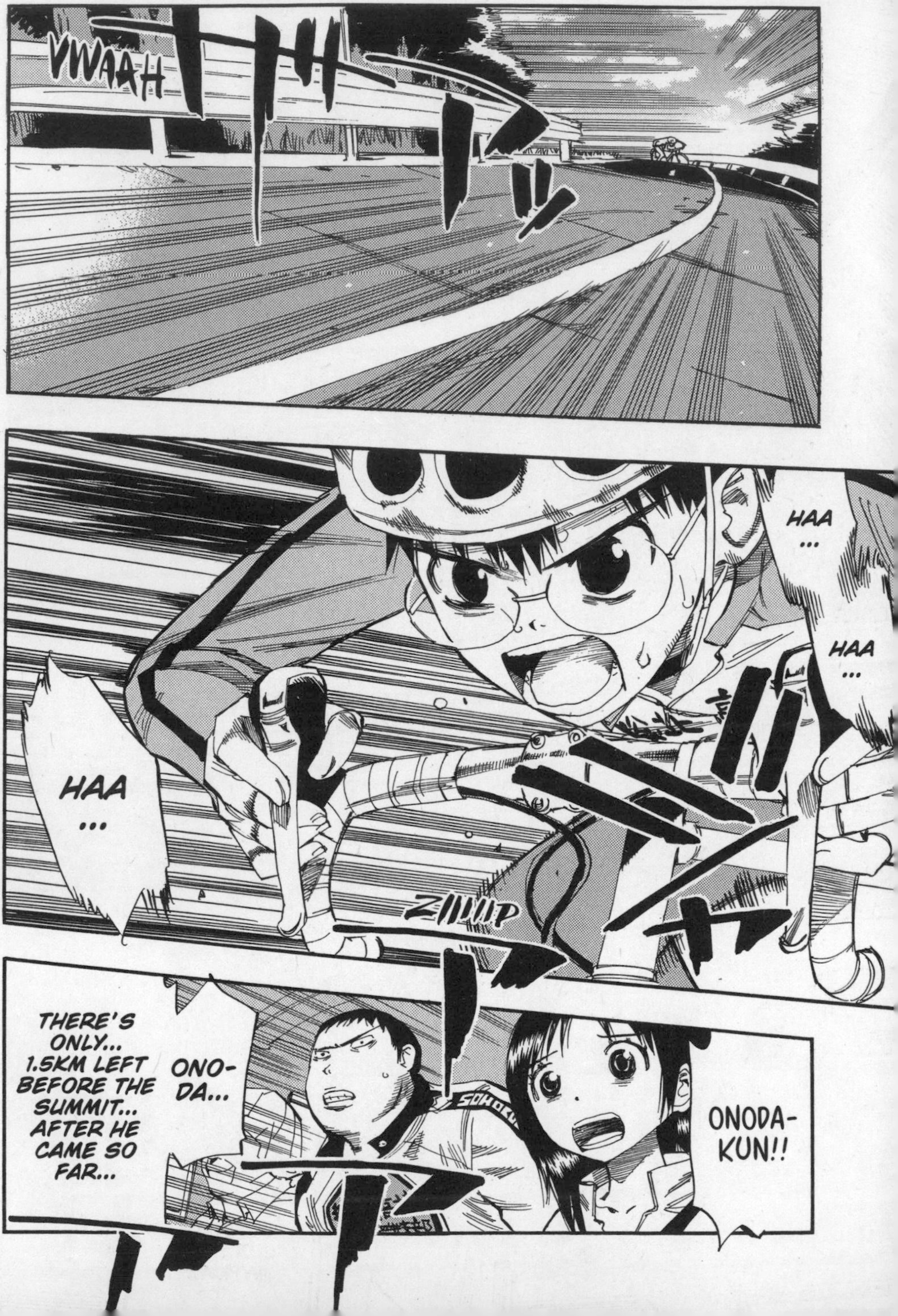
VWAAH
HAA ...
HAA ...
ZIIIIIP
HAA ...
ONODA-KUN!!
ONO-DA...
THERE'S ONLY... 1.5KM LEFT BEFORE THE SUMMIT... AFTER HE CAME SO FAR...

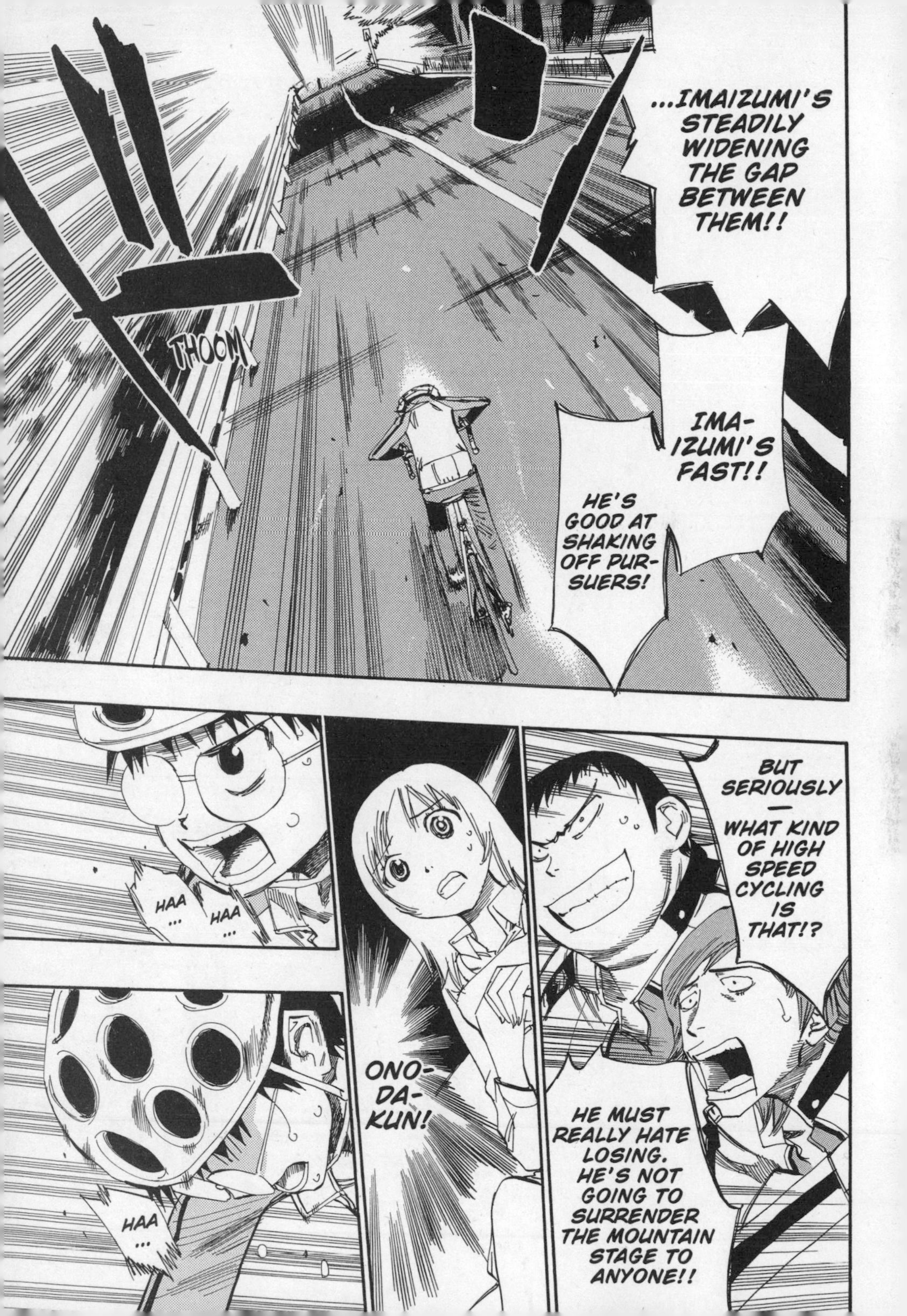
...IMAIZUMI'S STEADILY WIDENING THE GAP BETWEEN THEM!!
THOOM
IMA-IZUMI'S FAST!!
HE'S GOOD AT SHAKING OFF PUR-SUERS!
BUT SERIOUSLY— WHAT KIND OF HIGH SPEED CYCLING IS THAT!?
HE MUST REALLY HATE LOSING. HE'S NOT GOING TO SURRENDER THE MOUNTAIN STAGE TO ANYONE!!
ONO-DA-KUN!
HAA... HAA...
HAA...

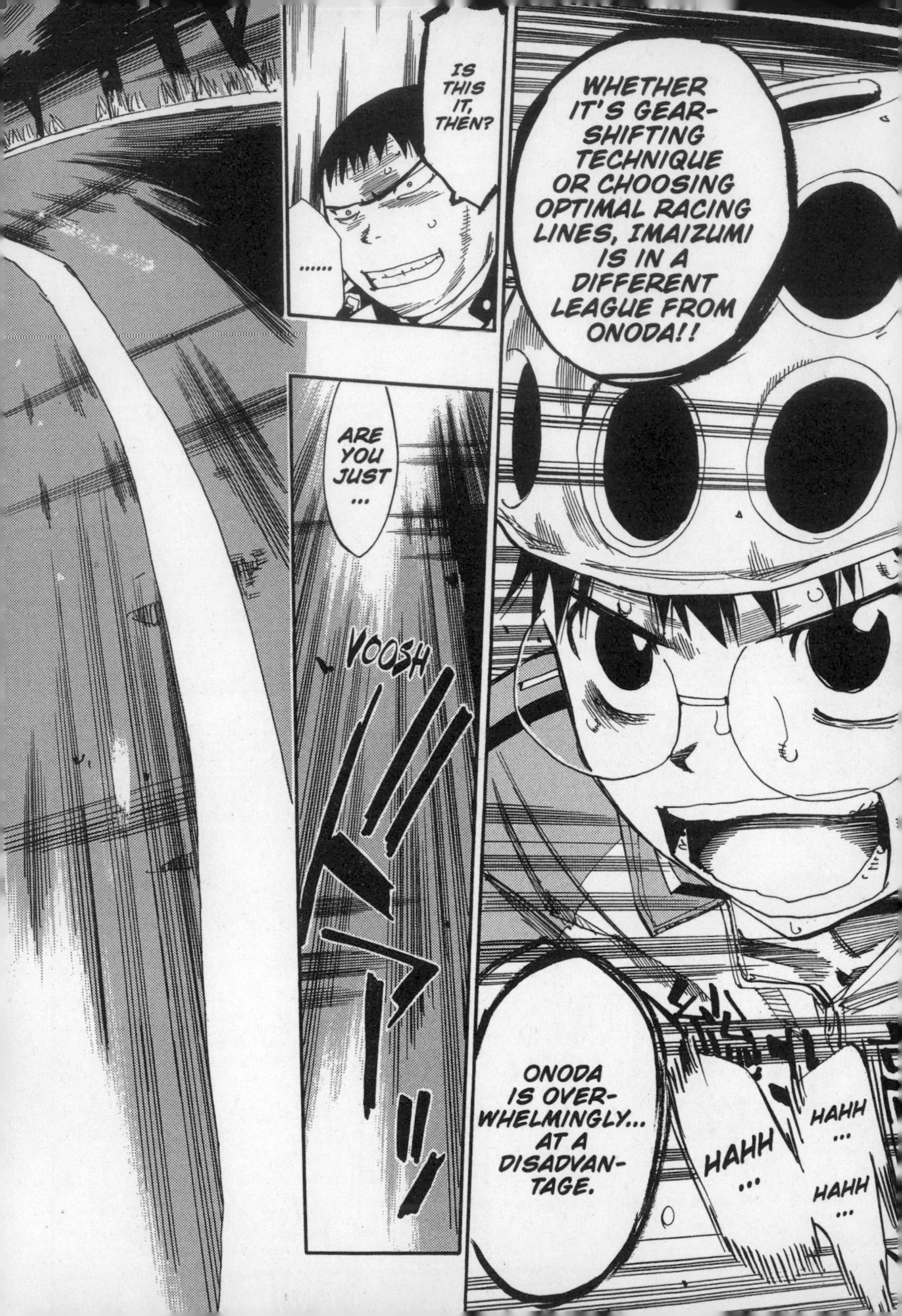
WHETHER IT'S GEAR-SHIFTING TECHNIQUE OR CHOOSING OPTIMAL RACING LINES, IMAIZUMI IS IN A DIFFERENT LEAGUE FROM ONODA!!
HAHH... HAHH...
HAHH...
ONODA IS OVERWHELMINGLY... AT A DISADVANTAGE.
IS THIS IT, THEN?
......
ARE YOU JUST ...
VOOSH

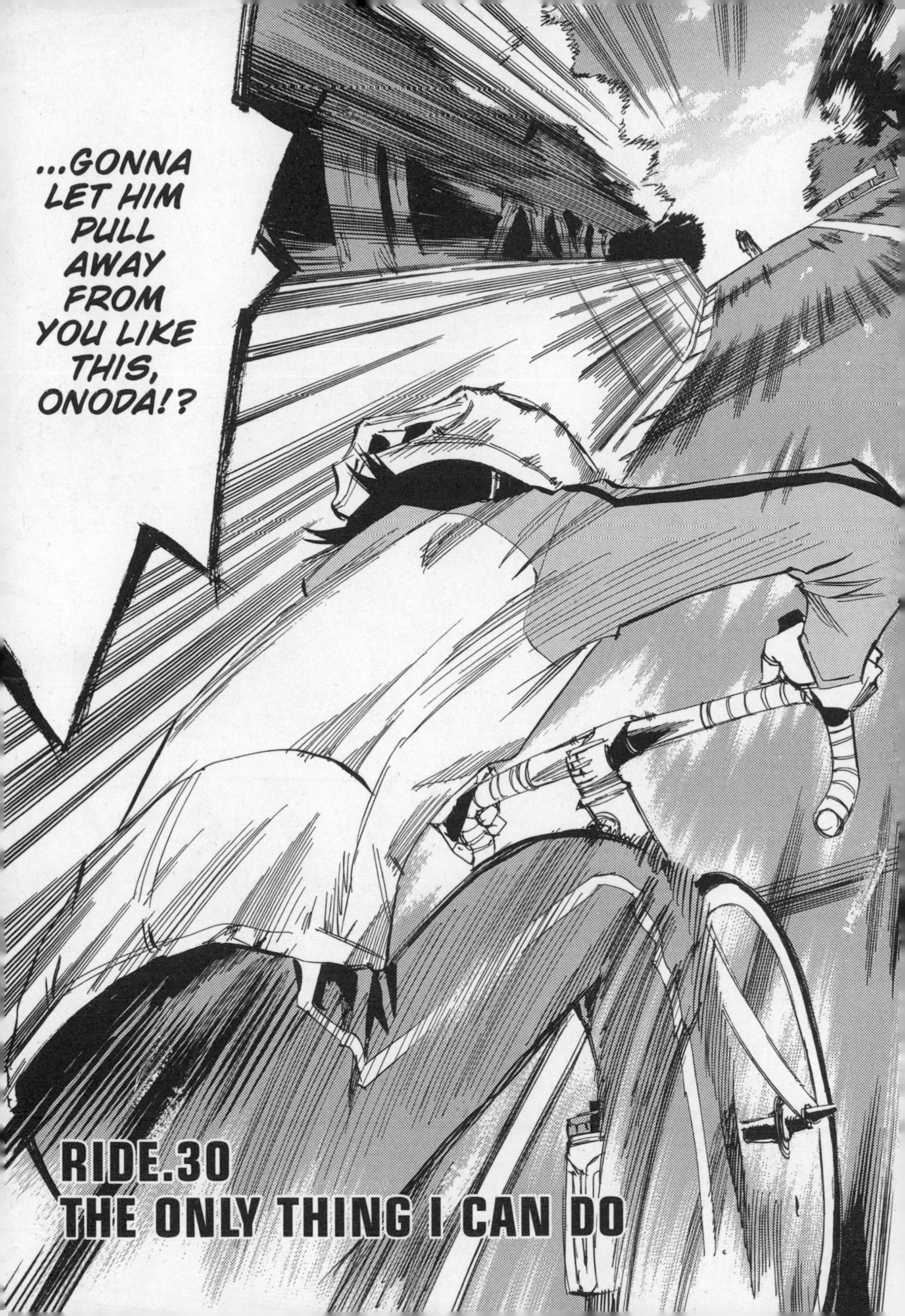
...GONNA LET HIM PULL AWAY FROM YOU LIKE THIS, ONODA!?
RIDE.30
THE ONLY THING I CAN DO

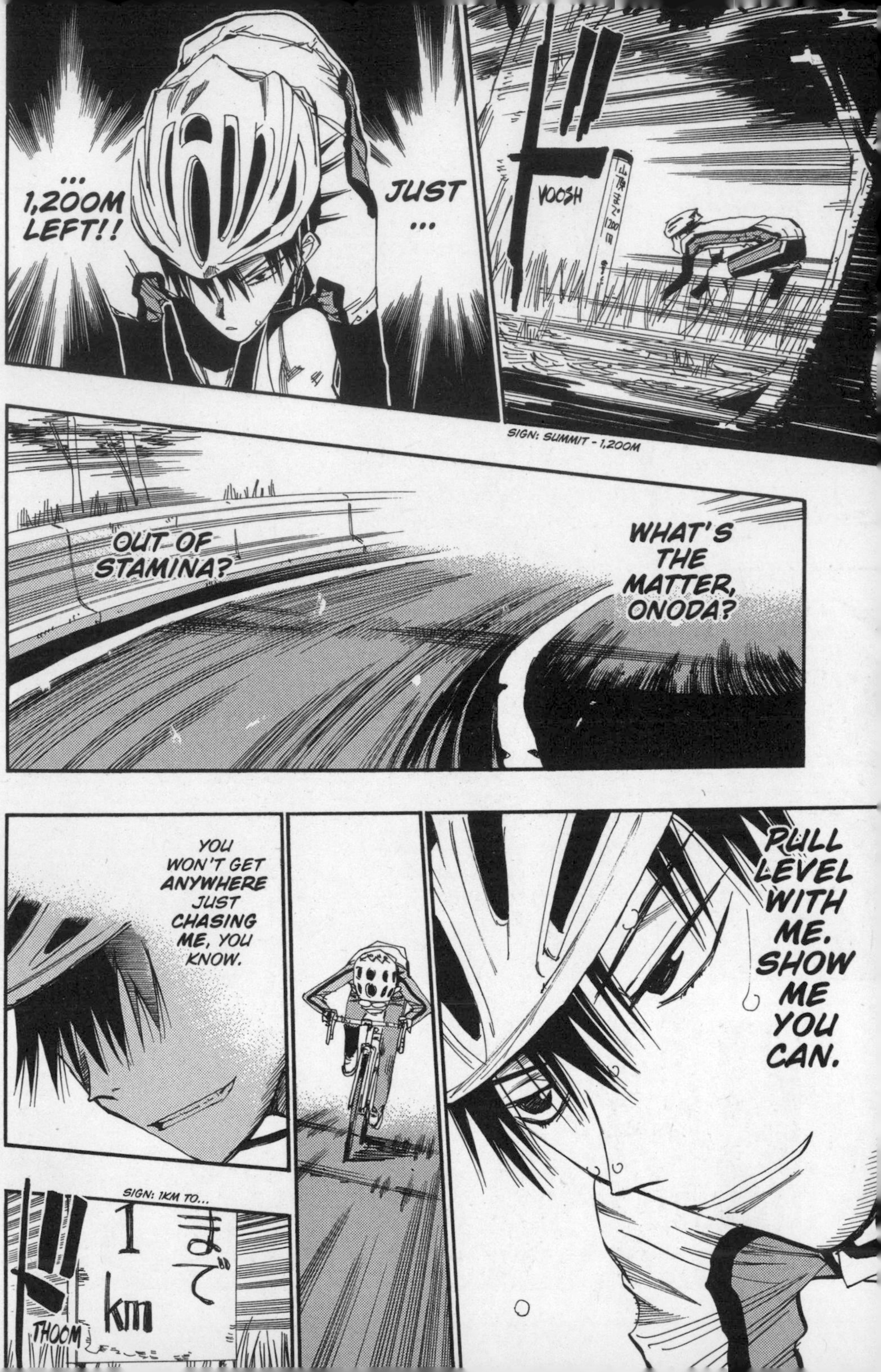
VOOSH
SIGN: SUMMIT - 1,200M
JUST ...
... 1,200M LEFT!!
WHAT'S THE MATTER, ONODA?
OUT OF STAMINA?
PULL LEVEL WITH ME. SHOW ME YOU CAN.
YOU WON'T GET ANYWHERE JUST CHASING ME, YOU KNOW.
SIGN: 1KM TO...
1km まで
THOOM

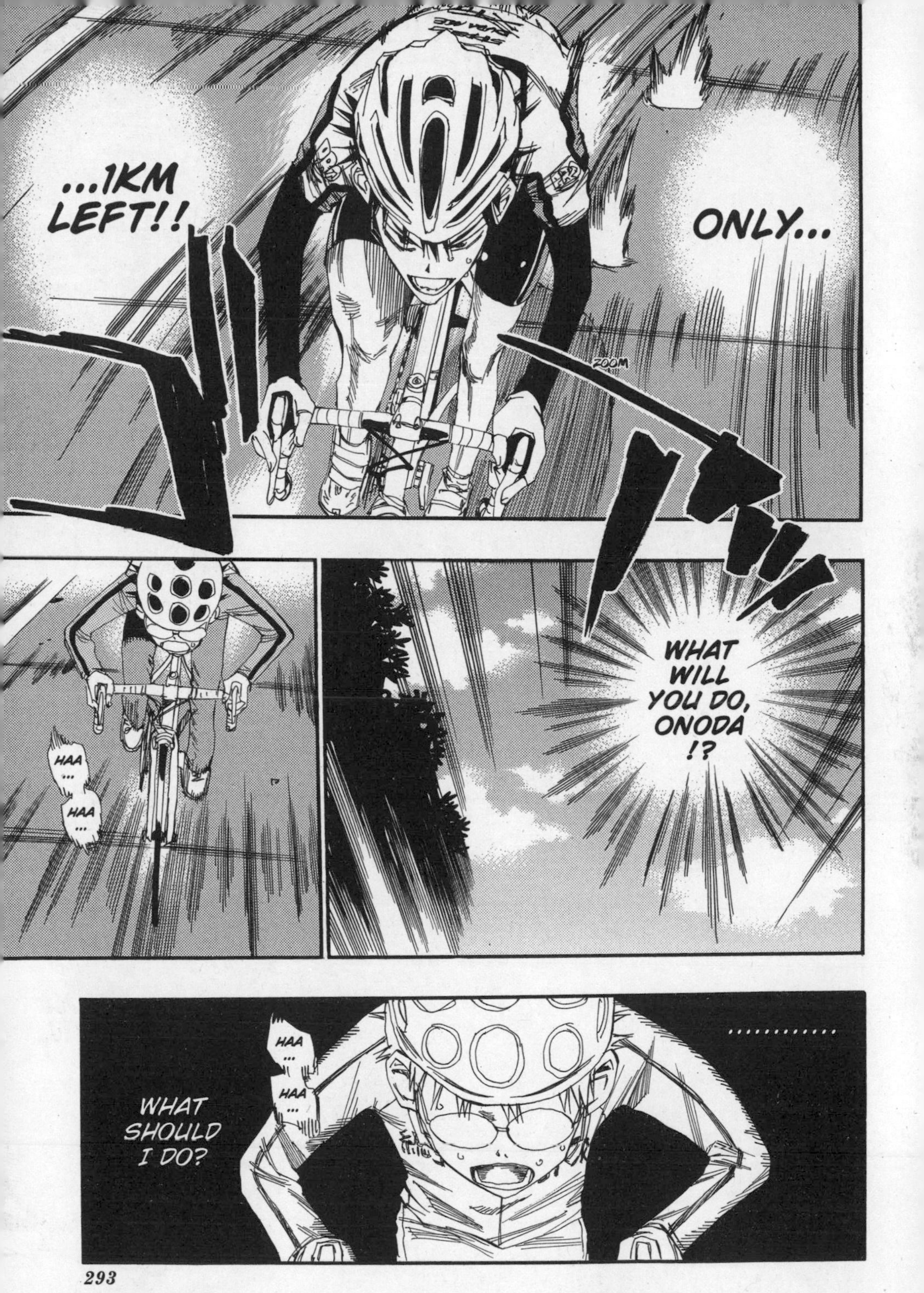
ONLY...
...1KM LEFT!!
ZOOM
WHAT WILL YOU DO, ONODA !?
HAA... HAA...
....
HAA... HAA...
WHAT SHOULD I DO?

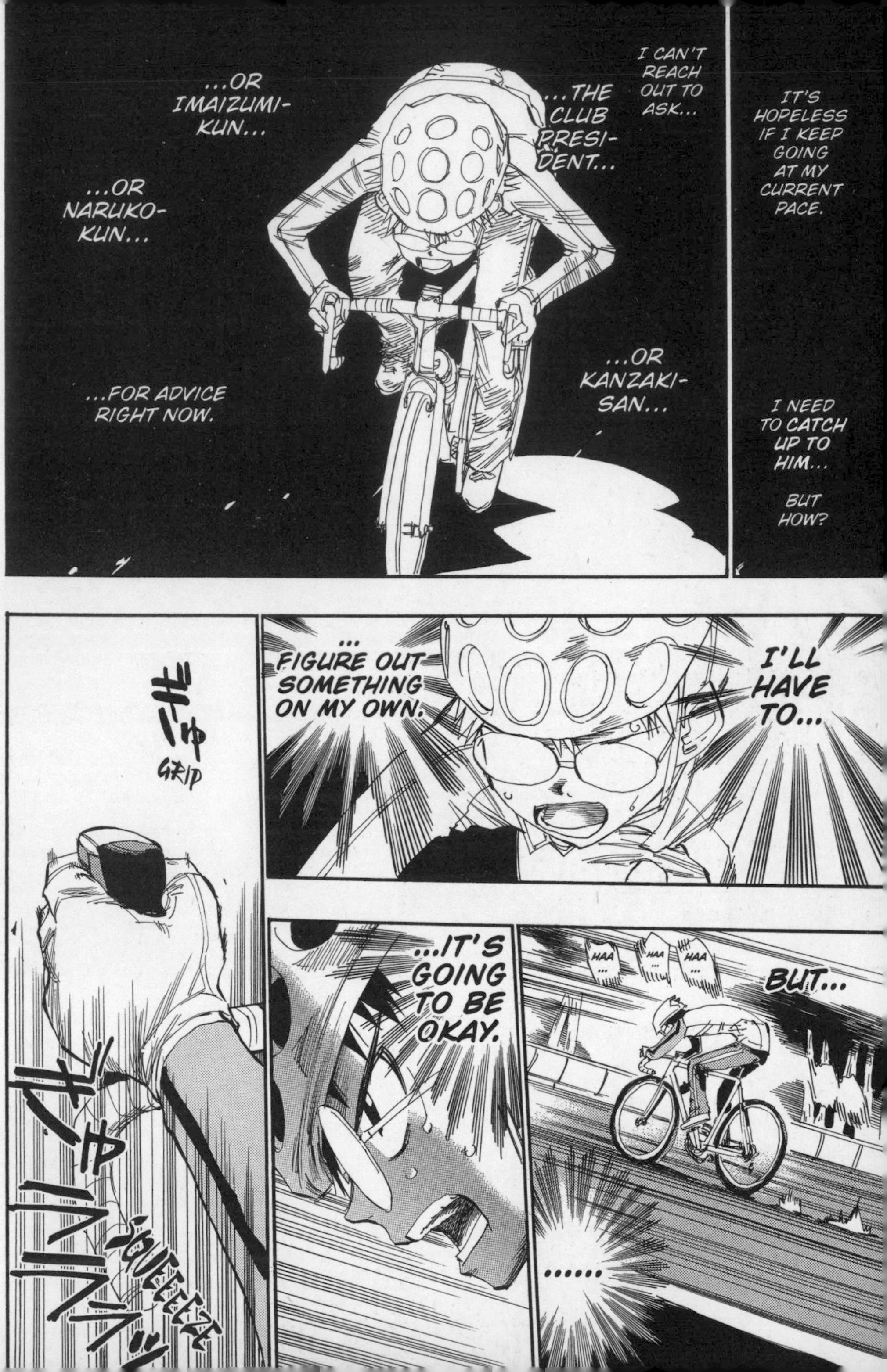
IT'S HOPELESS IF I KEEP GOING AT MY CURRENT PACE.
I NEED TO CATCH UP TO HIM...
BUT HOW?
I CAN'T REACH OUT TO ASK...
...THE CLUB PRESIDENT...
...OR IMAIZUMI-KUN...
...OR NARUKO-KUN...
...OR KANZAKI-SAN...
...FOR ADVICE RIGHT NOW.
I'LL HAVE TO...
...FIGURE OUT SOMETHING ON MY OWN.
BUT...
HAA...
HAA...
HAA...
......
...IT'S GOING TO BE OKAY.
ぎゅ
GRIP
SQUEEEEZE

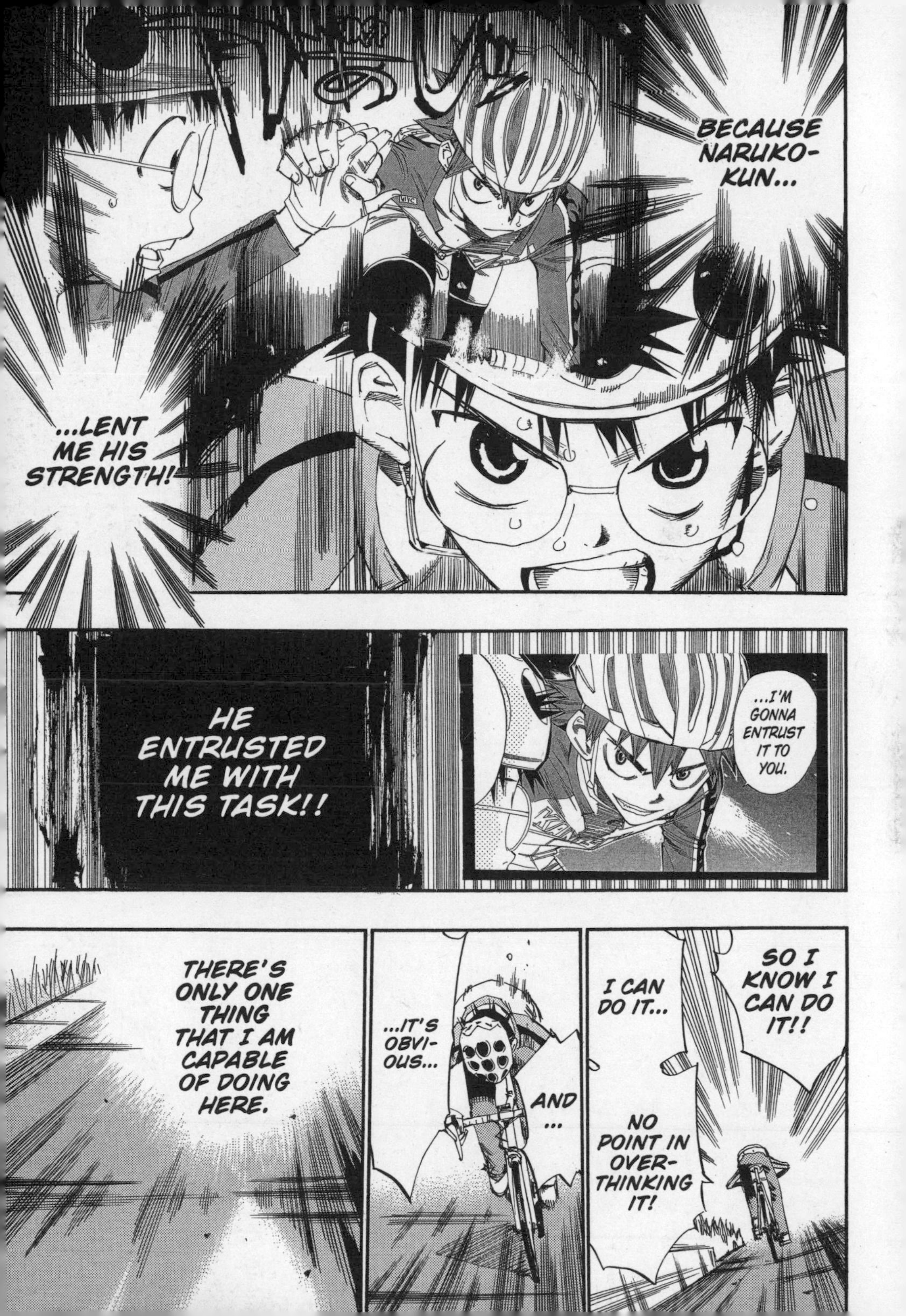
BECAUSE NARUKO-KUN...
...LENT ME HIS STRENGTH!
...I'M GONNA ENTRUST IT TO YOU.
HE ENTRUSTED ME WITH THIS TASK!!
SO I KNOW I CAN DO IT!!
I CAN DO IT...
NO POINT IN OVER-THINKING IT!
...IT'S OBVI-OUS...
AND ...
THERE'S ONLY ONE THING THAT I AM CAPABLE OF DOING HERE.

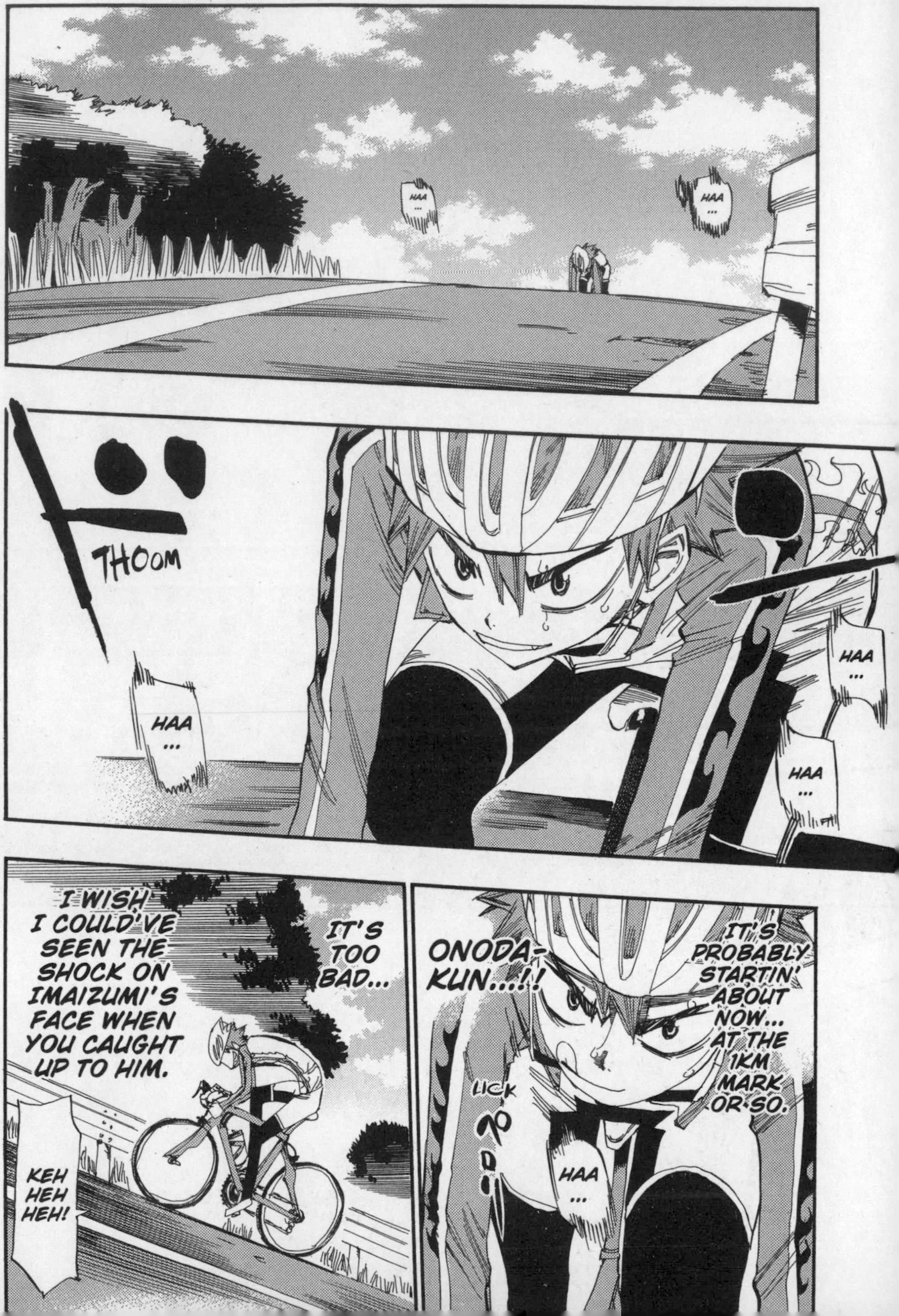
HAA...
HAA...
HAA...
HAA...
THOOM
HAA...
IT'S PROBABLY STARTIN' ABOUT NOW... AT THE 1KM MARK OR SO.
ONODA-KUN...!!
LICK
HAA...
IT'S TOO BAD...
I WISH I COULD'VE SEEN THE SHOCK ON IMAIZUMI'S FACE WHEN YOU CAUGHT UP TO HIM.
KEH HEH HEH!

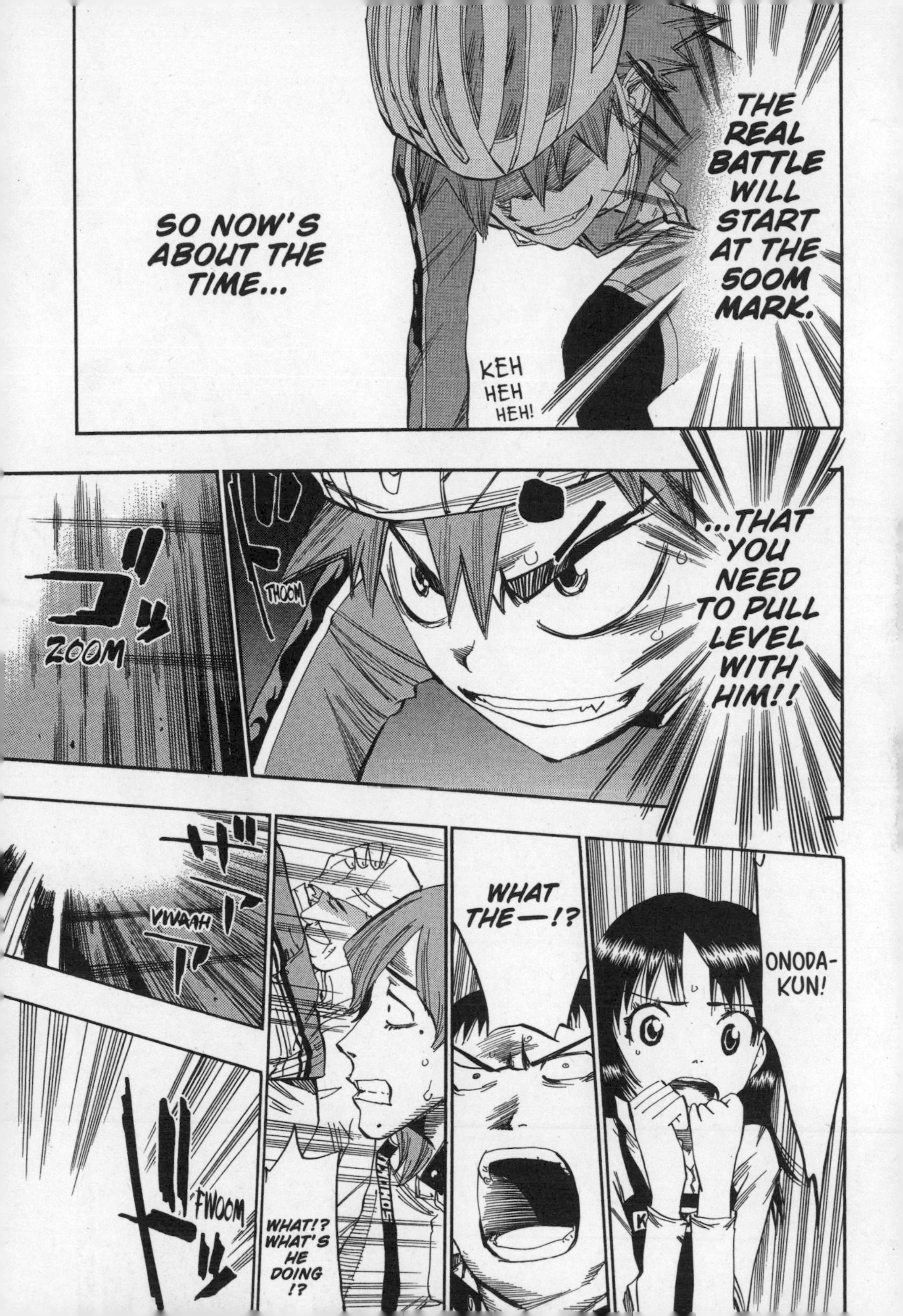
THE REAL BATTLE WILL START AT THE 500M MARK.
SO NOW'S ABOUT THE TIME...
KEH HEH HEH!
...THAT YOU NEED TO PULL LEVEL WITH HIM!!
THOOM
ZOOM
ONODA-KUN!
WHAT THE—!?
WHAT!? WHAT'S HE DOING !?
VWAAH
FWOOM

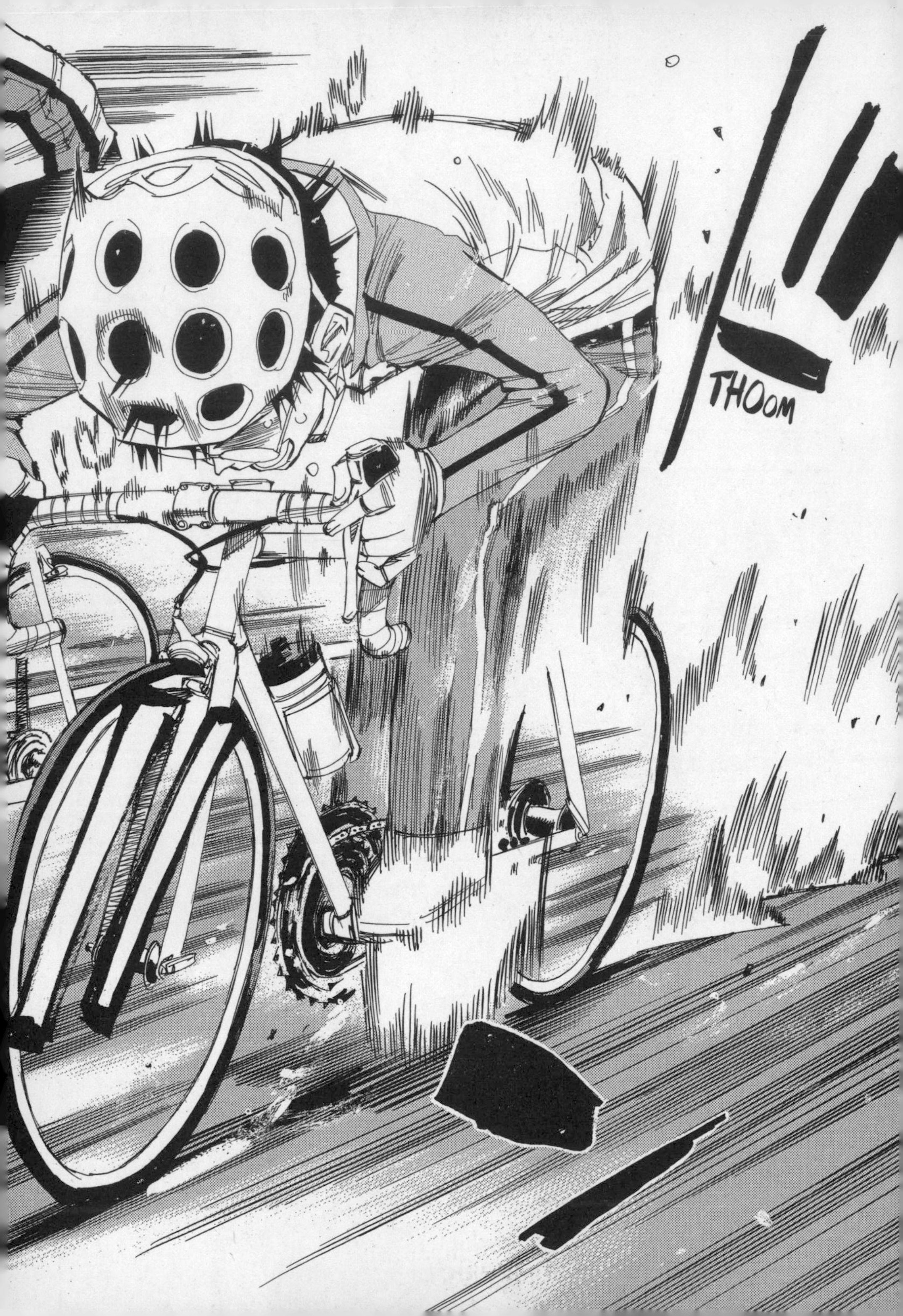
THOom

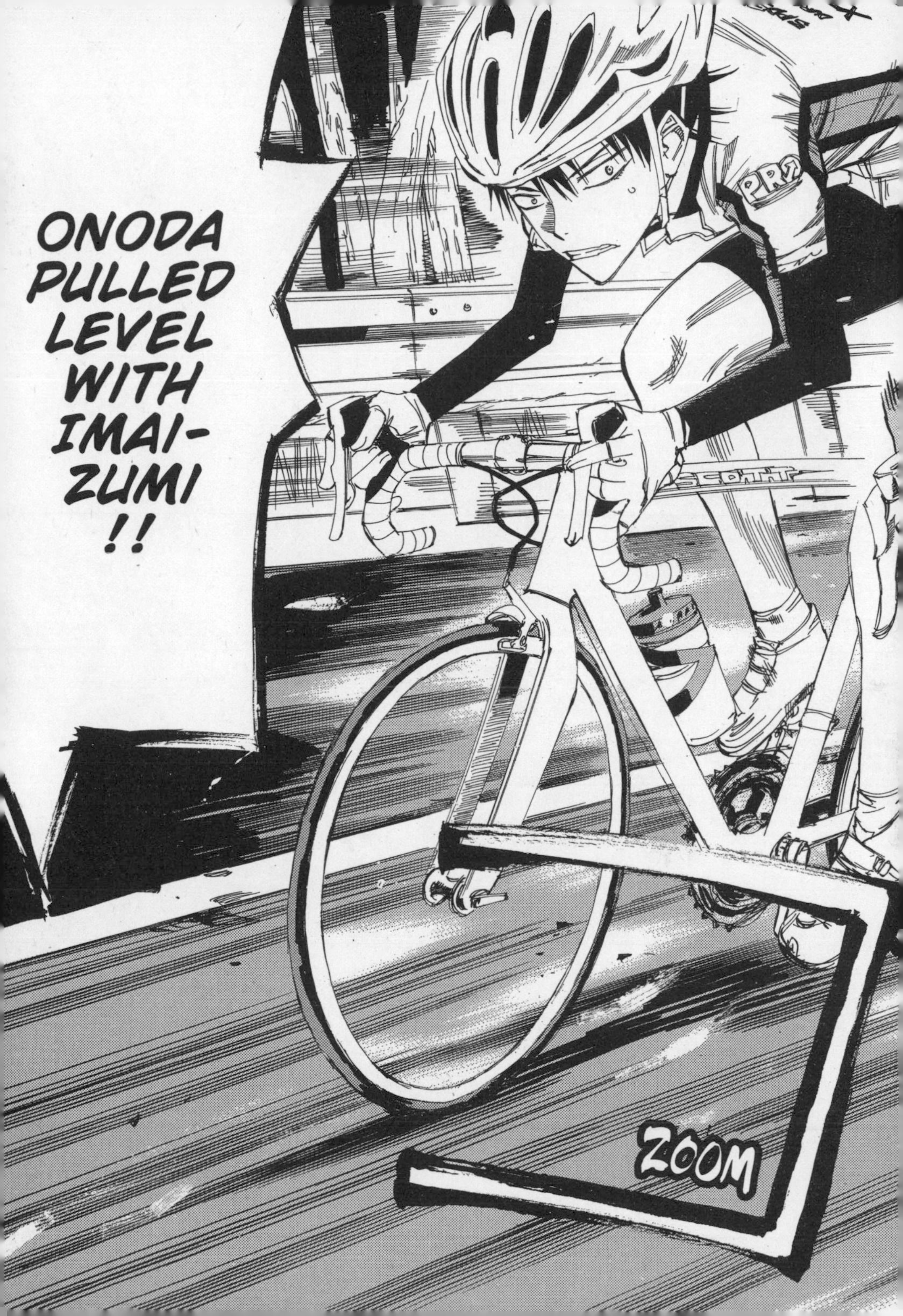
ONODA PULLED LEVEL WITH IMAI-ZUMI !!
ZOOM

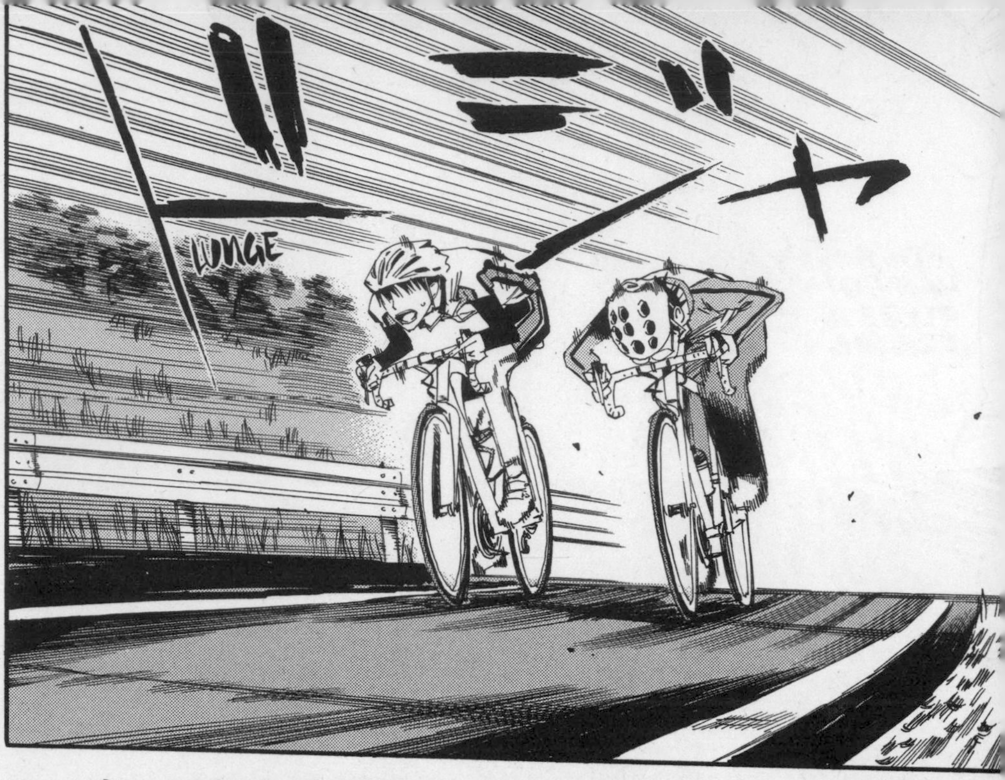
LUNGE
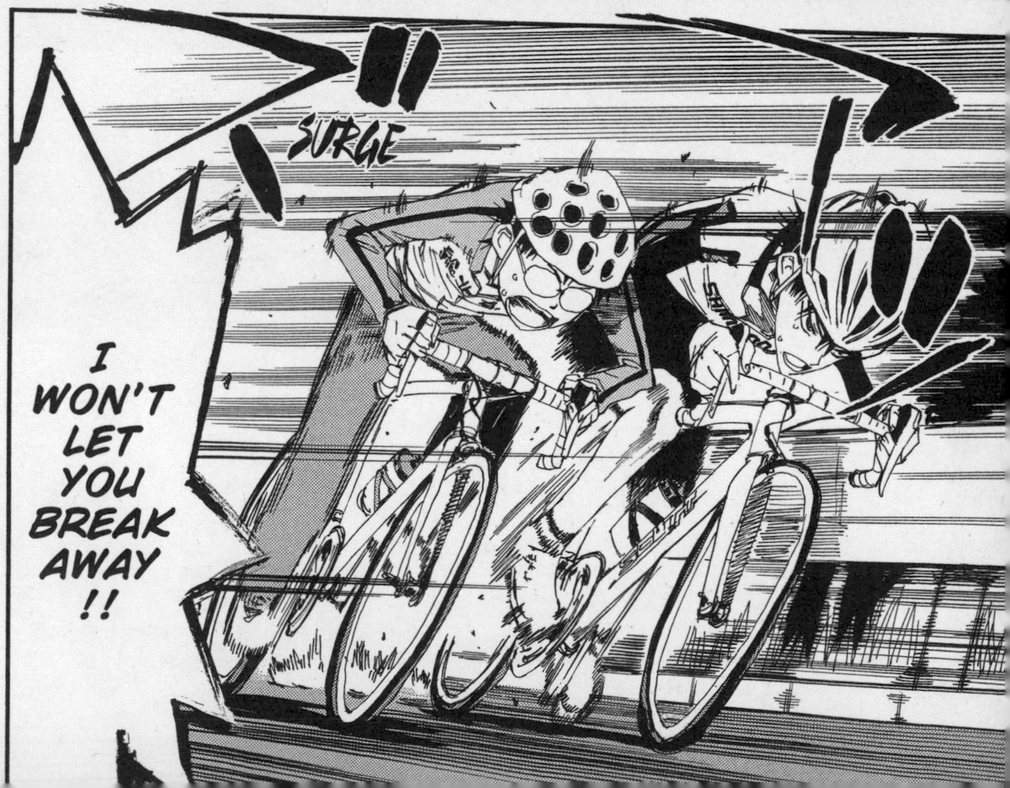
SURGE
I WON'T LET YOU BREAK AWAY!!

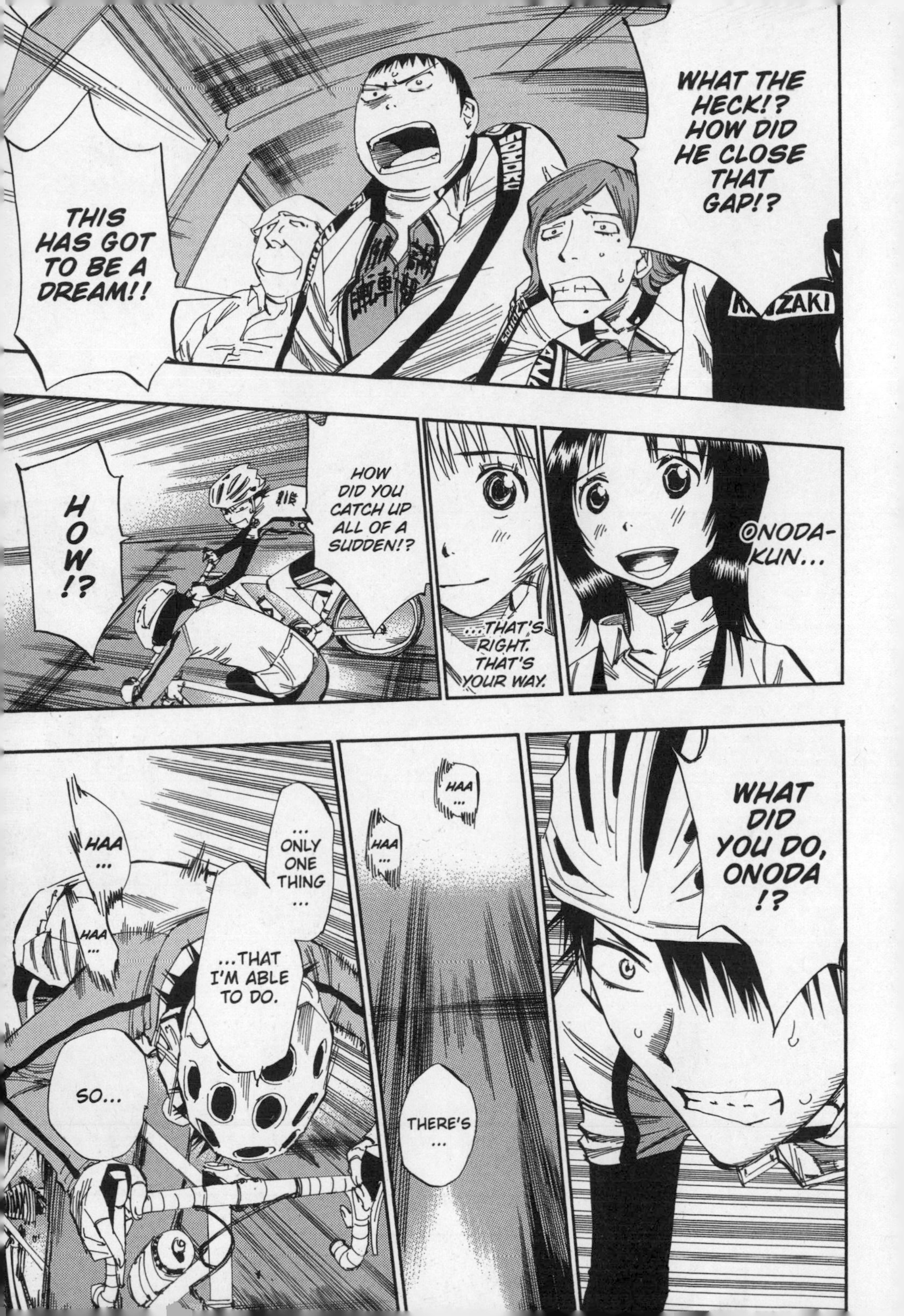
WHAT THE HECK!? HOW DID HE CLOSE THAT GAP!?
THIS HAS GOT TO BE A DREAM!!
ONODA-KUN...
...THAT'S RIGHT. THAT'S YOUR WAY.
HOW DID YOU CATCH UP ALL OF A SUDDEN!?
HOW!?
WHAT DID YOU DO, ONODA!?
HAA...
HAA...
THERE'S...
...ONLY ONE THING...
HAA...
...THAT I'M ABLE TO DO.
HAA...
SO...

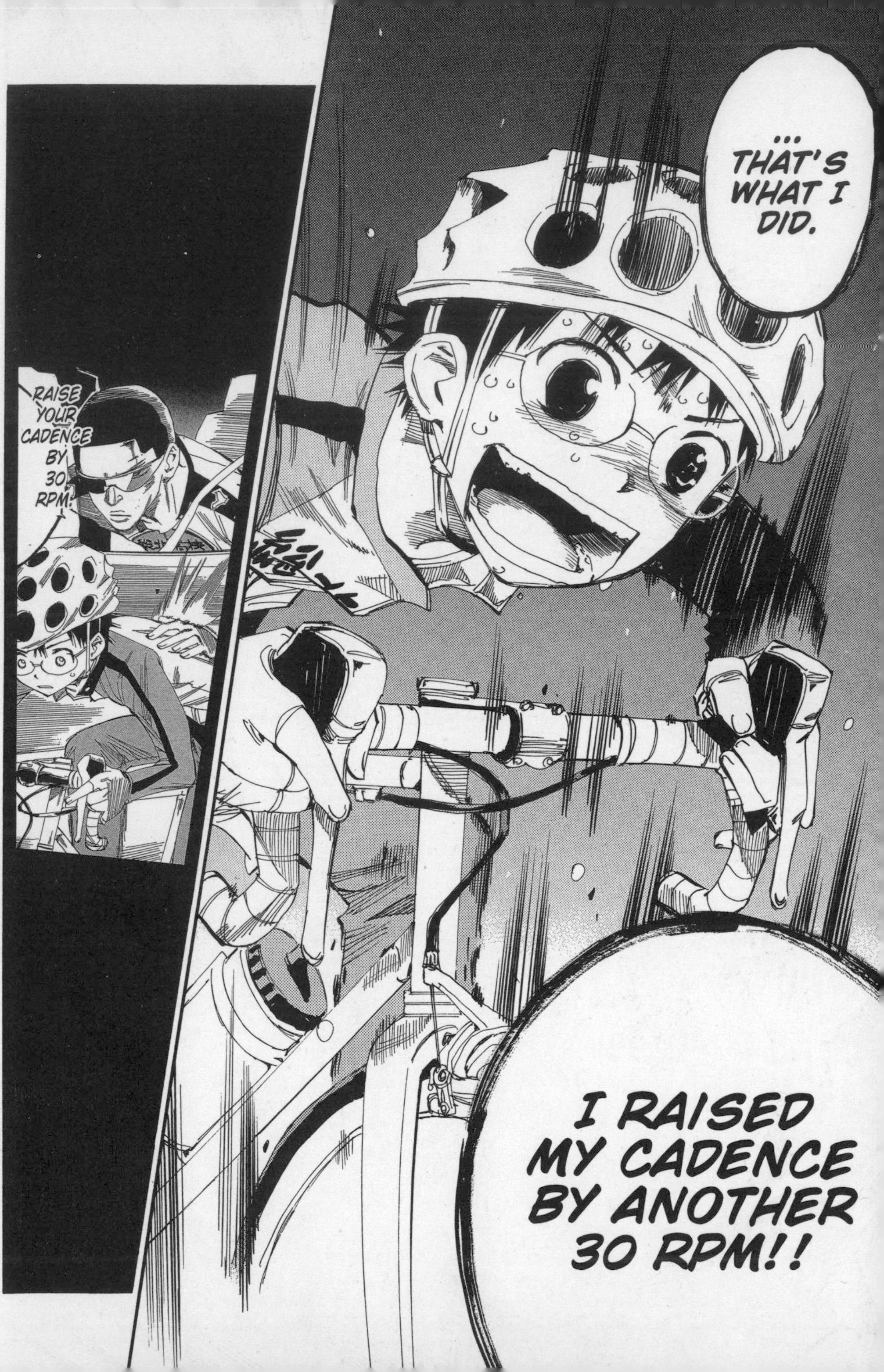
... THAT'S WHAT I DID.
I RAISED MY CADENCE BY ANOTHER 30 RPM!!
RAISE YOUR CADENCE BY 30 RPM!

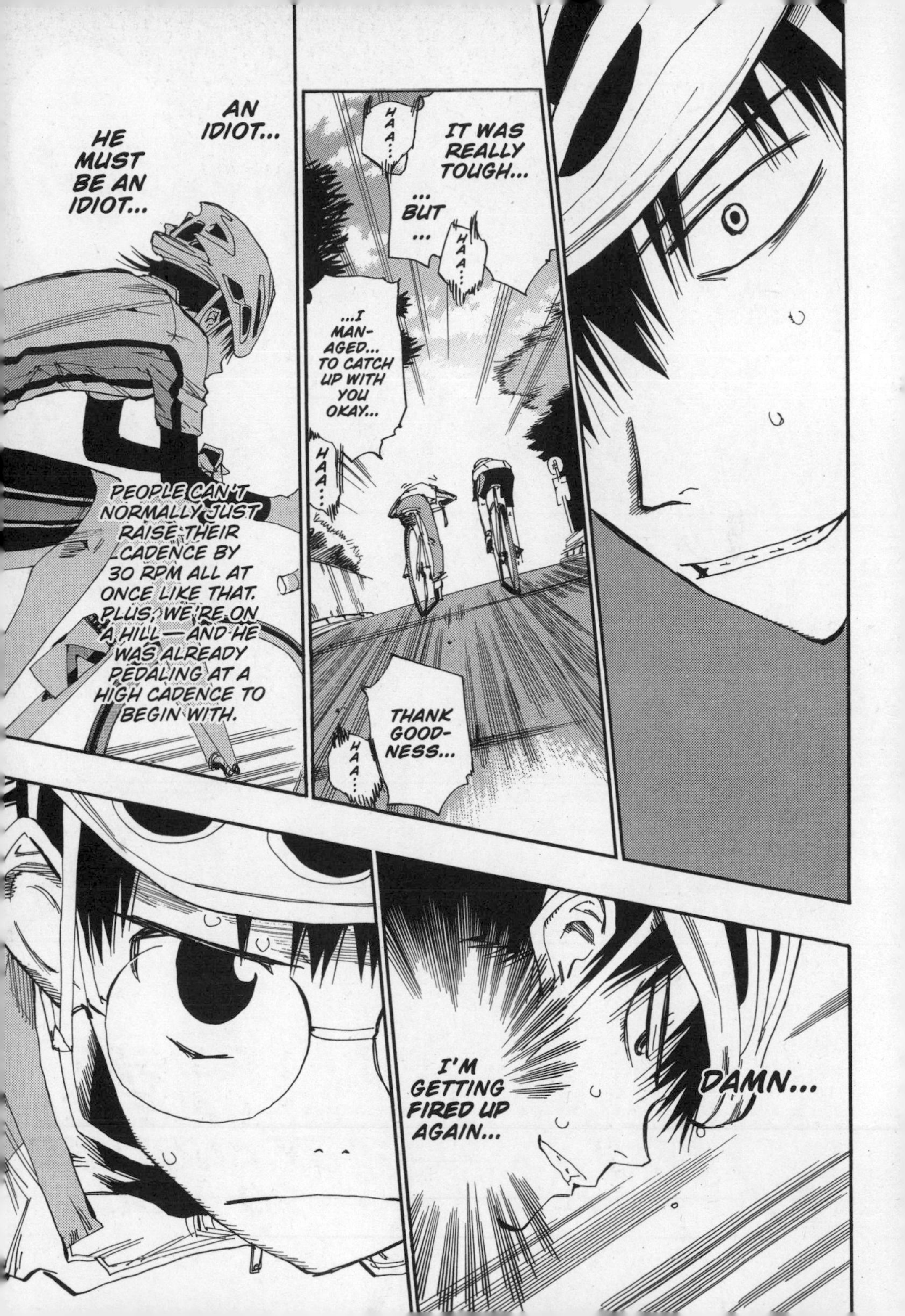
IT WAS REALLY TOUGH...
HAA...
...BUT...
HAA...
...I MANAGED... TO CATCH UP WITH YOU OKAY...
HAA...
THANK GOODNESS...
HAA...
AN IDIOT...
HE MUST BE AN IDIOT...
PEOPLE CAN'T NORMALLY JUST RAISE THEIR CADENCE BY 30 RPM ALL AT ONCE LIKE THAT. PLUS, WE'RE ON A HILL—AND HE WAS ALREADY PEDALING AT A HIGH CADENCE TO BEGIN WITH.
DAMN...
I'M GETTING FIRED UP AGAIN...

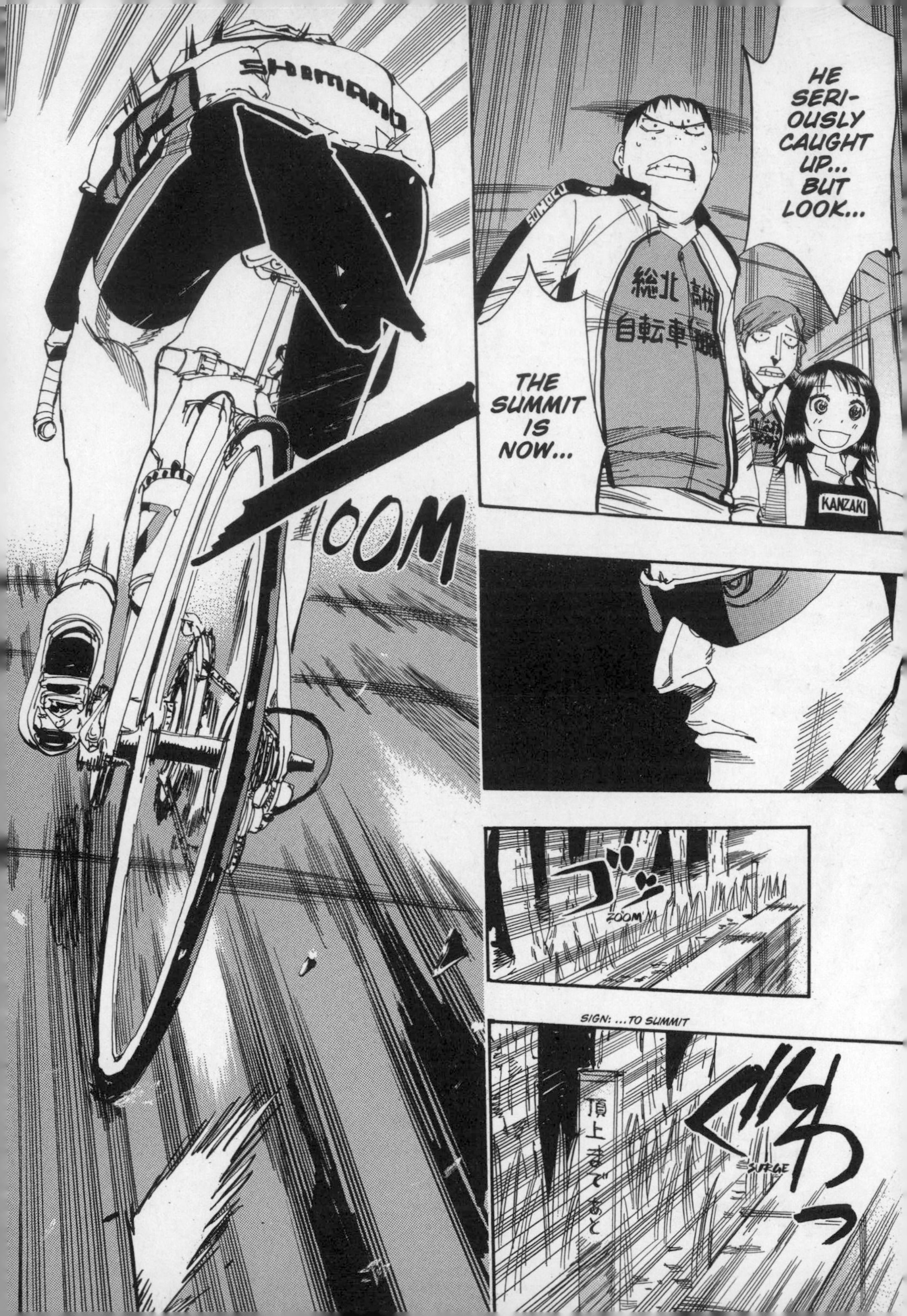
HE SERIOUSLY CAUGHT UP... BUT LOOK...
THE SUMMIT IS NOW...
KANZAKI
ZOOM
SIGN: ...TO SUMMIT
頂上まであと
SURGE
OOM

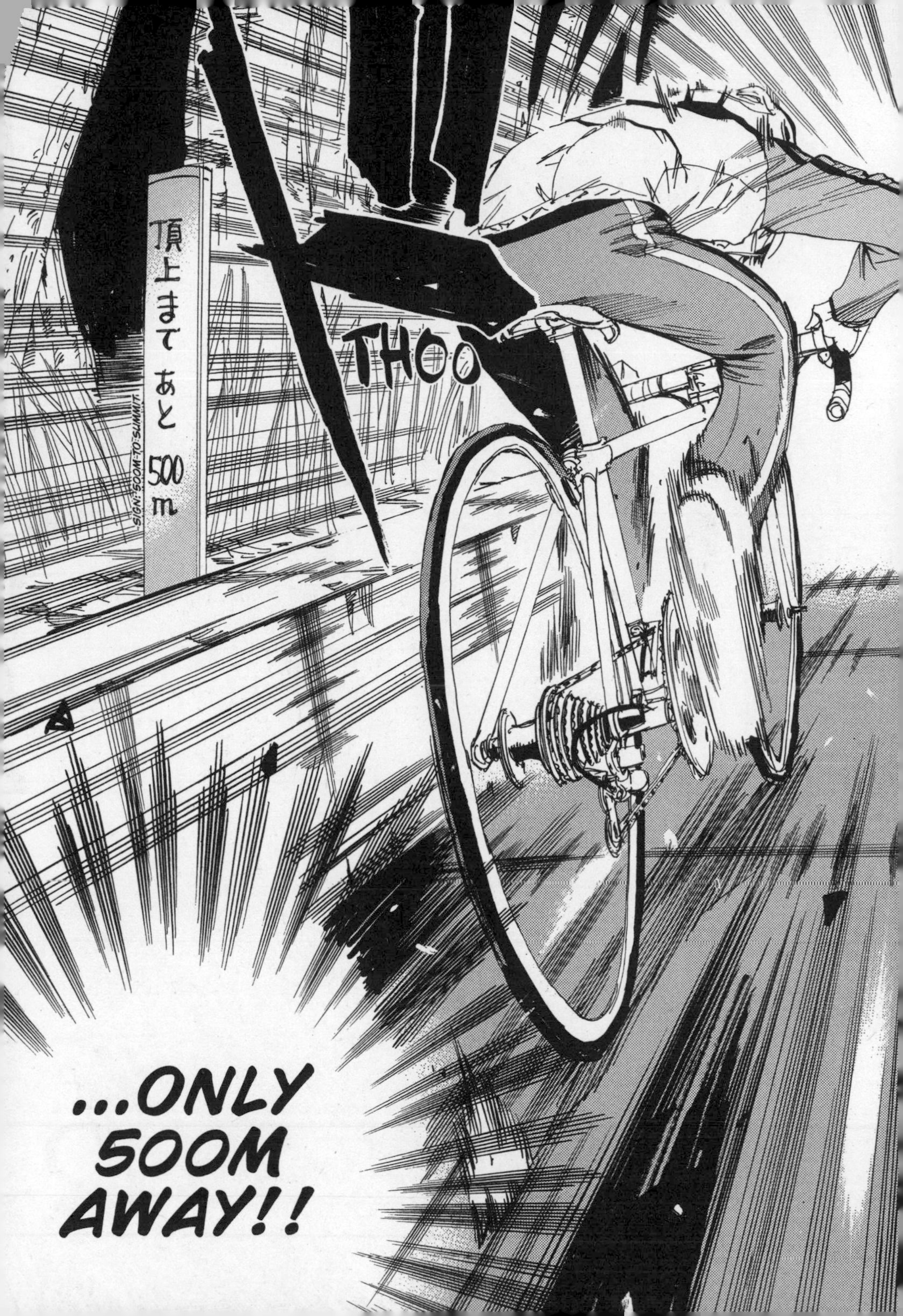
THOO
頂上まで あと 500 m
SIGN: 500M TO SUMMIT
...ONLY 500M AWAY!!

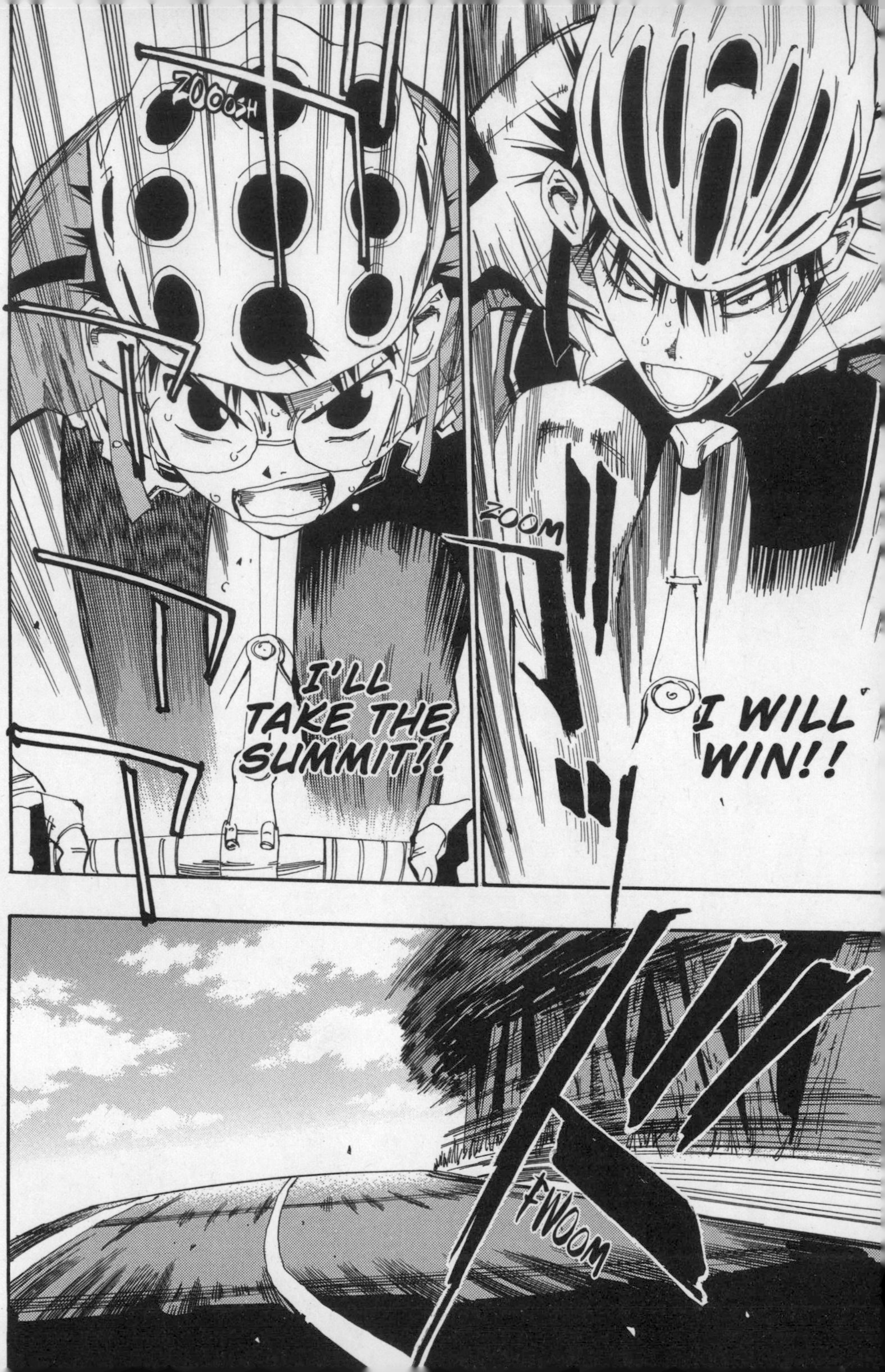
ZOOM
I WILL WIN!!
ZOOOSH
I'LL TAKE THE SUMMIT!!
FWOOM

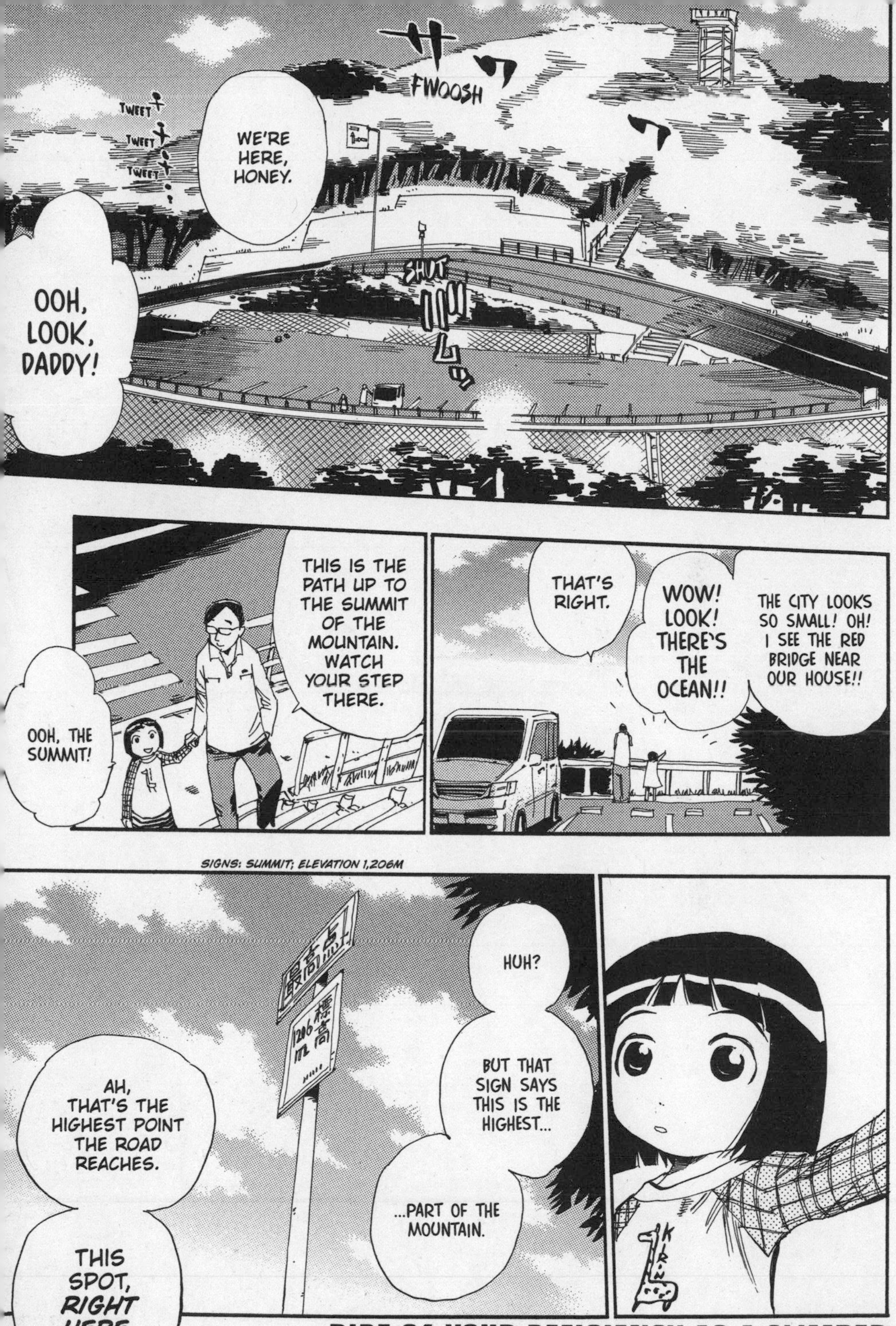
FWOOSH
SHUT
TWEET
TWEET
TWEET
WE'RE HERE, HONEY.
OOH, LOOK, DADDY!
WOW! LOOK! THERE'S THE OCEAN!!
THE CITY LOOKS SO SMALL! OH! I SEE THE RED BRIDGE NEAR OUR HOUSE!!
THAT'S RIGHT.
THIS IS THE PATH UP TO THE SUMMIT OF THE MOUNTAIN. WATCH YOUR STEP THERE.
OOH, THE SUMMIT!
SIGNS: SUMMIT; ELEVATION 1,206M
KIRIN
最高点
標高 1206m
HUH?
BUT THAT SIGN SAYS THIS IS THE HIGHEST...
...PART OF THE MOUNTAIN.
AH, THAT'S THE HIGHEST POINT THE ROAD REACHES.
THIS SPOT, *RIGHT HERE*.

RIDE.31 YOUR DEFICIENCY AS A CLIMBER

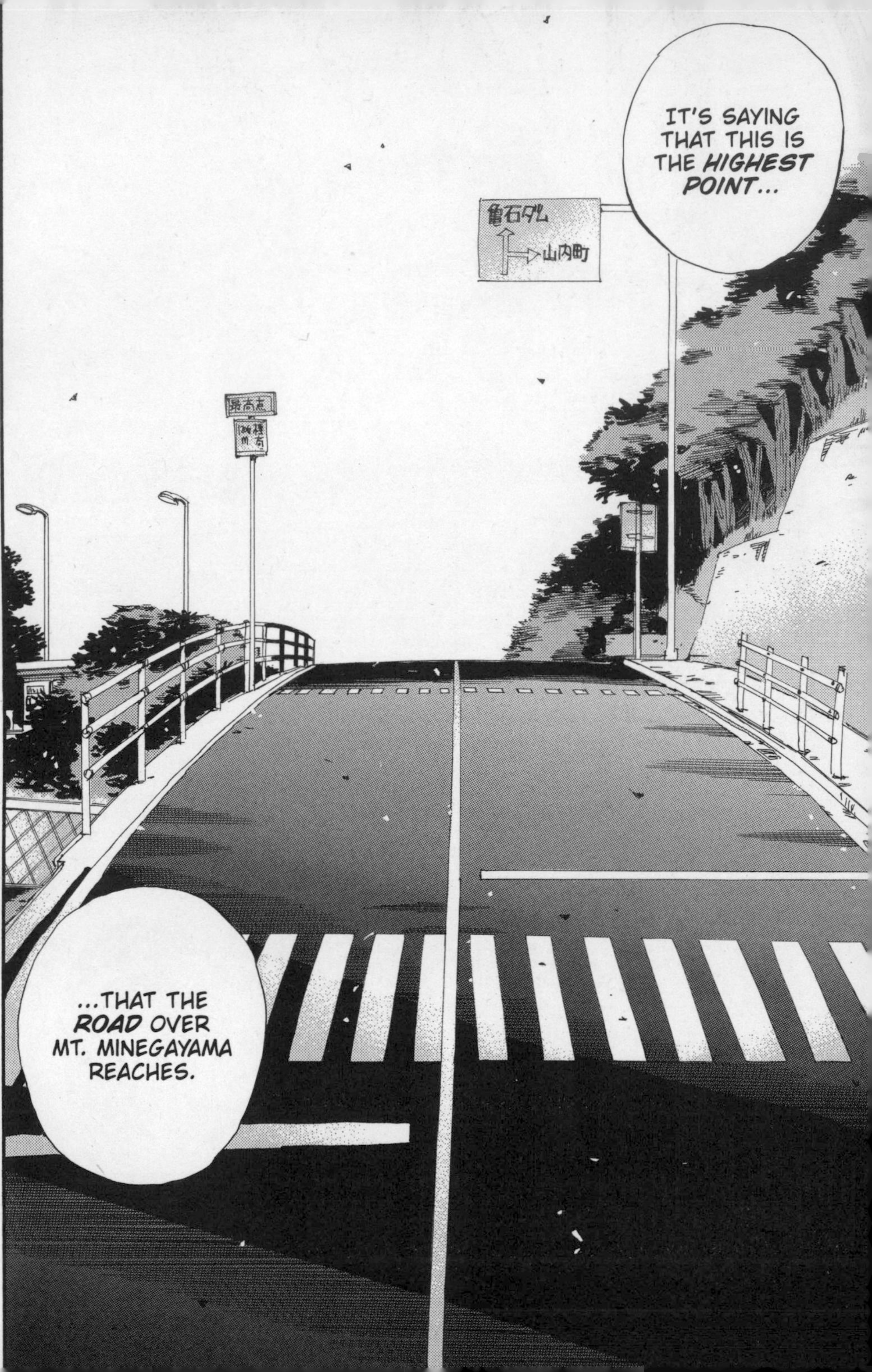

SIGNS: KAMEISHI DAM, YAMAUCHI CITY; SUMMIT, ELEVATION 1,206M

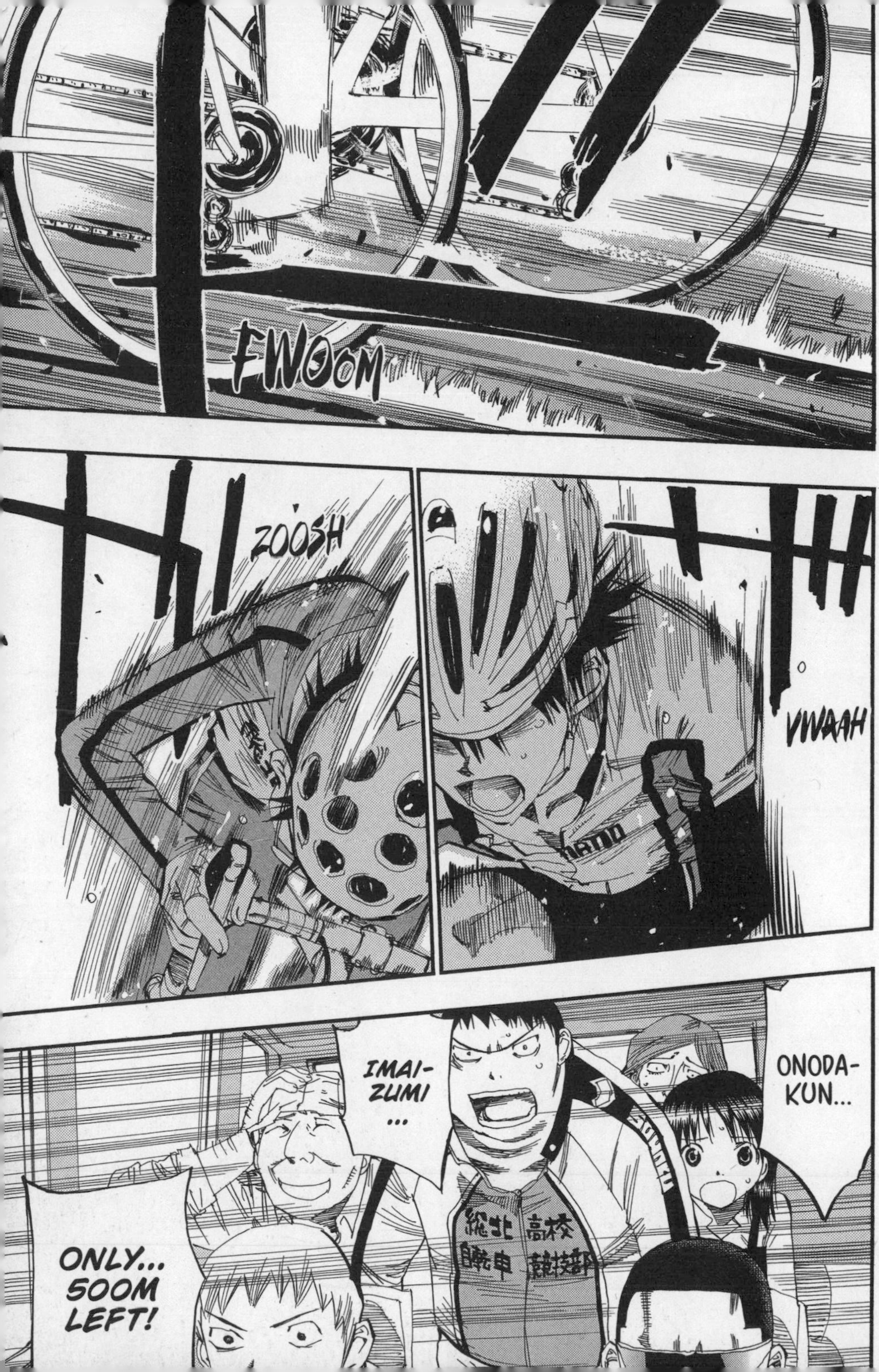
FWOOM
VWAAH
ZOOSH
ONODA-KUN...
IMAI-ZUMI ...
ONLY... 500M LEFT!

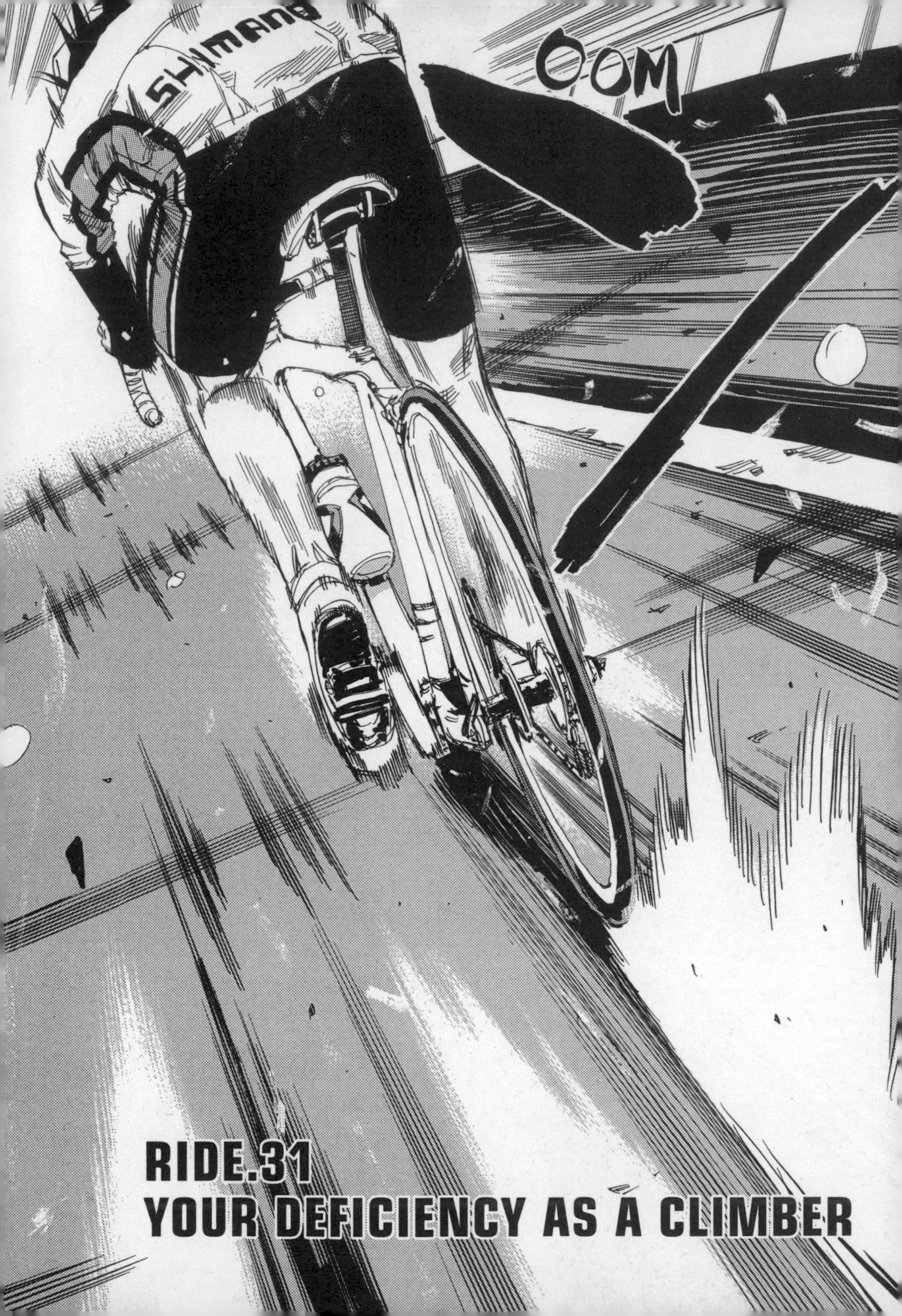
OOM
SHIMANO

RIDE.31
YOUR DEFICIENCY AS A CLIMBER

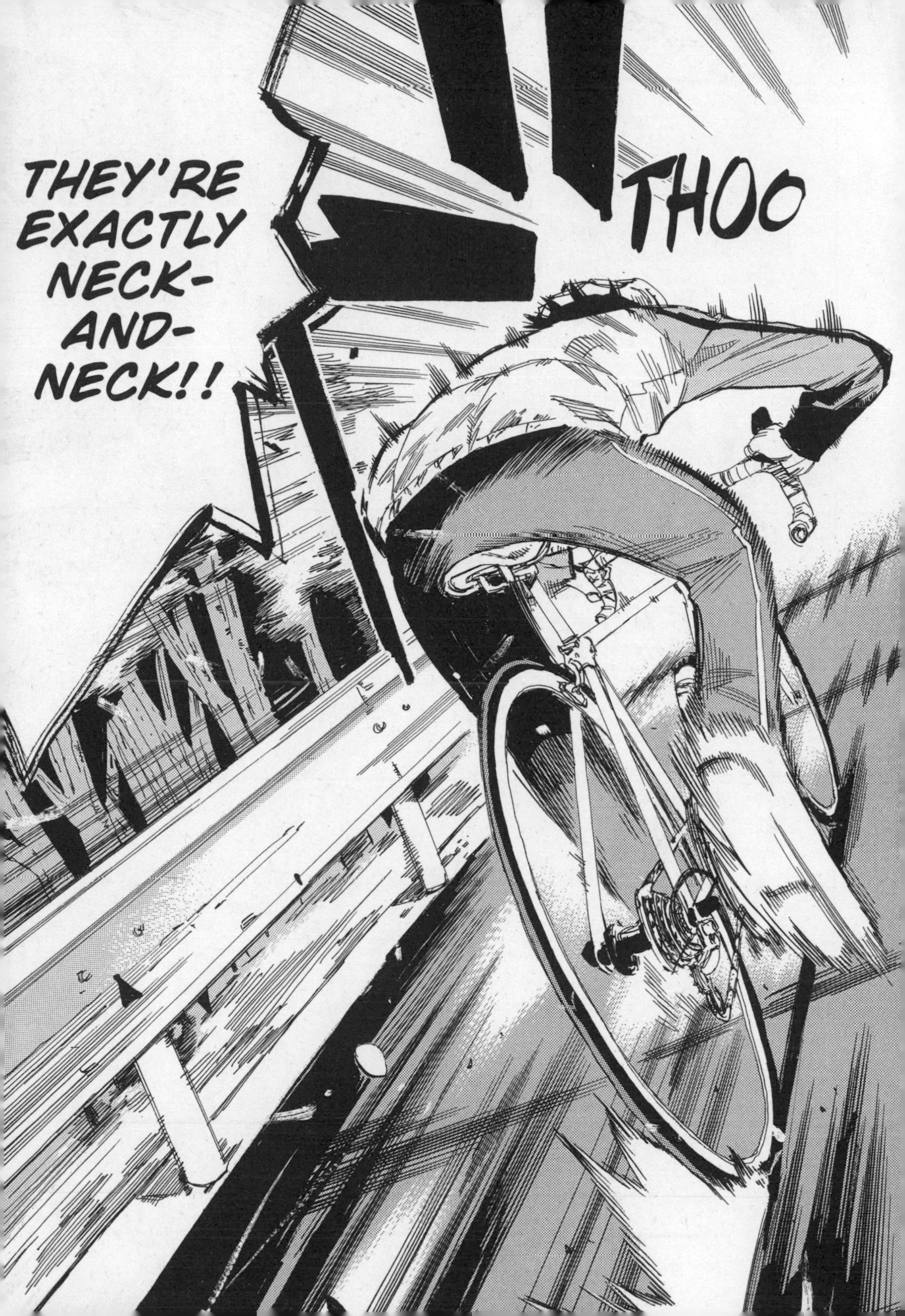
THEY'RE EXACTLY NECK-AND-NECK!!
THOO

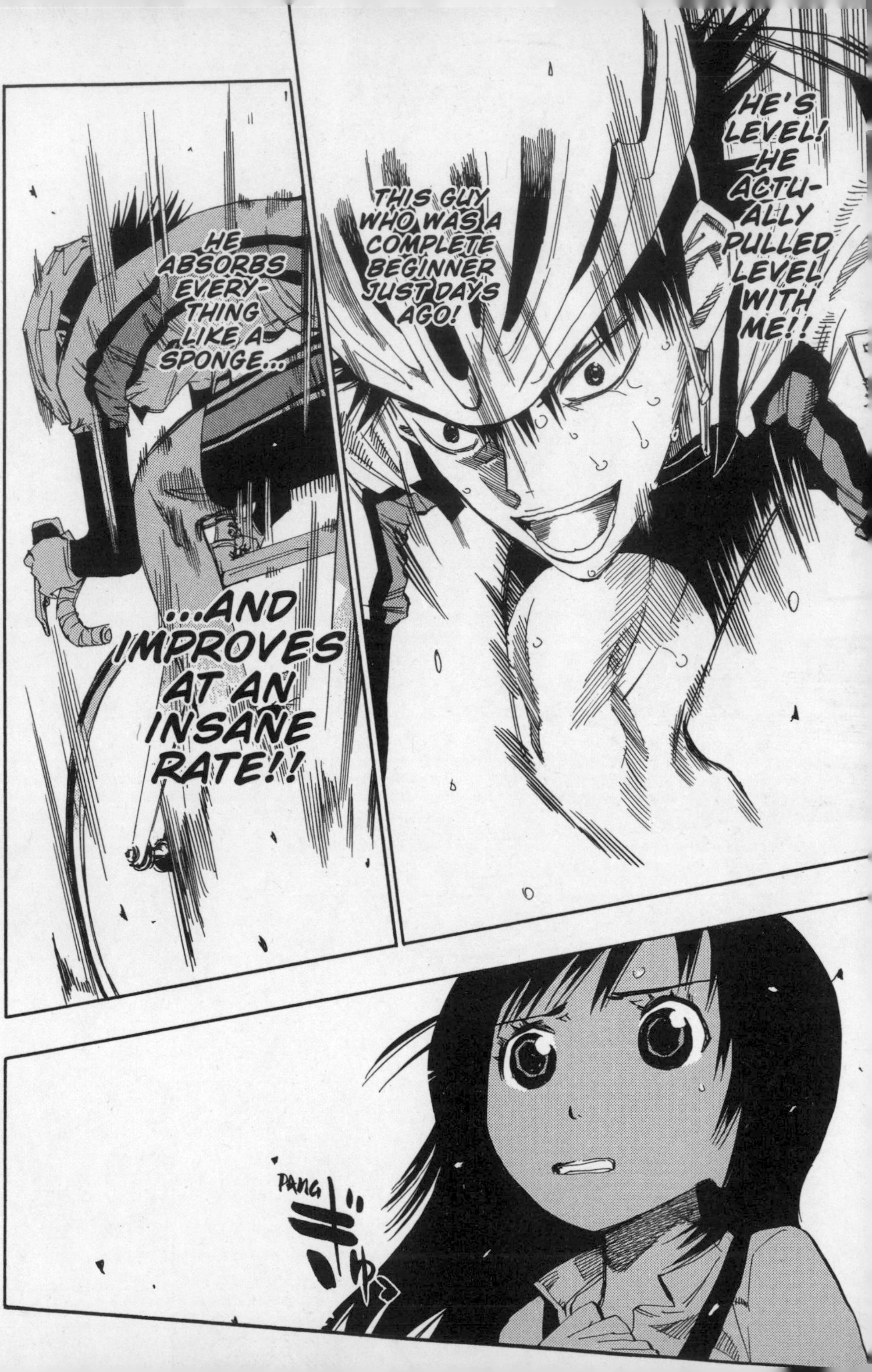
HE'S LEVEL! HE ACTU-ALLY PULLED LEVEL WITH ME!!
THIS GUY WHO WAS A COMPLETE BEGINNER JUST DAYS AGO!
HE ABSORBS EVERY-THING LIKE A SPONGE...
...AND IMPROVES AT AN INSANE RATE!!
PANG

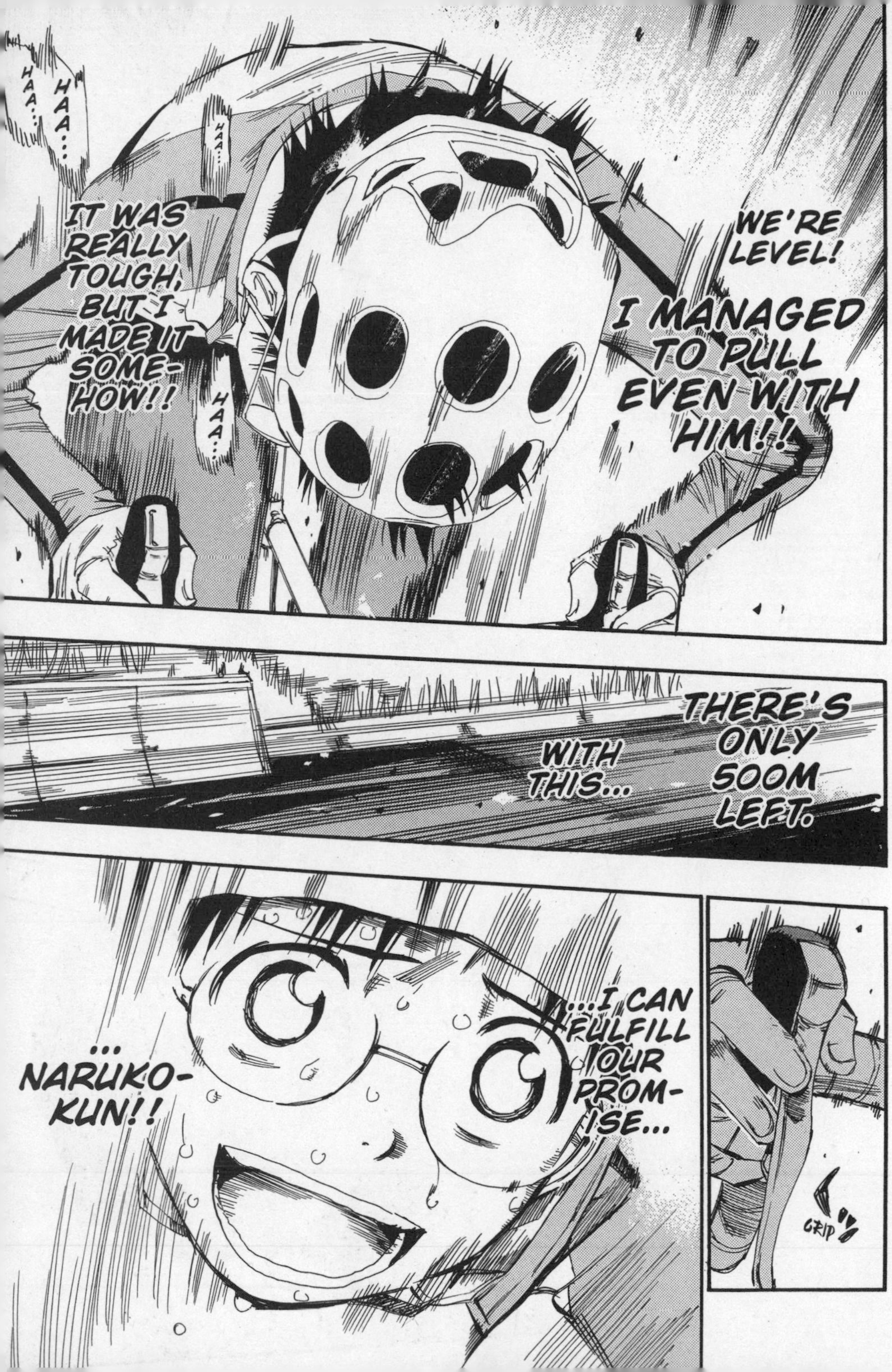
WE'RE LEVEL!
I MANAGED TO PULL EVEN WITH HIM!!
HAA...
HAA...
HAA...
HAA...
IT WAS REALLY TOUGH, BUT I MADE IT SOME-HOW!!
THERE'S ONLY 500M LEFT.
WITH THIS...
GRIP
...I CAN FULFILL OUR PROM-ISE...
...NARUKO-KUN!!

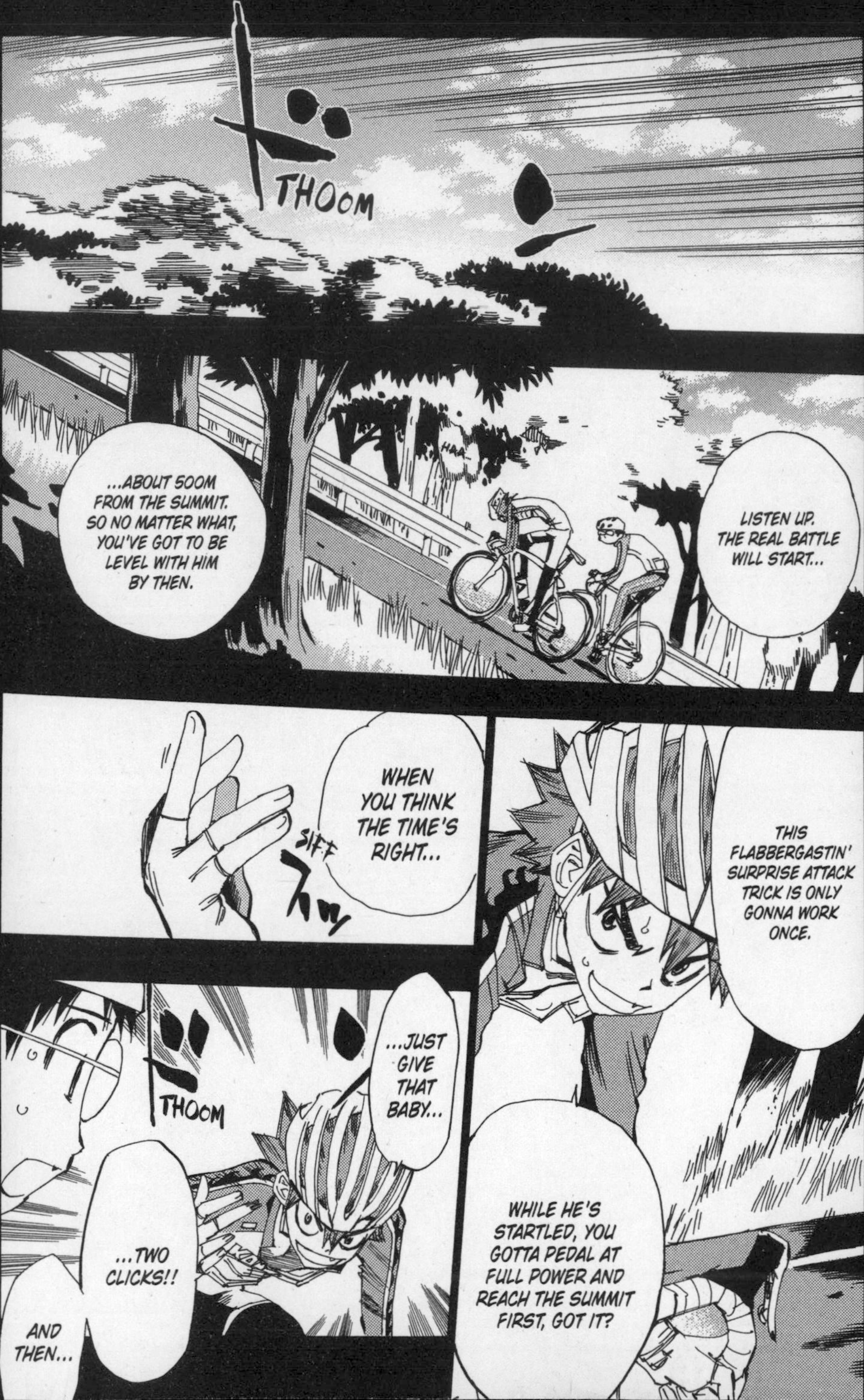
THOOM
LISTEN UP. THE REAL BATTLE WILL START...
HAA...
...ABOUT 500M FROM THE SUMMIT. SO NO MATTER WHAT, YOU'VE GOT TO BE LEVEL WITH HIM BY THEN.
THIS FLABBERGASTIN' SURPRISE ATTACK TRICK IS ONLY GONNA WORK ONCE.
WHEN YOU THINK THE TIME'S RIGHT...
SIFF
...JUST GIVE THAT BABY...
THOOM
...TWO CLICKS!!
AND THEN...
WHILE HE'S STARTLED, YOU GOTTA PEDAL AT FULL POWER AND REACH THE SUMMIT FIRST, GOT IT?

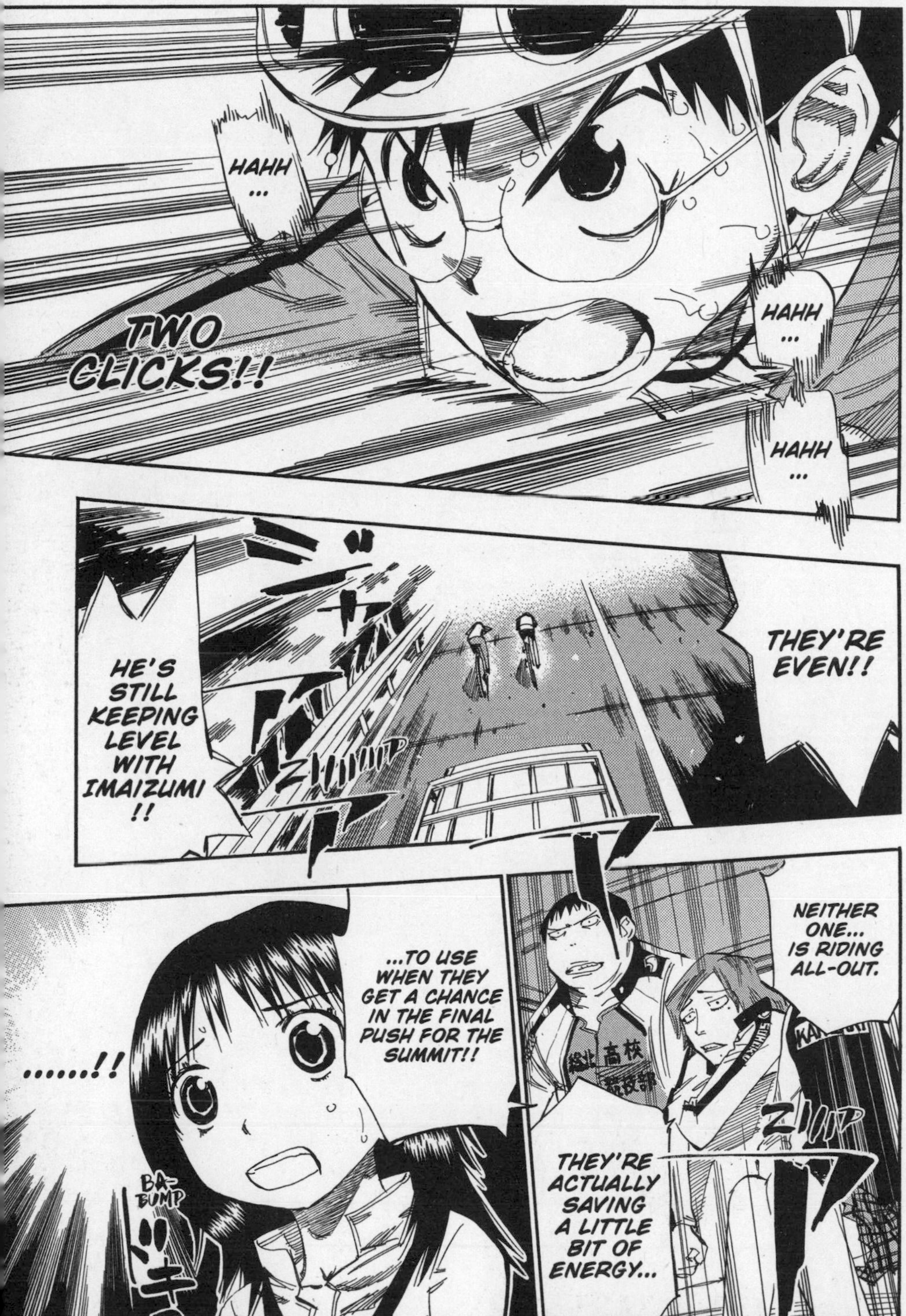
HAHH ...
HAHH ...
HAHH ...
TWO CLICKS!!
THEY'RE EVEN!!
HE'S STILL KEEPING LEVEL WITH IMAIZUMI !!
ZIIIIIIP
NEITHER ONE... IS RIDING ALL-OUT.
ZIIIP
THEY'RE ACTUALLY SAVING A LITTLE BIT OF ENERGY...
...TO USE WHEN THEY GET A CHANCE IN THE FINAL PUSH FOR THE SUMMIT!!
......!!
BA-BUMP

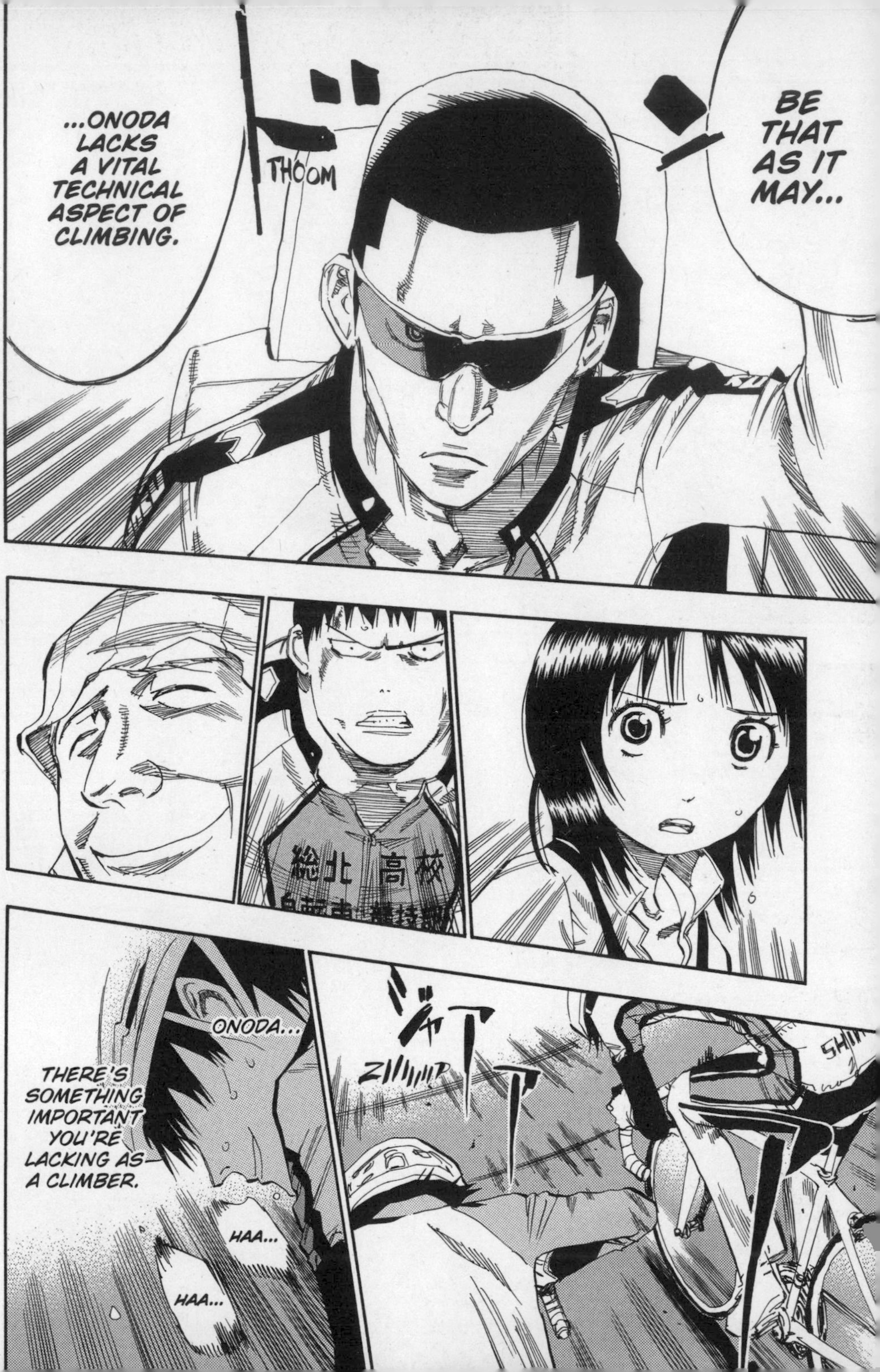
BE THAT AS IT MAY...
THOOM
...ONODA LACKS A VITAL TECHNICAL ASPECT OF CLIMBING.
総北 高校
ZIIIIIIP
ONODA...
THERE'S SOMETHING IMPORTANT YOU'RE LACKING AS A CLIMBER.
HAA...
HAA...

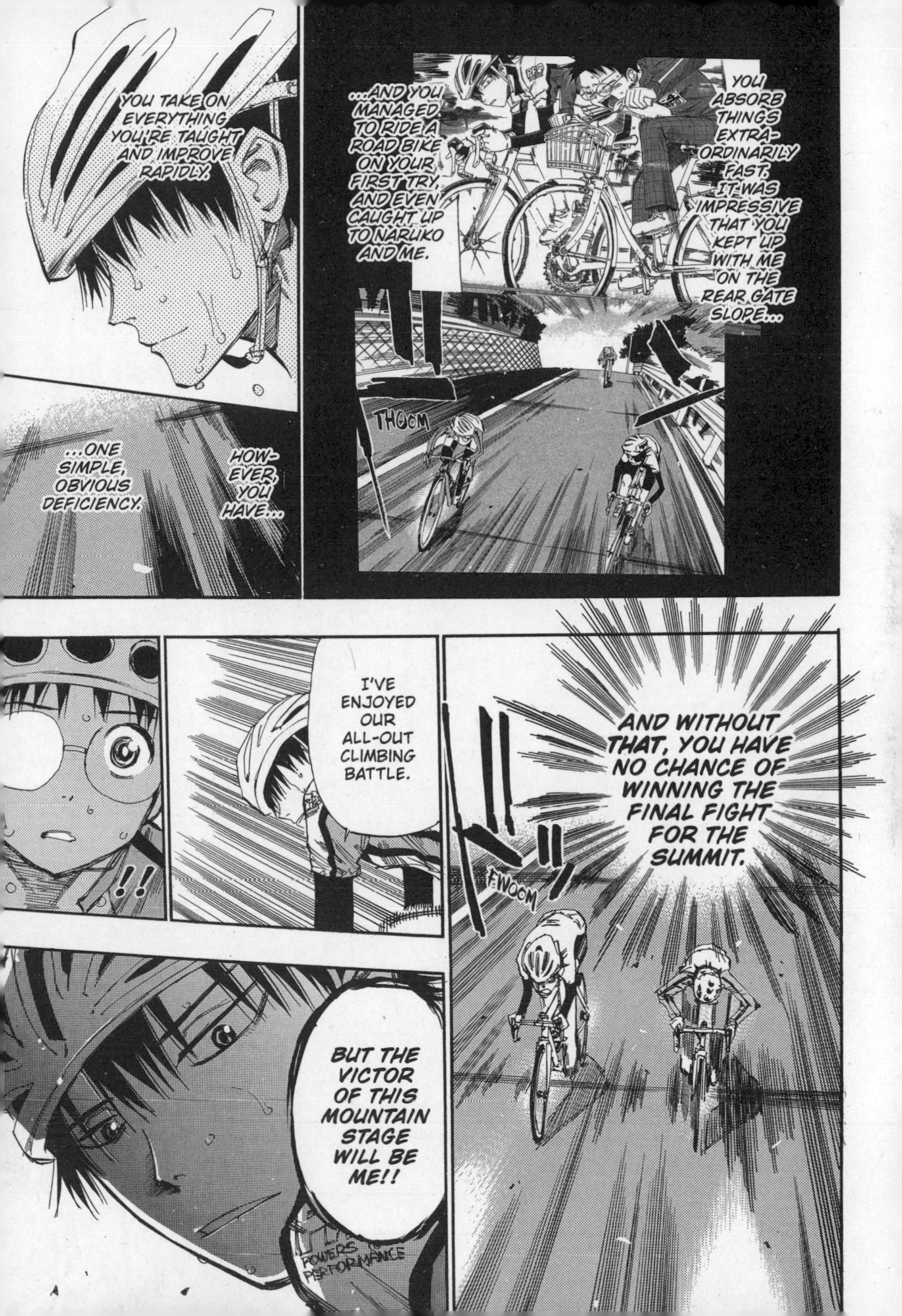
YOU ABSORB THINGS EXTRA-ORDINARILY FAST. IT WAS IMPRESSIVE THAT YOU KEPT UP WITH ME ON THE REAR GATE SLOPE...
...AND YOU MANAGED TO RIDE A ROAD BIKE ON YOUR FIRST TRY, AND EVEN CAUGHT UP TO NARUKO AND ME.
THOOM
YOU TAKE ON EVERYTHING YOU'RE TAUGHT AND IMPROVE RAPIDLY.
HOW-EVER, YOU HAVE...
...ONE SIMPLE, OBVIOUS DEFICIENCY.
AND WITHOUT THAT, YOU HAVE NO CHANCE OF WINNING THE FINAL FIGHT FOR THE SUMMIT.
FWOOM
I'VE ENJOYED OUR ALL-OUT CLIMBING BATTLE.
!!
BUT THE VICTOR OF THIS MOUNTAIN STAGE WILL BE ME!!
POWERS PERFORMANCE

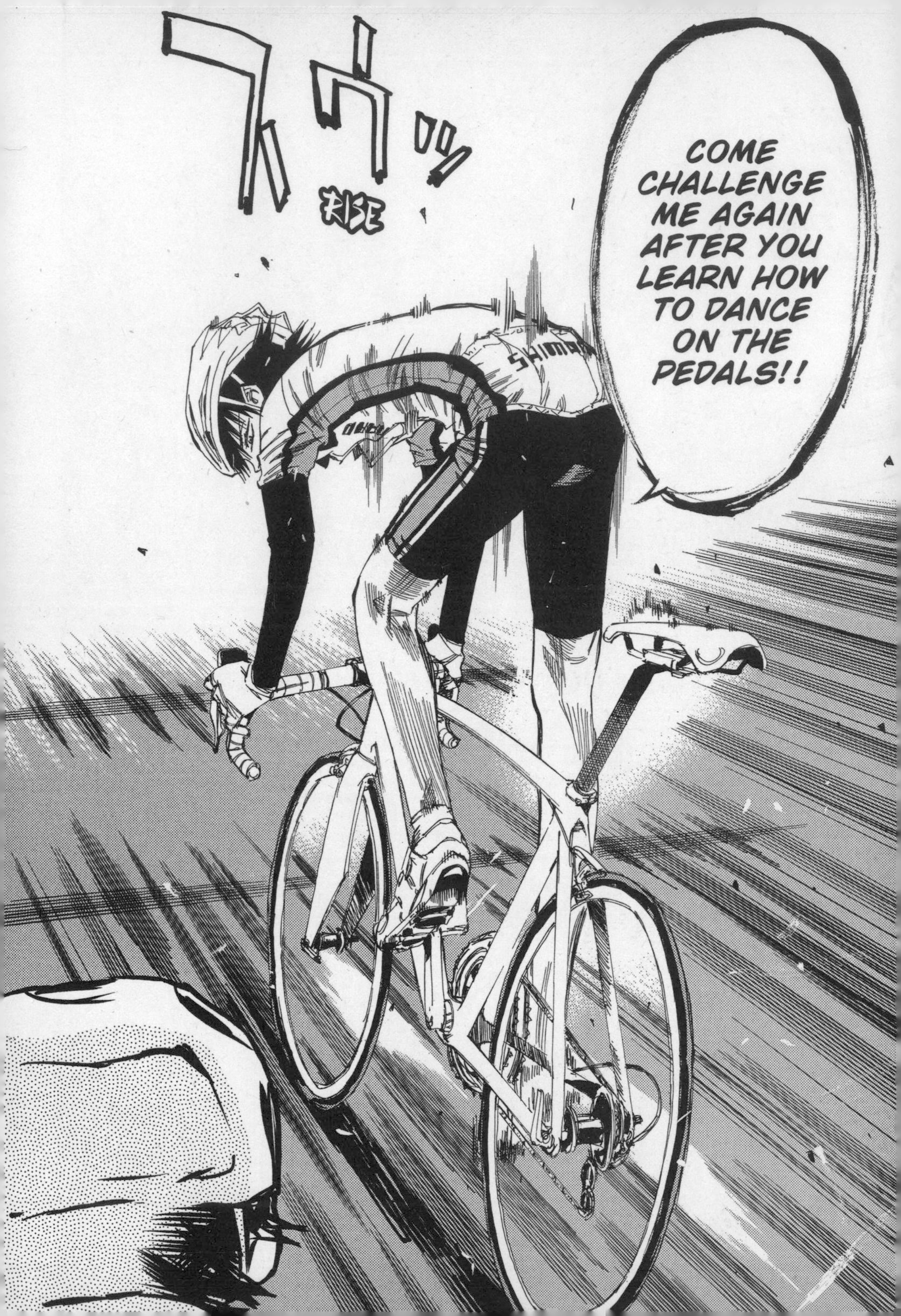
COME CHALLENGE ME AGAIN AFTER YOU LEARN HOW TO DANCE ON THE PEDALS!!
スウッ
RISE

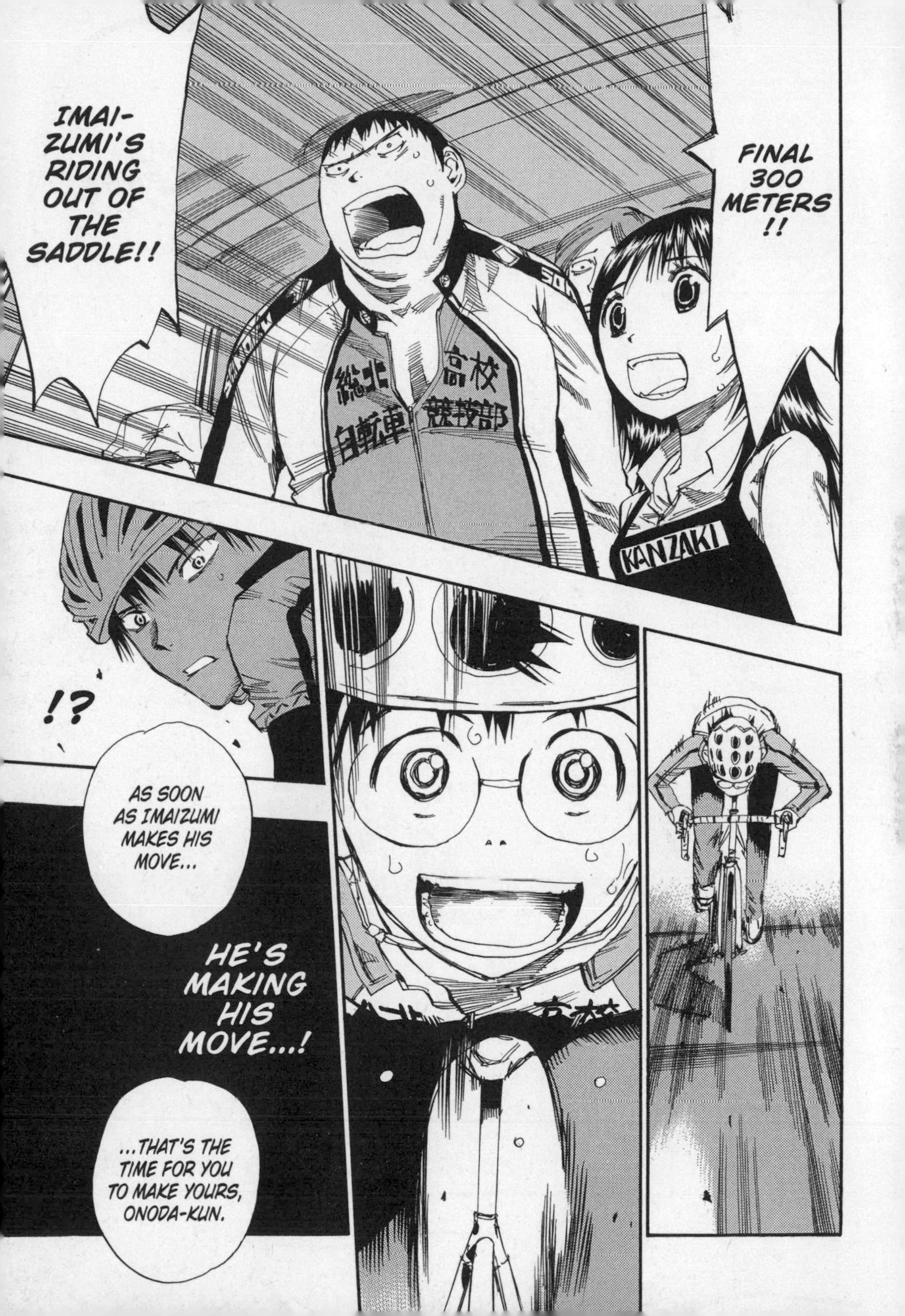
FINAL 300 METERS!!
IMAI-ZUMI'S RIDING OUT OF THE SADDLE!!
総北 高校 自転車 競技部
KANZAKI
HE'S MAKING HIS MOVE...!
!?
AS SOON AS IMAIZUMI MAKES HIS MOVE...
...THAT'S THE TIME FOR YOU TO MAKE YOURS, ONODA-KUN.

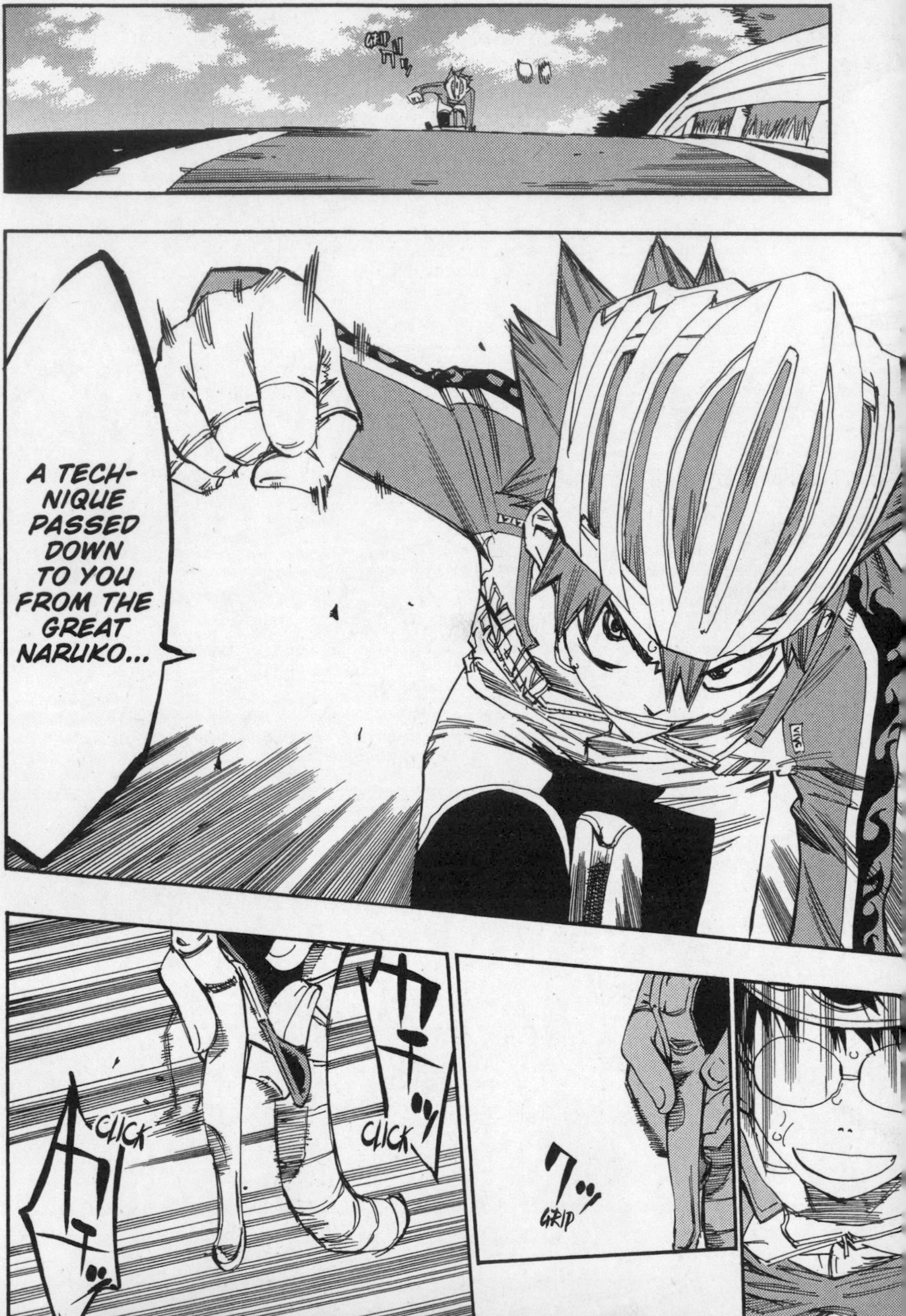
GRIP
A TECHNIQUE PASSED DOWN TO YOU FROM THE GREAT NARUKO...
GRIP
CLICK
CLICK

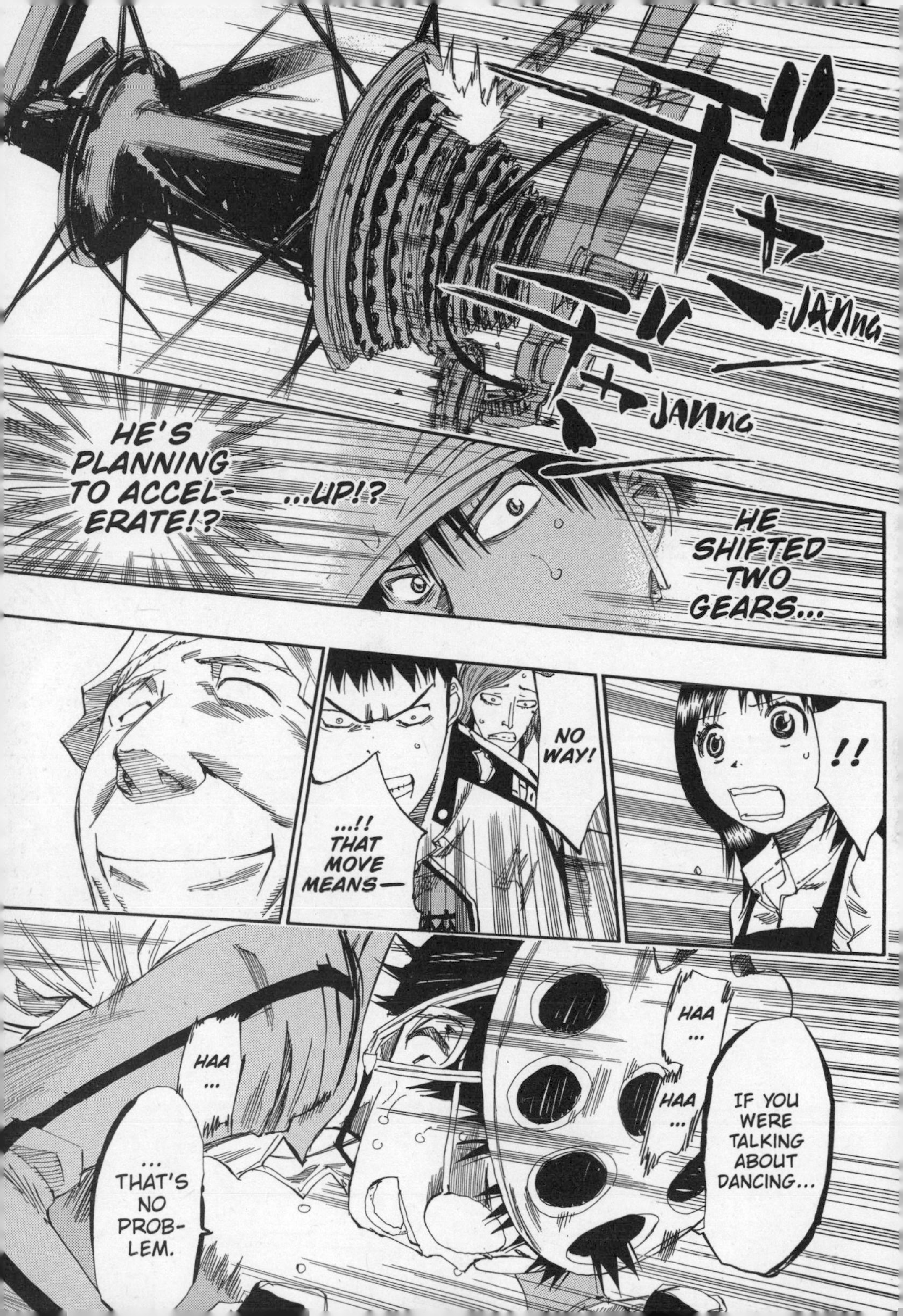
JANng
JANng
HE SHIFTED TWO GEARS...
...UP!?
HE'S PLANNING TO ACCEL-ERATE!?
!!
NO WAY!
...!! THAT MOVE MEANS—
HAA...
HAA...
IF YOU WERE TALKING ABOUT DANCING...
HAA...
...THAT'S NO PROB-LEM.

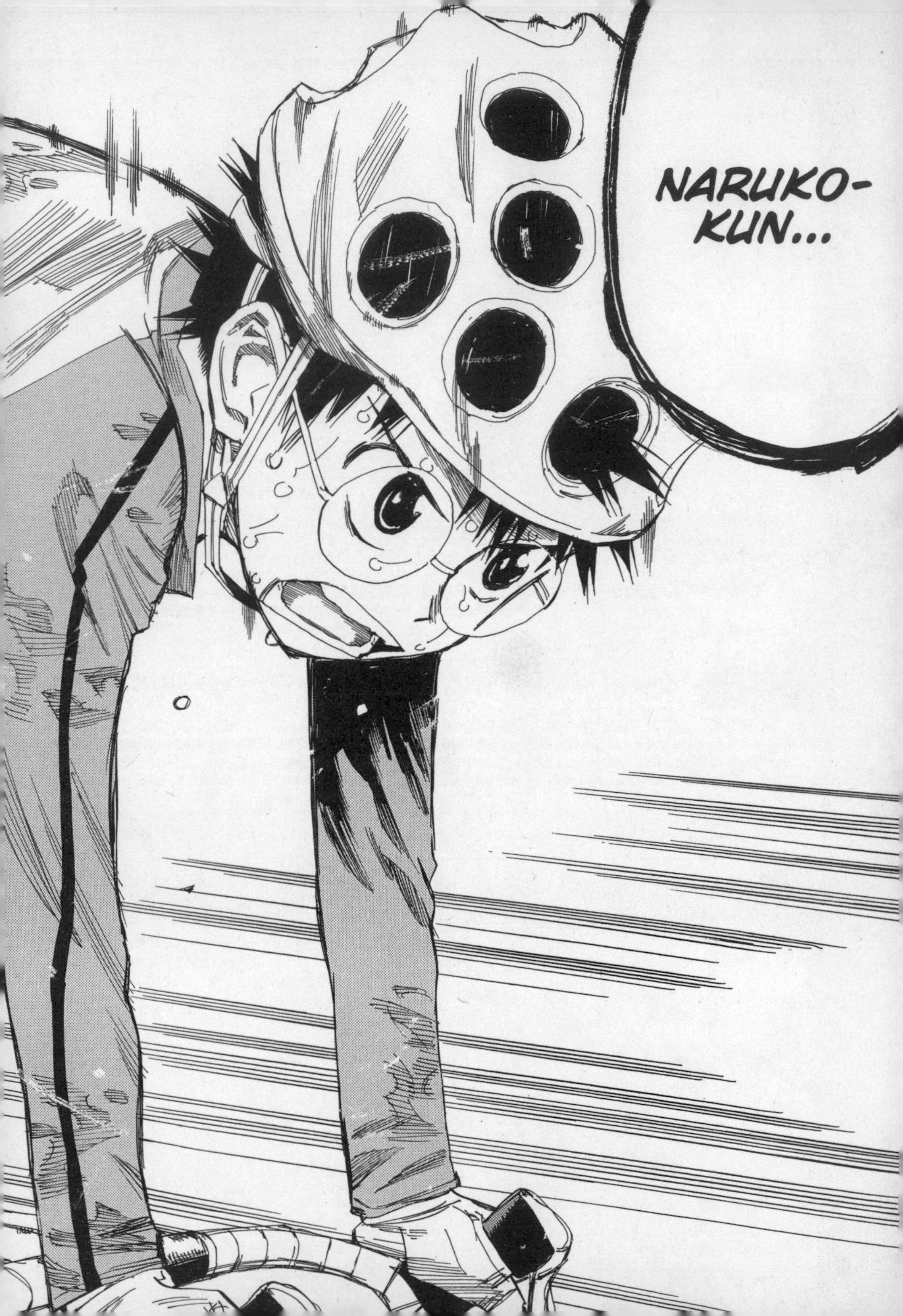
NARUKO-KUN...

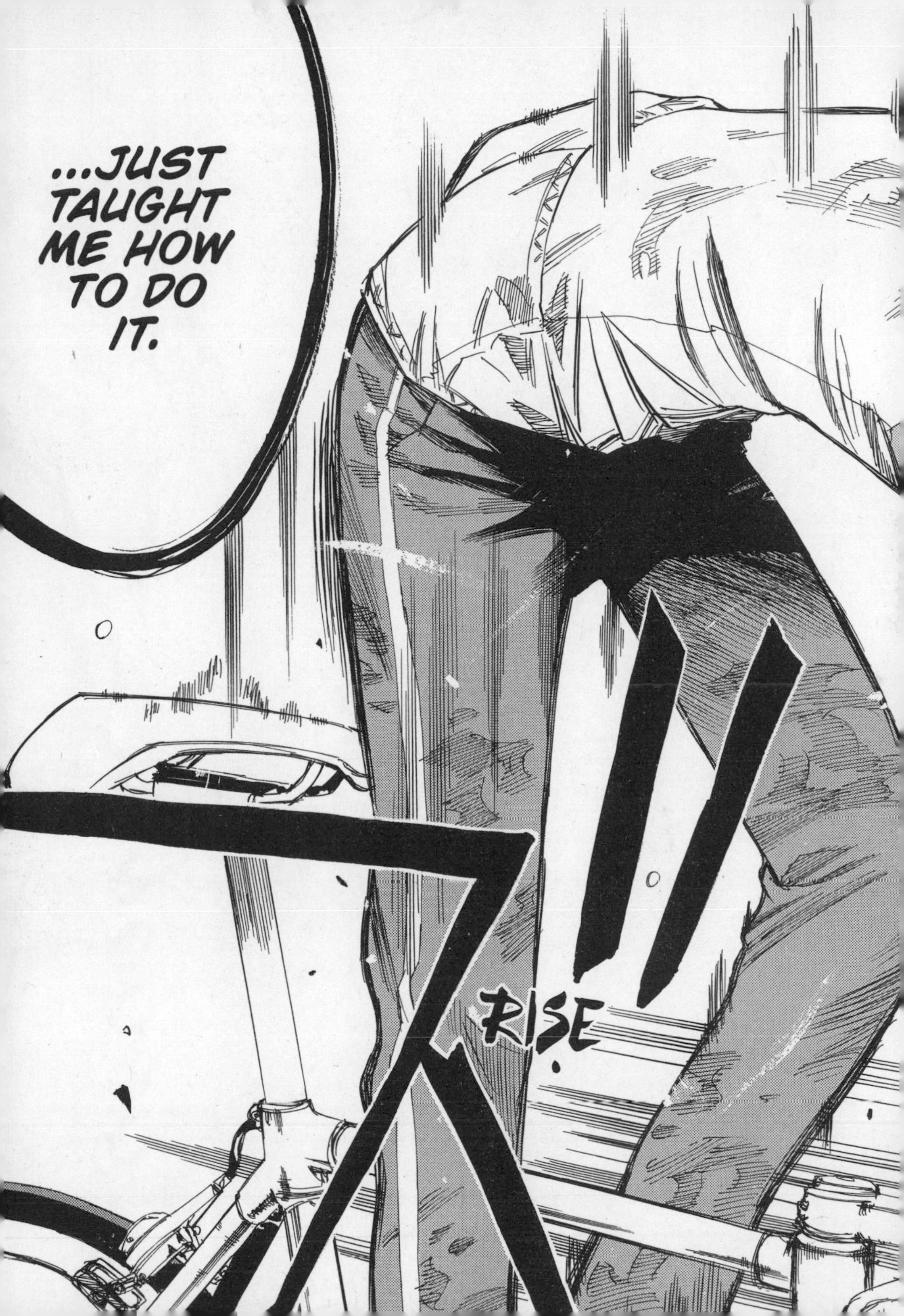
...JUST TAUGHT ME HOW TO DO IT.
RISE

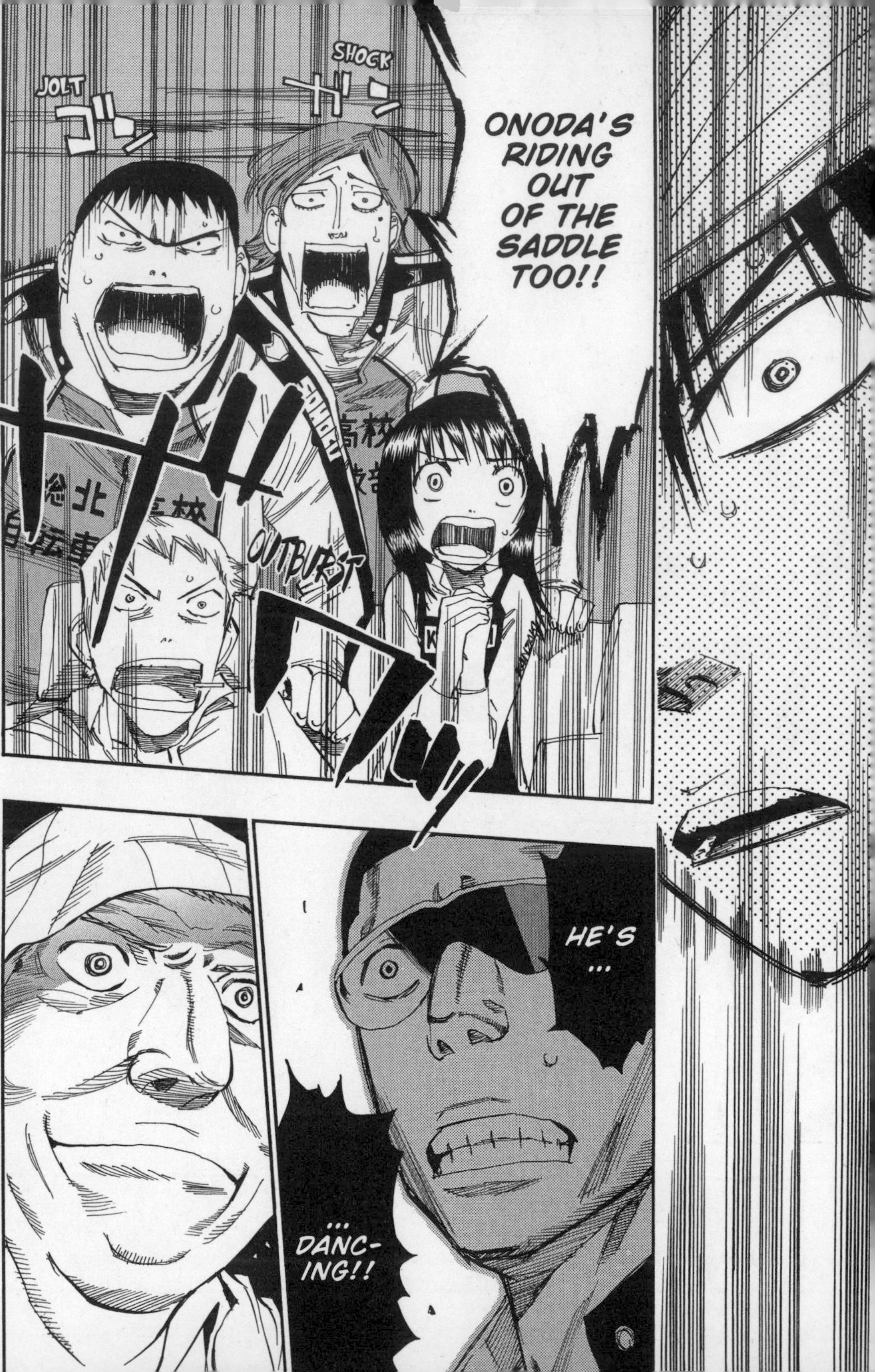
SHOCK
ONODA'S RIDING OUT OF THE SADDLE TOO!!
JOLT
OUTBURST
HE'S ...
... DANCING!!

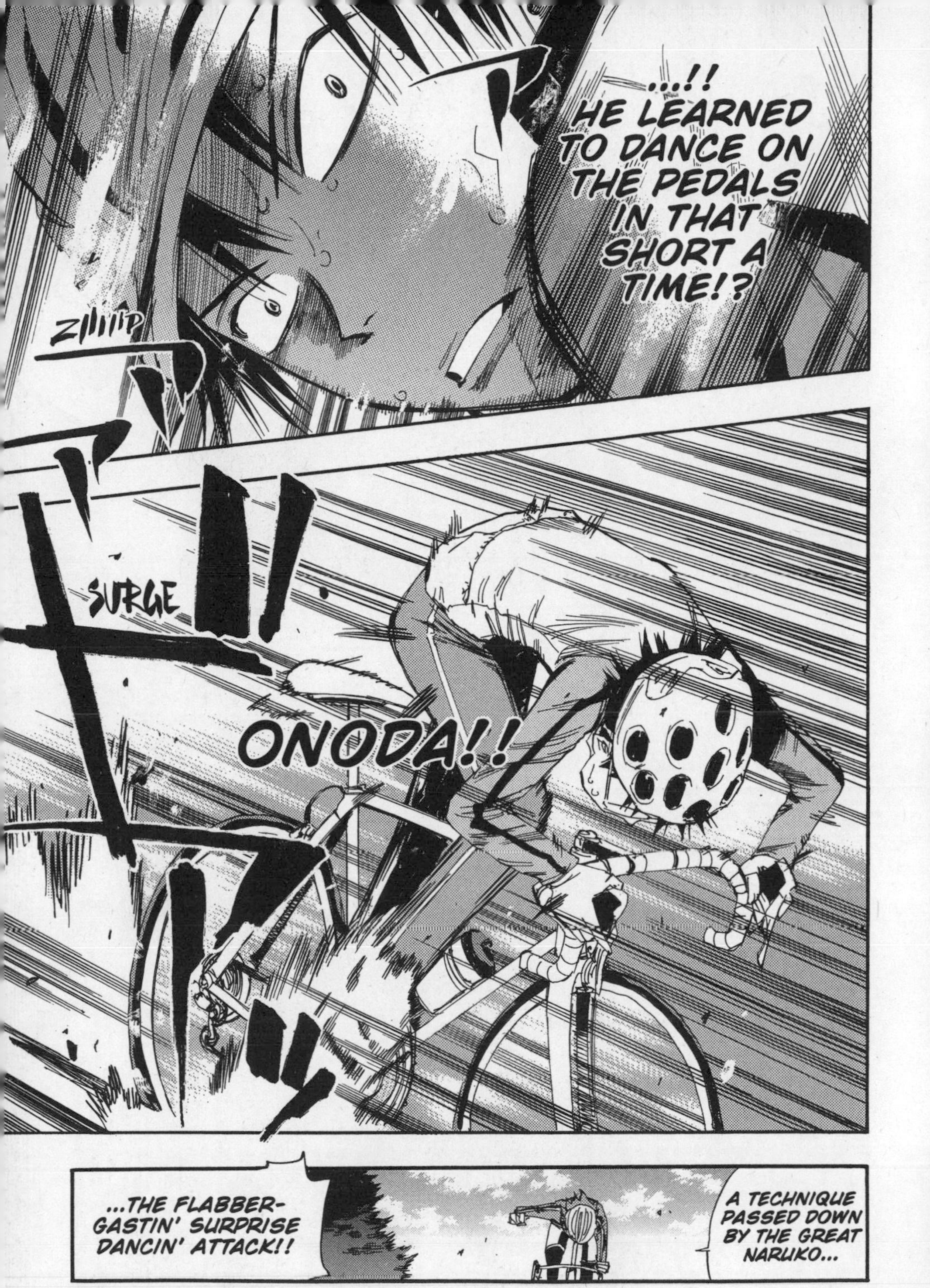
...!!
HE LEARNED TO DANCE ON THE PEDALS IN THAT SHORT A TIME!?
ZIIIIIP
SURGE
ONODA!!
A TECHNIQUE PASSED DOWN BY THE GREAT NARUKO...
...THE FLABBER-GASTIN' SURPRISE DANCIN' ATTACK!!

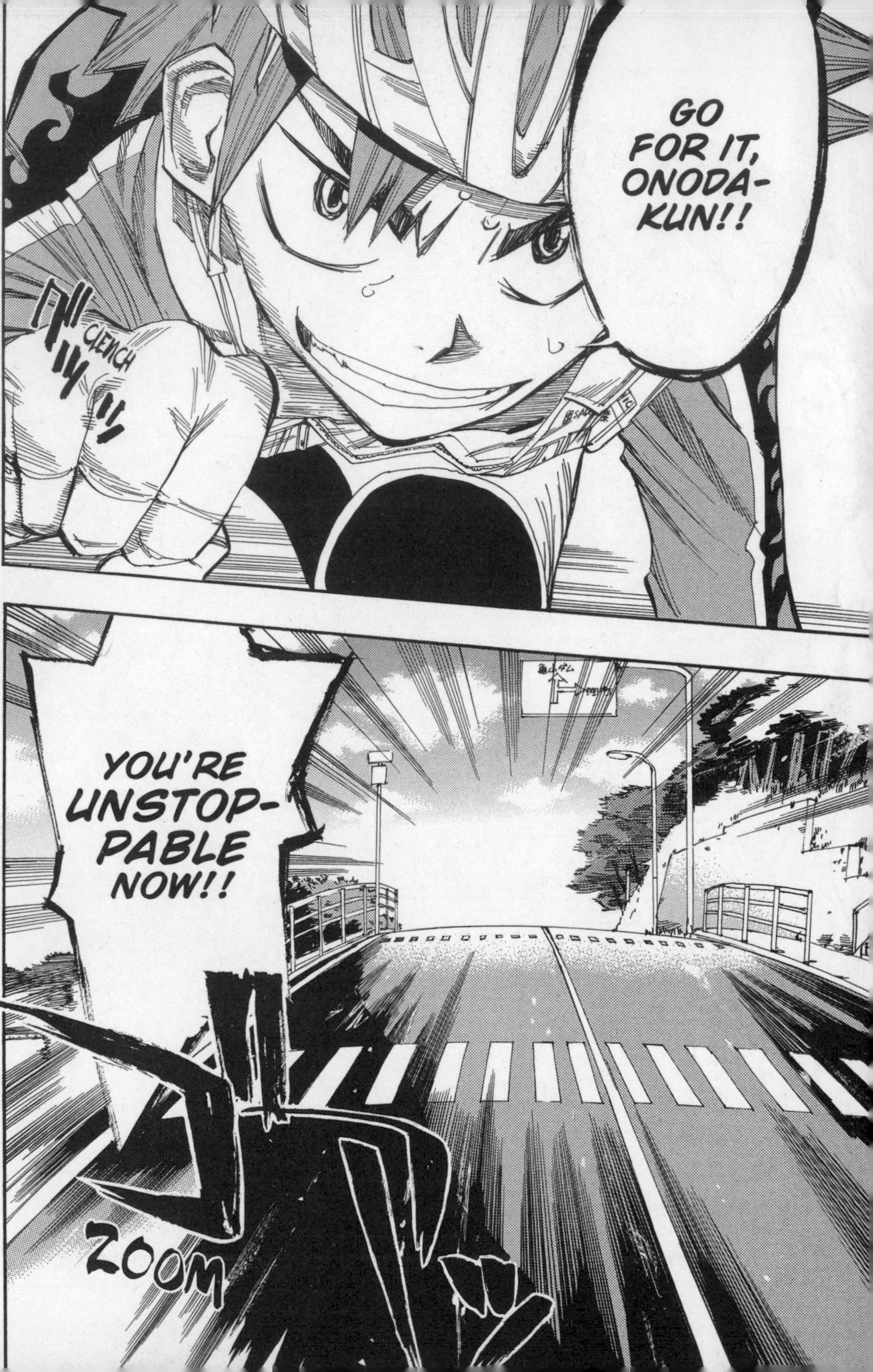
GO FOR IT, ONODA-KUN!!
CLENCH
YOU'RE UNSTOPPABLE NOW!!
ZOOM

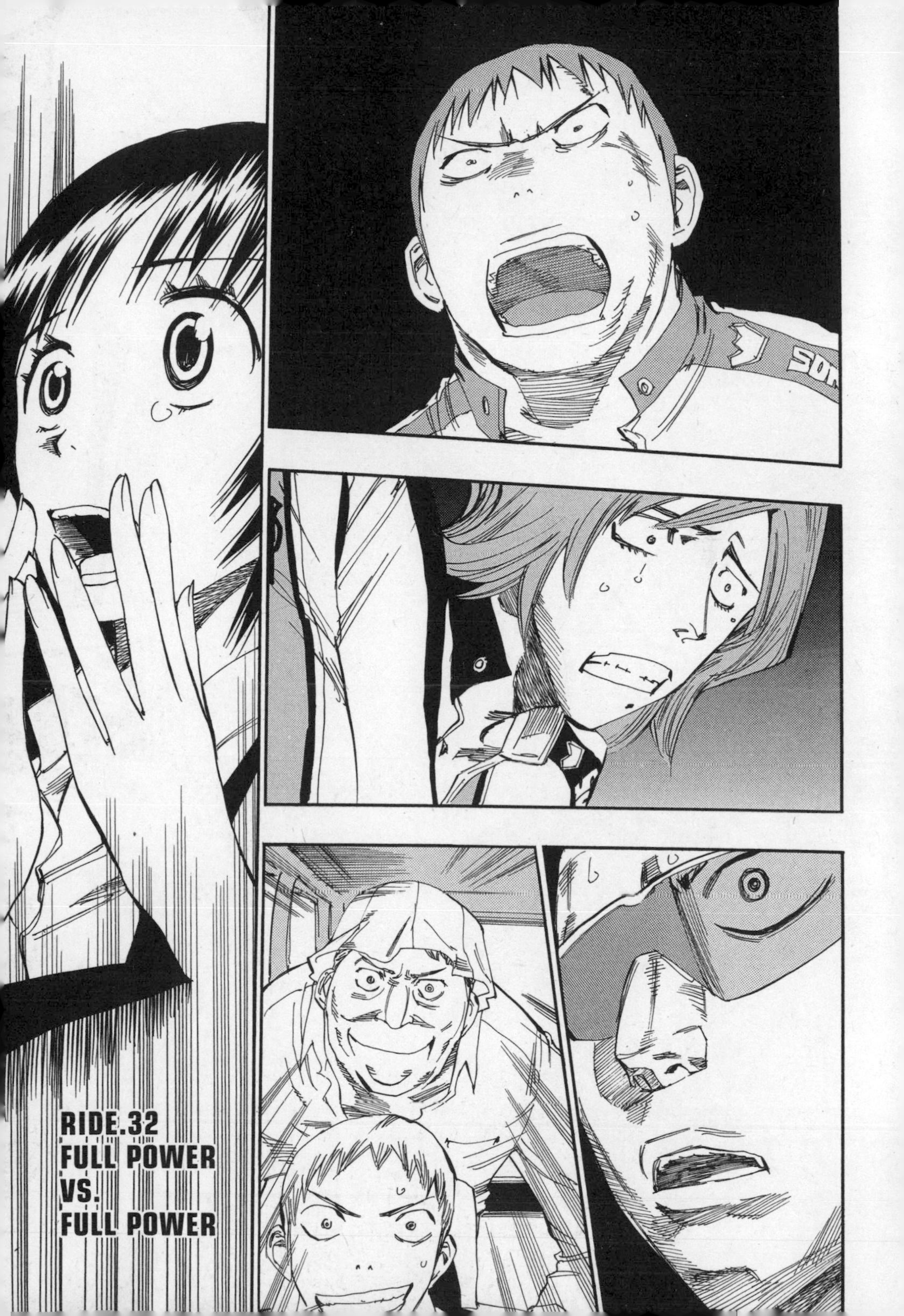
RIDE.32
FULL POWER
VS.
FULL POWER

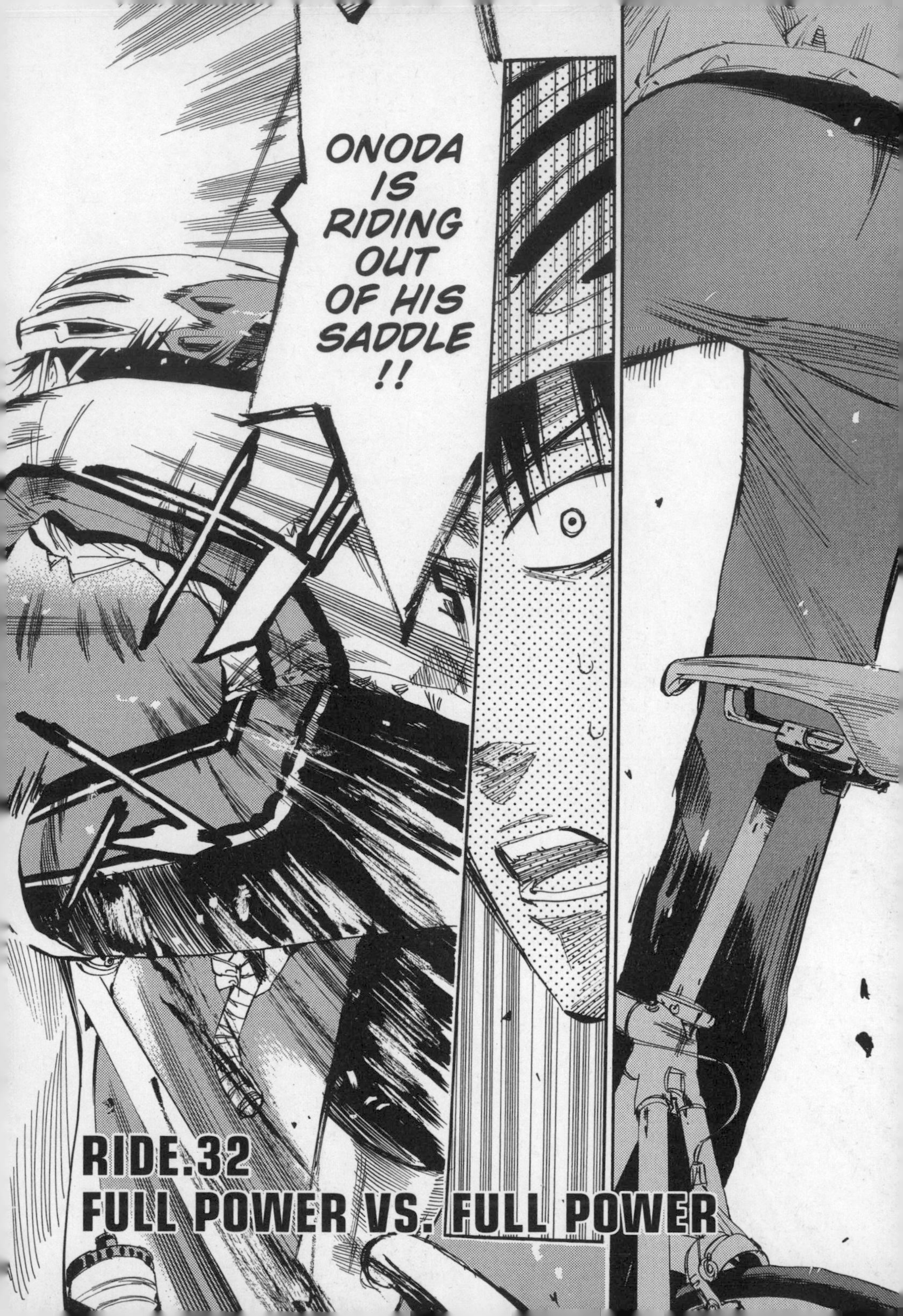
ONODA IS RIDING OUT OF HIS SADDLE !!
RIDE.32
FULL POWER VS. FULL POWER

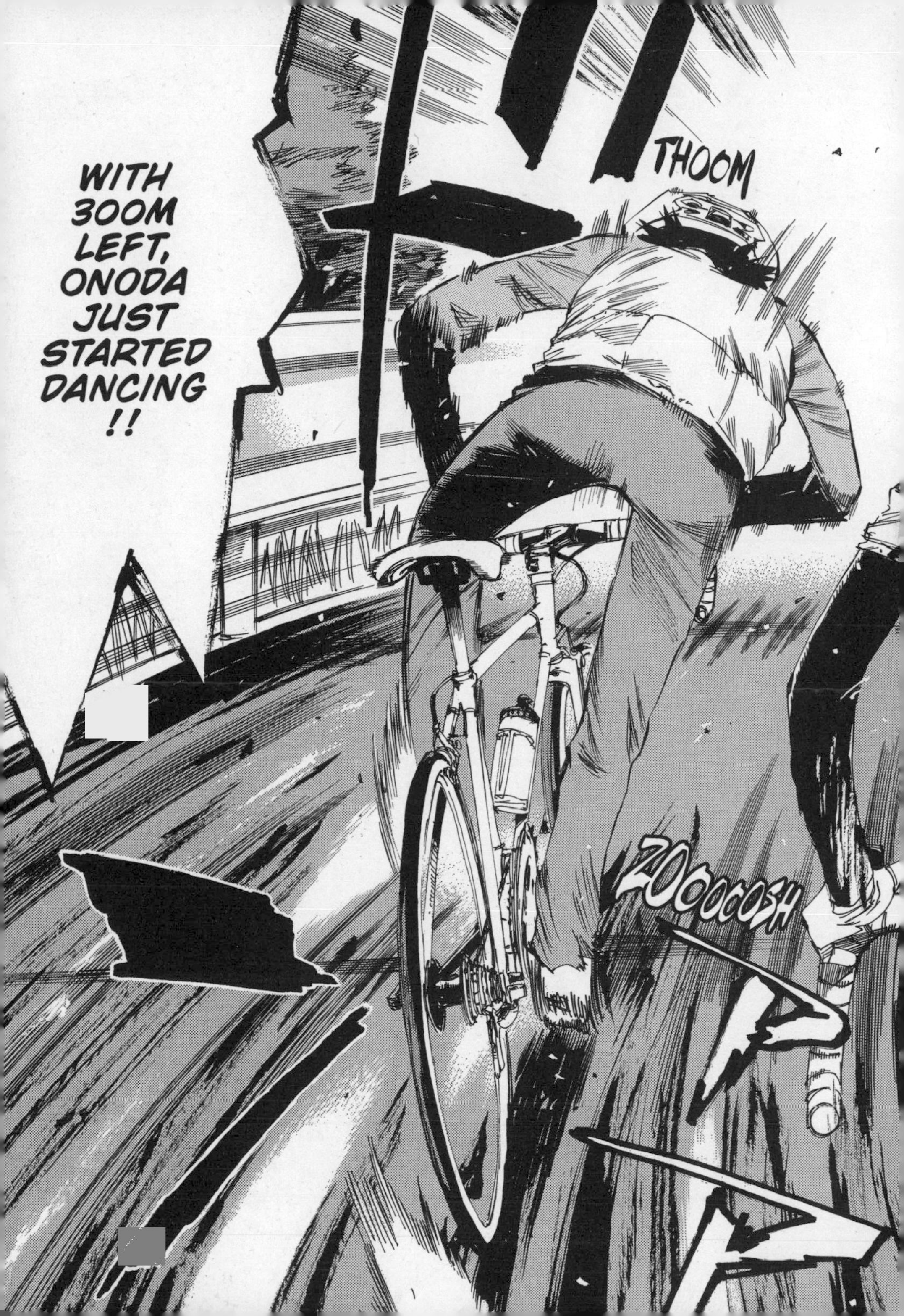
THOOM
WITH 300M LEFT, ONODA JUST STARTED DANCING!!
ZOOOOOSH

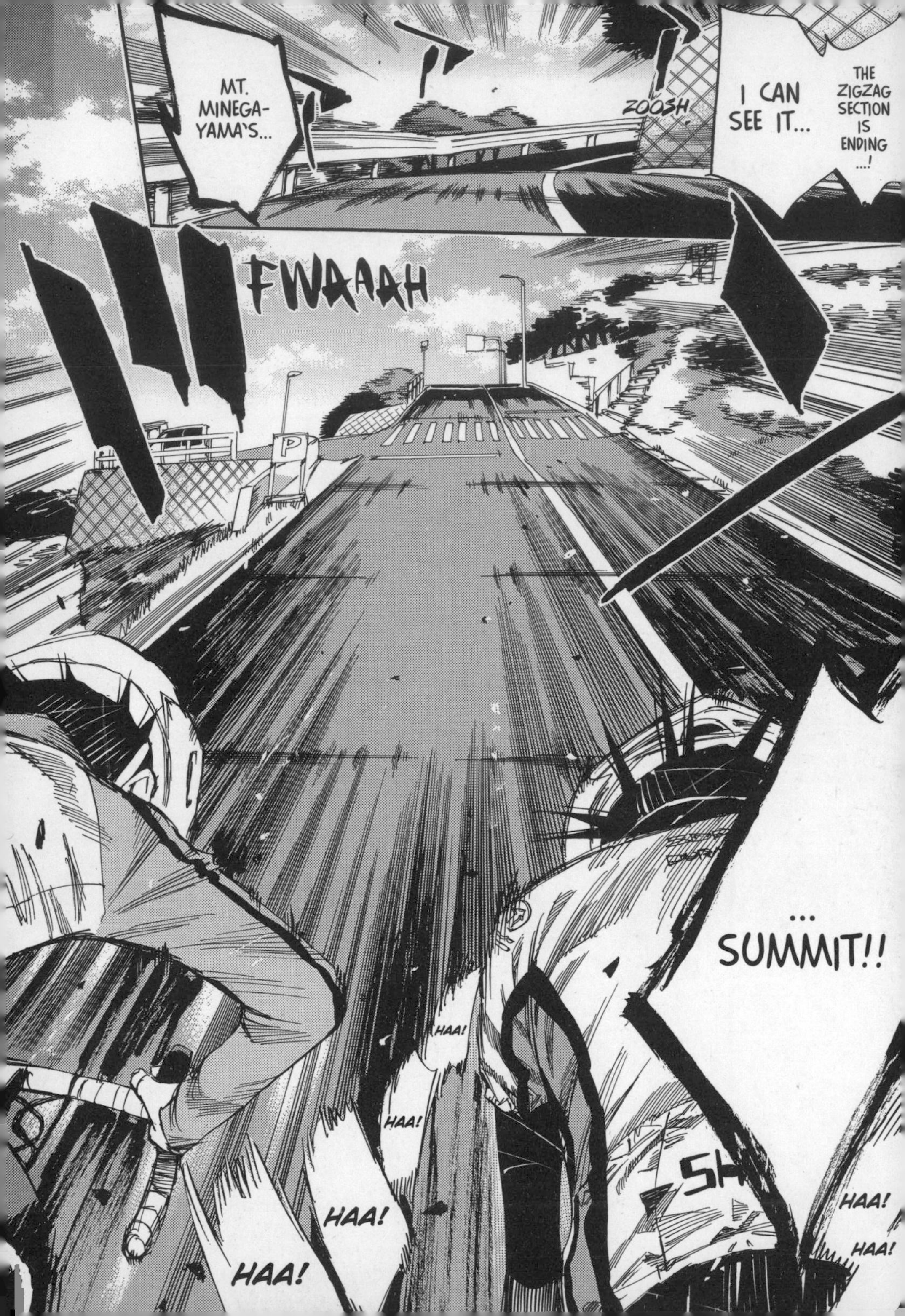

THE ZIGZAG SECTION IS ENDING ...!
I CAN SEE IT...
ZOOSH
MT. MINEGA-YAMA'S...
FWAAAH
... SUMMIT!!
HAA!
HAA!
SH
HAA!
HAA!
HAA!
HAA!
HAA!

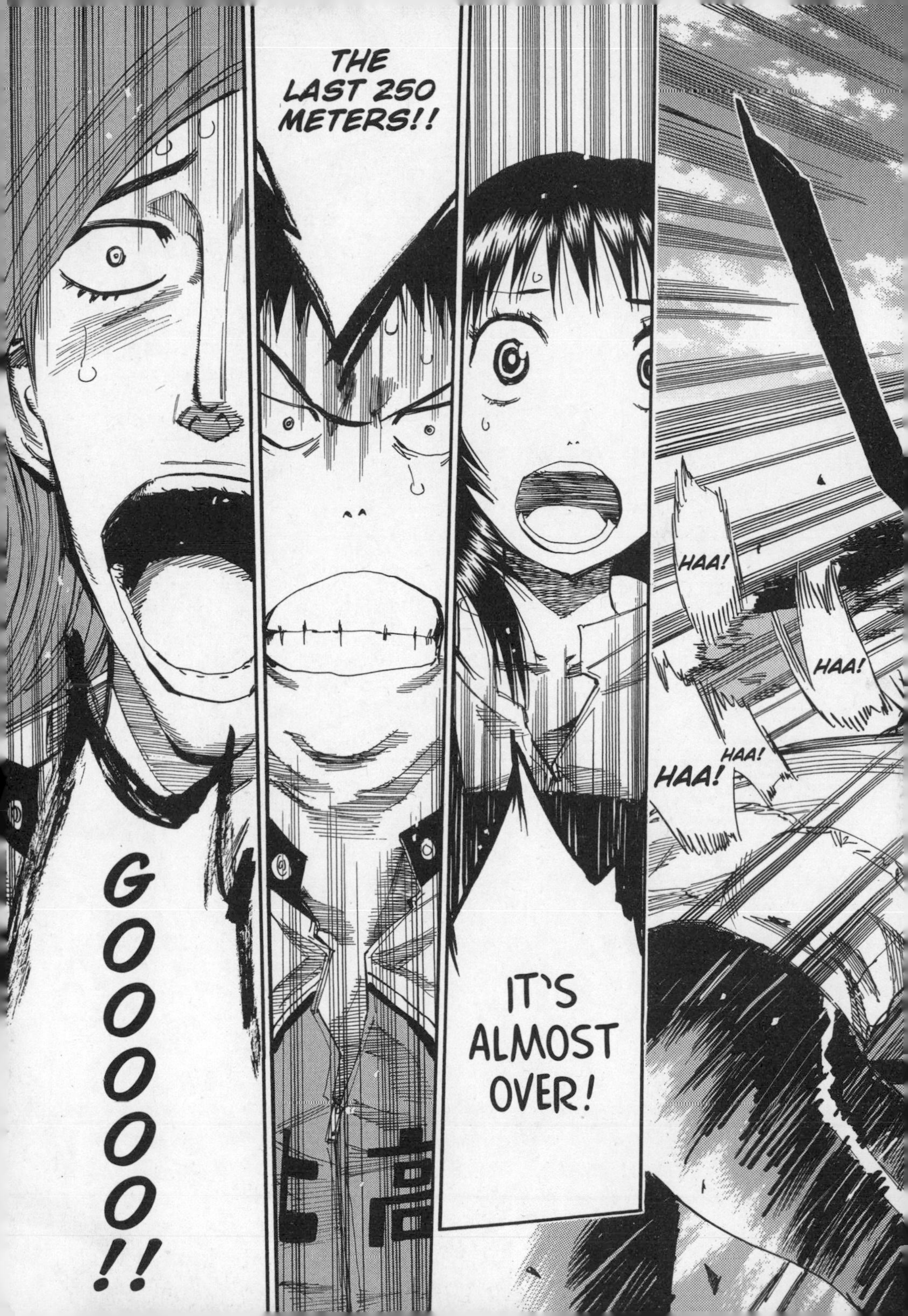
HAA!
HAA!
HAA!
HAA!
IT'S ALMOST OVER!
THE LAST 250 METERS!!
GOOOOO!!

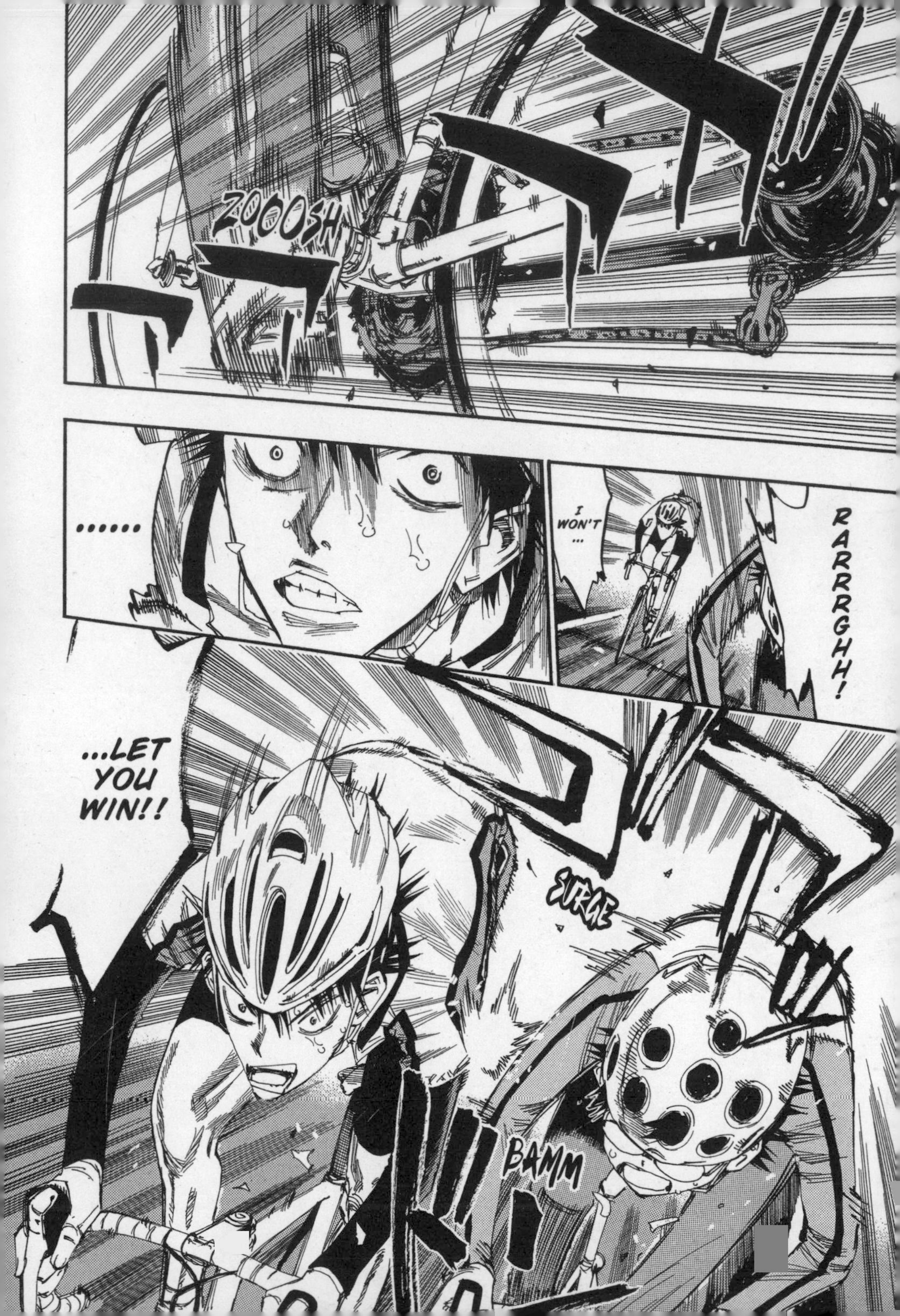

ZOOOSH
RARRRGHH!
I WON'T ...
......
...LET YOU WIN!!
SURGE
BAMM

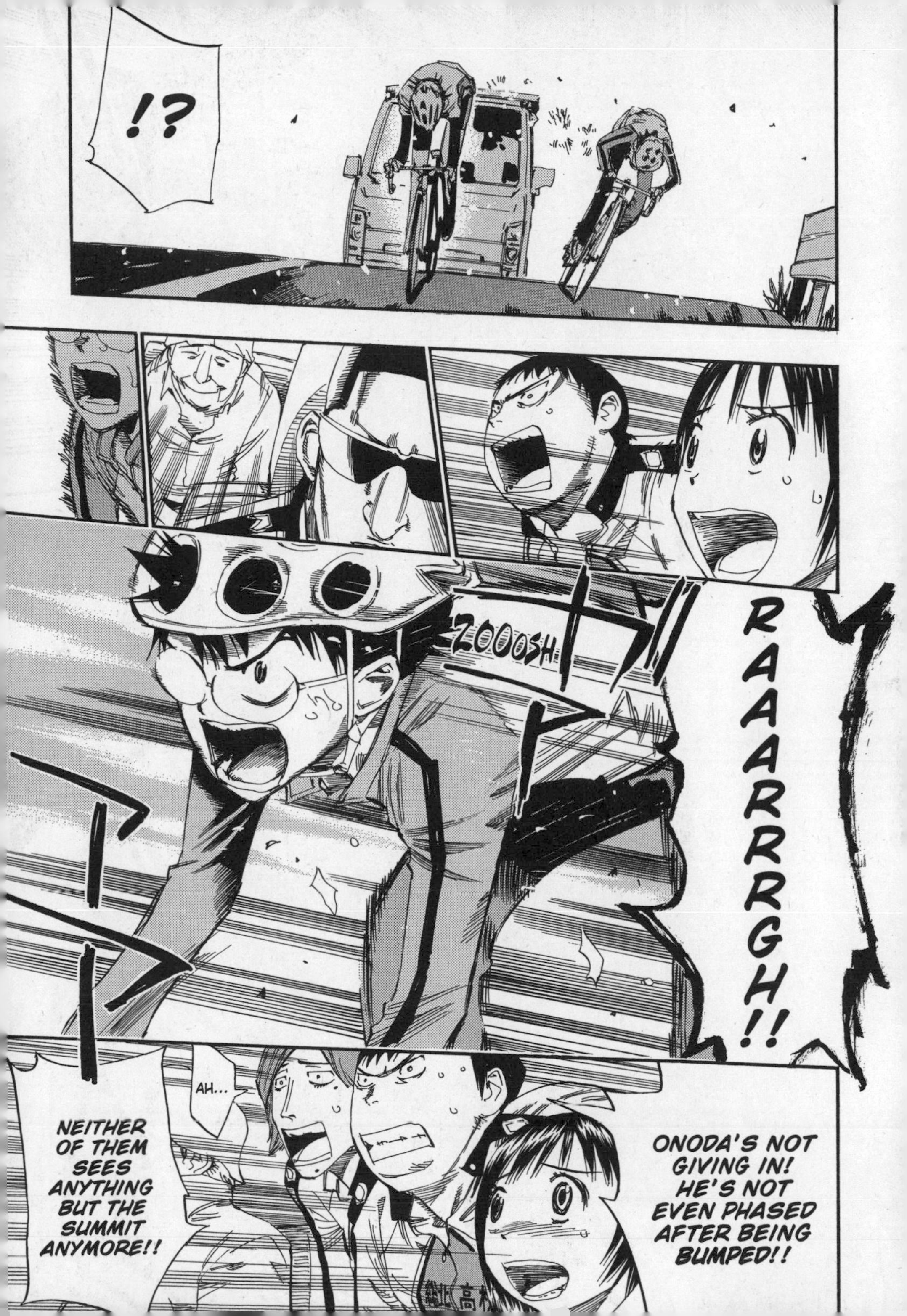
!?
RAAARRRGH!!
ZOOOSH
ONODA'S NOT GIVING IN! HE'S NOT EVEN PHASED AFTER BEING BUMPED!!
AH...
NEITHER OF THEM SEES ANYTHING BUT THE SUMMIT ANYMORE!!

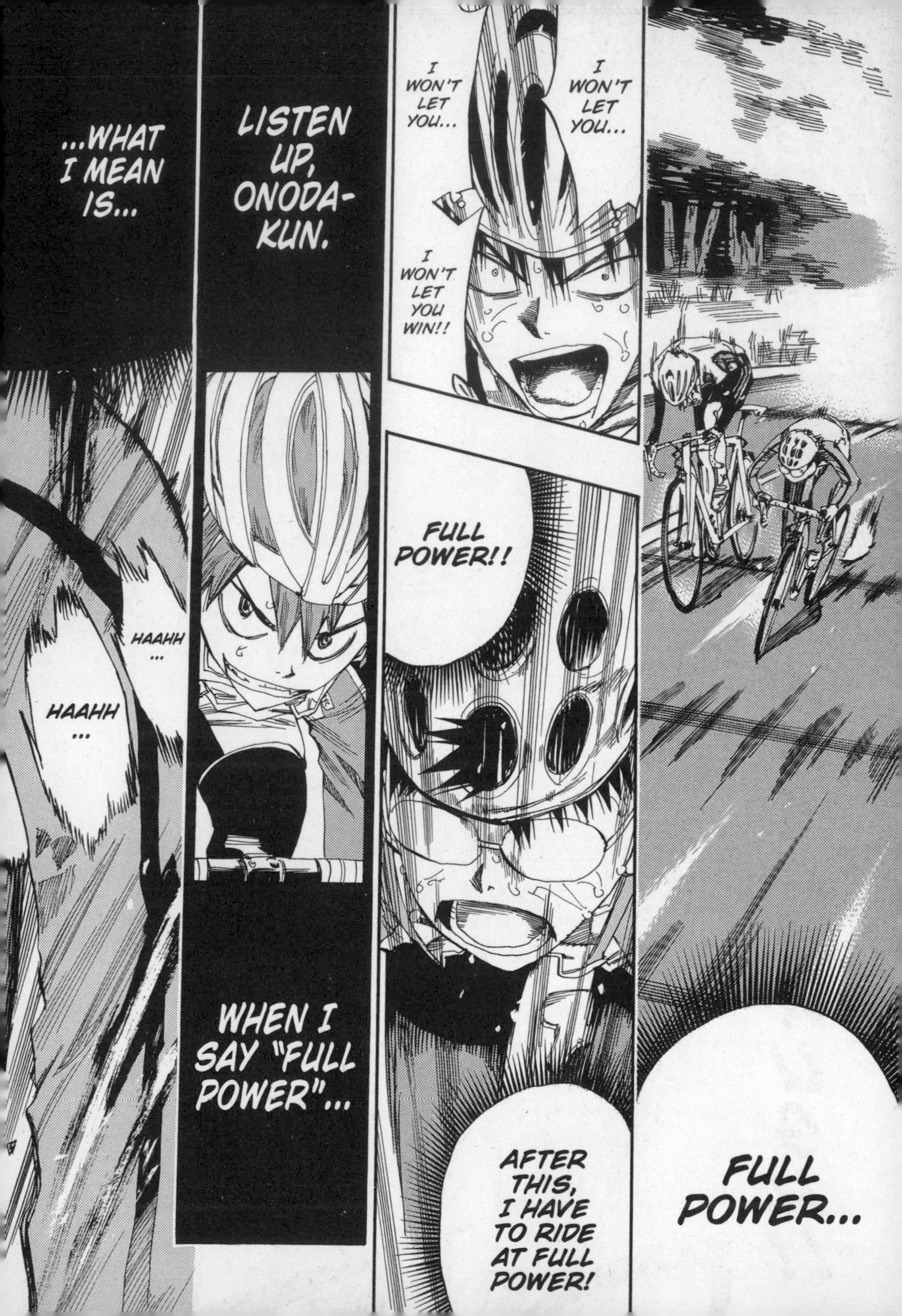
FULL POWER...
I WON'T LET YOU...
I WON'T LET YOU...
I WON'T LET YOU WIN!!
FULL POWER!!
AFTER THIS, I HAVE TO RIDE AT FULL POWER!
LISTEN UP, ONODA-KUN.
HAAHH...
WHEN I SAY "FULL POWER"...
...WHAT I MEAN IS...
HAAHH...

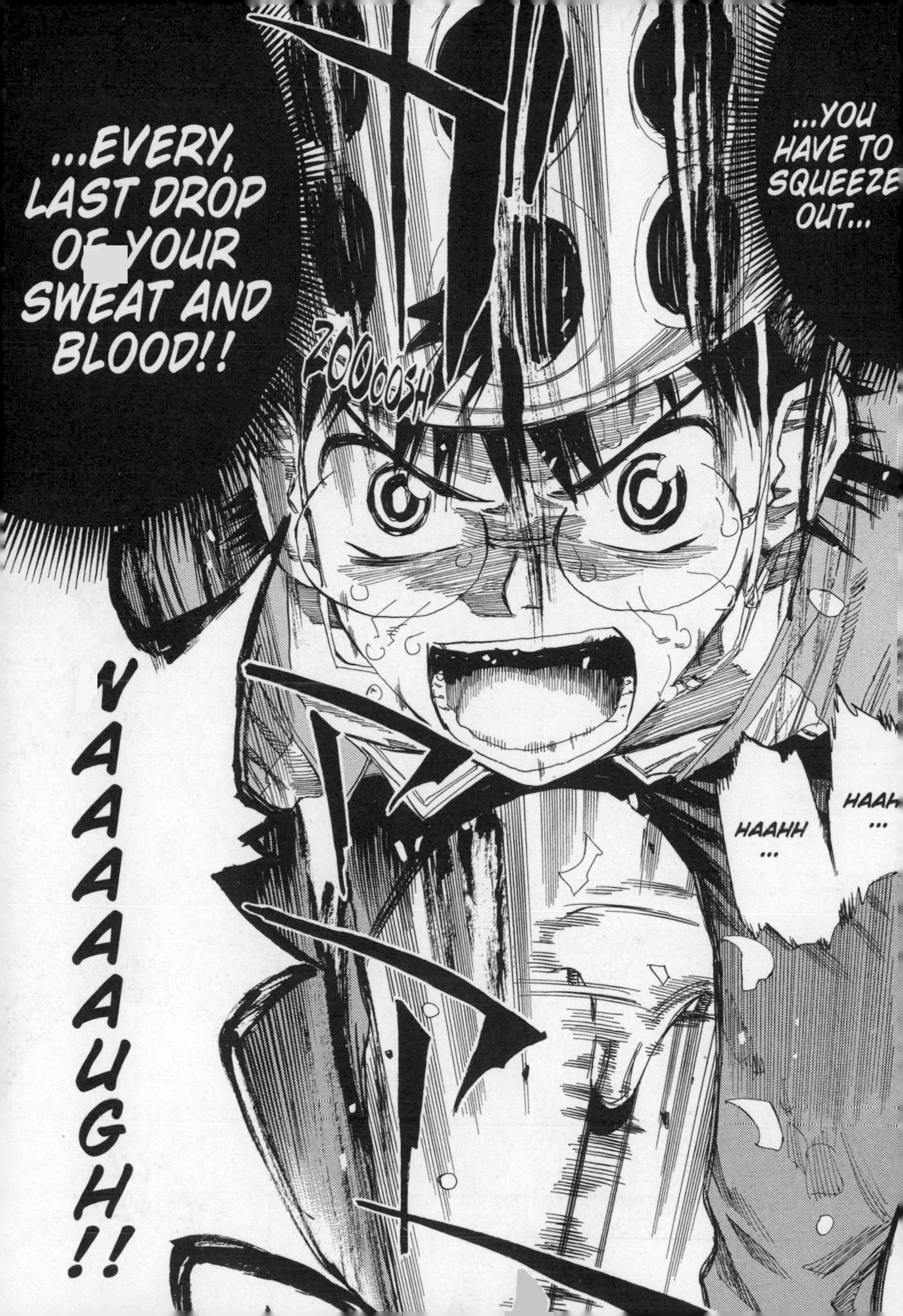
...YOU HAVE TO SQUEEZE OUT...
HAAH ...
HAAHH ...
ZOOOOSH
...EVERY, LAST DROP OF YOUR SWEAT AND BLOOD!!
NAAAAAUGH!!

AAAUUGHH!!

HAAH ...

HAAH ...

HAAH ...

HAAH ...

GO FOR IT, ONO-DAAAA!!!

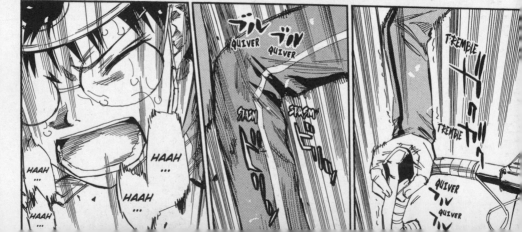

HAAH ...

HAAH ...

HAAH ...

QUIVER

QUIVER

TREMBLE

TREMBLE

QUIVER

QUIVER

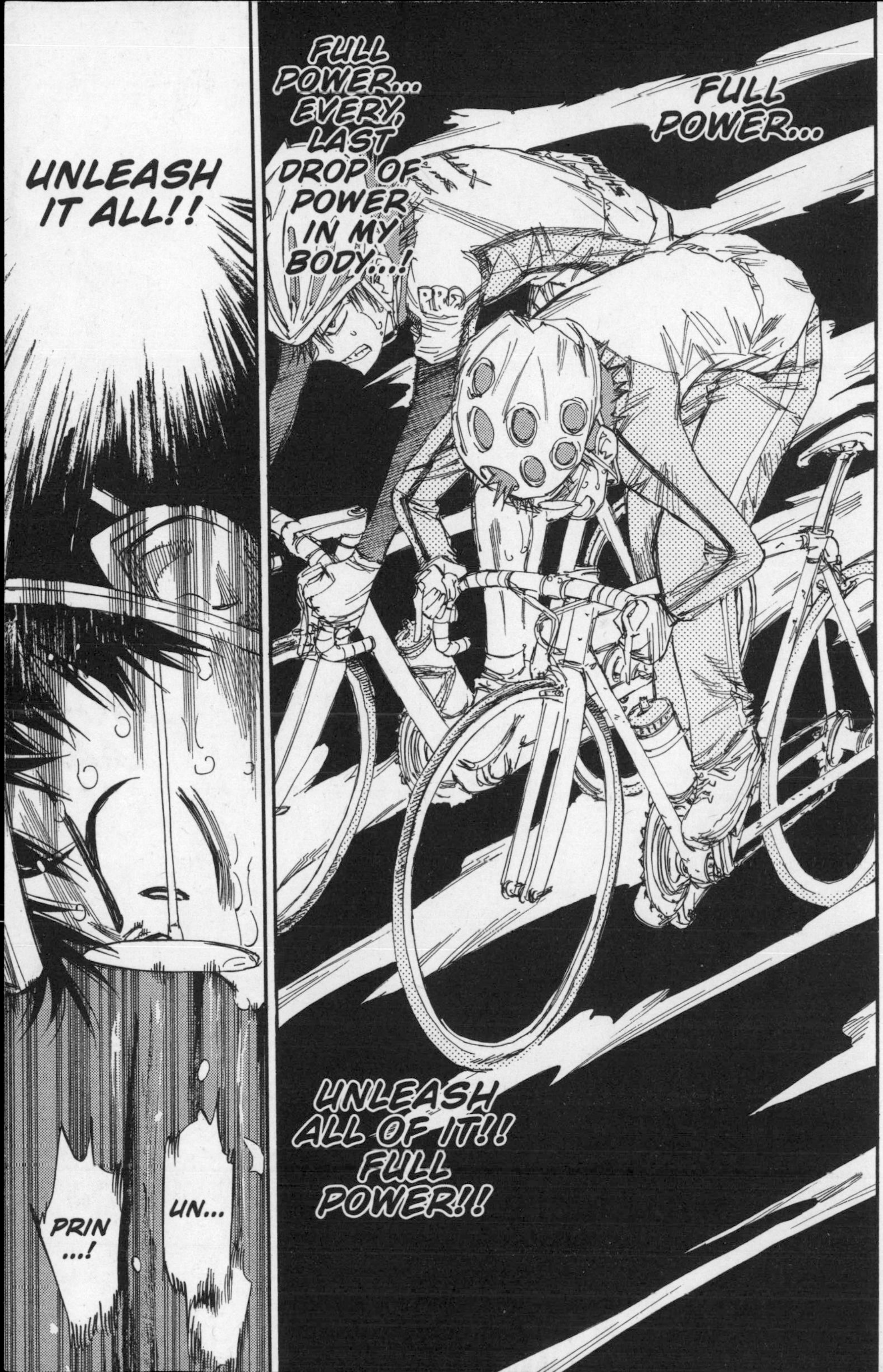
FULL POWER...
FULL POWER... EVERY, LAST DROP OF POWER IN MY BODY...!
UNLEASH ALL OF IT!! FULL POWER!!
UNLEASH IT ALL!!
UN...
PRIN ...!

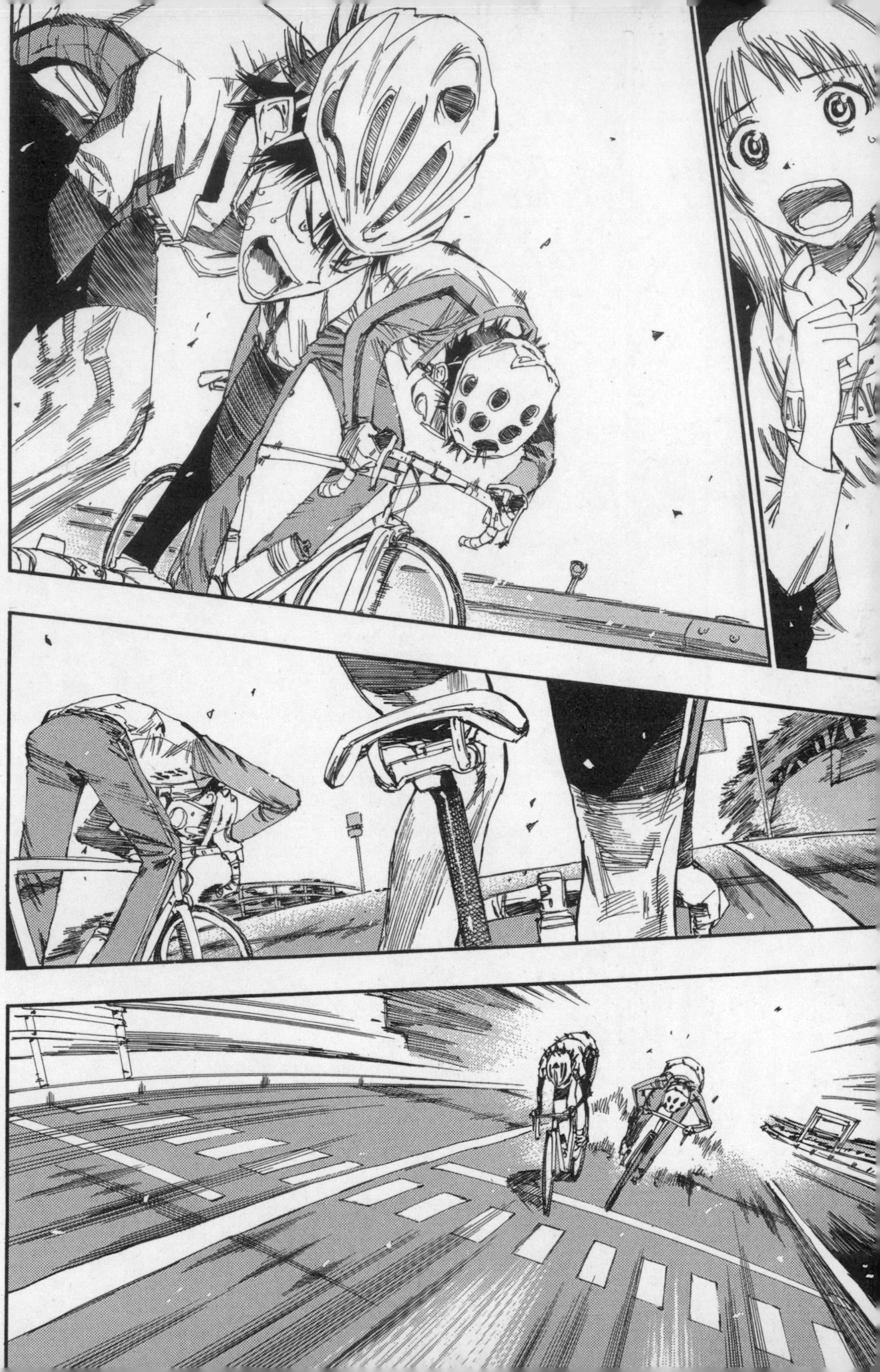

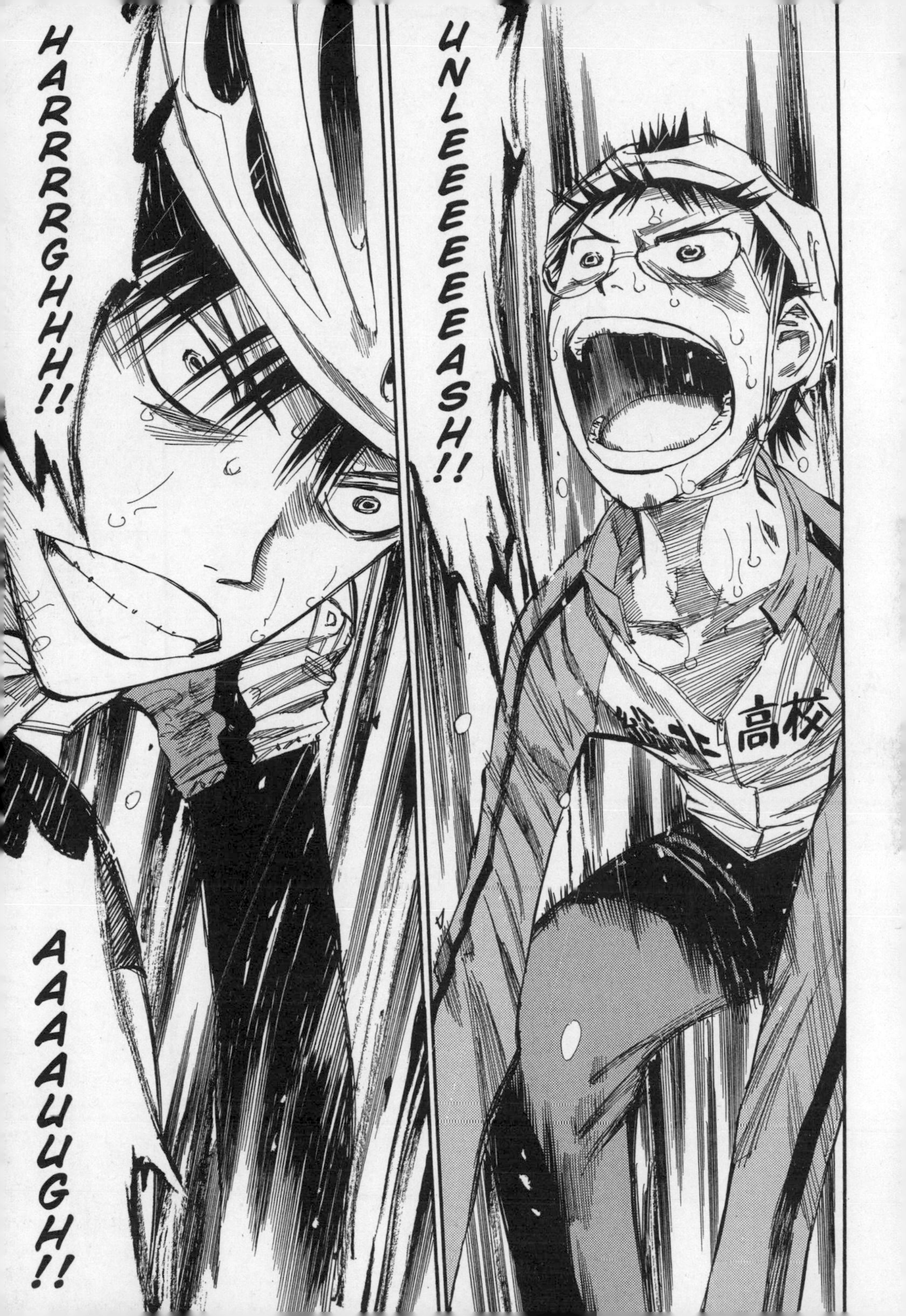
UNLEEEEEEASH!!
HARRRRGHHH!!
AAAAUUGH!!
高校

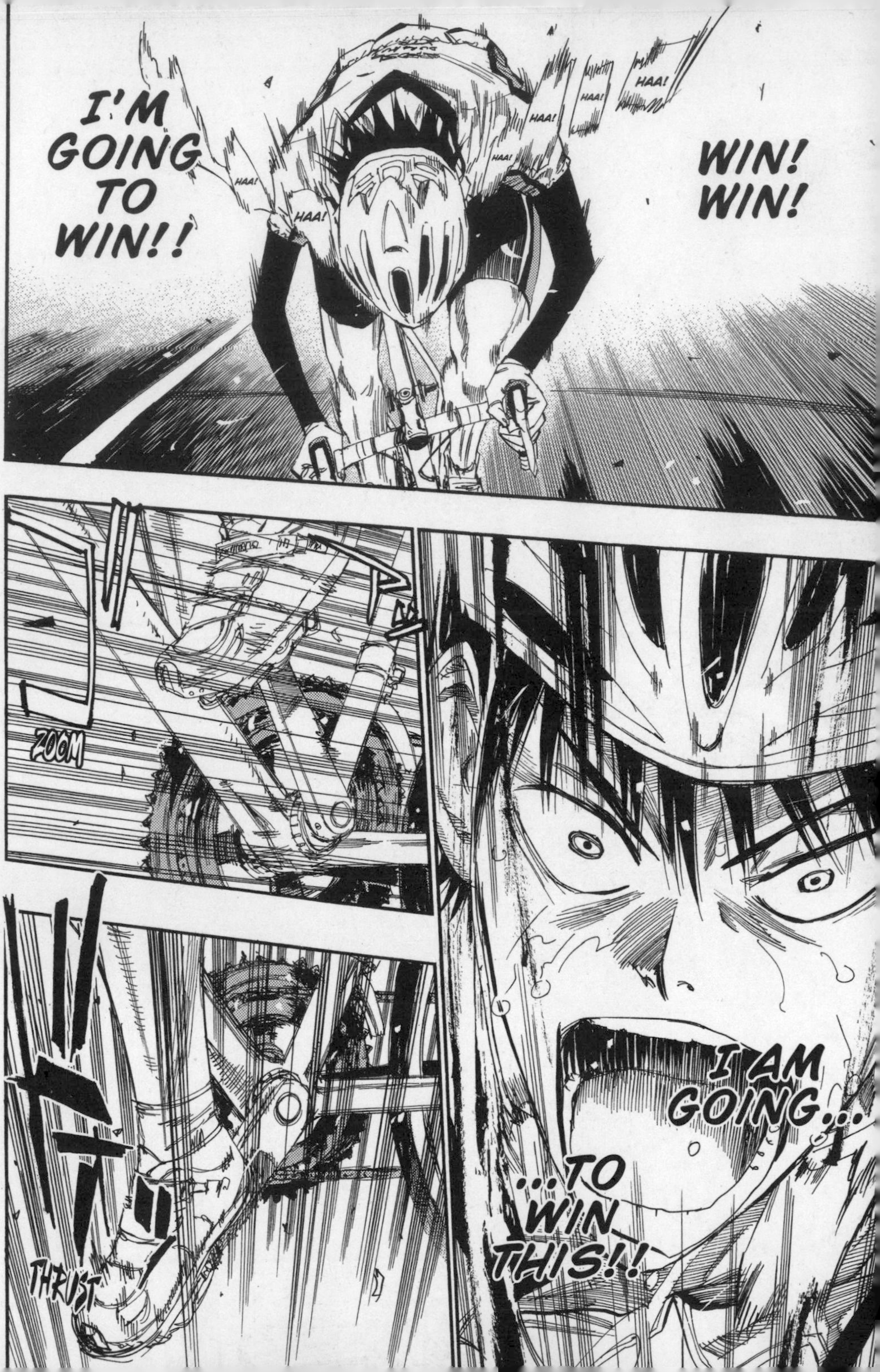

HAA!
HAA!
HAA!
WIN! WIN!
HAA!
HAA!
HAA!
I'M GOING TO WIN!!
I AM GOING...
...TO WIN THIS!!
ZOOM
THRUST

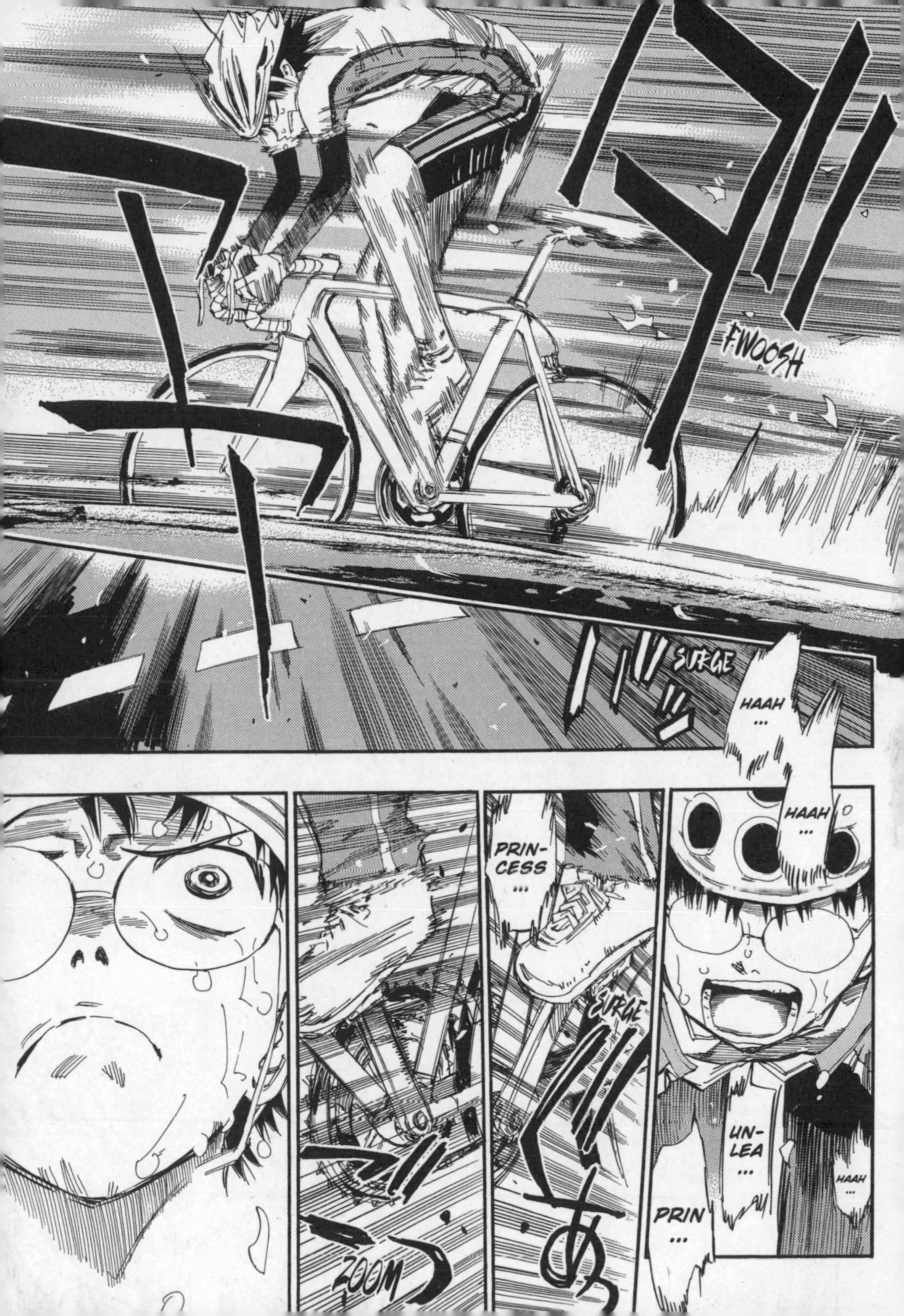
FWOOSH
SURGE
HAAH...
HAAH...
UN-LEA...
PRIN...
HAAH...
PRIN-CESS...
SURGE
ZOOM

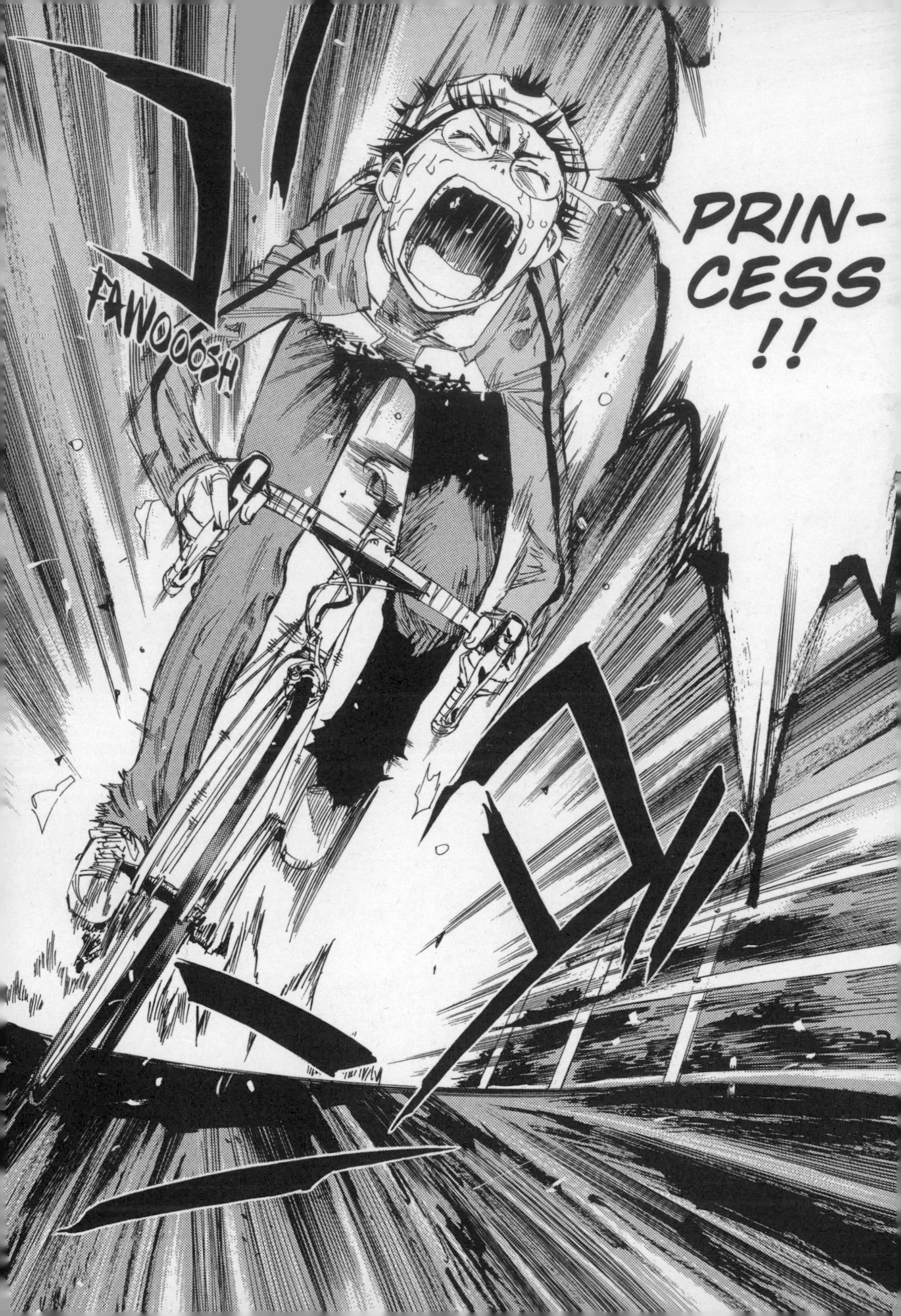
PRIN-
CESS
!!
FAWOOOSH

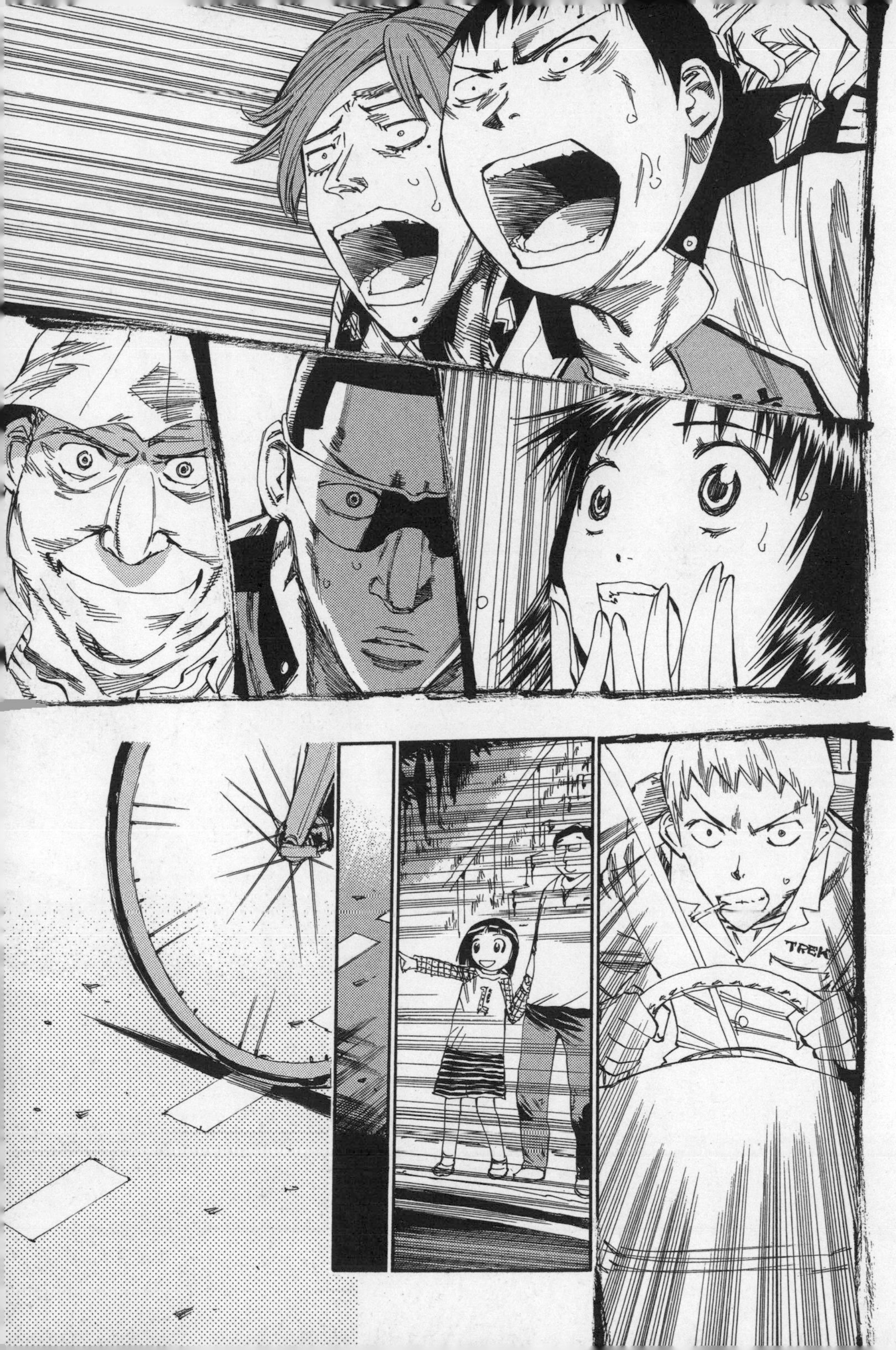
TREK

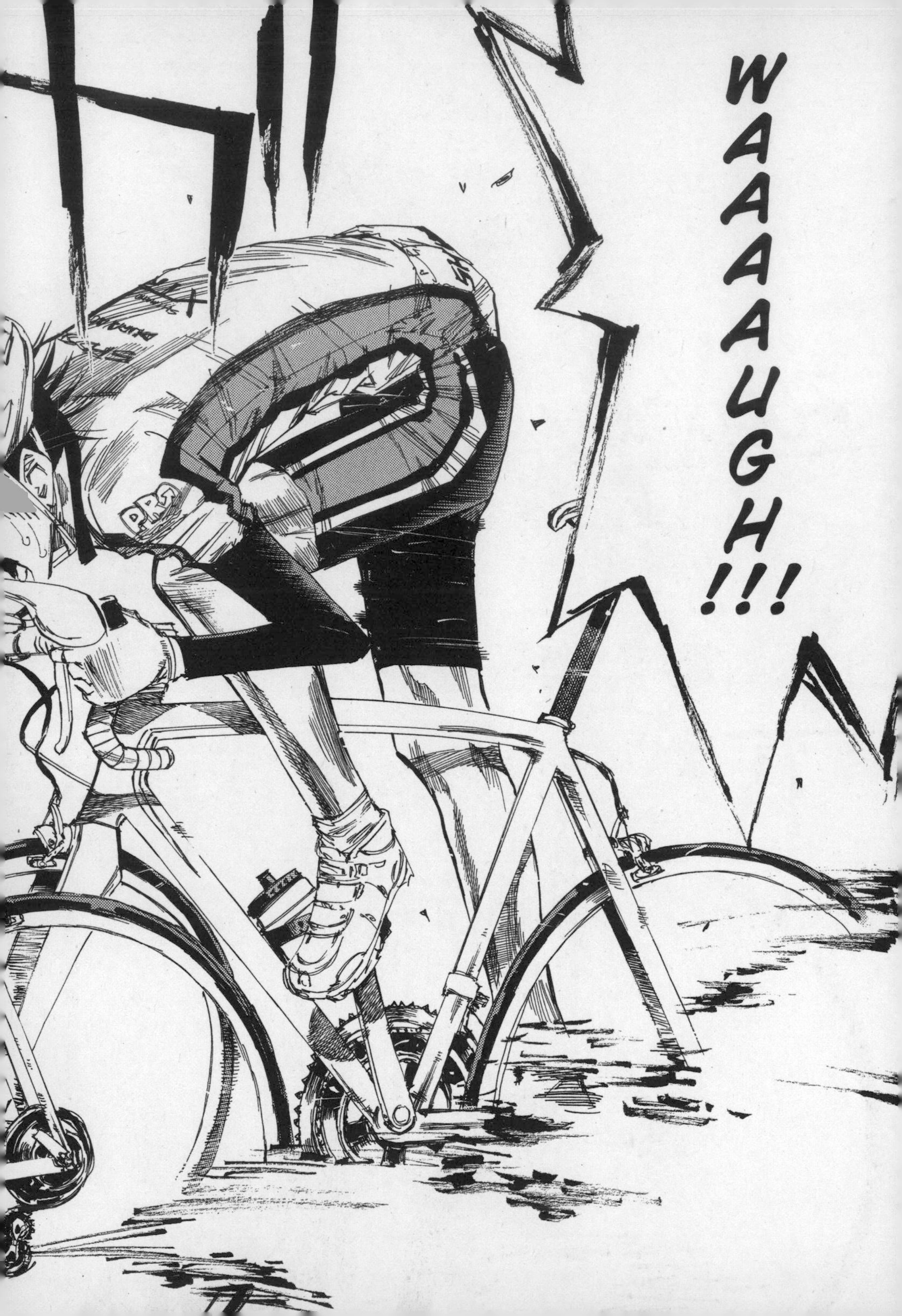
WAAAAAUGH!!!

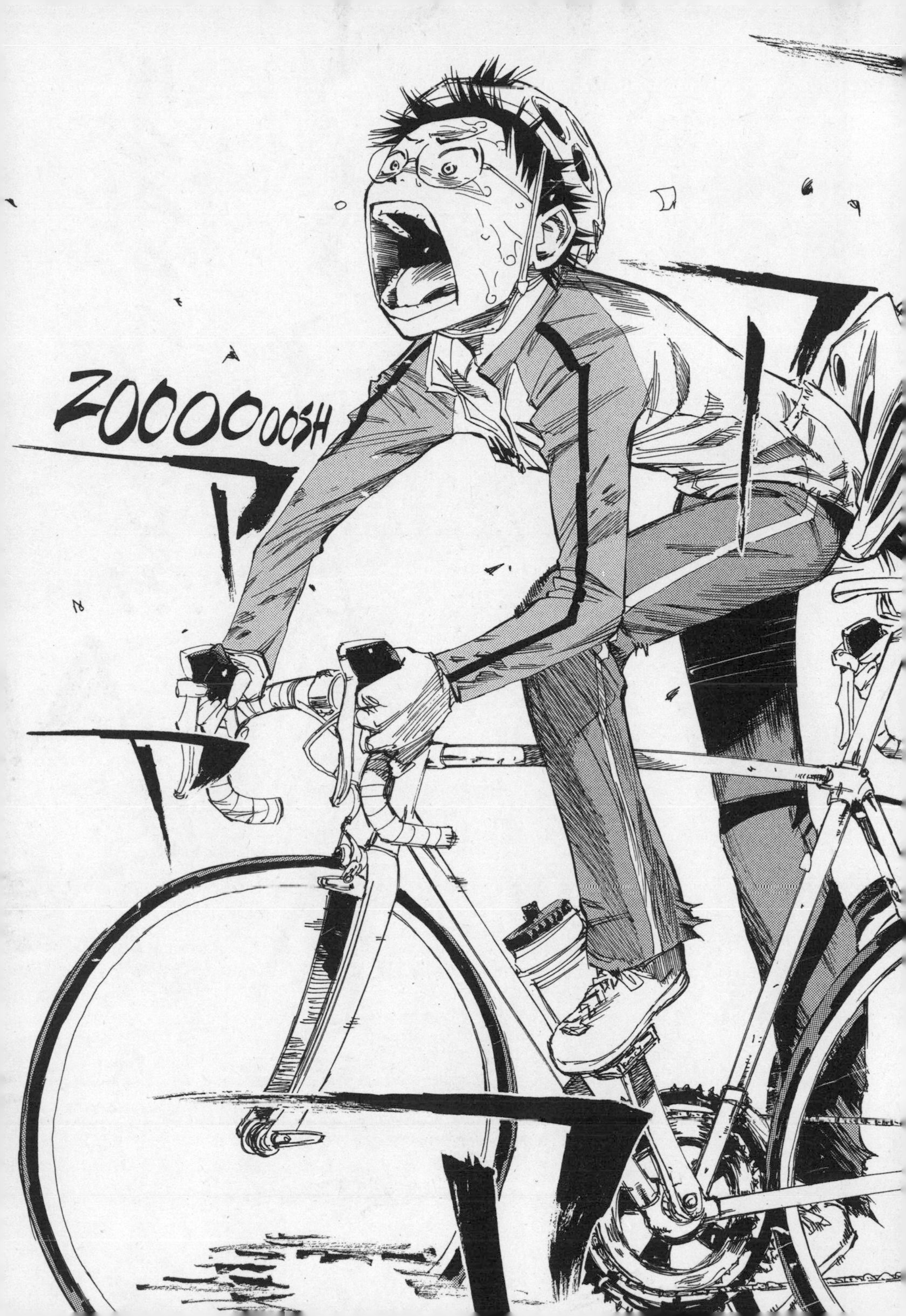
ZOOOOOOSH

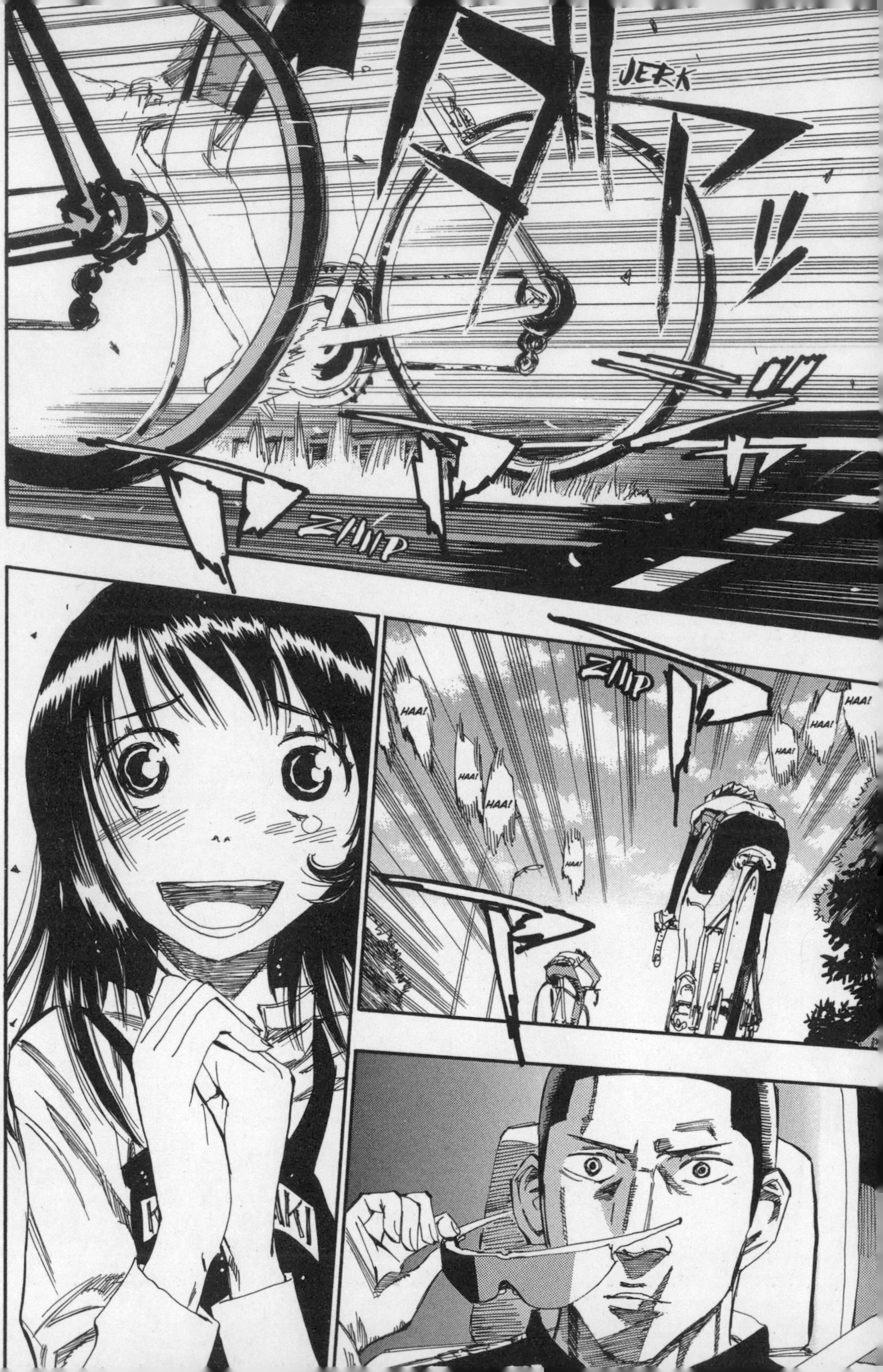
JERK
ZWIP
ZWIP
HAA!
HAA!
HAA!
HAA!
HAA!
HAA!
HAA!

RIDE.33 WINNER: ONODA!

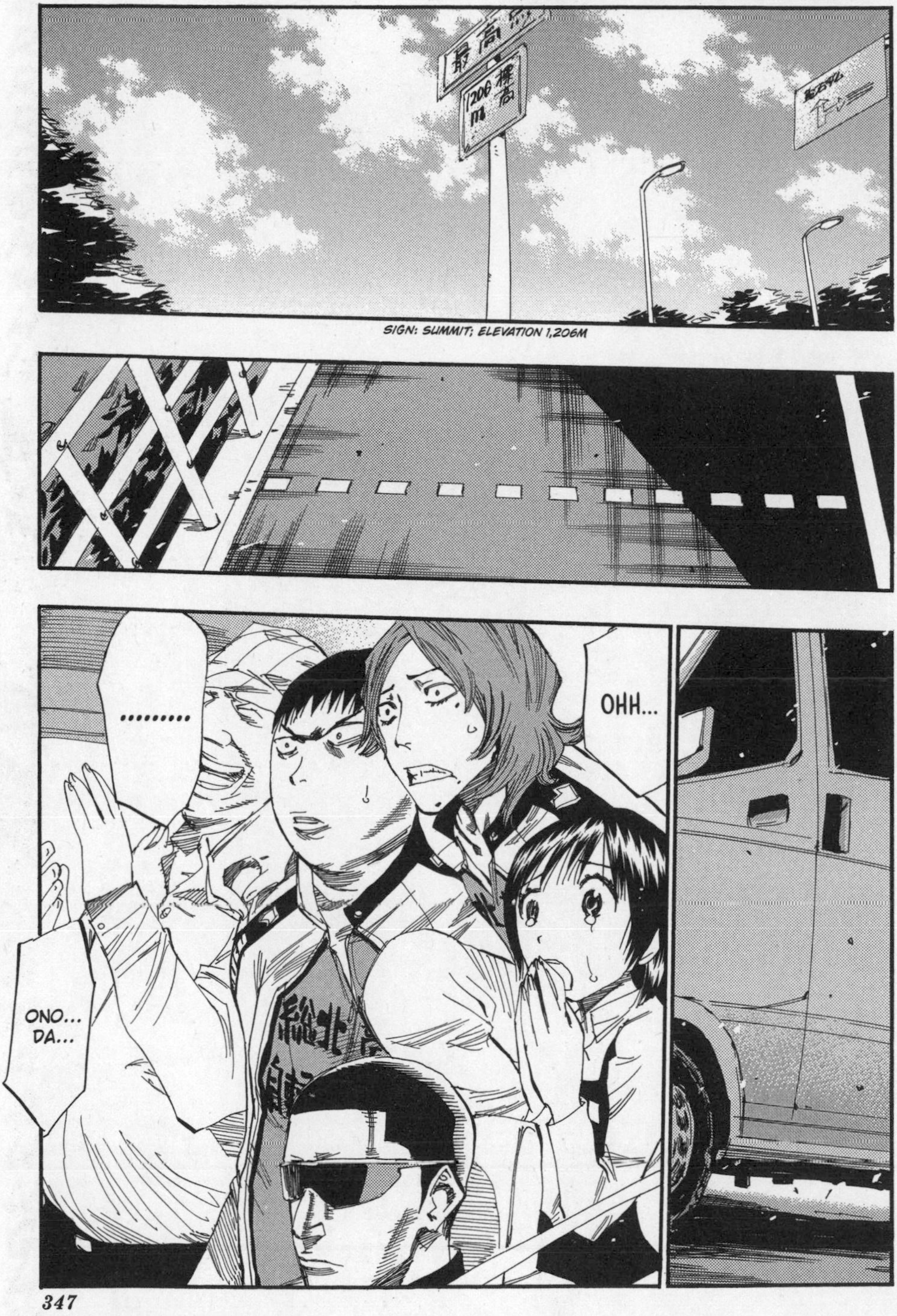
SIGN: SUMMIT; ELEVATION 1,206M
OHH...
....
ONO... DA...

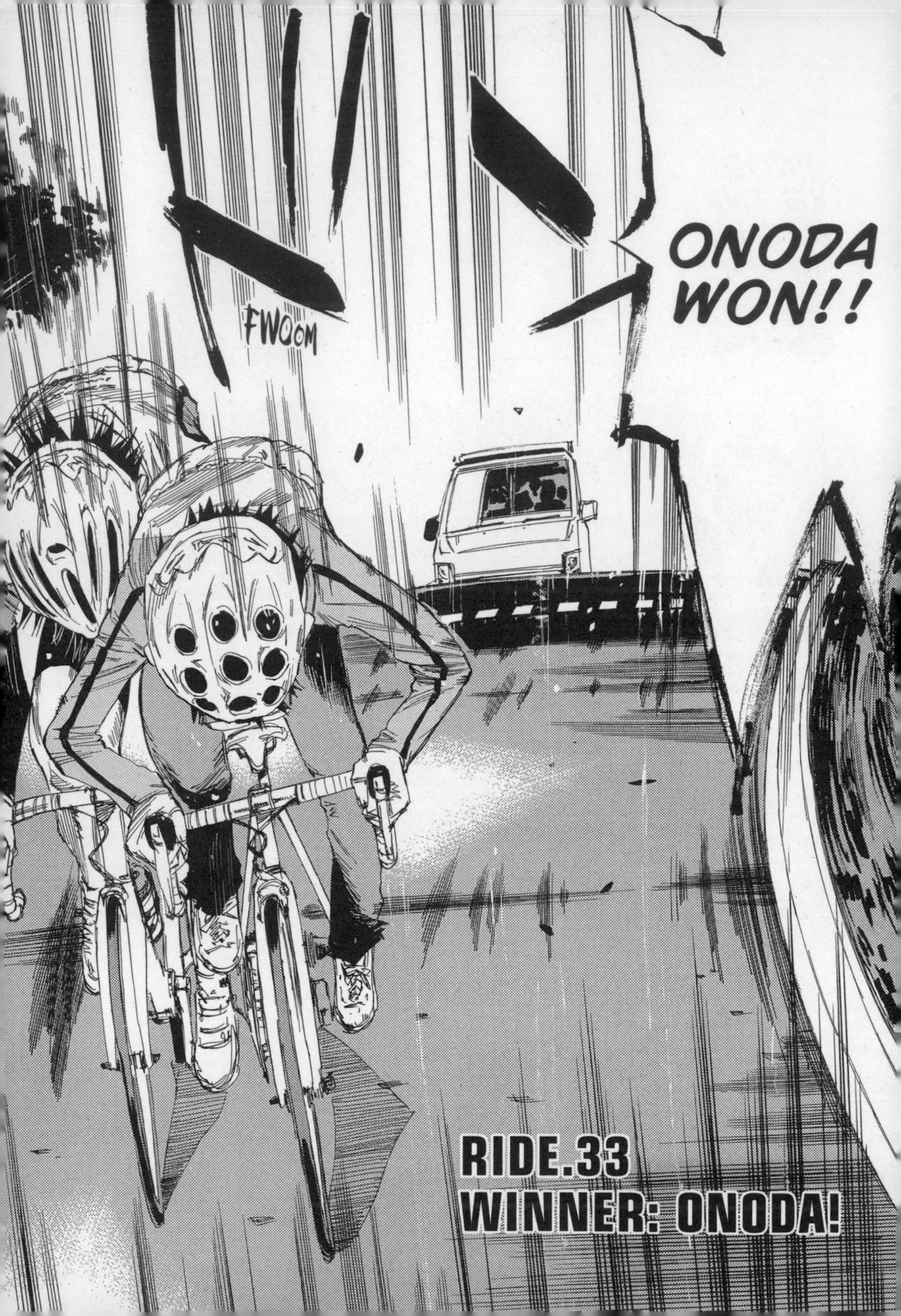
ONODA WON!!
FWOOM
RIDE.33
WINNER: ONODA!

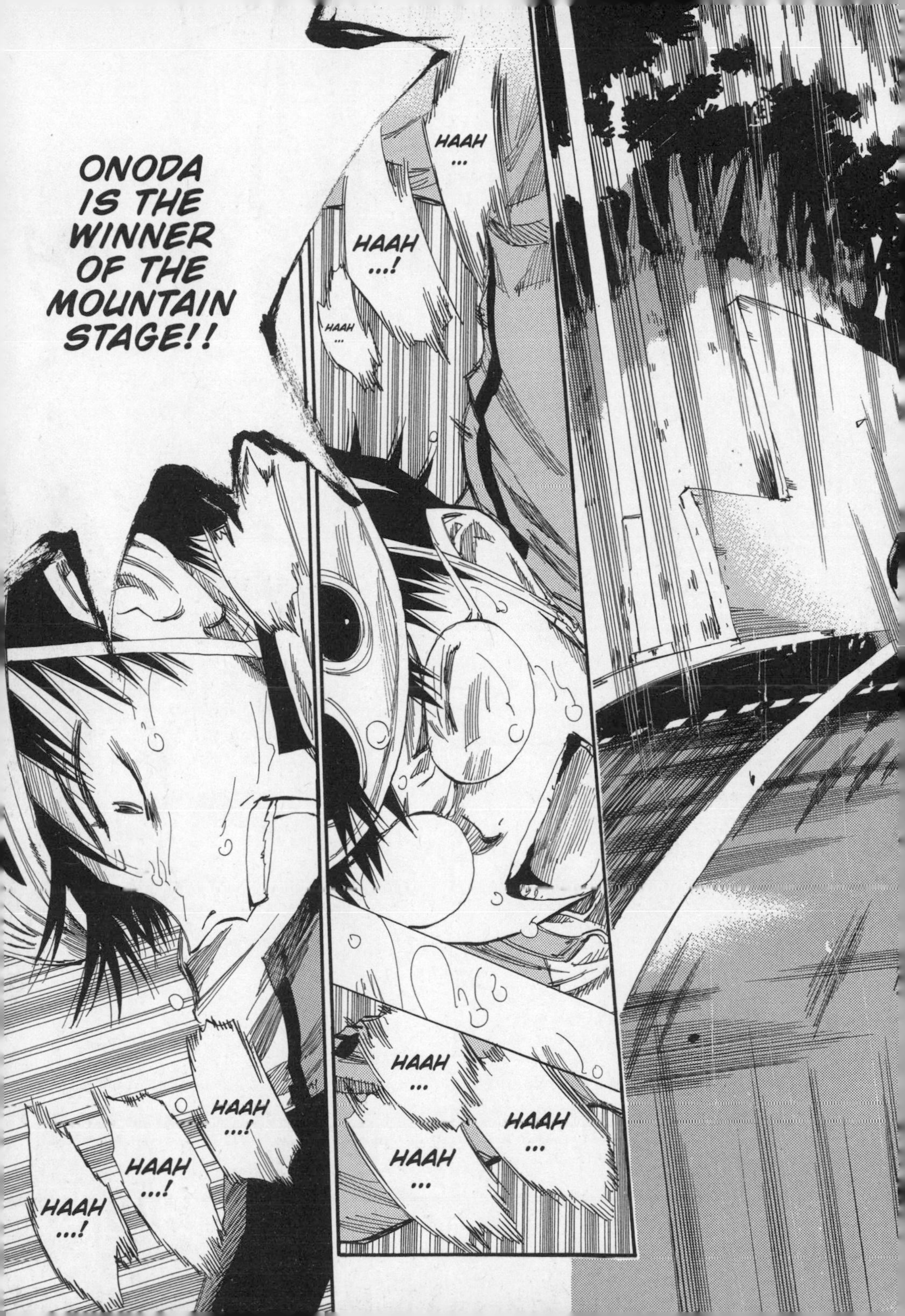
HAAH ...
HAAH ...!
HAAH ...
ONODA IS THE WINNER OF THE MOUNTAIN STAGE!!
HAAH ...
HAAH ...
HAAH ...
HAAH ...!
HAAH ...!
HAAH ...!

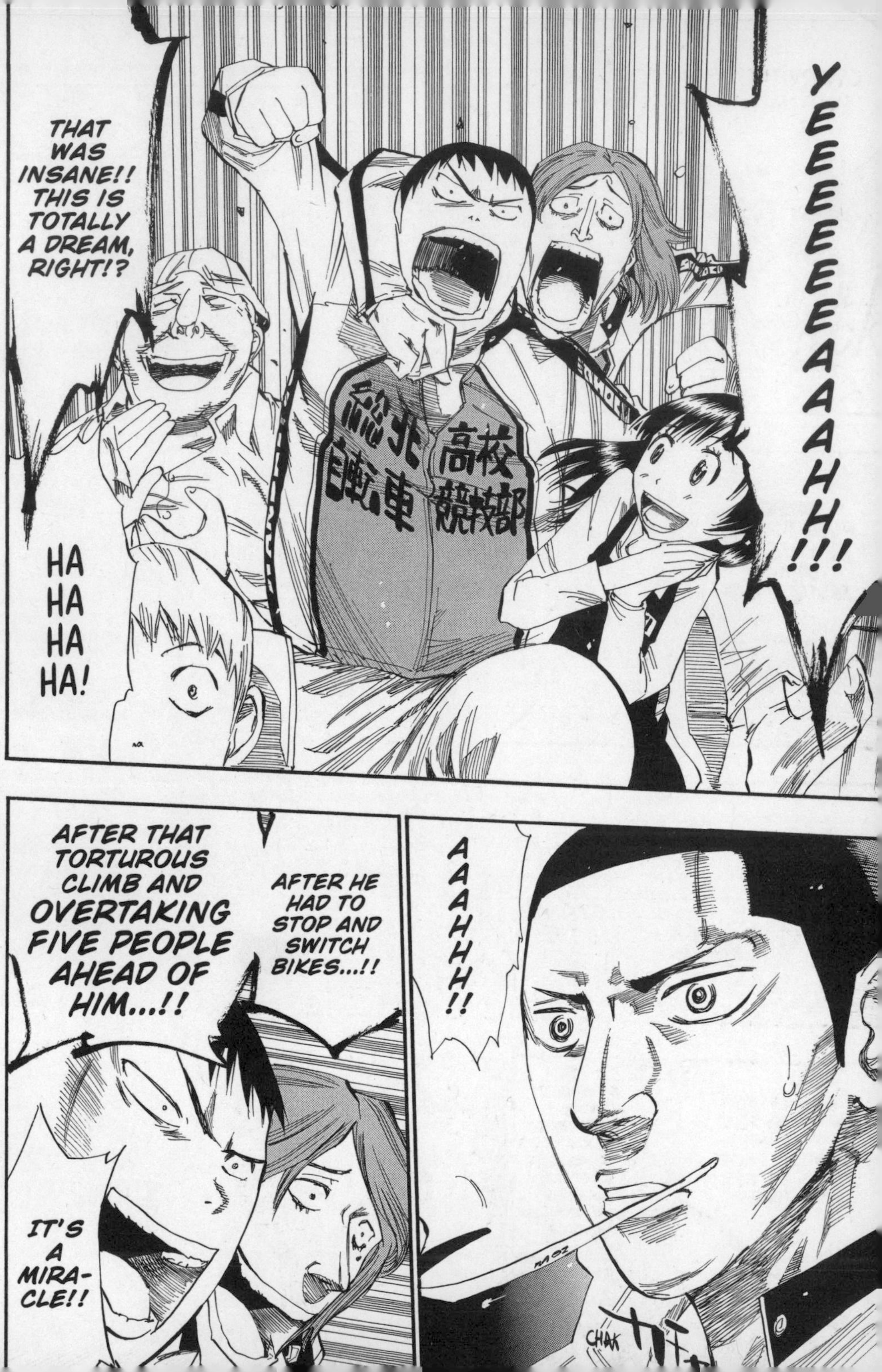
YEEEEEEAAAHH!!!
THAT WAS INSANE!! THIS IS TOTALLY A DREAM, RIGHT!?
総北高校
自転車競技部
HA HA HA HA!
AAAHHH!!
CHAK
AFTER HE HAD TO STOP AND SWITCH BIKES...!!
AFTER THAT TORTUROUS CLIMB AND OVERTAKING FIVE PEOPLE AHEAD OF HIM...!!
IT'S A MIRACLE!!

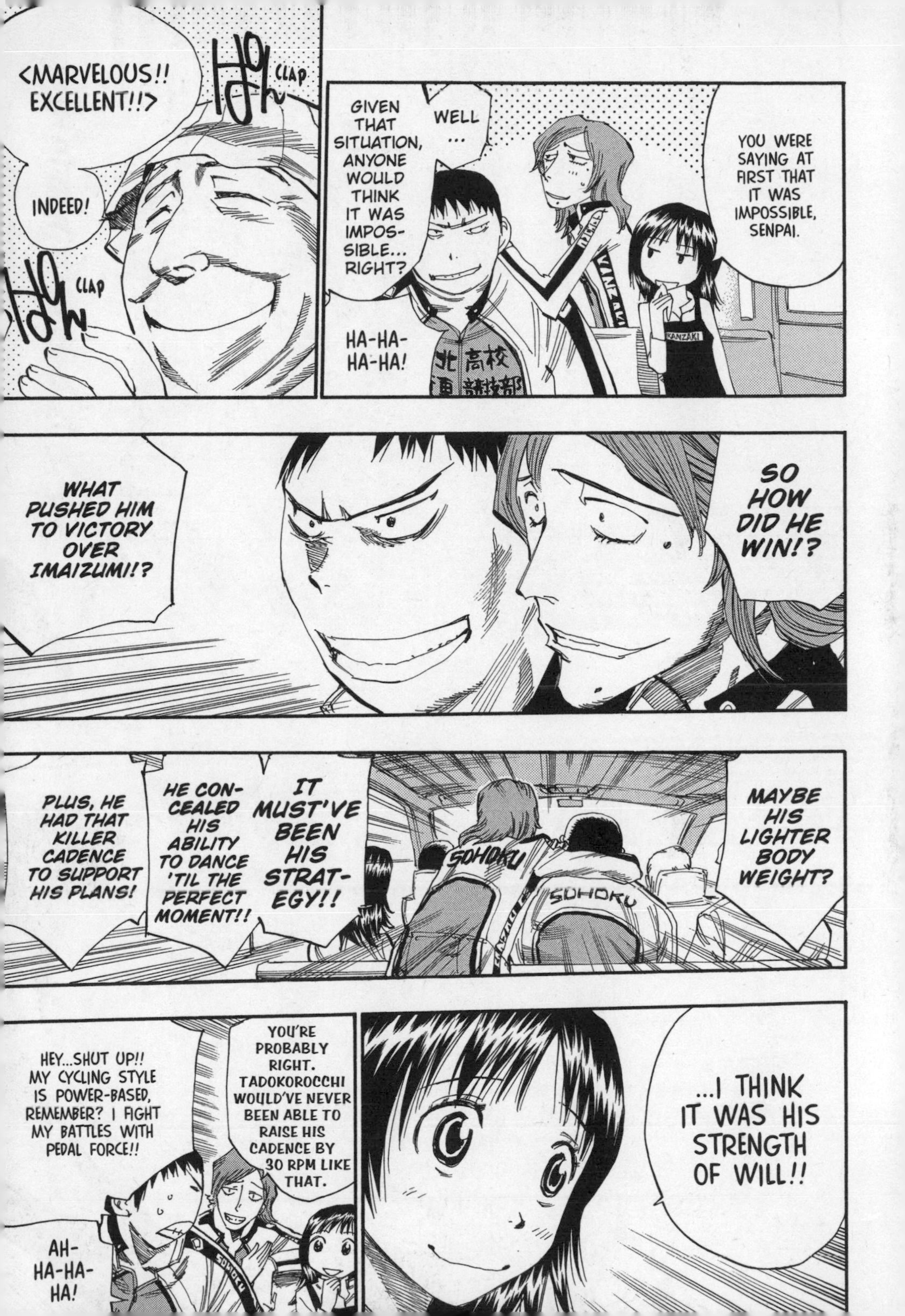
YOU WERE SAYING AT FIRST THAT IT WAS IMPOSSIBLE, SENPAI.
WELL ...
GIVEN THAT SITUATION, ANYONE WOULD THINK IT WAS IMPOSSIBLE... RIGHT?
HA-HA-HA-HA!
KANZAKI
<MARVELOUS!! EXCELLENT!!>
CLAP
INDEED!
CLAP
SO HOW DID HE WIN!?
WHAT PUSHED HIM TO VICTORY OVER IMAIZUMI!?
MAYBE HIS LIGHTER BODY WEIGHT?
IT MUST'VE BEEN HIS STRATEGY!!
HE CONCEALED HIS ABILITY TO DANCE 'TIL THE PERFECT MOMENT!!
PLUS, HE HAD THAT KILLER CADENCE TO SUPPORT HIS PLANS!
SOHOKU
SOHOKU
...I THINK IT WAS HIS STRENGTH OF WILL!!
YOU'RE PROBABLY RIGHT. TADOKOROCCHI WOULD'VE NEVER BEEN ABLE TO RAISE HIS CADENCE BY 30 RPM LIKE THAT.
HEY...SHUT UP!! MY CYCLING STYLE IS POWER-BASED, REMEMBER? I FIGHT MY BATTLES WITH PEDAL FORCE!!
AH-HA-HA-HA!

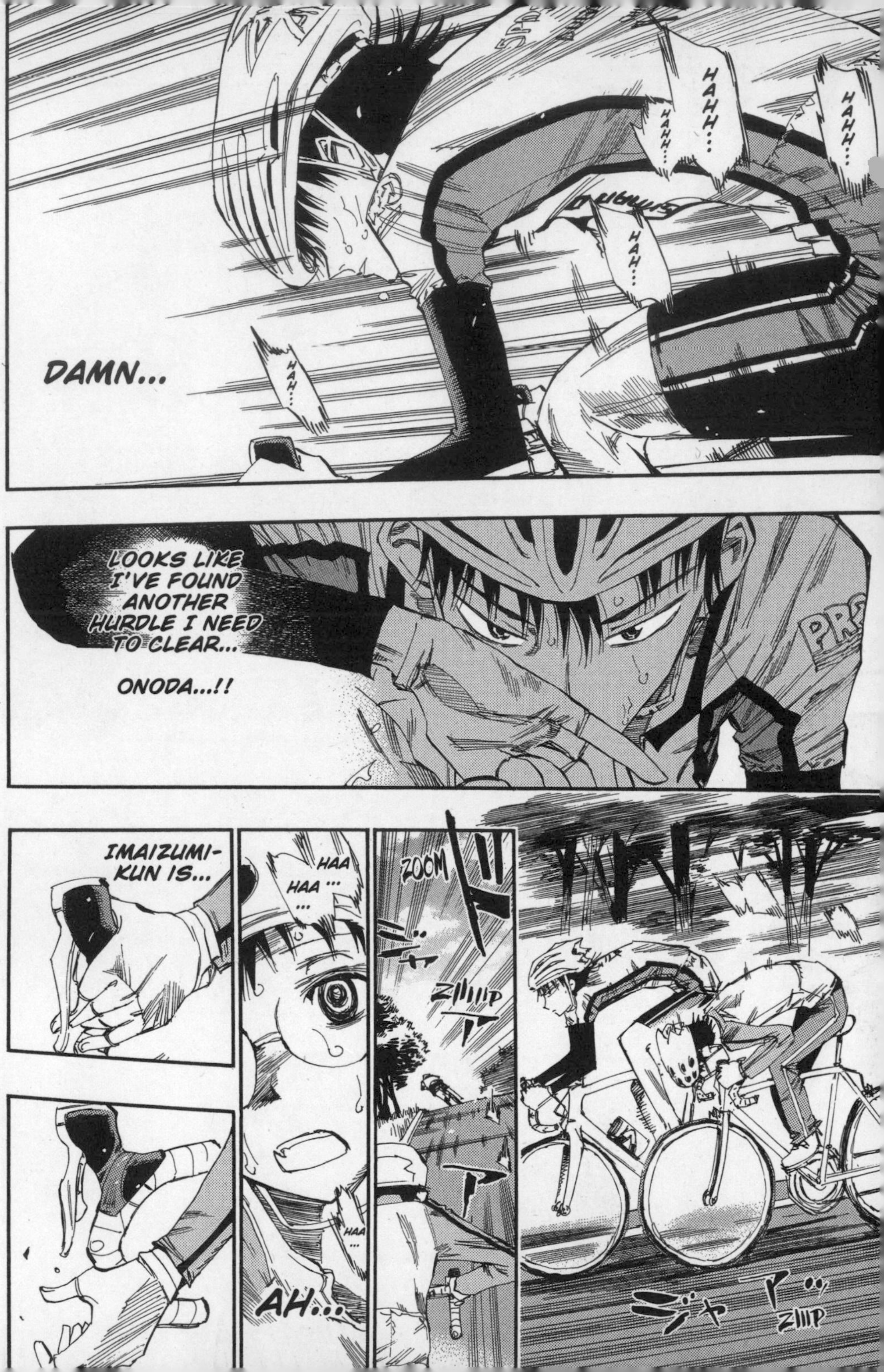
HAHH...
HAHH...
HAHH...
HAH...
HAH...
DAMN...
LOOKS LIKE I'VE FOUND ANOTHER HURDLE I NEED TO CLEAR...
ONODA...!!
ZIIIP
ZOOM
ZIIIIP
HAA
HAA ...
...
AH...
HAA ...
IMAIZUMI-KUN IS...

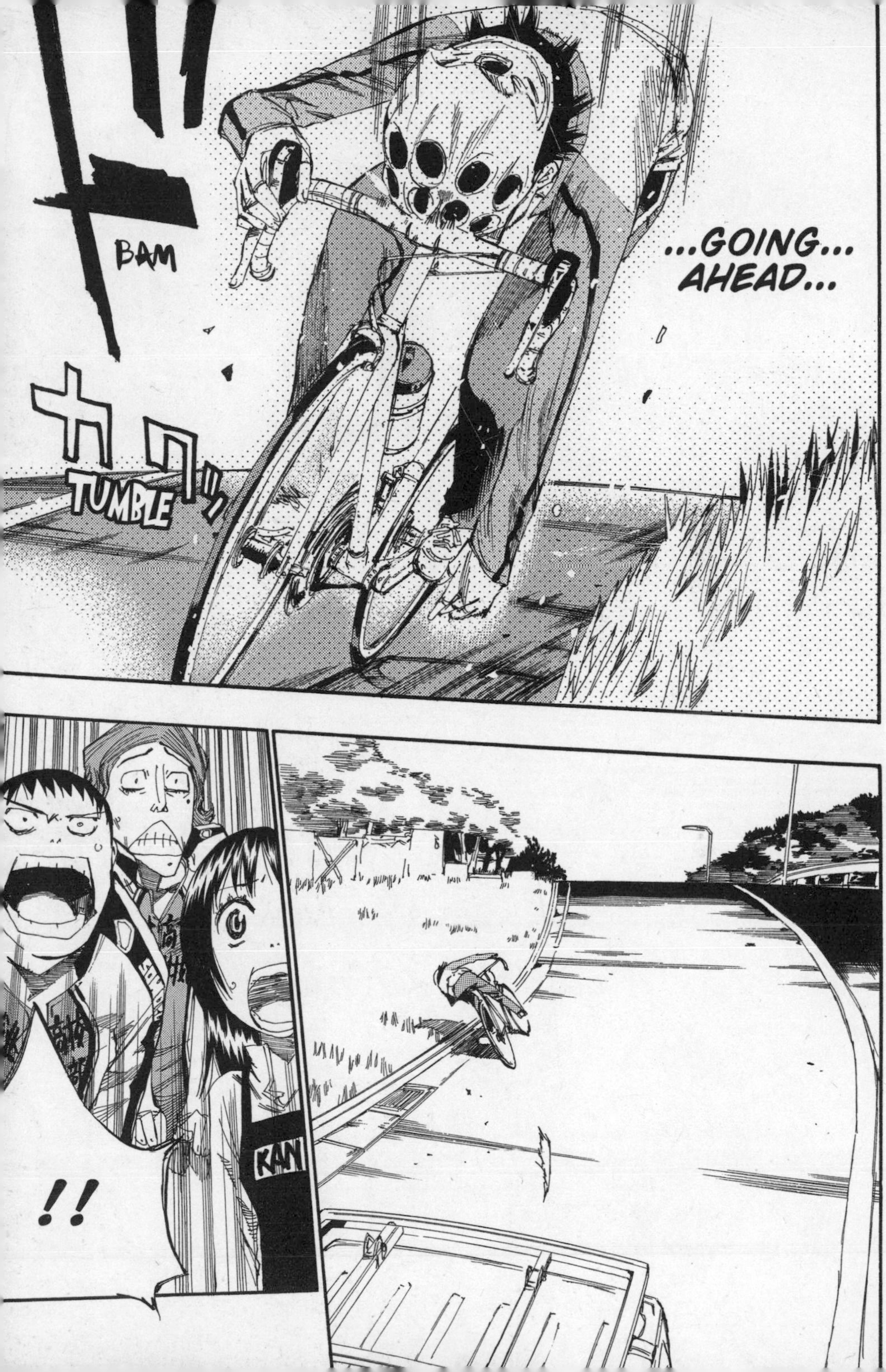
...GOING... AHEAD...
BAM
TUMBLE
!!

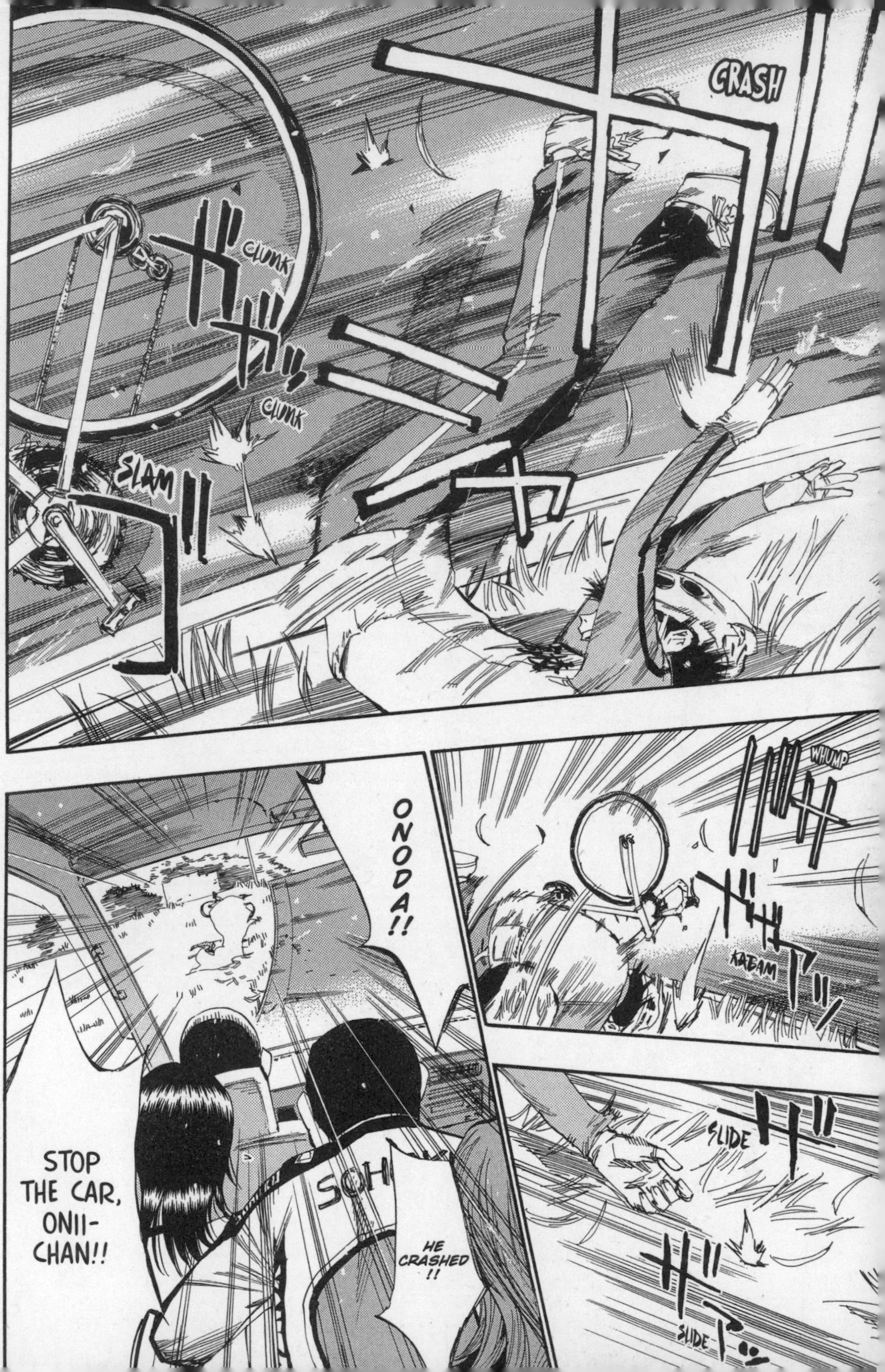
CRASH
CLUNK
CLUNK
SLAM
WHUMP
KABAM
SLIDE
SLIDE
ONODA!!
STOP THE CAR, ONII-CHAN!!
HE CRASHED!!
SOH

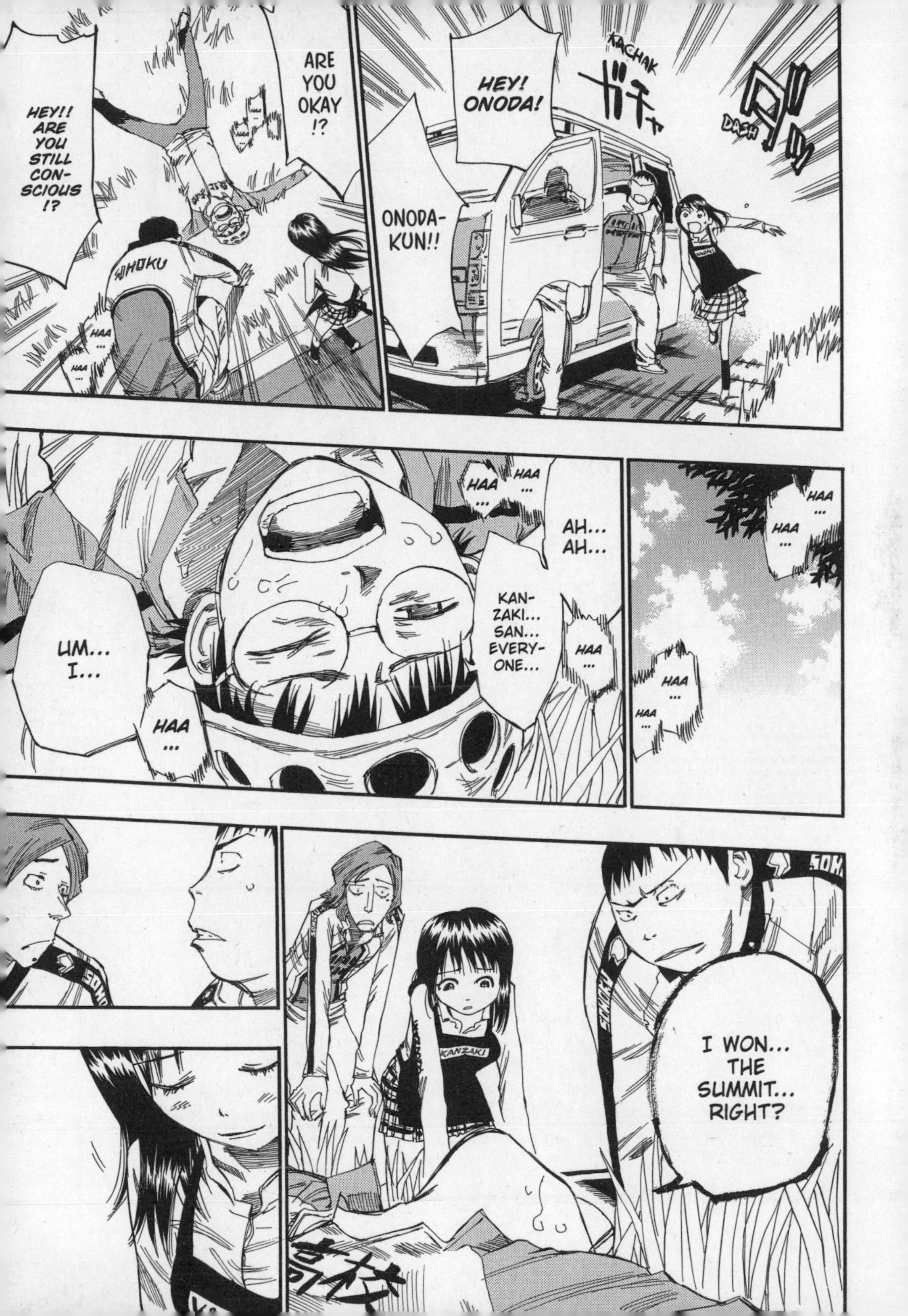
KACHAK
DASH
HEY! ONODA!
ONODA-KUN!!
ARE YOU OKAY !?
HAA ... HAA ...
HEY!! ARE YOU STILL CON-SCIOUS !?
HAA ...
HAA ...
HAA ...
HAA ...
HAA ...
HAA ...
HAA ...
HAA ...
HAA ...
AH... AH...
KAN-ZAKI... SAN... EVERY-ONE...
HAA ...
UM... I...
HAA ...
I WON... THE SUMMIT... RIGHT?

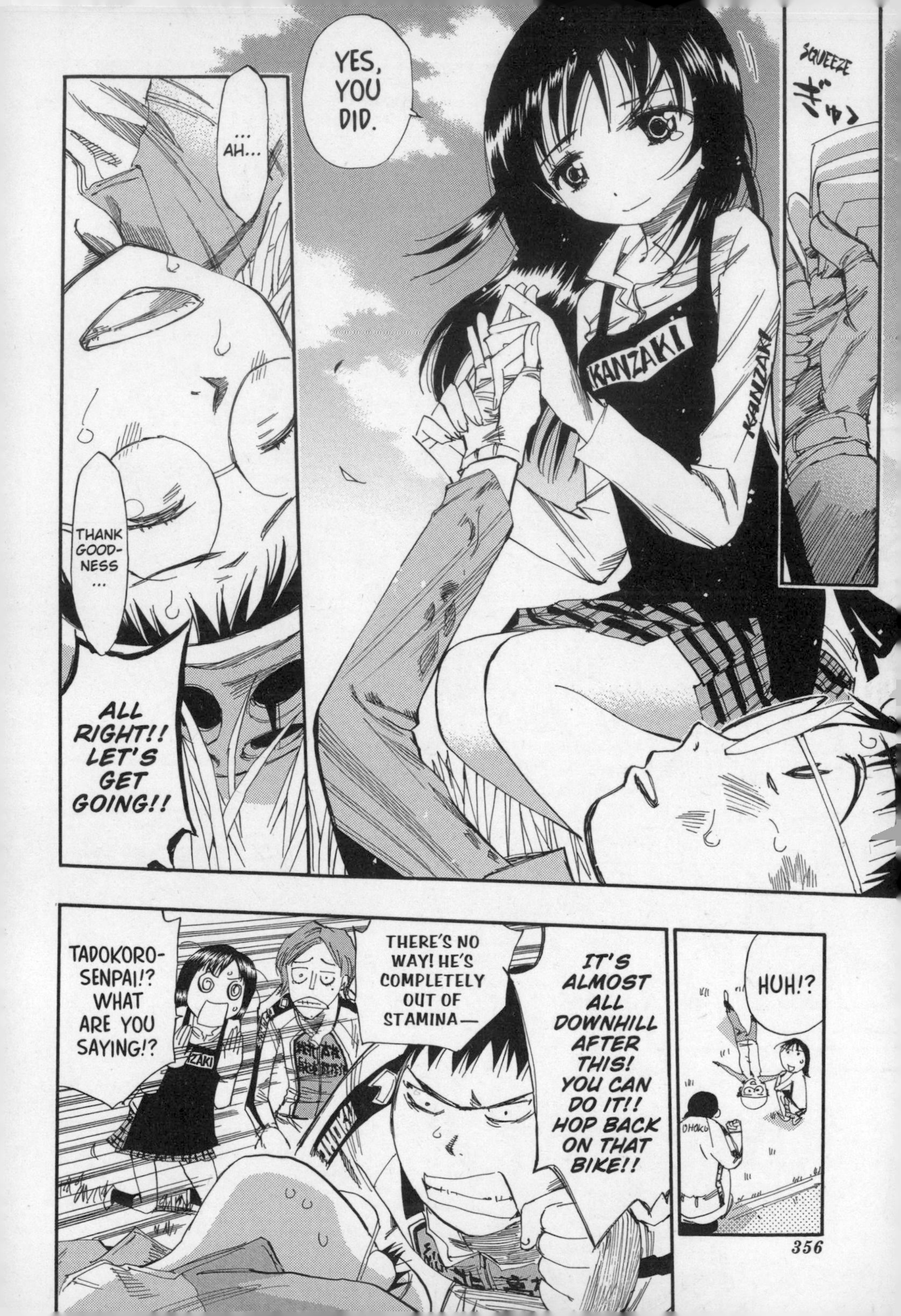
SQUEEZE
YES, YOU DID.
... AH...
THANK GOODNESS ...
ALL RIGHT!! LET'S GET GOING!!
HUH!?
IT'S ALMOST ALL DOWNHILL AFTER THIS! YOU CAN DO IT!! HOP BACK ON THAT BIKE!!
THERE'S NO WAY! HE'S COMPLETELY OUT OF STAMINA—
TADOKORO-SENPAI!? WHAT ARE YOU SAYING!?

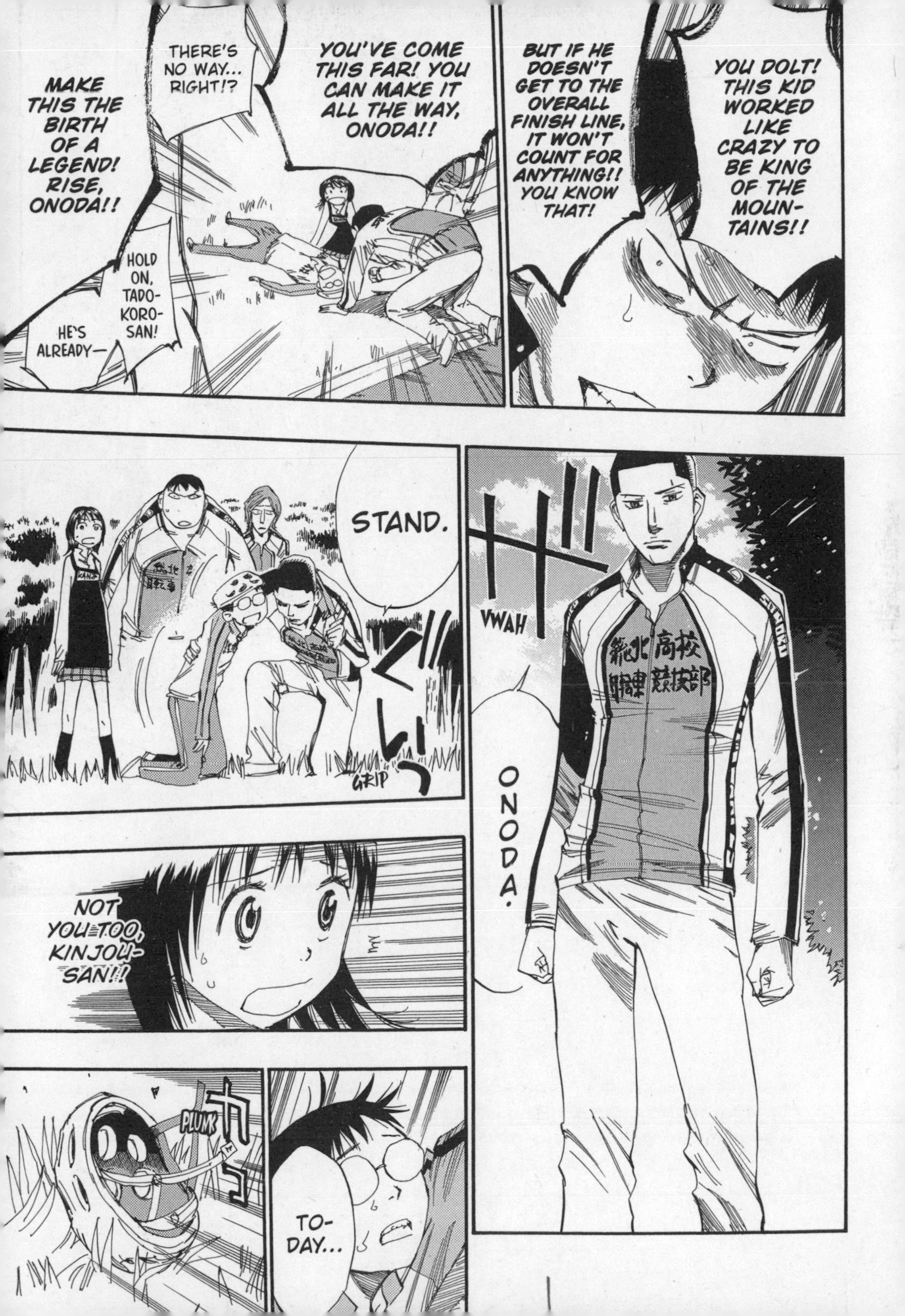
YOU DOLT! THIS KID WORKED LIKE CRAZY TO BE KING OF THE MOUNTAINS!!
BUT IF HE DOESN'T GET TO THE OVERALL FINISH LINE, IT WON'T COUNT FOR ANYTHING!! YOU KNOW THAT!
YOU'VE COME THIS FAR! YOU CAN MAKE IT ALL THE WAY, ONODA!!
THERE'S NO WAY... RIGHT!?
MAKE THIS THE BIRTH OF A LEGEND! RISE, ONODA!!
HOLD ON, TADOKORO-SAN!
HE'S ALREADY—
VWAH
ONODA.
STAND.
GRIP
NOT YOU TOO, KINJOU-SAN!!
TO-DAY...
PLUNK

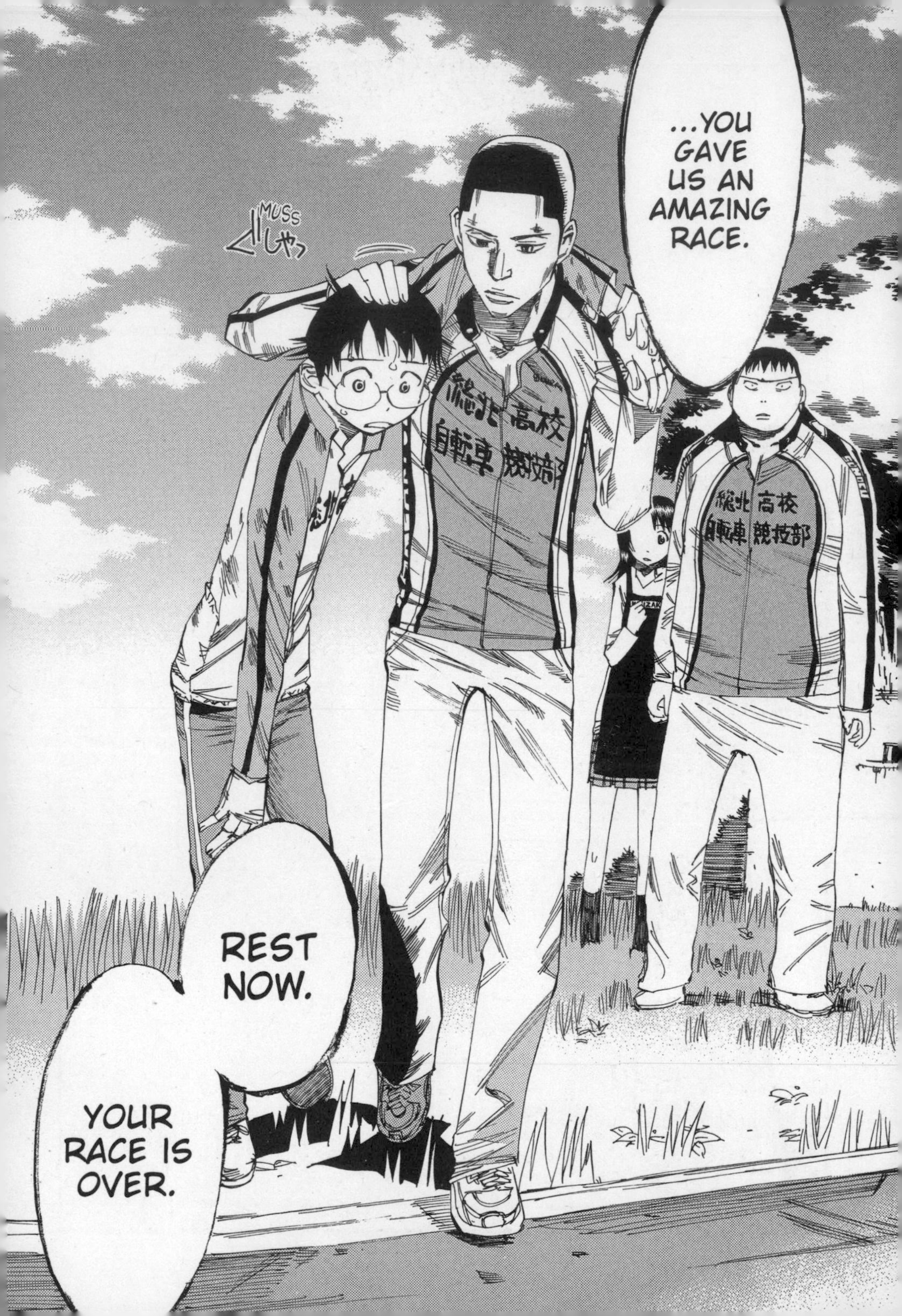
...YOU GAVE US AN AMAZING RACE.
MUSS
くしゃっ
総北高校 自転車競技部
REST NOW.
YOUR RACE IS OVER.

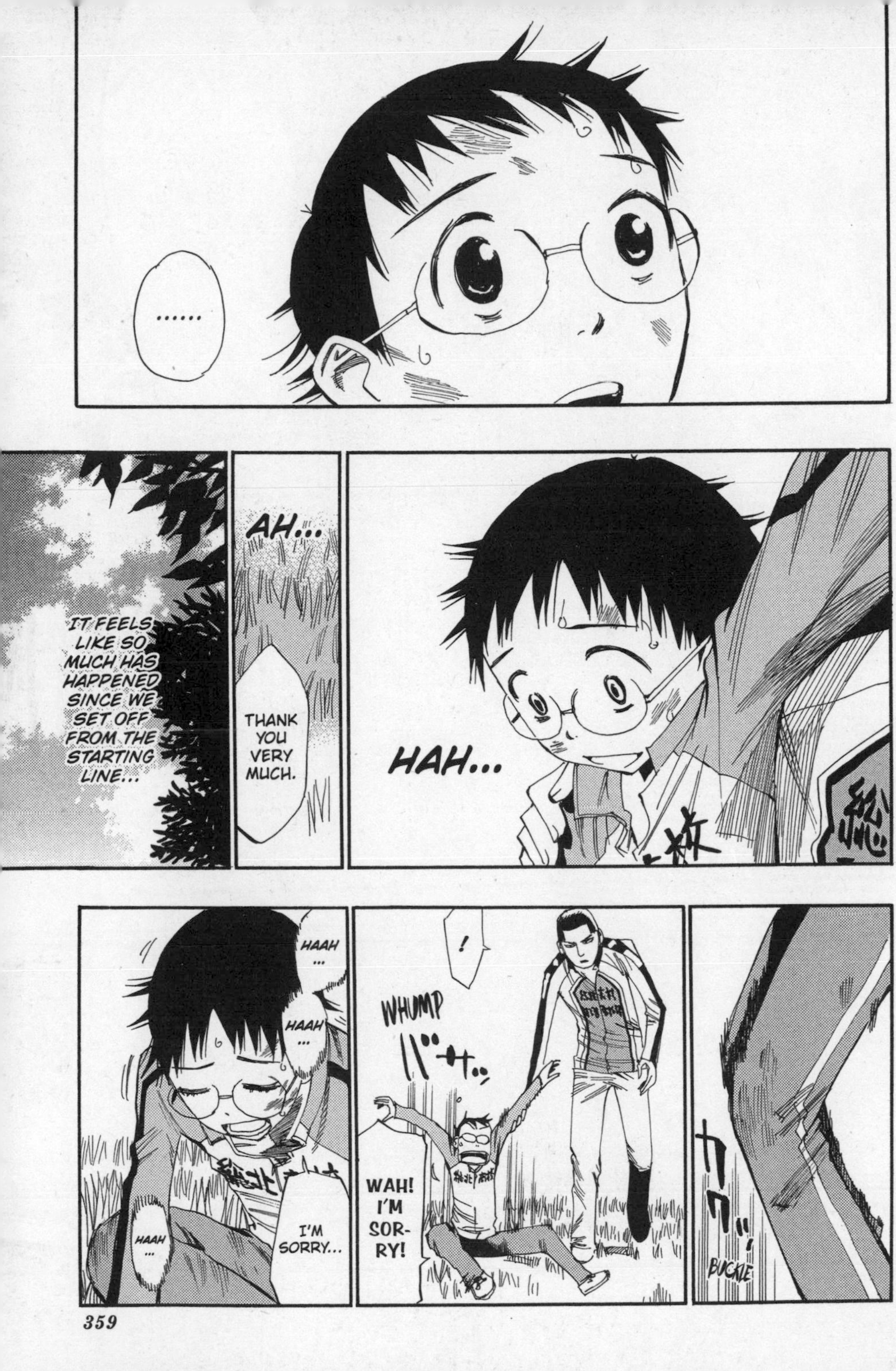
......
HAH...
AH...
THANK YOU VERY MUCH.
IT FEELS LIKE SO MUCH HAS HAPPENED SINCE WE SET OFF FROM THE STARTING LINE...
BUCKLE
!
WHUMP
WAH! I'M SORRY!
HAAH...
HAAH...
I'M SORRY...
HAAH...

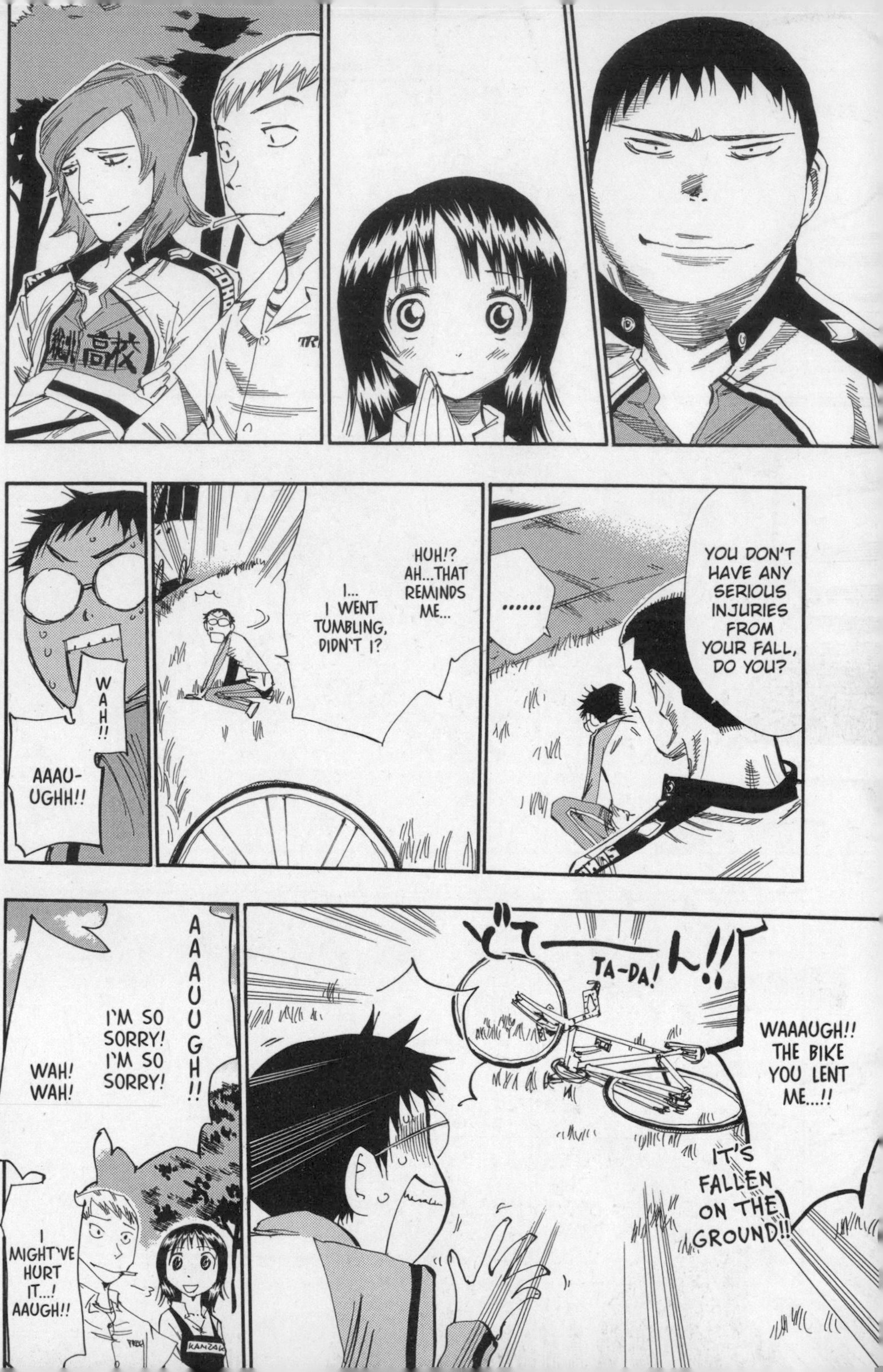

YOU DON'T HAVE ANY SERIOUS INJURIES FROM YOUR FALL, DO YOU?
......
HUH!? AH...THAT REMINDS ME...
I... I WENT TUMBLING, DIDN'T I?
WAH!!
AAAU-UGHH!!
どてーーん!!
TA-DA!
WAAAUGH!! THE BIKE YOU LENT ME...!!
IT'S FALLEN ON THE GROUND!!
AAAAUUGH!!
I'M SO SORRY! I'M SO SORRY!
WAH! WAH!
I MIGHT'VE HURT IT...! AAUGH!!

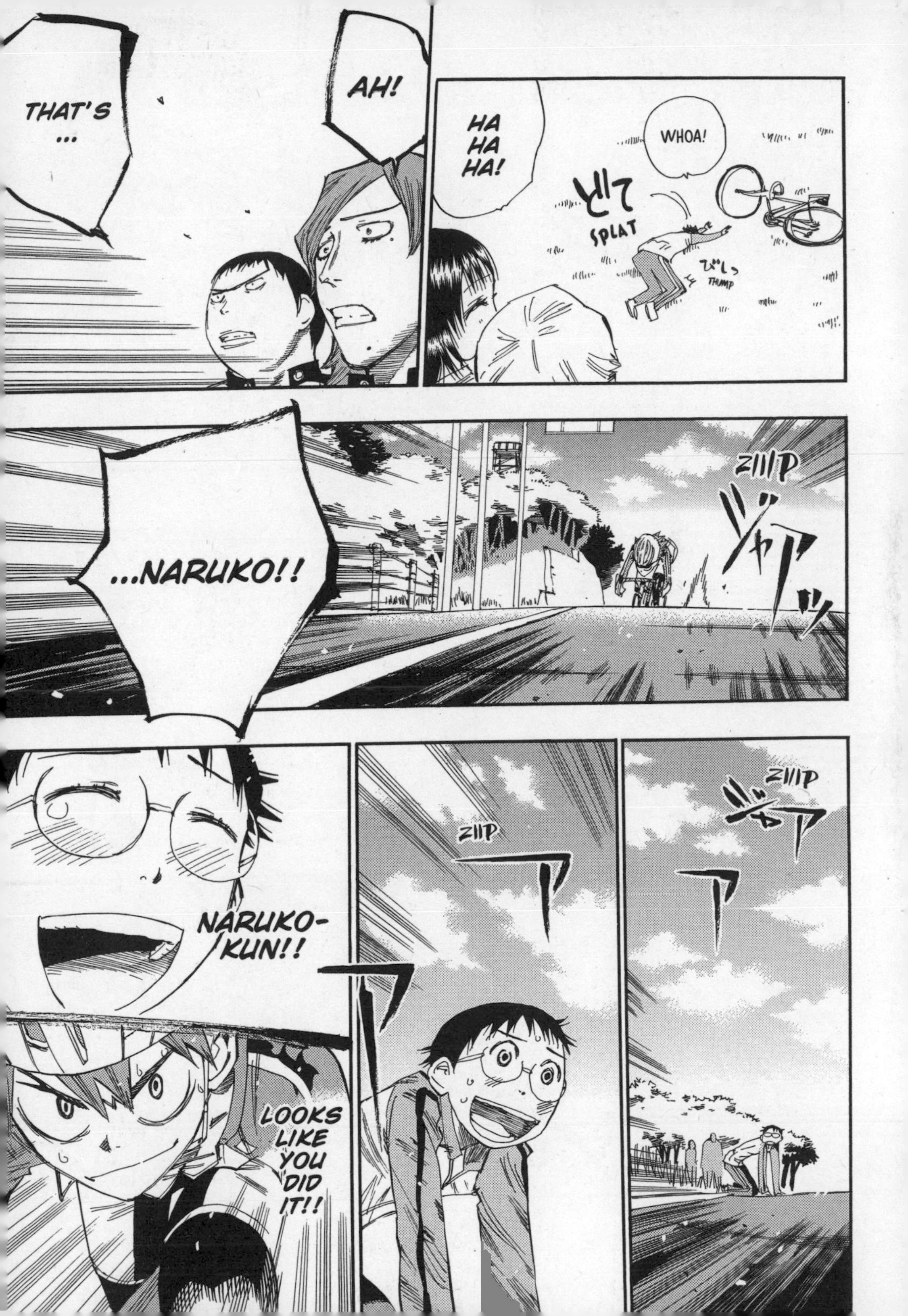
WHOA!
どて
SPLAT
びしっ
THUMP
HA HA HA!
AH!
THAT'S ...
ZIIP
ジャアッ
...NARUKO!!
ZIIP
ジャア
ZIIP
NARUKO-KUN!!
LOOKS LIKE YOU DID IT!!

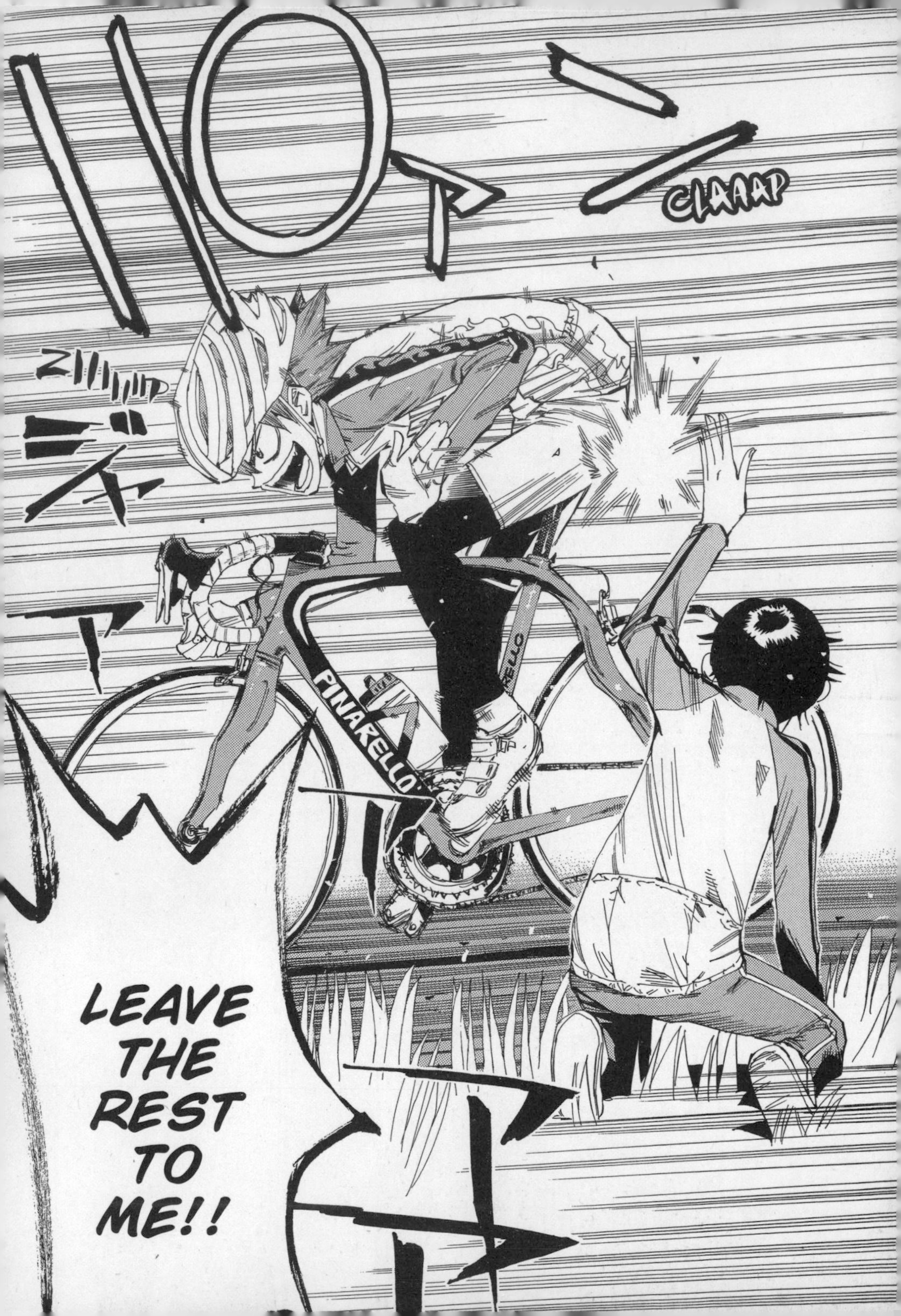
CLAAAP
ZIIIIIP
PINARELLO
LEAVE THE REST TO ME!!

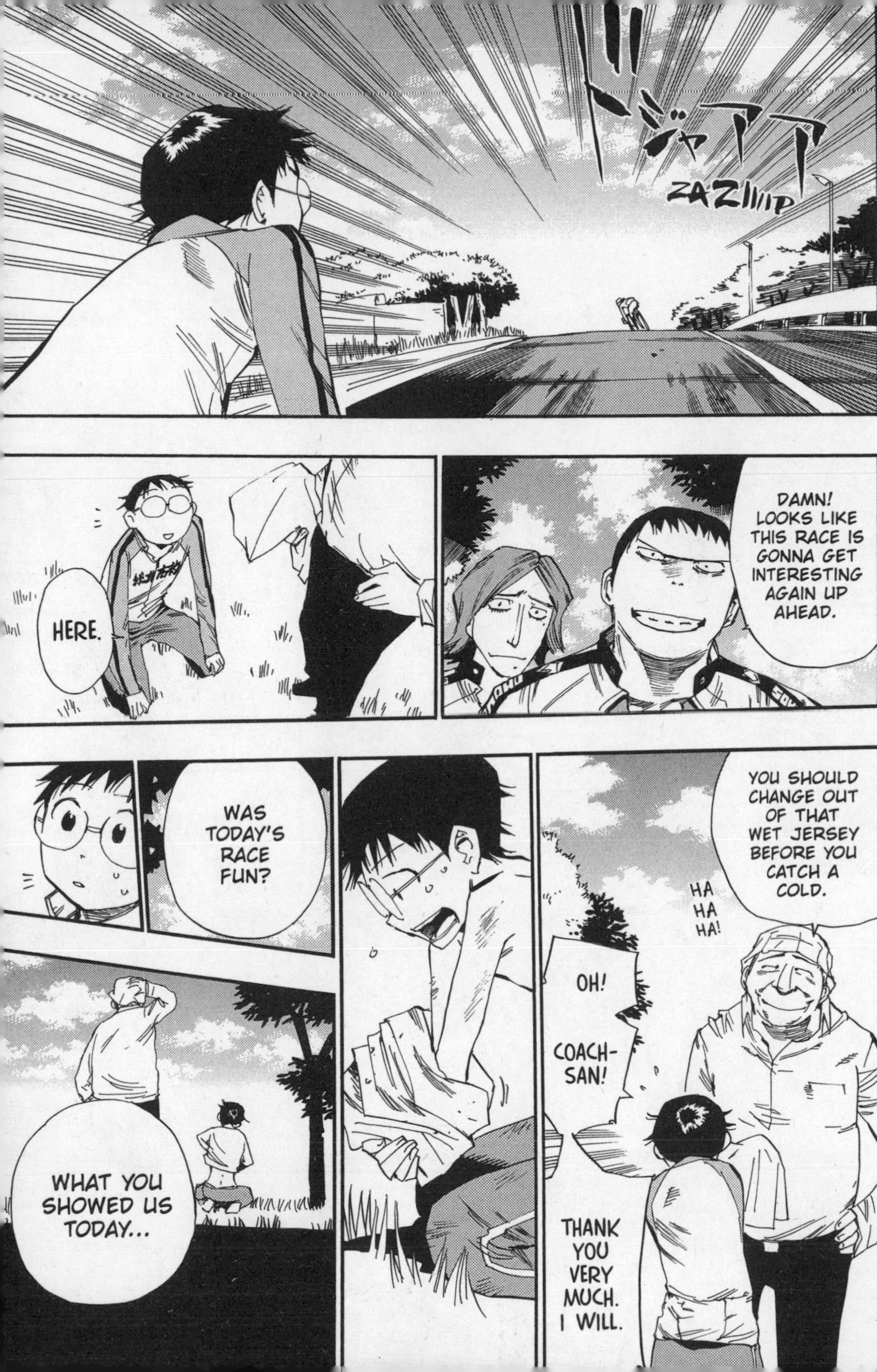
ジャアア
ZAZIIIIP
DAMN! LOOKS LIKE THIS RACE IS GONNA GET INTERESTING AGAIN UP AHEAD.
HERE.
YOU SHOULD CHANGE OUT OF THAT WET JERSEY BEFORE YOU CATCH A COLD.
HA HA HA!
OH!
COACH-SAN!
THANK YOU VERY MUCH. I WILL.
WAS TODAY'S RACE FUN?
WHAT YOU SHOWED US TODAY...

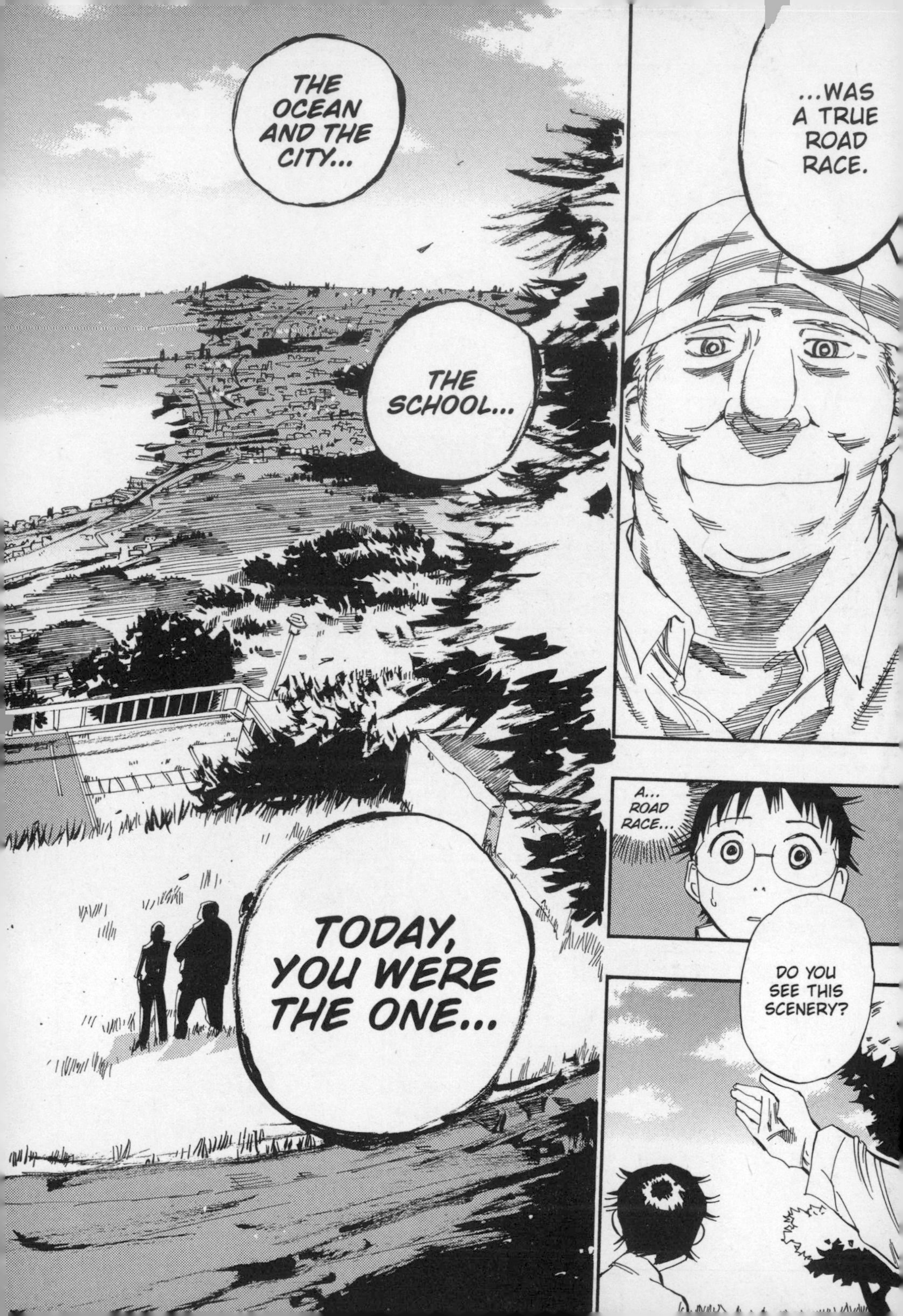
...WAS A TRUE ROAD RACE.
A... ROAD RACE...
DO YOU SEE THIS SCENERY?
THE OCEAN AND THE CITY...
THE SCHOOL...
TODAY, YOU WERE THE ONE...

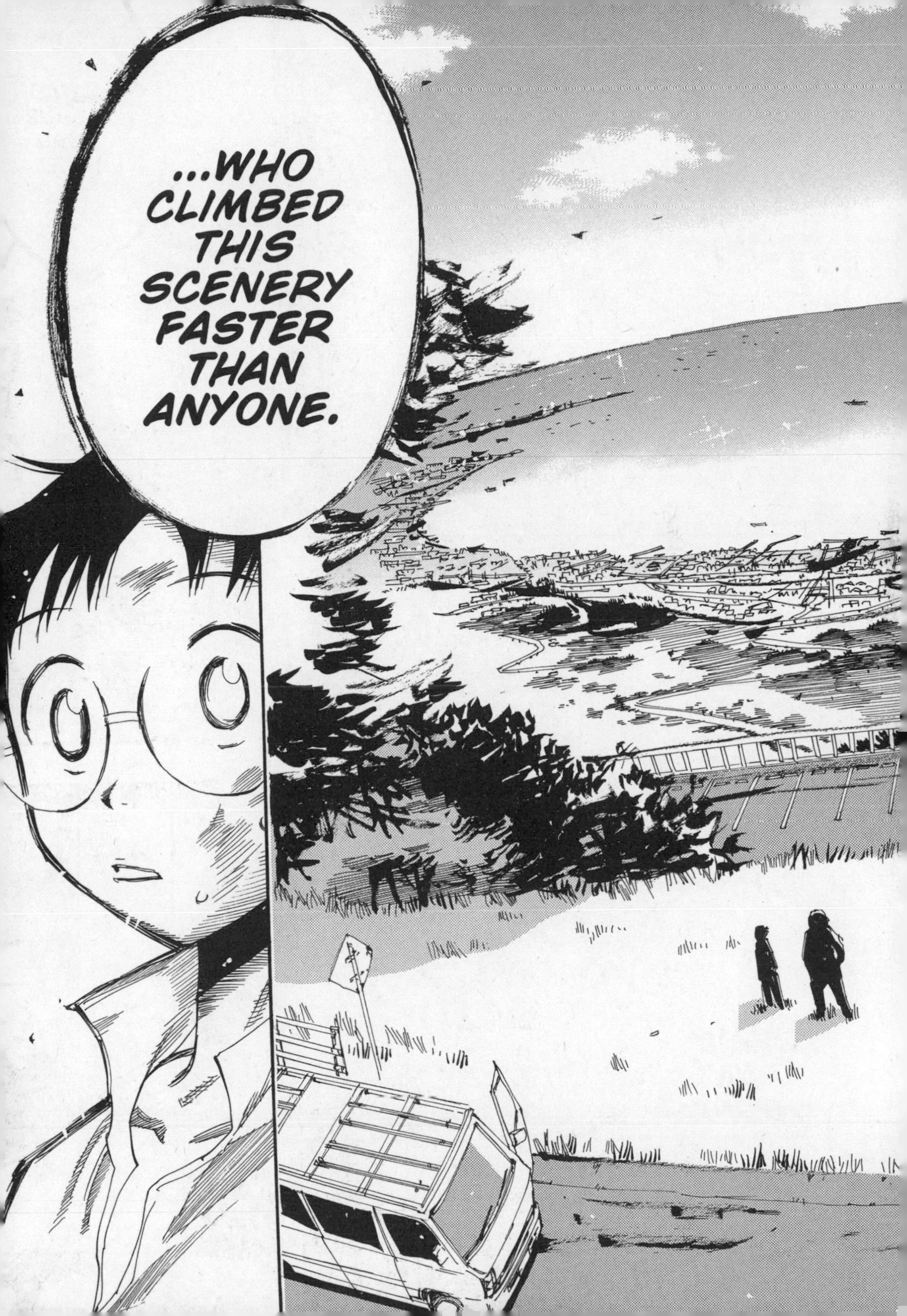
...WHO CLIMBED THIS SCENERY FASTER THAN ANYONE.

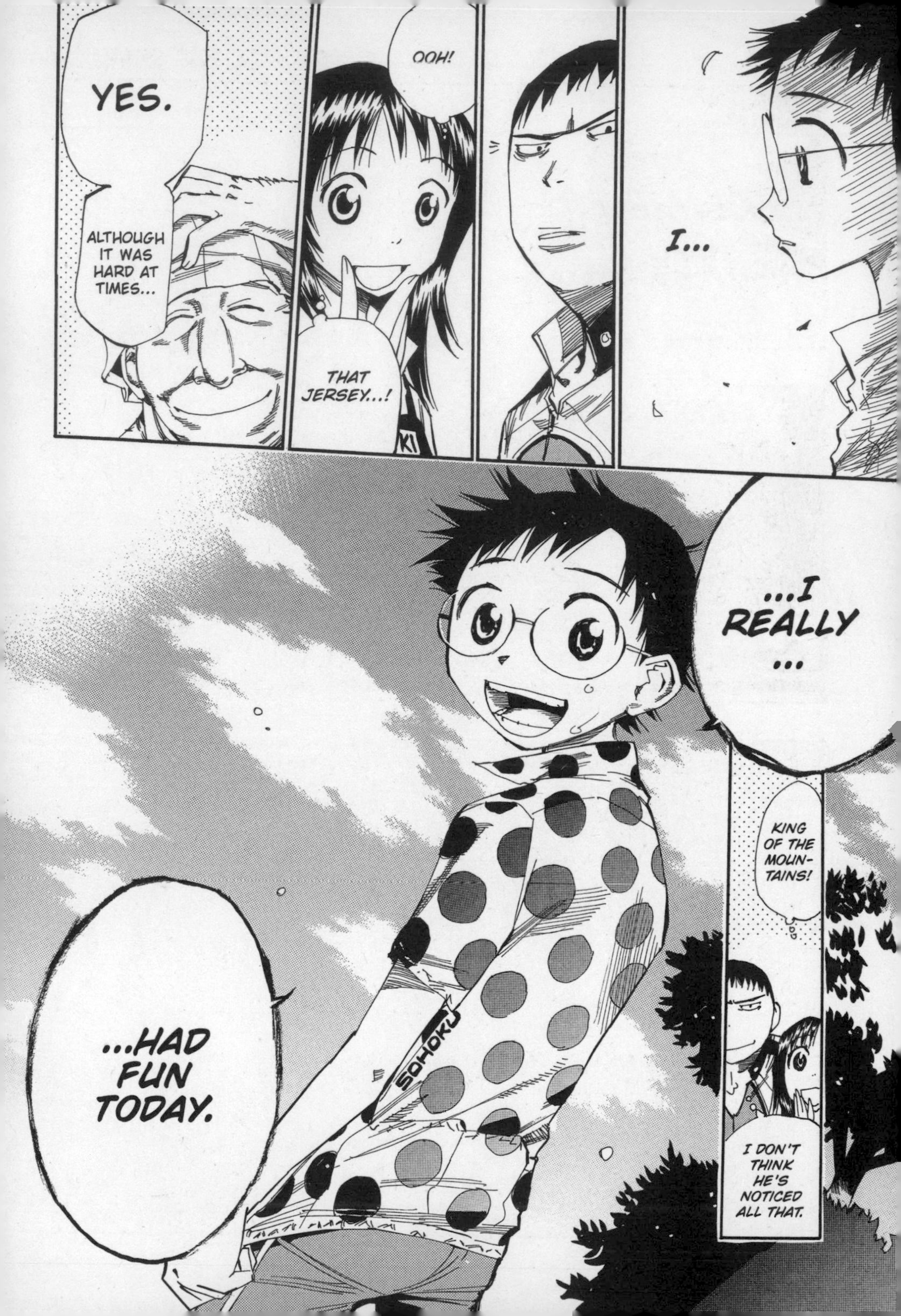
I...
OOH!
THAT JERSEY...!
YES.
ALTHOUGH IT WAS HARD AT TIMES...
...I REALLY ...
...HAD FUN TODAY.
SOHOKU
KING OF THE MOUN-TAINS!
I DON'T THINK HE'S NOTICED ALL THAT.

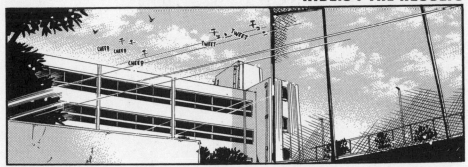

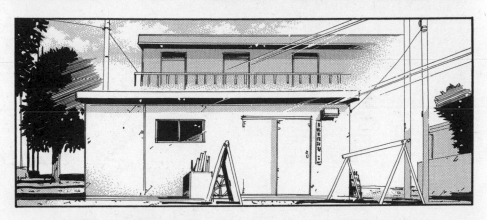

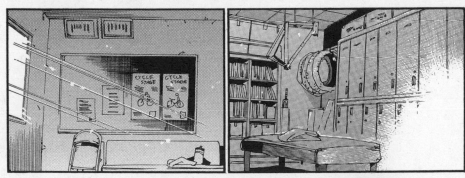

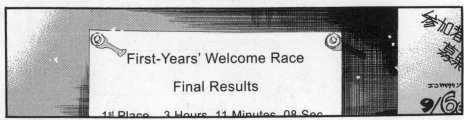

RIDE.34 THE RESULTS

TWEET
TWEET
CHEEP
CHEEP
CHEEP
CYCLE STAGE
CYCLE STAGE
First-Years' Welcome Race
Final Results
1st Place 3 Hours 11 Minutes 08 Sec

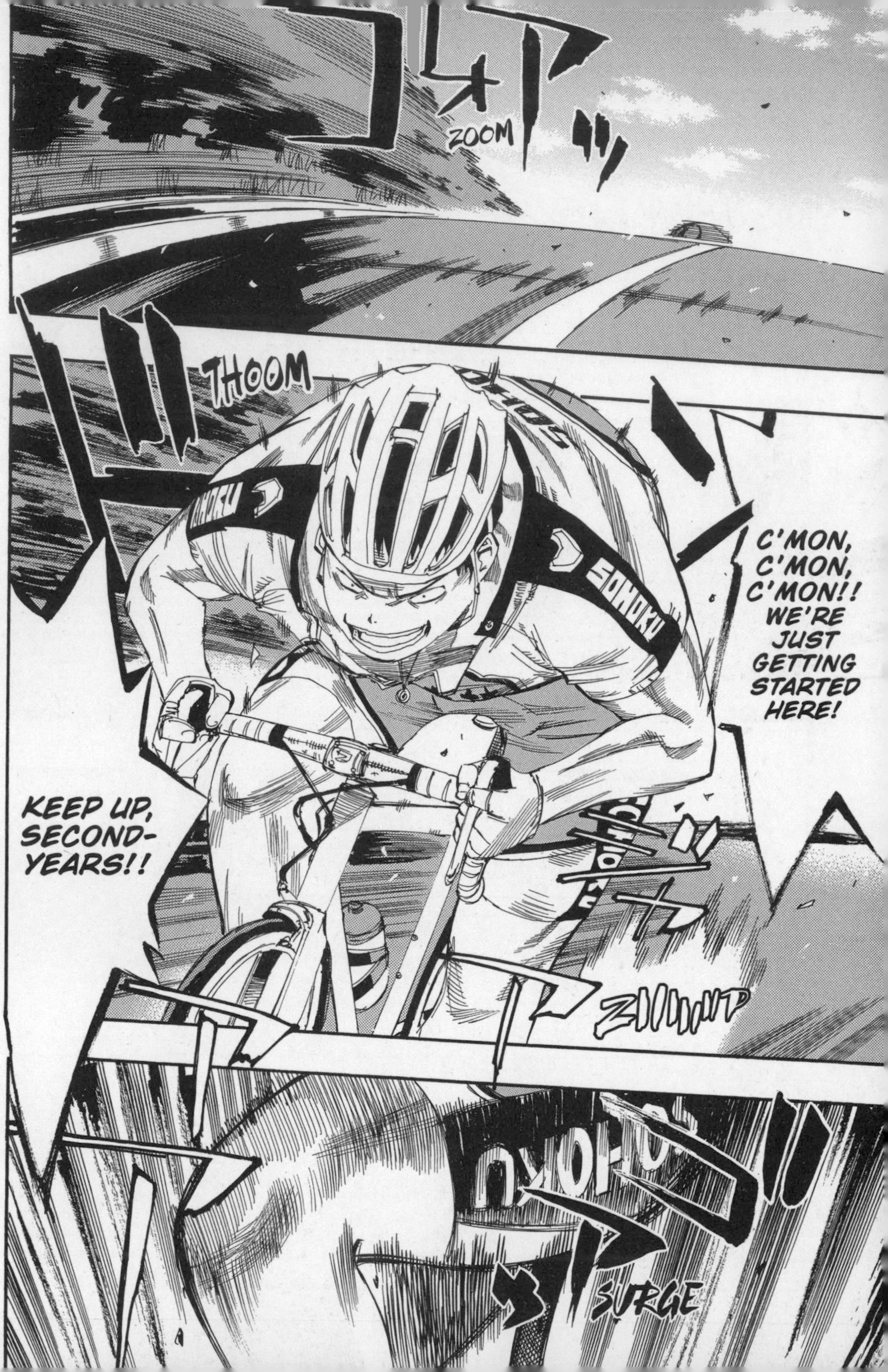
ZOOM
THOOM
C'MON, C'MON, C'MON!! WE'RE JUST GETTING STARTED HERE!
KEEP UP, SECOND-YEARS!!
ZIIIIIIIP
SURGE

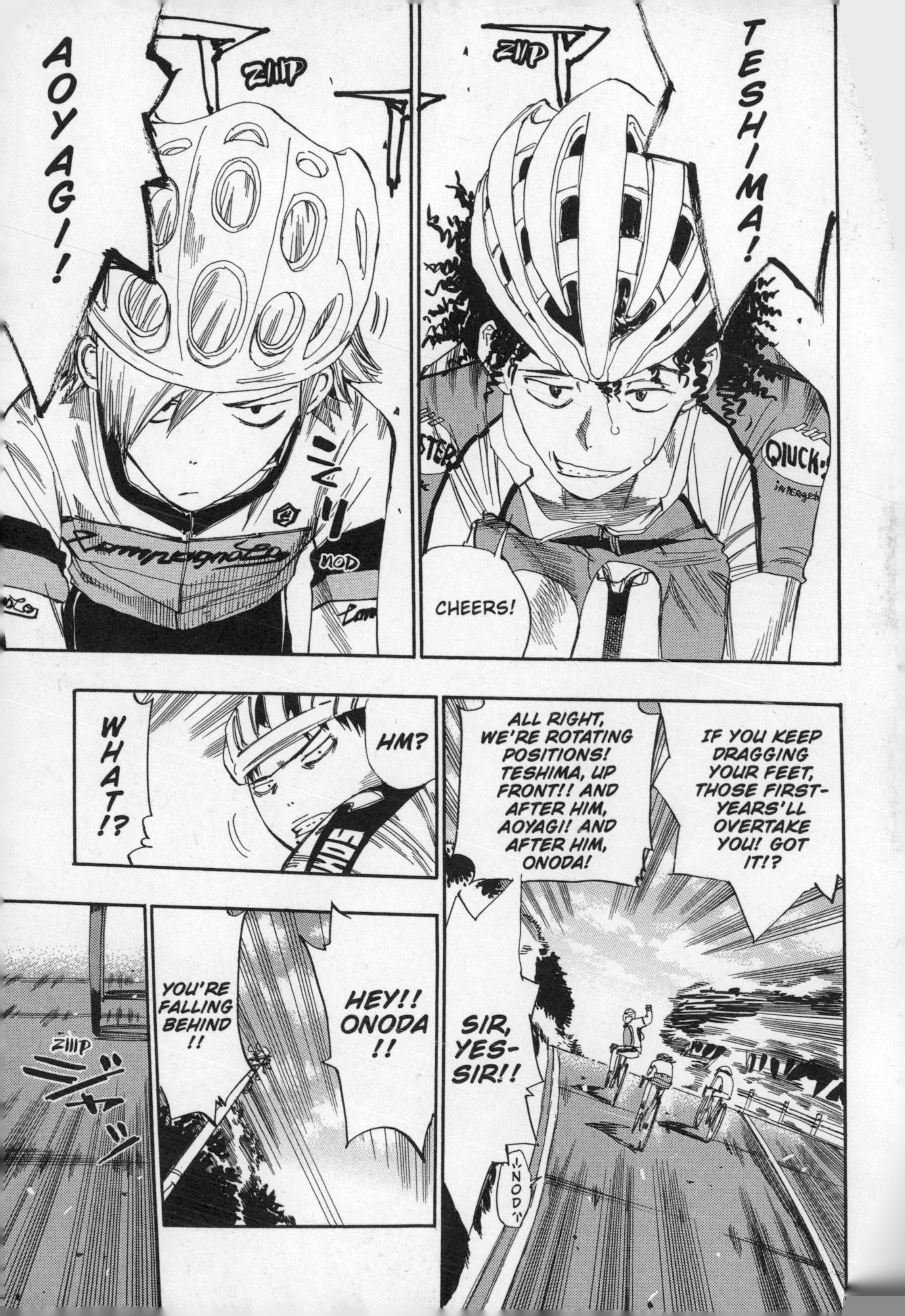
ZIIIP
TESHIMA!
CHEERS!
ZIIIP
AOYAGI!
NOD
IF YOU KEEP DRAGGING YOUR FEET, THOSE FIRST-YEARS'LL OVERTAKE YOU! GOT IT!?
ALL RIGHT, WE'RE ROTATING POSITIONS! TESHIMA, UP FRONT!! AND AFTER HIM, AOYAGI! AND AFTER HIM, ONODA!
HM?
WHAT!?
SIR, YES-SIR!!
NOD NOD
HEY!! ONODA!!
YOU'RE FALLING BEHIND!!
ZIIIP

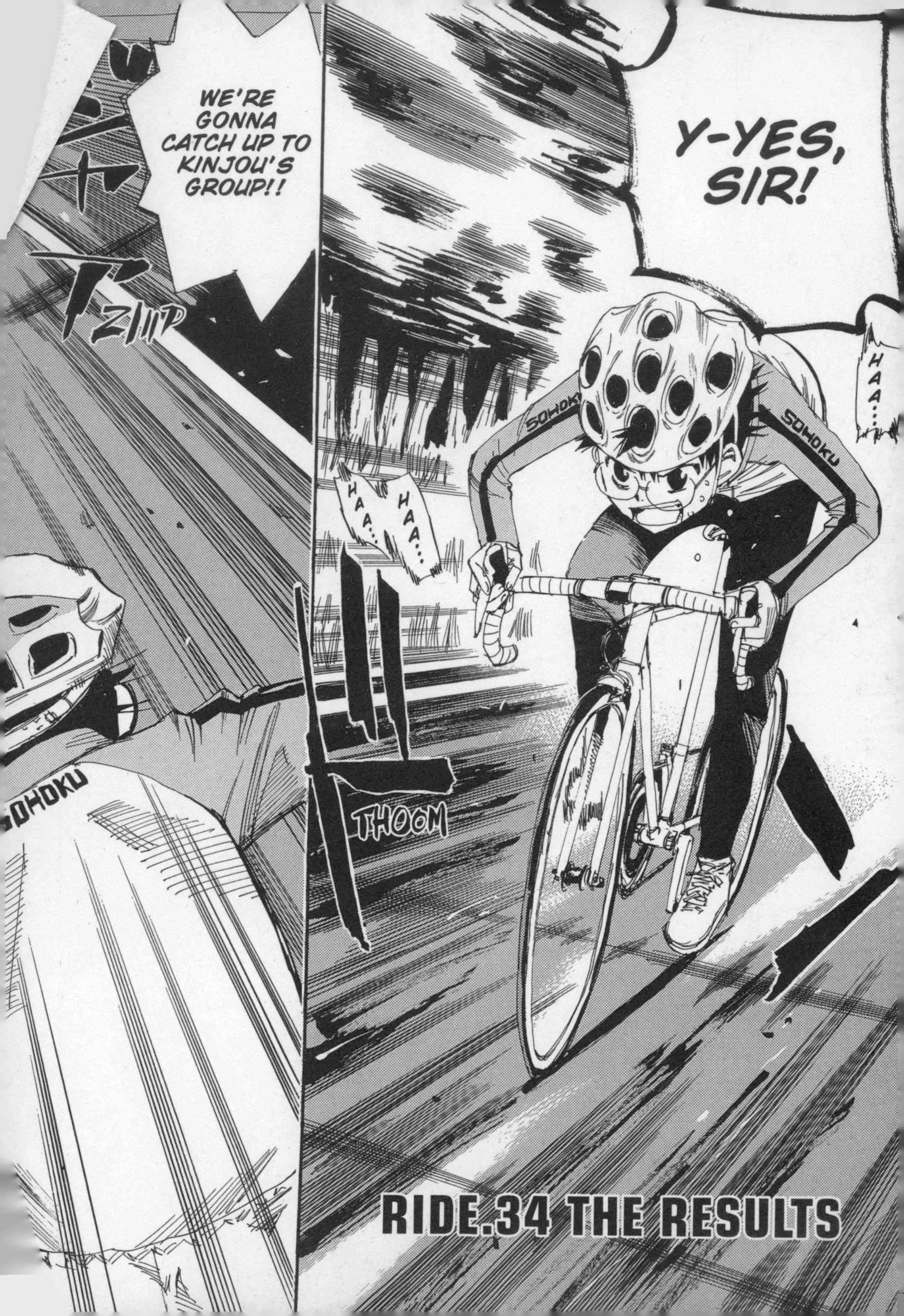
Y-YES, SIR!
HAA...
HAA... HAA...
THOOM
WE'RE GONNA CATCH UP TO KINJOU'S GROUP!!
ZIIIP

RIDE.34 THE RESULTS

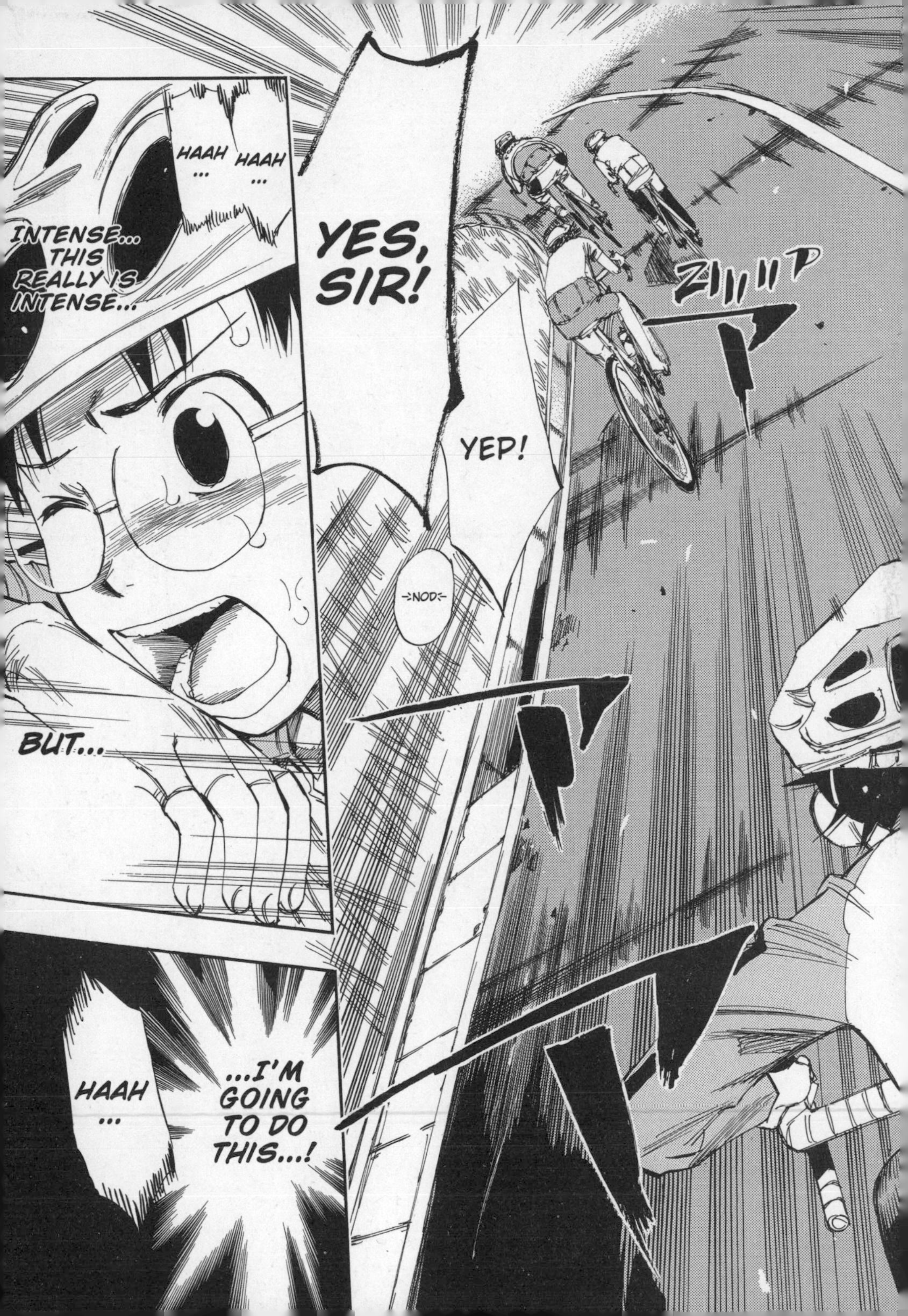
ZIIIIP
YES, SIR!
YEP!
NOD
HAAH... HAAH...
INTENSE... THIS REALLY IS INTENSE...
BUT...
...I'M GOING TO DO THIS...!
HAAH...

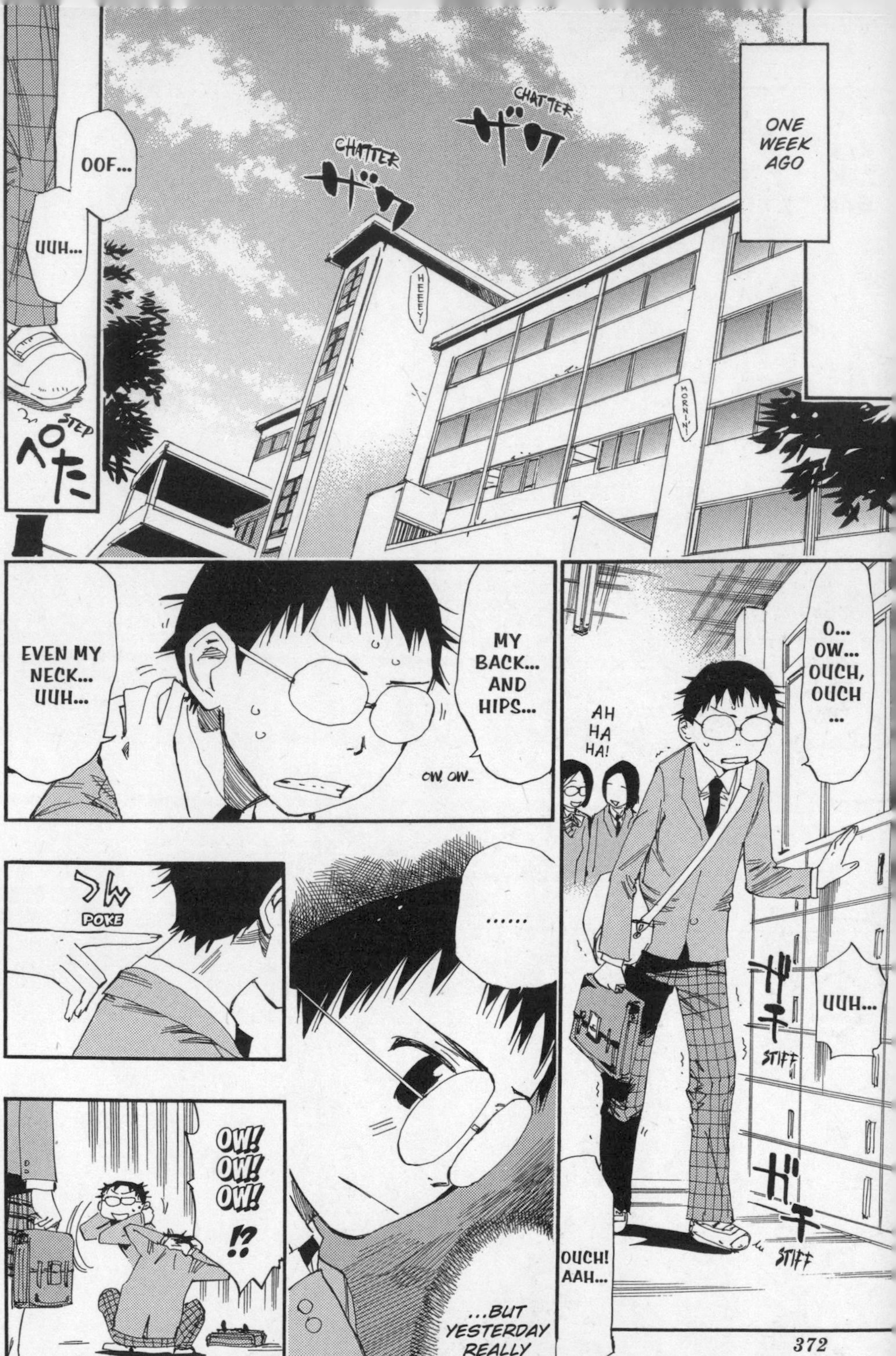

ONE WEEK AGO
CHATTER
CHATTER
HEEEY!
MORNIN'!
OOF...
UUH...
STEP
O... OW... OUCH, OUCH ...
AH HA HA!
STIFF
UUH...
STIFF
OUCH! AAH...
MY BACK... AND HIPS...
OW, OW...
EVEN MY NECK... UUH...
......
POKE
OW! OW! OW!
!?
...BUT YESTERDAY REALLY WAS...

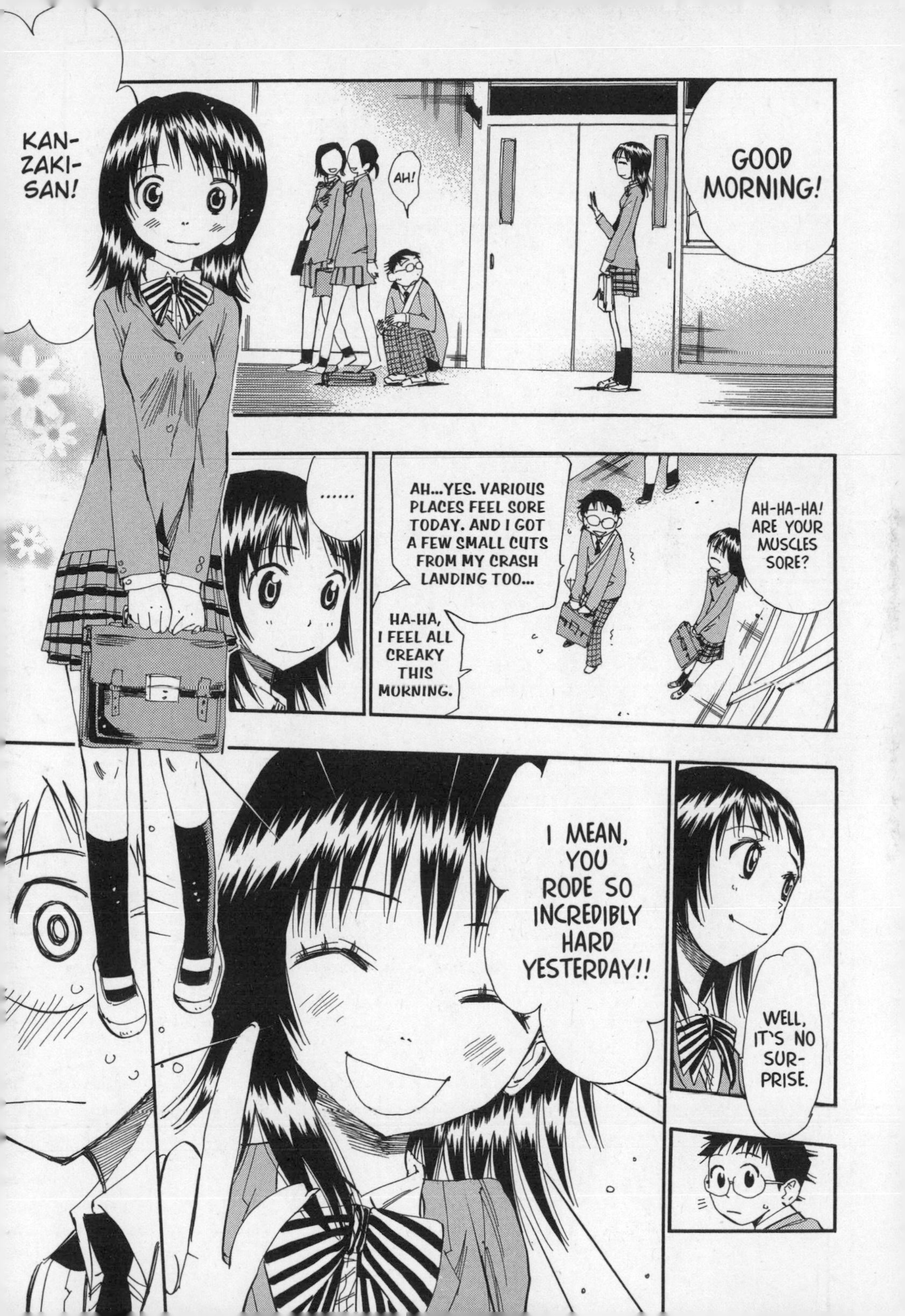
GOOD MORNING!
AH!
KAN-ZAKI-SAN!
AH-HA-HA! ARE YOUR MUSCLES SORE?
AH...YES. VARIOUS PLACES FEEL SORE TODAY. AND I GOT A FEW SMALL CUTS FROM MY CRASH LANDING TOO...
HA-HA, I FEEL ALL CREAKY THIS MORNING.
......
WELL, IT'S NO SUR-PRISE.
I MEAN, YOU RODE SO INCREDIBLY HARD YESTERDAY!!

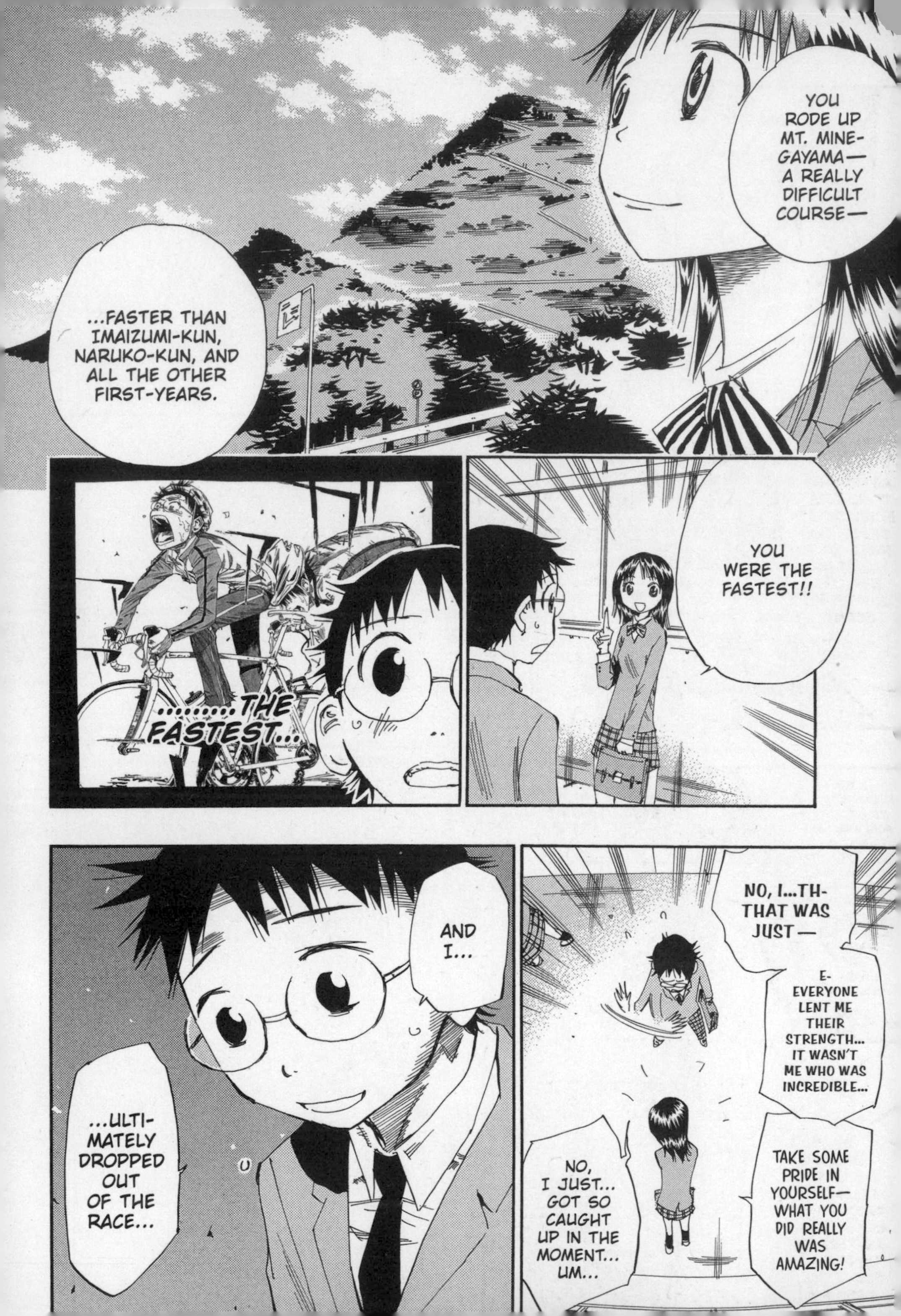
YOU RODE UP MT. MINE-GAYAMA—A REALLY DIFFICULT COURSE—
...FASTER THAN IMAIZUMI-KUN, NARUKO-KUN, AND ALL THE OTHER FIRST-YEARS.
YOU WERE THE FASTEST!!
........THE FASTEST...
NO, I...TH-THAT WAS JUST—
E-EVERYONE LENT ME THEIR STRENGTH... IT WASN'T ME WHO WAS INCREDIBLE...
TAKE SOME PRIDE IN YOURSELF—WHAT YOU DID REALLY WAS AMAZING!
NO, I JUST... GOT SO CAUGHT UP IN THE MOMENT... UM...
AND I...
...ULTIMATELY DROPPED OUT OF THE RACE...

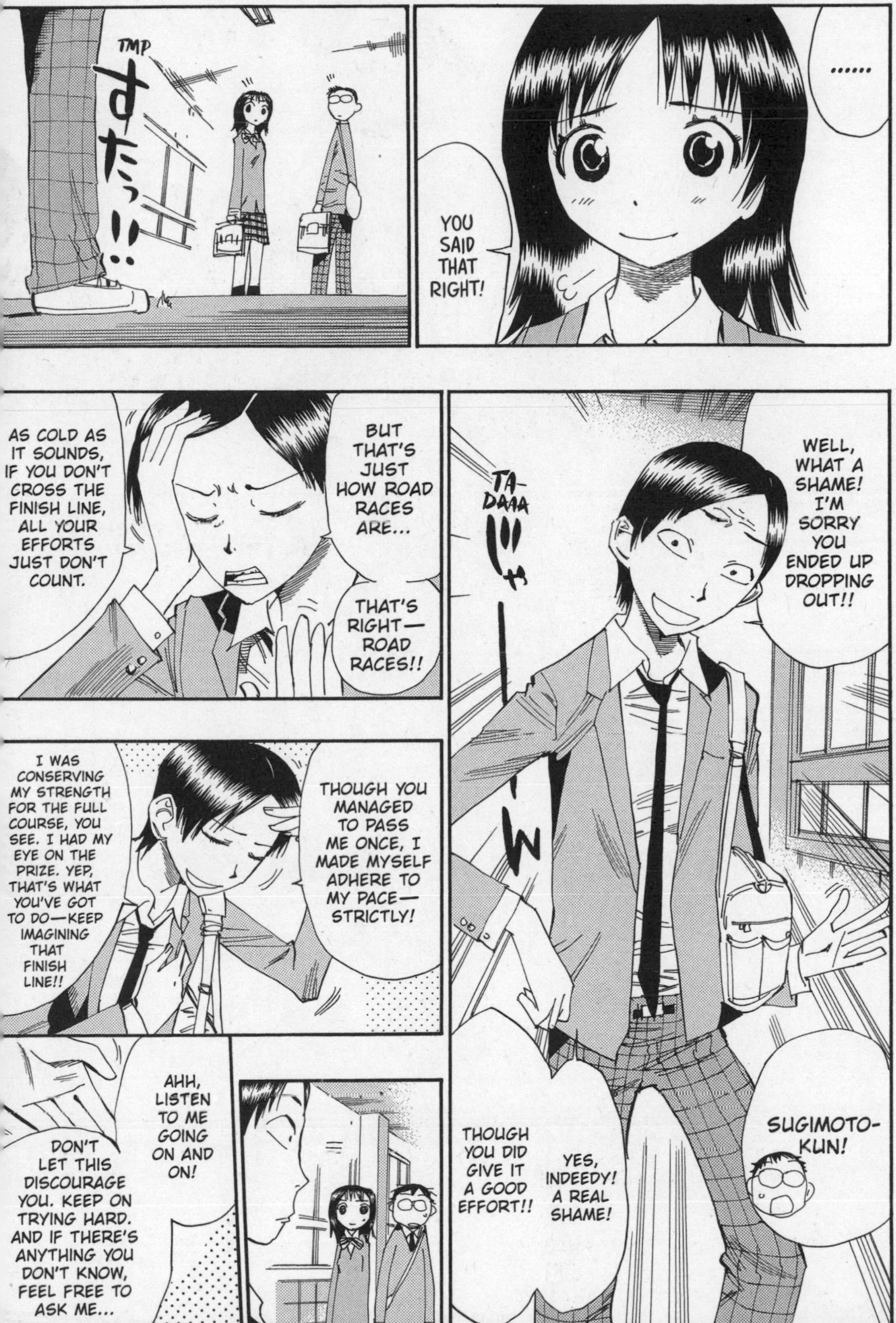
......
YOU SAID THAT RIGHT!
TMP
すたっ!!
WELL, WHAT A SHAME! I'M SORRY YOU ENDED UP DROPPING OUT!!
TA-DAAA
SUGIMOTO-KUN!
YES, INDEEDY! A REAL SHAME!
THOUGH YOU DID GIVE IT A GOOD EFFORT!!
BUT THAT'S JUST HOW ROAD RACES ARE...
AS COLD AS IT SOUNDS, IF YOU DON'T CROSS THE FINISH LINE, ALL YOUR EFFORTS JUST DON'T COUNT.
THAT'S RIGHT—ROAD RACES!!
THOUGH YOU MANAGED TO PASS ME ONCE, I MADE MYSELF ADHERE TO MY PACE—STRICTLY!
I WAS CONSERVING MY STRENGTH FOR THE FULL COURSE, YOU SEE. I HAD MY EYE ON THE PRIZE. YEP, THAT'S WHAT YOU'VE GOT TO DO—KEEP IMAGINING THAT FINISH LINE!!
AHH, LISTEN TO ME GOING ON AND ON!
DON'T LET THIS DISCOURAGE YOU. KEEP ON TRYING HARD. AND IF THERE'S ANYTHING YOU DON'T KNOW, FEEL FREE TO ASK ME...

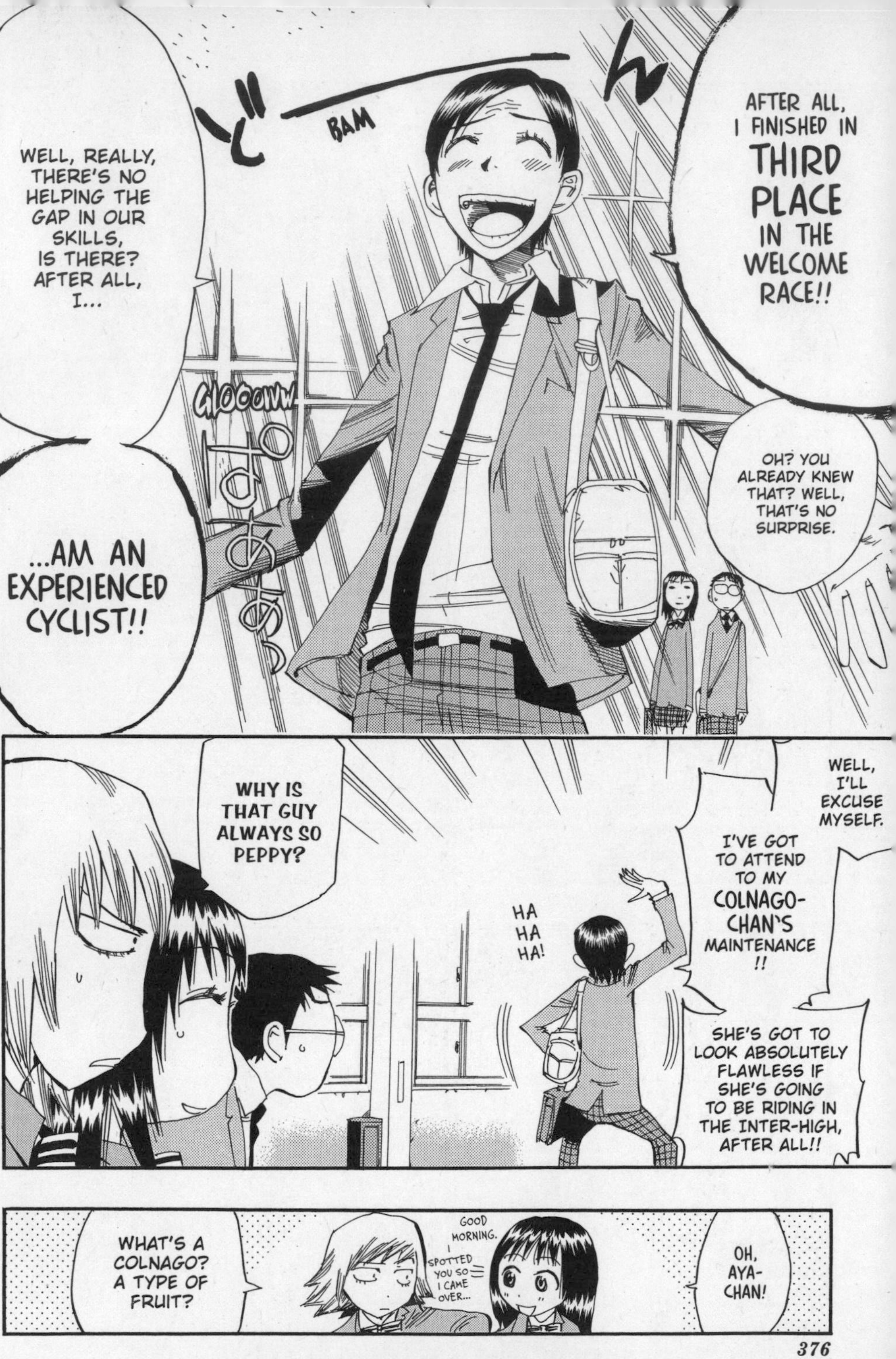
AFTER ALL, I FINISHED IN THIRD PLACE IN THE WELCOME RACE!!
BAM
OH? YOU ALREADY KNEW THAT? WELL, THAT'S NO SURPRISE.
WELL, REALLY, THERE'S NO HELPING THE GAP IN OUR SKILLS, IS THERE? AFTER ALL, I...
...AM AN EXPERIENCED CYCLIST!!
GLOOOWW
WELL, I'LL EXCUSE MYSELF.
I'VE GOT TO ATTEND TO MY COLNAGO-CHAN'S MAINTENANCE!!
SHE'S GOT TO LOOK ABSOLUTELY FLAWLESS IF SHE'S GOING TO BE RIDING IN THE INTER-HIGH, AFTER ALL!!
HA HA HA!
WHY IS THAT GUY ALWAYS SO PEPPY?
OH, AYA-CHAN!
GOOD MORNING.
I SPOTTED YOU SO I CAME OVER...
WHAT'S A COLNAGO? A TYPE OF FRUIT?

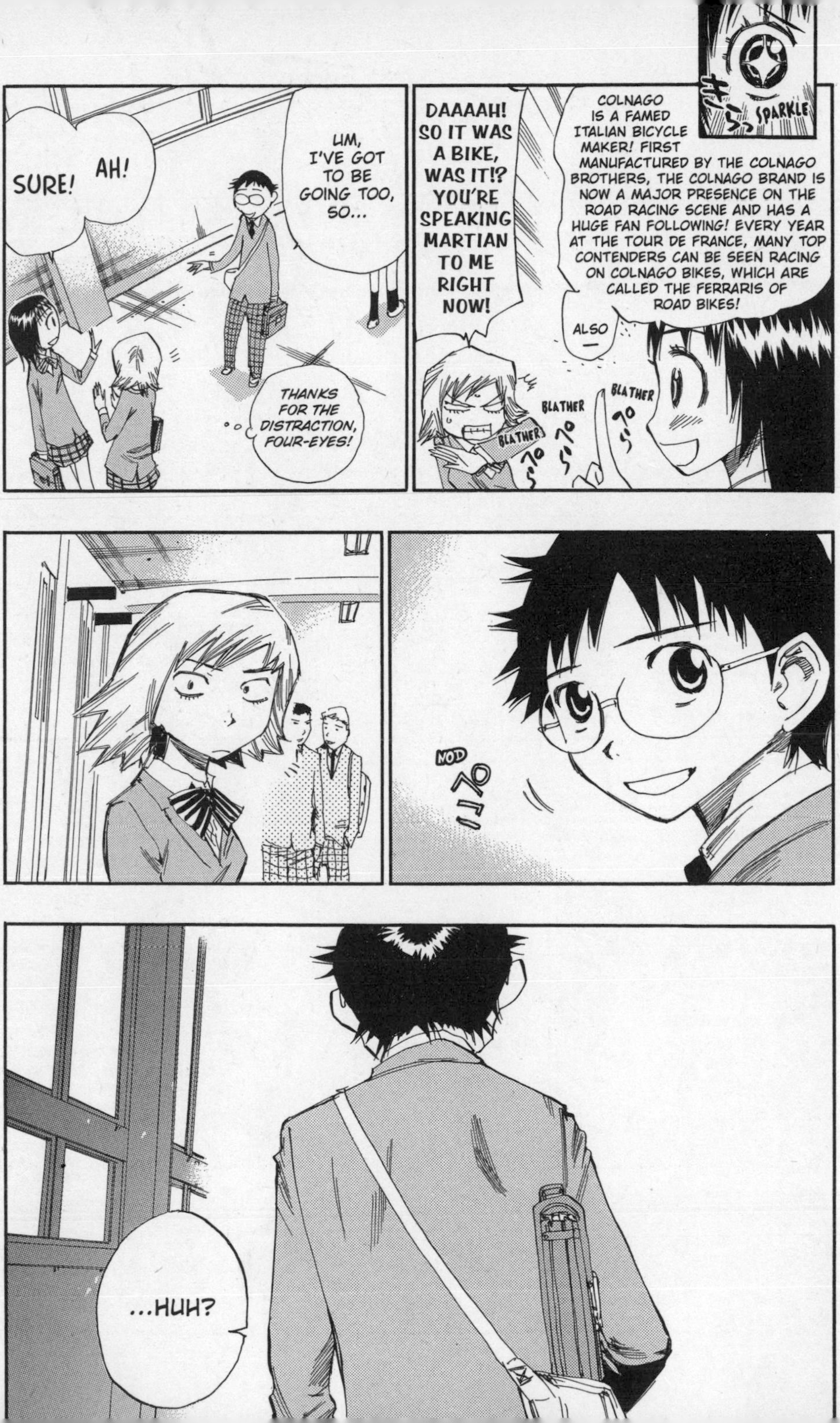
SPARKLE
COLNAGO IS A FAMED ITALIAN BICYCLE MAKER! FIRST MANUFACTURED BY THE COLNAGO BROTHERS, THE COLNAGO BRAND IS NOW A MAJOR PRESENCE ON THE ROAD RACING SCENE AND HAS A HUGE FAN FOLLOWING! EVERY YEAR AT THE TOUR DE FRANCE, MANY TOP CONTENDERS CAN BE SEEN RACING ON COLNAGO BIKES, WHICH ARE CALLED THE FERRARIS OF ROAD BIKES!
DAAAAH! SO IT WAS A BIKE, WAS IT!? YOU'RE SPEAKING MARTIAN TO ME RIGHT NOW!
ALSO—
BLATHER
BLATHER
BLATHER
UM, I'VE GOT TO BE GOING TOO, SO...
AH!
SURE!
THANKS FOR THE DISTRACTION, FOUR-EYES!
NOD
...HUH?

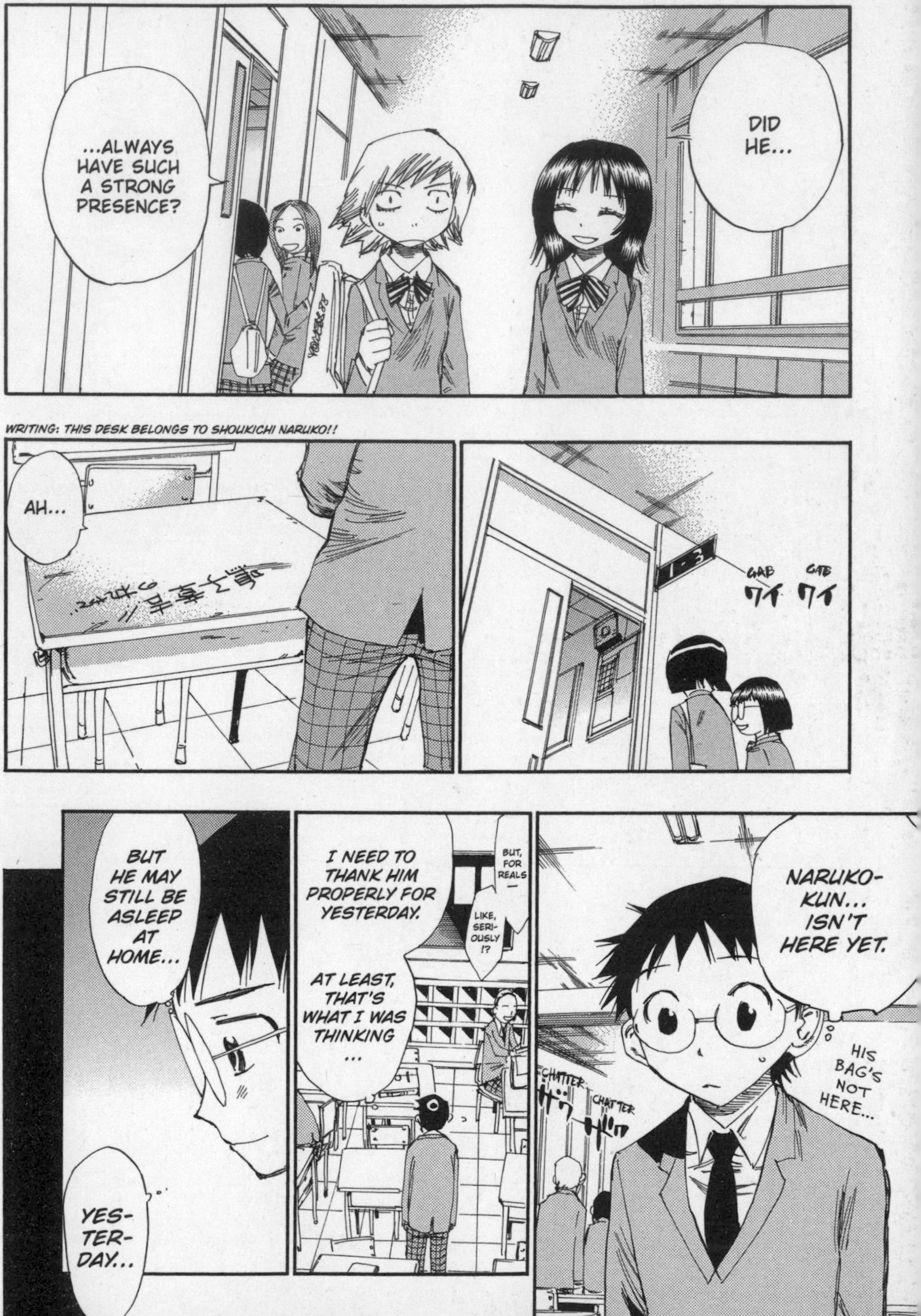
DID HE...
...ALWAYS HAVE SUCH A STRONG PRESENCE?
GAB GAB
WRITING: THIS DESK BELONGS TO SHOUKICHI NARUKO!!
AH...
NARUKO-KUN... ISN'T HERE YET.
HIS BAG'S NOT HERE...
CHATTER CHATTER
I NEED TO THANK HIM PROPERLY FOR YESTERDAY.
BUT, FOR REALS—
LIKE, SERIOUSLY!?
AT LEAST, THAT'S WHAT I WAS THINKING...
BUT HE MAY STILL BE ASLEEP AT HOME...
YES-TER-DAY...

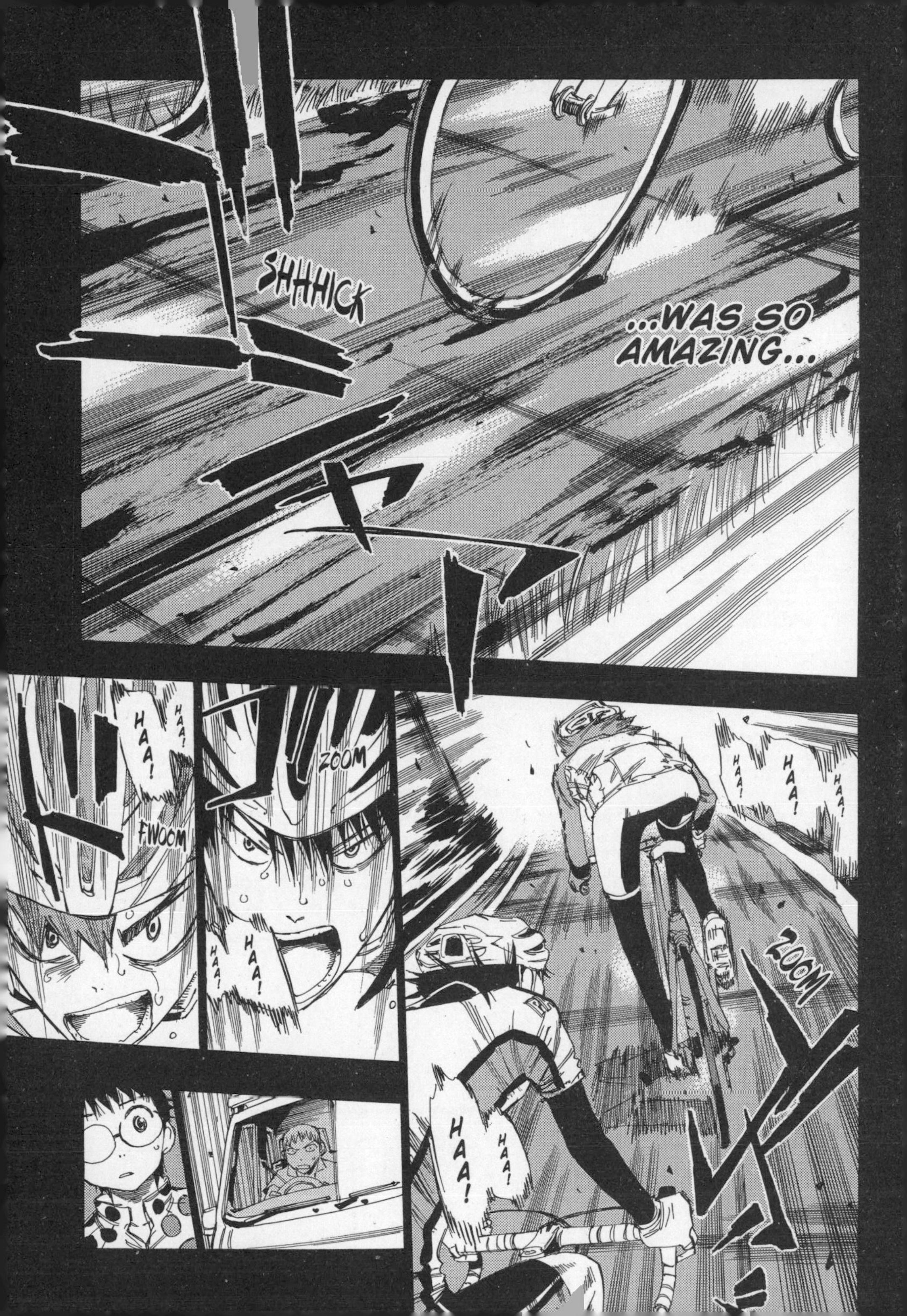
...WAS SO AMAZING...
SHHHICK
HAA!
HAA!
HAA!
ZOOM
HAA!
HAA!
ZOOM
HAA!
HAA!
HAA!
HAA!
FWOOM

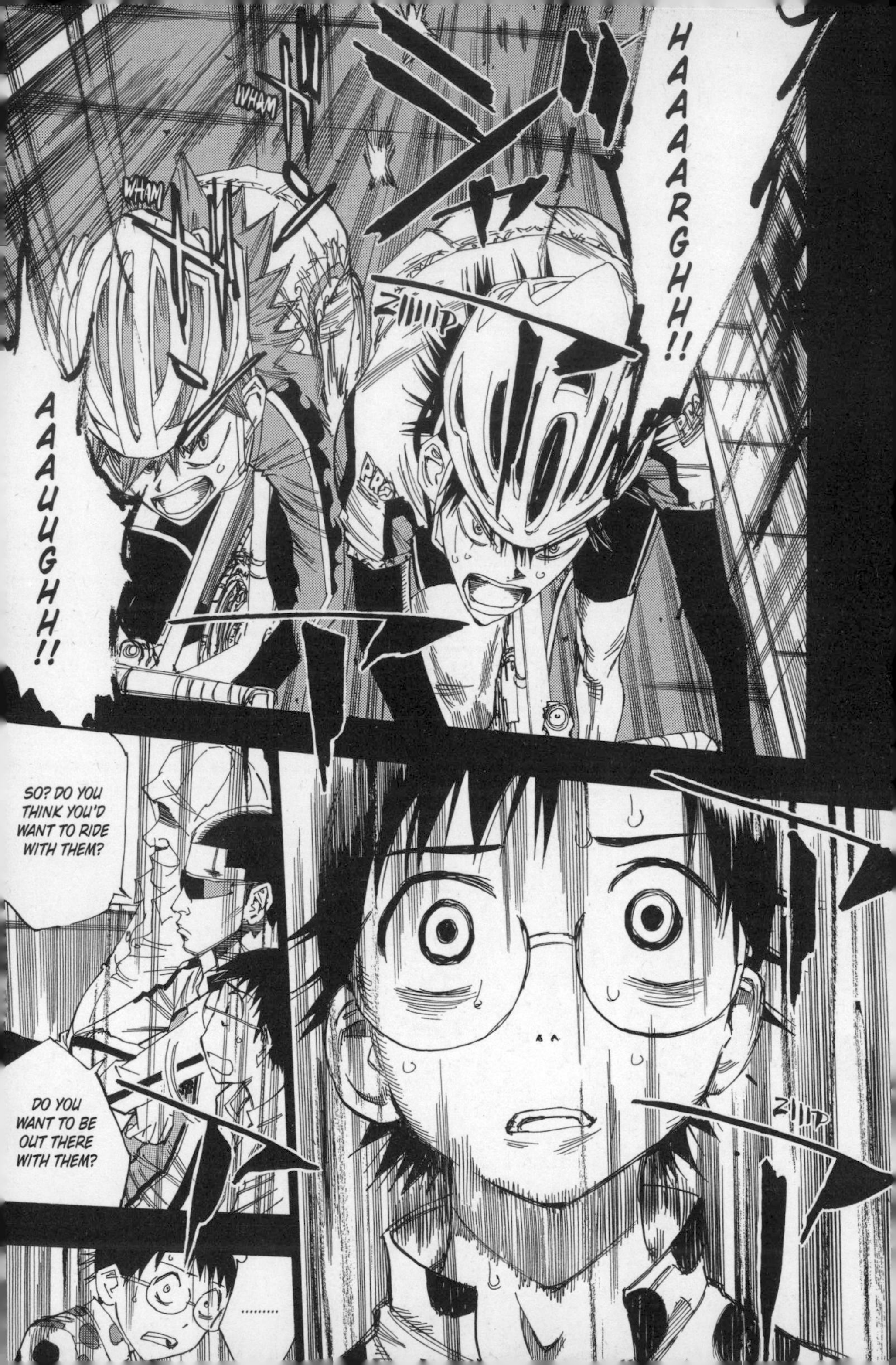
HAAAAARGHH!!
WHAM
ZIIIIP
WHAM
AAAAUUGHH!!
ZIIIP
SO? DO YOU THINK YOU'D WANT TO RIDE WITH THEM?
DO YOU WANT TO BE OUT THERE WITH THEM?
....

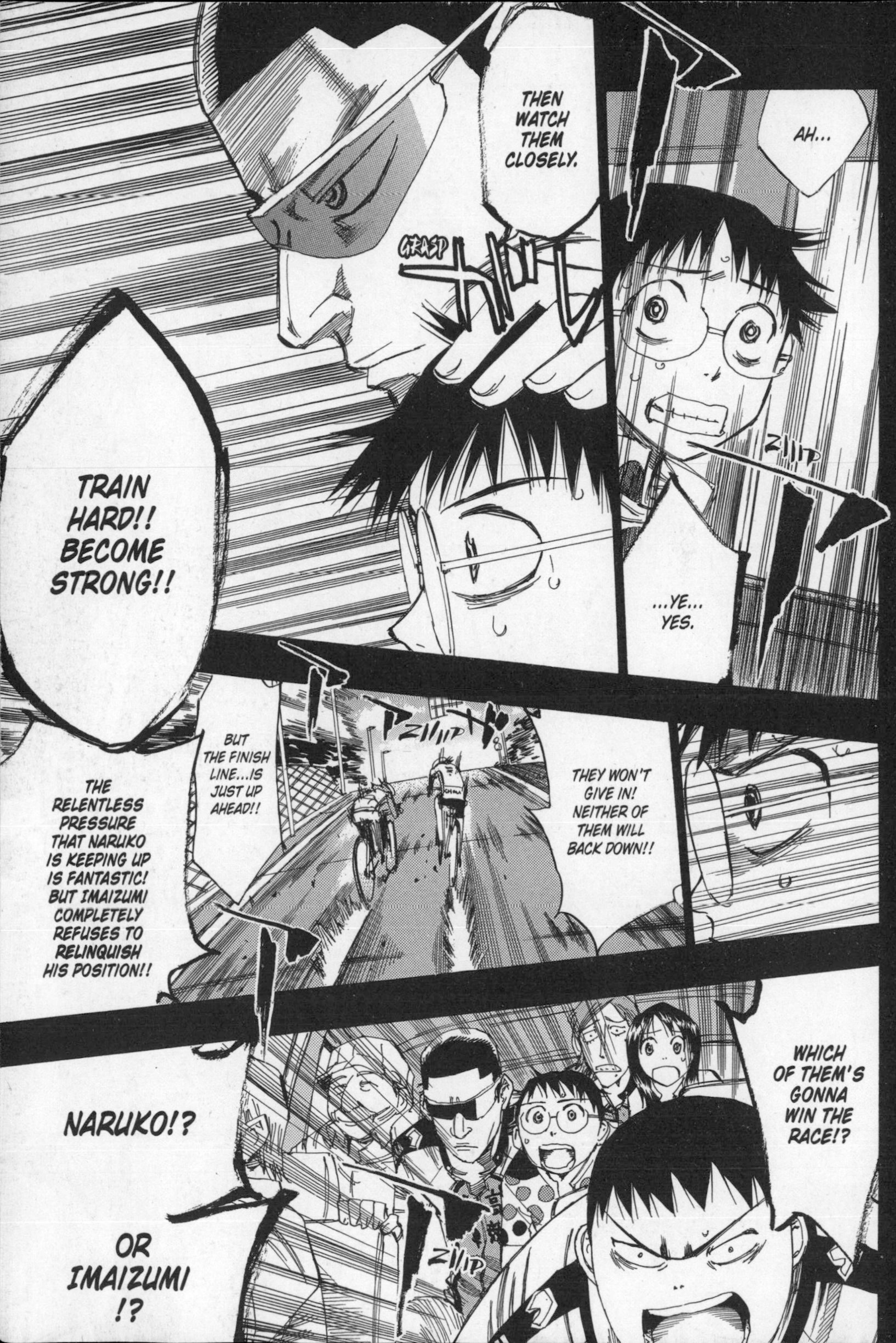
THEN WATCH THEM CLOSELY.
GRASP
AH...
ZIIIP
...YE... YES.
TRAIN HARD!! BECOME STRONG!!
THEY WON'T GIVE IN! NEITHER OF THEM WILL BACK DOWN!!
ZIIIP
BUT THE FINISH LINE...IS JUST UP AHEAD!!
THE RELENTLESS PRESSURE THAT NARUKO IS KEEPING UP IS FANTASTIC! BUT IMAIZUMI COMPLETELY REFUSES TO RELINQUISH HIS POSITION!!
WHICH OF THEM'S GONNA WIN THE RACE!?
ZIIIP
NARUKO!?
OR IMAIZUMI !?

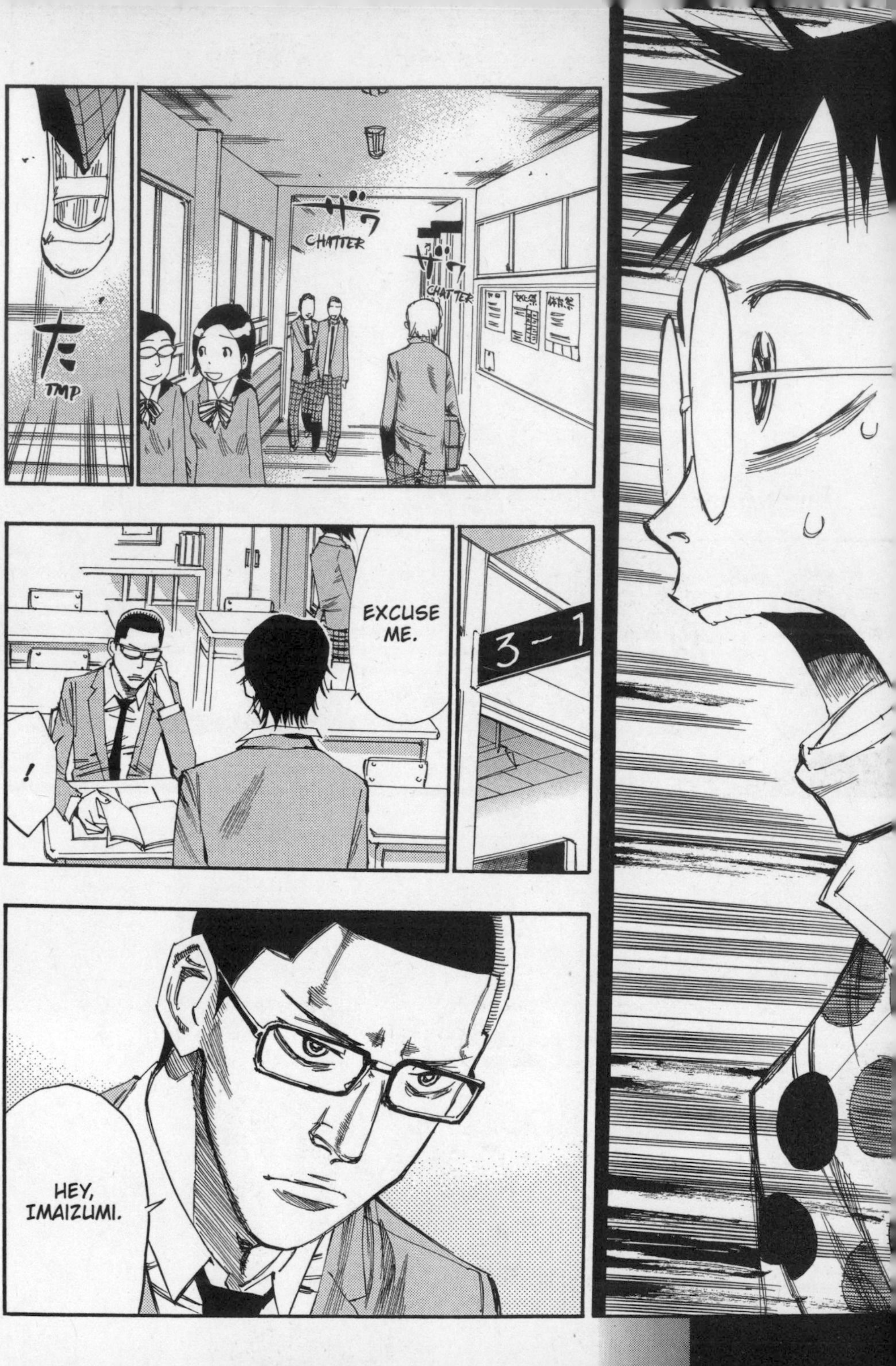

ザワ
CHATTER
ザワ
CHATTER
た
TMP
3-1
EXCUSE ME.
!
HEY, IMAIZUMI.

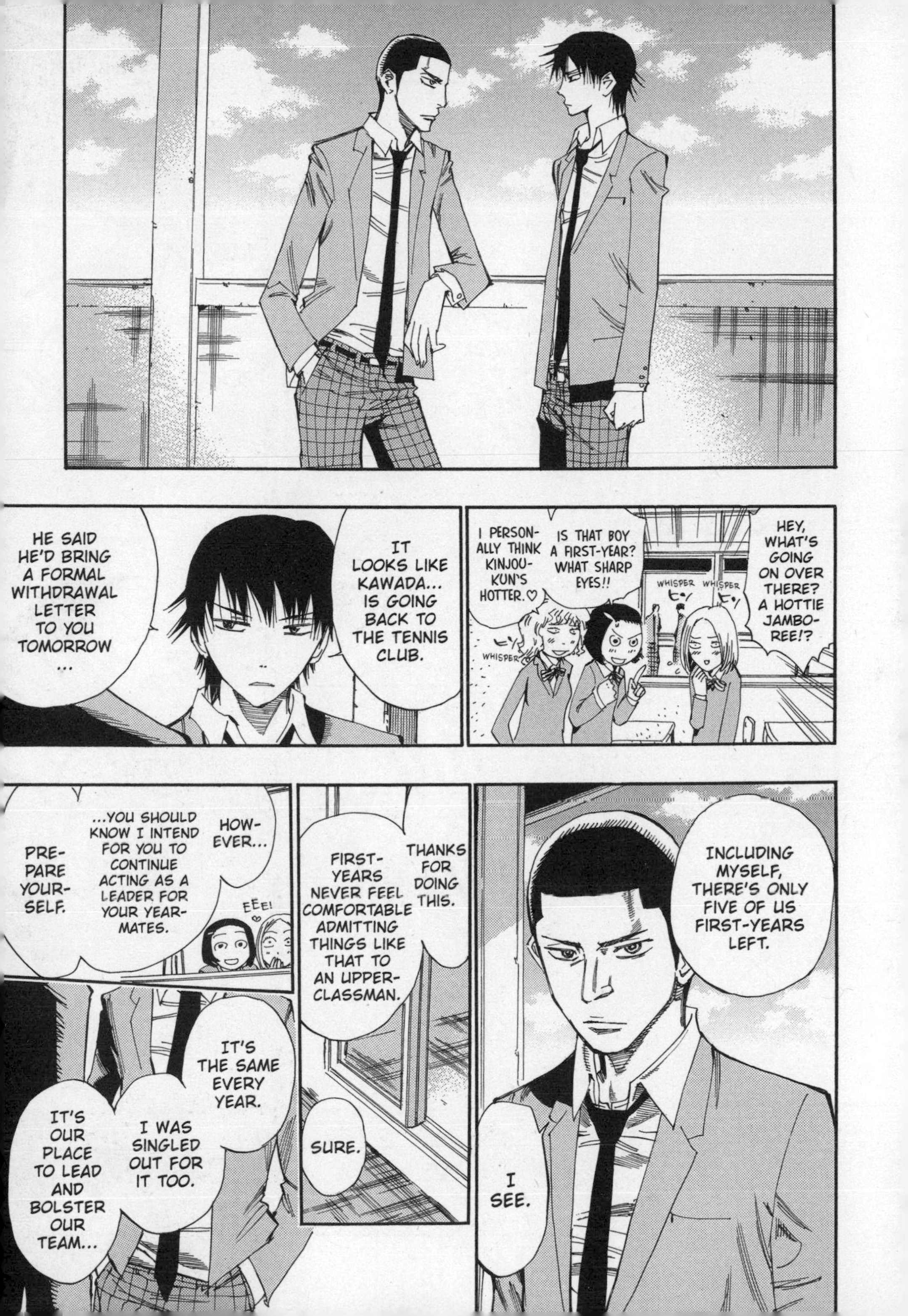

HEY, WHAT'S GOING ON OVER THERE? A HOTTIE JAMBOREE!?
IS THAT BOY A FIRST-YEAR? WHAT SHARP EYES!!
I PERSONALLY THINK KINJOU-KUN'S HOTTER.♡
WHISPER WHISPER
WHISPER
IT LOOKS LIKE KAWADA... IS GOING BACK TO THE TENNIS CLUB.
HE SAID HE'D BRING A FORMAL WITHDRAWAL LETTER TO YOU TOMORROW...
INCLUDING MYSELF, THERE'S ONLY FIVE OF US FIRST-YEARS LEFT.
I SEE.
THANKS FOR DOING THIS.
FIRST-YEARS NEVER FEEL COMFORTABLE ADMITTING THINGS LIKE THAT TO AN UPPERCLASSMAN.
SURE.
HOWEVER...
...YOU SHOULD KNOW I INTEND FOR YOU TO CONTINUE ACTING AS A LEADER FOR YOUR YEAR-MATES.
PREPARE YOURSELF.
EEE!
IT'S THE SAME EVERY YEAR.
I WAS SINGLED OUT FOR IT TOO.
IT'S OUR PLACE TO LEAD AND BOLSTER OUR TEAM...

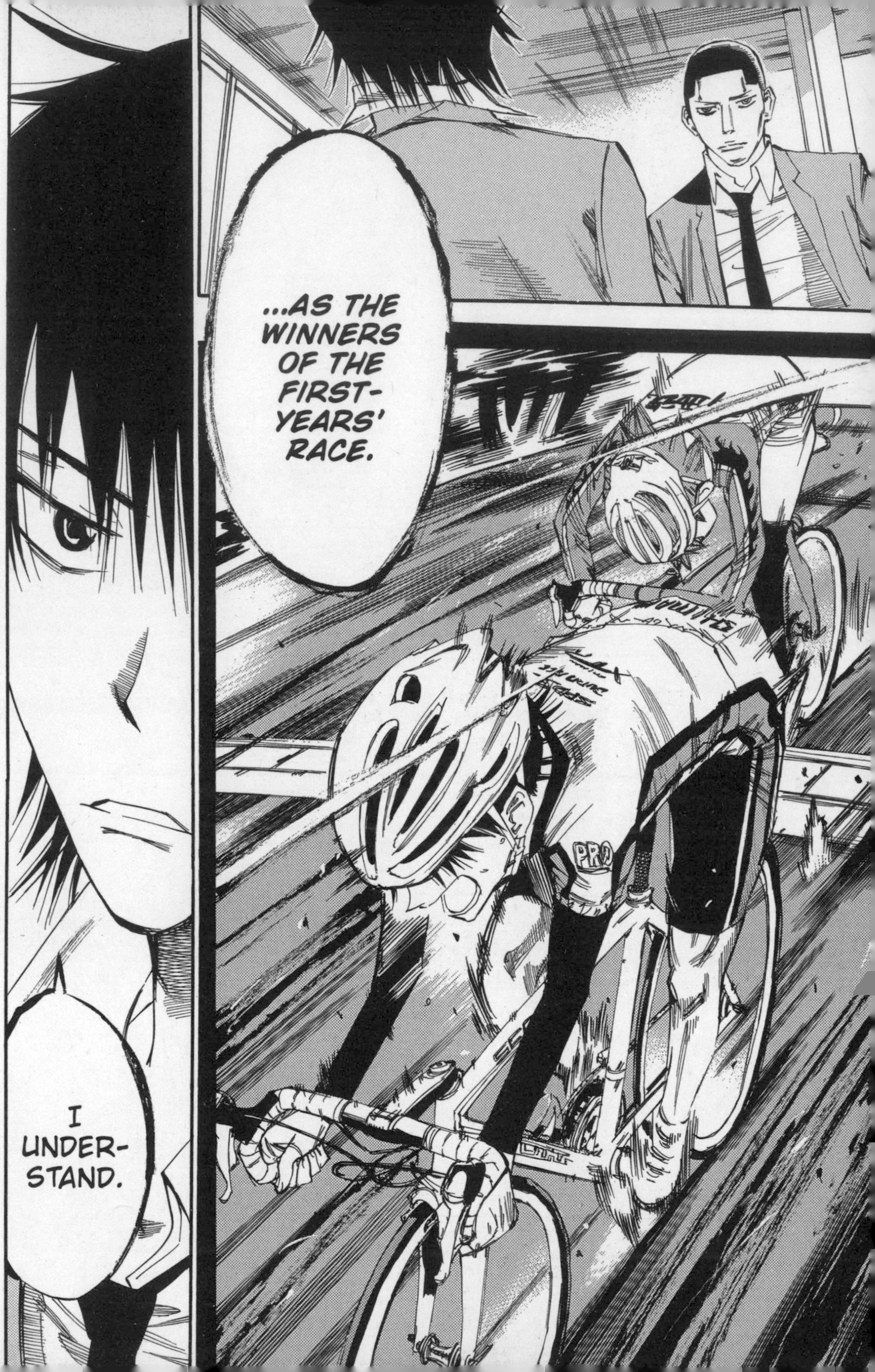
...AS THE WINNERS OF THE FIRST-YEARS' RACE.
I UNDER-STAND.

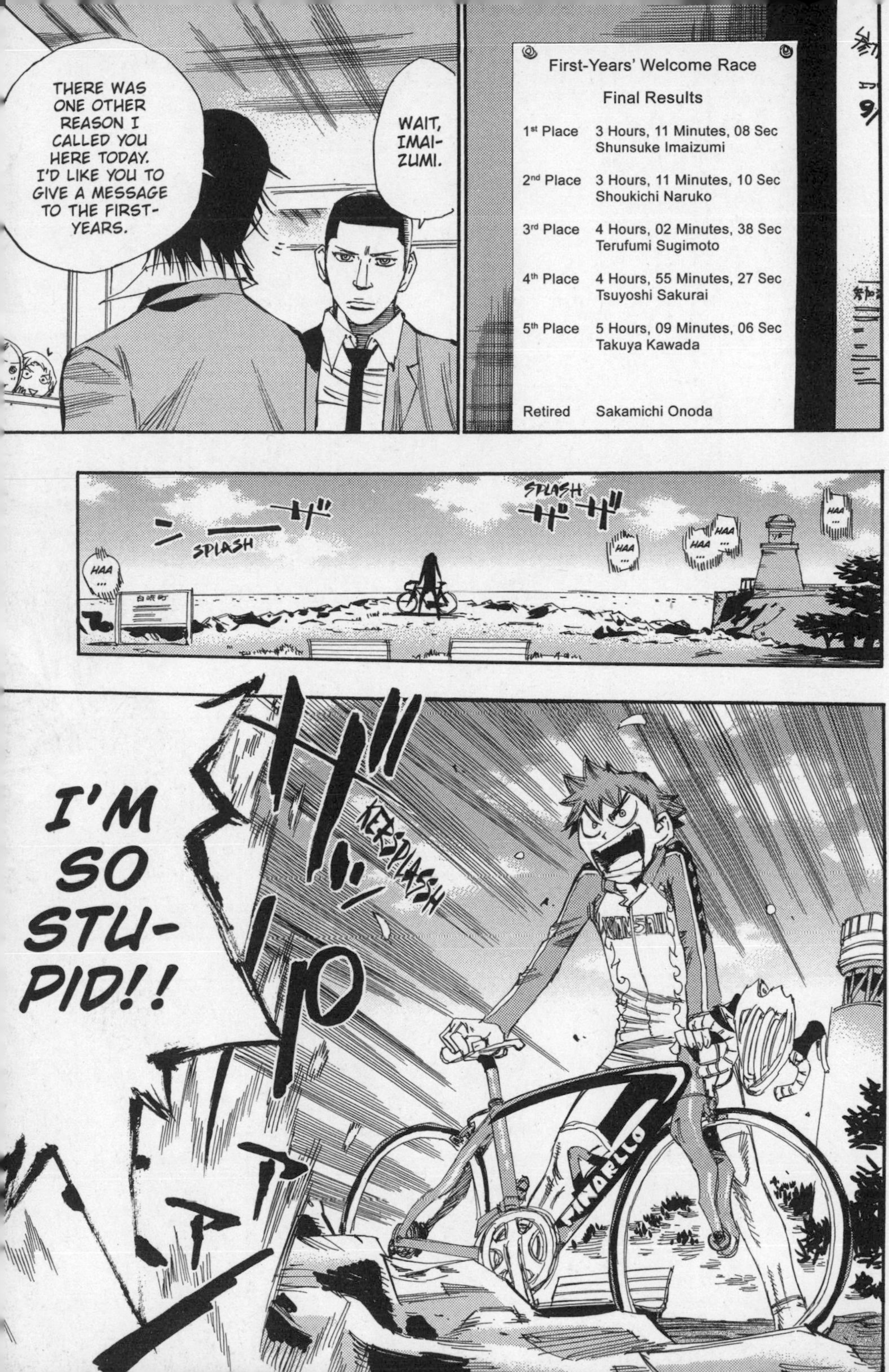
First-Years' Welcome Race
Final Results
1st Place 3 Hours, 11 Minutes, 08 Sec Shunsuke Imaizumi
2nd Place 3 Hours, 11 Minutes, 10 Sec Shoukichi Naruko
3rd Place 4 Hours, 02 Minutes, 38 Sec Terufumi Sugimoto
4th Place 4 Hours, 55 Minutes, 27 Sec Tsuyoshi Sakurai
5th Place 5 Hours, 09 Minutes, 06 Sec Takuya Kawada
Retired Sakamichi Onoda
WAIT, IMAIZUMI.
THERE WAS ONE OTHER REASON I CALLED YOU HERE TODAY. I'D LIKE YOU TO GIVE A MESSAGE TO THE FIRST-YEARS.
HAA...
HAA...
HAA...
HAA...
SPLASH
SPLASH
HAA...
KERSPLASSH
I'M SO STU-PID!!

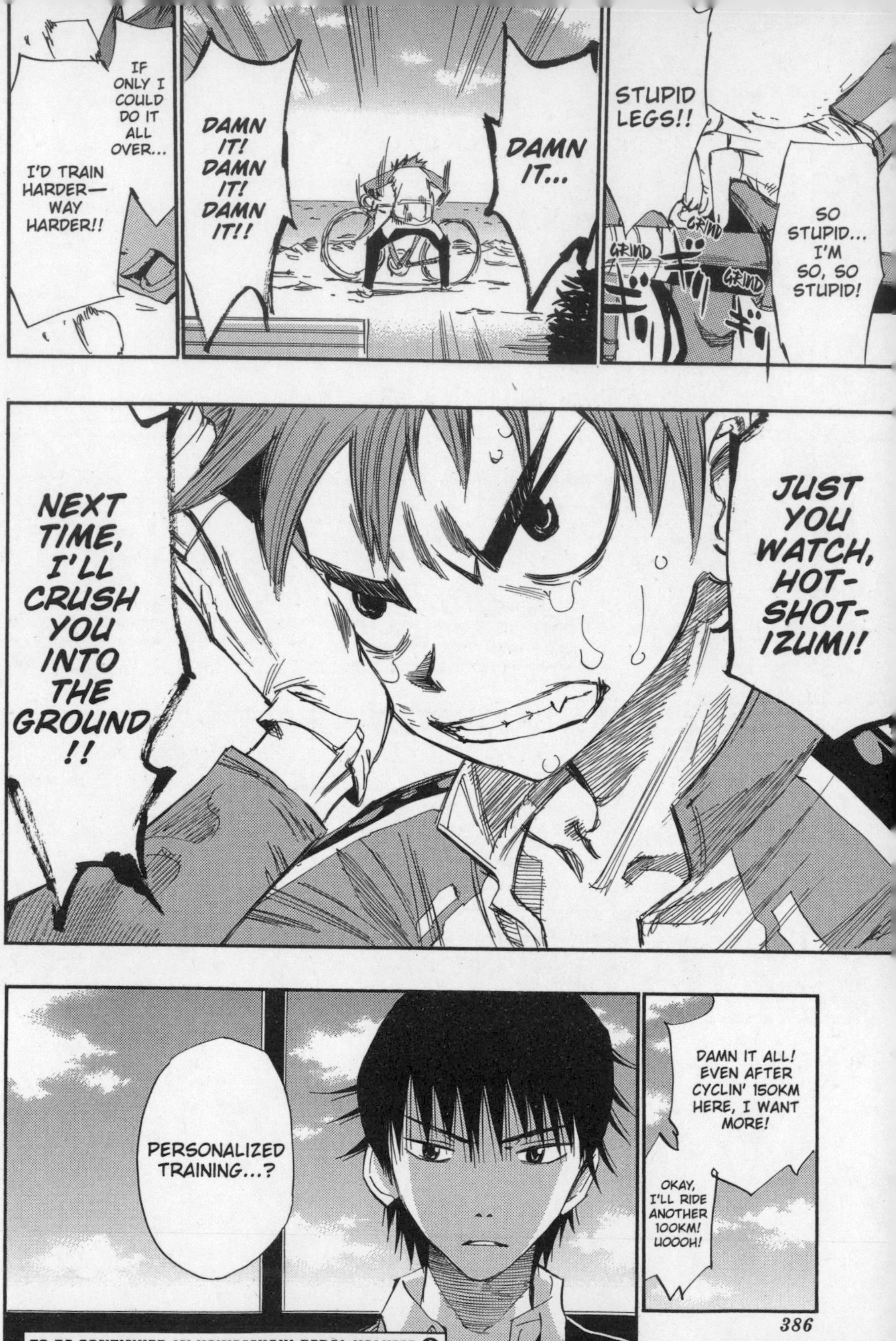

STUPID LEGS!!
GRIND
GRIND
GRIND
SO STUPID... I'M SO, SO STUPID!
DAMN IT...
DAMN IT! DAMN IT! DAMN IT!!
IF ONLY I COULD DO IT ALL OVER...
I'D TRAIN HARDER—WAY HARDER!!
JUST YOU WATCH, HOT-SHOT-IZUMI!
NEXT TIME, I'LL CRUSH YOU INTO THE GROUND!!
DAMN IT ALL! EVEN AFTER CYCLIN' 150KM HERE, I WANT MORE!
OKAY, I'LL RIDE ANOTHER 100KM! UOOOH!
PERSONALIZED TRAINING...?

TO BE CONTINUED IN YOWAMUSHI PEDAL VOLUME 3

YOWAMUSHI PEDAL ❷

WATARU WATANABE

Translation: Su Mon Han

Lettering: Lys Blakeslee

This book is a work of fiction. Names, characters, places, and incidents are the product of the author's imagination or are used fictitiously. Any resemblance to actual events, locales, or persons, living or dead, is coincidental.

YOWAMUSHI PEDAL Volume 3, 4
© 2008, 2009 Wataru Watanabe
All rights reserved.
First published in Japan in 2008, 2009 by Akita Publishing Co., Ltd., Tokyo.
English translation rights arranged with Akita Publishing CO., Ltd. Through Tuttle-Mori Agency, Inc., Tokyo.

Translation © 2016 by Hachette Book Group, Inc.

Yen Press
Hachette Book Group
1290 Avenue of the Americas
New York, NY 10104

www.hachettebookgroup.com
www.yenpress.com

Yen Press is an imprint of Hachette Book Group, Inc.
The Yen Press name and logo are trademarks of Hachette Book Group, Inc.

The publisher is not responsible for websites (or their content) that are not owned by the publisher.

Library of Congress Control Number: 2015960124

First Yen Press Edition: April 2016

ISBN: 978-0-316-35468-4

10 9 8 7 6 5 4 3 2 1

BVG

Printed in the United States of America

Hello! This is YOTSUBA!

Guess what? Guess what? Yotsuba and Daddy just moved here from waaaay over there!

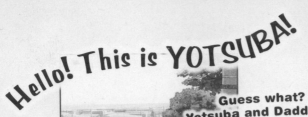

And Yotsuba met these nice people next door and made new friends to play with!

The pretty one took Yotsuba on a bike ride!
(Whoooa! There was a big hill!)

And Ena's a good drawer!
(Almost as good as Yotsuba!)

And their mom always gives Yotsuba ice cream!
(Yummy!)

And...
        And...
                OHHHH!

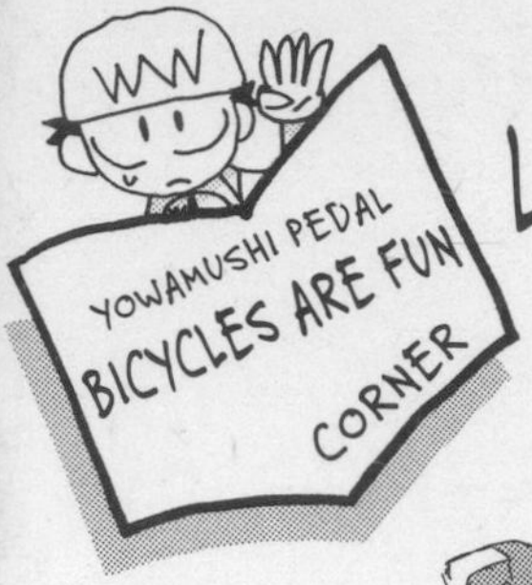
YOWAMUSHI PEDAL
BICYCLES ARE FUN
CORNER

LET'S EXPLAIN SOME STUFF

THOUGH THESE THINGS MAY SEEM OBVIOUS TO SOME...
FOR THE SAKE OF THOSE WHO DON'T KNOW, LET'S TALK ABOUT...

GEAR SHIFTERS

(THE MECHANISM THAT LETS YOU CHANGE GEARS)

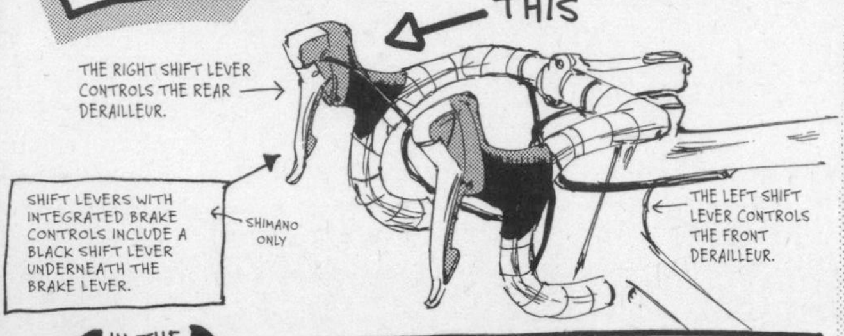
THIS
THE RIGHT SHIFT LEVER CONTROLS THE REAR DERAILLEUR.
SHIFT LEVERS WITH INTEGRATED BRAKE CONTROLS INCLUDE A BLACK SHIFT LEVER UNDERNEATH THE BRAKE LEVER.
SHIMANO ONLY
THE LEFT SHIFT LEVER CONTROLS THE FRONT DERAILLEUR.

GENERALLY, YOU GRAB ONTO THIS BLACK PART (THE "BRAKE HOOD") THAT KIND OF POPS UP LIKE THIS.

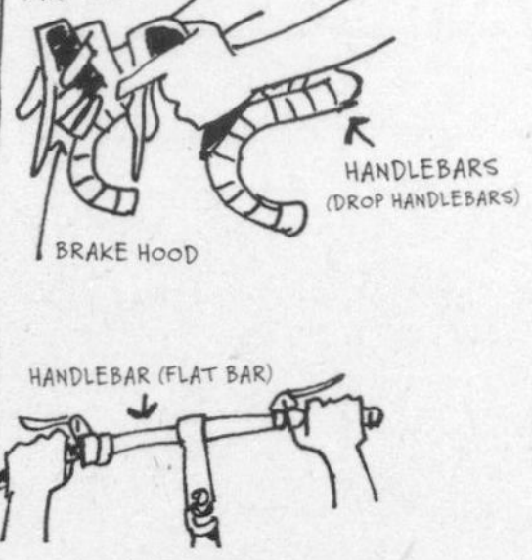
HANDLEBARS
(DROP HANDLEBARS)
BRAKE HOOD
HANDLEBAR (FLAT BAR)

WHEN RIDING AN MTB OR CITY BIKE, YOU HOLD ON TO THE HANDLEBARS. BUT ON A ROAD BIKE, YOU ACTUALLY GRIP THE BRAKE HOODS.

IN THE PAST...

SHIFTERS USED TO BE LOCATED DOWN HERE, SO YOU HAD TO KEEP TAKING YOUR HANDS OFF THE HANDLEBAR TO SHIFT GEARS.

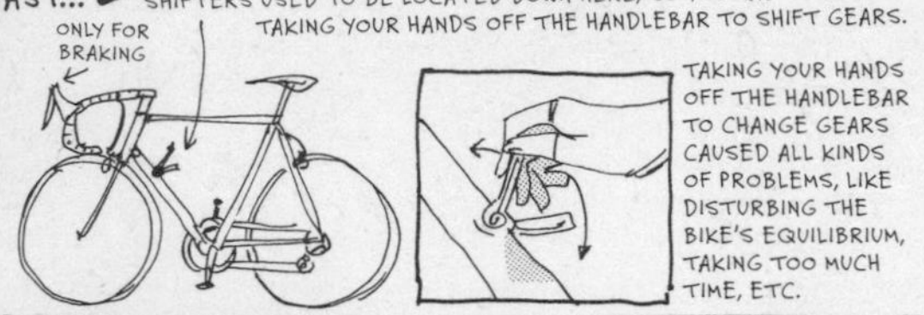
ONLY FOR BRAKING

TAKING YOUR HANDS OFF THE HANDLEBAR TO CHANGE GEARS CAUSED ALL KINDS OF PROBLEMS, LIKE DISTURBING THE BIKE'S EQUILIBRIUM, TAKING TOO MUCH TIME, ETC.

WHAT SOLVED ALL THESE PROBLEMS IN ONE FELL SWOOP WERE THE HANDLEBAR-MOUNTED SHIFTERS THAT ARE NOW UNIVERSALLY USED ON ROAD BIKES!! ADDING THE ABILITY TO SIMULTANEOUSLY BRAKE WHILE CHANGING GEARS IN A SINGLE CLICK WAS SO REVOLUTIONARY, THE TREND SPREAD THROUGHOUT THE WORLD WITH AMAZING SPEED (INCIDENTALLY, THE COMPANY THAT INVENTED THIS TECHNOLOGY WAS NONE OTHER THAN JAPAN'S OWN SHIMANO).

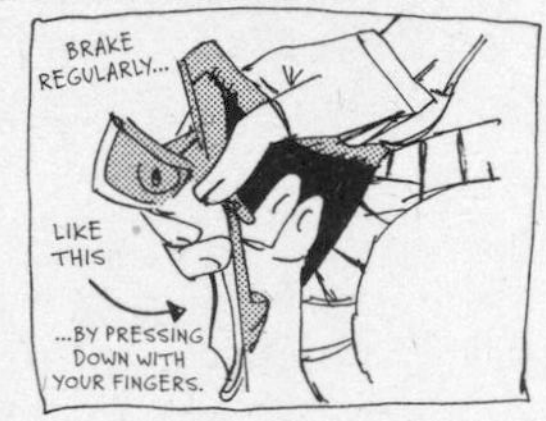
BRAKE REGULARLY...
LIKE THIS
...BY PRESSING DOWN WITH YOUR FINGERS.

HOW TO OPERATE (EXAMPLE)

① IF YOU CLICK YOUR RIGHT SHIFT LEVER TO THE LEFT, YOUR SPEED WILL INCREASE (SHIFTING TO A HEAVIER GEAR).

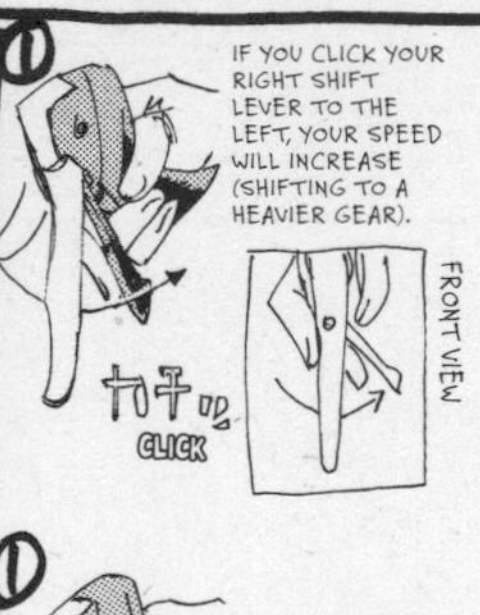
CLICK
FRONT VIEW

② IF YOU CLICK YOUR RIGHT BRAKE LEVER TO THE LEFT, YOUR SPEED WILL DECREASE (SHIFTING TO A LIGHTER GEAR).

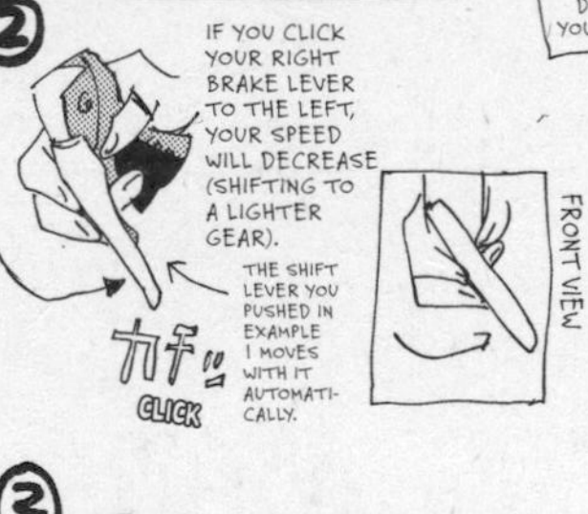
THE SHIFT LEVER YOU PUSHED IN EXAMPLE 1 MOVES WITH IT AUTOMATICALLY.
CLICK
FRONT VIEW

① IF YOU CLICK YOUR LEFT SHIFT LEVER TO THE RIGHT, YOUR SPEED WILL DECREASE (SHIFTING TO A LIGHTER GEAR).

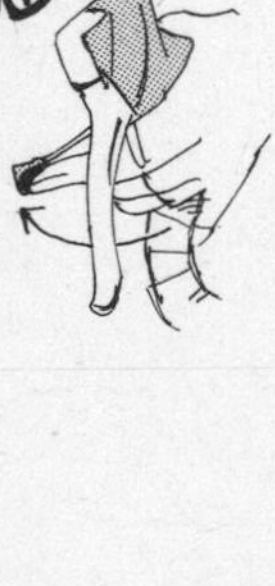

② IF YOU CLICK YOUR LEFT BRAKE LEVER TO THE RIGHT, YOUR SPEED WILL INCREASE (SHIFTING TO A HEAVIER GEAR).

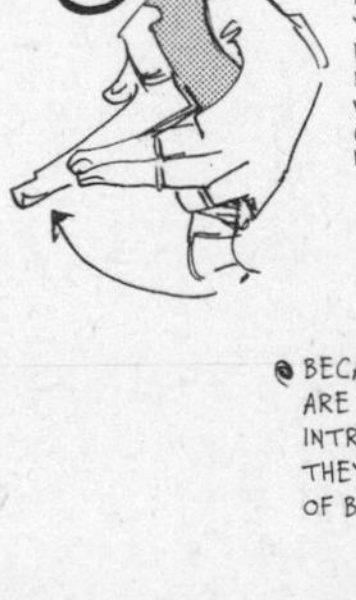

WARNING

SHIMANO'S SIGNATURE GEAR SHIFTER

I'M ONLY REFERENCING SHIMANO'S STI (SHIMANO TOTAL INTEGRATION) SHIFTING LEVERS IN MY EXPLANATION HERE. THERE ARE MANY OTHER MANUFACTURERS OF GEAR SHIFTERS, SUCH AS CAMPAGNOLO AND SRAM, ETC, SO PLEASE BE AWARE THAT THERE ARE SUBTLE DIFFERENCES IN THE MECHANICS OF SHIFTERS MADE BY DIFFERENT COMPANIES.

(INCIDENTALLY, CAMPAGNOLO'S SHIFTERS TEND TO LOOK LIKE THIS:)

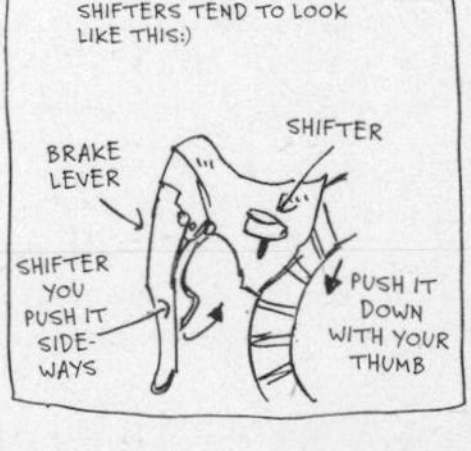
BRAKE LEVER
SHIFTER
SHIFTER YOU PUSH IT SIDEWAYS
PUSH IT DOWN WITH YOUR THUMB

- BECAUSE GEAR SHIFTERS ARE COMPRISED OF SO MANY INTRICATE MECHANISMS, THEY'RE ON THE PRICIER END OF BICYCLE PARTS.